Journeys

A HISTORY OF CANADA

SECOND EDITION

R. DOUGLAS FRANCIS
University of Calgary

RICHARD JONES

DONALD B. SMITH
University of Calgary

NELSON / EDUCATION

NELSON / EDUCATION

Journeys: A History of Canada, Second Edition

by R. Douglas Francis, Richard Jones, and Donald B. Smith

Associate Vice President, Editorial Director:
Evelyn Veitch

Editor-in-Chief, Higher Education:
Anne Williams

Executive Editor:
Laura Macleod

Executive Marketing Manager:
David Tonen

Senior Developmental Editor:
Linda Sparks

Photo Researcher/Permissions Coordinator:
Nicola Winstanley

Senior Content Production Manager:
Imoinda Romain

Production Service:
Newgen North America, Inc.

Copy Editor:
Rodney Rawlings

Proofreader:
Christine Gever

Indexer:
Grant Hackett

Production Coordinator:
Ferial Suleman

Design Director:
Ken Phipps

Managing Designer:
Franca Amore

Interior Design:
Dianna Little

Cover Design:
Rocket Design

Cover Image:
Walter J. Phillips, "York Boat on Lake Winnipeg," 1930, woodcut on paper, Collection of Glenbow Museum, Calgary, Canada, 53.1.7

Compositor:
Newgen

Printer:
Courier

Library and Archives Canada Cataloguing in Publication

Francis, R. D. (R. Douglas), 1944–

    Journeys: a history of Canada/ R. Douglas Francis, Richard Jones, Donald B. Smith. — 2nd ed.

Includes bibliographical references and index.
ISBN 978-0-17-644244-6

    1. Canada—History—Textbooks. I. Jones, Richard, 1943– II. Smith, Donald B., 1946– III. Title.

FC165.F73 2009   971
C2008-907655-9

ISBN-13: 978-0-17-644244-6
ISBN-10: 0-17-644244-8

Part and Chapter Opener Photo Credits Page 2: Courtesy of Lake Superior Provincial Park; Page 22: D.G.G. Kerr, ed., *A Historical Atlas of Canada* (Toronto: Thomas Nelson & Sons, 1961) p. 11; Page 24: Library and Archives Canada/C-001549; Page 50: Library and Archives Canada/C-43730; Page 74: *The Death of General Wolfe* (1727–59) [detail], c. 1771 (oil on panel). West, Benjamin 91738-1820)/Private Collection/Phillips, Fine Art Auctioneers, New York, USA/The Bridgeman Art Library; Page 94: Ville de Montreal. Gestion de documents et des archives; Page 96: Library and Archives Canada/C-004356; Page 118: Library and Archives Canada/C-011811; Page 142: M11588 *The Burning of the Parliament Building in Montreal* © McCord Museum; Page166: Library and Archives Canada, Acc. No. 1970-188-1928 W.H. Cloverdale Collection of Canadiana/C-041507; Page 168: Library and Archives Canada/C-092599; Page 194: 912.1.25: *Metis Encampment* (oil on canvas), 1848–1856; Kane, Paul; ROM2003_815_2. With permission of the Royal Ontario Museum © ROM; Page 214: Charles Gentile/National Archives of Canada/C-22626; Page 234: "Province House Ball, 1864" © Dusan Kadlec and Parks Canada; Page 236: George P. Roberts/Library and Archives Canada/C-000733; Page 262: Library and Archives Canada/C-052521; Page 280: Saskatchewan Archives Board #SPA R-B 1964(1); Page 302: Glenbow Archives, Calgary, Canada/NA-3205-11; Page 324: *Winnipeg Free Press*, October 23, 2002, pg A5. Reprinted with permission; Page 346: Photo courtesy of the late Bernice Loft, granddaughter of Ellen Loft; Page 370: Frederick Varley, *For What?* CW 19710261-0770 Beaverbrook Collection of War Art © Canadian War Museum; Page 372: Glenbow Archives /NA-1870-6; Page 392: Glenbow Archives /NA-1831-1; Page 418: Glenbow Archives, *Calgary Herald*, NA-2864-3445; Page 442: Vancouver Public Library/25644; Page 444: Library and Archives Canada/PA-111390; Page 466: R. Olsen/*Toronto Star*; Page 492: CP Photo (Jonathan Hayward); Page 514: CP Photo (Ryan Remiorz); Page 536: *Canadian Geographic*, January/February 2001, pp. 40–41. Photo courtesy of David Trattles; Page 558: CP Photo/*Toronto Star* (Frank Lennon); Page 582: CP Photo (Tom Hanson).

We wish to dedicate this second edition to our students over the years who have taught us so much.

Brief Contents

List of Maps xxi

Preface xxiii

CHAPTER 1   The First Peoples 2

PART ONE   Early European Settlement to 1760

CHAPTER 2   Early European Settlement and the Beginning
              of New France 24

CHAPTER 3   New France and Acadia, 1663–1760 50

CHAPTER 4   Struggle for a Continent 74

PART TWO   The Canadas, 1760–1864

CHAPTER 5   Quebec and Lower Canada, 1760–1840 96

CHAPTER 6   Upper Canada, 1791–1840 118

CHAPTER 7   The Union of the Canadas 142

PART THREE   Beyond the Canadas, to 1864

CHAPTER 8   Atlantic Canada, 1760–1864 168

CHAPTER 9   The Northwest to the 1860s 194

CHAPTER 10   The Pacific Coast to the 1860s 214

PART FOUR   Building the New Dominion, 1867–1914

CHAPTER 11   Confederation 236

CHAPTER 12 Consolidation of Confederation 262

CHAPTER 13 A "National Policy"? 280

CHAPTER 14 Conflicting Visions: 1867–1914 302

CHAPTER 15 Urban and Industrial Canada 324

CHAPTER 16 Social Reform and Culture: 1867–1914 346

PART FIVE   The Impact of Two World Wars and the Great
            Depression, 1914–1945

CHAPTER 17 Canada in the Great War 372

CHAPTER 18 The Interwar Years 392

CHAPTER 19 Canada in World War II 418

PART SIX   Modern Canada, 1945 to the Present

CHAPTER 20 Toward a More Affluent Society: 1945–1960 444

CHAPTER 21 Protest and Reform: The 1960s 466

CHAPTER 22 Aboriginal Canada: World War II to the Present . . . 492

CHAPTER 23 The Making of Modern Quebec 514

CHAPTER 24 Immigration and Multiculturalism 536

CHAPTER 25 Canada in the 1970s and 1980s: Constitution
            and Free Trade 558

CHAPTER 26 Contemporary Canada 582

Appendix: Canadian Prime Ministers since Confederation 607
Index 609

Contents

List of Maps xxi
Preface xxiii

CHAPTER 1   The First Peoples 2
Origin of the First Peoples of North America 3
Archaeological Hypotheses 4
Civilizations of the Americas 5
Classifying the First Nations 7
    Where Social Scientists Disagree: How Much Power Did Women Have in Northern
    Iroquoian Society? 15
Notes 18
Beyond the Book 18
Related Readings 19
Bibliography 19

PART ONE   Early European Settlement to 1760

Introduction 23

CHAPTER 2   Early European Settlement and the Beginning
                of New France 24
The Arrival of the Norse 25
The European Expansion in the Fifteenth Century 25
French Interest in the North Atlantic in the Sixteenth Century 26
European Fishers and Traders' Activities in the Sixteenth Century 28
    Community Portrait: The Basque Whaling Community of Red Bay, Labrador, 1550–1600 . 29
The Rise of the Fur Trade 32
Samuel de Champlain 32
The French in Acadia 34
The Founding of Quebec 34
The Company of One Hundred Associates 37
The Contributions of the French Religious Orders 38
New France in the Mid-1640s 39
The Missionaries' Arrival in Huronia 39
The Final Struggle between the Hurons and the Iroquois 43
    Where Historians Disagree: Why the Hurons Accepted Christianity 43
The Fall of Huronia and Its Impact on the French Colony 45
Renewed Iroquois Attacks on New France 46
Notes 47

Beyond the Book 47
Related Readings 48
Bibliography 48

CHAPTER 3   New France and Acadia, 1663–1760 50
The First Half-Century of Royal Government in Canada 51
The Obligations of the Seigneurs and the *Censitaires* 52
    Where Historians Disagree: The Nature of the Seigneurial System in New France 53
The Settlement of the St. Lawrence Valley 55
Colbert's Administrative Reforms 56
The Failure of Colbert's Plan for a "Compact Colony" 57
Economic Development after the Treaty of Utrecht 58
The Society of New France in the Eighteenth Century 59
The Habitants and Their Way of Life 61
The Church in New France 61
Education and Social Welfare 62
The First Nations Population 62
First Nations and African Slaves 63
The Rise of a *Canadien* Identity 63
The Rise of an *Acadien* Identity 64
Acadia Becomes Nova Scotia 64
Nova Scotia, between the Treaty of Utrecht and the Expulsion of the Acadians 66
The First Nations and the English 66
Britain's Growing Anxiety about the Acadians 66
The Expulsion of the Acadians 67
The Deportation Begins 67
The Destruction of Acadian Society 68
    Where Historians Disagree: The Expulsion of the Acadians: Was It Necessary? 68
Beyond the Book 71
Related Readings 72
Bibliography 72

CHAPTER 4   Struggle for a Continent 74
The English Challenge from the North 75
French Expansion to the North and West 75
The First Round of Conflict with the English Colonies, 1689–1713 76
New France's First Nations Allies 78
The Treaty of Utrecht and Its Aftermath 79
The Second Round of Conflict with the English Colonies, 1744–1760 80
Rivalry in the Ohio Country 82
The Fall of New France 84
New France's Final Year, 1759–1760 87
    A Historical Portrait: The Marquis de Montcalm 88
    Where Historians Disagree: Was Montcalm an Asset or a Liability for New France? 89
Notes 91

Beyond the Book 91
Related Readings 92
Bibliography 92

PART TWO The Canadas, 1760–1864

Introduction 95

CHAPTER 5   Quebec and Lower Canada, 1760–1840 96
Pontiac's Resistance and the Proclamation of 1763 97
Impact of the Royal Proclamation of 1763 on the Province of Quebec 98
Canadien Society in the Aftermath of the Conquest 99
The American Invasion 100
The French Canadians' Response to the American Invasion 101
The American Revolution and the First Nations 102
   Community Portrait: The Community of Odanak 103
Loyalist Immigration 105
The Constitutional Act of 1791 105
The Economic Revolution in the Early Nineteenth Century 107
Urban Life in Lower Canada 107
   Community Portrait: The St. Maurice Forges, an Early Industrial Community 108
Health Conditions 109
Rural Quebec 110
The Church 110
The Professional Elite 111
The Lower Canadian Rebellions, 1837–1838 112
Consequences of the Rebellions 113
Beyond the Book 115
Related Readings 116
Bibliography 116

CHAPTER 6   Upper Canada, 1791–1840 118
The Anishinabeg and Loyalist Settlement 119
   A Historical Portrait: David Ramsay 120
Loyalist Settlements 121
The Constitutional Act of 1791 121
A "Truly British" Colony 122
The First Nations: A Displaced People 123
The Growth of Settlement 125
Upper Canada Immediately after the War of 1812 128
The Aboriginal Peoples 129
Colonial Oligarchy: The Family Compact 130
Religious Disputes 130
   Community Portrait: The Children of Peace, Sharon, Upper Canada 131
Women in Upper Canada 133

Economic Growth and Conservation 134
Transportation 134
The Rise of a Reform Movement 135
The Upper Canadian Rebellion, 1837 136
    Where Historians Disagree: The Causes of the 1837 Rebellion in Upper Canada 136
Lord Durham's Report 138
Notes 139
Beyond the Book 139
Related Readings 140
Bibliography 140

CHAPTER 7   The Union of the Canadas 142
French Canadians and Union 143
The Commercial Empire of the St. Lawrence 144
The Rise of a Reform Coalition 145
The Arrival of Responsible Government 146
First Nations in the Canadas 148
The Advent of British Free Trade and Repercussions for the United Canadas 149
The Annexation Movement 149
From Transatlantic to Transcontinental Trade 150
Reciprocity with the United States 150
Politics in the 1850s and Early 1860s 153
Urban and Commercial Development 154
Social Developments 154
    Community Portrait: The Orange Community in Toronto's Cabbagetown 155
Religion 158
Education and Culture 159
Notes 162
Beyond the Book 162
Bibliography 163

PART THREE Beyond the Canadas, to 1864

Introduction 167

CHAPTER 8   Atlantic Canada, 1760–1864 168
New England's Outpost 169
Nova Scotia and the American Revolution 170
    Where Historians Disagree: Why Didn't Nova Scotia Join the American Revolution? 173
Loyalist Communities in the Maritimes 176
The Atlantic Economy from the Revolutionary War to the War of 1812 179
Economic Developments, 1815–1850 181
    Where Historians Disagree: The Timber Industry in Early New Brunswick:
    An Environmental Perspective 182
Saint John and Halifax 185

The Maritimes and the United States 185
Railways 186
The Population of Atlantic British North America 187
Women in the Maritimes 187
The First Nations in the Maritimes and Newfoundland 188
Political Changes in the Mid-Nineteenth Century 189
Notes 191
Beyond the Book 191
Bibliography 192

CHAPTER 9   The Northwest to the 1860s 194
The French and the English in the Interior 195
The Impact of the Europeans on the First Nations 196
The Fur Trade after the Fall of New France 197
The Emergence of the North West Company 197
    A Historical Portrait: George Nelson 198
Rivalry between the North West Company and the Hudson's Bay Company 199
The Rise of the Métis 200
    Where Historians Disagree: The First Nations' Role in the Fur Trade 200
The Red River Colony 202
The Establishment of the Selkirk Colony 203
Seven Oaks and Its Aftermath 204
Red River Society in the Mid-Nineteenth Century 204
The End of the Red River Colony's Isolation 205
The Plains First Nations in the Mid-Nineteenth Century 206
The Arrival of the Whisky Traders 207
The North West on the Eve of Canadian Settlement 207
Notes 210
Beyond the Book 210
Related Readings 211
Bibliography 211

CHAPTER 10   The Pacific Coast to the 1860s 214
The First Nations of the Northwest Coast 215
European Exploration of the Northwest Coast 216
The First Nations and the Maritime Fur Traders 217
The Joint Occupation of the Oregon Territory 218
James Douglas 220
    Where Historians Disagree: James Douglas's Contribution to British Columbia 223
The First Nations and the Impact of the Gold Rushes 225
British Columbia in the Mid-1860s 225
    Community Portrait: The Black Community of Victoria 226
The Union of the Two Colonies 228
Notes 230
Beyond the Book 230

Related Readings 231
Bibliography 231

PART FOUR   Building the New Dominion, 1867–1914

Introduction 235

CHAPTER 11   Confederation 236
The Impact of the American Civil War 237
Negotiating Confederation 238
   Community Portrait: The Charlottetown Conference as a Political Community 240
Opposition to Confederation in Atlantic Canada 243
External Pressures 244
Turning the Tide in New Brunswick 246
Final Negotiations 246
Politics 247
The Nature of Confederation 247
Canadian–British–American Relations 248
The Economy 248
Urbanization 249
Population 250
Social Life 251
   A Historical Portrait: Josiah Henson 251
Religion and Education 254
   Community Portrait: The Community of the Sisters of the Congregation of Notre Dame
   in the Late Nineteenth Century 255
Notes 258
Beyond the Book 258
Related Readings 259
Bibliography 259

CHAPTER 12   Consolidation of Confederation 262
The Nova Scotia Repeal Movement 263
The Canadian Acquisition of Rupert's Land 264
The Métis Resistance of 1869–1870 265
The Manitoba Act 266
The Wolseley Expedition 267
Relations with the First Nations 267
   Where Historians Disagree: Interpreting Treaties 1 to 7 in Western Canada 269
British Columbia Enters Confederation 271
An Unwilling Newfoundland and a Reluctant Prince Edward Island 275
Canadian Acquisition of the Arctic Archipelago 276
Notes 277
Beyond the Book 277
Bibliography 278

CHAPTER 13   A "National Policy"? 280

Emerging English-Canadian and French-Canadian Expressions of Nationalism . . . 281

Liberal Rule: 1873–1878 282

The National Policy of John A. Macdonald 283

Transcontinental Railways 284

  Where Historians Disagree: The National Policy 285

The Dominion's Strategy for the North West 290

  A Historical Portrait: Robert, a Barnardo Boy 294

Note 298

Beyond the Book 298

Related Readings 299

Bibliography 299

CHAPTER 14   Conflicting Visions: 1867–1914 302

The Provincial-Rights Movement in Ontario 303

Protest in Atlantic Canada 304

Discontent in the North West 305

  Where Historians Disagree: The Causes of the North-West Rebellion of 1885 306

Rising French-Canadian Nationalism 310

Cultural and Religious Feuds 311

Continentalism 314

Imperialism 315

The South African War 316

Growing French-Canadian Nationalism 317

Relations with the United States 318

The Naval Crisis 319

Note 321

Beyond the Book 321

Related Readings 321

Bibliography 322

CHAPTER 15   Urban and Industrial Canada 324

Canada's Economic Expansion 325

  Community Portrait: The T. Eaton Company: A Community Store 327

Economic Development in the East and West 329

Industrialization in Central Canada 330

The Uniqueness of Quebec's Industrial Development 331

  Where Historians Disagree: Industrial Growth in Quebec 332

The Impact of Industrialization 334

Urbanization 335

Working in the New Industrial Economy 337

Charitable and Social Institutions for the Working Class 339

Unions 339

Note 343

Beyond the Book 343

Related Readings 343
Bibliography 343

CHAPTER 16   Social Reform and Culture: 1867–1914 346

Social Gospel and Catholic Social Action 347
Educational Reformers 349
The Urban Reform Movement 350
Wilderness and Wildlife Conservation 350
Women and Social Reform 351
   Where Historians Disagree: Women and Reform 352
The Prohibition Movement 355
Canadian Culture 356
The Promotion of Canadian Culture 360
Popular Culture 361
Sport 362
Middle-Class Culture 363
Working-Class Culture 363
Aboriginal Culture 363
   Community Portrait: The Huron Community of Wendake 364
Notes 366
Beyond the Book 366
Related Readings 367
Bibliography 367

PART FIVE   The Impact of Two World Wars and the Great Depression, 1914–1945

Introduction 371

CHAPTER 17   Canada in the Great War 372

Canada Joins the War Effort 373
A "White Man's War" 375
The Nature of the Great War 376
The Interventionist State 377
Women and the War 378
Fighting on the Battlefields of Europe 378
"Invite Us to Your Councils" 380
Recruitment 380
National Disunity 380
The Conscription Crisis 382
Union Government and the Election of 1917 382
The War and Social Reform 383
Final Year of the War 384
   Community Portrait: The Canadian Corps: A Community of Soldiers 385
Demobilization 386

Notes 388
Beyond the Book 388
Related Readings . . . . , , , , , , , , , , , ... 389
Bibliography 389

CHAPTER 18   The Interwar Years 392
The Winnipeg General Strike 393
   Where Historians Disagree: The Winnipeg General Strike 394
New Postwar Political Leaders 397
Regional Protest 397
Advances to Nationhood 398
From Colony to Nation 399
The Economics of Adjustment 399
A Revolution in Transportation and Communication 400
Disillusionment and the Decline of Reform 400
Women in the 1920s 401
The Aboriginal Peoples 401
Labour in the 1920s 402
Cultural Developments 402
Popular Culture 403
Sports 404
The Advent of the Great Depression 404
The R.B. Bennett Government's Response to the Depression 405
Third Parties 407
Communists and Fascists 408
Labour in the Great Depression 408
Women in the 1930s 409
Mackenzie King's Government's Response to the Depression 410
Religion 411
Culture in the 1930s 411
Sport 412
Note 414
Beyond the Book 414
Bibliography 415

CHAPTER 19   Canada in World War II 418
Neutrality and Appeasement in the 1930s 419
Canada and the War against the Axis 420
   A Historical Portrait: Sir Frederick Banting and Pilot Joseph Mackey 421
Canadian–American Wartime Relations 421
The Wartime Economy 422
Women and the War Effort 423
The War and National Unity 424
French Canada and the War 426

Canada Intensifies Its War Effort 427
   Where Historians Disagree: Canadian Participation in the Land War
   in Northwestern Europe 429
The State's New Role 432
Federal–Provincial Relations: Toward Federal Supremacy 434
The Provinces in the War Years 434
Toward a New Internationalism 436
Notes 438
Beyond the Book 438
Related Readings 439
Bibliography 439

PART SIX   Modern Canada, 1945 to the Present

Introduction 443

CHAPTER 20   Toward a More Affluent Society: 1945–1960 444

Economic Nirvana in Canada? 445
   A Historical Portrait: Betty, Ruby, and the Others 447
Prosperity and Trade 449
A Government of Efficient Administrators 450
The Golden Age of Canadian Diplomacy 452
Yearning for Political Change 454
Labour Relations in Prosperous Times 455
The Status of Women 456
   Where Historians Disagree: Women and Unions in Postwar Canada 457
Higher Education 459
Culture: Canadian versus American 459
Notes 463
Beyond the Book 463
Related Readings 464
Bibliography 464

CHAPTER 21   Protest and Reform: The 1960s 466

Traditional Churches Questioned 467
Youth Protest 467
   A Historical Portrait: The Student Radicals at Sir George Williams University 470
A Cultural Renaissance 474
The Diefenbaker Government (1957–1963) 477
The Pearson Years (1963–1968) 479
A Changing Economy 482
Unequal Growth 482
Beginning of the Trudeau Era 485
The Canadian Centennial, 1967 487
Notes 488

Beyond the Book 488
Related Readings 489
Bibliography 489

CHAPTER 22   Aboriginal Canada: World War II to the Present . . . 492
The Yale–Toronto Conference on the North American Indian 493
The Aboriginal Peoples in Wartime 494
The Aboriginal Peoples of the North 495
A New Postwar Attitude toward the Aboriginal Peoples 495
From the "White Paper" of 1969 to the Constitution of 1982 497
First Nations Political Demands from the 1980s to the Present 499
The Royal Commission on Aboriginal Peoples 500
   Where Historians Disagree: The Debate over Indian Residential Schools, 1879–1986 . . . 501
Aboriginal Rights 503
Economic and Social Issues for Aboriginal Canada since the 1980s 505
The Métis, the Inuit, and the Federal Government 507
The Aboriginal North since the 1970s 508
Notes 511
Beyond the Book 511
Related Readings 512
Bibliography 512

CHAPTER 23   The Making of Modern Quebec 514
Quebec after World War II 515
The Quiet Revolution 517
Return of the Union Nationale to Power 518
The Debate over Language 519
A Polarized Quebec 520
The Growth of Nationalism 521
Quebec under the Parti Québécois 522
   Where Social Scientists Disagree: The Origins and Effects of Quebec's Language Legislation . 522
The 1980s: The Wheel Turns 524
Constitutional Impasse 526
Contemporary Politics 528
Language and Culture in Quebec Today 529
   A Historical Portrait: Céline Dion and the Global Village 531
The Environment 532
Notes 534
Beyond the Book 534
Related Readings 535
Bibliography 535

CHAPTER 24   Immigration and Multiculturalism 536
Postwar European Immigration, 1945–1957 537
   A Historical Portrait: The Immigrant Experience 538

Postwar Federal Immigration Policy 539
Canadian Responses to Postwar Immigration 540
An Evaluation of Postwar Immigration Policy 541
The Immigrant Experience in the 1960s and 1970s 542
Immigration in Recent Years 543
Reactions to Immigration 547
Multiculturalism 549
   Where Social Scientists Disagree: Evaluating Canada's Multicultural Policy 550
The Impact of Immigration 552
Notes 555
Beyond the Book 555
Related Readings 556
Bibliography 556

CHAPTER 25   Canada in the 1970s and 1980s: Constitution
             and Free Trade 558
The Trudeau Government 559
Change within Western Canada 560
Conservative Interlude 562
National Energy Program 562
The Constitution of 1982 563
The Progressive Conservatives in Power 565
The Great Free-Trade Debate 567
   Where Social Scientists Disagree: The Debate over Free Trade 568
Demography 569
The Changing Role of Women 571
Challenges for Labour 572
Cultural Concerns 572
New Challenges 576
The Environment 576
Notes 579
Beyond the Book 579
Related Readings 580
Bibliography 580

CHAPTER 26   Contemporary Canada 582
The Collapse of Consensus 583
The Chrétien Government 585
Canada and International Developments 587
Regional Imbalances 589
Population 591
An Aging Population 591
Health Care 592
Poverty 593
Gays and Lesbians 593

Women in the Workforce 594
Challenges for Labour 594
Spectator Sports . . . . , . . . 595
Cultural Development 595
   Community Portrait: Clayoquot Sound and the Environmental Movement:
   The "War in the Woods" 597
The Environment 599
Notes 604
Beyond the Book 604
Related Readings 604
Bibliography 605

Appendix: Canadian Prime Ministers since Confederation 607
Index 609

List of Maps

Canada between approximately 80 000 and 20 000 years ago 4

Canada about 12 000 years ago 4

Canada today 5

Aboriginal language families within the boundaries of present-day Canada 8

Aboriginal culture areas 9

Part of Mercator's Map, 1569 29

The St. Lawrence lowlands around 1600 33

Champlain's expeditions, 1604–1615 36

European beachheads in America, 1650 40

The St. Lawrence lowlands around 1640 42

Acadia in the mid-eighteenth century 65

European knowledge of northeastern North America in 1670 76

Declared French and English spheres of interest after the Treaty of Utrecht, 1713 81

The struggle for a continent: English and French fortifications, 1713–1758 85

Siege of Quebec, 1759 86

The American invasion of Canada, 1775–1776 101

The British colonies in North America, 1791 102

The Quebec boundary before and after the Quebec Act, 1774 106

Lower Canada during the Rebellions of 1837–1838 114

Upper Canada about 1800 124

Principal engagements in the War of 1812 127

Upper Canada in the early nineteenth century 129

Canadian railways and canals before Confederation 152

The Maritimes in the late eighteenth century 170

Loyalist settlement in the Maritimes before 1800 175

Prince Edward Island's proprietors 178

The Maritime economy in the mid-nineteenth century 180

The Maritimes in the mid-nineteenth century 185

The Anglo–American boundary dispute, settled by the Webster–Ashburton
Treaty in 1842 186

Early Newfoundland 188

Non-Aboriginals' knowledge of northern North America in 1795 199

Lord Selkirk's Grant 203

Non-Aboriginals' knowledge of northern North America in 1870 208

The British–American boundary settlement of 1818 219

Vancouver Island and British Columbia in the 1850s and 1860s. 223

Chief areas of settlement in Canada, 1867 250

Indian treaty areas, 1850–1930. 268

Canada's territorial evolution from a nation of four provinces (1867), to five (1870),
to seven (1873), and to nine (1905) 272–273

The original surveyed route and the final route of the CPR 288

Contested area in boundary between Ontario and Manitoba in 1882 304

Military operations in the North-West Rebellion, 1885. 308

The Alaska boundary dispute, 1903. 319

Canada at war, 1914–1917 376

Status of several northern land claims in 2000 509

Canada's francophone population, 2006 530

Distribution of Canada's population by province and territory, 2006 592

Preface

The word *history* refers to both the events of the past and the historian's study of those past events. Historians are well aware of how our understanding of the past changes and consequently what are considered "truths" today may well be questioned and challenged in the future. This explains why history is continually rewritten. This text contains the latest research on past events by specialists in the field. At the same time, we have retained earlier perspectives in the belief that the truth about the past is cumulative, later works building on the knowledge of earlier studies. In the Bibliography at the end of each chapter, we note the earlier major works as well as more current studies on the topics discussed.

Good history seeks a new perspective on a past event in hopes of better understanding its nature and significance. Thus historians challenge other historians' work, not just for the sake of argument but also on the belief that debate allows for a more accurate understanding of the past. In this textbook, "Where Historians Disagree" boxes highlight the major differing interpretations of some important events or movements in Canada's past.

Interpretations of past events change, as does the emphasis on what type of history should be studied. In the early accounts, historians emphasized political events and the actions of the major political figures on the assumption that politicians—usually "white" males—were the major shapers of Canada's history. More recently, social historians, interested in the role that the "average Canadian" played in our past, have challenged that assumption. A variety of new approaches to history, including women's, ethnic, Aboriginal, working-class, intellectual, military, and cultural history, now stand beside political history. We have also been conscious of the need to include the historical development and contribution of all groups in Canada's past—Aboriginal peoples, French-speaking and English-speaking Canadians, recent immigrants, women, and minority groups—realizing that together they make up our rich past.

In addition, historians continue to debate to what extent individuals are key actors in history, and in what way groups or society as a whole are the major forces. In the text, we have included boxes entitled "Historical Portrait" on famous and not-so-famous individuals in Canada's history as well as inserts on groups entitled "Community Portrait."

Historians are also aware of sequencing in history: that events follow in logical order of cause and effect. While history is much more than the memorization of dates and facts, these constitute the building blocks from which history is constructed. With this in mind, time lines appear at the beginning of each chapter highlighting the major events discussed by year to give a sense of chronology.

Professional historians construct their historical accounts predominantly on primary as opposed to secondary sources. *Primary sources* generally comprise evidence contemporary with the event or issue under study. *Secondary sources* are those written after the event or issue, very often by other historians. Primary sources are of two types: written and non-written. Written sources may be published or unpublished. Printed sources include published books, articles, government documents, census reports, memoirs, literature, and newspapers. Unpublished sources range from personal papers to diaries to church and other manuscript records. Historians use non-written sources in areas of history for which written sources are scarce or nonexistent. In the case of Aboriginal history, for example, oral accounts relayed from generation to generation allow access to the perspective of Aboriginal Canadians. Oral interviews are also popular in women's, working-class, and immigration history, for which written accounts are often limited. In some areas of social history, material artifacts can complement written sources. Some of the better known primary sources for chapter topics are available online, and these are listed in a "Beyond the Book" section at the end of each chapter.

Most of all, history should be enjoyable to read, bringing the past to life. History reaches out to a wide public that continues to have a fascination with what happened in the past. It also sheds light on present developments by putting current issues in a historical perspective. In this new edition, a subsection "Films & Novels" in each "Beyond the Book" identifies films and novels relevant to topics in the chapter. We also include a "Related Readings" section in almost every chapter that identifies useful articles in *Viewpoints: Readings in Canadian History*, edited by R. Douglas Francis and Donald B. Smith.

In conclusion, we have identified *diversity* as the organizing theme of this text. We have consciously used titles for our textbooks on Canada's history that are plural—*Origins, Destinies*, and *Journeys*—to point up the fact that there is no one dominant narrative or vision in the past. Rather, Canada's history has been made up of a host of people who have their own stories and who have in their own way contributed to that history. It is this plurality and diversity that together shape Canada's past and help explain Canada's multicultural society of today.

R. Douglas Francis
Richard Jones
Donald B. Smith

Acknowledgements

The authors wish to acknowledge the many Canadian historians who assisted them in the preparation of the six editions of *Origins: Canadian History to Confederation* and *Destinies: Canadian History since Confederation*, from which material for *Journeys: A History of Canada* has been taken. As well, we want to thank Ernest Levos, Canadian University College; Robynne Rogers Healey, Trinity Western University; Jeff Keshen, University of Ottawa; Ross Fair, Ryerson University; Lynn Berry, Thomson Rivers University; and Sarah Glassford and Jarett Henderson, both of York University, who reviewed the first edition of *Journeys* and offered helpful suggestions.

At Nelson, we benefited enormously from a dedicated and enthusiastic editorial team. In particular we wish to thank Laura Macleod, Linda Sparks, Imoinda Romain, and copy editor Rodney Rawlings. It was a pleasure to work with each of them. We also wish to thank our wives, Barbara Grant, Lilianne Plamondon, and Nancy Townshend, for their constant support throughout the writing of our textbooks, begun over a quarter of a century ago.

Journeys

A History of Canada

SECOND EDITION

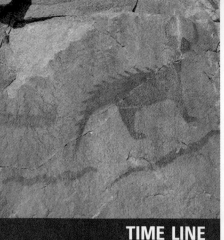

Chapter One

THE FIRST PEOPLES

70 000–14 000 years ago	A land bridge between North America and Siberia, known as Beringia, exists
c. 15 000 years ago	The glaciers begin to melt and to retreat
c. 12 000 years ago	A human settlement exists in the southernmost portion of the Americas, Monte Verde, Chile
10 000 years ago	Humans live throughout large sections of what is now Canada
5000 years ago	The glacial ice recedes to approximately its present northern position, and the climate becomes similar to today's
3500–2000 years ago	Civilizations develop in Mexico, Central America, and Peru
A.D. 1–500	Mound Builders' culture arises in Ohio
c. 500	The First Nations of southern Ontario begin to grow corn, resulting in the development of societies based on agriculture
c. 700–1000	Rise of Mississippian culture in the Mississippi valley
c. 1500	A variety of peoples reside within what is now Canada, with more than 50 languages, belonging to eleven separate linguistic families (one of these is Eskimo-Aleut, a family that includes Inuit, and ten First Nations language families)
c. 1730	The Plains people on what is now the Canadian prairies acquire the horse

The First Nations are the descendants of the original human inhabitants of the Americas. By international law they are the discoverers and sovereigns of its land. Many First Nations elders accept as a spiritual truth—one revealed in sacred stories, dreams, and visions—that their ancestors originated in the Americas. Oral traditions often place the Indigenous groups in their communities from the "beginning of time." Most archaeologists take another approach. They contend that early humans migrated to the Americas across the land bridge that then spanned the Bering Strait. The archaeologists disagree, however, as to when this migration first occurred, although consensus exists that the original inhabitants of North America lived on this continent at least 12 000 years before the Europeans' arrival. Dr. Eldon Yellowhorn, an archaeologist and a member of the Piikani First Nation in southern Alberta, welcomes the insights the scientific approach contributes: "A scientific perspective of antiquity may challenge traditional interpretations, but its also opens exciting possibilities for imagining the past."[1]

Origin of the First Peoples of North America

Spirituality and science are two different areas of discourse. Science concerns itself with the testing of information obtained from the observable natural world. The discussion that follows lies within the scientists' universe of discourse. For an exploration of explanations derived from legendary revelation readers must turn to studies that discourse on the spiritual universe.

On the basis of the weight of geological, biological, and archaeological evidence, archaeologists, some of whom are members of contemporary First Nations, argue that humans did not evolve independently in the Americas but migrated from Siberia.[2] A few archaeologists propose that other migrations occurred by sea, principally to South America from across the Pacific.

Archaeologists believe that *Homo habilis*, the first direct ancestor of modern-day human beings, appeared nearly 2 million years ago in Africa. A more advanced form, *Homo erectus*, followed, approximately 1.5 million years ago, in Asia, Africa, and Europe. About 100 000 years ago, *Homo sapiens neanderthalensis*, or Neanderthal man, emerged. As archaeologist Peter L. Storck writes: "Since the early twentieth century there has been little doubt in anthropological circles that the Americas were populated from Asia."[3] Physical evidence of hominid bones, dating back up to 40 000 years, have been found in Africa, Asia, and Europe, but not in the Americas. Physical and genetic data link Aboriginal peoples in the Americas to Asian populations. Thus, archaeologists conclude that the human species originated outside the Americas.

Most archaeologists believe that the early inhabitants of North America crossed from Siberia during the last Ice Age, when sea levels dropped and the continental shelf became exposed. This land bridge, known as Beringia, existed from 70 000 to 14 000 years ago. At one point, the expanse of open grassland and tundra was more than 2000 km wide. Beringia served as a highway for animals passing back and forth between Asia and the Americas. To date no evidence has been found of an ice-free corridor that may have existed along the eastern slope of the Rocky Mountains, thus providing the animals—and, later, humans—with a pathway southward. But an ice-free coastal corridor may have been present. Thus, human hunters, after crossing Beringia, may have travelled by water between the unglaciated pockets of land. Whether by foot or boat or a combination of the two, humans gradually advanced southward throughout North, Central, and South America, eventually crossing more than 15 000 km from Alaska to Patagonia, at the tip of South America. The possibility of human migration across the South Pacific from Polynesia to South America is regarded as most unlikely due to unfavourable ocean current and wind patterns, as well as an absence of adjacent islands. Again the obvious probability remains that humans entered the Americas from northeastern Siberia to Alaska. Canada's high Arctic was the last region to be populated, roughly 4000 years ago, as the ice retreated.

Canada between approximately 80 000 and 20 000 years ago. At this time, almost all of Canada was buried beneath a kilometre or more of glacial ice. A large ice-free area known as the Bering Land Bridge connected Siberia and Alaska. Animals and human hunters moved between the Old World and the New across this arctic landscape.

Map of Bering Land Bridge Photo © Canadian Museum of Civilization, Francis Back Collection, photo Harry Foster, 1989, image S98-10739

Canada about 12 000 years ago. At this time, the rapidly retreating glaciers were fringed by large lakes of glacial meltwater. The ancient beaches of some of these lakes reveal the remains of camps occupied by First Nations peoples who moved north to occupy the land that is now Canada.

Map of North America Photo © Canadian Museum of Civilization, Francis Back Collection, photo Harry Foster, 1989, image S98-10741

Archaeological Hypotheses

Scientists disagree as to when the migration from Siberia occurred. Supporters of the more controversial claims contend that humans possibly entered the Americas as early as approximately 100 000 years ago, although no incontrovertible evidence of such an early arrival exists. Most archaeologists place the earliest migration in a much more recent time span. They refer to sites, such as that at Monte Verde in south-central Chile, that show evidence of human occupation more than 12 500 years ago. (This, of course, indicates a human occupation of North America at least several thousand years earlier, if one accepts the northern migration route.) Most archaeologists accept as evidence only those artifacts found in sealed deposits with organic matter that can be radiocarbon-dated. In addition, they require evidence of distinctively styled artifacts. One example is the "fluted point," a stone projectile point with one or more flutes, or hollowed-out channels, that allowed for the attachment of the point to a wooden or bone shaft.

It has also been suggested that peoples who had adapted to a maritime way of life in the southern fringes of Beringia might have later travelled southward along ice-free pockets of land that opened up along the Pacific coast from what is now Alaska to Washington State.

By the "conservative" criteria, there are four Canadian sites—at Debert, Nova Scotia; at Vermilion Lakes, Banff National Park; at Charlie Lake Cave, north of Fort St. John, British Columbia; and Wally's Beach (St. Mary's Reservoir) in southwestern Alberta— that confirm the presence of humans in Canada at least 10 000 years ago.

Shortly before the period of human occupation in what is now Canada began, a drastic change in climate had occurred in the northern hemisphere. For reasons still not fully understood, the great ice sheets (more than 3 km thick) that once covered 97 percent of Canada began to melt. The runoff raised the sea level, causing the Beringian Plain to disappear and the Bering Strait to form.

The absence of ice sheets in formerly glaciated territories meant that wind and rainfall patterns shifted. Forests replaced grasslands, and deserts developed. Some animals now became extinct, especially large grazing animals such as mammoths (giant elephants), American camels, and a race of very large bison that foraged on the grasslands.

Civilizations of the Americas

About 5000 years ago, the ice receded to approximately its present northern position and the climate became similar to today's. The Bering Strait attained its present width of approximately 80 km, and land animals could no longer cross between Siberia and Alaska. People still made that journey, but no longer from Asia's inland centres; they were sea-mammal hunters and fishers who traded across the strait. The Indigenous peoples grew largely as a result of natural population increase, rather than migration. The study of their cultures and history is one of constant change over time as new technologies arrived, as the climate changed, and as subsistence strategies were altered.

From 3500 to 2000 years ago, the First Nations population of the Americas underwent major economic and social developments. The peak of technological and social complexity was achieved in present-day Mexico, Central America, and the Andes of Peru, where permanent communities had the highest population densities on the two continents. In central and southern Mexico, a series of great classical civilizations developed. The dominant one, the Aztec, emerged around 800 years ago. Agriculture (corn, beans, and squash) and rich sea resources formed the basis of these civilizations. Centres with temples and other large structures such as plazas, chiefs' houses, and highways, all constructed with carved and painted stone, appeared as well.

These civilizations developed without the aid of Europe's domesticated animals—horses, oxen, and donkeys. They had discovered the wheel (wheeled toys have been found in various parts of Mexico), but without animals for transport (other than the dog and, in the Andes, the llama) they had no use for it. They also lacked sufficient supplies of usable copper and tin, to allow for the replacement of stone tools. The Peruvians made a few tools from metal that had washed down in the streams, but in Mexico and Central America only stone tools existed.

Canada today.

Map of Canada Today Photo © Canadian Museum of Civilization, Francis Back Collection, photo Harry Foster, 1989, image S98-107342

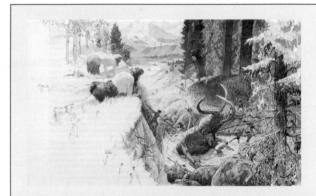

Canadian artist Franklin Arbuckle (1909–2001) drew this sketch of the hunt of a mammoth, used as an illustration in Selwyn Dewdney and Franklin Arbuckle, They Shared to Survive: The Native Peoples of Canada *(Toronto: Macmillan, 1975), p. 6.*

Despite the absence of the wheel and of metal tools, the Indigenous peoples of the Americas became well advanced in science and arts. The Maya in Central America, whose civilization flourished between 1700 and 1100 years ago, developed a sophisticated system of mathematics, applying the concept of zero 500 years before the Hindus did. The Maya, being knowledgeable about astronomy, outlined a 365-day annual calendar and plotted the cycle of the planet Venus. They calculated eclipses and recorded their calculations in a writing system that was both pictographic and phonetic. In the Andes, the Incas between 800 and 500 years ago developed irrigation systems, built bridges and roads, erected stone walls using enormous rocks cut to fit so tightly that a knife blade could not be pushed between two blocks, and did metalwork of the highest quality, in gold and silver. First Nations farmers developed more than 100 species of plants that are routinely farmed today, including two of the world's basic food crops: corn (maize) and potatoes (the other two are wheat and rice).

The Mound Builders

About 2000 years ago, immediately south of the Great Lakes, farming and a sedentary way of life replaced gathering and hunting in the Ohio and later the Mississippi valleys. The "Mound Builders" of the Ohio River valley (the Hopewell culture) constructed gigantic sculptured earthworks—some nearly 25 m high—in geometric designs, sometimes in the shape of humans, birds, or serpents.

Archaeologists have located thousands of mounds used as burial sites and have excavated several earthen-walled enclosures, including one fortification with a circumference of more than 5 km, enclosing the equivalent of 50 modern city blocks. The Ohio peoples developed, as did other groups, an extensive trading network. Archaeologists have found, among the artifacts in the burial mounds, large ceremonial blades chipped from obsidian (a volcanic glass) from deposits in what is now Yellowstone National Park in Wyoming; embossed breastplates, ornaments, and weapons made from copper nuggets from the Great Lakes; decorative objects cut from mica sheets from the southern Appalachians; and ornaments made from shells and shark and alligator teeth from the Gulf of Mexico.

The Mound Builders' culture evolved slowly, reaching its peak roughly 2000 years ago. The Ohio mounds may have influenced the building of the Serpent burial mounds on a point overlooking Rice Lake, near present-day Peterborough, Ontario. From approximately 1900 to 1700 years ago, the local people built the earthworks, 400 m long, 15 m across, and rising half a metre to a metre above the surface. Excavation has revealed numerous burials, with objects from afar— copper from western Lake Superior, silver from deposits in northern Ontario, and conch shell from the Gulf of Mexico. These findings confirm how extensive trading networks were.

About 1500 years ago the Ohio Mound Builders' culture declined, perhaps as a result of attacks by other nations or of severe changes in climate that undermined agriculture. A similar culture farther west, around present-day St. Louis, also based on agriculture, replaced that of the Mound Builders. It extended over most of the Mississippi watershed, from Wisconsin to Louisiana and from Oklahoma to Tennessee. The influence of the trading centre of Cahokia extended throughout most of North America. In its day it was the greatest settlement north of Mexico. From about 1300 to 800 years ago this Mississippian culture influenced the Aboriginal nations to the east. Indeed, its example led the Iroquoian-speaking peoples of the lower Great Lakes and the St. Lawrence valley to adopt agricultural techniques similar to those of the Mound Builders and the Mississippians.

Population Growth

Agriculture could support a larger population than hunting and gathering. The cultivation of as little as 1 percent of the land, in fact, could greatly increase the food supply. Recent estimates of the Aboriginal population of the Americas in the mid-fifteenth century indicate numbers as high as 100 million people, or approximately one-sixth of the human race at that time. The population north of Mexico may have reached 10 million before European contact. Aboriginal populations reached such numbers because they lived in a relatively disease-free zone. The Iroquoians, for instance, in present-day southern Ontario and southwestern Quebec, domesticated high-yield cereals and tubers, which allowed them to feed a large population. Approximately half a million people (the most widely accepted estimate) lived within the boundaries of present-day Canada.

The Fortress of Cahokia. Reconstitution by William R. Iseminger. Cahokia Mounds State Historic Site, Illinois.

Cahokia Mounds State Historic Site, painting by William R. Iseminger.

Roughly half of them lived along the Pacific coast, with its abundant and easily available resources, and in present-day southern Ontario and Quebec, where the Iroquoians practised farming.

The Europeans reduced the Indigenous populations dramatically by unintentionally exposing them to diseases new to the Americas. The Aboriginal population lacked defences against such contagious diseases as smallpox and measles. Environmental historian Alfred Crosby has written that "the initial appearance of these diseases is as certain to have set off deadly epidemics as dropping lighted matches into tinder is certain to cause fires."[4] Aboriginal healers had never before encountered these epidemic diseases. They could not combat them, nor could the Europeans, until the twentieth century—long after the First Nation population had been repeatedly devastated. After European contact, death rates in some areas of the Americas reached as high as 90–95 percent. By the early twentieth century, the entire First Nations population in Canada and the United States had been reduced to less than 1 million, or one-tenth of the estimated population at the time of European contact. Historian Olive P. Dickason has noted that in the seventeenth century, "the lands that appeared 'vacant' to the new arrivals were either hunting areas or else had been recently depopulated because of introduced epidemics."[5]

Classifying the First Nations

The First Nations population has been classified according to three distinct categories: linguistic, national, and cultural. None is satisfactory. A linguistic division in Canada reveals eleven separate indigenous language families. One is Eskimo-Aleut, the language spoken by the Inuit; the other ten are First Nations linguistic groups. Seven of them (Salishan, Tsimshian, Haidan, Wakashan, Tlingit, Kutenaian, and Athapaskan) are found in British Columbia. The Siouan speakers are found on the prairies and in the foothills of the Rockies. The Iroquoian speakers live in eastern Canada. The Algonquian (or Algonkian) linguistic family, the largest group, extends from the Atlantic coast to the Rockies. The Athapaskan language group can be found throughout the Yukon and the Northwest Territories and the northern sections of the four western provinces. As nearly as can be determined, the First Nations spoke about 50 different languages.

This linguistic classification unfortunately leads to the linking of widely disparate groups that had little in common except language. The language of one might differ as much from another as English from German or Portuguese from Romanian. Within the same linguistic family, groups often had different ways of life. The Mi'kmaq of the Maritimes and the Blackfoot of the Prairies, for instance, although separated by 4000 km, are joined in the Algonquian linguistic family. But they lived entirely different lives, totally unaware of each other's existence. Conversely, the Haidas of the Queen Charlotte Islands culturally resembled their mainland neighbours, the Tsimshians, in everything except their completely unrelated language.

To classify Canada's original inhabitants by political categories also poses problems. Nations—that is, groups of people bound by a common culture and language and acting as a unit in relations with their neighbours—certainly existed. But among some groups, the ties between the various bands were not strong. The more remote bands diverged considerably in dialect and, in some cases, had so thoroughly assimilated the customs of alien peoples around them that they lost all sense of political unity with their distant relatives.

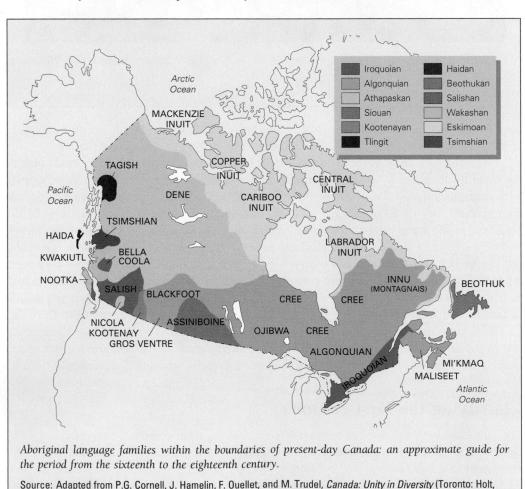

Aboriginal language families within the boundaries of present-day Canada: an approximate guide for the period from the sixteenth to the eighteenth century.

Source: Adapted from P.G. Cornell, J. Hamelin, F. Ouellet, and M. Trudel, *Canada: Unity in Diversity* (Toronto: Holt, Rinehart and Winston, 1967), p. 14.

Aboriginal Culture Areas

A better classification of Aboriginal North Americans is that by cultural areas because it recognizes how climate and regional resources influence the development of societies and technologies. According to this classification, Indigenous societies in Canada consisted of six culture areas: Northwest Coast, Plateau, Plains, Subarctic, Arctic, and Northeast. The cultural areas tend to coincide with ecological zones. None of these cultural areas stopped at what is now the Canada–U.S. border. What follows is a short overview of the six culture areas in what is now Canada, at approximately the eve of contact with the European newcomers over 500 years ago.

Aboriginal culture areas. Rather than being an authoritative representation of actual territories at any one time, this map should be regarded as a rough guide to contiguous groups that had or have similar cultures and histories.

Source: Based on *Handbook of North American Indians*, vol. 4, *History of Indian–White Relations* (Washington: Smithsonian Institution, 1988).

Gradually each band fitted itself to a culture area. They constantly adapted to new environmental conditions, especially climate change. The First Nations developed extensive trading networks. Warfare predated the European arrival, and they had elaborated codes of diplomacy. The peoples of northern North America belonged to a larger world than their own communities. The peoples of Aboriginal Canada were not isolated, but part of a hemisphere-wide civilization. Over time, Indigenous societies dynamically changed. As archaeologist Robert McGhee has written: "Native North American cultures were not fixed in ancient traditions, any more than were those of Old World peoples, and were remarkably flexible to change in response to new ideas or circumstances."[6]

The Northwest Coast

Archaeologists believe that the ancestors of the Aboriginal peoples of the Pacific coast had resided there for thousands of years before European contact. The linguistic complexity of the coastal region, with its nineteen distinct languages, suggests that it is an "old area," and thus the most likely starting point for migrations of successive groups to the east and south.

Yet, despite their different histories, the Northwest Coast peoples' ways of life resembled each others in many aspects. Evidence exists of wide-scale adaptation to a similar environment. All along the coast, groups shared knowledge and techniques. About 2500 to 1500 years ago, evidence exists that ranked societies had emerged, with ruling classes who maintained their position through lavish displays of their riches. Beginning about 1500 years ago Northwest Coast peoples took on increased cultural complexity. Artistic traditions became further elaborated. Warfare became common, with competition over important trade routes.

On the eve of European contact in the mid-eighteenth century, the coastal inhabitants relied on the abundant fish for their livelihood: herring, smelt, oolichan (candle-fish), halibut, and several species of cod. Salmon, which they speared, netted, and trapped in large quantities, then sun-dried or smoked, became their basic, year-round staple. In addition, they hunted sea mammals, such as whales, seals, sea lions, porpoises, and sea otters. Such an abundant food supply made the Pacific coast region the most densely populated area in Canada.

The Northwest Coast peoples used the giant cedars and firs of the coastal rain forest to build houses and to make dugout canoes and woodwork, such as carved boxes, bowls, dishes, and ladles. They lived the year round in villages located in sheltered island coves or on channels near the mouths of rivers. Each village was self-contained; but on occasion, particularly in times of war, several settlements joined together. Their communal activities included the *potlatch*, a large ceremonial feast, which they used to mourn the dead, to celebrate the investiture of new chiefs, or to mark the completion of a new house.

A hierarchical social structure based on wealth and heredity evolved with chiefs, nobles, and commoners. Social grading existed within each class. Below the commoners were slaves, who in some villages apparently made up a third of the population. Historian Olive P. Dickason observed that slaves "were usually prisoners of war, but sometimes individuals who had lost status

Canadian artist Franklin Arbuckle (1909–2001) drew this sketch of Pacific coast whale hunters, used as an illustration in Selwyn Dewdney and Franklin Arbuckle, They Shared to Survive: The Native Peoples of Canada *(Toronto: Macmillan, 1975), p. 132.*

because of debt; one could also be born into slavery, one of the few regions in North America where this happened. In any event, slaves had no rights of any kind and could be put to death at the will of their masters."[7]

The Plateau

The Plateau culture area, the smallest of the six regions, takes in the high plateau region between the Coast Range and the Rocky Mountains in the south-central interior of British Columbia. It extends southward through western Montana, Idaho, and eastern Washington and Oregon. The Canadian portion of the Plateau area is a region noted for its hot, dry summers and cold winters. In Canada the Plateau cultural area includes the Kutenai (or Kootenay) in the east, the Interior Salish in the west, and the Athapaskan-speaking groups to the north. These nations depended on salmon, and thus their populations were concentrated downriver, where the fish were most abundant. Their Northwest Coast neighbours influenced them greatly.

Over 8000 years ago the Plateau people took more sedentary ways, living in village sites. The western Plateau became a strategic trading area and the population, due to the major salmon runs, much denser than in the eastern Plateau. The villages along the Fraser River appear to have reached their greatest size about 2000 to 1000 years ago. In the eastern Plateau, after the arrival of the horse over 250 years ago, the resident Kootenay (Ktunaxa) had more contact with the Plains people. In dress, customs, and religion, the most easternly Plateau people came to resemble, in many ways, those on the Plains.

The Plains

East of the Plateau region lies the Plains (or Great Plains) culture area, the broad central region of North America west of the Mississippi and Red River valleys and east of the Rockies. The open grasslands, with tall grass in the east and short grass in the west, extend on a north–south axis from northern Alberta and Saskatchewan and western Manitoba to Texas. The region has a continental climate—hot, dry summers and cold winters.

Throughout the buffalo era, the northwestern Plains attracted Aboriginal communities from all directions. Knowledgeable and experienced, the First Nations pursued the vast herds. Often several local bands belonging to different First Nations formed a single encampment. Mixing, merging, and amalgamation were common. Relations between Indigenous communities spanned the spectrum from peaceful to hostile.

In the eighteenth century, First Nations belonging to three linguistic families lived on the Canadian Plains: the Algonquian, the Athapaskan, and the Siouan. As the Plains became a crossroads for many First Nations, a sign language developed to allow people to communicate. These Plains peoples specialized in the communal hunt of the buffalo, or bison, an animal that was central to their way of life. They ate its flesh and used the hide to make teepee covers, clothing, and robes. From the thick hide of the buffalo's neck they made shields, from the horns they fashioned spoons and drinking cups, and from the sinew they created thread and bow string. On the treeless Great Plains, dried buffalo dung provided fuel.

The Plains people hunted the buffalo on foot in small nomadic bands of roughly 50 to 100 people. Finding the buffalo required a knowledge of their migratory habits. Large herds existed in abundance, but one could go for days or weeks without seeing a single animal. Hunting also required considerable skill in approaching the animals because neither the lance nor the bow was effective against them except at close range. Buffalo also could run at speeds of over 50 km per hour, making it impossible for hunters on foot to run them down.

One of the most dramatic of the representations at the Agawa Pictograph Site is that of Mishipeshu, the great water lynx, from the Agawa pictograph site in Lake Superior Provincial Park, Ontario.

Courtesy of Lake Superior Provincial Park.

Over the millennia, the Plains people developed increasingly effective subsistence strategies. The drive became the best way of harvesting the herds. The Plains peoples lured the buffalo into corrals or pounds of poles and brush in small valleys where they could ambush them. Where the land was uneven, as in the foothills to the west, the ambush frequently took the form of a jump, where the hunters stampeded the animals over a cliff or steep cutbank.

One such location is Head-Smashed-In Buffalo Jump, a UNESCO World Heritage Site in the Oldman River valley, 130 km south of Calgary in southwestern Alberta. Used for at least 6000 and possibly for 9000 years, it is one of the oldest, largest, and best-preserved of all the buffalo jumps in North America. Evidence remains of several of the drive paths, marked by rock piles about a metre in diameter and a third of a metre high, stretching back, in one case, as far as 8 km from the cliff.

The arrival of the horse on the northern prairie in the early eighteenth century provides perhaps the most dramatic example of the ability of Plains people to adapt to new situations, to take advantage of new opportunities. The horse originally existed in the Americas, but then it disappeared, until reintroduced by the Spaniards into Mexico in the sixteenth century. Quickly the horse replaced the dog as the chief transporter of goods. The Plains peoples adapted the dog travois (two trailing poles on which was attached a platform or net for holding a load) for use with the horse. Their horse-drawn travois carried a load of 150 kg, in contrast to 35 kg pulled by a dog travois. As well, a horse could travel 20 km a day—twice as far as a dog. With the horse, the Plains peoples could take more than just the basic necessities as they moved from one hunting camp to another and keep extra suits of clothing, additional buffalo robes for winter, and more dried provisions. The horse transformed the buffalo hunt. Mounted hunters simply surrounded a buffalo herd, without having to drive it into an enclosure or over a cliff.

The Subarctic

To the north lies the Subarctic culture area, a sparsely populated region. A low-lying region covered with coniferous trees, it extends across the Canadian Shield, from the Labrador coast to the mouth of the Yukon River, covering over a quarter of present-day Canada. Its northern boundary is below the tree line. The winters are long and harsh, but the forests provide shelter for its human inhabitants. Members of two linguistic families lived in the Subarctic: in the west, the Athapaskan-speaking groups, or "Dene" (pronounced "de-ne" or "de-nay" and meaning "the people"); and in the east, the Subarctic Algonquians.

This area of vast northern forests remains one of the least-known of the archaeological areas in Canada, as small groups of hunters left few traces. The acidic soils of the Subarctic have reduced the hunters' remains to a few stone tools.

In the summer, on the eve of European contact, the Subarctic peoples lived in communal encampments of several hunting bands (about 100 people) situated at good fishing sites. In the autumn they divided into individual hunting bands of approximately 25 people, closely related either by family ties or by marriage, to hunt for food. A senior male directed the group and, in consultation with the other men, decided where and when they would hunt and camp. Many Dene and Algonquians relied on the moose, whose importance to them was comparable to that of the buffalo to the Plains peoples. Because of the thin distribution of game animals over vast areas of the boreal forest, the Subarctic human population was among the lowest in the world.

The Arctic

Immediately north of the Subarctic, above the tree line, lies the Arctic culture area. Today, this area includes much of Alaska, all of the Canadian North above the tree line, and Greenland. The region has one of the world's harshest climates. For about eight months of the year it remains snow-covered and its seas frozen.

Today, the various Inuit groups speak related languages, which suggests that these languages derived from a single ancestral tongue. Their languages also have similarities to those of the Chukchi, Koryak, and Itel'men peoples of northeastern Siberia. Racially as well, the Inuit resemble First Nations. This suggests that the Inuit originated in Asia.

About 4000 years ago, humans developed skills and technologies to hunt and to fish to enable them to survive winters on the treeless tundra of Arctic Canada. They constructed dogsleds, snow houses, and soapstone lamps. They killed sea mammals with harpoons attached to retrieving lines, and used barbed stone spears to fish and hunt birds. They also used the bow and arrow expertly. Although fewer species of animals exist in this region, they are relatively larger. In certain areas, migration and the availability of food lead to dense seasonal concentrations of many mammals, such as caribou, walrus, and seals.

About a thousand years ago, an Alaskan people, the Thule—the direct ancestors of the modern Inuit—entered the central Arctic. Four hundred years later, a sparse Thule population occupied most of Arctic Canada north of the tree line. In the relatively mild weather conditions at the time of their arrival, they were able to adapt their rich maritime hunting culture to the Canadian Arctic. They introduced many new items of technology for sea-mammal hunting. After perfecting the techniques of hunting on the open seas, they could even take the bowhead whale. The colder climate of the sixteenth century onward made this life untenable, and they developed the well-known classic Inuit culture. Modern Canadian and Greenlandic Inuit are descended from them.

The Northeast

The Northeast (or Eastern Woodlands) culture area extended roughly from the Atlantic to the Great Lakes, and north to the Subarctic. The Northeast Aboriginal peoples hunted a variety of large game, particularly deer, as well as smaller game. They also fished and gathered edible wild plants and roots. Dramatic changes followed when hunters in southern Ontario adopted the bow and arrow from the Ohio region, about 1500 years ago. Climate and soil conditions south of the Canadian Shield allowed some nations to grow corn, beans, and squash. Two linguistic families lived in the Northeast: the Algonquians, a migratory people primarily dependent on hunting and fishing; and the Iroquoians, a semi-nomadic and agricultural people. The Algonquians occupied the northern part of the region, while the Iroquoians inhabited much of present-day southern Ontario and neighbouring New York State.

The Algonquians

The Algonquian-speaking peoples were widespread on the eve of European contact. The Mi'kmaq (Micmac) lived in the Maritimes, and the closely related Maliseet (Malecite) in what is now western New Brunswick. North of the St. Lawrence and east of the St. Maurice River dwelt the

Montagnais (Innu). The Algonquins (Algonkins), the group that gave its name to the Algonquian linguistic family, lived in the Ottawa valley. (Note that the tribal name ends in "-quin" and that of the linguistic family in "-quian.") Still farther west lived the Nipissings on Lake Nipissing, the Ottawas (Odawa) on Manitoulin Island in Lake Huron, and the Ojibwas (Ojibways, Chippewas) around Lake Superior. The Beothuk, now extinct, lived in Newfoundland. They might have been Algonquian speakers, but the evidence is inconclusive.

Although many Algonquian groups grew crops, those north of the Great Lakes chiefly hunted and fished. During the winter they broke up into small independent family groups to hunt deer, elk, bear, beaver, and other animals. In the early spring families came together at maple groves to gather and boil the tree sap. In the summer by lakes and at river mouths, the women undertook agricultural work, while the men fished. During the fall they gathered wild rice, and, farther south, harvested corn.

Several winter hunting groups joined together for summer fishing. According to anthropologist Bruce Trigger, each fishing band had its own name, territory, and leader. The leader, however, had relatively little power or authority.[8] The men of these male-centred hunting groups usually married women from neighbouring bands, thus maintaining friendly ties. Adjacent bands, sharing a common language and customs, constituted a local community. Their unity was more cultural than political, since the band was the only clearly defined political unit. They traded extensively with their neighbours.

The Iroquoians

Initially, the Northeast peoples were hunters and gatherers, but gradually many in the area south of the Canadian Shield became Aboriginal farmers. Crops that originated in Mexico and Central America played an important role in the development of Iroquoian culture. About 1500 years ago, corn spread northward via the Ohio and Illinois areas to southern Ontario. It adapted to the shorter growing season and the more rigorous climate. Tobacco probably entered eastern Canada 2500 years ago, and beans about 1000 years ago. Beans, high in protein, partially freed the Iroquoians from having to supplement their corn diet with animal protein. This new food supply contributed to rapid population growth.

At first, small-scale gardening supplemented hunting and fishing, but later the opposite was true. By the time of European contact the Iroquoian farming nations of the lower Great Lakes depended on their crops for up to four-fifths of their food. Every 10 to 15 years, they moved their village sites as the soil and firewood became depleted. Iroquoian women assumed the tasks of planting, cultivating, and harvesting the crops, thus freeing the men for clearing the land for farming, and for hunting, fishing, trading, and warfare.

With the development of agriculture, larger First Nation confederacies formed. Two Iroquoian confederacies existed in the Great Lakes area at the time of European contact: the Huron, an alliance of four nations; and the Five (later Six) Nations or Iroquois. The territory of the Five Nations, or as they called themselves, the League of Hodenosaunee (People of the Longhouse), south of Lake Ontario, was more extensive than the lands of the Huron, south of Georgian

Canadian artist Franklin Arbuckle (1909–2001) drew this sketch of Iroquoian men building a new village with pallisade, used as an illustration in Selwyn Dewdney and Franklin Arbuckle, They Shared to Survive: The Native Peoples of Canada (Toronto: Macmillan, 1975), p. 65.

WHERE SOCIAL SCIENTISTS DISAGREE

How Much Power Did Women Have in Northern Iroquoian Society?

The question of women's authority in Iroquois society has long fascinated scholars. Much of the discussion centres on information provided by the Jesuits in their annual reports, or *Relations*, published from the early seventeenth century to the 1670s, and Jesuit writings in the early eighteenth century. Ethnologists a century ago noted that the Iroquois organized their societies on different lines than did the patrilineal western Europeans. The American ethnologist Lucien Carr, for instance, believed that Iroquois women controlled their societies. In 1884, he wrote that the Iroquois woman, "by virtue of her functions as wife and mother, exercised an influence but little short of despotic, not only in the wigwam but also around the council fire."[1] Another American ethnologist J.N.B. Hewitt, himself of Iroquois background (Tuscarora), agreed. In 1933, he wrote: "She indeed possessed and exercised all civil and political power and authority. The country, the land, the fields with their harvests and fruits belonged to her ... her plans and wishes molded the policy and inspired the decisions of council."[2]

Scholars in the mid-twentieth century returned to this topic, re-examining the same material but arriving at different conclusions. Anthropologist Cara E. Richards, for instance, argued that Iroquois women enjoyed little real power in the seventeenth century.[3] It was only in the eighteenth and nineteenth centuries, when population losses and other post-contact pressures necessitated a change to the early-seventeenth-century power structure, that women's power and influence prevailed.

In her book *Chain Her by One Foot: The Subjugation of Women in Seventeenth-Century New France*, Canadian sociologist Karen Anderson took a middle position arguing that before Huron contact with the French, equality existed between males and females. The Jesuit fathers, however, upset this balance by imposing Christianity and European standards on male–female relations. By 1650, Anderson notes, "Women, especially, had been profoundly changed, accepting the domination of their husbands and fathers." Elsewhere she emphasizes, "What is astonishing is how quickly women's status was changed once Christianity was established."[4]

Controversy had also centred on the sources that Anderson and others used: the Jesuit *Relations*. Anthropologist Judith K. Brown points out that "the Relations cover an extended period of time and are anecdotal rather than descriptive. They are the work of many authors, whose prime purpose was to describe not the customs they found, but their own missionary activities."[5]

In the 1970s, the Iroquoianist William N. Fenton and French-language specialist Elizabeth L. Moore made available an English translation of the early-eighteenth-century ethnological classic *Moeurs des sauvages amériquains, comparées aux moeurs des premiers temps* (1724) by Joseph-François Lafitau. While Lafitau's remarks on male–female relations apply to only one Iroquois community near Montreal, at a specific period of time, the 1710s, it is invaluable. The Jesuit missionary lived for nearly six years (1712–17) with the Christianized Iroquois converts at Sault St. Louis (later known as Caughnawaga or Kahnawake). He based his study on his own observations, information from another Jesuit who had worked in New France for over half a century, and on the Jesuit *Relations*. Lafitau summarized the status of Iroquois women in this manner: "Nothing is more real [...] than the women's superiority. It is they who really maintain the tribe, the nobility of blood, the genealogical tree, the order of generations and conservation of the families. In them resides all the real authority: the lands, fields and all their harvest belong to them; they are the soul of the councils, the arbiters of peace and war; they hold the taxes and the public treasure; it is to them that the slaves are entrusted; they arrange the marriages; the children are under their authority; and the order of succession is founded on their blood."[6]

Anthropologist Elisabeth Tooker added a fresh new geographical dimension to this topic in her 1984 essay, "Women in Iroquois Society." She emphasized the importance of the two different domains of Iroquois societies: the clearing—the domain of females; and the forest—that of males: "As the women did all the agricultural work of planting, tending, and harvesting of crops, the whole clearing (village and fields) also was regarded as the domain of women. The land beyond the clearing, the forest, was the domain of men."[7]

Over a hundred years after it began, the debate over the balance of power between Iroquois men and women in the seventeenth century continues. One of the most recent contributions to the discussion is Allan Greer's recent biography, *Mohawk Saint: Catherine Tekakwitha and the Jesuits* (Toronto: Oxford, 2005), a study of a woman of great influence among mid-seventeenth-century Christian Iroquois converts.

---

1. LucienCarr, "On the Social and Political Position of Woman among the Huron–Iroquois Tribes," *16th and 17th Annual Reports of the Trustees of the Peabody Museum*, 3, 3–4 (1884): 211; reprinted in WilliamGuy Spittal, ed., *Iroquois Women: An Anthology* (Ohsweken, ON: Iroqrafts, 1990), p. 13.

2. J.N.B.Hewitt, "Status of Women in Iroquois Polity before 1784," *Annual Report of the Board of Regents of the Smithsonian Institution for the Year Ending June 30, 1932*, p. 487; reprinted in Spittal, ed., *Iroquois Women*, p. 67.

3. Cara E.Richards, "Matriarchy or Mistake: The Role of Iroquois Women through Time," in V.F.Kay, ed., *Cultural Stability and Cultural Change*, Proceedings of the 1957 Annual Spring Meeting of the American Ethnological Society; reprinted in Spittal, ed., *Iroquois Women*, pp. 149–59. (The quote appears on p. 153.)

4. KarenAnderson, *Chain Her by One Foot: The Subjugation of Women in Seventeenth-Century New France* (London and New York: Routledge, 1991), pp. 52 and 162.

5. Judith K.Brown, "Economic Organization and the Position of Women among the Iroquois," *Ethnohistory*, 17, 3–4 (1970): 165, footnote 5; reprinted in Spittal, ed., *Iroquois Women*, p. 196.

6. Joseph-FrançoisLafitau, trans., *Customs of the American Indians Compared with the Customs of Primitive Times*, 2 vols. (Toronto: Champlain Society, 1974 and 1977), vol. 1, p. 69.

7. ElisabethTooker, "Women in Iroquois Society," in *Extending the Rafters: Interdisciplinary Approaches to Iroquoian Studies* (Albany: State University of New York Press, 1984), pp. 109–23; reprinted in WendyMitchinson et al., eds., *Canadian Women: A Reader* (Toronto: Harcourt Brace, 1996), p. 28.

Bay on Lake Huron. The languages of the Five Nations (from east to west: Mohawk, Oneida, Onondaga, Cayuga, and Seneca) were more distinct from each other than those of the Huron nations. Each member nation had its own council, which met in the group's largest village. The national councils sent representatives to the League, or Confederacy Council, which governed the confederacies. By the mid-1530s, another group of Iroquoians—neither Huron nor Iroquois—occupied the St. Lawrence River valley: the St. Lawrence Iroquoians.

The Iroquoian peoples lived in stockaded villages of up to 1500 inhabitants. From ten to thirty families belonging to the same clan lived together in "longhouses," some the size of half a football field in length, and consisting of a framework of saplings, often arched in a barrel shape, covered with sheets of bark. The Iroquoians divided the longhouses into apartments, occupied by closely related families. A corridor ran down the middle of the house, and families on each side shared fireplaces.

The core of any household consisted of a number of females descended from a common ancestor. When a man married, he moved to his wife's home, where authority was invested in an elderly woman. In Iroquoian society the older women had real social and political power. The matrons of the appropriate families elected the chiefs, who were men; these women could also vote out of office any chief who displeased them.

At the time of European contact, First Nations groups lived in six culture areas that parallel Canada's major environmental areas: the West Coast, the interior of British Columbia, the Prairies, the Canadian Shield, the eastern woodlands, and the Arctic. Linguistic diversity also existed, with more than 50 different languages being spoken in six culture areas. On the eve of European contact, the Aboriginal peoples had achieved full occupation and use of North America.

In each cultural area, nature and the availability of natural resources largely dictated the lifestyle of the particular groups. First Nations communities often traded across linguistic and cultural boundaries. These exchanges sealed political and social relationships. In some cases, hostile groups went to war against each other. Individuals considered themselves part of their family, their band, and their nation, but did not look upon all Aboriginal groups as one.

NOTES

1. EldonYellowhorn in Alan D.McMillan and EldonYellowhorn, *First Peoples in Canada* (Vancouver: Douglas & McIntyre, 2004), p. x.

2. AliceKehoe discusses this subject in her book *North American Indians: A Comprehensive Account*, 2nd ed. (Englewood Cliffs, NJ: Prentice-Hall, 1992), pp. 2–3; and in the 3rd ed. (Upper Saddle Creek, New Jersey: Pearson/Prentice-Hall, 2006), pp. 1–2; and also in her *America before the European Invasions* (London, England: Pearson Education, 2002), pp. 9, 20.

3. Peter L.Storck, *Journey to the Ice Age: Discovering an Ancient World* (Vancouver: UBC Press, 2004), p. 18.

4. Alfred W.Crosby, "Virgin Soil Epidemics as a Factor in the Aboriginal Depopulation in America," *William and Mary Quarterly*, 3rd series, 33 (1976): 290.

5. Olive P.Dickason, *Canada's First Nations: A History of the Founding Peoples from Earliest Times* (Toronto: McClelland & Stewart, 1992), p. 43.

6. RobertMcGhee, "Canada YIK: The First Millennium," *The Beaver*, December 1999/January 2000, p. 10.

7. Dickason, *Canada's First Nations*, p. 67.

8. Bruce G.Trigger, *The Indians and the Heroic Age of New France* (Ottawa: Canadian Historical Association, 1977), p. 6.

BEYOND THE BOOK

A Journey into Time Immemorial
http://www.sfu.museum/time/en/enter
Enter Xá:ytem, an Aboriginal village in the Pacific Northwest. Explore the culture and ways of life of the Stó:lō people who lived here hundreds of years ago in this fully immersive 3D environment.

Earliest Settlements in the Americas
http://www.sfu.museum/journey/en/05p_secondary/index.php
This site explores the first human settlements in North America. Leading historians and scientists are interviewed in videos playable on the site.

Echoes from the Past: Archaeology in Quebec
http://www.virtualmuseum.ca/Exhibitions/Echo/e_index.html
This site examines the archaeology and ecology of Quebec over the past several millennia. Cultural artifacts such as rock art sites are presented with vivid pictures.

The Architectural History of Early First Nations Cultures
http://thecanadianencyclopedia.com/index.cfm?PgNm=TCE&Params=A1ARTA0009249
The architecture of structures and homes can illustrate a great deal about a people's culture. First Nations architecture of the time before, and after, European contact is presented here.

Stones Unturned

http://www.civilization.ca/aborig/stones/engfrm.htm
A virtual exhibition of Aboriginal clothing, musical instruments, games, and toys from the Canadian Museum of Civilization. This site also contains brief descriptions and maps of the main First Nation language groups.

A History of Native Peoples of Canada

http://www.civilization.ca/archeo/hnpc/npint00e.html
Detailed histories of First Nation cultures in Canada spanning the time period of 12 000 to 1500 years ago.

Thule Excavation Site in the Arctic

http://anthropology.uwaterloo.ca/ArcticArchStuff/qkhn-12_1.html
This website describes the process of excavating a Thule house on Devon Island, Nunavut. Cultural artifacts found are presented with pictures and analysis.

When the World Began

Canada: A People's History—Episode 1, When the World Began. Directed by Andrew Gregg (CBC, 2000).

RELATED READINGS

R. Douglas Francis and Donald B. Smith, eds., *Viewpoints Readings in Canadian History* (Toronto: Thomson Nelson, 2007) contains an important article relating to this chapter: Harold E.L. Prins, "Children of Gluskap: Wabanaki Indians on the Eve of the European Invasion," pp. 4–23.

BIBLIOGRAPHY

Three valuable overviews by anthropologists include Alice B. Kehoe, *North American Indians: A Comprehensive Account*, 3rd ed. (Upper Saddle Creek, NJ: Pearson/Prentice-Hall, 2006); R. Bruce Morrison and C. Roderick Wilson, eds., *Native Peoples: The Canadian Experience*, 3rd ed. (Don Mills, ON: Oxford University Press, 2004); and Alan D. McMillan and Eldon Yellowhorn, *First Peoples in Canada* (Vancouver: Douglas & McIntyre, 2004). The best survey is Olive P. Dickason, *Canada's First Nations: A History of the Founding Peoples from Earliest Times*, 3rd ed. (Don Mills, ON: Oxford University Press, 2002); and her shorter work, *A Concise History of Canada's First Nations*, adapted by Moira Calder (Don Mills, ON: Oxford University Press, 2006). Useful overviews include Arthur J. Ray, *I Have Lived Here since the World Began: An Illustrated History of Canada's Native People* (Toronto: Key Porter Books, 1996; rev. ed. 2005); and Bruce G. Trigger and Wilcomb E. Washburn, eds., *The Cambridge History of the Native Peoples of the Americas: Volume 1, North America* (Port Chester, NY: Cambridge University Press, 1996).

Alice Kehoe provides an account of the development of human cultures in North America in *America before the European Invasions* (London, England: Pearson Education Limited, 2002). A popular account of the archaeological record is Robert McGhee's *Ancient Canada* (Ottawa: Canadian Museum of Civilization/Libre Expression, 1989). For a review of the human occupation of what is now Ontario just after the glaciers retreated, see Peter L. Storck, *Journey to the Ice Age: Discovering an Ancient World* (Vancouver: UBC Press, 2004).

Henry F. Dobyns, *Native American Historical Demography: A Critical Bibliography* (Bloomington: Indiana University Press, 1976) provides demographic information. For details on the impact of disease, consult Alfred W. Crosby, "Virgin Soil Epidemics as a Factor in the Aboriginal Depopulation in

America," *William and Mary Quarterly*, 3rd series, 33 (1976): 289–99, and his *Ecological Imperialism: The Biological Expansion of Europe, 900–1900* (Cambridge: Cambridge University Press, 1986). David Helge has challenged Dobyns's estimates on the magnitude of the demographic decline in *Numbers from Nowhere: The American Indian Contact Population Debate* (Norman: University of Oklahoma Press, 1998).

Short reviews of First Nation culture areas appear in Morrison and Wilson, *Native Peoples*; Kehoe, *North American Indians*; and McMillan and Yellowhorn, *First Peoples in Canada*. Very helpful are the well-researched essays included in Paul Robert Magocsi, ed., *Canada's Aboriginal Peoples. A Short Introduction* (Toronto: University of Toronto Press, 2002). Six volumes in the series *Handbook of North American Indians* (Washington, DC: Smithsonian Institution) are invaluable: vol. 1, David Dumas, ed., *Arctic* (1985); vol. 6, June Helm, ed., *Subarctic* (1981); vol. 7, Wayne Suttles, ed., *Northwest Coast* (1990); vol. 12, Deward E. Walker, ed., *Plateau* (1998); vol. 13, Raymond J. Demaillie, ed., *Plains* (2001); and vol. 15, Bruce G. Trigger, ed., *Northeast* (1978). A useful study of Aboriginal languages is Michael K. Foster's "Native People, Languages" in *The Canadian Encyclopedia*, 2nd ed., vol. 3 (Edmonton: Hurtig, 1988), 1453–56. On First Nations women consult the collection of essays edited by Mary-Ellen Kelm and Lorna Townsend, *In the Days of Our Grandmothers. A Reader in Aboriginal Women's History in Canada* (Toronto: University of Toronto Press, 2006).

The early maps in R. Cole Harris, ed., *Historical Atlas of Canada*, vol. 1, *From the Beginning to 1800* (Toronto: University of Toronto Press, 1987) are based on the most recent archaeological discoveries. This atlas contains a wealth of new information about the first inhabitants of present-day Canada. One of the best overviews on First Nations groups embracing change is Theodore Binnema's *Common and Contested Ground. A Human and Environmental History of the Northwestern Plains* (Norman: University of Oklahoma Press, 2001). For bibliographical information consult Shepard Krech III, *Native Canadian Anthropology and History: A Select Bibliography*, rev. ed. (Winnipeg: Rupert's Land Research Centre, University of Winnipeg, 1994). The First Nations constantly altered their ways of life to adjust to new ideas and conditions.

Part 1

EARLY EUROPEAN SETTLEMENT TO 1760

Anno Domino 1500 Gaspar Corterealis
Portogalensis navigavit ad has terras sperans
a parte Septentrionali invenire transitum ad
insulas Moluccas, perveniens autem ad fluvium
quem a devectic navibus vocant Rio nevada,
propter vigens frigus altius in Septentrionem
pergere destitit perlustravit autem litora
in meridiem usq ad C. Razo.
    Anno 1504 Britones primi invenerant litora
nove Francie circa ostia Sinus S. Laurentii
    Anno 1524 Joannes Verrazzanus Florentinus
nomine regis Gall Francisci primi ex portu
Diepa protectus Martii ad litus meridionale
noue Francie pervenit circum 34 gradum
latitud, atq inde versus orientem omne litus
perlustravit usq ad Britonium promontorium
    Anno 1534 duce classi Jacobo Cartier
lustrata fuit nova Francia & proximo
anno regi Gallie conquiri coepit.

Groenlant

Estotilant

C. de
terra f

Golfam de
Merofro

Terra
Corte
realis

Hoc fluvae
facilior est
navigatio
in Saguenai

Saguenai

Chasteaux
Belle ysle
C. Blanco di degrad abjs

Honguedo

y Iles

Sinus   S Laurentij
y della assumptione

y des oiseaux

Noua

Fran
Canada

France Rennfue

C. de Mommorancy

Terra de
bacallaos

C. de bona vista

Hochelay

y des trepures

G. de Chaleur

Hochela   ga

y. D'Orleans

S Pol
S Petro
S Joan

C. de Breton

C. de Razo

Chilaga

Mommorancy

Noro   mbega

Estane a
terra dus
Bretones

Arredonda

Norombega

y. de Juan esteuez

Moco
fa

Auac al   Ap alchen

C. de arenas

C. doblado

Santana

y. de g

INTRODUCTION

When western Europeans first crossed the North Atlantic in the fifteenth and sixteenth centuries, they entered a world remarkably different from that of Europe. The First Nations' ancestors had occupied what would become known as Canada for approximately five hundred generations. The two groups—First Nations and Europeans—interacted sometimes peacefully, more often through conflict, as they both sought to use the vast natural resources to their own advantage. Fish and furs brought the Europeans back annually, eventually leading the French to establish permanent settlements in what they called New France. French settlements prevailed in Acadia (the present-day Maritimes) and in Canada, as they called the St. Lawrence valley. New France was large in size, but in comparison with the colony of New England to the south, founded about the same time, the population remained quite small, numbering only 65 000 people at the time of the Conquest in 1760, almost 150 years after Champlain founded Quebec in 1608.

New France inherited French institutions, such as the French administrative and judicial systems, but because of differing geography and historical circumstances, they were modified to meet North American circumstances. Conflict with the Iroquois and English helped to forge a common identity among the French settlers. By the mid-eighteenth century, the contours of the Canadian and Acadian identities were evident. At its peak New France covered a vast territory in North America that included parts of present-day eastern, central, western, and northern Canada, as well as the valleys of the Ohio and Mississippi rivers down to the Gulf of Mexico. Being so vast and underpopulated by the French, the region was difficult to defend. The British conquest in 1760 ended the French regime in North America, but not the French fact in the St. Lawrence valley or in the Maritimes.

Chapter Two

EARLY EUROPEAN SETTLEMENT AND THE BEGINNING OF NEW FRANCE

TIME LINE

1001	Leif Eiriksson leads an expedition to northeastern North America from Greenland but within a decade the attempts to establish permanent Norse settlements fail
1497	Giovanni Caboto (John Cabot), an Italian navigator in the English service, lands in northeastern North America
1534	Jacques Cartier, on his first of three voyages for the king of France, enters the Gulf of St. Lawrence
1608	Champlain builds a fortified trading post at Quebec
1609	For the first time Champlain and the French clash with the Iroquois or Five Nations initiating a nearly century-long conflict
1642	Ville-Marie, later known as Montreal, is founded
1649	The fall of Huronia; the Iroquois defeat the Hurons in a quick military campaign
1667	Truce between the French and the Iroquois League of Five Nations; the beginning of two decades of peace

The strange boat amazed the Aboriginal hunters along the Labrador and Newfoundland coast. They believed that the world ended beyond the horizon and that they were the only inhabitants. Never before had anyone seen such a sight emerging from the edge of the world. Upon the small sea monster's back arose a tall leafless tree from which hung a gigantic white blanket. Around the tree stood ugly beings with facial hair and skin the colour of the underbelly of a fish. The year was approximately 1000 years ago, and the newcomers were the Norse. After an interval of nearly five centuries, other Europeans followed in quick succession: the English, the Portuguese, the French, the Spanish, and the Basques.

The absence of written source materials by the original inhabitants makes the narration of the Europeans' arrival a formidable task. Only a few Norse sagas, or adventure stories, passed on orally from generation to generation for about 300 years before being written down, and the occasional European explorer's journal exist for the period before 1600. Morris Bishop, the American author of a graceful and well-researched biography of Samuel de Champlain, founder of Quebec in 1608, put it best when he wrote, "In reading history one must always be impressed by the fact that our knowledge is only a collection of scraps and fragments that we put together into a pleasing design, and often the discovery of one new fragment would cause us to alter utterly the whole design."[1]

The Arrival of the Norse

From the ninth to the twelfth centuries, Scandinavia led the European sea powers. Its commercial empire extended from Russia in the east to Sicily in the south and Normandy in the west. The Norse occupied in the late tenth century small coastal areas on the southwestern coast of Greenland, as part of their voyages from the European mainland and Iceland. In the year 1001, Leifr (or Leif) Eiriksson assembled a crew of 35 and set out to explore the lands southwest of Greenland. He reached an attractive location with a moderate climate, which he named "Vinland" (Wineland) for its plentiful "wineberries" (probably wild red currants, gooseberries, or mountain cranberries). Scholars have placed Vinland at different locations between Labrador and Florida. In 1960, Helge Ingstad and his archaeologist wife, Anne Stine Ingstad, located the first known site of European settlement in North America, L'Anse aux Meadows, on the northeastern tip of the Great Northern Peninsula of Newfoundland. Today L'Anse aux Meadows, the only authenticated Viking site in northeastern North America, is designated a World Heritage Site by UNESCO.

For nearly 500 years, the Norse occupied Greenland. Their economy was based on raising stock, hunting, and fishing. They travelled to the west for timber from "Vinland," trading with the Inuit along the Greenlandic coast, and on Baffin and Ellesmere Islands. Hostile relations with the Aboriginal peoples, however, prevented permanent settlement.

The Greenland settlements prospered in the twelfth century, when an estimated 2000–4000 people, and perhaps as many as 6000, lived there. Then, in the thirteenth century, Greenland's climate became colder, which threatened agriculture. Furthermore, the settlements' prosperity, precariously built on the walrus-ivory trade, declined when the Portuguese imported African elephant ivory. As well, the Black Death of 1349 struck Norway and Iceland severely. The epidemic of bubonic plague killed one-third of the population—a loss that cost the Norse their command of the seas. Thereafter, the annual ship that brought vital supplies from Norway no longer appeared. By 1450, the Greenlandic settlements had disappeared.

The European Expansion in the Fifteenth Century

The Portuguese replaced the Scandinavians as the leading European sea power by the fifteenth century, as a result of their fast and efficient seagoing vessels known as *caravels* (their long, narrow ships with two masts). Curiosity and the desire to find a "New World," a better land than that in which they lived, led the Portuguese—and later the Spanish, French, English, and Dutch—to expand beyond Europe. Economic motives also played an important role. The Turks' capture in 1453 of Constantinople, the key city in Europe's trade with the Orient, caused a desperate search by the Europeans to find a new route to "the Indies," as China, Japan, Indonesia, and India were then collectively called, for spices and the riches of eastern and south Asia. As well, they came to convert the "heathen" to Christianity.

The English Cross the North Atlantic

When news of Columbus's first two Atlantic voyages to "Asia" in 1492 and 1493 reached England, King Henry VII sponsored his own expedition. In 1496, he chose John Cabot (Giovanni Caboto), an experienced Italian mariner, to lead it. The merchants of the English port of Bristol, anxious to secure direct access to the east, sponsored the expedition.

Cabot set sail in late May 1497. On June 24 he reached land, probably the eastern coast of Newfoundland. Here he planted the flags of England and his native Venice and claimed the territory for Henry VII. The Italian navigator also discovered that the nearby sea swarmed with fish by letting down and drawing up baskets weighted with stones, thus locating the great continental shelf of Newfoundland. These shallow areas, called "banks," are favourite breeding places of cod. Cabot also entered the Gulf of St. Lawrence, believing it to be a direct route to China and India.

Encouraged by this information, Henry VII sponsored a second voyage. In May 1498, Cabot sailed again from Bristol with five ships. Shortly out of port, one vessel turned back in distress to Ireland, but the other four were lost. Cabot's disappearance, followed shortly afterwards by the death of Henry VII, temporarily curbed English interest in the search for a Northwest Passage to the Orient. Nevertheless, John Cabot's first voyage announced England's interest in the Americas. The voyage also brought to Western Europe's attention the Grand Banks fishery. Possibly, Bristol fishers had fished the Grand Banks since the 1480s, but now their secret was out. Fishing—the first great European business in North America—had begun.

The Portuguese in the North Atlantic

Soon after Cabot came the Portuguese. Despite the dangers of navigating the uncharted North Atlantic, they annually fished the Grand Banks and the coastal waters of Newfoundland. Around 1520, the Portuguese made one attempt at permanent settlement, probably on the eastern coast of Cape Breton Island. After a year or so, difficulties arose with the local Aboriginal population, and the settlement—the first European settlement since the Norse—died out. After their colony's failure the Portuguese returned, not to settle, but to continue to fish the Grand Banks.

French Interest in the North Atlantic in the Sixteenth Century

Of all the western European powers in the early sixteenth century, France was the best situated to dominate northeastern North America. It had twice the population of Portugal and Spain together, and six times that of England. It also had more ocean-facing territory, at least as many seaports as England, and far greater wealth. Yet, due to its involvement in European conflicts, France did not become involved in North Atlantic exploration until 1524.

The French selected Giovanni da Verrazzano, an Italian navigator like Cabot, as the commander of their expedition in 1524. He searched the North American coast, from the Carolinas to Gaspé, for a westerly route to Asia. Despite his failure to find such a passage, France acquired a better understanding of the eastern North American coastline. France, however, did not follow up on Verrazzano's expedition, being preoccupied by their war against the Hapsburgs (the rulers of Austria, the Low Countries, and Spain).

The First of Jacques Cartier's Three Voyages, 1534

Jacques Cartier, a mariner from the northwestern port of Saint-Malo in Brittany, France, led a second French expedition a decade after Verrazzano's, in search of a passage to China and India. Cartier entered the Gulf of St. Lawrence and landed at present-day Prince Edward Island. Next, he sailed north to Chaleur Bay, which divides Quebec from New Brunswick, and met Mi'kmaq traders. Cartier's journal contains the first reference since the Norse sagas to a trading exchange between the Indigenous peoples and Europeans—initiated by the Aboriginals. They "set up a great clamour and made frequent signs to us to come on shore, holding up to us some furs on sticks," a clear indication that they had already participated in a previous exchange, or exchanges.

As the French moved north to Gaspé, they encountered Iroquoians who came from the interior to fish. Unaccustomed to trading with Europeans, they brought no furs with them. The French first presented "knives, glass beads, combs, and other trinkets of small value" to the Iroquoians to win their friendship, and then kidnapped two sons of the chief, Donnacona. They took them back to France to learn French, and to serve as guides on the next voyage.

It was standard practice among early Europeans in the Americas to capture the inhabitants and take them back to Europe as proof of having reached the new lands. Often, the First Nations persons perished on the voyage across the Atlantic; those who survived the journey often died in Europe. They fell victim to illnesses that did not exist in the Americas and to which they had not developed immunities. In this instance, Taignoagny and Domagaya, Donnacona's sons, lived and assisted Cartier in his next expedition.

Cartier's Wintering Over in "Canada," 1535–1536

In 1535, Cartier returned with three ships and sailed up the St. Lawrence to the village of Stadacona (present-day Quebec), the home of his guides. The French mariner recorded a word that they used to refer to their home: "They call a town, *Canada*."[2] En route, Cartier gave the name "St. Lawrence" to a cove at which the French stopped, after the Christian martyr whose feast day it was (August 10). The entire gulf and the great river later obtained the same name.

The Iroquoians at Stadacona initially saw the French as powerful and valuable trading partners. But, by travelling upriver without Donnacona's permission, Cartier interfered with the Stadaconans' trading rights. In addition, the French who had been left behind built a small fort during Cartier's absence—an act that infringed on the Stadaconans' land rights, which the French did not recognize.

The winter, much longer and colder in Canada than in France, proved a nightmare for the French. To add to the sailors' problems, scurvy, a disease caused by insufficient vitamin C in the diet, broke out. Twenty-five men (one-quarter of Cartier's crew) died before the French learned the Aboriginal cure for the disease: boiling the bark and leaves of the *annedda* (white cedar) to make a brew with a high content of ascorbic acid (vitamin C).

Despite the Stadaconans' help, Cartier remained antagonistic to Donnacona and his people. Anxious to obtain more information about the lands in the interior, particularly the rich "kingdom of the Saguenay" that Taignoagny and Domagaya had spoken of, the French mariner kidnapped both of them, their father Donnacona, and three of his principal supporters. The French believed this fabulous land to be a second Mexico, rich in gold and silver. (In reality, the stories of the Saguenay probably referred to copper deposits around Lake Superior.) After promising to return his hostages the following year, Cartier left in the spring of 1536. Four children presented to Cartier by Donnacona and the chief of a neighbouring village left as well. The ten Aboriginal captives never saw "Canada" again.

Cartier entered Saint-Malo in July 1536, having been away for over a year. Although the French sea captain had not discovered great wealth, he had nonetheless made some important contributions to European knowledge of North America. He proved that Newfoundland was an island, charted much of the Gulf of St. Lawrence, and recorded in his journal the existence of a great river flowing from deep in the interior.

The Cartier-Roberval Expedition, 1541–1543

War between France and Spain delayed Cartier's third voyage to "Canada" until 1541. This time, he took with him 150 French settlers to found a colony. Cartier also sought to locate the famed "kingdom of the Saguenay." Very little information has survived regarding the settlement that winter, but it was later reported that the First Nations killed at least 35 settlers. By the spring, Cartier had had enough and returned to France. As initially planned, Cartier's superior, Jean-François de La Rocque de Roberval, would come in 1542, to reinforce the initial settlement. He did, but Cartier was gone. Roberval and his 200 settlers spent a terrible winter at the site of Cartier's encampment. An inscription on a French map of 1550 explains the reasons for Roberval's departure the following summer: "It was impossible to trade with the people of that country because of their austerity, the intemperate climate of said country, and the slight profit." (Just recently, in 2005, a team of Quebec archaeologists found the site of Cartier's and Roberval's fort at Cap Rouge, now an eastern suburb of Quebec City.)

During the French Wars of Religion (1562–1598), France left Canada to its Aboriginal inhabitants. French fishers, whalers, and traders continued to come in great numbers to northeastern North America, but France did not attempt colonization again for another half-century. The harsh climate, hostile relations with the Aboriginal peoples, and the failure to find gold gave the French a poor image of Canada.

European Fishers and Traders' Activities in the Sixteenth Century

European fishers maintained contact with Newfoundland. Between March and October of each year, large fishing fleets—Portuguese, Basque, French, and English—gathered on the Grand Banks. They supplied the markets of western Europe and the Mediterranean with the "beef of the sea" (cod). The Newfoundland fishery had become big business by the mid-sixteenth century. With an estimated 10 000 individuals visiting annually, it provided a livelihood for twice as many fishers as did the fisheries of the Gulf of Mexico and the Caribbean combined, where the great Spanish fleets sailed.

The success of the Newfoundland cod fishery initially depended on the harvesting of salt left by the evaporation of seawater. This salt, more uniform in quality, was better than the mineral variety for curing fish. France, Spain, and Portugal produced an abundance of "solar salt," but England, with less sunshine, did not. This hurt England in the age of the "green fishery," the term sailors used to describe a method of salting fish immediately upon catching them, then transporting them back to Europe for drying. To compensate for the lack of solar salt, the English developed "dry fishing"—drying their lightly salted fish before returning home. The sun-cured codfish lasted indefinitely if kept dry, and could be reconstituted by soaking it in water.

Estimates of the number of English ships involved in Newfoundland expeditions around the year 1600 vary from 250 to 400, and the number of men from 6000 to 10 000. These expeditions made good England's claims to the Avalon Peninsula on Newfoundland's east coast, the location of the best English fishing and processing sites. Just to the west, in the region of the Strait of Belle Isle, which separates Newfoundland and Labrador, the Basques were active.

The Basque Whaling Stations

From their homeland in the border region of France and Spain, Basque whalers joined the cod fishers in the early sixteenth century. The south coast of Labrador became the first region of northeastern North America to undergo extensive exploitation by Europeans. Europe's first commercial whalers came prepared to set up a long-distance fishery. Whaling stations flourished in the Strait of Belle Isle for half a century. Sixteenth-century Europeans treasured whale oil as a fuel for lamps, an all-purpose

Part of Mercator's Map, 1569.

D.G.G. Kerr, ed., *A Historical Atlas of Canada* (Toronto: Thomas Nelson & Sons, 1961), p. 11.

lubricant, an additive to drugs, and a major ingredient of scores of products, such as soap and pitch. At its peak, the fishery employed about 2000 men, who remained in Newfoundland–Labrador waters for six months each season, from June until January.

COMMUNITY PORTRAIT

The Basque Whaling Community of Red Bay, Labrador, 1550–1600

In the mid-1970s, Selma Barkham, a researcher employed by the Public Archives (now the Library and Archives Canada), discovered a forgotten chapter of Canadian history. While it had long been known that Basque whalers had hunted off the Labrador coast, the extent of their operations, and the location of their whaling stations, were not known. While examining wills, lawsuits, mortgages, and insurance policies in Basque archives in Spain, Barkham came across substantial information on a whale fishery in the Strait of Belle Isle, separating Labrador from the northern tip of Newfoundland. The Strait

was an ideal location for whale hunting, as it acted as a funnel through which migrating whales passed in great numbers.

Barkham made a preliminary investigation of the southern Labrador coast with James Tuck, an archaeologist from Memorial University of Newfoundland, and several other scientists in the summer of 1977. All along the coast they found evidence that the Basques had been in the region. At several locations they located red patches on the beaches, the remains of the imported red roof tile used by the Basque whalers for their buildings. Tuck returned in the summer of 1978 to excavate the most promising site, Saddle Island in Red Bay, one of the finest harbours in the Strait of Belle Isle. On the harbour side of the island he found fragments of old stone walls stained with a black material, later identified as burnt whale oil. The archaeologist had discovered the remains of the ovens where whale blubber was tried (boiled down) into oil. During future visits to Saddle Island, Tuck and his team located additional evidence of Basque activity. They located the remains of houses and of the workshops where the coopers (barrel-makers) constructed the barrels to ship whale oil.

In 1978, Robert Grenier, head of marine archaeology for Parks Canada, began underwater investigations that greatly complemented Barkham's archival research and Tuck's archaeological work on Saddle Island. He discovered the well-preserved remains of a sunken Basque ship only 30 m offshore of the Saddle Island station. It had gone down in a squall with a load of nearly 1000 barrels of whale oil. Subsequent investigations in the icy waters led to the location of the ship's compass, anchor, rudder, and loaded swivel gun. In 1979, the Historic Sites and Monuments Board of Canada designated the forgotten Basque whaling station of Red Bay a site of national historic interest.

Red Bay appears to have been the Basque whalers' favourite whaling station. Normally about ten galleons arrived in Red Bay every summer in the late sixteenth century. Depending on a ship's tonnage, crews ranged from 50 to 120 men. During the whaling season, the men harpooned whales from small open whale boats. Once killed, the dead whales were towed back to the galleon left moored in the harbour. After the men removed large strips or slabs of blubber, they hauled it ashore. At the whaling station they rendered it into whale oil in huge ovens or tryworks, containing several ovens, sheltered by roofs of red tile brought to Red Bay for that purpose.

The graves located at Red Bay reveal that the tradespeople were sturdy and relatively young. Basque males of all ages, some as young as 11 or 12, joined the whaling expeditions. The captains hired in the late winter and early spring. They did not allow females to join their crews. Each crew member had to produce, at personal expense, essential items, such as clothing, suitable for great variations in climate. The Basque crews earned shares in the season's catch rather than fixed salaries. Constant upward mobility allowed individuals to climb the shipboard hierarchy and, with special training, to become harpooners or pilots themselves. For food the ships brought large amounts of cider, wine, and ship's biscuit. At Red Bay the men enjoyed a diet based largely on cod and salmon, with an occasional piece of caribou or a wild duck.

Between mid-June and early July the whaling ships left for Labrador. An average Atlantic crossing in the sixteenth century normally took a month. Basque whalers commonly stayed in Labrador well into the winter, returning to Spain by the end of January, by which time the Strait of Belle Isle normally had frozen over. Their residency in Labrador in winter required solid buildings, so the Basques imported large amounts of Iberian tile for their construction.

The whaling effort at stations such as Red Bay proved so effective that it led to a massive depletion in northwestern Atlantic whale stocks. Another factor that helped to put an end to the Basque Labrador whale fishery by the end of the sixteenth century was the ill-fated Spanish Armada of 1588, the attempted Spanish naval invasion of Britain, a

An artist's reconstruction of Basque galleons riding at anchor in Red Bay, Labrador, the largest whaling port on the Strait of Belle Isle. Smoke billows forth from the massive stone tryworks built by the Basques to render blubber into whale oil. Painting by Richard Schlecht.

"Discovery in Labrador: A 16th-Century Basque Whaling Port and Its Sunken Fleet," *National Geographic*, 168, 1 (July 1985): 42–43.

disaster that claimed many Basque ships and sailors' lives. One written source indicates that perhaps another contributing factor was Aboriginal resistance, particularly by the Inuit. In any event, the Basque whaling community at Red Bay vanished shortly after the beginning of the seventeenth century.

FURTHER READING

Selma Barkham, "The Basques: Filling a Gap in Our History between Jacques Cartier and Champlain," *Canadian Geographical Journal*, 96, 1 (February/March, 1978): 8–19.

Robert McGhee, "Chapter 10. The Grand Bay," *Canada Rediscovered* (Ottawa: Canadian Museum of Civilization, 1991), pp. 141–53.

Jean-Pierre Proulx, *Basque Whaling in Labrador in the 16th Century* (Ottawa: National Historic Sites, Parks Services, 1993).

James A. Tuck and Robert Grenier, *Red Bay, Labrador: World Whaling Capital, A.D. 1550–1600* (St. John's, NF: Atlantic Archaeology Ltd., 1989).

English Activity in the North Atlantic and Arctic

England sponsored a number of expeditions north of Newfoundland in the late sixteenth and early seventeenth centuries. In 1576, Martin Frobisher, 37 years old and a mariner of great repute, sailed northerly in search of a Northwest Passage to India and China. Off southern Baffin Island, the English navigator encountered Inuit, who came to trade meat and furs for metal objects and clothing. The Inuit showed that they were no strangers to European ships by doing gymnastic exercises in the ship's rigging. They wanted to trade, indicating that they had already encountered vessels of the Newfoundland fishing fleet. Frobisher himself discovered they had already acquired iron when, in a skirmish with the Inuit, he was struck by an iron-tipped arrow.

Frobisher failed to find a passage to the Orient on this first journey and on two subsequent voyages in 1577 and 1578. Ten years later, John Davis followed up on Frobisher's work in three successive summers (1585–1587), but also without success. The necessary maritime technology for the penetration of the Arctic Archipelago simply did not exist in the late sixteenth century. It was as impossible a goal for that age as a landing on the moon would have been for the nineteenth century.

The Rise of the Fur Trade

Jacques Cartier's three voyages established a French claim to the Gulf of St. Lawrence, but international recognition of France's claim would come only with successful occupation. In the early 1580s the fur trade led to France's return, and to its permanent occupation of the St. Lawrence valley. In the Gulf of St. Lawrence and along the Atlantic coastline, the fur trade began as a byproduct of the fishing industry. Fur coats, muffs, wraps, gloves, fur-trimmed garments, and most important, wide-brimmed beaver hats all commanded high prices. Fur proved an ideal product for the European traders. By returning each year to the same locality, the French established good trading relationships with the local First Nations. In the 1580s, French merchants sent out ships commissioned solely to trade for furs.

One story later recorded by the Jesuit Fathers indicates the initial Algonquian impression of French drinking and eating customs. In the early 1630s Pierre Pastedechouan, an Algonquian, who had learned French after five years' study in France, told this story to Father Paul Le Jeune, who repeated it in his order's 1633 annual report, or *Relation*, back to France. His elderly grandmother told him that after the first Innu men in her community boarded a French vessel they reported back that the "Frenchmen drank blood and ate wood, thus naming the wine and [sea] biscuits."

The trade, that began modestly, so increased in volume that by the early seventeenth century many of the Algonquians on the Atlantic coast had lost much of their self-sufficiency. The fur trade transformed coastal groups from hunters and fishers into trappers. Prior to European contact, the Mi'kmaq lived more than half the year on the coast, as the sea supplied as much as 90 percent of their diet. Now they spent long periods each year hunting inland for fur-bearing animals. This change in their traditional activities affected their winter diet. No longer did they accumulate their usual summer food stores. Instead they relied partly on the dried foods they received in trade.

Tadoussac, at the mouth of the Saguenay River, became France's principal trading centre on the Gulf of St. Lawrence. Pre-existing trading networks led from there to Hudson Bay and the Great Lakes. In the mid-1580s, as many as 20 vessels at a time called at Tadoussac in the summer.

Samuel de Champlain

Much had changed in the St. Lawrence valley since Cartier's journeys. On the official French expedition to the St. Lawrence valley in 1603, Samuel de Champlain, who kept the journal of the voyage, saw large numbers of Algonquian-speaking groups at Tadoussac and small groups at several encampments along the St. Lawrence; but the Iroquoian-speaking peoples of the St. Lawrence valley had mysteriously left. Champlain, a competent ship's captain, and on this expedition the cartographer, thus begins his long association with the St. Lawrence River valley. Over the course of the following 32 years, he would cross the Atlantic 22 times, travel 35 000 km, and camp on the banks of the St. Lawrence throughout all seasons of the year.

Unfortunately, we have only hypotheses, and no complete accounts, of the St. Lawrence valley from the time of Cartier's voyages in the mid-sixteenth century to Champlain's visit in 1603. Canadian economic historian Harold Innis believed that eastern Algonquian nations drove out the St. Lawrence Iroquoians.[3] They had obtained iron weapons before the St. Lawrence Iroquoians, which gave them a technological advantage in warfare.

In the 1970s, Bruce Trigger, an anthropologist who has done extensive research on the ethnohistory of northeastern North America, advanced another theory.[4] Trigger speculates that the landlocked New York Iroquois wanted European trade goods, but found them difficult to obtain from either the Saint Lawrence Iroquoians or the Algonquians. Consequently, the Iroquois raided and dispersed their neighbours, the St. Lawrence Iroquoians, some of whom may have moved west to join the Hurons on Georgian Bay on Lake Huron. Archaeologists, Trigger states, have established that European goods reached all of the New York Iroquois groups by 1600. These, he surmises, must have been largely obtained as booty from the St. Lawrence Iroquoians. Although both explanations for the disappearance of the St. Lawrence Iroquoians are plausible, insufficient data prevents definite conclusions. It is also possible that European diseases, inadvertently introduced by Cartier and the French, wiped out these people.

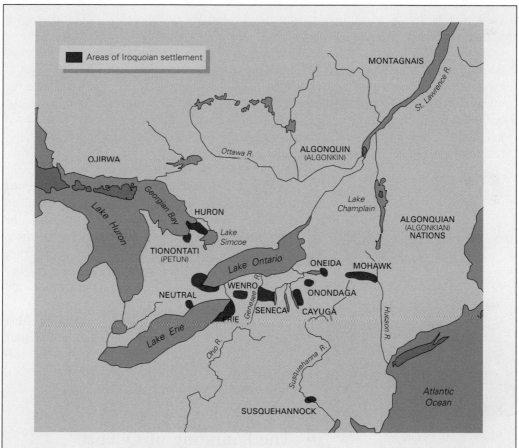

The St. Lawrence lowlands around 1600.

Source: Based on Bruce G. Trigger, *Natives and Newcomers* (Montreal/Kingston: McGill-Queen's University Press, 1985), p. 150.

The French in Acadia

Today we take it for granted that Quebec, founded in early July 1608, was the natural site for France's first permanent settlement in present-day Canada. But actually the French initially rejected this location. From 1604 to 1607 they searched elsewhere for the best place to establish a colony. They sailed south to the present-day Maritime provinces, a region with a climate milder than that of the St. Lawrence region and one potentially rich in minerals. They also searched for a more southerly location for the colony in the hope that they might still find a route to Asia.

Their first winter on a small island near the mouth of the St. Croix River, now on the border between Maine and New Brunswick, proved catastrophic; roughly half of the expedition of 79 died of scurvy. After their second summer exploring the coastline, the French stayed the winter of 1605–1606 on the south coast of what is now Nova Scotia. Their colony at Port-Royal became the first European agricultural settlement in what is now Canada. The French continued to explore the coastline the following summer and then wintered again at Port-Royal, but decided not to stay. After three years of considerable expenditures, unsuccessfully searching for mineral resources and the Northwest Passage, the French realized the area's limitations. The expedition could not enforce its fur-trade monopoly along the winding and indented coasts of the Maritimes. Ironically, the very year that the French left Acadia (the name given to the area of what is now Maine, New Brunswick, Nova Scotia, and Prince Edward Island), the English established their first permanent settlement at Jamestown in Virginia.

The French did return to Acadia, but only in the early 1630s did they make a serious attempt to establish a French colony there. Many of the settlers came from the west coast of France, near the Atlantic port of La Rochelle. Labourers skilled in harvesting salt joined the contingent of several hundred colonists. In Acadia, rather than clear the forested upland areas, they built dikes to reclaim the fertile marshland that the Bay of Fundy's strong tides flooded twice daily. To ensure the effective drainage of the diked marshlands, the Acadians also constructed a system of drainage ditches, combined with an *aboîteau* (a hinged valve in the dike itself), which allowed fresh water to run off the marshes at low tide and at the same time prevented salt water from flowing onto the diked farmland when the tide rose. For two to four years, the Acadians let snow and rain wash away the salt from the tidal marshes. At the end of that period they planted crops on the fertile, stone-free plains. As they reclaimed land from the sea, they encroached on Aboriginal lands, but nothing to the extent of the farming frontier in New England to the south. After the 1630s further emigration from France was quite limited, but the Acadian colony thrived in the mid-seventeenth century, and increased in number, thanks to natural increase.

Acadians repairing a dike in the early eighteenth century. This re-creation by Azor Vienneau is based on archaeological and historical evidence.

History Collection, Nova Scotia Museum; artist Azor Vienneau. Based on archaeological evidence from Belleisle, N.S/NSM 87.120.2

The Founding of Quebec

In July 1608 Samuel de Champlain, who had been a member of the Acadian expedition, returned to the St. Lawrence valley, to found a fur trading post from which the French could control access to the interior and prevent competition from other traders. This time Champlain served as the leader of the expedition. At the point where the St. Lawrence narrows before widening out again, and in the shadow of a towering cliff, Champlain constructed a *habitation*, a collection of wooden buildings built in the form of a quadrangle and surrounded by a stockade and moats. He called it Quebec—Kebec being the Algonquian word for "strait" or "narrow passage." Champlain's *habitation* became the heart of the first permanent and continuous French settlement in Canada. It is ironic that while Champlain selected an Algonquian name for his post, he never bothered to learn any of the First Nation languages. Neither did he ever obtain a full understanding of the Aboriginal peoples among whom he had settled.

In hindsight, one might ask why the Algonquians welcomed the French permanent trade settlement at Quebec. Like other Europeans, the French did not recognize the First Nations' rights to the land. They officially claimed the St. Lawrence valley for France on the basis of Jacques Cartier's "discovery" of it. And, as a Christian nation, the newcomers assumed they had the right to occupy non-Christians' lands. In 1627, for instance, they simply granted all of North America then not occupied by a Christian prince to the newly created Company of One Hundred Associates.

The First Nations of northeastern North America regarded the land as theirs. Each Algonquian band around Tadoussac and Quebec, for example, occupied a specific territory; the boundaries were well known to them and usually well defined by recognizable geographical features. Fortunately for the French, however, they had entered a war zone. The Algonquians welcomed the French traders because they saw them as potential allies who possessed muskets. They could use help against the Iroquois raiders. The fur trade post at Quebec also ensured that they could obtain badly needed iron goods, at advantageous rates.

Early French–Aboriginal Relations

No sooner had the French established Quebec and concluded an economic alliance with the Algonquians than the First Nations asked Champlain to form a military one. As the French depended on these nations for furs, they complied. In 1609, Champlain and the French joined the Algonquians and some Hurons, their Iroquoian-speaking allies in the interior, in an attack on the Iroquois to the southwest. The French firearms so frightened the Iroquois that they lost the battle at the lake the French named Lake Champlain. The next summer, the French and their First Nation allies again defeated an Iroquois war party near the mouth of the Richelieu River.

The Franco–Algonquian alliance proved invaluable to the French. The Algonquians taught the French how to adapt to winter, and supplied them with invaluable geographical information about the interior. The French learned the value of birchbark canoes, and when the waterways froze, of toboggans and snowshoes. As well, they relied on First Nations hunting bands for food.

In 1610, Champlain arranged an exchange with the Hurons. He sent Étienne Brûlé, a young Frenchman, to live with them. In return, Champlain took

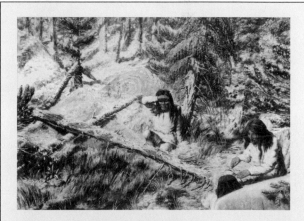

Indian Preparing Birch Bark Map for Professor Hind, *by Henry Youle Hind, 1861–1862. A scene from a mid-nineteenth-century expedition across what is now northern Quebec and Labrador. For more than three centuries, Europeans relied on the Aboriginal peoples for geographical information about the Americas.*

J. Ross Robertson Collection/Toronto Reference Library/T31956.

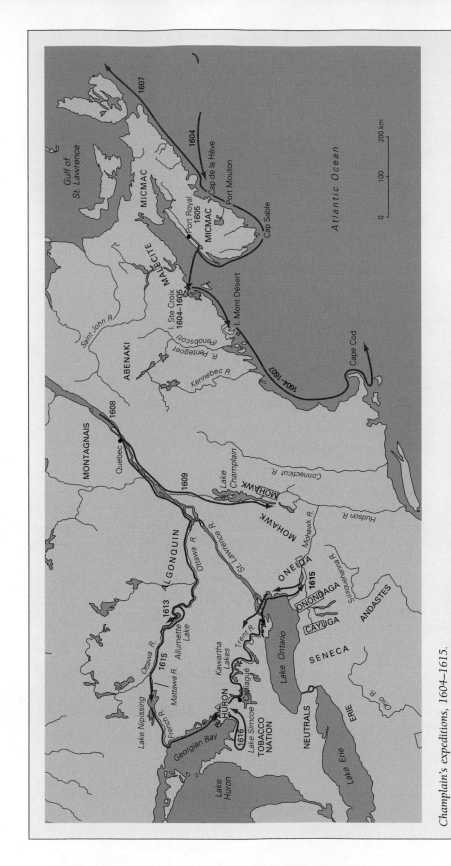

Champlain's expeditions, 1604–1615.

Source: D.G.G. Kerr, ed., *A Historical Atlas of Canada* (Toronto: Thomas Nelson & Sons, 1961), 16–17.

Savignon, brother of a Huron headman and roughly the same age as Brûlé, into his custody. Brûlé became the first of the *coureurs de bois* (literally, "runners of the woods"), the individuals who lived with the First Nations and reinforced France's economic and political alliance with the Algonquians and Hurons.

From Brûlé and Savignon the French learned about the Huron Confederacy, an alliance of several Iroquoian-speaking nations with a population of up to 30 000 on Lake Huron. The Hurons' trading area extended as far west as Lake Superior and as far north as James Bay. Huron, in fact, was the trading language of the entire Upper Great Lakes.

Champlain made his last journey into the interior in the summer of 1615, for the purpose of strengthening the Franco–Huron alliance. While in Huronia, Champlain concluded friendship treaties with individual Huron leaders, affirming French support in their wars—provided that the Hurons continued to trade with the French. By joining a large war party of Hurons and Algonquians against the Iroquois, he convinced the Hurons of his support. Henceforth, the French could live securely as guests among their Huron allies. By the 1620s, the Hurons supplied from one-half to two-thirds of the furs obtained by the French.

The Company of One Hundred Associates

New France grew slowly. During the winter of 1620–1621, no more than 60 people lived at Quebec. Thanks to the cooperation of the Aboriginal peoples, the fur trade required few Europeans. Furthermore, no incentive existed for Europeans to settle and farm in the northern colony. To whom would French farmers in New France have sold their produce? No market existed. In contrast, the English colony of Virginia, with its tobacco-based economy, had 2000 inhabitants by 1627, or twenty times New France's population. Even the newly established Dutch colony of New Netherlands in the Hudson River valley had 200 settlers by 1625.

In 1627, the French government, observing the success of other European settlements in America, decided to end New France's total dependency on furs. Cardinal Richelieu, Louis XIII's prime minister, sponsored a new company called the *Compagnie des Cent-Associés* ("Company of One Hundred Associates"), which obtained working capital from 100 investors to develop and exploit New France's resources and to encourage Roman Catholic missionary activity. In return for its trade monopoly, the company promised to bring out 4000 settlers, all French and Roman Catholic, within 15 years and to promote missions to the First Nations.

Unfortunately for New France, the project began at the worst possible time: war had just broken out between France and England. In 1627 the English seized Tadoussac and captured the French ships bringing 400 settlers to New France. In 1629, the English attacked Quebec itself. Cut off from France and their provisions long exhausted, Champlain and his starving garrison surrendered in July 1629. Champlain and the garrison left Quebec. For three years, the St. Lawrence remained closed to the French, which meant heavy losses for the Company of One Hundred Associates, losses from which it never really recovered. Only in 1632 did the English leave Quebec. Champlain returned to New France and undertook one last initiative: he founded a fur-trading post above Quebec in 1634 at Trois-Rivières.

Champlain deserves full credit for establishing New France, their Laurentian colony in northeastern North America. The French leader served, in effect if not in title, as New France's governor. Through his numerous alliances with the Algonquians and Hurons, managed by young French *coureurs de bois*, he kept the tiny trading post of Quebec alive. Rightly, he is considered "the founder of New France." With Champlain's death on Christmas Day, 1635, the effective leadership of the fur-trading colony passed into the hands of the religious orders, particularly the Jesuits.

The Contributions of the French Religious Orders

In the sixteenth century, France was rent by civil strife between Catholics and Protestants, or Huguenots. The Catholic majority in France fought back. The Roman Catholic church launched a "Counter-Reformation," first to root out the corruption in the Catholic church, and then to win back those lost to Protestant heretics. The Society of Jesus (commonly known as the Jesuits), the papacy's most expert missionaries, led the struggle. Other groups, such as the Ursulines, a female teaching order, followed them. Both the Jesuits and the Ursulines extended their mission to convert non-Christians throughout the world.

Champlain wanted the neighbouring Algonquians on the St. Lawrence to convert to Christianity, form settlements, and farm, as the French did. Ultimately he hoped that the French and the Christianized First Nations would amalgamate, through intermarriage, into a single people. The first French missionaries assigned the task of transforming the Aboriginal peoples into a French people were the Récollets, a branch of the Franciscan Friars. At first they believed the task would be relatively easy, but the Récollets quickly learned that the First Nations had no desire to assimilate into French society. Their seminary soon closed for lack of students and funds.

The Jesuit Order and the Ursulines

In an attempt to solve their financial problems, the Récollets sought to collaborate with the Jesuits, a wealthy and powerful order founded by Ignatius Loyola a century earlier. From 1625 to 1629, the Jesuits assisted the Récollets in establishing missions in New France. This highly disciplined order, renowned for its ability to attract able candidates, often of high rank, was also known for its willingness to assume the most dangerous tasks. Thanks to their *Relations*, or annual reports back to France, we know a great deal about their activities in New France.

In 1632, Cardinal Richelieu gave the Jesuits a monopoly over the Canadian mission field. Their work then began in earnest. Yet when they opened a school for Aboriginal children, they encountered the same problems as the Récollets had. Enlisting First Nation students proved difficult as parents often refused to let their children attend. The priests had to give presents to the families to gain students for the seminary. Many students ran away, and others became ill and died. The deaths increased the parents' resistance to their children's schooling, as did the French custom of physically punishing children, a practice foreign to the Aboriginal peoples' approach to child rearing.

The arrival of the Ursuline nuns in Quebec in 1639 marked the beginning of their outreach to the First Nations. The Jesuits invited them to Christianize and to "civilize" the young Aboriginal girls. But the Ursulines, despite determined efforts on their part, had little success. In 1668 Marie de l'Incarnation, founder of the Ursuline Order in New France, wrote, "We have observed that of a hundred that have passed through our hands we have scarcely civilized one. We find docility and intelligence in these girls but, when we are least expecting it, they clamber over our wall and go off to run with their kinsmen in the woods, finding more to please them there than in all the amenities of our French houses."[5]

The Jesuits Bring Indentured Workers to New France

The church, in effect, became the second industry of the colony. The Jesuits, Ursulines, and the Hospital nuns came in number to serve the Aboriginal peoples and in turn brought out *engagés*, or indentured workers, on three-year contracts, to help them. These newcomers created a market for agricultural produce in the colony. Upon being discharged, many returned to France, rather than stay on in a land that had little to offer in terms of security or creature comforts, with its formidable winters, heavily forested land to clear, and shortage of marriageable women. But some *engagés* stayed and cleared farms.

The Founding of Montreal

The Société de Notre-Dame de Montreal, a group of fervent French Roman Catholics, planned a mission settlement remote and independent from the main settlement at Quebec. It believed that once it had built a church, a school, and a hospital, the First Nations would come, and accept Christianity. The organizers chose the island of Montreal, at the crossroads of the Ottawa and the St. Lawrence Rivers, a location that could be easily reached by the Algonquian-speaking nations. Paul de Chomedey de Maisonneuve, a 33-year-old career soldier, led the first forty settlers to establish what they hoped would become a model Christian community. In mid-May 1642 they founded Ville-Marie, the future Montreal.

The first settlers farmed on the grassy areas where villages of the Laurentian Iroquoians once stood. The only sizable influx of new settlers, 100 in all, arrived in 1653. Despite an initial burst of enthusiasm, the outpost grew slowly. Chronic underpopulation remained a problem until the late 1660s. Two factors prevented the colony's expansion: the Société's quick loss of enthusiasm for its missionary enterprise, and the repeated raids by the Iroquois, who resented the founding of a French village in their northern hunting grounds. In 1663 the Sulpicians, another French religious order, took over the direction of the settlement and became the *seigneurs* of the island of Montreal.

New France in the Mid-1640s

In 1645—a decade after Champlain's death—the French colony in the valley of the St. Lawrence remained quite marginal. It contained only 600 residents and a few hundred *engagés*. Clerical intervention in the 1630s had helped, but the colony's population still remained smaller than that of a single large Iroquoian village.

The Missionaries' Arrival in Huronia

At the time of French–First Nations contact in the seventeenth century, the Hurons and the Iroquois were at war. A desire for war honours and prestige contributed to the hostility. Participation in a war party, if successful, raised a man's standing in his clan and village. It increased the chances of an advantageous marriage and hopes of one day becoming a village leader. Moreover, the necessity of avenging the dead led to more warfare, since the Iroquois and the Hurons believed the souls of the dead could not rest in peace until they had been avenged. This led to an escalation of the feud between the two hostile groups.

With the arrival of the Europeans, economic motives joined those of prestige and the blood feud as causes of Aboriginal warfare. Both the Iroquois and the Hurons needed a steady supply of furs to buy European trade goods. By the 1620s, the Hurons had

A rare photo of an Iroquois trail, taken a century ago in the territory of the Seneca, near Conesus Lake, New York. Generally, the paths followed the ridges, where the forest was not so thick.

National Anthropological Archives/Smithsonian Institution/947A.

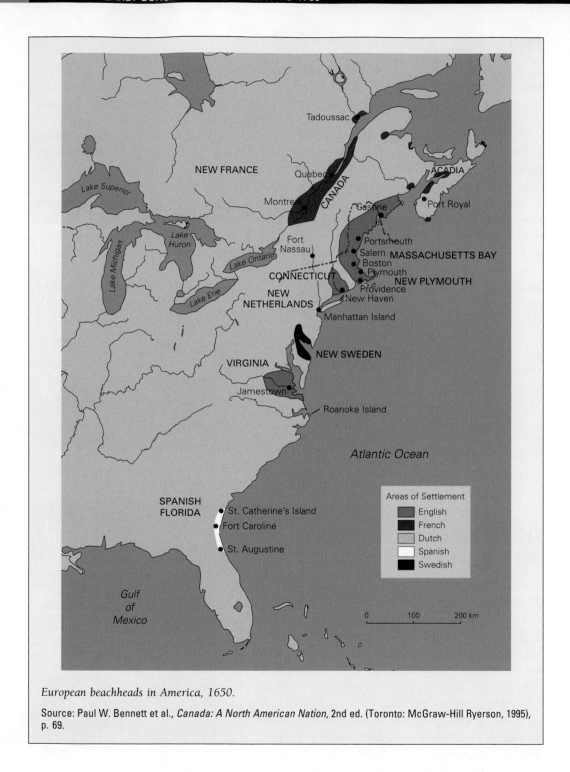

European beachheads in America, 1650.

Source: Paul W. Bennett et al., *Canada: A North American Nation*, 2nd ed. (Toronto: McGraw-Hill Ryerson, 1995), p. 69.

become the principal economic partners of the French, exchanging furs for corn and European goods with the neighbouring Algonquians, who, in turn, traded as far north as James Bay and along the shores of Lakes Michigan and Superior. As elsewhere on the continent, the fur trade and the goods that it brought enriched Huron culture. The Hurons began to decorate their pottery with more elaborate patterns and to use iron knives to make more intricate bone carvings.

The Jesuits and the Hurons

After establishing their economic alliance with them, the Hurons gave the French permission to send Roman Catholic priests to Huronia, first Récollets in 1615 and then Jesuits in 1627. As a condition for renewing the Franco–Huron alliance after the English occupation of Quebec in 1632, the French insisted that the Hurons allow Jesuits to live in Huronia. Reluctantly, they agreed. In 1634, Jean de Brébeuf and two companions reopened the Huron mission. Dressed in black gowns, wearing broad-brimmed black hats, and with iron chains and black beads hanging from their belts, the "Black Robes" went from village to village to spread the Christian gospel. The Hurons met them with apprehension and a growing fear, particularly after the outbreak of European diseases.

The Jesuit order put great effort into building up its mission. They mastered the Huron language and then communicated their ideas to the would-be converts. They also used nonverbal methods: pictures of holy subjects or of the sufferings of lost souls; religious statues; coloured beads as prizes for successful memorization; ceremonies, chants, and processions on holy days and on such occasions as baptisms, marriages, and funerals. They decorated the churches with crosses, bells, and candles, creating a colourful visual display.

Cultural Differences between the Hurons and the French

In this initial period the Jesuits made some progress, but the gulf between the two societies remained enormous. For the Hurons, the very meaning of existence was to maintain harmony with nature. They considered humans equal, not superior, partners to other entities in the natural world. Their sacred stories explained their perception of the universe: the relationship between humanity and the earth, between people and animals, between the sun and the moon, between sickness and health. Christianity differed from the Hurons' religion in viewing the world as provisional and preparatory to the afterlife. John Webster Grant, the Canadian religious historian, wrote that if the First Nations religious symbol was the circle, the Christians' "might well be an arrow running from the creation of the world through God's redeeming acts in history to the final apocalypse."[6]

To gain an audience among the Hurons, the Jesuits emphasized the similarities between the Hurons' faith and their own. They pointed out that both believed in a supernatural power that influenced their lives, one that the Hurons located in the sun or sky and the Jesuits in heaven. Both Huron shamans and Roman Catholic priests encouraged personal contact with the supernatural. At puberty, every young Huron man was expected, through fasting and a vision quest, to find his own guardian spirit. The Jesuits also encouraged spiritual quests and valued fasts and vigils. The common reliance on prayer revealed a shared conviction that divine power controlled warfare, caused rain or drought, and gave health or disease. Finally, both Jesuits and Hurons accepted the idea of an afterlife; for the Hurons it was a pleasant place where life continued essentially as on earth, and for Christians it was heaven.

Common elements aside, the two religions had enormous differences, such as the Christian insistence that only one deity ruled the universe. This conflicted with the Hurons' belief in many supernatural beings. Furthermore, the Hurons had nothing remotely close to the Jesuits' concepts of the Trinity and the Incarnation. Marriage was another controversial issue. The Jesuits found the Hurons' sexual behaviour aberrant. Among the Hurons, divorce was easy and frequent, in contrast with the Jesuits' ideal of the indissolubility of marriage. Since Huron children by custom belonged to the mother, divorce did not endanger family stability. The Hurons also failed to see lifetime marriage as superior to their own customs. Moreover, they could not understand the Jesuits' practice of celibacy and sexual self-denial.

The two cultures also disagreed on issues of human sinfulness and the need for salvation. Although the Hurons distinguished between good and evil, they had no concept similar to the missionaries' idea of universal guilt, of a fundamental inadequacy in human nature. Like most

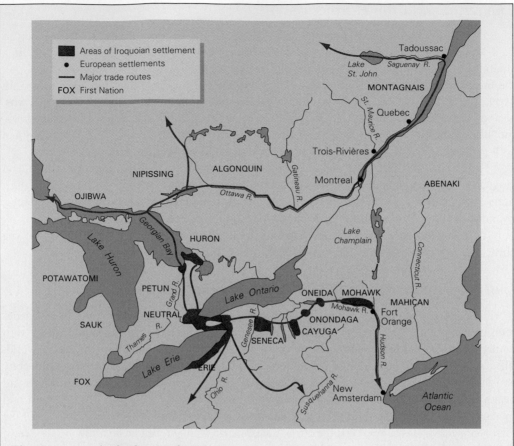

The St. Lawrence lowlands around 1640.

Source: Adapted from Bruce G. Trigger, *Natives and Newcomers* (Montreal/Kingston: McGill-Queen's University Press, 1985), p. 228.

Aboriginal North Americans, the Hurons believed that almost all people would experience the same pleasant afterlife, regardless of how they had lived on Earth. For the Jesuits, there was both a heaven and a hell. The only way to escape hell was through Christianity. This concept of a place of torment proved very difficult to convey to the Hurons.

The Jesuits tried to convince the Hurons of the worthiness of biblical standards. They insisted that the Hurons curtail easy divorce, marry for life, and end their undue reliance on dreams. To the Hurons, the missionaries threatened to subvert the very customs and beliefs essential to successful hunting, good health, and survival.

New Epidemics Strike Huronia

The French brought with them more than European trade goods and a Christian missionary message. Unknowingly, they brought European diseases that devastated the Hurons and their neighbours. By 1639 smallpox raged throughout Huronia, killing more than half the Huron population and reducing their numbers to 10 000. Since old people and children died in the greatest numbers, the Hurons lost much of their traditional religious knowledge, which tended to be the preserve of the elderly, and suffered a shortage of warriors in the next decade with the deaths of so many children.

By the late 1630s, the Hurons concluded that the Jesuits were sorcerers who brought disease. The Hurons recognized three major sources of illness: natural causes, unfulfilled desires of a person's soul (alleviated by a form of dream-fulfilment), and witchcraft. Not surprisingly, the Hurons blamed the new diseases on their visitors, since the Jesuits alone seemed immune to the diseases. The Jesuits' celibacy also suggested that the "white shamans" nurtured great supernatural power for the purposes of witchcraft. Furthermore, they seemed to cause death by their rituals: after they touched sick babies with drops of water, many died.

As the epidemics spread, the Hurons' fear of the Jesuits increased, and they denied them entry into their longhouses and villages. The Hurons harassed and threatened the Jesuits. On at least two occasions, in 1637 and 1640, general Huron councils discussed the death penalty for the missionaries, or at least the possibility of forcing "the sorcerers" to return to Quebec. Yet they pursued neither course of action. Many of the leading chiefs realized that the Hurons depended on the French for European hardware and dry goods and that now they could not live without them. Thus, trading relations with the French forced the Hurons to tolerate the missionaries.

Huron Christian Converts

In the early 1640s, conversions increased. Several factors contributed to this. No doubt the Jesuits' repeated explanations of the two faiths' common themes helped, and the Jesuits' unquestioned bravery during the Iroquois attacks influenced others to convert. Simple economics also influenced many Huron traders. French traders and government officials accorded Aboriginal Christians far greater honour and gave them additional presents at Quebec and Trois-Rivières. Another incentive to convert came from the French policy of selling guns only to First Nations people who were baptized. By 1646, the Christian Huron community numbered 500 and was growing.

The Final Struggle between the Hurons and the Iroquois

At a time when disease had weakened them and the growth of a Christian faction reduced their internal cohesion, the Hurons faced their greatest military threat from the Iroquois, who now searched for new sources of furs. The Huron country bordered the fur-rich areas around the upper Great Lakes that the western Iroquois wanted to exploit. The Iroquois also coveted the hunting grounds of southern Ontario.

Guns made the Iroquois a formidable foe. By 1639, they obtained firearms from English traders in the Connecticut valley and then directly from Dutch traders on the upper Hudson River. The longer and heavier Dutch guns were superior to those that the French sold to their Christian converts. Thus equipped, the Iroquois could raid the nations to the north much more easily than before.

WHERE HISTORIANS DISAGREE

Why the Hurons Accepted Christianity

In the 1640s an extraordinary event occurred; large numbers of Hurons in good health accepted Christianity. Before 1639, the Jesuits' attempts to Christianize the Hurons met with limited success, mostly with individuals who were on the point of death, yet by 1648 they had converted several thousand people. Had it not been for the

Iroquois defeat of the Hurons in 1649–1650 and their subsequent dispersal, the Jesuits' dream of establishing a Roman Catholic Huronia might have been realized. The massive conversion of Hurons to Christianity in the last years of Huronia has recently aroused new interest among historians.

The impact of disease offers one explanation for the Hurons' sudden receptiveness to Christianity. From 1635 to 1640, a series of epidemics carried away more than half the population. The Hurons lost many of their most skilful leaders and craftspeople, and this had the effect of increasing their dependence on trade with the French. Anthropologist Bruce G. Trigger, in his article "The French Presence in Huronia," identified the economic motives, among other factors, that led many Hurons to convert. They sought, through conversion, "to receive preferential treatment in their dealings with traders and officials in New France," and in particular, to be able to secure guns, which were given only to converts. In fact, as Trigger points out, "in 1648, when only 15 percent of the Hurons were Christian, half of the men in the Huron [trading] fleet were either converts or were preparing for baptism."[1]

Trigger's secular explanation of the Jesuits' success in his later two-volume work[2] greatly annoyed historian Lucien Campeau, a Jesuit. Referring to Trigger's work as "*malheureusement biaisée et peu exacte sous l'aspect historique*" [unfortunately biased and not very historically accurate], Campeau wrote a full account of his order's work among the Hurons in order to prove that the Hurons understood the Christian message as it was preached to them and that this message was the primary reason for their conversion.[3] In reply, Trigger pointed out that Campeau had failed to examine the most recent ethnohistorical research in preparing his study. Moreover,

he was too ready to accept, uncritically and at face value, the Jesuits' account of their mission work. "What we have here is splendid hagiography but very old-fashioned historiography."[4]

Biography can be useful in humanizing historical controversies such as this by putting a human face on the discussions. Yet, in the case of the Hurons, the would-be biographer faces incredible obstacles. As Trigger has written, "For the majority of Indians whose names have been preserved, only a few isolated events are recorded and even a skeletal life history of such individuals remains beyond our grasp."[5] Fortunately, however, Trigger was able to use the Jesuit *Relations* to provide an account of the Christian convert Joseph Chihoatenhwa.[6] Expanding upon Trigger's sketch, John Steckley, an anthropologist and student of the Huron language, has completed a short biography.[7] In Chihoatenhwa's case, economic factors apparently played very little part in his decision to accept Christianity, as he traded with the neighbouring Petuns and not with the French. Steckley argues, as does Trigger, that Joseph Chihoatenhwa converted in 1637 for reasons deep within his First Nations culture. "As a Christian, Chihoatenhwa did have, or believed he had, a source of power on which he could draw, a spiritual source not unlike that upon which a pre-contact Huron shaman could rely.... The priest appeared to have an effective medicine when no other was forthcoming; a preventative or cure which Chihoatenhwa accepted much [as] he would have in earlier times accepted the curing vision or dream of a powerful shaman."[8]

Historians, anthropologists, and ethnohistorians radically differ about the causes of the Hurons' conversion to

Christianity, but all agree on the importance of the phenomenon and on the richness of the Jesuits' descriptions of their efforts to convert the Hurons.

1. Bruce G. Trigger, "The French Presence in Huronia," *Canadian Historical Review*, 49 [1968]: 134; reprinted in R. Douglas Francis and Donald B. Smith, eds., *Viewpoints: Readings in Canadian History* (Toronto: Thomson Nelson, 2007), p. 37.

2. Bruce G. Trigger, *The Children of Aataentsic: A History of the Huron People to 1660*, 2 vols. (Montreal/Kingston: McGill-Queen's University Press, 1976).

3. Lucien Campeau, *La Mission des Jésuites chez les Hurons, 1634–1650* (Montreal: Éditions Bellarmin, 1987), p. 18.

4. Bruce G. Trigger, "Review of *La Mission des Jésuites chez les Hurons, 1634 1650* by Lucien Campeau," *Canadian Historical Review*, 69 (1988): 102.

5. Trigger, *The Children of Aataentsic*, vol. 1, p. 22.

6. Ibid., vol. 2, pp. 550–51, 565–67, 594–95, 598–601.

7. One of the three biographies included in John Steckley's *Untold Tales: Three 17th Century Huron* (Ajax, ON: R.A. Kerton, 1981).

8. Steckley, *Untold Tales*, pp. 9–10.

In 1648, Bruce Trigger estimates the Iroquois had more than 500 guns, while the Hurons probably had no more than 120.[7] These guns were crude, awkward to handle, and in many ways little better than the bow and arrow, but their thunderous noise and their ability to inflict mortal wounds made them a source of terror. They also increased their owners' self-confidence.

The Fall of Huronia and Its Impact on the French Colony

In mid-March 1649, a large Iroquois army struck a small Huron village, killing or capturing all but 10 of the 400 inhabitants. They then used the village as a base camp to destroy other settlements. Over the course of the campaign, several hundred Hurons died or were captured. The Iroquois took prisoner and tortured to death Fathers Jean de Brébeuf and Gabriel Lalemant. The attacks threw the surviving settlements into chaos. The Hurons, seeing their position as untenable, burned their villages and deserted them. Hunger and contagious diseases claimed many Huron refugees, who spent the winter on Christian Island, in Georgian Bay. A small number of survivors eventually accompanied the Jesuits to Quebec, where the order established a fortified mission for them on Île d'Orléans, just east of the town. Others joined the Algonquians to the north. In the next few years, a number of Hurons voluntarily joined the Iroquois. The Hurons' dispersal marked the end of Huronia.

The fall of Huronia led to Iroquois attacks on other Iroquoian-speaking peoples. The urgency behind this warfare appears to be a result of the severe depopulation from epidemics after the mid-1630s. Economic motives played a part, but the demand for captives to replace their deceased relatives played an equally important role. The Five Nations' subsequent victories over the Hurons' neighbours to the west, the Petuns, and to the south, the Neutrals, greatly disrupted the fur trade.

In the long run, however, the dispersal of the Hurons helped New France's economy. Because the Hurons could no longer supply food to the northern Algonquians, the latter became a new market for the colony's farmers. By 1653, the French *coureurs de bois* had also replaced the vanquished Huron intermediaries in the fur trade. They went inland to live with the Algonquians of the upper Great Lakes, or the "Ottawa," as the French called them, and to take their furs to New France.

Renewed Iroquois Attacks on New France

The early 1650s were difficult years for the colony. The Iroquois's use of guerrilla war tactics, their avoidance of open combat in favour of ambush, and the speed and unexpectedness of their attacks demoralized many colonists in the three tiny French settlements. Only with the outbreak of war between the Iroquois and the Eries to the west did New France obtain a five-year truce with the Iroquois in the mid-1650s. However, fighting resumed in 1658. Fortunately for the French, their population had increased by this time: the population had tripled, from 1050 permanent French residents in 1651 to nearly 3300 by 1662, thanks largely to new farming opportunities. From their Algonquian allies they also began to master guerrilla warfare tactics.

Security finally came for the habitants when, in 1663, King Louis XIV elevated the tiny colony to a royal province of France. Two years later he dispatched the Carignan-Salières regiment, over 1000 strong. In 1666, the French made two overland attacks on the Iroquois in present-day New York State. The Iroquois, who at the time were involved in a war with the Susquehannock (Iroquoian-speaking First Nations living in present-day Pennsylvania), made peace with the French in 1667. Twenty years of peace followed, during which the colony greatly advanced. It took lasting form in the years of Royal Government.

Early contact between Europeans and the First Nations in northeastern North America led to the development of the fur trade. The Europeans dealt with, to use the description of archaeologist Robert McGhee, "the most easterly representatives of a hemispheric civilization that had achieved full occupation and use of the American continents."[8] At the beginning of the seventeenth century, the European presence in what is now Eastern Canada remained marginal. The establishment in the early seventeenth century of French settlement in the St. Lawrence valley, and a French presence in Acadia, did allow for further advances by the French. The impact of new diseases wreaked havoc among the First Nations, weakening them at the moment of greater French expansion in the mid-seventeenth century.

NOTES

1. Morris Bishop, *Champlain: The Life of Fortitude* (Toronto: McClelland & Stewart, 1963 [1948]), p. 26.

2. H.P. Biggar, ed., *The Voyages of Jacques Cartier* (Ottawa: King's Printer, 1924), p. 245. For an important discussion of other possible origins of the word "Canada," see Olive P. Dickason, "Appendix 1: Origin of the Name 'Canada,'" in *The Myth of the Savage and the Beginnings of French Colonialism in the Americas* (Edmonton: University of Alberta Press, 1984), pp. 279–80.

3. Harold Innis, *The Fur Trade in Canada: An Introduction to Canadian Economic History* (rev. ed., Toronto: University of Toronto Press, 1956), p. 15.

4. Bruce G. Trigger, *Natives and Newcomers: Canada's 'Heroic Age' Reconsidered* (Kingston and Montreal: McGill-Queen's University Press, 1985), pp. 144–48.

5. Marie de l'Incarnation, *Word from New France: The Selected Letters of Marie de l'Incarnation.* Translated and edited by Joyce Marshall (Toronto: Oxford University Press, 1967), p. 341.

6. John Webster Grant, *Moon of Wintertime: Missionaries and the Indians of Canada in Encounter since 1534* (Toronto: University of Toronto Press, 1984), p. 24.

7. *Trigger, Natives and Newcomers*, 262.

8. Robert McGhee, "Canada Y1K: The First Millennium," *The Beaver*, December 1999/January 2000, p. 17.

BEYOND THE BOOK

Where Is Vinland?
http://www.canadianmysteries.ca/sites/vinland/whereisvinland/indexen.html
This site details the history of where Vinland has been believed to be, and presents arguments in favour of, and against, historically proposed locations.

National Historic Site: L'Anse aux Meadows
http://whc.unesco.org/pg.cfm?cid=31&id_site=4
An interactive, 360 degree panography of the L'Anse aux Meadows National Historic site. Click on "WHTour" in the Links section to view.

World Health Organization: Smallpox
http://www.who.int/mediacentre/factsheets/smallpox/en
Information about the historical significance and pathology of smallpox from the World Health Organization.

Encounters
http://www.champlain2004.org/html/encounter.html
Digitized primary sources detailing the first interactions between First Nations and European peoples in Canada. Site contains many digitized reports first made by European explorers when documenting their experiences. See also sections regarding daily life in New France.

Champlain Society

http://link.library.utoronto.ca/champlain/search.cfm?lang=eng
The digital collections of the Champlain Society contain numerous early primary source accounts of European contact with the First Nations, including Samuel de Champlain's voyages in New France. Browse the database by subject, and select, for example, "Canada—Discovery and exploration," "New France—Discovery and exploration."

The Jesuit Relations

http://puffin.creighton.edu/jesuit/relations
Translated and transcribed versions of *The Jesuit Relations and Allied Documents*, a very important source of knowledge of the history of New France and interactions between Aboriginal peoples and emigrated settlers.

Adventurers and Mystics

Canada: A People's History—Episode 2, Adventurers and Mystics. Directed by Claude Lortie and Serge Turbide (CBC, 2000).

Claiming the Wilderness

Canada: A People's History—Episode 3, Claiming the Wilderness. Directed by Serge Turbide and Claude Lortie (CBC, 2000).

RELATED READINGS

R. Douglas Francis and Donald B. Smith, eds., *Viewpoints: Readings in Canadian History* (Toronto: Thomson Nelson, 2007), contains the following article relevant to this chapter: Bruce G. Trigger, "The French Presence in Huronia: The Structure of Franco–Huron Relations in the First Half of the Seventeenth Century," pp. 24–48.

BIBLIOGRAPHY

Well-written summaries of the early European explorers' accounts include Samuel Eliot Morison, *The European Discovery of America: The Northern Voyages, A.D. 500–1600* (New York: Oxford University Press, 1971); Daniel J. Boorstin, *The Discoverers: A History of Man's Search to Know His World and Himself* (New York: Random House, 1983); and Robert McGhee, *Canada Rediscovered* (Ottawa: Canadian Museum of Civilization/Libre Expression, 1991). The primary texts are available in David Quinn, ed., *New American World: A Documentary History of North America to 1615*, 5 vols. (New York: Arno Press, 1979). The *Dictionary of Canadian Biography*, vol. 1, *1000–1700* (Toronto: University of Toronto Press, 1966), contains biographical portraits. It is now available online: www.biographi.ca. Ralph T. Pastore provides a bibliographical guide to the secondary literature in his essay "Beginnings to 1600," in M. Brook Taylor, ed., *Canadian History: A Reader's Guide*, vol. 1, *Beginnings to Confederation* (Toronto: University of Toronto Press, 1994), pp. 3–32.

Marcel Trudel provides an overview of the period in *The Beginnings of New France, 1524–1663* (Toronto: McClelland & Stewart, 1973). A shorter summary appears in W.J. Eccles, *The Canada Frontier, 1534–1760* (Toronto: Holt, Rinehart and Winston, 1969). His later work, *France in America*, rev. ed. (Markham, ON: Fitzhenry & Whiteside, 1990 [1972]), also contains information on the early French colonies in the Caribbean as well as New France and Acadia. Two well-written biographies of Champlain are available: Morris Bishop, *Champlain: The Life of Fortitude* (Toronto: McClelland & Stewart, 1963 [1948]); and Samuel Eliot Morison, *Samuel de Champlain: Father of New France* (Boston: Little, Brown, 1972). Bibliographical guides include Jacques Rouillard, ed., *Guide d'histoire du Québec du régime français à nos jours: Bibliographie commentée* (Montreal: Éditions du Méridien, 1991); and Thomas Wien, "Canada and the Pays d'en haut, 1600–1760," in M. Brook Taylor, ed., *Canadian History: A Reader's Guide*, vol. 1, *Beginnings to Confederation* (Toronto: University of Toronto Press, 1994), pp. 33–75.

For First Nations affairs, see Bruce G. Trigger's *The Children of Aataentsic: A History of the Huron People to 1660*, 2 vols. (Montreal/Kingston: McGill-Queen's University Press, 1976), and his *Natives and Newcomers: Canada's "Heroic Age" Reconsidered* (Montreal/Kingston: McGill-Queen's University Press, 1985). Denys Delâge's *Bitter Feast: Amerindians and Europeans in Northeastern North America, 1600–64*, trans. Jane Brierley (Vancouver: University of British Columbia Press, 1993), also provides a complete overview. Arthur J. Ray, *Indians in the Fur Trade* (Toronto: University of Toronto Press, 1974), reviews economic aspects of early Aboriginal–European contact. A good overview of early French–First Nation relations is the chapter "The Native People and the Beginnings of New France" in John A. Dickinson and Brian Young's *A Short History of Quebec*, 3rd ed. (Montreal/Kingston: McGill-Queen's University Press, 2003), pp. 3–27. For an historical geographer's review of early European contact and settlement, see the chapter by Cole Harris, "The Northwestern Atlantic, 1497–1632," in his *The Reluctant Land. Society, Space, and Environment In Canada before Confederation* (Vancouver: UBC Press, 2008), pp. 20–51. Emma Anderson's *The Betrayal of Faith. The Tragic Journey of a Colonial Native Convert* (Cambridge: Harvard University Press, 2007), is a biography of Pierre Pastedechouan, an early-seventeenth-century Algonquian convert to Christianity. A good short summary of the Jesuits' contact with the Hurons is contained in Henry Warner Bowden, *American Indians and Christian Missions* (Chicago: University of Chicago Press, 1981), pp. 59–95.

For excellent maps of early European exploration see: R. Cole Harris, ed., *Historical Atlas of Canada,* vol. 1, *From the Beginning to 1800* (Toronto: University of Toronto Press, 1987); and Derek Hayes, *Historical Atlas of Canada: Canada's History Illustrated with Original Maps* (Vancouver: Douglas and McIntyre, 2002).

VUE DE QUEBEC,
Capitale du Canada.

Fleuve S? Laurent

Chapter Three

NEW FRANCE AND ACADIA, 1663–1760

TIME LINE

1663	Louis XIV makes New France a royal province under his direct control
1682	The first term of office of the Comte de Frontenac, the best-known governor of New France; he also served from 1689 to 1698
1686	The number of French settlers in present-day Nova Scotia grows to 800
c. 1700	The ratio between males and females in New France becomes evenly balanced
1713	In the Treaty of Utrecht, France cedes Acadia to England; the beginning of 30 years of peace in the St. Lawrence valley
1720	France begins the construction of its fortress Louisbourg on Île Royale (Cape Breton Island)
1755	The expulsion of the Acadians begins
1760	Of the 67 000 European inhabitants in the St. Lawrence valley, 10 percent lived in the Trois-Rivières district, with the remainder divided equally between the Quebec and Montreal regions

In 1661, Louis XIV became king of France. He created an absolute monarchy in which all authority descended from him ("*L'état c'est moi*," he said in his famous phrase). The "Sun King," as he became known, ruled France for the next half-century, until his death in 1715. The new monarch sought to create a dynamic French presence in North America by making New France a *province de France*, a colony directly under his personal rule. Jean-Baptiste Colbert, the minister of the marine, or to use the modern term, minister of colonies, worked to strengthen the colony's economic infrastructure. He also introduced new political institutions that would last nearly a century. The French colony in the St. Lawrence valley truly took form in the period of Royal Government. In contrast, however, the colony of Acadia received little attention.

The French used the name "Acadia" to distinguish the eastern or maritime part of New France from the valley of the St. Lawrence, which they called Canada. Under French rule, Canada and Acadia remained separate colonies. Just where Acadia ended and Canada began was never clearly defined, but certainly Acadia included present-day Maine, New Brunswick, Nova Scotia, and Prince Edward Island. Acadia had the misfortune of being located in a war zone between the English- and French-dominated areas.

The First Half-Century of Royal Government in Canada

Colbert dreamed of making Canada into a much more self-reliant, defensible colony, with a prosperous agricultural base and its own basic domestic industries. The minister wanted it to become a "compact colony," one centred in the St. Lawrence valley, without unnecessary forts and outposts on the periphery. He also opposed western expansion. Colbert's first objective was to strengthen the colony militarily. In the mid-1660s, he dispatched regular troops to New France, the Carignan-Salières regiment. When the Iroquois made peace in 1667, Colbert began his mission to transform the St. Lawrence valley into a profitable and well-populated colony.

The Reform of the Seigneurial System

In fashioning the French colony in the St. Lawrence valley, the minister of the marine reformed the system of land holdings. The system used was similar to the feudal system in France. Peasant settlers, or *censitaires*, depended on *seigneurs*, or lords (or, more appropriately, squires or gentry), in turn themselves vassals of the king. Title to all the land rested with the king, who granted fiefs, or estates, as he saw fit. The soil belonged to the seigneur, but the mineral or subsoil rights and all oak trees on the property belonged to the monarch. Landowners who acquired large domains and who did nothing to improve them lost their lands to more energetic seigneurs.

In 1627, the Company of One Hundred Associates gained legal and seigneurial rights over the territory of New France. The company in turn granted to favoured individuals—usually nobles or religious bodies such as the Jesuits, the Ursulines, or the Sulpicians—large tracts of land, called *seigneuries*, along the St. Lawrence between Quebec and Montreal. In return for their rectangular estates fronting on the river and usually extending into the foothills behind, the seigneurs undertook to bring out the *censitaires* (or *habitants*, to employ Canadian usage), who in turn paid them rent and dues.

Under royal government, the *intendant*, among his other administrative duties, granted seigneuries and supervised the seigneurial system. On his arrival in 1665, Jean Talon, the first intendant of New France, implemented Colbert's plan. He made actual occupancy a condition of all future grants. Talon and his immediate successors also kept the size of the seigneuries relatively small to prevent the rise of a class of large landowners who might challenge royal authority. Nearly 200 seigneuries were open for settlement by 1715, most of them along the St. Lawrence from Montreal to below Quebec.

The Obligations of the Seigneurs and the *Censitaires*

Both the seigneurs and the *censitaires* had obligations to fulfil under the seigneurial system. The seigneurs had to clear some of their seigneury, maintain a manor house, and reside there or have a responsible person living there throughout the year. They had to make land grants of up to 80 ha to any genuine settlers who applied. Finally, on part of their land, they had to establish a flour mill for the use of their *censitaires*. Some seigneurs also maintained a court of law to settle minor disputes.

The *censitaires*, or habitants, also had responsibilities. They had to build their own house, clear their land, and pay their seigneur the *cens* (a small cash payment) and *rentes* (another money payment). Together, these two charges amounted to less than one-tenth of a *censitaire*'s annual income. They had to take their wheat to the seigneurial mill, paying the seigneur one sack of flour out of every fourteen for this privilege. In a few seigneuries, the seigneur had the *droit de corvée* (right to forced labour), usually three days per year, determined in the contract with the *censitaire*. As well, the *censitaires* were required by the Crown to work without pay for a day or two a year, doing general maintenance work on any seigneurial roads or bridges. In return for their grant of land, the habitants had to maintain the portion of road that passed through their farms. If they met these requirements, they became virtual owners of their land, which they could pass on to their children. If they sold their land outside their families, however, they had to pay the seigneur a portion of the money they obtained, somewhat like a real-estate sales tax.

Under Royal Government, the settlers became part of a well-organized social unit and gained title to a tract of land. In time, the seigneur built a manor house, a church, and a mill on the seigneury. Many seigneurs in pioneer times lived and worked as their habitants did, and this blunted the social distinctions that had prevailed in France between lord and peasant. Later, social distinctions became important as the seigneuries became heavily settled and the opportunity for social mobility declined.

The Growth of Settlement

To help populate the seigneuries, Colbert and Jean Talon worked to correct a social imbalance in the colony: the abundance of eligible bachelors and the shortage of French women. In Montreal in 1663, for example, there was only one marriageable woman for every eight eligible men. Colbert sought French women to immigrate to the colony who were strong enough for work in the fields and who had a good

Thomas Davies (c. 1737–1812), an English military artist, completed this painting of Château-Richer on the Côte de Beaupré, east of Quebec City, in 1787. It offers an excellent view of a mature rural landscape along the St. Lawrence River in the late eighteenth century. The wooden enclosures in the river and the tidal marshes are traps for eels. Note the long strip farms reaching back into the interior from the individual farm houses by the river.

Thomas Davies A *View of Château-Richer near Quebec in Canada*, Taken in 1788, 1788 Photo © National Gallery of Canada. National Gallery of Canada, Ottawa moral character. At first the French Crown selected orphanage girls, but when they proved not to be rugged enough, it recruited young, healthy country girls. A number of the *filles du roi* ("daughters of the king") were not much older than sixteen. The king provided substantial dowries —"the king's gift"—usually consisting of clothing or household supplies. The state sent out nearly 800 *filles du roi* between 1663 and 1673.

WHERE HISTORIANS DISAGREE

The Nature of the Seigneurial System in New France

French-Canadian historians have debated the nature of the seigneurial system in New France for more than a quarter of a century. Earlier historians, such as François-Xavier Garneau, held that the system was neither harsh nor oppressive. According to them, the institutions that France established in the St. Lawrence valley, including the seigneurial system, had been purified in the new setting, their negative aspects removed by the French Crown. In 1899, historian Benjamin Sulte suggested that the seigneur in New France was not an exploiter but a "colonization agent."[1] This traditionalist interpretation of New France as an open, egalitarian society dominated in Quebec until the mid-twentieth century.

A new, critical view of the seigneurial system emerged in the 1960s and 1970s. In 1974, Louise Dechêne published a meticulous local study of the Montreal area that pointed to the oppressive nature of the seigneurial system in the late seventeenth century.[2] She thus sided with fellow historian Fernand Ouellet, who, in his numerous writings from the 1960s to the 1980s, argued that eighteenth-century New France was a class-bound society. Both Dechêne and Ouellet maintained that seigneurial practices in the St. Lawrence valley conformed to French patterns. In some cases, the customs in Canada were more outdated than those in France. As Ouellet wrote in 1981, "In brief, the ancien régime society that had developed in the St. Lawrence valley, far from being a modernized or purified version of that of the mother country, was in a sense more archaic."[3]

Anglophone historians have divided equally on the seigneurial system. R. Cole Harris, for instance, agreed with traditionalist French-Canadian historians. He questioned the interpretation that farmers in New France occupied a position comparable to that of peasants in rural France during the last two centuries of pre-revolutionary France. "Rural Canada provided relative opportunity (cheaper land and higher wages) for ordinary people, and relative disincentive (higher labour costs, land of little value, and weak markets) for a landed elite."[4] Harris argued that the rural population of New France was independent and self-reliant, and that it had opportunities for upward mobility. To a certain extent, the late W.J. Eccles, the leading anglophone historian on New France, in the 1970s and 1980s, sided with the traditionalists. He wrote, "The seigneurs were little more than land settlement agents and their financial rewards were not great."[5]

Historian Allan Greer has challenged the traditionalists' viewpoint, He contends that "exploitation, domination, and the clash of interests were characteristics of rural Canada since the early years of the French regime."[6] More recently, he elaborated further: "By the end of the French regime, a substantial proportion of the surplus production, that is, of the grain not needed to keep family members alive, was being siphoned off by the colony's seigneurs. All in all, seigneurial exactions did tear a significant chunk out of the habitant household economy."[7]

1. Benjamin Sulte, "Le Système seigneurial," in *Mélanges historiques*, vol. 1 (Montreal: 1918), p. 80; cited in Serge Jaumain and Matteo Sanfilippo, "Le Régime seigneurial en Nouvelle-France: Un débat historiographique," *The Register*, 5, 2 (Autumn 1984): 227.

2. Louise Dechêne, *Habitants et marchands de Montréal au XVIIe Siècle* (Paris: Les Edition Plons, 1974).

3. Fernand Ouellet, "The Formation of a New Society in the St. Lawrence Valley: From Classless Society to Class Conflict," in Jacques A. Barbier, ed. and trans., *Economy, Class and Nation in Quebec: Interpretive Essays* (Toronto: Copp Clark Pitman, 1991), p. 33; originally published in French in the *Canadian Historical Review*, 62, 4 (1981): 407–50.

4. R. Cole Harris, in the new preface to *The Seigneurial System in Early Canada: A Geographical Study*, 2nd ed. (Montreal/Kingston: McGill-Queen's University Press, 1984), p. xix.

5. W.J. Eccles, *The Canadian Frontier 1534–1760* (Toronto: Holt, Rinehart and Winston, 1969), p. 68.

6. Allan Greer, *Peasant, Lord, and Merchant: Rural Society in Three Quebec Parishes, 1740–1840* (Toronto: University of Toronto Press, 1985), p. xiv.

7. Allan Greer, *The People of New France* (Toronto: University of Toronto Press, 1997), p. 38.

The girls, kept under supervision in one place, chose their husbands themselves, usually within two weeks after arrival. A young man in search of a wife had to declare his possessions and means of livelihood to the "directress" in charge of the girls. To encourage marriage, the government fined bachelors and denied them trading rights. Thus, men sought brides, and women had a good deal of choice. Usually they immediately wanted to know whether the suitor had a farm.

Even if the young man had built a home, a difficult life awaited these women, whose marriage contract bound them for life. They faced relentless work in clearing and maintaining their new family farms. In New France women toiled in the fields alongside the men. The severity of Canadian winters with their extreme cold also came as a shock. In northern France, snow covered the ground for a few days, at most.

Fortunately, though, by the time the *filles du roi* arrived, the French settlers had learned to adjust to winter conditions. They now slaughtered animals at the onset of winter and hung the meat in icy cellars. By eating fresh meat and the past season's vegetables through the winter, they escaped scurvy. They also now constructed houses in ways that improved heat retention and heating efficiency, by digging cellars first and by putting fireplaces in the centre of the houses. In addition, they built roofs with steep angles that readily shed the snow. In the late seventeenth century, the settler introduced another improvement: iron fireboxes that produced four times more heat than conventional fireplaces. They built larger barns to store fodder for the winter and to keep domestic animals inside during the coldest weather.

To make the settlers' lives easier, Colbert sent livestock to Canada at the Crown's expense. The first horses arrived in 1665. The First Nations, who had never seen such animals, called them the "moose of France." Horses thrived in the colony. The habitants developed a particular fondness for them, and by the eighteenth century even the poorest settler tried to keep one. By the 1720s, there was one horse for every five settlers.

French Immigrants by Sex and Decade, 1608–1759

PERIOD	MEN	WOMEN	TOTAL
Before 1630	15	6	21
1630–1639	88	51	139
1640–1649	141	86	227
1650–1659	403	239	642
1660–1669	1075	623	1698
1670–1679	429	369	798
1680–1689	486	56	542
1690–1699	490	32	522
1700–1709	283	24	307
1710–1719	293	18	311
1720–1729	420	14	434
1730–1739	483	16	499
1740–1749	576	16	592
1750–1759	1699	52	1751
Unknown	27	17	44
Total	**6908**	**1619**	**8527**

Source: R. Cole Harris, ed., *Historical Atlas of Canada*, vol. 1, *From the Beginning to 1800* (Toronto: University of Toronto Press, 1987), plate 45. Reprinted by permission of the University of Toronto Press Incorporated.

In the first years of Royal Government, the Crown sent several thousand men, mostly indentured labourers, and women to Canada. Many died from disease, either on the voyage or in the colony itself. A number returned to France. Nonetheless, New France's population grew rapidly from roughly 3000 in 1663 to almost 10 000 a decade later. Most settled along the St. Lawrence River from below Quebec to Montreal, and they cleared more land east of Montreal along the Richelieu River.

The Settlement of the St. Lawrence Valley

Throughout the French regime, the St. Lawrence River remained the colony's main thoroughfare, both in summer by canoe or small boat and in winter by sleigh over the ice. Frontage along the water highway was always most sought after. In addition, the settlers wanted to be close to one another, within hailing distance of their neighbours, in the event of Iroquois attacks. Around Quebec, the shores of the St. Lawrence already looked like one sprawling, unending village street, with the habitants' whitewashed farmhouses huddled close together. The narrow farms extending back from the river were often twenty times as long as they were wide.

New France achieved significant population growth from 1663 to 1672. The women sent out in Colbert's great wave of immigrants married and produced large families. In the late seventeenth century, the state encouraged births by offering what might be viewed as Canada's first baby bonuses. Couples with ten or more living children received a substantial gift of money. The sexes became evenly balanced in New France. By 1700, women were an average age of 22 when they were married, an age seven years higher than it had been 40 years earlier! Their spouses tended by 1700 to be older; the males averaged 28 years of age. Despite disasters, such as the smallpox epidemic of 1701 which killed 1000 people, New France's rapid population increase continued. It doubled every 25 years, almost entirely as a result of the high birth rate rather than immigration. The fact that women married earlier than their European counterparts effectively gave them more child-bearing years.

In the colony's early years, women gave birth to eight or nine children on average (after 1700, the figure dropped to seven). One out of every five children, however, died before the age of one; hence the average "completed" family in the eighteenth century consisted of 5.65 children per couple. Midwives delivered babies at home. A new mother might have a woman friend stay for a week or so after the birth, and her own mother usually stayed with her for at least a month.

Colbert's Administrative Reforms

To mark New France's new status as a royal colony, Colbert established administrative structures identical to those already existing in the provinces of France. At the top was the king, Louis XIV. He, however, delegated enormous powers to his ministers, particularly to Colbert. In effect, the government of New France resided with the minister of the marine, assisted by his *commis*, or secretary (the equivalent of a twenty-first-century deputy minister in Canada).

In the political structure of Royal Government, the governor general held supreme authority. Almost without exception from the nobility or the military, he ensured that the other officials discharged their responsibilities honestly and efficiently. He had undisputed control over military and diplomatic affairs. Probably the most celebrated occupant of the post in the late seventeenth century was the Comte de Frontenac (1672–1682 and 1689–1698), who spent much of his time dealing with the First Nations and with the English colonies.

The intendant—the official responsible for justice, public order, and finance—was the second-ranking official in the colonial hierarchy. A skilled administrator with a good educational background and, usually, extensive legal training, he ran most of the daily affairs of New France. He managed the budgets of both the army and the colony. The intendant headed the police and looked after road construction and maintenance. He was also responsible for the construction and maintenance of fortifications.

The bishop played a role in the political life of the colony, even though the powers of the office were significantly reduced after 1663. When the Sovereign Council was first established, the bishop ranked directly behind the governor. Thus, the first bishop, François de Laval, initially shared with the governor the responsibility of selecting the other council members from among the leading colonists. But after Laval clashed with the governor, he lost this right. Thereafter, the bishop's influence declined, and his attendance at the council became infrequent. The Crown respected the social and religious role of the church, but opposed any political authority it might claim. The minister of the marine instructed the governor and the intendant to subordinate the church to the authority of the state. After 1663, the king nominated the bishop and contributed 40 percent of the colonial church's finances in order to control the church.

The Sovereign Council, after 1703 known as the Superior Council, both made laws and heard criminal and civil cases. The members of the tribunal sat around a large table, with the governor, bishop, and intendant at the head—the governor in the centre, the bishop on the governor's right, and the intendant on the governor's left. As the amount of litigation in the colony increased, the council restricted itself to legal functions, and the intendant enacted legislation. In 1664 the law for the area around Paris, the so-called Custom of Paris (*coutume de Paris*), officially became the colony's legal code. Today's Civil Code in Quebec evolved from this "law of Canada."

Colbert also established the office of captain of militia. In 1669, the intendant organized the entire male population between the ages of 16 and 60 into militia units. He formed a company in each parish and appointed a captain from among the most respected habitants to command it. The office carried with it no salary, but it brought considerable status and prestige; the captains became the most influential men in their communities. In addition to drilling the militia, supervising their equipment, and leading them in battle, the captains acted locally as the intendant's agents, communicating his regulations and ordinances to the habitants and seeing

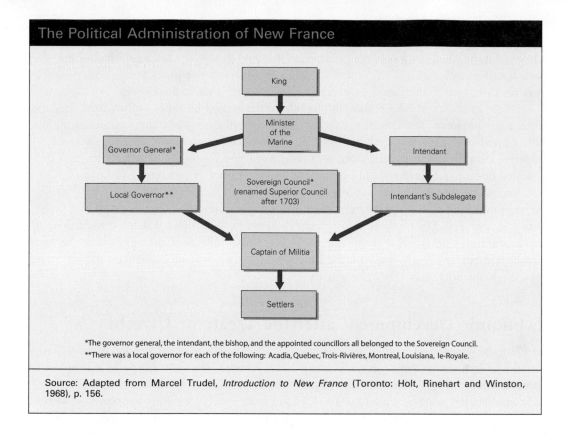

The Political Administration of New France

*The governor general, the intendant, the bishop, and the appointed councillors all belonged to the Sovereign Council.
**There was a local governor for each of the following: Acadia, Quebec, Trois-Rivières, Montreal, Louisiana, le-Royale.

Source: Adapted from Marcel Trudel, *Introduction to New France* (Toronto: Holt, Rinehart and Winston, 1968), p. 156.

that they were carried out. They also directed the *corvées* for work on bridges and roads. During a *corvée*, even the local seigneur came under the militia captain's command. This new office thus prevented the seigneurs from becoming too powerful.

Colbert made no provision for local self-government. New France had no municipal governments, nor mayors or town councils. Furthermore, people could not call a meeting or arrange a public assembly. Government came from above, not from below. Even the magistrates of the Sovereign Council were appointed and paid stipends, and were, therefore, dependent on the governor and the intendant. The only elected office in the late seventeenth century (and for the remainder of the French regime) was that of church warden. Yet a little flexibility did exist. Occasionally the governor and the intendant consulted the public on issues of general interest. They called together seventeen assemblies between 1672 and 1700.

The Failure of Colbert's Plan for a "Compact Colony"

Having set up a new administrative structure, Colbert sought capable men to fill the senior posts to build a self-reliant colony, or a "compact colony," in the St. Lawrence valley. Intendant Jean Talon, a man of about 40 who had previously been an intendant in France, began investigating New France's economic possibilities—discovering what the soil would grow, surveying the forests, and sponsoring expeditions to search for minerals. He also tried to develop a shipbuilding industry in the colony. The Crown sent skilled ship carpenters, tarmakers, blacksmiths, and foundry workers, as well as the necessary supplies. Three ships were built, but the industry never became profitable. The imported skilled workers demanded high wages, iron had to be imported, and the industry required heavy capital outlays. In the end, ships cost much more to build in Canada than in France, and the program was curtailed.

New France also failed to develop a large overseas trade with the West Indies. Ships out of New France could sail south only in the summer months—the hurricane season in southern waters. They had to run the gauntlet of English vessels in wartime. As well, the Canadians had to compete with New England mariners, who could sell wheat and fish at lower prices year-round. For these reasons, then, New France failed to secure a foothold in the West Indies market.

Of the industries in New France, fishing offered the greatest promise. Colbert subsidized the necessary equipment. But Canadian fishers faced several disadvantages, the foremost being the failure to establish salt works in the colony. This meant a reliance on France for a supply of salt. In addition, French merchants in France sent their ships directly to the Grand Banks, and they returned directly to France without ever landing in New France or purchasing Canadian fish.

One of Talon's enterprises succeeded: the brewery at Quebec. Cheap beer brewed in the colony proved popular. Unfortunately for Colbert's hopes, everything Canada produced, except furs and beer, could be obtained more cheaply elsewhere. When Jean Talon left the colony in 1672, the industries he had promoted died. The Crown allocated no more funds because France had begun a costly war with the Dutch. New France depended solely on the fur trade, which remained its main economic activity.

Economic Development after the Treaty of Utrecht

In 1713, the British and French signed the Treaty of Utrecht, which ended a period of roughly two decades of continuous warfare in northeastern North America. The welcome peace inaugurated a three-decade-long truce. This "30 years of peace" finally enabled New France to consolidate itself economically and socially. This time the French government successfully supported economic initiatives in New France. The number of flour mills in the colony increased by 50 percent between 1719 and 1734. The fishing industry also grew, with fish and seal oil becoming export products. Tanneries were established at Quebec, Lévis (opposite Quebec), and Montreal.

The Crown also improved transportation. In 1737, the intendant completed the "Chemin du Roi" (King's Highway), which connected Montreal and Quebec for the first time. It greatly facilitated travel. A return trip by water from Montreal to Quebec might take several weeks, while a coach trip over the King's Highway could be completed in as little as nine days. The highway opened up new lands north of the St. Lawrence to settlement. It also became the colony's lifeline in the summer of 1759, when the British fleet gained control of the St. Lawrence.

Private citizens also worked to develop the colony's industrial resources. Beginning in the 1720s, local contractors established small shipyards along the St. Lawrence. The intendant assisted in establishing state-owned shipyards. He also encouraged the building of large ships, even though Canada's resources were better suited for small ones. In the 1740s, for example, the royal shipyard at Quebec constructed nine warships. The labour costs were too high, however, and in the 1750s the shipyard cut back to only five naval vessels.

In 1729, François Poulin de Francheville established Canada's first heavy industry, the St. Maurice Forges, or ironworks, 15 km north of Trois-Rivières. But by 1741, as a result of serious technical errors and lax administration, the company declared bankruptcy. The Crown, which had given large subsidies, now took control. Production under royal administration fluctuated greatly from year to year, but for a few years profits were reported. The ironworks employed about 100 workers, who produced sizable quantities of cooking pots, pans, and soup ladles, as well as cannons and cannonballs. They also made the first Canadian stoves.

By 1700, agriculture replaced the fur trade as the leading economic activity in New France, with three out of four Canadian families involved in farming. This greatly changed the colony's economic structure. Between 1706 and 1739, the Canadian population increased 250 percent and the amount of land under cultivation increased 430 percent. Wheat accounted for about

View of Quebec, about 1730. Note the Fort, "A"; the Cathedral, "E"; the Hotel Dieu, "G"; and the Bishop's Residence, "H."

Library and Archives Canada/C-43730.

three-quarters of the cultivated farmland, so the colony became self-sufficient in wheat and flour. (Wheat, in fact, made up one-third of the colony's exports by the 1730s.) The habitants also grew peas, oats, rye, barley, buckwheat, and maize. Surprisingly, the vegetable that in the early nineteenth century became the staple food of the habitants' diet was not yet grown in the colony: the English introduced the potato to the St. Lawrence valley after 1760.

Market conditions limited the production of produce and the growth of livestock. The towns of New France were not large, and many town dwellers kept their own gardens and livestock. But, in the eighteenth century, an increase in the population and the opening of an export market improved the situation. Flour, biscuits, and peas were exported regularly to the new French fortress at Louisbourg on Île Royale (now Cape Breton Island) as well as to the French West Indies.

The unlimited supply of land and the high productivity of the new soil discouraged farmers from applying the intensive agricultural methods then commonly used in France, where land was scarce and expensive. When the good land became exhausted, the farmers cleared more with no concern for conservation. They avoided elaborate crop rotations, heavy manuring, and selective breeding of their cattle.

The Society of New France in the Eighteenth Century

During the eighteenth century, about one-quarter of New France's inhabitants resided in towns. At the end of the French regime, in 1760, nearly 8000 people lived in Quebec, with Montreal having only one-half of Quebec City's population. Quebec was the seaport and administrative capital, Montreal was a secondary town on the westernmost edge of French settlement. Trois-Rivières remained a small service centre with fewer than 1000 inhabitants.

From the St. Lawrence, the church spires, the religious communities' residences, the governors' and intendants' homes, the stone warehouses along the waterfront, gave the towns of New France an impressive look. But appearances were deceiving. Well into the eighteenth century, pigs rooted among the refuse citizens dumped in the narrow streets. On a few streets open sewers carried garbage down to the river during heavy rains and the uncobbled streets became quagmires. There was no street lighting.

Royal officials and military officers dominated life in Quebec, Montreal, and Trois-Rivières. In terms of social ranking, these senior administrators stood at the top. The metropolitan French predominated in the Sovereign Council and held the top positions in the civil-service hierarchy. At the local level Canadian-born judges dominated.

The military formed a vital part of the community, especially considering that the St. Lawrence valley had enjoyed only 50 years of complete freedom from war in the course of New France's 150-year existence. Every year, the Crown spent large sums for the maintenance of about 1500 regular French soldiers in New France, many of whom were stationed in the towns. Most of the soldiers were billeted in private homes. Within the army, tension arose between the French and the Canadian-born officers. Canadian leaders enjoyed greater popularity with the Canadian troops than did the metropolitan French officers. Unlike the French soldiers, Canadian troops had adapted to, and preferred, a different type of warfare—what in the twenty-first century would be called guerrilla warfare.

The metropolitan French controlled the profitable wholesale trade. They had the necessary funds and contacts to obtain adequate supplies in France. These French merchants provided most of the imported manufactured goods at Louisbourg and at Quebec. French Canadians dominated in smaller-scale trading. In the eighteenth century, scores of small partnerships participated in the fur trade. The companies usually consisted of three or four partners who obtained a three-year lease on the trade at a particular fur-trading post, and shared in the profits or losses according to the percentage of the capital they had invested. The partners obtained trade goods from the large Montreal merchants, usually on credit at 30 percent interest. These Montreal merchants in turn marketed the furs through their agents at home in France.

Women in eighteenth-century New France frequently ran small businesses that sold cloth, clothes, furs, brandy, and utensils. During their husbands' absences in the interior, the fur traders' wives and daughters often looked after their stores and accounts. A number of widowed merchants' wives continued their husbands' businesses. Throughout New France, married women shared in the work of their husbands. At busy times of the year, they helped in the fields. In the urban areas, artisans' and merchants' wives assisted their spouses. Both rural and urban women often kept the family accounts and managed the servants (if there were any) or the apprentices, in the case of artisans.

The colony had about 2000 trades workers by the 1740s. The most numerous in the construction industry were carpenters and masons; in transportation,

A French-Canadian couple in their Sunday clothes.

Ville de Montréal. Gestion de documents et des archives.

navigators and carters; and in the food industry, bakers and butchers. As a rule, crafts workers owned all their own tools and worked in small workshops attached to their homes. The French authorities often accused Canadian workers of being headstrong and insubordinate; their self-confidence and independence were frowned upon by the administrators from Old France, where the average person had little, if any, personal freedom or opportunity for personal advancement.

The Habitants and Their Way of Life

The habitants made up the largest group in the colony. By the 1740s, the oldest seigneuries had two (in some cases, three) rows of farms stretching back from the river. The habitants' lots, or *rotures*, were rectangular and generally had a ratio of width to length of one-to-ten. The habitants paid no direct taxes, apart from the occasional tax for local improvements, whereas in France the peasants paid between one-third and one-half of their income in taxes. In addition, the habitants paid only half the rate for the church tithe that was required at the time in northern France.

The majority of the habitants apparently ate well. They enjoyed almost daily pork and game, particularly venison and wild hare. Gradually, though, wild game came to be relied on less and less as it became harder to obtain near the settled areas. The pig remained a mainstay of the habitants' diet, because it was inexpensive to keep (it would eat anything from acorns to kitchen scraps) and because, as the old folk saying in both France and New France put it, "You can eat everything but the squeal." Fish formed part of the core diet of the French settlers, as did buckwheat, a hardy cereal used to make bread, pancakes, and porridges. Maple syrup was used for sweetening.

Vegetables from the garden, particularly peas and fèves (the large tough-fibred beans from Normandy that were brought to the St. Lawrence valley), were favourites. Dried peas and beans could be stored for years and then made into tasty soups. And because legumes absorbed the flavour of either smoked or salted pork fat well, the habitants frequently used pork in their recipes for pea soup and baked beans.

The *Canadiens* also enjoyed such fruits as apples, plums, and cherries. Apple trees, brought from the northwest of France, thrived in the cool, moist Canadian climate. Wild fruits, especially raspberries, red and black currants, and cranberries, were to be had for the picking.

As for beverages, wealthy habitants could obtain expensive tea and coffee from the traders. Milk, in contrast, was cheap and plentiful. Cider was drunk at all meals. The well-to-do could afford wine imported from France, while the habitants drank the cheaper beer brewed in the colony or, indeed, beer that they brewed themselves.

Farmers in New France detested being called "peasants." As the Finnish visitor Pehr Kalm noted in 1749, "The gentlemen and ladies, as well as the poorest peasants and their wives, are called Monsieur and Madame." The habitants had more personal freedom than did their counterparts in France. The royal officials in New France repeatedly complained that the independent-minded Canadians always pleased themselves and paid little attention to the administrators' directives.

The Church in New France

During the years of royal government, and particularly during the years of the great migration from France in the late 1660s and early 1670s, the church suffered from a shortage of priests. As late as 1683, the intendant reported that three-quarters or more of the habitants heard mass only four times a year. This problem remained until well into the nineteenth century.

The frequent *ordonnances* of the intendant directed to the inhabitants of the parishes with priests provide proof of the independence of many *Canadiens* from the clergy. The ordinances prohibited walking out of church as soon as the priest began his sermon, standing in the lobby arguing, brawling during the service, and even bringing dogs into church.

The clergy did, however, enjoy the respect of the community for what today would be called social services. During the early history of New France, the clergy were actively involved in teaching, nursing, and other charitable work. In 1760, the nearly 100 diocesan or parish priests in the colony were assisted by 30 Sulpicians (a religious order that had begun work in the colony in 1657), 25 Jesuits, 24 Récollets (who had returned in 1670), and more than 200 nuns belonging to six religious communities. The clerically administered social institutions endured, in many cases, into the twentieth century.

Education and Social Welfare

The church controlled schooling in the colony, and all the religious communities assumed some responsibility for education. Urban dwellers benefited most from the schools, as most schools were located in the major towns. The Quebec Seminary ran the Petit Séminaire, the most important elementary school in the colony. The Jesuit College at Quebec provided male students with a postsecondary education equivalent to that which could be obtained in a provincial town in France. The Congrégation de Notre-Dame and the Ursuline order established elementary schools for girls in the larger centres.

The church also provided welfare services and maintained charitable institutions. To help pay for these institutional services and for their hospitals, the church held initially about one-tenth of the seigneurial lands in the St. Lawrence valley, and by the 1750s about one-quarter of the land. In 1760, more than one-third of New France's population lived on church seigneuries, providing the clergy with substantial revenue.

The seminary in Quebec trained Canadian priests at its theological college. During the eighteenth century, Canadians increasingly staffed the parishes in New France. By 1760, Canada had about 100 parishes, most of them run by diocesan clergy, about four-fifths of whom were Canadian. Tensions, however, existed between the Canadian-born clergy at the lower levels of the church's administration and the French-born clergy who dominated at the top.

The First Nations Population

In many regards New France was a multicultural society, with a considerable First Nations population and an African community. In the Montreal area the "mission" First Nations outnumbered the French settlers from the 1670s to the 1710s. Several thousand First Nations people lived in four major *réductions*, or missions, in the St. Lawrence valley in the late seventeenth and early eighteenth centuries: the Hurons at Lorette, near Quebec; the Abenakis from present-day Maine at Saint-François, east of Montreal; and the Iroquois at Sault St. Louis (Kahnawake), and the Lake of Two Mountains (Kanesatake or Oka), both west of Montreal. The Catholic missionaries did not insist on Aboriginal amalgamation with French civilization. As long as First Nation customs did not conflict with Christianity, they were accepted.

These First Nations communities acted as a buffer against Iroquois and English invaders. But their existence had an unanticipated side-effect. It speeded up the expanding contraband fur trade between New France and the American colonies, in which both the Roman Catholic Iroquois and the Abenakis participated. The "mission" First Nations did not consider themselves subjects of French law. As the French needed the resident First Nations for protection and assistance in their raids against the English, they could not antagonize them by rigorously enforcing French laws.

First Nations and African Slaves

A slave class existed in Canada to help meet an acute labour shortage. From the late 1680s, Aboriginal slaves from the upper Mississippi valley began arriving in New France on a regular basis. Other First Nations sold these *panis*, or Pawnees (the name of a single nation, was used despite the fact that the slaves were taken from many other groups as well), to the French. Africans captured during raids on the English colonies or brought in from the French West Indies also increased the number of slaves in the colony. The few African slaves were sold at an average price twice as high as that received for the more numerous Aboriginal captives, because Africans had greater resistance to disease than did the First Nations. Montreal, the centre of New France's fur trade, had the largest number of slaves in the colony—several hundred by the mid-eighteenth century.

The Canadians traded slaves like cattle, at the marketplace and at auctions. Three-quarters of the slaves lived in towns, where they worked mainly as domestic servants. The governors owned slaves: Rigaud de Vaudreuil, governor from 1703 to 1725, owned 11 slaves, while the Marquis de Beauharnois, in office from 1726 to 1746, owned 27. But the biggest slave owners were merchants, traders, and the clergy. First Nations and African slaves also worked at the convents and hospitals operated by nuns in Quebec and Montreal.

Marie-Joseph Angélique's revolt against her enslavement is one of the best-known incidents in the early history of Montreal. On the evening of April 10, 1734, the woman in her mid-twenties allegedly set fire to the house of her owner. The fire spread quickly, and within minutes Montreal became a fiery inferno. The blaze, Montreal's worst disaster since the Iroquois attacks, destroyed 46 houses, as well as the hospital. Captured by the authorities, she was tried and sentenced to die. Angélique was hanged, her body burned, and her ashes thrown into the wind.

While no exact census of New France's slave population exists, local records reveal that approximately 3600 slaves lived in the colony from its origin to 1759; of these, about two-thirds were First Nations, and one-third were African. They lived short lives: for Aboriginal slaves, the average age at death was about 18, and for Africans, 25.

The Rise of a *Canadien* Identity

By the early eighteenth century, the colonists called themselves *Canadiens*. Some families had already resided in Canada for two or three generations. A new French people, self-confident and increasingly conscious of their separation from the French in France, emerged. As well, the regional dialects of France eventually died out in the St. Lawrence valley, as the newcomers from various areas of France intermingled, settling together in one area and speaking a common French language. They spoke *canadien-français*, a language with its own distinct expressions to describe Canadian realities—for example, *poudrerie* (drifting or powdering of snow), *cabane à sucre* (a cabin used at maple sugar time), and First Nations words such as *canoë* and *toboggan*. By the

An artist's imaginative re-creation of Angélique trying to escape from the fire and from Montreal.

Painting by Alan Daniel in Janet Lunn and Christopher Moore, THE STORY OF CANADA (Toronto: Lester Publishing/Key Porter Books, 1992), p. 67.

mid-eighteenth century, the Acadians (the majority of whom lived under British rule, after the Treaty of Utrecht of 1713 ceded mainland Nova Scotia to England) had also become a people distinct from both the Canadians and the French.

The Rise of an *Acadien* Identity

In Acadia the descendants of the immigrants of 1632 intermarried and developed a tightly knit community. The population doubled every 20 years, a faster rate than in New France. By 1670, the colony had a population of about 500. The absence of war, famine, or epidemics (such as typhoid, smallpox, and cholera) contributed to the rapid population increase.

Blood ties, common beliefs, and a system of mutual aid and solidarity united these first Europeans in Acadia. They developed their own speech patterns in an amalgam of various French dialects—with some English and a few First Nation words—that merged and adapted into a single new language that reflected the Acadians' distinctive way of life and their need for a special vocabulary to describe it.

Although Port-Royal was Acadia's largest settlement, there were other small outlying communities on the Bay of Fundy and along the eastern coastline of present-day Nova Scotia. With the addition of about 40 families brought out after 1671, the population grew to more than 800 by 1686.

By the end of the seventeenth century, the Acadians had established themselves in the region's fertile marshlands. Wheat and peas became their principal field crops. Every farm included a plot of vegetables. Most farms had a small orchard of cherry, pear, and apple trees. Most farmers had cattle and sheep. Their pigs roamed freely in the forest behind their houses. The Acadians produced small agricultural surpluses to trade for items they did not make or grow themselves. They traded mainly with New England, rather than Canada or France.

In Acadian society, the family and the church, rather than the seigneurial system that dominated Canadian society, became the most powerful institutions. In the St. Lawrence valley the intendant enforced the seigneurial system, but in Acadia no such official existed. Acadia became much more egalitarian than Canada with its clearly stratified society.

The inhabitants often sought the advice of their priests, who acted as unofficial judges in the disputes that arose among them. But the clergy did not rule the settlements. As in New France in the late seventeenth and eighteenth centuries, the Acadian clergy had limited authority over the populace.

Relations with the Aboriginal Peoples

At first the Acadians enjoyed good relations with the Mi'kmaq, in part because they used only small portions of the tidal flats. Unlike the New England settlers, who antagonized the First Nations by seizing their lands and clearing away the forests, the Acadians initially posed little threat. Indeed, a few Acadian men married Aboriginal women. But, as the Acadian population increased, it began to compete with the Mi'kmaq for the same natural resources.

Acadia Becomes Nova Scotia

New England wanted political as well as economic control over Acadia. When war broke out in Europe in 1689, the New Englanders seized Port Royal, and held on to Acadia for seven years until 1697, when France regained the colony. With the outbreak of war in Europe in 1702, Acadia again became easy prey for seafaring raiders from New England. The Acadians held their

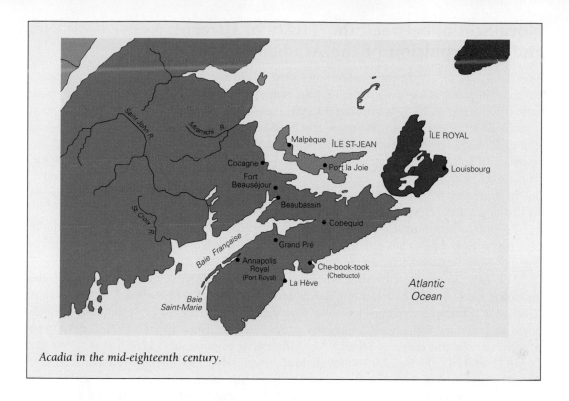

Acadia in the mid-eighteenth century.

own with little help from France, until 1710. With the fall of Port Royal in mid-October, the colony again fell into English hands. Finally the Treaty of Utrecht in 1713 put to rest the question of ownership of the peninsula. Acadia became Nova Scotia. France did retain Île Royale (Cape Breton Island), where it began in 1720 to build a fortified town to protect the Gulf of St. Lawrence. They called their new fortress Louisbourg.

Anxious to establish a strong colony there, the French tried to attract the Acadians. The Acadian community sent representatives to inspect the lands on Cape Breton, but the delegates reported negatively on the rocky soil. Few Acadians liked the idea of having to leave their rich farmlands and comfortable houses to pioneer once again. From the English vantage point, French immigration to Cape Breton would only reinforce the French presence there and weaken Nova Scotia, which would lose successful farmers and their livestock. The British also feared that the Acadians might destroy their homesteads and the restraining dikes as they left.

The English administrators of Nova Scotia did insist that the Acadians become British subjects by swearing an oath of allegiance. The Acadians insisted on remaining neutral. As a border people between two rival empires, the Acadians wanted to proceed cautiously. In particular, they feared reprisals from the Mi'kmaq, firm allies of the French, if they appeared to ally themselves with the British.

Finally, in 1717, the Acadians worked out the terms on which they would remain under British government: they would have the right to practise their Catholic faith and the right to maintain neutrality in future wars against France. In 1730 the British agreed to their terms, and required in return only that the Acadians take this mild oath:

> *I sincerely promise and swear on my faith as a Christian that I will be utterly loyal, and*
> *will truly obey His Majesty King George the second, whom I recognize as the sovereign*
> *lord of Acadia or Nova Scotia. May God so help me.*

Nova Scotia, between the Treaty of Utrecht and the Expulsion of the Acadians

After the Treaty of Utrecht the Acadians prospered. Their high birth rate and longevity led to a phenomenal population increase. In 1711, there were approximately 2500 Acadians; in 1750, more than 10 000; and in 1755, more than 13 000 (Louisbourg excluded). The Acadian population spread into settlements along the present-day New Brunswick shoreline, as well as Île Saint-Jean (Prince Edward Island) and even into areas of present-day Nova Scotia that had been surveyed and reserved for future English immigration. Then, in 1744, war broke out between England and France once again. The conflict lasted four years, and during it the English captured Louisbourg. But the peace treaty of 1748 restored the status quo. The English returned Louisbourg to France, an act that angered the New Englanders who, at great expense and loss of life, had captured it.

England consequently felt obliged to fortify Nova Scotia, to make it a proper counterbalance to Louisbourg. Now they sought to make the Acadians into completely trustworthy subjects, and to populate Nova Scotia with Protestant settlers.

The new governor, Edward Cornwallis, transported 2000 colonists to the port the Mi'kmaqs knew as *Che-book-took* (at the biggest harbour), a name the English rendered as "Chebucto." Cornwallis renamed it Halifax, after the Earl of Halifax, the president of the English Board of Trade and Plantations, which was a committee of Crown appointees in London who handled the administration of Britain's North American colonies until 1768.

In 1750–1751, the British also brought in approximately 1500 "foreign Protestants," largely Germans, whom they settled at Lunenburg on the south shore of the peninsula, within easy reach of Halifax. Lunenburg became the first British settlement in Nova Scotia outside Halifax, the new seat of government. Cornwallis introduced British institutions and laws to Nova Scotia, and fortified the new settlement to equal the strength of Louisbourg. These measures, together with the construction of roads to the Acadian settlements and the introduction of a large English garrison, completely changed the balance of power in the colony. Simultaneously, the French strengthened their position in what is now New Brunswick.

The First Nations and the English

The French had maintained their alliance with the Mi'kmaq and Maliseet (from present-day western New Brunswick) in the hope of using them against the English. The Mi'kmaq needed little encouragement, since they were resentful of English encroachments on their hunting grounds. In addition, unlike the French, the British had refused to give them annual gifts in return for the use of their land. The English seldom took the Mi'kmaqs into account when the question of land ownership arose. As far as they were concerned, France had ceded its title to the land with the Treaty of Utrecht in 1713, and it belonged to Britain.

Years of Mi'kmaq raids and harassment followed the Treaty of Utrecht, with many of the attacks against the British taking place at sea. (The Mi'kmaqs had purchased European longboats after their first contact with French fishers.) They captured dozens of English trading and fishing boats in the course of these attacks. With the outbreak of war between England and France in 1744, the Mi'kmaq raids against the British in Nova Scotia reached a new level of intensity. In wartime the French paid the First Nations for English scalps, just as the English paid for the scalps of First Nation enemies and of any Acadian French fighting beside them.

Britain's Growing Anxiety about the Acadians

As frontier incidents and Mi'kmaq raids increased, Cornwallis became ever more doubtful of the Acadians' loyalty to Britain in the event of another war. In 1749 the governor commanded them to swear an oath of unconditional allegiance to Britain or risk deportation. But when the Acadian delegates replied negatively to Cornwallis's ultimatum, he did not expel them. This convinced the majority of the Acadians that he had, like other English governors before him, accepted their "neutral" status.

When Charles Lawrence became lieutenant governor of Nova Scotia in 1753, the Acadians expected the situation to remain the same. This time, however, they were wrong. First and foremost, Colonel Lawrence was a soldier. Like most soldiers, he knew only allies and enemies, not "neutrals." To him, the Acadians posed a definite threat in the event of another full-scale war between France and Britain.

The Expulsion of the Acadians

The outbreak of war in North America in 1754 and a serious British military defeat outside Fort Duquesne in the Ohio country in 1755 totally altered the military situation. Governor Lawrence now fully turned his attention to the Acadian question.

In July, Lawrence ordered representatives of the Acadians to appear before the Halifax Council, which advised the governor. The council, dominated by military officers, insisted on an ironclad oath from the Acadians that they would support Britain in the event of war. (The council may have had ulterior motives in setting such strict terms: some of the twelve council members were perhaps eyeing the Acadians' rich lands along the Bay of Fundy; there were profits to be made in the evacuations, as well as in the resettlement of New Englanders in Nova Scotia.)

On July 23, two days before the first Acadian delegates from the villages arrived, the news of General Braddock's catastrophic defeat near Fort Duquesne reached Halifax. Casualties approached 40 percent, and the British commander himself had been killed. Nova Scotia's need for the Acadians to make a declaration of unequivocal allegiance to Britain, to recognize themselves as unconditional subjects of the British Crown, became all the more urgent.

The Acadian delegates pointed out that they had always been loyal to George II and agreed to present all their firearms to the English as proof of their loyalty. They were prepared to abide by the oath they had sworn earlier, but not to take a new one. They asked for consideration as a neutral people, pointing out that between 1713 and 1755 they had never fought for France. Throughout the discussion, none of the delegates foresaw the catastrophe impending if they refused to swear the required oath. They underestimated the determination of Lawrence's council.

The final confrontation came on July 28. After hearing the delegates one last time, the council reached a decision. It endorsed the deportation of all Acadians under British jurisdiction who had refused to take the unqualified oath. Now, in the general hysteria after Braddock's defeat, the British prepared to remove them. The Acadians' fate passed into the hands of 2000 hostile, anti-Catholic New England militiamen working under the instructions of Lieutenant Governor Lawrence.

The Deportation Begins

The deportation began immediately after the council's decision. Lawrence attempted initially to prepare carefully for the evacuation, providing adequate cabin space on the ships and ample provisions for the duration of the journey. But, in the end, the evacuation proved brutal and poorly planned. The English first herded the Acadians together at their settlements, then dispersed most of them among the Thirteen Colonies and sent some to England. Lawrence's troops burned houses and barns to deprive those who escaped of shelter. Within hours, the work of more than a century of toil had become ashes.

The Destruction of Acadian Society

The expulsion destroyed Acadian society. It broke up communities and dispersed closely knit families. An estimated 2000 Acadians fled to Île Saint-Jean (Prince Edward Island). The refugees outnumbered the original Acadian residents on the island three to one. The exodus brought confusion to Île Saint-Jean. Many Acadian refugees came with only the clothes on their backs. Starvation was widespread as the islanders had enjoyed only one good harvest over the previous five years. But, despite the hardships, the Acadian refugees felt that this life was preferable to that of banishment from the Maritimes. After the fall of Louisbourg in 1758, however, the British landed on the island and began to deport all the Acadians they could capture.

Many died, victims of malnutrition and exposure in the deportations from the Maritimes. Storms at sea, a shortage of food and drinking water, and poor sanitary conditions meant that many ships lost more than one-third of their Acadian passengers. The expulsions continued for seven years, until 1762. Approximately 7000 were deported in 1755, alone. By the time the policy ended in 1762, the British had exiled perhaps another 3000 Acadians.

The British military occasionally sent ships from the same village to different destination points. Inevitably, family members were separated. Massachusetts, New York, Pennsylvania, Maryland, Virginia, the Carolinas, and Georgia all received Acadians. For the most part, the Americans provided support and tried to settle the exiles in various small towns and villages,

WHERE HISTORIANS DISAGREE

The Expulsion of the Acadians: Was It Necessary?

Canadian historians have long discussed the necessity and the degree of cruelty of the British expulsion of the Acadians in 1755. The controversy owes as much to the complexity of the question and the contradictions in the evidence as to differing perspectives. As historian Naomi Griffiths wrote: "Acadian history 1710–1755 provides endless questions of fact and interpretation, problems about what actually happened and whether it was brought about intentionally or not.... As the years lead on to 1755, the problems which divide historians multiply, and the events of the expulsion itself have been so diversely treated that one sometimes wonders whether the authors are writing about the same events."[1] Some condemn the English; others believe the Acadians themselves were to blame for their misfortunes. A third group contends that interference from Quebec and Louisbourg resulted in the tragedy.

The argument that the deportation was necessary was still being made in the 1950s. As late as 1956, popular historian Joseph Lister Rutledge summarized this position: "If ever a conquered people were treated with consideration by their captors, it was the Acadians.... The net result was generous and understanding treatment for people who represented a very stubborn breed indeed. This conquered people retained their land and freedom and the assurance of the exercise of their religion. The loyalty oath required of them was generous to a fault."[2]

Several English-language writers have argued that the expulsion should be seen solely as a military operation necessary for Nova Scotia's defence. Archibald McKellar MacMechan, professor of English at Dalhousie University, for instance, wrote as follows in

1913: "Before passing judgement on the men who conceived and executed this removal of an entire population, it should be remembered that they acted as did Louis XIV in expelling the Huguenots from France and the United States in expelling the tories. All were precautionary measures dictated by the need of national self-preservation; and they were regarded by those who took them as imperative in a dangerous crisis. Lawrence acted like the commander of a fort expecting a siege, who levels trees and houses outside the walls in order to afford the enemy no shelter and to give the garrison a clear field of fire."[3]

Most French-language historians have rejected the arguments advanced in defence of the expulsion. In the 1920s, French historian Émile Lauvrière noted of Governor Lawrence's actions, "only a criminal soul could devise such a plot in all its details."[4] French-Canadian writer and Roman Catholic priest Henri Beaudé (who wrote under the pseudonym of Henri d'Arles) considered the deportation order entirely undeserved and "conceived in hate, a prejudice of race and religion."[5]

While not overlooking the cruelty of the expulsion, two English-language historians have tried to understand more fully the British decision to evict an entire people. In 1979, Naomi Griffiths wrote that the imposition in 1755 of a "declaration of unequivocal allegiance to British interests" was "reasonable enough" because war with France had begun.[6] Historian Stephen E. Patterson has commented as well on the circumstances, or the context, in which the deportation occurred: "It took place in a time of war, a bitter war between inveterate enemies for whom possession of Nova Scotia had become symbolic of their power and prestige in the international world."[7]

A recent resolution, passed unanimously in June 2002 in the Quebec National Assembly, proves, however, that intense feelings remain on this issue. The Quebec legislators expressed their support for the Acadian people in Canada's demand, "that the British Crown officially recognize the historical wrongdoing in the deportation of their ancestors."[8] In mid-December 2003, the governor general of Canada officially acknowledged the Acadian expulsion in a royal proclamation. It acknowledged the wrongs done to the Acadians during the expulsion. It also stated that, beginning in 2005, and then annually thereafter, July 28 would become a commemorative day to mark the deportation.

1. Naomi Griffiths, ed., *The Acadian Deportation: Deliberate Perfidy or Cruel Necessity?* (Toronto: Copp Clark, 1969), p. 3.

2. Joseph Lister Rutledge, *Century of Conflict* (Toronto: Doubleday, 1956), p. 409. *Century of Conflict* was published in the popular Canadian History Series, edited by Thomas B. Costain.

3. Archibald McKellar MacMechan, in A. Shortt and A.G. Doughty, eds., *Canada and Its Provinces*, vol. 13. (Toronto: Glasgow Brook, 1914), p. 98.

4. N.E.S. Griffiths, "The Acadians," in the *Dictionary of Canadian Biography*, vol. 4, *1771–1800* (Toronto: University of Toronto Press, 1979), p. xxvi.

5. Henri d'Arles [Henri Beaudé], *La déportation des Acadiens* (Montreal: Bibliothèque de l'Action française, 1918), pp. 21–26, translated and quoted in Griffiths, *The Acadian Deportation*, p. 156.

6. Griffiths, "The Acadians," p. xxvi.

7. Stephen E. Patterson, "1744–1763: Colonial Wars and Aboriginal Peoples," Ch. 7 of Phillip A. Buckner and John G. Reid, eds., *The Atlantic Region to Confederation: A History* (Toronto: University of Toronto Press, 1994), p. 145.

8. Rhéal Séguin, "Britain Made a Mistake with Acadians, Quebec says," *The Globe and Mail*, June 14, 2002.

but these efforts proved largely unsuccessful. Despite all prohibitions to the contrary, the Acadians, footsore and half-clad, wandered from town to town, looking for family and friends. They remained outsiders in the communities where they were settled. Their mortality rate in the American colonies was high. An estimated one-third of those deported died from diseases that had been practically unknown to them before 1755—smallpox, typhoid, and yellow fever. Eventually, after the British permitted the Acadians to resettle in Nova Scotia, a steady stream returned, an estimated 3000. But since New Englanders now owned their farms they could not regain their land. The majority of the returned Acadians went to present-day New Brunswick where there was vacant land. Buffeted about for a generation from 1755 to the late 1780s, a number of Acadians settled in Louisiana. Today it is home to more than a million descendants of the Acadians. As the Acadians spread across the Louisiana bayous and prairies, their neighbours shortened the French name "Acadien" to "Cadien," and eventually to "Cajun."

By 1754, the St. Lawrence valley colony had truly become a New France, a new community in Canada. Particularly from the mid–seventeenth century onward, the French had become *Canadiens*, with an outlook that separated them more and more from the metropolitan French. Despite their common French origins and shared Roman Catholic faith, emerging cultural differences also existed between the Acadians and the Canadians. The Acadians had become a people distinct from both the Canadians and the French by the mid–eighteenth century, but the events of 1755 made them a people in exile. It is tragic that the first European immigrant group to establish itself successfully in the present-day Canada's Maritime provinces received such treatment. The horrors of the deportation of the Acadians strengthened the resolve of the *Canadiens* in the late 1750s to resist the British invaders in the St. Lawrence valley, who, if victorious, might also attempt to expel them.

BEYOND THE BOOK

Education in New France

http://www.champlain2004.org/html/07/07_e.html
Digitized letters and records regarding the educational system in New France,
especially the role of the Church.

France in America

http://memory.loc.gov/intldl/fiahtml/fiahome.html
"France in America" is a cooperative project of the Library of Congress and the
Bibliothèque nationale de France. The first part of the site, launched in Paris in May
2005, explores the history of the French presence in North America and the interactions
between the French and American peoples from the 16th to the early 19th centuries.

Angélique and the Burning of Montreal

http://www.canadianmysteries.ca/sites/angelique/accueil/indexen.html
This site details a fire that struck Montreal in 1734, and the person who was blamed for
causing it, Marie-Joseph Angélique, an African-Canadian slave. But was she guilty?
Transcribed documents from the time explore this issue.

Military Life

http://www.phmc.gc.ca/cmh/en/page_165.asp?flash=1
What was the daily life of soldiers in New France like? This website presents the
military recruiting methods of the time, how soldiers were paid, and other topics.

The Acadians

http://www.cbc.ca/acadian
An overview of Acadian past and contemporary history. Contains articles on the
Acadian Flag, National Acadian Day, and provides links to present-day Acadian
organizations.

1755: L'Histoire

http://www2.umoncton.ca/cfdocs/etudacad/1755/index.cfm?lang=en
This site contains digitized articles and pictures of Acadian individuals and families
from the era of expulsion to today. Acadian cultural works and art are also featured.

Champlain Society

http://link.library.utoronto.ca/champlain/search.cfm?lang=eng
For primary sources on Acadia from the Champlain Society, browse the database by
subject and select "Acadia."

Expulsion: The Story of Acadia

Drawn from the series *Canada: A People's History, Expulsion: The Story of Acadia* (CBC,
2006) is a dramatic documentary of the dislocation of the Acadians.

Pélagie-la-Charette

Antoine Maillet, *Pélagie-la-Charette* (1979), translated by Philip Strafford (Don Mills, ON:
General, 1983). An historical novel about the journey of the widow Pélagie LeBlanc who,
in the 1770s, leads her people back from their exile in the American South to Acadia.

RELATED READINGS

In R. Douglas Francis and Donald B. Smith, eds., *Viewpoints: Readings in Canadian History* (Toronto: Thomson Nelson, 2007), the articles by Naomi Griffiths, "The Golden Age: Acadian Life, 1713–1748", pp. 64–75; and by Elizabeth Mancke, "Imperial Transitions," pp. 75–93, relate to the Acadian sections of this chapter.

BIBLIOGRAPHY

Allan Greer provides a good introduction to the social history of New France in *The People of New France* (Toronto: University of Toronto Press, 1997); also consult John A. Dickinson and Brian Young, *A Short History of Quebec*, 3rd ed. (Montreal/Kingston: McGill-Queen's University Press, 2003), pp. 3–104. More detailed treatments include W.J. Eccles, *Canada under Louis XIV, 1663–1701* (Toronto: McClelland & Stewart, 1964); and Dale Miquelon, *New France, 1701–1744* (Toronto: McClelland & Stewart, 1987). Other works include W.J. Eccles, *The Canadian Frontier, 1534–1760* (Toronto: Holt, Rinehart and Winston, 1969), and his *France in America*, rev. ed. (Markham, ON: Fitzhenry & Whiteside, 1990). A number of important articles by W.J. Eccles have been reprinted in his *Essays on New France* (Toronto: Oxford University Press, 1987). Peter N. Moogk's *La Nouvelle France: The Making of French-Canada—A Cultural History* (East Lansing: Michigan State University Press, 2000), a series of exploratory articles on various aspects of French-Canadian culture before 1760, is invaluable. Cole Harris covers both New France and Acadia, in *The Reluctant Land. Society, Space, and Environment In Canada before Confederation* (Vancouver: UBC Press, 2008), pp. 137–230.

For the activities of women in New France consult Micheline Dumont et al., *Quebec Women: A History* (Toronto: Women's Press, 1987); and "Women in New France," Ch. 2 of Alison Prentice et al., *Canadian Women: A History* (Toronto: Harcourt Brace, 1996), pp. 33–57. Jan Noel's *Women in New France* (Ottawa: Canadian Historical Association, 1998), contains an up-to-date bibliography. A fascinating literature now exists on Angélique, the slave woman accused of causing the great 1734 fire in Montreal; a full study is Afua Cooper's *The Hanging of Angélique: Canada, Slavery and the Burning of Montreal* (Toronto: HarperCollins, 2006).

Biographies of prominent individuals in Canada and Acadia appear in the *Dictionary of Canadian Biography*, vols. 1–4 (Toronto: University of Toronto Press, 1966, 1969, 1974, 1979). It is now also available online: www.biographi.ca. Two valuable bibliographies on New France's and Acadia's history, particularly their social and economic pasts, are Thomas Wien's essay on Canada in M. Brook Taylor, ed., *Canadian History: A Reader's Guide*, vol. 1, *Beginnings to Confederation* (Toronto: University of Toronto Press, 1994), pp. 33–75; and, in the same volume, Barry Moody's on Acadia, pp. 76–111. For valuable maps of the St. Lawrence colony, consult R. Cole Harris, ed., *Historical Atlas of Canada*, vol. 1, *From the Beginning to 1800* (Toronto: University of Toronto Press, 1987). Naomi Griffiths has written two good summaries of Acadian history: *The Acadians: Creation of a People* (Toronto: McGraw-Hill Ryerson, 1973); and *The Contexts of Acadian History, 1686–1784* (Montreal/Kingston: McGill-Queen's University Press, 1992). Jean Daigle's account, "Acadia, 1604–1763: An Historical Synthesis" in Jean Daigle, ed., *The Acadians of the Maritimes* (Moncton: Centre d'études acadiennes, 1982), pp. 17–46, is very useful. Various opinions on the issue of the expulsion appear in Naomi Griffiths, ed., *The Acadian Deportation: Deliberate Perfidy or Cruel Necessity?* (Toronto: Copp Clark, 1969). T.G. Barnes provides a good historiographical review in his "Historiography of the Acadians' *Grand Dérangement*, 1775," *Quebec Studies*, 7 (1988): 74–86.

Maps of Acadian marshland settlement and of the Acadian deportation and return appear in R. Cole Harris, ed., *Historical Atlas of Canada*, vol. 1, *From the Beginning to 1800* (Toronto: University of Toronto Press, 1987). For a complete overview of Acadia in the seventeenth and eighteenth centuries, consult the early chapters of Phillip A. Buckner and John G. Reid, eds., *The Atlantic Region to Confederation: A History* (Toronto: University of Toronto Press, 1994).

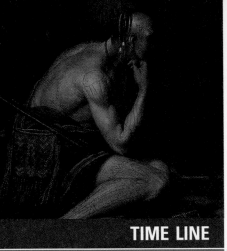

Chapter Four

STRUGGLE FOR
A CONTINENT

TIME LINE

1670	Establishment of the Hudson's Bay Company
1697	War between England and France
1701	Great Peace with the Iroquois
1713	War between England and France resumes
1713	Signing of the Treaty of Utrecht; France gives up her claim to Hudson Bay and Newfoundland, and cedes "Acadia" to England
1756	Beginning of the Seven Years' War
1759	Wolfe's victory on the Plains of Abraham, leading to the fall of Quebec
1760	The British conquer New France and establish a military government until the signing of the peace treaty in 1763, which ends the war

At approximately the same time as the French settled Quebec, England established its first colonies in North America: Virginia in 1607, Newfoundland in 1610, and Massachusetts in 1620. Others followed on the Atlantic seaboard, and in 1664 the Dutch colony of New Netherlands passed into English hands and was renamed New York. The English also sponsored expeditions into Hudson Bay. Henry Hudson in 1610–1611 first located the immense body of water the size of the Mediterranean Sea. A little more than half a century later, an English company established a string of fur-trading posts around Hudson Bay. Conflict between England and France arose in the late 1680s, when the two empires confronted each other in the North American interior. The struggle continued, with several interludes of peace, until 1760, when the French forces capitulated at Montreal.

The English Challenge from the North

English interest in finding the Northwest Passage revived in the early seventeenth century. In June 1610, Henry Hudson entered an icebound strait previously noted (in the 1570s and 1580s) by English Arctic explorers Martin Frobisher and John Davis. Both the strait and the inland sea into which it led were later named after him. Although Hudson and his men spent a terrible winter on the east coast of James Bay, they continued their search for the Northwest Passage the following spring. Hudson's crew mutinied and seized him, his son, and seven others, and set them adrift. Nothing is known of Henry Hudson's fate.

Other English expeditions followed until 1631, when it became clear that, even if the Northwest Passage existed, it would not be a commercially viable trade route. Since both the Dutch and the English had already begun to make the longer but less hazardous journey around Africa to India and China, the lure of the Northwest Passage diminished.

Ironically, two renegade French traders, Pierre-Esprit Radisson and Médard Chouart Des Groseilliers ("Mr. Radishes" and "Mr. Gooseberry," as the English called them), who had found no support in New France for their plan to expand their operations into the rich fur country south of Hudson Bay and James Bay, directed the English to that area. In 1668, a group of English merchants under the patronage of Prince Rupert, a cousin of King Charles II, sponsored Groseilliers's expedition, which was to winter on Hudson Bay and return with a cargo of fur. The enterprise proved so successful that in 1670 Charles II gave the Hudson's Bay Company exclusive trading rights and property ownership to "Rupert's Land," all the lands within the area drained by the rivers flowing into Hudson and James Bays (nearly half the area of Canada today).

French Expansion to the North and West

The English now threatened New France's fur trade from two sides: New York and Hudson Bay. The collapse of the French trading system with the Hurons in 1649 had left a vacuum and greatly facilitated the English dominance of Hudson Bay. In response, the French in the early 1670s sent overland expeditions to Hudson Bay, Lake Superior, and the Mississippi River.

Frontenac, who became governor in 1672, openly promoted further westward expansion into the Mississippi valley. His ally was René-Robert Cavelier de La Salle, a daring and ambitious fur trader, who in 1682 reached the Mississippi delta. He raised the royal arms of France and claimed all the land drained by the Mississippi River and its tributaries for the king of France. He named the huge valley Louisiana, after Louis XIV. La Salle attempted to found a colony in Louisiana, but his efforts ended in failure—and his assassination in 1687—although the French established a successful settlement 20 years later.

In the mid-1670s, Montreal traders built Michilimackinac at the junction of Lakes Michigan and Huron, which became the starting point for the fur trade along the upper

Mississippi River and beyond Lake Superior. Soon the French built trading posts from the Ohio River to Lake Superior and north to Hudson Bay. A mixed First Nations and French (Métis) population arose at these western posts, particularly at the larger centres like Michilimackinac, and later Green Bay and Detroit. First Nations, Métis, and Canadians lived as neighbours. They shared cultural traits and developed a new trade language, accommodating words and expressions from Aboriginal languages and from French. Historian Richard White describes the new culture as "the middle ground."[1]

The First Round of Conflict with the English Colonies, 1689–1713

Frontenac's successors faced an increasingly difficult military situation in the 1680s. After the French ended their truce with the Iroquois in the mid-1680s, the Five Nations, with the encouragement of the English, resumed their raids on New France. Few in number and scattered over a vast area, the French realized the importance of cooperation with their Algonquian allies. The *coureurs de bois* now became the colony's greatest strength, as they linked New France with its Aboriginal allies in the interior.

The Iroquois raid in 1689 on Lachine, a settlement just west of Montreal, sent in retaliation for earlier French attacks, led to a new round of conflict between the French and the Iroquois, and their allies, the English colonies. Sent back to New France as governor in 1689, Frontenac launched French-Canadian and First Nations guerrilla raids against the English settlements. At Schenectady, New York, and Salmon Falls, New Hampshire, the French and First Nation

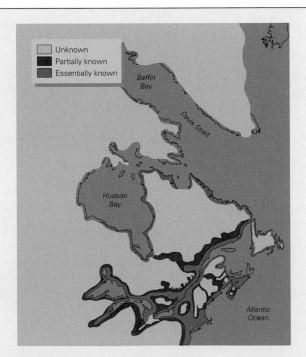

European knowledge of northeastern North America in 1670.

Source: Adapted from Richard I. Ruggles, *A Country So Interesting: The Hudson's Bay Company and Two Centuries Of Mapping, 1670–1870* (Montreal/Kingston: McGill-Queen's University Press, 1991), p. 27.

raiding parties broke into homes. They scalped men, women, and children and took (in the raids between the 1690s and 1713, and then again between 1744 and the fall of New France in 1760) hundreds of prisoners. They brought them back to the Aboriginal communities or to the French settlements in the St. Lawrence valley. While many eventually returned to New England, others (particularly those taken as young children) refused to leave, and remained with their new First Nation or French-Canadian families.

The Great Peace with the Iroquois, 1701

A major break in the unity of the League of the Iroquois came in the late seventeenth century. The presence of Jesuit priests in their villages during the truce weakened the Iroquois, especially from 1668 to 1686. The priests attracted war captives, who had previously encountered missionaries and others, to move from the Iroquois villages in present-day New York State to their mission on the island of Montreal (later moved to the Lake of Two Mountains, at Oka, in 1717), and to Sault St. Louis (Caughnawaga, now Kahnawake) southwest of Montreal. By 1700, an estimated two-thirds of the Mohawks, the most easterly of the Five Nations or Iroquois Confederacy, lived in the Montreal area. In the early 1690s, Iroquois from the Montreal area fought beside the French against the League Iroquois.

The French settlers (by necessity now skilled in the techniques of guerrilla warfare), together with 1500 regular troops sent from France, and mission Iroquois from around Montreal, gained the upper hand against the League Iroquois in the mid-1690s. By 1693, the Five Nations were suffering very heavy losses as a result of both war and disease. In the face of the Algonquians' attacks, they could no longer maintain their forward position on the north shore of Lake Ontario. Their numbers fell from more than 10 000 in the 1640s to less than 9000 at the turn of the century, despite the massive adoptions of other Iroquoians. In 1700 the League Iroquois made an offer to the French, who convened a council with them at Montreal.

The Iroquois south of Lake Ontario made peace with the French and their Algonquian allies in August 1701. First Nation representatives travelled to Montreal for the ratification of the treaty. To ensure that the Iroquois continued to serve as a buffer between the English colonies and New France, the French allowed them to continue to trade some northern furs with the English. (The Christian Iroquois at Kahnawake became the intermediaries in the lucrative Albany–Montreal trade route.) In turn, the Five Nations promised their neutrality in any future colonial war between France and England. The Great Peace ended the Iroquois wars that had menaced New France for decades. But in 1701, the very year that New France's long conflict with the Iroquois ended, war broke out again with England, after a short four-year truce.

France's New North American Strategy, 1701

France developed a new North American strategy in 1701 and held to it for the remainder of the French regime. With a glut of furs in France, the fur trade no longer was of any real economic benefit. But rather than retreat from the Great Lakes and the Mississippi valley, the French chose to stay in order to keep the First Nations in the French alliance and thus prevent English expansion into the West. As a result, the French retained their fur-trading empire for strategic rather than economic reasons. They paid no more attention to Colbert's idea of a "compact colony" on the banks of the St. Lawrence. Instead, the French began preparations for a chain of posts linking the Great Lakes to the Gulf of Mexico. Louis XIV also ordered the building of a new settlement, to be named *Détroit* ("the straits"), at the narrows between Lakes Erie and Huron. Detroit would bar English access to the northwest and maintain French control of the upper Great Lakes. With their Aboriginal allies, the French planned to contain the English within the coastal strip between the Alleghenies and the Atlantic.

New France in Wartime

In the struggle with the English between 1689 and 1713, marked only by four years of peace from 1697 to 1701, New France had three limitations. First, it had a small population in comparison with the English colonies, being outnumbered by nearly 20 to 1. A second weakness lay in New France's precarious economy. Only one export industry existed—the heavily subsidized fur trade—and it was extremely vulnerable in wartime when the transport of furs from the interior could be cut off. The relatively small scale of its agriculture, vulnerable to disruption in wartime, constituted its third weakness. Even in good years, the habitants produced only a small surplus. In wartime, they had a deficit, because militia service took farmers off the land. War also meant increased dependence on France for food and war materials at a time when the sea lanes to and from France became exposed to English attack.

The French colony did, however, have a number of strengths. It had effective political leadership. Royal government in 1663 had left New France with a unified command structure in times of war. Subject only to annual review, the governor had complete control over the marshalling of the colony's resources, its negotiations with the First Nations, and the planning of its war strategy. Nature had provided New France with a second strength: natural defences. The Adirondacks of New York, the Green Mountains of Vermont, and the White Mountains of New Hampshire and Maine all protected the French colony from a direct attack from the south. Two of the three gateways to the St. Lawrence—the river itself (closed half of the year by ice) and the Hudson River–Lake Champlain–Richelieu River waterway—could be sealed. Quebec commanded the St. Lawrence River, and a system of forts existed on the Richelieu River (later complemented by French fortifications at the southern end of Lake Champlain). Only the western approach from Lake Ontario remained open. Inadvertently the Iroquois had built up the third strength of the French, by teaching the habitants the techniques of guerrilla warfare. A cadre of tough and versatile French raiders had emerged from the wars with the Iroquois in the Illinois country—individuals who subsequently became Frontenac's most valued troops in his raids against English frontier settlements in New England and New York.

New France's First Nations Allies

New France's Aboriginal allies constituted her fourth great asset. The French had very close trading (and, hence, military) ties with the Abenakis from Maine, many of whom had sought refuge in Canada at Odanak (St. François) and Bécancour. These Catholic converts now joined the other First Nations groups in the St. Lawrence valley, living beside the French. The "mission" First Nations included the Iroquois near Montreal: at Kahnawake (Caughnawaga), Kanesatake (Oka), and Akwesasne (St. Regis); as well as the Algonquian-speaking peoples at Kanesatake, and the Hurons at Lorette (Wendake) near Quebec. The close French allies, who numbered approximately 4000 individuals in the mid-eighteenth century, helped to protect the St. Lawrence valley. The French "mission" First Nations formed an alliance network known as the Seven Nations of Canada. Anxious not to antagonize these allies, the French left them with a surprising degree of independence. They were, for example, largely excluded from the application of the French legal system.

New France also had alliances with the Great Lakes Algonquians: the Ojibwa, Ottawa, Potawatomi, Miami, and Illinois. Canadian fur traders and fort commanders cultivated the friendship of the Great Lakes Algonquians by giving them gifts and presents. While the English benefited from the Five Nations' support in the 1680s and 1690s, the majority of the Aboriginal groups in northeastern North America sided with the French.

Division among the English Colonies

The French also benefited from divisions within the English colonies. A great deal of friction existed in English America, arising in part from differences in origin and religion. Thus the numerical superiority of the English colonies was more apparent than real. Furthermore, as not all the colonies felt threatened by the French, not all were prepared to fight. The colonies of the Carolinas, Virginia, Maryland, and Pennsylvania, for instance, believed themselves quite safe behind their mountain barriers. New York and Massachusetts shielded Rhode Island and Connecticut. In the north, only two highly populated colonies—Massachusetts and New York—supported the struggle.

Of the two English colonies that fought New France, New York might have proved Canada's match had the colony's non-Aboriginal population not been divided in the 1690s between the descendants of the original Dutch colonists and the new English settlers. The Dutch in the north showed little enthusiasm for offensive operations in the name of the English king, and consequently New York posed little threat to New France. Massachusetts, though, did launch a naval attack on Quebec in 1690.

Two Disastrous English Naval Expeditions

Two English attempts to seize Quebec by naval attack failed. In 1690 Sir William Phips of Massachusetts took command of a naval expedition of more than 30 vessels with 2300 men. Fortunately for the survival of Canada, Phips's ships took two months to reach Quebec from Boston: en route, smallpox broke out and swept through his ranks. He also faced a determined French defence force at Quebec. When Phips demanded that Frontenac surrender, the governor informed the invader that he would obtain his reply "from the mouths of my cannon and muskets." Having arrived at Quebec late in the season, and fearing entrapment in the ice during a lengthy siege, Phips withdrew. Frontenac's blistery response had its intended effect. After Phips's retreat grateful residents of Quebec named the newly built parish church at Place Royale, Notre-Dame-de-la-Victoire.

The English failed again to take Quebec 21 years later, at the end of the first round of the Anglo–French struggle for northeastern North America. In 1711, Sir Hovenden Walker organized an armada of some 7500 troops, while an additional force of 2300 troops worked their way up the Lake Champlain route by land. New France thus faced an invasion force equal to half the total French population of the St. Lawrence valley. Once again, disaster struck the invaders. In fog and gales at the mouth of the St. Lawrence, the English lost ships and nearly 900 men. The Walker expedition turned back. Quebec's thankful citizens rejoiced by renaming the little church in the lower town—this time, Notre-Dame-des-Victoires, in honour of both victories. (A church still stands on this site today.)

The Treaty of Utrecht and Its Aftermath

The Treaty of Utrecht in 1713 settled the war that had been waged in Europe as well as in northeastern North America. By the end of the struggle, the French in North America had gained ground. They occupied York Factory, the most important Hudson's Bay Company post on Hudson Bay. They retained Detroit and their forts on the Great Lakes. The establishment of Louisiana had consolidated their position in the Mississippi valley. Yet the peace treaty did not reflect these strengths.

At the bargaining table at Utrecht, New France paid for Louis XIV's European losses. France had to make concessions, and the French monarch made them in North America. France ceded all claims to Newfoundland, except for fishing rights on the north shore, and renounced its claims on Hudson Bay. The French recognized British suzerainty over the

Iroquois Confederacy and surrendered control over what the English called Nova Scotia, handing the major French Acadian settlements over to the English. Thus, without losing a single major battle, the Canadians were defeated in the Treaty of Utrecht.

Military Preparations, 1713–1744

France's forfeiture of Acadia and Newfoundland proved a serious setback for New France. But the French still held Île Royale (Cape Breton Island), whose cod fishery was worth more to France's economy than the entire fur trade of New France. In an attempt to redress the strategic situation, they began in 1720 the construction on Île Royale of the military fortress of Louisbourg. It also served as the administrative centre for both Île Royale and Île St-Jean (Prince Edward Island). Although essentially a garrison town, Louisbourg also became an important fishing port and trading centre between France, Quebec, and the West Indies. As one of the busiest seaports in colonial America—fourth after Boston, New York, and Charleston—it was visited in the 1740s, on average, by 130 to 150 vessels every year. By the 1740s, its year-round population was 2500 to 3000. Soldiers made up about one-quarter of the population in the 1740s, and in the 1750s they constituted nearly one-half.

To protect the major towns in the St. Lawrence valley, Governor Philippe de Rigaud de Vaudreuil built fortifications at Quebec and Montreal. The French also strengthened their military position on the Great Lakes and on Lake Champlain. They built Fort Saint-Frédéric on Lake Champlain, at the narrows of the lake near its southern end to close off the main invasion route into Canada from New York.

The War against the Fox

While strengthening their military position on the Great Lakes, the French became involved in an Aboriginal war west of Lake Michigan. The Fox nation, wishing to retain their position as intermediaries in the fur trade, prevented the French from making direct contact with the Dakota (Sioux), the Fox's neighbours and enemies immediately to the west. Friction with the French turned into open warfare from 1714 to 1717. The first campaigns checked the Fox only temporarily, and conflict broke out again in 1728. For the first and only time in the Great Lakes area, the French incited neighbouring nations to kill off the Fox. This annihilation policy, however, proved impossible. In 1737 the French authorities conceded the futility of continued military action and granted the Fox a pardon.

The strength of the French in the interior rested on the "gift diplomacy" they so skilfully practised. Each year at Detroit, Niagara, Michilimackinac, and other posts around the Great Lakes and Lake Winnipeg, the French gave their Aboriginal allies gifts of guns, ammunition, and supplies. The First Nations regarded the annual gifts as a form of rent for the use of the land on which the French forts stood and also as a fee for the right to travel across their territory. They controlled their lands and limited the French to the confines of their trading posts, and to their towns and settlements in the St. Lawrence valley.

The Second Round of Conflict with the English Colonies, 1744–1760

Apart from the war with the Fox to the west and the Mi'kmaq raids against the British in Nova Scotia, peace prevailed in the period 1713–1744. This tranquillity ended in 1744 with the outbreak of war in Europe between France and England. The New England business community welcomed

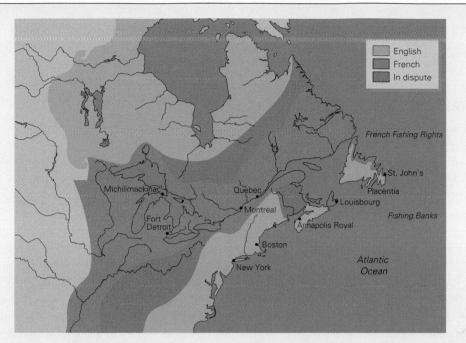

Declared French and English spheres of interest after the Treaty of Utrecht, 1713. Beyond the palisades of the French and English forts, the Aboriginal peoples controlled the interior.

Source: Adapted from P.G. Cornell, J. Hamelin, F. Ouellet, and M. Trudel, *Canada: Unity in Diversity* (Toronto: Holt, Rinehart and Winston, 1967), p. 38.

the opportunity to attack Île Royale. If it fell, they could secure a monopoly of the North Atlantic fisheries.

Governor William Shirley of Massachusetts organized an expedition of 4000 New Englanders to capture Louisbourg. In spite of the many years spent on construction, the walls on the town's southern and northern flanks remained extremely weak. The French also lacked adequate provisions and munitions. The attackers bombarded the town heavily for nearly seven weeks, reducing it to ruins. Without help from France, the defenders surrendered.

Louisbourg's fall caused great anxiety in Canada. It revealed the precariousness of France's position in the interior. It also opened the gates of the St. Lawrence, clearing the way to Quebec. Fortunately for New France, England could not mount an invasion of Quebec in 1745, as their control of Scotland was threatened. Only after their defeat of Charles Edward Stuart (Bonnie Prince Charlie) and his insurgent Highlanders at Culloden Moor in April 1746, did they have troops to send elsewhere.

France, realizing the importance of Louisbourg, attempted to retake it in the summer of 1746. The invasion, however, proved to be one of the most unfortunate ever undertaken by the French. Scurvy and smallpox took their toll. Nearly 600 of the 7000 soldiers died and another 1500, stricken with disease, could not fight. The force returned to France without having attained a single one of its objectives.

England's possession of Louisbourg continued to hurt the French. It prevented supplies of ammunition and trade goods, so badly needed for the Aboriginal trade, from reaching the interior. This led to the defection of many of France's Great Lakes First Nations allies. Fortunately, hostilities with England ceased in 1748 and the French rushed trade goods to the interior, ending the First Nations' hostility.

France now knew that without its leading Atlantic port it would lose the interior of North America, and perhaps the St. Lawrence valley as well. During the peace treaty negotiations at Aix-la-Chapelle in 1748, France therefore sacrificed its conquests in the Netherlands as well as the city of Madras in India in order to regain Louisbourg.

Rivalry in the Ohio Country

The Treaty of Aix-la-Chapelle in 1748 proved no more than a glorified ceasefire. The next clash came in the Ohio country. In 1753 the Marquis Duquesne, the new governor of New France, made French control of the Ohio River, the natural highway to the West, a top military priority. He sent a French military expedition to clear a route from Lake Erie to the forks of the Ohio River. The following year he commanded French soldiers to build Fort Duquesne at the forks of the river (at the site of present-day Pittsburgh, Pennsylvania).

In early 1754, Virginia's governor sent George Washington, a 22-year-old militia officer, and a number of Aboriginal allies to expel the French from the Ohio. Washington's party ambushed a small French detachment in the Ohio country. Washington then withdrew to Fort Necessity, about 100 km from Fort Duquesne. The French retaliated with a force of 500 French, Canadians, and First Nations. They attacked the Virginians and soon overpowered them. The French allowed Washington and the Virginians to return home, but their defeat brought all the wavering Aboriginal bands into the French alliance. These skirmishes, in essence, began the Seven Years' War, two years before the first shots were fired in Europe.

New France at the Outset of the Seven Years' War

By the mid-1750s, New France had built up its military strength considerably. The population of Canada tripled after 1713, to more than 55 000 in 1755, thus enlarging the militia. As well, settlers cleared new farmland along the Richelieu River, southeast of Montreal; along the Ottawa River, northwest of Montreal; and along the Chaudière River, south of Quebec, providing additional food for the army. In addition, extensive road building allowed expansion back from the waterfront, thereby facilitating better communication.

Many weaknesses existed, however. First, New France's elongated frontier was a liability; for example, it took a year to exchange letters between Quebec and New Orleans. To protect French interests, the Crown built a string of forts from Louisbourg to Fort Duquesne, but many of these outposts were simply trading posts grown into wooden forts. Second, Canadian control of the interior depended on the precarious support of the Great Lakes First Nations. Third, although the population of New France had increased to more than 55 000, the population of the American colonies now exceeded 1 million. American settlement extended nearly 200 km from the coastline. Fourth, although the 8000 militia of the colony could be called up quickly, few of them knew the guerrilla techniques that their grandfathers and great-grandfathers had mastered. Fifth, the growing friction between the French and the Canadian-born in the army officers' ranks weakened New France.

A sixth weakness of New France lay in its economy. Although agricultural productivity had improved, the colony still could not feed its more than 6000 regular troops, as well as varying numbers of First Nations and militia who had to be supplied in wartime. Another problem existed as well: the need for farm labour to harvest crops made it impossible for the French to go on lengthy offensives.

More troubling than all these shortcomings was the new unity of the American colonies. The coordination of strategy under a British commander-in-chief did much to draw the English colonies together. In addition, the colonists wanted to defeat New France in order to end the border raids and to gain access to the rich farmlands of the Ohio valley. The English colonists had a labour-force advantage of roughly 20 to 1 over the *Canadiens*. The foodstuffs available to them were enormous. In 1755, the governor of Pennsylvania claimed that his colony alone produced enough food to provide for an army of 100 000.

New France's Successes, 1754–1757

In its early years, despite their advantages, the war for North America went badly for the British. In 1755, General Edward Braddock planned a four-pronged offensive aimed at taking four French forts: Duquesne, Niagara, Saint-Frédéric, and Beauséjour (on the Isthmus of Chignecto, between present-day Nova Scotia and New Brunswick). Braddock took command of the assault on Fort Duquesne with a strike force of 1000 regulars and 1500 colonial troops. It took two months for the force to make its long march over the mountains. As they travelled they constructed a road, a technique of war totally foreign to the French and Aboriginal allies, who valued speed and the surprise attack. The advance column of 1450 men had high spirits when they finally arrived within 15 km of Fort Duquesne. Then came the ambush at the Monongahela River. The French and their First Nation allies unleashed a barrage of gunfire at the scarlet-coated regulars and blue-coated Virginians, inflicting 1000 casualties. They killed Braddock and destroyed his army.

Upon receiving news of the defeat at Fort Duquesne, the British postponed their expedition against Fort Niagara. Meanwhile, in their attack on Fort Saint-Frédéric in the Lake Champlain area, they did no better than a draw. The newly appointed Canadian-born governor, the Marquis de Vaudreuil, immediately built Fort Carillon at the northern end of Lake George. Carillon, so named because it was located where the falling waters produced the sound of bells, became New France's first line of defence for the St. Lawrence valley.

The Anglo-Americans scored their only clear-cut success in Acadia. In June 1755, the British took Fort Beauséjour and, with it, French Acadia. On the grounds of military necessity, the British authorized the deportation of the Acadians in late July. They captured and expelled nearly 10 000 Acadians, who numbered approximately one-sixth of the population of New France.

With the exception of their loss of Fort Beauséjour, the French and their First Nation allies humiliated the larger English colonies and the British army in 1755. Governor Vaudreuil wanted to keep up the momentum. In 1756, he sent out more than 2000 Aboriginal warriors and Canadians in raids from Fort Duquesne. The Canadian guerrilla bands caused so much terror in Virginia and Maryland that these two colonies stayed out of the war until 1758, fearing that the raids might trigger slave uprisings. The French gained control of the Great Lakes by capturing Fort Oswego, at the eastern end of Lake Ontario, in 1756. The following year Vaudreuil attempted to take Fort William Henry, south of the French stronghold of Carillon (or Ticonderoga, as the English called it). This was a greater challenge, as Fort William Henry—unlike Oswego—lay at the end of a short and easy supply line and could be reinforced speedily from Albany. In addition, grain shortages proved to be severe and persistent in Canada, and the limited provisions would not permit a long siege of the English fort.

A reconstruction by Edwin Willard Deming of General Braddock's defeat by the French and their Aboriginal allies at the Battle of Monongahela, 1755.

State Historical Society of Wisconsin/WHi (X3) 29984.

A final problem surfaced: a growing rift arose between Governor Vaudreuil and the Marquis de Montcalm, the new French military commander in Canada. When Fort William Henry fell, Vaudreuil wanted to march against Fort Edward, the English post on the Hudson River, 25 km to the south, but Montcalm opposed such a strategy. He wanted to concentrate French and Canadian troops in the St. Lawrence valley in order to protect Montreal and Quebec against the next English invasion. The French ministry resolved the dispute in late 1758 by putting Montcalm in command over Vaudreuil in military matters.

Britain Gains the Upper Hand

The entire aspect of the war changed in 1757 with the accession of William Pitt the Elder, the self-styled saviour of the British empire, to the prime ministership of England. He inspired the nation to make a greater effort, and made the American war and the conquest of Canada his major objectives. The British offensive of 1758 aimed at the same four localities as that of 1755, but on this occasion, the results proved quite different.

Several factors explain the improvement in England's fortunes. First, Pitt decided in 1758 to commit large numbers of regular soldiers to America, men reliable under fire in set-piece European-style battles. Second, by 1758 the Royal Navy had effectively blockaded France to prevent "escapes" of French support squadrons to Canada. Finally, Pitt greatly increased Britain's financial commitment to the war. More men, more ships, and more money made a significant difference in British fortunes in 1758 and 1759.

France's Reverses in 1758

The first English objective in 1758 was to retake Louisbourg. On account of the effectiveness of the British blockade on France, Louisbourg lacked the protection of a fleet. The British, with their attack force of approximately 27 000, believed that Louisbourg had to be taken quickly if Quebec was to be captured in the same season. Although outnumbered three to one, however, the defenders held out for seven weeks—just long enough to rule out an expedition against Quebec before winter arrived.

The successful French defence at Carillon also prevented an attack on Canada in 1758. Montcalm faced an English army of 15 000 with only 3500 men. Yet Montcalm won. But the French success had its price. Indirectly, it cost the French both Fort Frontenac on Lake Ontario and Fort Duquesne in present-day Pennsylvania. Since Fort Frontenac, with its small garrison and inadequate walls, could not be defended against an English attack, the French themselves destroyed the important post in August 1758. They also blew up Fort Duquesne and retreated. The English renamed the site "Pittsburgh," after their prime minister.

The largest single explanation for the English success in 1758 was the Royal Navy. It allowed the English colonies to obtain troop reinforcements and supplies, while also blockading New France. In 1759, New France faced odds of nearly three to one in ships, four to one in regular soldiers committed to North America, and ten to one in money.

The Fall of New France

In 1759, Pitt concentrated all his efforts on taking the French colony. With the great resources England had in America, it could attack both Quebec and Carillon in equal strength. New France, by contrast, with limited resources, had to concentrate its defence forces in the most vital area, Quebec. At the capital, white-haired men and beardless boys turned out to defend their homeland. They feared the fate of the Acadians: deportation. The Franco–Canadian army at Quebec numbered approximately 15 000 defenders, an impressive force in a colony of only about 60 000.

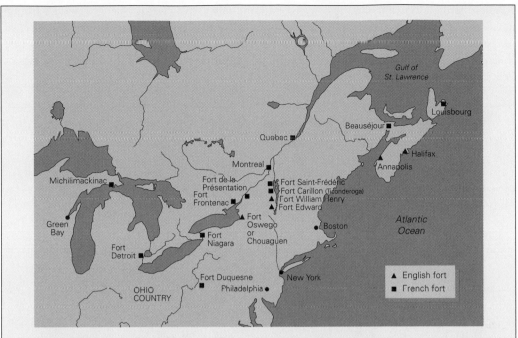

The struggle for a continent: English and French fortifications, 1713–1758.

Source: Adapted from Marcel Trudel, *Introduction to New France* (Toronto: Holt, Rinehart and Winston, 1968), p. 88.

The defenders at Quebec faced several defensive problems in the summer of 1759. First, the city walls on the western side facing the Plains of Abraham had no gun emplacements, seriously weakening the city's defence. Second, the French made a monumental error: they left undefended the south bank of the river opposite the city. Worse still, under cover of this fire, the Royal Navy could transport its ships up the river beyond Quebec. In effect, the British army could land either above or below Quebec for an assault on the walled town.

All that summer, inland French-held garrisons fell into enemy hands. By the end of June 1759, the British had reoccupied Fort Oswego. Fort Niagara succumbed to a British attack in late July. Rather than see the British take Fort Rouillé, France's small outpost in the area that the First Nations called Toronto, the French burned it to the ground. (An obelisk on the grounds of Toronto's Canadian National Exhibition marks the fort's location.) The French now lost control of Lakes Ontario and Erie, and the Ohio country. In addition, they abandoned Forts Carillon and Saint-Frédéric and retreated northward to the head of Lake Champlain.

James Wolfe at Quebec

James Wolfe, a 32-year-old professional soldier who had performed well at Louisbourg, commanded the British invasion force of some 13 500 men against Quebec. Though an excellent battalion commander, he had never led an army before. Moreover, at the time of the attack on Quebec, Wolfe looked ill and indeed he was. Frequently in pain, he was often depressed to the point of despair.

The Canadian historian C.P. Stacey aptly called James Wolfe a "Hamlet-figure"—because of his enormous difficulty making up his mind.[2] Only after several weeks of indecision did he decide to strike Montcalm and his forces at Montmorency, just east of Quebec. Wolfe's frontal attack on the French army's entrenchments failed, and the British retreated. The English commander spent the remainder of the summer systematically devastating the parishes around Quebec. On the south shore of the St. Lawrence, the British destroyed a thousand buildings as well as the French Canadians' harvest.

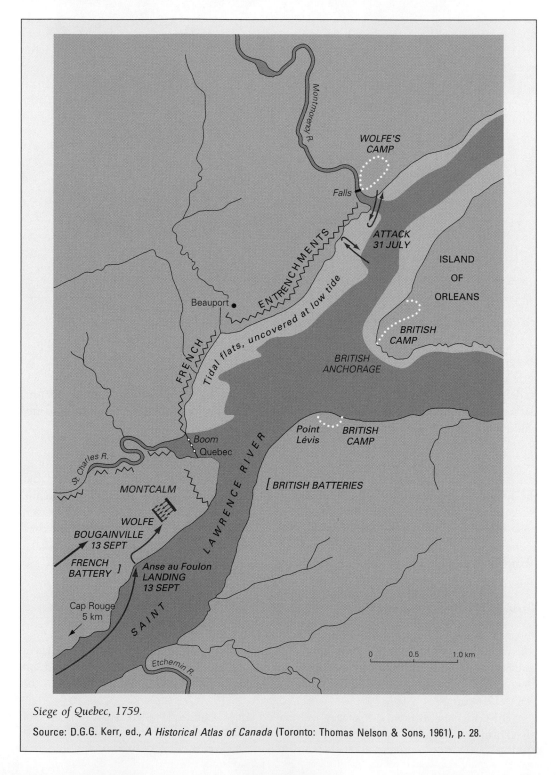

Siege of Quebec, 1759.

Source: D.G.G. Kerr, ed., *A Historical Atlas of Canada* (Toronto: Thomas Nelson & Sons, 1961), p. 28.

The Battle of the Plains of Abraham

Wolfe knew he had to obtain a foothold on the north shore and then force Montcalm into an open, European-style battle. Fortunately, he found a small cove, Anse au Foulon (now known in English as Wolfe's Cove), from which a narrow path led up the steep, 65 m cliffs. Believing that an invasion force could not climb the heights on the tiny path, the French had left it lightly guarded. Equally surprisingly, the French had failed to establish a password for a French convoy expected to bring supplies on the night of September 12. As well, Montcalm believed the British attack would come on the other side of the city or at its centre—never at Anse au Foulon to the west. Thus, the British achieved complete surprise.

The French sentries on the shore believed that the boats gliding past them belonged to the French convoy expected that night. (In fact, the convoy had been cancelled.) The British commander placed his few French-speaking officers in the forward vessels; in the dark, they answered the sentries' challenges satisfactorily. A half-hour before dawn on September 13, the British landed. Three waves of landing ships reached the shore in total darkness. The advance party, two abreast, then walked up the steep pathway and, without detection, gained the summit of the cliffs.

A series of risks paid off for Wolfe: the difficult naval landing succeeded and his advance guard of Scottish Highlanders overpowered the French post, securing a foothold on the cliffs. If the French sentries had identified the British in time, they could have sounded the alarm and easily eliminated the advance guard as they climbed the cliffs.

By daybreak, Wolfe had deployed 4500 highly trained British troops on the Plains of Abraham, the grassy field close to the unarmed western walls of the citadel. At this point, Montcalm made a fatal mistake. Instead of waiting for Colonel Louis-Antoine de Bougainville to arrive with his 3000 regulars stationed at Cap Rouge, about 15 km upstream, he attacked. The decisive battle lasted less than half an hour. Wolfe was ready: to ensure accurate and concentrated fire power, he had deployed three-quarters of his men in a single line confronting the French. The British held their fire until the French army was within 40 m of them. Then the British officers gave the order, "Fire." The muskets roared, and a second volley followed, breaking the French attack and causing the French army to retire in disorder. Wolfe, leading a picked force of grenadiers, was shot down and died on the battlefield. In the confusion after Wolfe's death, the French army retreated up the St. Lawrence by a circuitous route. Mortally wounded in the battle, Montcalm died the next morning from wounds received in battle. Both sides suffered about 650 casualties. On September 18, Quebec, short of provisions and soldiers and weakly fortified, surrendered.

New France's Final Year, 1759–1760

New France's fate was not decided on the Plains of Abraham. The loss of Quebec proved a serious blow to the French, but they still controlled the rest of the St. Lawrence valley and their army remained intact. Ironically, the decisive battle for New France was a naval battle fought at Quiberon Bay, off the coast of France. The Royal Navy's destruction of the French fleet meant that France could not send, even if it wished to do so, a reserve force to save Canada. The success of the French army's offensive against Quebec in the spring of 1760 depended on the dispatch of a French armada, with fresh troops and supplies. But help would not arrive.

Before the ice left the rivers in April, the Chevalier de Lévis, Montcalm's successor as French commander, marched his 7000 troops to Quebec. James Murray, the British commander, had experienced a terrible winter, in which scurvy had reduced his garrison to only 4000. Lévis defeated him at Ste. Foy, immediately west of the city (near the site of Université Laval today). This battle proved bloodier than that of the Plains of Abraham, with about 850 casualties on the French side and nearly 1100 on the English side.

A HISTORICAL PORTRAIT

The Marquis de Montcalm

Louis-Joseph de Montcalm was born in 1712 at the Château of Candiac in the south of France, near Montpellier. He came of a noble background. The Montcalm family had turned Protestant during the sixteenth century. When the persecution of French Protestants intensified in the mid-1680s, Montcalm's uncle took refuge in the Protestant stronghold of Geneva, Switzerland, while his father converted to Catholicism and thus was permitted to inherit the family's confiscated estates.

At the age of 20, Louis-Joseph began his active military career. In 1736 he married Angélique Talon de Boulay, whose family had powerful connections at court, which, no doubt, helped her husband to obtain his rapid promotions. Before his call to Canada in 1756 he fought in eleven European campaigns and was wounded five times. In the intervals between campaigns he spent much of his time at Candiac, with his wife and children (four of the ten children died in infancy). He truly loved his wife. Just four months before the fateful battle on the Plains of Abraham, he wrote to her: "I think that I should have given up all my honours to be back with you, but the king must be obeyed; the moment when I shall see you again will be the finest of my life. Good-bye, my heart, I believe I love you more than ever."

As the commander of French regular soldiers (*troupes de terre*) in New France, Montcalm was subordinate to Governor Vaudreuil, who directly controlled the colonial troops (*troupes de la marine*) and the militia, as well as relations with the First Nations allies. The two men did not get along at all. Montcalm viewed the Canadian-born governor as a civilian playing at war. In turn, Vaudreuil found Montcalm pompous and arrogant. Despite their differences, New France won three great battles from 1756 to 1758: Oswego (1756), William Henry (1757), and Carillon (1758).

Montcalm advocated a cautious strategic policy, whereas the Canadian-born Vaudreuil favoured boldness. The French general wanted all of New France's forces withdrawn from the interior and concentrated in the St. Lawrence valley. But Vaudreuil refused to abandon the outer defence lines.

The threat of a massive British invasion of the St. Lawrence valley in 1759 led the king to intervene. He made Montcalm supreme commander, responsible for all French forces at Quebec, in 1758. The marquis was a brave and experienced soldier, but at the important battle of the Plains of Abraham on September 13, 1759, he made the mistake of rushing forward, without waiting for nearby reinforcements, to fight the British on the Plains. He paid with his life for that serious tactical error. Mortally wounded in the battle, Montcalm died at the age of 47 in the early morning of September 14. He was buried by torchlight that evening, in a shell crater under the floor of the Ursuline chapel. The Church of the Ursulines was the only church in Quebec not completely destroyed by shellfire.

Lévis then proceeded to besiege Quebec. But short of ammunition and supplies, Lévis—and all of New France—prayed for French ships to reach Quebec. Unfortunately for New France, it was English, not French, ships that arrived first at Quebec in mid-May. Lévis had to abandon his plans to retake Quebec. The rest of the year's operations were a foregone conclusion. General Jeffery Amherst, British Commander-in-Chief in America, advanced toward Montreal from the south, with a huge invasion army.

At Montreal that September, Lévis and 2000 troops confronted 17 000 British and American troops. The French capitulated on September 8, 1760, and the British took possession of Montreal. Canada passed into British hands.

In 1760, the imperial conflict for mastery of northeastern North America ended. France lost New France essentially because of the low ranking it assigned the colony. Half a century earlier, at the Treaty of Utrecht, it had traded New France's gains in North America to win back lost territory in Europe. During the Seven Years' War, Europe, the Caribbean, and India remained France's priorities. Compared to England and the Thirteen Colonies, France supplied little assistance to New France in the late 1750s. The flippant line by Voltaire in *Candide* (1759) that the North American conflict was over "a few acres of snow," best summarizes France's attitude.

WHERE HISTORIANS DISAGREE

Was Montcalm an Asset or a Liability for New France?

Historians have long debated the abilities of Montcalm as a military leader. Nineteenth-century French-Canadian historians like François-Xavier Garneau and the Abbé J.B.A. Ferland had little use for him. Vaudreuil, the first Canadian-born governor of New France, is their hero, active and energetic—in contrast to the apathetic, defeatist Montcalm. But the late-nineteenth-century American historian Francis Parkman favoured Montcalm over Vaudreuil, adding to the debate. Then, in the early twentieth century, the French-Canadian historian Thomas Chapais stepped forward to defend the French general. In *Le Marquis de Montcalm*, a full-length biography published in 1911, Chapais argued that Montcalm had energy, courage, and ability. He also loved, not detested, the Canadian people. Up until the 1950s, both French- and English-Canadian historians regarded the book as thorough, objec-

tive, and well researched. Montcalm's reputation was intact when Lucien Bouchard, a future sovereigntist premier of Quebec, attended secondary school. Years later Bouchard remembered his history lessons in the 1950s: "There was the battle of Wolfe against Montcalm. That was the big thing. We spent weeks on that. The battle, before the battle, during the battle, after the battle. The sense of loss and sadness and mourning. It was so sad when Montcalm died—we didn't care much about Wolfe."[1]

Chapais's study was eventually challenged. In 1955, Guy Frégault, one of the first university-trained French-Canadian historians, published a lengthy study, in which he questioned the competence of Montcalm.[2] English-Canadian historian W.J. Eccles later supported Frégault in his denunciations of the French general. In his negative sketch of Montcalm,[3] Canadian military historian George F.G. Stanley added balance to the discussion when he wrote: "Criticism of Montcalm, two centuries later, may smack of hindsight—that wonderful advantage possessed by historians over people about whom they write." Stanley, however, then added, "but even Montcalm's contemporaries were similarly critical."[4] The best summary on the subject is probably that of C.P. Stacey, who wrote in the postscript to the *Quebec, 1759: The Siege and the Battle*, "The last word will never be said on the remarkable happenings at Quebec in 1759."[5]

1. Lucien Bouchard, quoted in Jeffrey Simpson, *Faultlines: Struggling for a Canadian Vision* (Toronto: HarperCollins, 1993), p. 279.

2. Guy Frégault, *La guerre de la conquête* (Montreal: Fides, 1955); translated by Margaret M. Cameron, as *Canada: The War of the Conquest* (Toronto: Oxford University Press, 1969).

3. W.J. Eccles, "Louis-Joseph de Montcalm, Marquis de Montcalm," *Dictionary of Canadian Biography*, vol. 3, *1741–1770* (Toronto: University of Toronto Press, 1974), pp. 458–69.

4. George F.G. Stanley, *New France: The Last Phase 1744–1760* (Toronto: McClelland & Stewart, 1968), p. 233.

5. C.P. Stacey, *Quebec, 1759: The Siege and the Battle* (Toronto: Macmillan, 1959), p. 167.

NOTES

1. See Richard White, *The Middle Ground: Indians, Empires, and Republics in the Great Lakes Region, 1650–1815* (Cambridge: Cambridge University Press, 1991).

2. C.P. Stacey, *Quebec, 1759: The Siege and the Battle* (Toronto: Macmillan, 1959), p. 171.

BEYOND THE BOOK

Treaty of Utrecht

http://www.canadiana.org/ECO/mtq?display=9_03428+0034
A digitized copy of the 1713 Treaty of Utrecht.

Fortress of Louisbourg

http://www.pc.gc.ca/apps/dci/src/3d_e.asp?what=site&sitename=lb&theme
=dc&btn_state=Text%20only
A vivid virtual tour of the eighteenth-century French Fortress of Louisbourg, as it existed then.

The Battle of the Plains of Abraham

http://www.champlain2004.org/html/11/14_e.html
Digitized primary source documents relating to the Battle of the Plains of Abraham.

Louisbourg Grenadiers

http://www.militaryheritage.com/quebec1.htm
The transcribed account of a Sergeant Major in James Wolfe's forces, describing the months leading up to the Battle of the Plains of Abraham, the battle, and the days after it.

The Plains of Abraham: Tactical Positions

http://www.masshist.org/maps/2739_Atlas_16/2739_Atlas_16.html#
A digitized, interactive version of a tactical map drawn in 1759 depicting British and French forces in the St. Lawrence River at the time of the Battle of the Plains of Abraham.

Early Images of Canada: Military

http://www.collectionscanada.gc.ca/earlyimages/index-e.html
A database of scanned illustrations from seventeenth- and eighteenth-century books about Canada. Suggested search terms: "Battles" and "Fortifications."

Battle for a Continent

Canada: A People's History—Episode 4, Battle for a Continent. Directed by Serge Turbide (CBC, 2000).

The Light in the Forest

Conrad Richter, *The Light in the Forest* (New York: Knopf, 1953; many editions in paperback since 1953). An historical novel that tells the story of a young American taken captive at age four by the Delaware, who adopted him into the Nation. He considered himself to be a Delaware (Lenni Lenape), even after his forced return to his own people as a young man.

RELATED READINGS

Two articles are included in R. Douglas Francis and Donald B. Smith, eds., *Viewpoints: Readings in Canadian History* (Toronto: Thomson Nelson, 2007), that deal with this topic: W.J. Eccles, "The Battle of Quebec: A Reappraisal," pp. 98–105; and Allan Greer, "The Fall of New France," pp. 119–124.

BIBLIOGRAPHY

For an overview of French expansion into the interior of North America and New France's conflict with the English colonies, see the following works by W.J. Eccles: *The Canadian Frontier, 1534–1760* (Toronto: Holt, Rinehart and Winston, 1969); *France in America*, rev. ed. (Markham, ON: Fitzhenry & Whiteside, 1990); and *Essays on New France* (Toronto: Oxford University Press, 1987). For a bibliographical guide see: Thomas Wien, "Canada and the Pays d'en haut, 1600–1760," in M. Brook Taylor, ed., *Canadian History: A Reader's Guide*, vol. 1, *Beginnings to Confederation* (Toronto: University of Toronto Press, 1994), pp. 33–75.

Excellent volumes on the military events of the late seventeenth and eighteenth centuries include I.K. Steele, *Guerillas and Grenadiers: The Struggle for Canada, 1689–1760* (Toronto: Ryerson Press, 1969), and his more recent book, *Warpaths: Invasions of North America* (New York: Oxford University Press, 1994); George F.G. Stanley, *New France: The Last Phase, 1744–1760* (Toronto: McClelland & Stewart, 1968); C.P. Stacey, *Quebec, 1759: The Siege and the Battle* (Toronto: Macmillan, 1959); and Guy Frégault, *Canada: The War of the Conquest*, trans. Margaret M. Cameron (Toronto: Oxford University Press, 1969). Other important works include Fred Anderson, *The Crucible of War: The Seven Years' War and the Fate of the Empire in British North America, 1754–1766* (New York: Vintage, 2000); and William M. Fowler, Jr., *Empires at War: The Seven Years' War and the Struggle for North America* (Vancouver: Douglas & McIntyre, 2005).

The first four volumes of the *Dictionary of Canadian Biography* (Toronto: University of Toronto Press, 1966–1976) contain important biographical sketches. It is now also available online: www.biographi.ca. Stephen Brumwell has written the first full-length biography of James Wolfe to appear in nearly half a century, *Paths of Glory. The Life and Death of James Wolfe* (Montreal: McGill-Queen's University Press, 2006). Summaries of the two respective armies in the 1750s appear in vol. 3 of the *Dictionary of Canadian Biography*; see the essays by W.J. Eccles, "The French Forces in North America during the Seven Years' War," pp. xv–xxiii; and C.P. Stacey, "The British Forces in North America during the Seven Years' War," pp. xxiv–xxx.

Two overviews of the history of Louisbourg are J.S. McLennan, *Louisbourg from Its Foundation to Its Fall, 1713–58* (Halifax: Book Room, 1990 [1918]); and the short, up-to-date booklet by Terry Crowley, *Louisbourg: Atlantic Fortress and Seaport* (Ottawa: Canadian Historical Association, 1990).

Important books on the Iroquois and the Great Lakes First Nations include Daniel K. Richter, *The Ordeal of the Longhouse: The Peoples of the Iroquois League in the Era of European Colonization* (Chapel Hill: University of North Carolina Press, 1992); Richard White, *The Middle Ground: Indians, Empires, and Republics in the Great Lakes Region, 1650–1815* (Cambridge: Cambridge University Press, 1991); and Gilles Havard, *The Great Peace of Montreal of 1701: French–Native Diplomacy in the Seventeenth Century* (Montreal/Kingston: McGill-Queen's University Press, 2001). For background on the Aboriginal involvement in the Seven Years' War, see D. Peter MacLeod, *The Canadian Iroquois and the Seven Years' War* (Toronto: Dundurn Press, 1996).

Valuable maps depicting events of the Seven Years' War and the battles for Quebec, 1759–60, are contained in R. Cole Harris, ed., *Historical Atlas of Canada*, vol. 1, *From the Beginning to 1800* (Toronto: University of Toronto Press, 1987).

Part 2

THE CANADAS, 1760–1864

INTRODUCTION

Quebec became Britain's first new colony in 1763. Considering the upheaval of the Conquest, the French adjusted well to British rule. By 1791, they retained their Catholicism, the seigneurial system, and their language.

The British government shifted its Quebec policy three times between 1760 and 1815. In the Proclamation of 1763, the British aimed to assimilate the French. When immigration of New Englanders to Quebec after the Conquest did not occur in significant numbers, the British government realized the advantages of winning over the French-Canadian population and publicly recognized French-Canadian institutions in the Quebec Act of 1774. Then in the 1780s, a large number of Loyalists from the south settled in Quebec. The Constitutional Act of 1791 led to the creation of Upper Canada out of the western portion of the Province of Quebec as a new Loyalist homeland.

Upper Canada's first governor, John Graves Simcoe, aimed to make Upper Canada a "model British colony" in hopes of attracting more Loyalists. They did come, although more often in search of cheap land than from loyalty to Britain. On the eve of the War of 1812, probably four-fifths of the population of Upper Canada was of recent American origin. The American invasion led many of these American immigrants to identify with their new home.

Both Canadas experienced a population boom between 1815 and 1967. In Upper Canada, the increase was due to large-scale immigration from the British Isles. In Lower Canada, the population growth among the French Canadians resulted from a high birth rate. Whatever immigration did occur into Lower Canada was English-speaking, heightening tension between the two cultural groups.

Population growth in the Canadas coincided with a period of economic prosperity, based on external trade. Until 1849, most trade occurred with the mother country; the colonies supplied the raw materials in return for British manufactured goods. Once Britain dismantled its mercantile system in favour of free trade in the late 1840s, the British North American colonies looked increasingly to the United States, especially during the period when the Reciprocity Treaty was in effect between 1854 and 1866, as a trade partner. Later, the British North American colonies looked to trading among themselves—one of the factors leading to Confederation. Prosperity in the Canadas was also due to industrialization, symbolized by railroads, factories, and manufacturing centres in the growing towns and cities.

Politically, the period begins with the struggle for responsible government: that the governor and his appointed council be responsible to the elected Assembly. Opposition to this idea led to rebellion in both the Canadas. The British government commissioned Lord Durham to investigate the rebellions and suggest solutions. Durham's most contentious recommendation was union of the Canadas, which took place in 1841. What developed was a *modus vivendi*, by which moderate political leaders from the two Canadas worked together to achieve responsible government in 1849.

Chapter Five

QUEBEC AND LOWER CANADA, 1760–1840

TIME LINE

1760	The British proclaim military rule over Quebec, in effect to 1763
1763	A royal proclamation creates a vast "Indian Territory" south of the Great Lakes and establishes governmental institutions for Quebec
1774	The Quebec Act extends Quebec's boundaries, modifies the structures of the colony's government, and bestows official recognition upon the Roman Catholic church and the seigneurial system
1775	American armies invade Quebec; but the arrival in 1776 of British reinforcements forces an American retreat
1783	The Treaty of Paris ends the war between Britain and the United States; peace returns to North America
1791	The Constitutional Act divides the Province of Quebec, by executive order, into the separate provinces of Upper and Lower Canada
1837	Rebellion against the British colonial authorities breaks out in Lower Canada
1839	In his report, Lord Durham recommends the union of Upper and Lower Canada

With thousands of British troops massed at the gates of Montreal in early September 1760, the Marquis de Vaudreuil, governor general of New France, saw no sense in continuing the struggle. The French capitulated on September 8, 1760. Two weeks later General Amherst, the British commander, proclaimed military rule over Quebec, which remained in effect until 1763. The British Conquest thus became a reality, at least militarily.

The Treaty of Paris, signed in 1763, formally ended the Seven Years' War. The following year, civil rule began. The three military districts of Montreal, Trois-Rivières, and Quebec were united into the Province of Quebec, with James Murray as governor. Britain faced a difficult dilemma. It now administered a large French population in North America whose loyalty would naturally be doubtful in the event of renewed war with France. The new colonial masters therefore hoped that the French population might be quickly assimilated, with the anticipated arrival of large numbers of English-speaking Protestant immigrants. But rather than move north to Quebec, with its harsh climate and "foreign" population, New England migrants headed west to more fertile lands. The assimilationists' program, to be outlined in the Royal Proclamation of 1763, was doomed from the beginning.

Pontiac's Resistance and the Proclamation of 1763

With the return of peace, the First Nations question also posed a problem for Britain. Pontiac, an Ottawa chief in the Detroit region, organized a pan-Indian confederacy that mounted a formidable Aboriginal resistance to the British. The First Nations resented settler encroachments on their lands around the Great Lakes. Dissatisfaction also arose from another source—a fundamental difference in French and English policy toward the Aboriginal peoples. The French practised "gift diplomacy," the custom of making generous annual payments to First Nations people. In contrast, the English in the Thirteen Colonies preferred treaties or one-time-only purchases for the First Nations' lands.

In May 1763, Pontiac and his confederacy attacked British garrisons and frontier settlements throughout the upper Mississippi and Ohio River basins. The First Nations of the Upper Great Lakes captured every British post west of Niagara with the exception of Detroit, killing or taking captive an estimated 2000 settlers. Several factors finally led the First Nations to make peace. First, the key fort of Detroit still remained in English hands. Also, by autumn the Aboriginal peoples had to resume their hunting to bring in winter food supplies. Then came word of the peace treaty between the French and the English, signifying that Pontiac could not expect French military aid from Louisiana. In addition, old rivalries resurfaced, destroying the unity of the First Nations' alliance. By late 1764, British military expeditions succeeded in quelling lingering Aboriginal opposition.

The resistance justified British plans, already drawn up, to satisfy First Nation grievances. The Proclamation of 1763, issued by the British in October, at the height of the resistance, set aside a huge reserve west of the Allegheny Mountains. The British agreed not to colonize First Nations territory without prior purchase by the Crown and the consent of the affected band. Colonial governors were forbidden to make any land grants to colonists or to survey within the area of the reserve. London alone was to manage trade relations with the First Nations.

How the French and English forces might have appeared on the day of capitulation at Montreal, September 8, 1760. Canadian artist Adam Sherriff Scott (1887–1980) painted this scene two centuries after the event.

Scott, Adam Sherriff/National Archives of Canada/C-11043.

The Royal Proclamation of 1763 became the first legal recognition by the British Crown of Aboriginal rights. Events soon showed, however, that the policy was unenforceable without a substantial British military presence in the interior. In defiance of the British government, thousands of land-hungry Americans began to push over the mountains into First Nations' land, notably the fertile Ohio country.

Impact of the Royal Proclamation of 1763 on the Province of Quebec

In creating the "Indian Territory," the Royal Proclamation drastically reduced Quebec's territory to a rough quadrilateral along both sides of the St. Lawrence River, extending from what is today eastern Ontario to Gaspé. It also provided the new province with governmental institutions, among them a council to assist the governor.

Other stipulations in the Royal Proclamation referred directly to the *Canadiens*. They gave good reason to worry about the future: for one thing, as Roman Catholics, the *Canadiens* were to be excluded from all offices. Elected assemblies were promised, with a view to attracting English Protestant immigrants from the New England colonies. While awaiting the expected wave of settlers that would permit the British to remake Quebec into an English colony, those few English-speakers already living in Quebec could rely on "the enjoyment of the benefit of the laws of our realm of England." It was left to the colonial governors in Quebec to deal with the practical realities and to find appropriate compromises.

In practice, French civil law and the role of the Roman Catholic church remained largely intact in the new province. The fact that very few English-speakers came north forced Governor Murray to authorize Roman Catholic barristers to practise in the courts. Murray also adopted a pragmatic attitude toward the Catholic church. He realized that, even with all the support of the colonial administration, the handful of Protestants in the conquered colony had no chance of converting the *Canadiens*. He also judged that the church enjoyed considerable influence with the habitants. By avoiding any open oppression of Roman Catholics and rewarding loyal priests, the British administration, Murray reasoned, might even be able to rally the church's support. Thus, he made no attempt to close the churches. Instead, he and his officials simply kept a watchful eye on their activities and administration.

The most delicate problem that had to be solved was the replacement of Bishop Pontbriand, who died in 1760. The British government instructed Murray not to re-establish the "Popish hierarchy." But when the New Englanders failed to come north, the governor needed someone with whom he could deal as the leader of French-Canadian society. Murray, an aristocrat, believed that such a leader should come from the church. He was thus ready, in spite of London's directives to the contrary, to accept a "superintendent of the Romish religion." Murray made known his preference for Jean-Olivier Briand, vicar general of the diocese of Quebec, who had shown great respect for British authority. The Quebec cathedral chapter then nominated Briand for the position. In June 1766, six years after Pontbriand's death, the Canadian church at last had a new leader. With a bishop installed, priests could now be ordained.

Cooperation with the British brought the church obvious benefits. Bishop Briand, for example, even obtained an annuity from the governor for his "good behaviour." But the British exacted a high price for their concessions. After all, the governor had effectively chosen the bishop, and this marked a significant limitation of ecclesiastical authority. The governor used the church to communicate with the general population and to keep French Canadians loyal to the government. Priests made government announcements from the pulpits and on church steps.

Canadien Society in the Aftermath of the Conquest

Although British rule of Quebec immediately after the Conquest hardly proved a golden age for French Canadians, their survival was possible. Pressures on the land in the old seigneurial region along the St. Lawrence were not yet intense, and new concessions could be had with relative ease. Nor did the habitants feel threatened by an increase in the "foreign," English-speaking population: excluding soldiers, the barely 500 British in the colony in 1765 hardly posed a threat to the 70 000 *Canadiens*. Moreover, the presence of British troops prevented any serious uprising among the French Canadians, especially at a time when they could not expect any help from France.

In general, both Murray and his successor Guy Carleton, appointed in 1768, showed favour toward the seigneurs, believing that they had great influence with the habitants. Recognizing that the "nobles" had been deprived of "their honours, their privileges, their revenues and their laws," Guy Carleton recommended that the British show them sympathy in return for their loyalty. London agreed, and by 1771 additional royal instructions had been issued to ensure the perpetuation of the seigneurial system.

Urban Life

The degree of satisfaction among urban dwellers remains difficult to judge. Even the term "urban" must be put in context. Barely 20 percent of the Province of Quebec's citizens lived in towns, and even the largest of these were tiny communities by today's standards. Quebec, the largest centre, had scarcely more than 7000 inhabitants in 1765; Montreal had barely 5000. Beyond the new borders, the Detroit area contained perhaps another 2000 *Canadiens*.

Although these townspeople had access to certain goods and services that their country cousins lacked, they suffered important disadvantages. Wageworkers, for example, had to contend with the seasonal nature of much of the available employment. Disease and fire also caused untold misery. Epidemics due to contaminated water supplies and poor hygiene took many lives, especially among the old and the very young.

In the urban areas, particularly Quebec, several hundred merchants were involved in a wide variety of commercial pursuits, including the fur trade. Many of these merchants were French-speaking. Some, however, were English-speaking, having arrived after the Conquest from Britain or the American colonies. This group quickly carved out for itself an important place in the local economy; indeed, research shows that British investments in the fur trade as well as in other sectors appear to have surpassed French investments by the early 1770s.

The Quebec Act

For Britain, security in North America was paramount. The Quebec Act of 1774, which spelled out Britain's new policy, extended Quebec's frontiers into the Ohio region. The British hoped that this boundary extension would end the virtual anarchy and ferocious competition among traders that plagued the territory. Quebec's economy depended far more on furs than did New York's, and giving the West to Quebec would thus preserve the economic balance.

The Quebec Act retained the application within Quebec of English criminal law. In civil matters, the act put into law the significant concessions that Governors Murray and Carleton had already made to the seigneurs. In particular, it reintroduced French civil law with regard to property. This was an attempt to resolve the uneasy co-existence of two completely different legal systems. The return of French civil law enraged the English-speaking merchants but pleased the seigneurs. Britain now legally confirmed the existence of the seigneurial system and gave it a much-needed boost through the restoration of seigneurial dues.

Finally, this new constitution for Quebec substantially modified the province's political structure. It established an appointive Legislative Council that could make laws with the governor's consent. The governor could suspend or remove councillors. Significantly, these councillors could now be Roman Catholics.

Reaction to the Quebec Act

While satisfied with the colony's new boundaries, the English merchants were furious that Parliament denied them the elective assembly for which they had so often petitioned. The higher clergy and seigneurs, in contrast, were pleased. They saw the Quebec Act as a veritable charter of French-Canadian rights as well as a vindication of their dominant role in society. But, for the habitants, the legal recognition given to the tithe and seigneurial dues was surely disappointing. Nevertheless, restoration of their system of colonization, which enabled the habitants to obtain land without having to purchase it, no doubt pleased them.

Not surprisingly, the extension of Quebec's boundaries embittered the Americans. They viewed it as a hostile measure that effectively continued to seal off the West, which had been officially closed since the Proclamation of 1763. They also bitterly resented the recognition that the Quebec Act bestowed on the colony's despised "papists" by conceding "the free exercise of the religion of the Church of Rome" and by firmly recognizing the right of the Roman Catholic church to collect tithes. The "tyrannical act" figured prominently among the grievances of the Americans when they launched their rebellion in April 1775, three weeks before the Quebec Act was officially proclaimed.

The Quebec Act showed that the British believed the Roman Catholic church and the seigneurial class were powerful and held considerable sway over the *Canadiens*. There was no quick way in which to Anglicize and Protestantize a colony that had attracted but a few hundred English-speaking Protestant immigrants, largely merchants. Not that the British rejected assimilation as their ultimate aim; it was simply not a realistic policy in 1774. A year later, with the outbreak of revolution to the south, it became even less feasible. Eventually, with the arrival of thousands of Loyalists who cast their lot with Britain, the hopes of the assimilationists revived. But for the moment, Quebec's population remained overwhelmingly French-speaking and Roman Catholic.

The American Invasion

From the early 1770s, American radical propaganda denouncing British tyranny, lauding elective institutions, and proclaiming the people's rights and liberties circulated widely in Quebec. American agents roamed the countryside, appealing to the French Canadians to choose between making the rest of North America their "unalterable friends" or their "inveterate enemies."

The Continental Congress in Philadelphia decided early in the revolutionary war to invade Canada in order to prevent the British from concentrating their forces there and then sweeping southward into the Thirteen Colonies. In September 1775, General George Washington's armies advanced into Quebec by way of Lake Champlain and Maine. Both the clergy and the seigneurs upheld the traditional order that the American revolutionaries threatened. They urged the habitants to support the British cause and, indeed, to enlist. Few came forward.

Governor Guy Carleton abandoned Montreal to the invading Americans, but succeeded in defending Quebec against the American assault that came in the early morning of December 31. In May 1776, a fleet of British ships sailed up the St. Lawrence, and the ill-equipped and demoralized Americans hastily departed.

The following year the British conceived a plan to crush the revolt by striking down from Quebec to New York City, thus gravely weakening their resistance, by dividing the rebellious

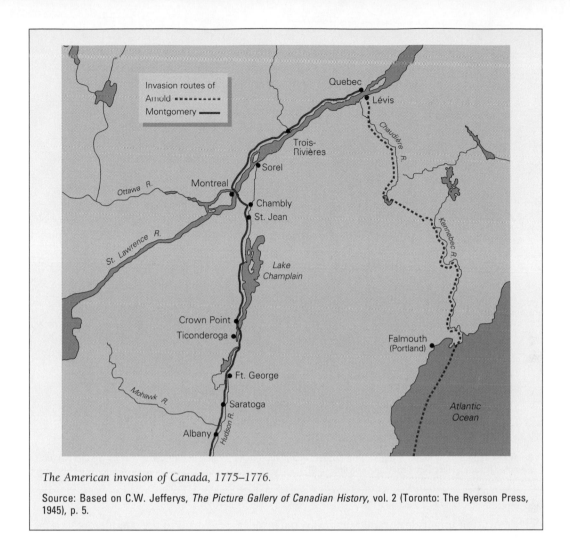

The American invasion of Canada, 1775–1776.

Source: Based on C.W. Jefferys, *The Picture Gallery of Canadian History*, vol. 2 (Toronto: The Ryerson Press, 1945), p. 5.

colonies in two. These hopes were dashed when a numerically superior American force surrounded and defeated the British at Saratoga, north of Albany, New York. Thereafter, the British launched no more large-scale expeditions southward from the St. Lawrence.

The alliance of France with the American colonies in February 1778 changed the face of the war. A secret clause of the arrangement stipulated, however, that France would not invade Canada or Acadia; the Americans wanted no restoration of New France. Louis XVI, for his part, wanted to weaken British power by assisting the Thirteen Colonies in gaining their independence, but he did not favour an American conquest of Canada. Indeed, he hoped that a British Canada, by posing a continual threat to the Americans, would ensure the latter's dependence on France. Clearly, neither France nor the United States wished the other to possess Canada.

The French Canadians' Response to the American Invasion

During the American expedition into Canada, some people, often English-speaking merchants, welcomed the invading revolutionaries with enthusiasm. Some habitants, for their part, also seem to have given support to the Americans. No doubt many habitants listened receptively to the Americans' denunciations of tithes and seigneurial rents, both firmly established by the

The British colonies in North America, 1791.

Source: Adapted from Ralph Krueger, Ray Corder, and John Koegler, *This Land of Ours: A New Geography of Canada* (Toronto: Harcourt Brace Jovanovich, 1991), p. 130.

Quebec Act. But linguistically and religiously, the invaders were akin to the conquerors, not the conquered. There was little love lost for the *Bastonnois*, or "people of Boston," as the French Canadians called the Americans. In general, the habitants felt little interest in this struggle, and preferred to keep their neutrality as long as possible. When American fortunes improved and American soldiers paid good prices in coin for supplies, the habitants sympathized with them. But when the invaders failed to take Quebec and the long winter siege dragged on, and—even worse—when they began to pay for their provisions with paper money or simply not at all, their popularity fell, precipitously.

The American Revolution and the First Nations

Like the *Canadiens*, the Aboriginal peoples, particularly the Six Nations, were threatened and cajoled by both sides. At the beginning of the American Revolution, the Six Nations Confederacy council declared its neutrality in what it perceived as a "family feud" between the British and their American offspring. Later on, however, the Confederacy split on the issue of involvement.

Thanks largely to the efforts of Mohawk war chief Joseph Brant, the Mohawks and some Senecas supported the British. The Onondagas and the Cayugas, though, declared their neutrality, while many Oneidas and Tuscaroras, as well as some of the Iroquois in the Montreal area, showed a preference for the Americans. In 1779, however, American troops under General John Sullivan invaded the Six Nations territory, indiscriminately punishing the

Iroquois by burning crops and destroying villages. These attacks on the hitherto neutral Onondagas and Cayugas brought them over to the British side. One thousand Iroquois warriors retaliated by burning and pillaging American farms throughout the immense territory between the Ohio and Mohawk rivers.

The cost of the involvement proved heavy: the Iroquois League, now several hundred years old, collapsed, and the Mohawks lost their lands along the Mohawk River in central New York State and elsewhere. Peace came, first in preliminary fashion at the end of 1782 and finally in September 1783 with the Treaty of Paris. The First Nations were not mentioned in the treaty.

Britain's Iroquois allies felt completely betrayed, as they had prevented American control of much of northern New York and Pennsylvania. To appease them the British purchased vast tracts of land from the Mississaugas, as the British called the Ojibwa (Anishinabeg) on the north shore of Lake Ontario. The British then gave part of this territory, a long narrow strip of land along the Grand River, to the Six Nations. England's defeat led 2000 Iroquois to abandon their homelands and migrate to the western section of the Province of Quebec that would become Upper Canada.

COMMUNITY PORTRAIT

The Community of Odanak

Often overlooked in discussions of the Aboriginal history of the St. Lawrence valley in the eighteenth century are the Algonquian-speaking communities, one of the most prominent being the Abenaki of Odanak. Located on the banks of the St. Francois River, near Sorel, just east of Montreal, "Odanak" means "at the village" in the Algonquian language of the Abenaki. The name "Abenaki" itself is an alteration of "Wabanaki," meaning "and of the dawn," or "country lying to the east." Here today live descendants of the original inhabitants of the northern and central New England states. The community of Odanak was one of four major Roman Catholic mission stations in the St. Lawrence valley, in the French regime, along with Lorette (Hurons) at Quebec, Kahnewake (Iroquois), and Kahnesatake (Iroquois and Algonquian), in the Montreal area. It was a community of great ethnic diversity.

The majority of the Abenaki at Odanak arrived in New France as refugees from northern New England's Indian Wars. Apparently the Soroki nation originally constituted a majority in the refugee community, founded in the early eighteenth century. But Odanak was swept by smallpox in 1730, and the losses in the raids to the south proved great. Then another important nation, the Abenaki proper, arrived and gained predominance in the community. In total, the members of perhaps as many as twenty Algonquian-speaking First Nations made their way as refugees from the encroaching American settlements to the south. At Odanak they all gradually lost their separate identities. As the majority, the Abenaki proper gave their name to the others in the community.

Abenaki war parties went forth from the St. Francois River against the "Bastoniak" (people from Boston), as the Abenaki called the New England settlers. These loyal French allies served the French to the end of the French regime. Odanak warriors joined other First Nations and the French in the ambush of British General Braddock in 1755, and fought beside the French at Quebec in 1759. In retaliation for their repeated raids on New England settlements, the British made an assault on the "St. Francis Indians" a priority in 1759. Only weeks after their victory on the Plains of Abraham, a company of American frontier rangers led by Major Robert Rogers made a surprise attack on Odanak, during which they burned the village church and all the houses to the ground, and killed Abenakis at random.

In his report to General Amherst, the British Commander, Major Rogers claimed his rangers killed 200 Abenaki, but French sources state that only 30 died. What explains the discrepancy? Anthropologist Gordon Day's investigation of Abenaki oral traditions helped demystify the event. Two hundred years after the horrific raid a vivid oral memory of it remained with several of the eldest members of the community. After evaluating the oral memories with the same degree of care used in documentary analysis, he identified a valuable addition to our knowledge of the raid. At Odanak in the late 1950s he spoke with several elderly people who remembered traditions told to them as children by their grandparents, themselves born in the early nineteenth century. According to these informants, a First Nations person serving with the American forces came to the village the night before the attack to give warning. This allowed the community to move their children, women, and old people into places of safe refuge (hence Rogers's overestimation of Abenaki losses). The Odanak Abenaki regrouped shortly thereafter and the next year raided an American settlement in New Hampshire.

Peace came late that year, and they re-established their village at the same location on the banks of the St. François.

Strangely it was to this same First Nation village that Rev. Eleazar Wheelock sent recruiters in 1774 to obtain students for his Moor's Indian Charity School at Hanover, New Hampshire (today's Dartmouth College). Normally Odanak would have had nothing to do with the detested "Bastoniak," who had occupied the Abenaki homeland. But at the time of their visit an individual then in office as a principal chief proved very sympathetic: Joseph-Louis Gill, "The White Chief of the Abenakis," the son of two New England captives. Gill was of European descent only in a biological sense. In the early eighteenth century the Abenaki had captured two English children, a boy and a girl, from the New England coast. Adopted into Abenaki families at Odanak, and raised as Abenakis and as Catholics, these captives later married at Odanak where they lived their entire lives. Joseph-Louis, the eldest of their seven children, became a chief in the community around 1750. His first wife, an Abenaki woman, died during Rogers's raid; his second wife was French Canadian. During the British regime he met with the British authorities in 1764 to complain of encroachments by settlers in the Odanak area on the Abenakis' hunting territories. Toward the end of his life, Gill became prayer leader at Odanak, which meant he was the most important person in the Odanak church after the Catholic missionary.

Although a staunch Roman Catholic, Gill wanted his family to obtain an education, even if the welcoming school was Protestant and in "Bastonki," as the

Abenakis called New England. The chief sent four of his relatives to Dartmouth. Although none of the Abenaki young men he sent to the school converted to Protestantism, several Abenaki students from Odanak did, after Chief Gill's death in 1798. These Protestant Abenaki and their converts in the community added an additional layer of complexity to the already multiethnic Aboriginal community, made up of descendants of approximately twenty First Nations.

FURTHER READING

Thomas M. Charland, "Joseph-Louis Gill, Known Also as Magouaouidombaouit," *Dictionary of Canadian Biography*, vol. 4, *1771–1800* (Toronto: University of Toronto Press, 1979): 293–94.

Gordon M. Day, "Oral Tradition as Complement," *Ethnohistory*, 19, 2 (Spring 1972): 99–107.

Gordon M. Day, "Western Abenaki," in Bruce G. Trigger, ed., *Handbook of North American Indians*, vol. 15, *Northeast* (Washington: Smithsonian Institution, 1978), pp. 148–59.

Loyalist Immigration

During and after the revolution, thousands of Loyalists, bitterly denounced as un-American by the victorious revolutionaries, fled north. Many came to Quebec from upper New York and New England. The arrival of the Loyalists encouraged those British administrators who wanted to make Quebec into an English-speaking colony. For the first time since the Conquest, a significant contingent of English-speaking immigrants settled in the province. Quebec's population of British origin increased to at least 10 percent of the total non-Aboriginal population, estimated at about 160 000 in 1790.

Guy Carleton, now Lord Dorchester, had commanded the evacuation of nearly 30 000 Loyalists from New York City in 1782–1783. He had developed a great sympathy for them, and subsequently showed a much more English outlook during his second tour of duty as governor of Quebec from 1786 to 1796. Dorchester himself no longer believed that Quebec was destined to remain predominantly French Canadian "to the end of time."

While the church showed little interest in the colony's constitutional future, the English-speaking merchants discussed it with increasing urgency. They wanted a Legislative Assembly, preferably controlled by the province's tiny English-speaking minority. Many French-Canadian merchants and professionals also desired an Assembly, since the French, as the majority, hoped to control this part of government.

The Constitutional Act of 1791

The British government drew up the new constitution, the Constitutional Act of 1791. At the same time, the Province of Quebec was divided by executive order into two sections, the provinces of Upper and Lower Canada, with the upper part possessing an English-speaking Loyalist majority.

The Constitutional Act of 1791 established an elective Legislative Assembly in each of the Canadas. Besides giving a voice to the population, this body could raise money through taxes for local expenditures, thus reducing the burden on the imperial treasury. At the same time, wary of what had happened in the American colonies, London placed the Assembly under strong executive control that would apply restraint if the people's representatives got out of hand. A lieutenant governor was to be appointed in each province. He would name the members of the Legislative Council, the upper house. The Legislative Council's membership was intended eventually to be hereditary, like that of the British House of Lords. Thus, the "right men"—landowners—would be assured of a place in power. The Executive Council, also composed of appointed officials, would be the governor's personal cabinet. The governor enjoyed extensive veto powers and a measure of financial autonomy, thanks to the revenues from the Crown lands set aside by the Constitutional Act of 1791. Both the appointed executive branch and the elected Assembly possessed considerable powers and frequently used them to thwart each other's will.

On account of property qualifications in England at this time, relatively few people there (less than 3 percent of the population) could vote in elections. Essentially the same qualifications applied in Lower Canada, but because of that colony's very different social structure, the great majority of non-Aboriginal male farmers, or habitants, obtained the right to vote. Still, suffrage was far from

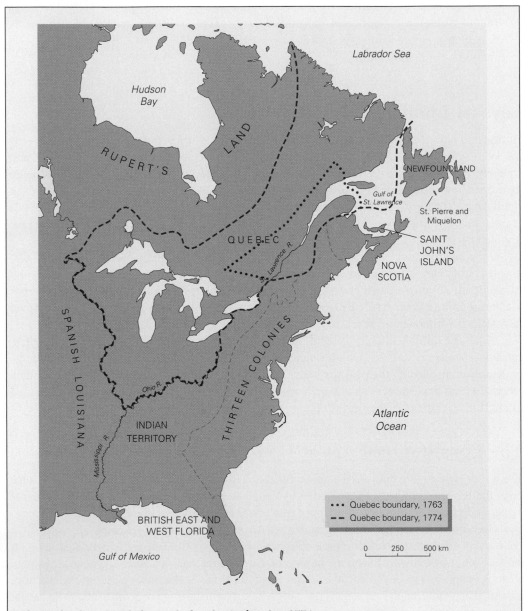

The Quebec boundary before and after the Quebec Act, 1774.

Source: Based on *The Integrated Atlas: History and Geography of Canada and the World* (Toronto: Harcourt Brace, 1996), p. 114.

universal. Most urban labourers and domestics were disqualified because they neither owned property nor paid sufficient rent. The property qualification eliminated most women from the rolls, although it was only in 1834 that the Assembly of Lower Canada specifically disenfranchised women.

After the Proclamation of 1763 and the Quebec Act of 1774, Quebec obtained, with the Constitutional Act of 1791, its third constitution in less than 30 years. The American Revolution and the arrival of thousands of Loyalists made change imperative. Certain Lower Canadian groups, such as the seigneurs, the professionals, and the merchants, thought that they could use the new institutions profitably. Most disappointed as a group were Lower Canada's 10 000 English. The Constitutional Act of 1791 led to their separation from the growing English-speaking population in the new colony of Upper Canada. Moreover, the English-speaking inhabitants of what now became Lower Canada obtained few of the reforms for which they had agitated and did not even succeed in getting the Quebec Act repealed. Nevertheless, regardless of political changes, the English merchants' economic power continued to increase. In the 1790s, in fact, they had reason to be optimistic about the future.

The Economic Revolution in the Early Nineteenth Century

At the end of the eighteenth century, Quebec entered a period of intense, if uneven, economic growth, as Britain's industrialization and urbanization created new markets for the colony's foodstuffs and resources. The fur-trade era drew to a close, as profits slumped because of declining demand for furs overseas and ruinous competition at home.

The rise of the timber industry offset the decline of the fur trade in Lower Canada. By 1810, wood products accounted for three-quarters of Quebec's exports (and the fur trade only one-tenth). Britain needed wood, especially to build ships. Napoleon's control of northern Europe from 1808 to 1810 cut Great Britain off from its traditional Baltic suppliers. As a result, Britain's imports of timber from Lower Canada and other North American colonies increased significantly. The British government doubled import duties on foreign, but not colonial, timber. This effectively guaranteed a highly profitable monopoly to colonial suppliers.

Other sectors of the economy experienced significant, though less spectacular, growth. Ships were built at nearly 80 localities along the St. Lawrence River. Quebec City had the biggest shipyards, and much of their production went overseas to Britain. Sawmills, candle and soap manufacturers, textile factories, flour mills, and an expanding construction industry contributed to this growth. Banks, beginning with the Bank of Montreal in 1817, were established to supply credit to new enterprises and commercial ventures.

Urban Life in Lower Canada

Lower Canada's rapidly expanding population provided the labour needed for the increased resource exploitation and manufacturing. Thanks largely to a birth rate that stayed slightly above 50 per 1000 throughout the period, as well as to substantial immigration from Britain, the population quintupled, rising from about 160 000 in 1790 to 890 000 in 1851. As early as the 1830s, demographic pressures resulted in increasing numbers of French Canadians emigrating to the United States in search of the land or work they could not find at home.

Lower Canada's two major cities developed rapidly as centres of both wealth and poverty. In the early 1800s, the population of Quebec City grew at an annual rate of more than 5 percent. The Lower Town, around the seaport, was bustling, noisy, and dirty. Fires were frequent throughout the city and took a heavy toll. Montreal also grew quickly. By the late 1830s it had overtaken Quebec, the administrative and ecclesiastical capital, and become British

North America's premier city, with a population of 37 000. Citizens of French origin constituted only a minority of its residents. Well over half of the city's anglophones were Irish immigrants, most of them poor labourers who settled in industrial areas near the port. Increasingly, Montrealers settled in the suburbs. Wealthy British residents built palatial residences with gardens on the verdant slopes of Mont Royal.

COMMUNITY PORTRAIT

The St. Maurice Forges, an Early Industrial Community

A few kilometres north of Trois-Rivières, Quebec, the tourist can spend a few pleasant and instructive hours visiting the Forges du Saint-Maurice National Historic Site. Set in rolling countryside along a small stream that drops through a gully to the St. Maurice River just below, it features the large reconstructed *Grande Maison*, the Master's House, built in 1738, and a modern blast-furnace interpretive centre describing the iron industry's early development, from 1730 until 1883.

The Forges constituted a remarkable legacy from the era of New France. Already in this early period, the Forges produced large quantities of munitions for the army. After the British conquered New France, they soon realized the importance of the ironworks and made certain that masters and skilled employees continued working and did not return to France. The British also used corvées to force the habitants to cut wood for charcoal.

The Forges attained their maximum development in the first decades of the nineteenth century, using wood charcoal in the process of ore reduction rather than the more modern, more efficient coke-fuelled technology. The ore used was bog ore, found in the form of nodules close to the surface in swampy areas. The Forges employed 400 people directly and also provided work for the surrounding population, hired to collect, prepare, and transport raw materials as well as products and goods.

Work "campaigns," during which the blast furnace operated without interruption, lasted six to eight months. The pig iron that was produced by the blast furnace was taken to the forges where blacksmiths fashioned tools and implements, pots and kettles, stoves, and munitions including cannonballs. From the 1850s, the Forges sold huge quantities of iron to the railway industry.

For most of the company's productive life, the Forges were state-owned, marking the great importance that the French, British, and finally Canadian governments accorded to this industry. Until 1863, the state granted the Forges free access to vast timber and ore resources, a privilege that ensured profitability. When this privilege was withdrawn, and when the plant was forced to pay the real costs of raw materials, it soon collapsed under an increasing debt load.

Mathew Bell, a Scottish merchant, was master of the Forges from 1793 until 1846, when the government sold the enterprise. The government set very favourable terms for the tenants, who could run the business for their profit. Bell used his influence as a member of the Assembly and then as a legislative councillor to ensure that the Forges disposed of adequate reserves of land for procuring raw materials, including 10 000 cords of wood annually. Bell's monopolistic control of huge tracts of land provoked substantial criticism. The Assembly even accused him in one of the Ninety-Two Resolutions in 1834 of having been unduly and illegally favoured by the Executive.

The community that grew up around the Forges had a population of about 400 people, mostly workers and their families. Five generations of workers lived on the site, with fathers often passing on their trade to their sons. Skilled workers and craftsmen lived in houses, while the families of unskilled labourers inhabited more modest tenements. Most workers had kitchen gardens, and kept livestock and poultry. The village boasted a chapel while the Grande Maison contained a well-stocked store.

The St. Maurice Forges constituted the first industrial village in Canada's history, its character defined by its industrial vocation and its population of skilled workers. The community that grew up around the Forges was a precursor of the numerous mining and forestry communities that developed later, particularly in northern regions of Canada.

FURTHER READING

Michel Bédard, André Bérubé, and Jean Hamelin, "Mathew Bell," *Dictionary of Canadian Biography*, vol. 7, *1836–1850* (Toronto: University of Toronto Press, 1988): 70–75.

Roch Samson, *The Forges du Saint-Maurice: Beginnings of the Iron and Steel Industry in Canada, 1730–1883* (Quebec: Les Presses de l'Université Laval and the Department of Canadian Heritage—Parks Canada, 1998), p. 10.

Communications stimulated Montreal's growth. In 1836, Canada's first railway, linking St. Jean, on the Richelieu River, and hence Lake Champlain, to La Prairie, on the south shore of the St. Lawrence opposite Montreal, was inaugurated. Goods destined to and coming from increasingly prosperous Upper Canada passed through the port of Montreal.

Most workers were unskilled. Many labourers had to spend more than half their earnings simply to feed their families. Prior to the 1830s, there were no unions, and legislation passed in 1802 authorized fines and prison sentences for striking employees. Over one-quarter of the women of Lower Canada appeared to have been in the labour force in 1825, a figure higher than that at the end of the nineteenth century. They toiled in a wide variety of occupations. Many were weavers. Others made soap, candles, and dresses. A census taken in 1825 showed that Montreal had female innkeepers, mercers, blacksmiths, and coachmakers. Some women earned money by taking in boarders, providing meals for them, and washing their laundry. Convents began to train a few women as teachers. Many female labourers found jobs as domestics, work that began at dawn and finished when the family went to bed. By 1820, about one family in five in Quebec City employed at least one servant.

Health Conditions

In the early decades of the nineteenth century, disease posed a serious and constant threat to public health, particularly in the towns, with their filthy living conditions and relatively concentrated populations. In 1832, the first of a series of cholera epidemics provoked a wave of panic among Canadians. The disease, transmitted mainly through contaminated water supplies, had spread from the delta of the Ganges River in India across Europe to Britain. Its attacks were sudden, extremely painful, and very often fatal; death came within 48 hours, a result of complete dehydration of the victim's body. No known cure existed.

The arrival in Canada of large numbers of immigrants, very often indigents from Ireland, caused much concern to the French Canadians living in the St. Lawrence valley. The Irish had been migrating in large numbers to Lower Canada since 1815, although most went on to Upper Canada or to the United States. Some 50 000 arrived in 1831. They were steerage passengers who had spent weeks on the boats, in filthy conditions, and often near starvation. Worried about the threat these immigrants posed to public health, the government of Lower Canada established a quarantine station on Grosse Île, a small island in the upper St. Lawrence River downstream from Quebec.

Conditions in Lower Canadian towns greatly contributed to the spread of infection. Houses were dirty and overcrowded, yards and streets were piled with refuse, and towns had open sewers. People emptied the remains of animal pens and latrines into the streets. Pigs and other animals ran loose. Slaughterhouses, often located in residential districts, dumped their waste into open water. In early spring 1832, the health board of Quebec City tried to force residents to clean up streets, houses, and yards. They were ordered to "scrape, wash and cleanse their premises and carry away all filth." Such regulations proved unenforceable in the face of public indifference, if not outright hostility.

Cholera struck Quebec City at the end of the first week in June 1832. Hospitals overflowed with victims, while hundreds more lay in tents on the Plains of Abraham. Many panic-stricken residents fled to rural areas, often carrying the disease with them. To prevent despair, church bells were no longer rung for the dead. Police had to be called to enforce the rapid burial of the deceased. By the end of October, 7500 residents of Quebec and Montreal—more than one-tenth of the population of each city—had died.

Rural Quebec

Nineteen out of twenty French Canadians in the early nineteenth century lived in rural areas, where they practised subsistence farming. Yet rural Quebec also underwent change. Thanks to the good harvests and high wheat prices of the 1790s and early 1800s, many habitants accumulated small surpluses of wheat that they sold to grain merchants for export abroad. For a short time, habitants saw their living conditions improve.

But yields varied enormously, and after 1815, crop failures became more frequent again. The productivity of even the best lands tended to drop after decades of cultivation without fertilization. New lands that had been opened up for colonization, especially those near the Canadian Shield, proved rocky and infertile. Crop diseases and insects posed a constant threat. Historians agree that the 1830s witnessed a rapid deterioration of economic conditions, with famine reported in 1837.

The Church

During this period, two groups vied to obtain influence and prestige among the habitants: the Roman Catholic church, implacably hostile to republican and liberal ideals; and a new professional elite composed of notaries, lawyers, and doctors. The professionals endorsed increasingly nationalistic ideas, particularly on political issues, and tended to be critical of the church; their forum became the colony's Assembly.

At the turn of the nineteenth century, the church's position in Lower Canada was far from assured. In spite of what clerical historians have written about the habitants' profound religiosity, Quebec was not a theocratic society, and the clergy were neither very influential nor dominant. Contemporary accounts detail the spread of religious indifference and even of anticlericalism, particularly among the bourgeoisie.

To increase its influence within French-Canadian society, the church needed more clergy. Indeed, at this time, it faced a veritable crisis: the number of priests declined from about 200 in 1760 to only 150 in 1790 and then increased to somewhat more than 300 by the time of the rebellion—but the population had grown from 70 000 to 500 000 in the same period. During his tenure as bishop of Quebec from 1806 to 1825, Monseigneur Joseph-Octave Plessis encouraged the establishment of classical colleges and succeeded in increasing the number of vocations.

The church's major triumph in these years was the achievement of independence from government dictates. Until the 1830s, the government interfered with the nomination of bishops, although with declining success. By 1840, ecclesiastical nominations became purely a church concern.

Church leaders were skilful diplomats who exploited every opportunity to assert the church's independence while at the same time giving the government full cooperation and assuring British authorities of their unbending loyalty. International events provided the church with new opportunities to demonstrate loyalty. The clergy had vigorously opposed the "anti-Christian" French Revolution that broke out with the storming of the Bastille prison in Paris on July 14, 1789. Horrified by the Reign of Terror that soon set in (which included Louis XVI among its victims), Canadian prelates issued strong condemnations. Then, while Napoleon's military campaigns provoked new suspicions of all things French, the War of 1812 gave the church a welcome opportunity to preach loyalty through pastoral letters and sermons. Led by the clergy, loyal French Canadians praised the exploits of Charles-Michel de Salaberry and his militia, who forced a numerically far superior American force to retreat at the battle of Châteauguay in 1813.

The rise of the church in the early years of the nineteenth century took place partly at the expense of the colonial government, and partly at the expense of the new professional elite. The professional class was the church's only serious rival in the struggle for support and influence among the French-speaking population. The Rebellion of 1837 brought this conflict to a head and decided its outcome in the church's favour. By 1840 French Canada's clerical elite was poised to enter a golden age that lasted for more than a century.

The Professional Elite

Many of the members of the new professional class were sons of small farmers. Politics became an outlet for this group's ambitions. Espousing liberal, democratic, and, ultimately, republican ideals, the group sought government reform through enlarging the powers of the lower house and curtailing those of the executive. These professionals were well aware of Lower Canada's colonial status and of French Canadians' lesser role in the economy and in government. They associated the interests of French Canada with those of their own class. Not surprisingly, they framed their declarations of battle in the name of the French-Canadian nation.

This new middle class aspired to replace the seigneurs and, to a degree, compete with the clergy as leaders of French Canada. Many of its members viewed the seigneurs as exploiting the habitants when they raised seigneurial *rentes*. The French-speaking seigneurs also appeared as collaborators who bowed to the British to gain lucrative appointments and pensions. Many notaries and lawyers also condemned the church for its support of Britain. Some were openly anticlerical, espousing the ideals of the French Revolution and American democracy. The professionals defended traditional agriculture and denounced the threat of commercial capitalism, but, as political radicals, they called for greater autonomy for the colony and some even favoured rebellion.

Understandably, the French-speaking professionals who formed the backbone of the Parti canadien had increasingly hostile relations with the British merchants. The merchants wanted to control Lower Canada's political institutions in order to introduce new laws to promote economic growth, commerce, and transportation. Some even demanded the abolition of the seigneurial system. Naturally, they accused the Assembly's French-speaking majority of systematically blocking necessary change. One solution they put forth was the union of the two Canadas, a measure intended to reduce the influence of the French.

Assembly versus Governor

The Rebellion of 1837 marked the failure of the Constitutional Act as a system of government for Lower Canada. Actually, the Act's weaknesses had been apparent for at least a generation. Since the turn of the century, the increasingly French and Parti canadien–dominated Assembly had sought to strengthen the elective part of government and to weaken the all-powerful executive, whose members were appointed in London and Quebec.

The causes of the Rebellion of 1837 in Lower Canada were more complex than in Upper Canada because of Lower Canada's ethnic division. In part, this struggle pitted the English against the French, since Lower Canada's tiny English-speaking minority dominated the Executive Council and the Assembly represented the province's French-speaking majority. Yet the deterioration of French–English relations in the colony and the increasingly violent rhetoric on both sides did not prevent a small group of English-speaking Quebeckers from supporting the Patriotes, such as brothers Wolfred and Robert Nelson. Both supporters of reform, they endorsed Patriote demands for an executive that would be responsible to the Assembly.

In an effort to strengthen its role in government, the Assembly sought greater control of the colony's finances. The question of provincial revenues had produced a deadlock in relations between the Assembly and the governor by the 1820s. Louis-Joseph Papineau led the attack. Foremost among the leaders of the Parti canadien (called the Parti patriote after 1826), Papineau entered the Assembly in 1809 and became its speaker in 1815. He had many contradictions. As a seigneur himself, Papineau defended the values of tradition, nation, and family. Yet his education and political career had acquainted him with liberal thought. As the political crisis deepened after 1830, Papineau's early esteem for British institutions evolved into admiration for republicanism and American-style democracy. Liberal in his religious views, he nevertheless viewed the Roman Catholic church as an important national institution, and he attended mass to set an example for his tenants.

On the financial issue the British parliament adopted what it hoped would be perceived as a compromise solution. It gave the Assembly control of all expenditures on the condition that it agree to pay the civil list each year—that is, to pay for the civil administration of the colony, including the salaries of civil servants. But the mood among the Patriotes remained uncompromising. In 1834 they drew up the Ninety-Two Resolutions, in part a denunciation of the composition of the appointed Legislative Council and of its tendency to block legislation adopted by the elected Assembly.

In March 1837 the English government issued the Ten Resolutions that announced an end to conciliation. In its series of resolutions the Colonial Office refused all of the Assembly's Ninety-Two Resolutions. They authorized the government of Lower Canada, if necessary, to pay its administrative costs from the tax revenues without the Assembly's approval. There would be no elective Legislative Council, thus preserving the English-speaking minority's political influence. The Executive Council, representing wealth and enterprise, would, as before, continue to be responsible to the governor alone, not to the Assembly.

The Lower Canadian Rebellions, 1837–1838

When they received news of Russell's resolutions, the Patriotes altered their tactics, since Britain apparently would not yield. Throughout the tense days of summer and autumn 1837, Patriote leaders prepared for armed resistance. They staged assemblies and collected funds. At a public assembly at St. Charles on the Richelieu River east of Montreal, attended by perhaps 4000 people, Patriote orators called for revolt. The meeting adopted resolutions that included a declaration of independence.

When the government issued warrants for their arrest, the principal Patriote leaders, Papineau included, fled to the countryside east of Montreal. After an initial skirmish at St. Denis on November 23, which the Patriotes won, the British troops momentarily withdrew, awaited their second column, and then advanced. The fierce combat that ensued on November 25 at neighbouring St. Charles, in which Patriote forces were led by Wolfred Nelson, proved catastrophic for the rebels. Between 50 and 150 Patriotes died, while the British lost only three men. Poorly armed civilians proved no match for well-trained British regulars led by professional officers. Prisoners were then rounded up and sent to jail in Montreal. Throughout the St. Denis and St. Charles area, British troops also torched 20 houses and barns, adding to the atmosphere of terror.

Having pacified the Richelieu valley, Sir John Colborne, the former governor of Upper Canada who had just become commander-in-chief of all British troops in the Canadas, turned his attention to the area north of Montreal. News of the Patriotes' defeat at St. Charles only hardened Dr. Jean-Olivier Chénier, the local resistance leader, in his determination to "die fighting rather than surrender."

A reconstruction by Henri Julien of the hanging of five Patriotes on January 18, 1839: Joseph-Jacques Robert, François-Xavier Hamelin, Pierre-Théophile Décoigne, and Ambroise and Charles Sanguinet. The British, during the rule of the Special Council, executed 12 Patriotes and sent 58 to the penal colonies in Australia for their part in the 1838 uprising.

Library and Archives Canada/C-20295.

When Colborne approached St. Eustache in December 1837, Chénier and a number of his followers took refuge in the church and other buildings. Some 70 Patriotes, including Chénier, died by gunfire or were burned to death. In total, 250 men died in battle in Lower Canada, in the Richelieu valley, and at St. Eustache, in late November and December 1837. The victory won, the British imprisoned the rebel leaders they could catch and initiated a policy of home-burning throughout the St. Eustache district.

By the time news of the insurrection reached London, just before Christmas, many of the rebel leaders had found asylum in the United States, where they attempted to muster support and regroup. Indeed, in February 1838, Robert Nelson led an incursion across the border. As provisional president of Lower Canada, he declared Canada's independence from Britain before fleeing back to safety on the American side. In November 1838 the British easily turned back Patriote raids from across the American border, ending the Rebellions.

Consequences of the Rebellions

To govern Lower Canada after it had suspended the colony's constitution, Britain set up a Special Council composed of members of the English-speaking minority and a few strongly loyalist French Canadians. During the rebellions, it suspended civil liberties and legal rights. Then it set up a police force in Montreal as well as a rural police force to pacify the habitants.

For the long term, London addressed the Canadian problem by forming a royal commission under Lord Durham to visit both Lower and Upper Canada. Durham's concerns for economic development made him sympathetic to the Lower Canadian British merchants' views. They emphasized the ethnic aspect of the conflict. In his report, submitted in 1839, Durham drew attention to the "deadly animosity" between French and English: "I found two nations warring in the bosom of a single state; I found a struggle, not of principles, but of races." A union of the two Canadas would yield a slight English majority, which immigration would further reinforce. Durham

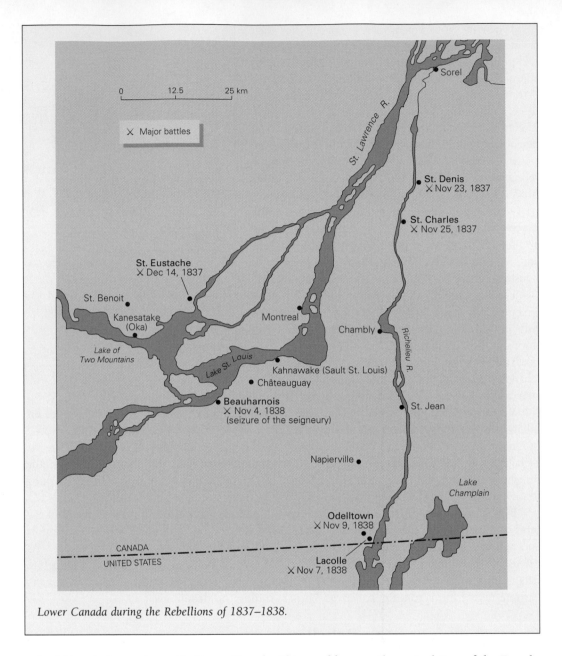

Lower Canada during the Rebellions of 1837–1838.

voiced his solution: union with Upper Canada. This would assure the assimilation of the French, ending forever the resurgence of ethnic conflict in Lower Canada.

From the Conquest to 1791 Quebec obtained three constitutions: the Royal Proclamation of 1763, the Quebec Act of 1774, and the Constitutional Act of 1791. The turmoil of the Rebellions of 1837–1838 led to a fourth: the Act of Union of 1840. The colony of Lower Canada lost its own government and was to be joined to Upper Canada in a union that the great majority of the French Canadians did not want. The avowed purpose of joining the two Canadas, as expressed by Lord Durham, British parliamentarians, and Lower Canadian merchants, was to break the power of French Canada and eventually to assimilate it. The advocates of the Union of the Canadas proved to be poor prophets.

BEYOND THE BOOK

The Treaty of Paris

http://www.yale.edu/lawweb/avalon/paris763.htm
A digitized copy of the Treaty of Paris, 1763.

The Quebec Act, 1774

http://www.canadiana.org/ECO/PageView/48786/0003?id=7f1ab5cd834af05f&size=2
A digitized copy of the Quebec Act of 1774.

Aboriginal Peoples and the English Government

http://www.champlain2004.org/html/12/11_e.html
Digitized letters documenting negotiated agreements between First Nations peoples
and the English during the Seven Years' War.

Changed Lives

http://www.champlain2004.org/html/12/13_e.html
The conflicts that led to the conquest of New France by the English resulted in much
upheaval to the lives of ordinary citizens, as documented by letters and records here.

Documents of the Rebellions of 1837 and 1838

http://www.canadiana.org/citm/specifique/rebellions_e.html
This site contains digitized primary source documents about the times before, during,
and after the 1837/38 rebellions. Included are Louis-Joseph Papineau and his
colleagues' Ninety-Two Resolutions, and the Rebellion Losses Bill of 1849.

Aftermath of the Rebellions

http://www.mccord-museum.qc.ca/en/keys/webtours/GE_P1_1_EN
A richly illustrated exhibit regarding life in the Canadas following the 1837/38
rebellions.

Rebellion and Reform

Canada: A People's History—Episode 7, Rebellion and Reform. Directed by Peter Ingles
(CBC, 2001).

Arundel

Kenneth Roberts, *Arundel* (New York: Doubleday, 1929; numerous printings ever
since). An historical novel that recounts the excitement of the American invasion across
northern Maine to take Quebec in 1775.

Drums along the Mohawk

Walter D. Edmonds, *Drums along the Mohawk* (Boston: Little, Brown and Company,
1936; numerous printings ever since). An interesting fictional account of the American
Revolution's impact on the Mohawk Valley's inhabitants in what is now New York State,
a struggle that resulted in the exile of both non-Aboriginal and Iroquois Loyalists
northward, at its conclusion.

RELATED READINGS

R. Douglas Francis and Donald B. Smith, eds., *Viewpoints: Readings in Canadian History* (Toronto: Thomson Nelson, 2007), contains the following articles relevant to this chapter: José Igartua, "A Change in the Climate: The Conquest and the *Marchands* of Montreal," pp. 105–18; and Allan Greer, "The Fall of New France," pp. 119–24.

BIBLIOGRAPHY

Although first published more than half a century ago, A.L. Burt, *The Old Province of Quebec* (Toronto: McClelland & Stewart, 1968 [1933]) remains the standard general work on the post-Conquest decades. Hilda Neatby incorporated new research into her book *Quebec: The Revolutionary Age, 1760–1791* (Toronto: McClelland & Stewart, 1966). An excellent study of the framing of British policy toward Quebec is Philip Lawson, *The Imperial Challenge: Quebec and Britain in the Age of the American Revolution* (Montreal/Kingston: McGill-Queen's University Press, 1989). For a study of the evolution of justice and the legal system, see Donald Fyson, *Magistrates, Police and People: Everyday Criminal Justice in Quebec and Lower Canada, 1764–1837* (Toronto: University of Toronto Press and the Osgoode Society for Canadian Legal History, 2006). James H. Lambert provides bibliographical references for the period from 1760 to 1867 in "Quebec/Lower Canada," in M. Brook Taylor, ed., *Canadian History: A Reader's Guide*, vol. 1, *Beginnings to Confederation* (Toronto: University of Toronto Press, 1994), pp. 112–83.

A brief synthesis of the rebellions is available in English in Jean-Paul Bernard, *The Rebellions of 1837 and 1838 in Lower Canada*, Historical Booklet 55 (Ottawa: Canadian Historical Association, 1996). Allan Greer challenges earlier analyses of the events of 1837 and their origins in *The Patriots and the People: The Rebellion of 1837 in Rural Lower Canada* (Toronto: University of Toronto Press, 1993). Joseph Schull, *Rebellion: The Rising in French Canada, 1837* (Toronto: Macmillan, 1971) is an older, popular treatment. Jacques Monet, *The Last Cannon Shot: A Study of French Canadian Nationalism, 1837–1850* (Toronto: University of Toronto Press, 1969) contains useful material on both the rebellion and its aftermath.

Fernand Ouellet reviews economic aspects of the period in *Economic and Social History of Quebec, 1760–1850* (Toronto: Macmillan, 1980); and *Lower Canada, 1791–1840: Social Change and Nationalism* (Toronto: McClelland & Stewart, 1979). Ronald Rudin provides a short review of Quebec's embryonic English-speaking community in *The Forgotten Quebecers: A History of English-Speaking Quebec, 1759–1980* (Quebec: Institut québécois de recherche sur la culture, 1985). For material pertaining to women in Lower Canada in the early nineteenth century, see Micheline Dumont et al., *Quebec Women: A History* (Toronto: Women's Press, 1987), pp. 31–59. The major individuals of these years all have biographies in various volumes of the *Dictionary of Canadian Biography*. It is now also available online: www.biographi.ca.

The following two books provide a good introduction to the Aboriginal history of the period: Gregory Evans Dowd, *A Spirited Resistance: The North American Indian Struggle for Unity, 1745–1815* (Baltimore: Johns Hopkins University Press, 1992); Richard White, *The Middle Ground: Indians, Empires and Republics in the Great Lakes Region, 1650–1815* (Cambridge: Cambridge University Press, 1991).

Useful maps of the St. Lawrence valley in the late eighteenth and early nineteenth centuries appear in the first two volumes of the *Historical Atlas of Canada*, vol. 1, R. Cole Harris, ed., *From the Beginning to 1800* (Toronto: University of Toronto Press, 1987); and vol. 2, R. Louis Gentilcore, ed., *The Land Transformed, 1800–1891* (Toronto: University of Toronto Press, 1993).

Chapter Six

UPPER CANADA, 1791–1840

TIME LINE

1791	The Constitutional Act of 1791 is followed by the division of the Province of Quebec into Upper Canada and Lower Canada
1792	John Graves Simcoe arrives as the first lieutenant governor of Upper Canada
1812–1814	The War of 1812
1813	Tecumseh, the great First Nations leader, dies at the battle of Moraviantown
1824	William Lyon Mackenzie begins his newspaper, *The Colonial Advocate*, at Queenston, Upper Canada
1829	Welland Canal opens for navigation between Lake Ontario and Lake Erie
1837–1838	William Lyon Mackenzie leads an unsuccessful rebellion against British rule Battle of the Windmill near Prescott, Upper Canada

In 1774, the Province of Quebec included the territory north of the Great Lakes and immediately south of the Canadian Shield. The only European settlement of any size was located on the outskirts of present-day Windsor, where French-Canadian farmers who supplied Fort Detroit, just across the river, had settled farms. The remainder of the whole western portion of the Province of Quebec remained one continuous forest.

The American Revolution led to the creation of Britain's first inland colony in 1791. John Graves Simcoe, commander of the Queen's Rangers (a Loyalist corps) in the revolution became the first lieutenant governor of Upper Canada. He spent four years constructing the framework for a colony intended to be the ideal home for Loyalists. In the end, Americans in search of cheap land, not Loyalists, formed the majority of the settlers, outnumbering the Loyalists four to one at the beginning of the War of 1812. Yet, thanks to a strong British and First Nation military resistance the northern colony avoided American conquest.

From 1815 to 1840 Upper Canada's population quadrupled, from less than 100 000 to more than 400 000. Immigration accounted for much of this increase. Some of the new immigrants came from the United States, but most arrived from the British Isles: northern Irish Protestants, southern Irish Roman Catholics; Lowland and Highland Scots; Welsh and English. The newcomers settled the land; established and refined political, social, and educational institutions; contributed to the colony's economic growth; and participated in its political movements. The British immigrants, with the exception of some Catholic Irish, worked to develop a sense of loyalty to Britain. These newcomers brought British customs and attitudes that eventually mixed, in the years to follow, with those of the settlers already there to create a unique Upper Canadian character.

The Anishinabeg and Loyalist Settlement

The Proclamation of 1763 had recognized the Great Lakes area as First Nations country; hence, the Aboriginal peoples had to surrender that land to the Crown before Loyalist settlement could proceed. Until the early 1780s, three nations lived in what is now southern Ontario: the Ojibwas (Chippewas), the Ottawas (Odawas), and the Algonquins—the three Algonquian nations who called themselves the "Anishinabeg," meaning true human beings.

Sir Frederick Haldimand, the governor of Quebec from 1778 to 1784, arranged for the purchase of the land from the Mississaugas, as the British called the Ojibwa along the north shore of Lake Ontario. Why did the Mississaugas make agreements with the British? First, they did so because they relied on the traders' European goods and on the gifts that the English had given them annually since the suppression of Pontiac's resistance. Second, it appears that they did not believe they were selling the land once and for all. The Aboriginal pattern of land ownership and use differed from that of the British. Among the Great Lakes Algonquians, an individual family could use a recognized hunting ground, fishing place, or maple sugar bush, but as soon as the family ceased to go there, it reverted to the collective ownership of the entire band. Most likely, the Anishinabeg regarded the initial transactions as ones with tenants for the use of the land as long as they practised good behaviour. Third, the Mississaugas had a small population of about 1000, divided into a dozen or more separate bands along the 500 km of lakefront. They could have resisted their British and Iroquois allies only with great difficulty. Thus, weakly organized, reliant on European trade goods, and believing that they would receive presents in perpetuity for the use of their land, the Mississaugas agreed to the proposals.

A HISTORICAL PORTRAIT

David Ramsay

In the 1790s David Ramsay, fur trader, revolutionary war soldier, guide—and Indian-killer—was one of the best-known individuals in Upper Canada. The colonial administrators and the Loyalist settlers respected him. In contrast, Joseph Brant, the Mohawk leader, regarded him as an "unworthy rascal." A number of the Mississaugas tolerated him—although he once killed and scalped eight Anishinabeg, including a woman and two children—because he provided a link with the dominant settler society. That the Mississaugas had to rely on this dangerous, unstable man, simply because he knew their language, shows their isolation from the British officials, and from the incoming settlers.

What little is known about Ramsay's early life comes from a land petition that he submitted to Governor Simcoe and from notes made by a British traveller, Captain Patrick Campbell, whom Ramsay guided in 1792 from Niagara to New York. Taking great interest in his fellow Scot's adventures, Captain Campbell stayed up with him one whole night to record his story, which he accepted completely because, as he wrote in his *Travels in North America*, "His honesty and fidelity is so well known, that he is entrusted with sums of money to any amount without requiring any token or receipt for the same." Ramsay claimed that he came from the town of Leven, Fifeshire, Scotland. As a young man he joined the crew of the British warship Prince of Orange, serving in the sieges of Louisbourg in 1758 and Quebec in 1759. After the Seven Years' War, he entered the Great Lakes fur trade, operating out of Schenectady, New York.

The details of Ramsay's life confirm that he might have been a psychopath. He spent the winter of 1771–1772 on the north shore of Lake Erie with his 17-year-old brother, who had just arrived from Scotland. Ramsay alleged that he had been forced, in self-defence, to kill several Aboriginal people who, in a drunken state, attacked them. Sir William Johnson, the Indian Superintendent for the northern colonies, had a different account. Johnson argued that Ramsay deserved "Capital punishment." He dismissed Ramsay's argument of self-defence because "the Indians, whenever they meditate mischief, carefully avoid Liquor." But Johnson also realized that a jury would acquit him. As he wrote to an Indian Department assistant: "I don't think he will Suffer, had he killed a Hundred." Johnson was correct. In September 1773, a Montreal jury released Ramsay for "want of Evidence." Ramsay's brother, the only eyewitness of the killings present at the trial, supported his brother's story of self-defence. No Mississaugas were present.

After his military service with the Royal Navy on the Atlantic coast during the American Revolution, Ramsay went back to live among the First Nations people whose relatives he had killed a decade earlier. He learned to dress like them, to live like them, and to speak their language. Why he did so remains a mystery, especially as his dislike of them in no way appears to have diminished. He told Campbell, for example, in describing the killings of 1771–1772: "After killing the first Indians, I cut lead, and chewed above thirty balls, and above three pound of Goose shot, for I thought it a pity to shoot an Indian with a smooth ball." Although in the late 1780s and early 1790s he received death threats from some Mississaugas, he remained among them.

Why did the Mississaugas tolerate him? First, they did so probably because Ramsay followed their custom. He "covered the graves" of the murdered, paying a certain number of gifts to the relatives of those that he had killed. Secondly, and more important, a number of Mississaugas saw him as a valuable ally, perhaps their only ally. This "eccentric white man," as the Mississauga Methodist minister Peter Jones later described him, forwarded their grievances to the government. In a petition sent in their name to Governor

Simcoe in the winter of 1793, for instance, Ramsay outlined the settlers' encroachments on their hunting territories and fishing grounds.

David Ramsay claimed that the Mississaugas in 1789 gave him a large tract of land at the mouth of the Twelve Mile (Bronte) Creek, between present-day Hamilton and Toronto, as a gift. He stated that he and his heirs would allow the Mississaugas to use the land, to hunt and fish, and to plant orchards there, "forever as they now are or until they are half white. (But no black mixture allowed to inherit the above land)." The government never recognized the gift, but it did give Ramsay two substantial land grants elsewhere in Upper Canada, that were together roughly 500 ha in size. Ramsay died in New York City in 1810.

Loyalist Settlements

In 1785, approximately 7500 Loyalists (5500 non-Aboriginal and 2000 Iroquois Loyalists) lived in what is now present-day southern Ontario. By 1791, the number had risen to perhaps 30 000. New settlements had been established throughout the area that extended north from the St. Lawrence up the Ottawa River to the Rideau River. They were spread over 15 km around the Bay of Quinte and formed a narrow strip along the Lake Ontario shore from the Bay of Quinte to York (now Toronto), where farms extended 25 km up Yonge Street. Settlers, mostly from rural New York and Pennsylvania, now occupied the narrow strip of good land below the escarpment around the Niagara peninsula and part way up the Lake Erie shoreline. From the concessions along the front of the Detroit River, settlement began to move along the south shore of Lake St. Clair, and into the lower Thames River valley.

The early Upper Canadian Loyalists came from many ethnic backgrounds, but most belonged to the same economic and social class—a humble one. Not until the wave of immigration from New Brunswick in the 1790s did Upper Canada receive what might be termed a Loyalist elite, composed of families such as the Robinsons, the Jarvises, and the Ryersons.

The Constitutional Act of 1791

The Constitutional Act of 1791 brought the colony of Upper Canada into existence. It provided for freehold tenure and free land. (Settlers paid only the fees for issuing and recording land titles.) The legislation also set aside the equivalent of one-seventh of all lands granted in the future for "the Support and Maintenance of a Protestant Clergy." Unfortunately, the act failed to make explicit just what constituted the "Protestant Clergy"—the Church of England only, as it was the established, or state-recognized, national church in England—or the Church of

On a Bush Farm near Chatham, Upper Canada, 1838, *by Philip John Bainbrigge. Side by side, pioneer men and women shared in clearing the land, constructing log houses, and planting, tending, and harvesting the crops.*

Library and Archives Canada/C-011811.

Scotland and other Protestant denominations as well? This caused confusion and controversy. Initially, for instance, the provincial government interpreted the phrase to refer only to the Church of England. In addition, the British government set aside another seventh of all lands as Crown reserves; the revenues from the sale or rental of these lands were to be used to fund the colonial government.

A "Truly British" Colony

John Graves Simcoe, an energetic and enthusiastic military officer in the revolutionary war, then in his late thirties, became Upper Canada's first lieutenant governor. He wanted to make Upper Canada a centre of British power in North America. To him, "democracy" and "republicanism" were wicked words. Believing that many in the new republic to the south remained actively loyal to England, he attempted to win Americans back to their old allegiance. He was convinced that a new colony with "a free, honourable British Government" would remind Americans of what they had lost in leaving the empire and of the benefits of returning to it.

The governor wanted to create a hierarchical society like that which existed in England. He firmly believed in the established Church of England. In his model British colony, the Anglican Church alone would enjoy the right of performing marriages. Reluctantly Simcoe agreed that justices of the peace in remote areas might conduct marriage ceremonies, provided they followed the Anglican ritual. Only in 1798 was the right to solemnize marriages extended to Lutheran, Calvinist, and Church of Scotland ministers. Methodists remained excluded until 1831. The Upper Canadian administration regarded the Methodists, particularly the Methodists from the United States, with great suspicion, because they remained affiliated with the American parent church until 1828. The American Methodists had formed an independent Methodist church in the United States immediately after the American Revolution, separating themselves from their British co-religionists.

Simcoe put the new colony on a firm military footing. The British government allowed him to raise an infantry corps of 425 officers and men, the Queen's Rangers (the name of his old Loyalist regiment in the revolution), to protect Upper Canada. The first governor contributed to the establishment of a road system in the colony. In 1793 he ordered the construction of a military road from Burlington Bay to the Thames River, which he named Dundas Street after Henry Dundas, then the secretary of state in the English cabinet. Simcoe believed that a second military road should be built from York to Lake Simcoe, to ensure rapid communication with the upper lakes. It was begun in 1796. The governor called this road Yonge Street after Sir George Yonge, the British secretary of war.

Initially Simcoe established his headquarters at Newark (now Niagara-on-the-Lake), only later changing it to York (Toronto). Then he called for elections to the Legislative Assembly. The legislature created a judicial system. William Osgoode, a well-regarded English lawyer, became chief justice, with responsibility for the Court of King's Bench, the new superior court of civil and criminal jurisdiction. Within each district Simcoe created surrogate courts and a provincial court of probate. At a lower level, meetings for the courts of quarter sessions were organized. The justices of the peace presided over these and performed as well a wide range of administrative and judicial duties. At the township level the justices of the peace enjoyed considerable power. Township officials in Upper Canada were appointed, not elected as they were in New England.

The Slavery Question

While the majority of African-American Loyalists and slaves went to Nova Scotia after the revolution, some slaves, perhaps as many as 500, were brought to Upper Canada. Slavery, however, did not prosper in a northern area such as Upper Canada. Crops such as cotton, which required a cheap, plentiful labour force, were ruled out by the short Canadian growing season. Furthermore, owners had to feed, clothe, and house slaves throughout a long and unproductive winter. Finally, many Upper Canadians, including Simcoe, found slavery abhorrent.

Under the governor's direction, the Assembly adopted a bill in 1793 that abolished slavery but freed not one single slave. It stated that slaves already in Upper Canada had to remain slaves until death, but all children born after the act's passage would become free at the age of 25. Furthermore, no additional slaves could be brought to Upper Canada. After 1793, slavery steadily declined in the colony.

Simcoe left Upper Canada in mid-1796. While serving as governor, he experienced many disappointments. While he may have considered the colony as something approaching the centre of the universe, the British government did not. It turned down his expensive schemes to build up Upper Canada economically and militarily. His proposal to create a provincial university also received little support, as did his attempt to establish the Church of England in the colony under a bishop's tutelage. In addition, he failed in his attempt to promote a hierarchical society in Upper Canada, based on large land grants. Nevertheless, he did succeed in putting the colony on a firm military footing, in establishing a legal framework for Upper Canada, and in organizing its early transportation system. The provincial holiday held on the first Monday in August is known as Simcoe Day in Toronto, in his honour.

Loyalist Women in Early Upper Canada

During the American Revolution, female Loyalists displayed exceptional courage. They took charge of their families and farms during their husbands' absences. Many had been harassed or persecuted. The insurgents had stolen their property and seized their homes, and in some cases jailed them. They had travelled, in many cases, with very young children through difficult wilderness to British refugee camps. Even here their struggles did not end. As historian Janice Potter writes, once behind British lines, "They had to fit once again into a patriarchal power structure in which their inferiority and dependence were assumed."[1] Men remained the decision-makers, the women and children being expected to follow their directions. A married woman had no legal identity separate from that of her husband. Some Loyalist women did submit claims for compensation to Britain after the war. Without fail, however, the all-male adjudicators of Loyalist claims awarded much more, proportionally, to men than to women.

The First Nations: A Displaced People

By 1796, the Aboriginal peoples understood that the treaties meant the denial of a right of way across cleared fields, and if they camped on the settlers' lands, the farmers shot their dogs. The elders told the young people, such as Kahkewaquonaby (Sacred Feathers, known in English as Peter Jones), that when the British first came, they "asked for a small piece of land on which they might pitch their tents; the request was cheerfully granted. By and by they begged for more, and

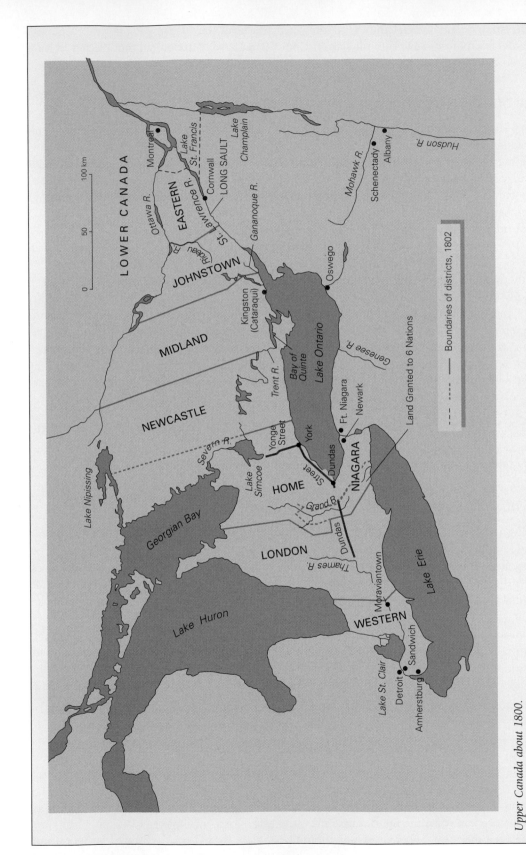

Upper Canada about 1800.

Source: Gerald M. Craig, *Upper Canada: The Formative Years 1784–1841* (Toronto: McClelland & Stewart, 1963), p. 45.

more was given them. In this way they have continued to ask, or have obtained by force or fraud, the fairest portions of our territory." Between 1805 and 1818, the Crown successfully pressured the Mississaugas to sell their last remaining tract, between Toronto and the head of the lake (present-day Hamilton). In two separate agreements, the British acquired the desired land.

Other tragedies followed for the First Nations. Between the 1790s and the 1820s, smallpox, tuberculosis, and measles killed almost two-thirds of the Mississaugas at the western end of the lake. The band's population in that area dropped to 200 in the 1820s, down from more than 500 a generation earlier. The Iroquois also experienced difficult times in the 1790s and 1800s, as land sales took away much of their territory on the Grand River. Chief Joseph Brant endorsed these sales, for he welcomed non-Aboriginal settlers to the Grand River to teach the Iroquois European agricultural techniques. Not all his followers agreed. Many objected to the presence of the outsiders who, by 1798, controlled two-thirds of the Six Nations' original grant on the Grand River.

The Growth of Settlement

Upper Canada's non-Aboriginal population continued to grow in the 1790s and in the decade following, not at the phenomenal rate of the 1820s and 1830s, but still substantially. Many were "late Loyalists," or individuals of non-Loyalist backgrounds who came in search of cheap land. Among the immigrants to Upper Canada were members of religious sects commonly called the "Plain Folk," because they believed in a pure religion and plain dress. They included Quakers, Mennonites, and Dunkards (a small group of Baptists who practised adult baptism by "dunking" the individual in water). By 1812, settlers lived on all the vacant townships along the north shore of Lake

Ontario and on several townships on Lake Erie as well. Although few roads existed, the waterways allowed for the dispersal of settlement along an 800 km front in a period of less than 20 years.

On the eve of the War of 1812, the population of Upper Canada reached 75 000. Scattered along the St. Lawrence River and Lakes Ontario, Erie, and St. Clair, the settled areas rarely extended more than a few kilometres into the interior. The work of establishing farms and clearing new land took much of the settlers' time. The newcomers from the United States outnumbered the Loyalists and the British immigrants four to one. Like the Acadians of Nova Scotia a century earlier, these Americans lived in a British colony without really belonging to it. The War of 1812 led to enormous pressures on them to choose sides.

The War of 1812

Many Great Lakes First Nations already knew the side they would support in any future Anglo-American conflict. In the first decade of the nineteenth century, Tecumseh, a Shawnee chief, and his brother, a religious leader, assembled a formidable Aboriginal confederacy. In 1811, Tecumseh was at open war with the Americans. Many Ohioans, Tennesseeans, and

Old Fort Erie with the Migrations of the Wild-Pigeon in Spring, April 12, 1804, by Edward Walsh (1766–1832). In her diary entry for November 1, 1793, Elizabeth Simcoe commented that passenger pigeons were so numerous in Upper Canada in the spring and autumn that, at times, they darkened the entire sky. The pioneers put a stop to that. On both sides of the border, settlers trapped, clubbed, and shot the pigeons by the millions. The last recorded sighting of passenger pigeons in Ontario was in 1902. The last known passenger pigeon in North America died in 1914 in a zoo in Cincinnati, Ohio.

952.218: *Old Fort Erie with the Migration of Wild Pigeons*; Walsh, Edward; ROM2006_7733_1. With permission of the Royal Ontario Museum © ROM.

Kentuckians suspected—incorrectly—that the British continued to encourage and finance the First Nations raids. Many aggressive and intensely patriotic Americans judged it time to attack the British in the Canadas. At the same time, American "war hawks," anxious to begin a war with Britain, argued that the United States could use the opportunity to seize Upper Canada.

Two direct provocations by Britain led many Americans, including President James Madison, to support the pro-war group. In 1812, Napoleon's Continental System, which forbade trade with Great Britain on the part of France, her allies, and neutrals, closed all of western Europe, except Portugal, to British goods. Britain retaliated by imposing a naval blockade on France, preventing all ships, including American vessels, from trading with France. Officially neutral in the struggle, the Americans called for freedom of the seas. What right had England to board American ships on the high seas and prevent them from trading with countries on the continent? Madison considered this act the first provocation.

Without regard for neutral rights, British cruisers stopped and searched American ships on the North Atlantic. The British looked for British deserters who had gone over to American vessels to obtain higher wages, better food, and better working conditions. The Royal Navy seized thousands of sailors, alleging that they were British deserters. If a man produced his easily obtained certificate of American naturalization, the English ignored it, as their government did not recognize the right of a British subject to transfer allegiance to another country. "Free Trade and Sailors' Rights" became the cry of many Americans.

Forced, as he put it, to choose between war and degradation, Madison sent a message of war to Congress on June 1, 1812. Congress agreed and declared war against Britain.

Throughout the first year of the war, the Americans believed that Upper Canada's American population would welcome them as liberators. Had not the majority of Upper Canada's population only recently arrived from the United States? Thomas Jefferson assured Americans that the conquest of Upper Canada would be a "mere matter of marching." This proved not to be the case at all.

Major General Isaac Brock, who had fought in the French wars in Europe and had then been stationed in North America, deserves much of the credit for Upper Canada's success in 1812. Before the war, Brock had built up the province's fortifications, trained the provincial militia, and maintained good relations with the First Nations. As soon as war broke out, he took the offensive.

The Aboriginals' military contribution helps to explain Brock's success. For the Great Lakes First Nations, war did not break out in 1812; they had fought American frontiersmen for generations. Welcoming the outbreak of the second Anglo–American War in 1812, Tecumseh and hundreds of warriors joined the British in Upper Canada. At the outset, they assisted a small British force to take Michilimackinac, the leading fur-trading post in the Upper Great Lakes. Then they helped to cut the Americans' communication lines to Detroit, effectively winning that fort for the British. The fall of Detroit led to the embarrassing loss of all American territory west of Lake Erie.

Brock's unexpected victory at Detroit in August restored confidence among the loyal population that Upper Canada could be defended. He proved it again in October at Queenston Heights, but this time at the cost of his life: he was hit as he led a charge up the face of the heights. The attack, however, succeeded after 500 Iroquois joined 1000 British regulars and 600 Upper Canadian militia to retake the strategic heights. The British victors captured 900 American prisoners. Having lost one army at Detroit, the Americans lost another on the Niagara frontier.

The Campaigns of 1813 and 1814

The Upper Canadians' worst moment in the war came in the spring and summer of 1813, when the gains of 1812 were reversed. The Americans twice briefly occupied York and launched a second invasion of the Niagara peninsula, forcing the British to withdraw to Burlington Heights

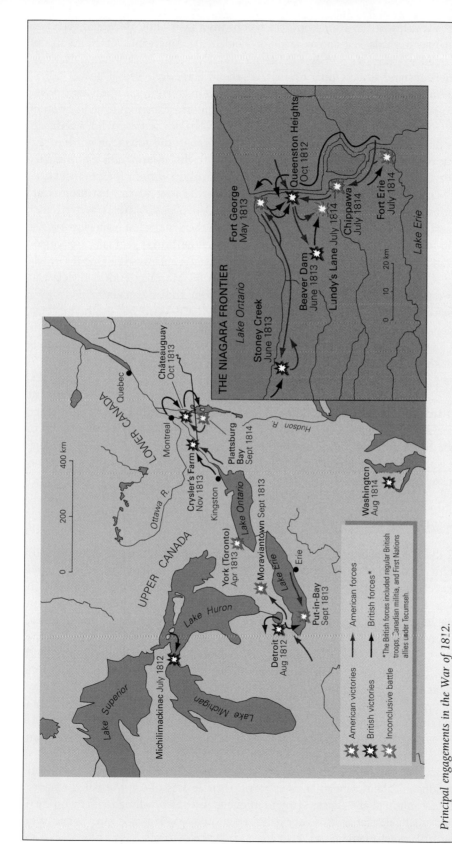

Principal engagements in the War of 1812.

Source: Based on *The Integrated Atlas: History and Geography of Canada and the World* (Toronto: Harcourt Brace, 1996), p. 114.

at the head of the lake (present-day Hamilton). Desertions from the militia grew, and even two members of the Upper Canada Legislative Assembly joined the Americans. Only a surprise attack by British regular troops at Stoney Creek, immediately south of Burlington Heights, dislodged the Americans and saved Upper Canada. A second battle followed at Beaver Dams, where Iroquois from the Montreal area and from the Six Nations territory at the Grand River ambushed the Americans. The attackers benefited from vital information about the location of the American troops received from Laura Secord, a 37-year-old settler, who overheard American officers discussing their invasion plans. Slipping through the American cordon, she took a roundabout route to the British–First Nations camp with this information. Shortly after the Iroquois victory at Beaver Dams, the American invaders withdrew from the peninsula.

While their Niagara campaign in 1813 ended in failure, the Americans, that same year, proved successful in the Detroit sector of the conflict. The Americans' fortunes revived after their naval forces obtained control of Lake Erie. The British then withdrew from Detroit. At Moraviantown, on the Thames River, the Americans defeated the British regulars, the Upper Canadian militia, and the First Nations. The Americans held on to southwestern Upper Canada until the end of the war. That fall, their two-pronged attack on Montreal ended in defeat at Crysler's Farm in eastern Upper Canada, and at Châteauguay in Lower Canada.

Tecumseh was killed at Moraviantown on October 5, 1813. With his death, his First Nation confederacy collapsed. The link between the British and the Aboriginal peoples of the American Midwest was broken. Never again in the lower Great Lakes area did the First Nations constitute a serious military threat.

After Moraviantown, the battle lines consolidated for the remainder of the war. On July 25, 1814, the British defeated the Americans' last great attempt to capture Upper Canada, at Lundy's Lane in the Niagara peninsula. Lundy's Lane was the site of the bloodiest battle of the War of 1812. The six-hour battle lasted until darkness, and each side lost over 800 men. Although each side claimed victory, at the end of the battle the Americans had failed to dislodge the British. They withdrew, ending their final offensive in Upper Canada. The peace treaty was signed on December 24, 1814.

Upper Canada Immediately after the War of 1812

The War of 1812 did not change the boundaries of Upper Canada. The peace treaty essentially confirmed the status quo. But, in one respect, the war had a very profound effect on Upper Canada: the unsuccessful and destructive attacks of 1812–1814 engendered anti-American sentiments among a number of non-Loyalist settlers. Ironically, the American invasion contributed to the work that Simcoe had begun—the promotion of a loyalty to Upper Canada.

After 1815, growing numbers of British settlers arrived in the colony. The end of the Napoleonic Wars best explains the migration. Peace brought economic depression and unemployment to Great Britain. It curtailed the army's demand for manpower, and, at the same time, made overseas travel less dangerous. Postwar Britain encouraged emigration. From the government's perspective, it reduced the population pressure in Britain, provided relief from social unrest, and facilitated expansion and control of its empire. The British government in the late 1810s and early 1820s assisted the exodus with generous aid, similar to that first given the Loyalists.

In the mid-1820s, however, the British government stopped aiding emigrants, as private charitable associations and landowners, anxious to rid their estates of impoverished tenants, now provided at least minimal assistance. Many immigrants were also willing to come on their own, without government assistance, to escape a desperate situation. This was especially true of the victims of the Irish potato famine in the 1830s and 1840s.

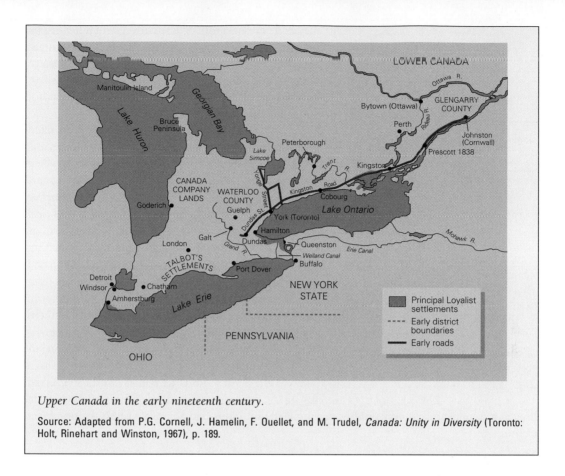

Upper Canada in the early nineteenth century.

Source: Adapted from P.G. Cornell, J. Hamelin, F. Ouellet, and M. Trudel, *Canada: Unity in Diversity* (Toronto: Holt, Rinehart and Winston, 1967), p. 189.

Upper Canadian landowners, such as Colonel Thomas Talbot, also assisted immigrants in the hope of profiting from government incentives for settlement and land development. Talbot eventually accumulated an estate of nearly 30 000 ha, making him one of the largest landholders in Upper Canada. In return, he contributed to the transformation of more than 200 000 ha of forest into 3000 farm lots in southwestern Upper Canada. His extensive road system made his lands more accessible and hence more valuable.

In 1826, the British government itself created the Canada Company, the first large-scale Canadian land company. The Canada Company purchased over 400 000 hectares of land, consisting of Crown reserves and the huge Huron Tract (the latter in southwestern Upper Canada on the shores of Lake Huron). The Company founded the towns of Goderich, in the Huron Tract, and the town of Guelph in another of its parcels of land east of the Tract.

The Aboriginal Peoples

The land for the immigrants came from the First Nations peoples, who, by 1815, were already outnumbered ten to one by non-Aboriginals. After the War of 1812, the First Nations in Upper Canada made seven major land surrenders, opening up much of present-day southern Ontario for settlement. In 1818, the government of Upper Canada changed the method of purchasing the land, offering to make annual payments or annuities in perpetuity, an arrangement that was preferable for the government to a simple one-time payment. Although by this time the First Nations realized that these land-sale agreements were final and irreversible, they lacked the strength in numbers to resist the proposed cessions. In addition, settled areas now divided the

The Mississauga village on the Credit River during the winter of 1826–1827. The houses, just built, were dressed log cottages with two rooms, of the type erected as a second house by settlers who had been on their farms for 5 to 10 years. Two families occupied each home, and each family had its own room. Originally, 20 of these two-family houses were built.

Egerton Ryerson, *The Story of My Life*, ed. J. George Hodgins (Toronto: William Briggs, 1883), p. 59.

bands from one another, a situation which deterred a united response. Finally, groups like the Mississaugas were influenced by the government's oral promise to help them adjust to farming—a promise not fulfilled, in the case of the Mississaugas at the western end of Lake Ontario, until the mid-1820s.

First Nations migrated north from the United States to settle in Upper Canada. They came to escape the American government's removal policy, which dictated that First Nations east of the Mississippi must move west of the river. Several thousand Anishinabeg took up residence in Upper Canada in the 1830s and 1840s. Most of the Oneida, one of the Iroquois nations remaining in New York State after the American Revolution, also migrated around 1840 and purchased land on the Thames River west of London. Apart from Governor Francis Bond Head's unsuccessful attempt in 1836–1837 to relocate the Anishinabeg of southern Ontario (the Ojibwas, Odawas [Ottawas], and Potawatomis) to Manitoulin Island—a proposal they vigorously opposed—the government of Upper Canada allowed the First Nations to remain on their reserved lands, or reserves. Here they were encouraged to farm in the hopes that they would be acculturated and ultimately assimilated into the dominant society.

Colonial Oligarchy: The Family Compact

During the years 1815–1840, a small, tightly knit elite popularly known as the "Family Compact" ruled Upper Canada. Through political patronage they appointed likeminded people to the local centres, thus creating or recognizing already-existing, smaller oligarchies throughout the province.

At the centre of the Family Compact stood John Strachan, cleric and educator, as a leading adviser to the governors of Upper Canada. Around Strachan gathered a group of whom many were his former pupils. Members of this "old boys' network" had strikingly similar backgrounds and views. About half of the Family Compact consisted of descendants of the original Loyalist families. The other half included British immigrants who, like Strachan, had come in the early years of the colony.

Their role in the defence of the province during the War of 1812 heightened their British patriotism. They believed, first, that Upper Canada's strength came from its imperial connection. Secondly, they wanted power to remain in the hands of the governor and his appointed advisers. Thirdly, they wanted the established Church of England to give a "moral underpinning to society." Finally, this elite believed in the economic progress of the province—to be directed by themselves—through commerce, canal building, settlement schemes, and banks.

Religious Disputes

The first challenge to the Anglicans' ecclesiastical monopoly came from the Presbyterians. As the established Church of Scotland, this major Protestant denomination demanded a share of the clergy reserves, which consisted of one-seventh of the land in each township for the support of a "Protestant clergy." In 1829, the Colonial Office authorized their inclusion. The Executive Council denied the Methodists the same right. Since Methodism had come into Upper Canada from the United States, Family Compact members suspected it of having radical republican sympathies. Thus, the Methodists had to fight for a portion of the clergy reserves.

The Methodists counterattacked through Egerton Ryerson, a 23-year-old preacher of Loyalist background, who wrote a thundering reply in 1826. Raised in a prominent Anglican family but converted to Methodism, Ryerson upheld the educated quality of the itinerant preachers, denied that Methodists held republican views, and challenged the legality of Strachan's position that the Church of England was the established church in the province. So began the public career of Egerton Ryerson. For a half-century he would maintain a position of prominence in education and politics in Upper Canada.

Other Protestant denominations and religious sects appeared in the province. Baptists, Quakers, Dunkards, Millerites, Campbellites, Christian Universalists, Mormons, and German-speaking Amish created greater religious pluralism. With the arrival of substantial numbers of Irish Catholics, the Roman Catholic Church also strengthened its position.

COMMUNITY PORTRAIT

The Children of Peace, Sharon, Upper Canada

In 1801, David Willson left Pennsylvania with a group of fellow members of the Society of Friends, or Quakers, to establish a new community in Upper Canada based essentially on Quaker values and beliefs. His vision for the new community came to him in the form of a dream. He dreamt of a poor man who could not find lodging in the city where he wanted to locate, and so moved on to the lake in front of the city, where he built a magnificent church in the shape of a house. The church, which was flooded with the light of God, served as a refuge for the poor and outcasts of society. He envisioned the community that formed around the church as "the New Jerusalem" in the wilderness of Upper Canada, comparable to the Israelites in the Promised Land.

Willson and a small band of followers broke away from the Quakers in 1812 to form an independent community known as the Children of Peace, or sometimes referred to as "Davidites" after their

founding father. They settled in East Gwillimbury, Upper Canada, north of York (Toronto), around the village initially known as Hope and then, in 1841, changed to the biblical name "Sharon." Here they established independently owned farms (unlike the Quakers, who held property in common), but farms that could only be handed down to family members or sold to fellow community members. As well, members of the sect practiced a form of "moral economy" that differed from the capitalist economy in that it was based on a spirit of cooperation and mutual assistance, and guided by the golden rule: "Do unto others as you would have them do unto you."

The community was united through a close-knit ancestry, common religious beliefs, and their communal lifestyle. It was, in the words of one analyst of the community, "less a physical community than a community of spirit." The Temple of Peace, a beautiful three-story, foursquare building, inspired by the biblical Solomon's temple and in the shape of a house as in Willson's dream, became the focal point of the community. There were four entrances to the Temple, one door in the middle of each side so as to allow people to enter, as Willson noted, "from the east and the west, the north and the south on equal and the same footing." Men, women, and children were to enter as equals. In the centre of the Temple was the Altar in the shape of Noah's Ark. It was held up by four pillars inscribed with the words Faith, Hope, Love, and Charity, symbolizing the four cardinal virtues that guided the community. A magnificent organ—one of the first in Upper Canada—graced the sanctuary; unlike the Quakers, the Children of Peace saw music as an important expression of their faith. Besides a place of worship, the Temple served as a meeting place where monthly all members of the community met to discuss common concerns, to work out mutual agreements, and to collect alms for the poor.

It was their commitment to help the poor, which extended beyond their own community to the larger community of Upper Canada and even the world at large, that linked the Children of Peace to the wider world and insured that their community would not become isolated and inward-turning. The Children of Peace established the first shelter for the homeless in the province, and the first credit union, known as the Charity Fund, from which anyone in need could borrow money. As well, they created the first producer cooperative in Canada, known as the "Farmer's Storehouse Company." Situated in downtown Toronto next to the market square, it offered an alternative marketing centre to Toronto's competitive and individualistic merchant approach.

Some of the Children of Peace members got involved in political reform, hoping this would lead to social reform. They supported William Lyon Mackenzie's rebellion in 1837. Two members died in battle. After the failed rebellion, some members of the community organized "Durham meetings," organized to support reform based on Lord Durham's *Report*. Unfortunately, involvement by some members in the rebellion split the community, and it never regained its original cohesion. Still, the community continued to operate until 1889, when it disbanded.

The community of the Children of Peace was one of the few success stories of alternative community life to that of the mainstream in nineteenth-century Upper Canada. Its significance lies not in the fact that it failed, but that it lasted for over three-quarters of a century as a successful community known for its charity, cooperative spirit, communal values, and Christian beliefs.

Temple of the Children of Peace, photo taken around 1860.

Aurora Museum, acc., no. X81.36.18.

FURTHER READING

Mark Fram and Albert Schrauwers, *4Square: An Introduction to the Sharon Temple National Historic Site* (Toronto: Coach House Books, 2005).

W. John McIntyre, *Children of Peace* (Montreal/ Kingston: McGill-Queen's University Press, 1994).

Albert Schrauwers, *The Children of Peace and the Village of Hope, 1812–1889* (Toronto: University of Toronto Press, 1993).

Women in Upper Canada

Women played an integral role in British North American society in the early-to-mid-nineteenth century, although their importance was seldom acknowledged publicly. Their responsibilities consisted mainly of childbearing, childrearing, and social assistance to others, as well as "domestic employment," which included such tasks in the home as cooking, cleaning, sewing, knitting, spinning, and weaving, in addition to outdoor work, such as taking care of the poultry and the barnyard, the vegetable garden, and fruit-growing—freeing the men and boys to work in the fields. When her husband was away, a farm wife often assumed complete responsibility for outdoor work. Beyond the immediate family obligations, some women took in sewing or laundry, or boarders, or were seamstresses, keepers of inns or taverns in their homes, or schoolteachers within their homes.

Women were regulated and restricted by rules, traditions, customs, and laws made by male social elites, church leaders, government officials, and legal authorities. The concept of "domesticity" was taking hold in upper-middle-class families in the early-to-mid-nineteenth century. It was premised on the belief in a differentiation between women and men in work and lifestyle, with women restricted essentially to the private sphere of the home and family and men to the public sphere of the workplace.

British common law defined women as subordinate to their husbands, fathers, and even brothers. In the eyes of the law, husband and wife constituted one person—the husband. That meant a wife did not have the legal right to sign a "contract" or to run her own business without her husband's permission. A married woman did have the right of a dowry, a lifetime interest in one-third of her husband's property. But even when and where the law was operative, it only applied upon the death of the husband, and not in instances of separation or marriage breakdown. As well, it could be overridden, since the husband had the right to dispose of the family property to whomever he chose as heir, which in most cases was a son, or even a grandson or son-in-law over a wife or a daughter. Divorce was possible but difficult, since in Upper Canada it required a special act of the legislature.

Christian law criminalized abortion and forbade infanticide. The murder of a child was punishable by death, although the ruling was seldom applied. It was considered "criminal" to conceal the birth of a "bastard," a child born out of wedlock. As noted in *Canadian Women: A History*, all of the laws "affecting sexuality, marriage, and motherhood might be regarded as evidence of new kinds of intrusions into women's lives, as male lawgivers attempted to reinforce or reinterpret traditional male control over, as well as their protection of, women in a changing world."[2]

Despite such restrictions, some women played active roles in education and religion. Some became schoolteachers in tax-supported schools. By 1851, women constituted almost one-fifth of "common" schoolteachers in Upper Canada. They were most often in rural schools, where few male teachers were available, or in districts where financial constraints necessitated hiring a female teacher, since she could be hired for "half the price." Women were also active in the Sunday school movement and in missionary societies, both of which played a social and educational role. Women were still refused entry into medical and law schools, and into the ministry. A few women did preach and prophesy, especially in the evangelical religious denominations, but even here they could not become ministers because this would imply gender equality. The one possible exception consisted of Quaker women, considered separated from but equal to men.

Some women were able to exercise their vote in general elections in the early nineteenth century in Upper Canada. But in 1849, a Reform government passed a law excluding women from the franchise in both the Canadas. Still, in the first half of the nineteenth century, politicians' wives played an active role "behind the scenes." Isabel Mackenzie, for example, fought as hard against the

Tory elite as her husband, William Lyon Mackenzie. Women were also involved in distributing and signing petitions for political change. Women in Upper Canada exercised considerable social power, even if they lacked official authority.

Economic Growth and Conservation

The mass immigration of 1815–1840 contributed to economic growth. During this period, Upper Canada became a thriving, complex, and viable society based on an exchange economy, both export and domestic, and financed by both capital and credit. The expansion rested to a large extent on wheat farming, although timber rivalled wheat as the major export staple of Upper Canada. In the Ottawa valley, with its rich forests of pine and oak and the region's easy access to the St. Lawrence, lumbering, not farming, became the primary industry. The timber trade was a byproduct of farming, since settlers had to clear the forests before farming the land.

The early settlers transformed the landscape of Upper Canada ecologically. In general, they had little interest in conservation or in the long-term management of land. They sought only to maximize short-term profits. Thus, they came to see the forests as a monolith to push back.

In the name of "progress," settlers and woodsmen cut down trees at an astonishing rate. A contemporary witness, journalist William Smith, noted the determination by which settlers cleared the Oak Ridges Morraine, north of Toronto: "the universal Canadian practice has been followed in clearing the land, that of sweeping away everything capable of bearing a green leaf. The new settlers look upon trees as enemies."

While such frenzied forest-cutting resulted in a host of productive farms that greatly boosted the economy of Upper Canada, "progress" came at a price: the loss of a large segment of the eastern woodlands as well as the animals, and birds that lived in these wooded areas. Some of the cleared areas were at the headwaters of rivers, which resulted in soil erosion that caused tonnes of silt to pour into streams that flowed into Lake Ontario. Thus, the water ecology was adversely affected, along with the fish and aquatic animals. Atlantic salmon, for example, lost their spawning grounds, and by the mid-nineteenth century no longer migrated in vast numbers up the St. Lawrence River. The last Atlantic salmon were caught in Ontario in the 1890s. (A century later, in 1988, the Ontario Ministry of Natural Resources began reintroducing the fish to Lake Ontario.)

By the 1850s, over one-third of the forested areas of southern Ontario had been destroyed. Within the next generation, three-quarters were gone, and by 1914 and the outbreak of World War I, over 90 percent.

The Road between York and Kingston, Upper Canada, 1830, *a watercolour by James Pattison Cockburn (1779–1847), a British army officer, shows the density of the early Upper Canadian forests.*

Library and Archives Canada/C-12632.

Transportation

Wheat and timber required transportation networks. Aboriginal trails soon became roads, giving greater accessibility. The settlers built road systems in the

Huron Tract beside Lake Huron, in the Talbot settlement south of London, in the Ottawa valley and the Kingston area. Around York, a road system soon connected the capital to outlying regions dependent on it for trade. Canal-building followed.

The British government paid for Upper Canada's first megaproject: the Rideau Canal, to link Bytown (Ottawa) with Kingston for defence purposes. It opened for public use in 1832. The construction of the province's second megaproject, a canal bypassing Niagara Falls and linking Lake Ontario to Lake Erie, began at roughly the same time as the Rideau Canal. It opened, however, three years earlier, in 1829. The incentive behind construction of the Welland Canal was strictly commercial.

The Rise of a Reform Movement

In the 1820s, Upper Canada had become polarized into conservative and reform camps. Led by the Family Compact, the conservatives favoured British monarchical ties, appointed Legislative and Executive Councils, and a hierarchical society free of political opposition. Their ideology was premised on a strong central government. Economically, they favoured the construction of canals and the establishment of banks, both of which they believed would advance the commercial well-being of the province. The conservatives obtained strong support from newly arrived middle- and upper-class British immigrants.

The Reform members of the Assembly opposed conservative policies. They tended to be "late Loyalists," or recent poorer British immigrants who favoured an elected Legislative Council, or upper house, and an Executive Council responsible to the Assembly rather than to the governor. Economically, the Reformers endorsed policies that promoted agriculture. In large measure they represented the farmers of the central and western areas of the province. They often opposed commercial enterprises such as canal-building and banks, which they saw as costly and of limited benefit to farmers. In short, there had developed in Upper Canada a situation roughly parallel to that in Lower Canada. One could class many of the conservatives in both the Canadas as "reactionary" politically, but "progressive" economically; and the Reformers as "radical" politically, but "reactionary" economically.

The Move to Rebellion

In the mid-1830s, William Lyon Mackenzie, a radical who had arrived in Upper Canada from Scotland in 1820, gradually favoured a Republican form of government, having visited the United States during the Jacksonian era. Mackenzie's views, however, were not representative of the majority of Reformers. A rift in Reform ranks had developed by the mid-1830s between a moderate wing led by Robert Baldwin and a radical wing under Mackenzie. The moderates desired to preserve Upper Canada's allegiance to the monarchy and its ties to the British empire, and did not want the American form of elective government that Mackenzie advocated, favouring instead the British plan of responsible government—a government responsible to the Assembly. To the moderate Reform politicians who had spent years dissociating reform from republicanism, Mackenzie was an acute embarrassment.

Mackenzie and his followers underestimated completely the strength of Upper Canadian conservatism, as well as the moderate Reformers' opposition to rebellion. In his recently created newspaper, *The Constitution*, begun symbolically on July 4, 1836, Mackenzie cited the American Revolution as justification for overthrowing the government. A group of his followers issued a Toronto Declaration closely modelled on the American Declaration of Independence.

Economic and social forces contributed to unrest in the province. In 1836, an economic downturn occurred throughout the Western world. In Upper Canada, this recession led to tight bank credit and even a recall of loans, which hit farmers especially hard. Such action intensified Mackenzie's already deep distrust of banks. News of the uprising of Lower Canadian Patriotes under Louis-Joseph Papineau further encouraged the Upper Canadian rebels.

The Upper Canadian Rebellion, 1837

In early December about 500 poorly-clad and -armed rebels gathered at Montgomery's Tavern on Yonge Street (just north of present-day Eglinton Avenue in Toronto). Government supporters quickly defeated them. Mackenzie's ill-conceived and ill-fated rebellion was over. With a price on his head, he managed to escape to the United States, while some of his followers were captured.

From across the border, the rebel leaders planned further attacks on the government of Upper Canada. Mackenzie found support in the United States among those Americans who saw the rebellion as a Canadian version of the American Revolution—an attempt to end British tyranny. Other Americans saw the uprising as an opportunity for the United States to annex Upper Canada. Some American supporters simply saw participation in a counterattack as an opportunity for looting.

Small, unsuccessful attacks followed along the border. The most serious counterattack occurred at the Battle of the Windmill along the St. Lawrence River near Prescott. In November 1838, 200 invaders barricaded themselves in an old windmill until they were forced to surrender. By the end of the Rebellion of 1837–1838, the Upper Canadian authorities jailed more than 1000 people on suspicion of treason. Nearly 100 of them were sent to the convict settlements in Australia (more than 70 of these individuals were Americans) and 20 were hanged.

WHERE HISTORIANS DISAGREE

The Causes of the 1837 Rebellion in Upper Canada

Amateur historians were the first to write about the Rebellion of 1837 in Upper Canada. They were both partisan and emotional in their approach, because of their closeness to the incident in both time and circumstance. Charles Lindsey, the son-in-law of William Lyon Mackenzie, the leader of the rebellion, blamed the Family Compact's refusal to compromise for driving the moderate Mackenzie to rebellion. In a two-volume work on the rebellion, journalist-cum-historian J.M. Dent challenged Lindsey's view and depicted a diabolical and extreme Mackenzie who led the colony to an unnecessary struggle.[1] These writers all believed the cause of the rebellion to be political—a classic struggle

between "democracy" and "privilege." This Liberal interpretation of history held sway in the late nineteenth and early twentieth centuries. During the 1920s, a decade in which Canada moved toward autonomy, a new liberal-nationalist school of historical writing saw the rebellion as an attempt to gain independence from Britain. The rebellion became an important event on the road from "colony to nation."

In the midst of the economic upheaval of the Great Depression of the 1930s, an economic interpretation of the rebellion appeared. Historian Donald Creighton depicted the rebellion in Upper Canada as a struggle between agrarian interests, represented by Mackenzie and his followers, and commercial interests, which controlled the appointed Executive and Legislative Councils. "The rebellions were," Creighton wrote, "the final expression of that hatred of the rural community for the commercialism of the St. Lawrence."[2] Creighton strengthened his economic argument by pointing out that the rebellions broke out in Upper Canada after a succession of crop failures that had brought farmers to the point of starvation and bankruptcy.

Other historians have more recently argued that economic distress was not really at the root of the rebellion. Historian Colin Read pointed out in *The Rebellion of 1837 in Upper Canada* that "the rebels were, for the most part, well-settled members of a reasonably prosperous agrarian society." He saw "no single cause or grand overriding explanation" for their participation. Short-term economic dislocation played a part, as did more individual motivations based on family loyalties or personal friendships and animosities: "So too did specific political grievances as well as the general reform perception that the world was ordered too much in the interests of the few, too little in the interests of the many."[3] The rebels' ignorance of the military strength of the loyalist militia also was a contributing factor, according to Read.

Intellectual historians depict Mackenzie as a man of ideas, who drew his inspiration and his direction from reform movements in both Britain and the United States, for greater public participation in government. They see the rebellion in Upper Canada as part of the general reform impulse. R.A. MacKay notes: "Few public men in Canadian history have so represented the spirit of their age as did William Lyon Mackenzie, and particularly during the pre-Rebellion stage of his career.... On both sides of the Atlantic the new wine of liberty and democracy was bursting the old bottles of restriction and privilege.... In the 1820's and 1830's William Lyon Mackenzie was the principal purveyor of these wines of liberty to the backwoods colony of Upper Canada."[4]

In the 1960s, social historians questioned whether the rebellion in Upper Canada was a class struggle. Marxist historian Stanley Ryerson interpreted the rebellion as a bourgeois-democratic revolution caused by oppression and led by men who were fighting for the cause of popular liberty. "Workers ... made up nearly half, and farmers over 40 per cent of the victims of oppression: a significant indication of the social forces that were engaged in action."[5] Fellow Marxist historian Leo Johnson saw the roots of the rebellion in an inequitable system of land grants designed at the time of Governor Simcoe to create a landed gentry class at the expense of the ordinary farmer. The rebellion was a fight between two different views of land ownership held by two different classes of people.[6]

Read challenges the image of the Upper Canadian rebellion as a "people's revolution." Using the less-known Duncombe uprising in the London area, Read concludes: "There is no basis for arguing that the rebels comprised a clearly disadvantaged sector of society and hence were driven to arms by economic despair or the prospect of plunder." What did distinguish rebels from loyalists, according to Read, was the large number of rebels who were either American-born or born to American parents and who "may well have retained or adopted the deep American dislike of Britain and have been more willing to rebel, hoping to sever the provincial ties to Great Britain."[7] This ideological split was the real cause of the rebellion.

The debate continues, with no interpretation emerging as definitive. The net result, however, is a richer and deeper understanding of the 1830s in Upper Canada, the decade out of which the Rebellion of 1837 arose.

1. J. M. Dent, *The Story of the Upper Canadian Rebellion*, 2 vols. (Toronto: C. Blackett Robinson, 1885).

2. Donald Creighton, *The Empire of the St. Lawrence: A Study in Commerce and Politics* [1937]. Reprint with Introduction by Christopher Moore (Toronto: University of Toronto Press, 2002), p. 316.

3. Colin Read, *The Rebellion of 1837 in Upper Canada* (Ottawa: Canadian Historical Association, 1988), p. 18.

4. R.A. MacKay, "The Political Ideas of William Lyon Mackenzie," *Canadian Journal of Economics and Political Science*, 3 (1937): 1.

5. Stanley Ryerson, *Unequal Union: Confederation and the Roots of Conflict in the Canadas, 1815–1873* (Toronto: Progress Books, 1968), p. 131.

6. Leo Johnson, "Land Policy, Population Growth and Social Structure in Home District, 1793–1851," *Ontario History*, 63 (1971): 41–60.

7. Colin Read, *The Rising in Western Upper Canada, 1837–38: The Duncombe Revolt and After* (Toronto: University of Toronto Press, 1982), pp. 207, 208.

Lord Durham's Report

The Rebellion of 1837 in Upper Canada was a minor affair from a military standpoint. Simply put, the majority of Upper Canadians did not support revolution. But together with the more extensive uprising in Lower Canada, the troubles in Upper Canada convinced Britain of the need to investigate the causes of the unrest. The British cabinet sent out one of its most gifted politicians, Lord Durham, to inquire into the affairs of the colony and report back to the British government. Durham spent only five months in the Canadas, most of the time in Lower Canada. But he made one short visit to Upper Canada.

The Durham Report of 1839 made two very important recommendations. First, it advised that the colonial governor should choose his closest advisers, the members of the Executive Council, from the majority party in the Assembly and abide by the wishes of these elected representatives. Although Durham did not call this "responsible government," it nonetheless came to be known as such. Second, the Report recommended union of the two Canadas. Durham saw such a union of the Canadas as the nucleus of an eventual amalgamation of all the British North American colonies, which he highly favoured, and as a necessary precursor to the assimilation of the French Canadians. The British government accepted union but rejected responsible government.

By the terms of the Act of Union of 1840, the capital of the new Province of Canada became Kingston. English was recognized as the only official language of the Assembly. The united province assumed Upper Canada's debt. And the Assembly consisted of 84 members—42 from Upper Canada and 42 from Lower Canada. Upper Canada officially ceased to exist. Instead, the area became known as Canada West, part of a larger union of English and French Canadians.

Simcoe's years in Upper Canada marked the beginning of a new British American colony in the interior of the continent. Thanks largely to British military and First Nation support in the War of 1812, it escaped American conquest in the War of 1812. The years 1815 to 1840 witnessed a transformation in Upper Canada. Large-scale immigration, chiefly from the British Isles, added some 300 000 people, greatly extended the areas of settlement, and gave the colony a decidedly Upper Canadian orientation, one that rejected violent political change and endorsed the imperial connection.

NOTES

1. Janice Potter, "Patriarchy and Paternalism: The Case of the Eastern Ontario Loyalist Women," *Ontario History*, 81 (1989): 20.

2. Alison Prentice et al., *Canadian Women: A History*, 2nd ed. (Toronto: Harcourt Brace, 1996), p. 91.

BEYOND THE BOOK

Joseph Brant

http://thecanadianencyclopedia.com/index.cfm?PgNm=TCE&Params=A1ARTA0000959
A biography of Mohawk First Nations Chief Joseph Brant (Thayendanegea).

Who Was Molly Brant?

http://www.carf.info/kingstonpast/mollybrant.php
A detailed, illustrated biography of Molly Brant, sister of Joseph Brant.

The Loyalist Six Nations

http://www.canadiana.org/ECO/PageView/91942/0080
This document by John Graves Simcoe formally grants a reserve along the Bay of Quinte to the Six Nations. The land had been purchased from the Mississauga people.

Enslaved Africans in Upper Canada

http://www.archives.gov.on.ca/english/exhibits/slavery/index.html
This exhibit presents the lives of four African individuals who in the 1790s were slaves in Upper Canada. Primary-source letters and photographs detail their lives.

The War of 1812 in the Western District

http://209.202.75.197/digi/war1812/indexflash.htm
Details the events and effects of the War of 1812 in the Western District of Ontario. Letters from citizens and soldiers are presented.

Peace and Conflict: The War of 1812

http://www.histori.ca/peace/page.do?pageID=336
Journal entries, speeches, images, and maps relating to the participants of the War of 1812.

Welland Canal

http://www.thecanadianencyclopedia.com/index.cfm?PgNm=ArchivedFeatures&Params=A2139
A detailed, illustrated history of the Welland Canal, which linked Lake Erie and Lake Ontario. Before this canal, a portage was required to cross the two lakes.

A Question of Loyalties

Canada: A People's History—Episode 5, A Question of Loyalties. Directed by Laine Drewery (CBC, 2000).

Chiefs

Chiefs (Galafilm Inc., 2002). A documentary and reenactment of the lives of five First Nations chiefs, including Joseph Brant.

RELATED READINGS

Two articles deal with Upper Canada in this time period in R. Douglas Francis and Donald B. Smith, eds., *Viewpoints: Readings in Canadian History* (Toronto: Thomson Nelson, 2007): E. Jane Errington, "Reluctant Warriors: British North Americans and the War of 1812," pp. 128–36; and Cecilia Morgan, "'Of Slender Frame and Delicate Appearance': The Placing of Laura Secord in the Narratives of Canadian Loyalist History," pp. 136–48.

BIBLIOGRAPHY

The best overview of Upper Canadian society remains Gerald M. Craig, *Upper Canada: The Formative Years, 1784–1841* (Toronto: McClelland & Stewart, 1963). For a guide to the historical literature in general, see Bryan D. Palmer, "Upper Canada," in M. Brook Taylor, ed., *Canadian History: A Reader's Guide*, vol. 1, *Beginnings to Confederation* (Toronto: University of Toronto Press, 1994), pp. 184–236. Peter A. Baskerville has written a useful overview of all of Ontario's history, *Ontario: Image, Identity and Power* (Toronto: Oxford University Press, 2001).

For information on the Loyalists who settled in Upper Canada, see Bruce Wilson, *As She Began: An Illustrated Introduction to Loyalist Ontario* (Toronto: Dundurn Press, 1981); and Janice Potter-MacKinnon, *While the Women Only Wept: Loyalist Refugee Women in Eastern Ontario* (Montreal/Kingston: McGill-Queen's University Press, 1993). Economic issues are examined in Douglas McCalla's *Planting the Province: The Economic History of Upper Canada, 1784–1870* (Toronto: University of Toronto Press, 1993).

The experience of the Six Nations in early Upper Canada is reviewed in Charles M. Johnston, ed., *The Valley of the Six Nations: A Collection of Documents on the Indian Lands of the Grand River* (Toronto: Champlain Society, 1964). For a discussion of the Ojibwas see Peter S. Schmalz, *The Ojibwa of Southern Ontario* (Toronto: University of Toronto Press, 1990); Donald B. Smith, *Sacred Feathers: The Reverend Peter Jones (Kahkewaquonaby) and the Mississauga Indians* (Toronto: University of Toronto Press, 1987); and Janet Chute, *The Legacy of Shingwaukonse: A Century of Native Leadership* (Toronto: University of Toronto Press, 1998).

A short summary of the War of 1812 appears in Carl Benn, *The War of 1812* (New York: Routledge, 2003). Fuller overviews are Victor Suthren, *The War of 1812* (Toronto: McClelland & Stewart, 1999); and Mark Zuehlke, *For Honour's Sake: The War of 1812 and the Brokering of an Uneasy Peace* (Toronto: Knopf Canada, 2006). Valuable studies of the First Nations in the War of 1812 include John Sugden, *Tecumseh: A Life* (New York: Henry Holt, 1997); and Carl Benn, *The Iroquois in the War of 1812* (Toronto: University of Toronto Press, 1998).

Helen Cowan, *British Emigration in British North America: The First Hundred Years*, rev. and enlarged ed. (Toronto: University of Toronto Press, 1961), best describes the experience of immigrating to British North America from Britain. A shorter version is Helen Cowan, *British Immigration before Confederation* (Ottawa: Canadian Historical Association, 1968). Two books that review the experience of African Canadians in Upper Canada include: Robin Winks's *The Blacks in Canada*, 2nd ed. (Montreal/Kingston: McGill-Queen's University Press, 1997); and Peggy Bristow et al., *"We're Rooted Here and They Can't Pull Us Up": Essays in African Canadian Women's History* (Toronto: University of Toronto Press, 1994).

Carol Wilton has written an important political study, *Popular Politics and Political Culture in Upper Canada, 1800–1850* (Montreal/Kingston: McGill-Queen's University Press, 2000). On the background to the Rebellions of 1837/38, William Kilbourn's biography of William Lyon Mackenzie, *The Firebrand* (Toronto: Clarke Irwin, 1956; reprint, Toronto: Dundurn Press, 2008) is a lively account. Colin Read's *The Rebellion of 1837 in Upper Canada* (Ottawa: Canadian Historical Association, 1988) remains very useful.

For early maps of Upper Canada, see R. Louis Gentilcore and C. Grant Head, eds., *Ontario's History in Maps* (Toronto: University of Toronto Press, 1984); and consult R. Louis Gentilcore, ed., *Historical Atlas of Canada*, vol. 2, *The Land Transformed, 1800–1891* (Toronto: University of Toronto Press, 1993). Valuable portraits of early Upper Canadian figures appear in the *Dictionary of Canadian Biography*, vol. 4, *1770–1800*; vol. 5, *1800–1820*; and vol. 6, *1821–1835* (Toronto: University of Toronto Press, 1979, 1985, 1987); also available online at www.biographi.ca.

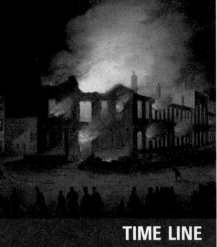

Chapter Seven

THE UNION OF THE CANADAS

TIME LINE

1840	The Union of the Canadas comes into effect
1846	Britain establishes free trade
1849	Lord Elgin sanctions the Rebellion Losses Bill; English-speaking protesters burn the Parliament building in Montreal Manifesto of the Annexation Association published The Anglican-affiliated King's College becomes the nonsectarian University of Toronto
1852	Toronto Stock Exchange opens Université Laval founded in Quebec City
1854	Emergence of the Liberal–Conservative alliance Treaty of Reciprocity between British North America and the United States
1857	"Rep by Pop" becomes the main plank of Reform party's platform Ottawa selected as Canada's capital
1859	Completion of the Victoria Bridge over the St. Lawrence River at Montreal

The Act of Union adopted by the British parliament in July 1840 joined the two Canadas, now renamed Canada East and Canada West. The union had a short but stormy life, which ended with the realization of a larger British North American Confederation in 1867.

Although ultimately a failure, the union could boast important successes. The government adopted laws providing for the education of children in both sections of the colony. As railway fever swept the nation's business community in the 1850s, solicitous politicians oversaw a multitude of costly construction projects. The railways transformed the agricultural, commercial, and urban character of the province. After Britain, the world's industrial pioneer, adopted free trade in the mid-1840s, the government fostered increased trade relations with the United States by negotiating a Reciprocity Treaty covering natural products. In 1854, it finally abolished the seigneurial system in Canada East and even found a solution to the contentious clergy reserves question in Canada West. According to political scientist S.J.R. Noel, "The overall record of governmental accomplishment compares favourably with that of any other era, either before or since."[1]

The union years also saw the end of constant feuding between the Legislative Assembly and the governor. Within ten years after the failure of the rebellions, London accepted the principles of responsible government. Henceforth, the governor governed less; his executive councillors or cabinet ministers, who were responsible to the Assembly, made decisions in his place. With the coming of responsible government, traditional elites were largely replaced by the new commercial and industrial elites, to whom many of the new brand of politicians were closely allied.

In addition, many English-speaking and some French-speaking Canadian historians argue that, in the Union period, French- and English-speaking politicians found common ground on which to cooperate in solving many major political questions. The need to construct a *modus vivendi* also helped restrain ethnic and religious bigotry.

French Canadians and Union

Britain originally intended to use union of the Canadas to punish the French and assure their subjugation, if not their eventual demise, as a linguistic group. Certainly the conditions of union constituted a severe blow for Lower Canada in general and for French Canadians in particular. English became the sole official language of parliamentary documents. The elective Assembly had an equal number of representatives from both halves of the colony, even though in 1841 the population of largely French-speaking Canada East was 40 percent greater than that of English-speaking Canada West.

The Act of Union also made Upper Canada's heavy debt burden the responsibility of the Province of Canada as a whole. Upper Canada could no longer by itself finance costly transportation facilities like roads and canals; only union with the virtually debt-free Lower Canada could strengthen its position. Union would bring in higher revenues because the United Canadas could raise tariffs, a measure that Lower Canada, where most goods from Europe entered, could no longer block. Pleasing Montreal's English-speaking merchants, it would also recognize that the two Canadas formed a common economic bloc.

Lord Sydenham

Charles Poulett Thomson, Lord Durham's successor as governor general of Canada in 1839, wanted to put Canada on a sound financial footing to attract development capital. He also hoped that substantial British immigration would diminish the political and economic influence of French Canadians. A masterful strategist, Thomson convinced most political groups in Upper Canada to agree to political union. He did not have to convince Lower Canada, which would have no say in the matter.

On September 13, 1842, LaFontaine gave his maiden speech in the assembly of the Province of Canada. Immediately one of the executive councillors from Canada West rose and asked him to speak in English. LaFontaine then made his famous reply: "I am asked to pronounce in another language than my mother tongue this first speech that I have to make in this House. I distrust my ability to speak English. But I must inform the honorable members that even if my knowledge of English were as intimate as my knowledge of French, I should nevertheless make my first speech in the language of my French-Canadian compatriots, if only to protest against the cruel injustice of the Union Act in trying to proscribe the mother tongue of half the population of Canada. I owe it to my compatriots; I owe it to myself." Cited in English translation in Mason Wade, The French Canadians, *vol. 1 (2 vols., Toronto: Macmillan, 1968), p. 239.*

Library and Archives Canada C005961.

The union was officially inaugurated in Montreal on February 10, 1841, establishing a single government and legislature. Most French Canadians, though, were defiant and bitter. They certainly had no reason to trust the assurances of the anti-French Thomson, now Lord Sydenham. Moreover, the union simply had too many elements that they found objectionable. Unyielding opposition appeared to be the only path open to them.

Well aware of French-Canadian hostility, Sydenham worked to assure the election of a maximum number of English-speaking members in Canada East by gerrymandering riding boundaries to eliminate French votes from certain districts and by staging polls in English localities situated far from French-speaking towns. He also used British troops as well as Irish construction labourers to intimidate French-speaking voters in the open voting (the secret ballot was established only in 1874). Not surprisingly, the governor won a comfortable working majority in United Canada's first legislature. Sydenham was now in a position to be his own prime minister.

Sydenham's heavy-handed tactics actually improved the chances for fruitful collaboration between Reformers in Canada East and Canada West. In Canada West, such prominent Reform leaders as Robert Baldwin assured former patriote Louis-Hippolyte LaFontaine in Canada East that, in return for cooperation in working toward responsible government, they would assist French-Canadian efforts to rid the union of objectionable features such as official English unilingualism. LaFontaine and most other French-Canadian leaders finally concluded that French Canada could obtain more by accepting union than by continuing to oppose it.

The Commercial Empire of the St. Lawrence

The economic life of the Province of the Canadas, as was true of the other British North American colonies at the time, was based on the production and exporting of "staple" resources such as fish, furs, timber, and wheat to markets in Britain and the United States. The British desired two staples readily available in the United Canadas: timber and wheat. British shipbuilders needed square-hewed timber, made from Canadian white and red pine, for the masts of sailing ships. Britain also wanted lumber for construction. Wood became British North America's most valuable export commodity, making up nearly two-thirds of the value of the colonies' exports to Britain by the 1840s. But the lumber industry remained vulnerable to fluctuating demand in Britain, reduced British tariffs which aided lumber exporters in the Baltic region, and overproduction.

Within the Canadas, a second commodity—wheat—rivalled timber. After 1840, a combination of good weather and increased hectarage due to rapid settlement of the rich farmland of Canada West greatly increased total production. Improved transportation lowered costs and reduced insurance rates. Canada West became one of the chief suppliers of wheat to feed industrial Britain's growing urban population.

Transportation

Exporting staples such as wheat and timber required a sophisticated transportation system. By the early 1850s, a comprehensive road system linked Windsor to Montreal, with branches northward to towns on Lake Huron and to Bytown (Ottawa).

More important for transportation was the canal system linking Lake Erie with Montreal and the Atlantic Ocean. During the 1840s, the government widened and deepened existing canals such as the Welland and the Lachine canals to accommodate larger steamboats. It also built new canals, notably between Montreal and Prescott, at the head of navigation above the St. Lawrence rapids. The St. Lawrence–Great Lakes route now rivalled the Erie–Hudson River route, and Montreal could compete with New York as the major exporting and importing centre for the North American continent.

The Rise of a Reform Coalition

Major political transformations also took place during the Union's first decade. In the early 1840s, Tories and Reformers stood out within Canada West's broad political spectrum. Basically, Tories vaunted their loyalty to the Crown and to the British connection. In their view, responsible government could only weaken ties with Britain, because it challenged the authority of the colonial governor. Tory supporters included business interests, numerous professionals, and the many that benefited from government patronage. Many working-class Irish Protestant immigrants also supported the Tories; in return for Tory largesse, the Orange Order provided, notably in Toronto, the "votes and strong arms needed in the rough and tumble polling process of the day."[2]

Lord Durham's endorsement of responsible government in 1839 gave Reformist ambitions a powerful boost. In order to prove their loyalty, Reformists kept their demands within the framework of the British constitution and British traditions. That the Crown act in nonpartisan fashion was accepted British practice, they asserted. They also reminded their opponents that party government existed in Britain. Reformists denounced the abuses linked to the government's distribution of patronage, although later, when they took power, they would prove themselves to be equally ardent practitioners in the art of dispensing favours.

An alliance between Reformers and French seemed natural, in view of the traditional political goals of both groups and the growing personal friendship between Baldwin and LaFontaine. It took time to establish this common front, however. Many so-called Reformers did not want to oppose the government, as the French Canadians had done, for fear of compromising the public-works projects promised for their districts by Sydenham. Only after Sydenham's death in 1841 did they return to Baldwin's leadership.

Sir Charles Bagot and Sir Charles Metcalfe, Sydenham's successors as governor, walked a tightrope in attempting to govern the colony without the aid of representatives of the French Canadians, who formed half the united province's population. Yet both were Conservatives and strong believers in the British connection, and, in trying to appease the supposedly disloyal and rebellious French, they risked losing support among the English-speaking of both Canadas. In addition, the governors had difficulty persuading the British government to renounce at least any immediate hopes for assimilation of the French.

In 1845, Governor Metcalfe asked the British parliament to amend the Act of Union to end the proscription of French as an official language. At first, the Colonial Secretary vehemently disagreed: the Act of Union was designed "to promote the amalgamation of the French and English races," he reminded the governor, and to authorize bilingualism would be to abandon this goal. Three years later, implicitly agreeing that its linguistic policy was unrealistic, the British government gave French official recognition.

The Arrival of Responsible Government

The most important single factor in bridging the ethnic gulf during the 1840s was the arduous, but ultimately successful, struggle for responsible government. In 1840, recognition of this principle still appeared far off. The Act of Union concentrated enormous power in the hands of the colonial governor, appointed by London. The governor, in turn, appointed for life the members of the upper house, or Legislative Council. He could also reward his supporters, since he had the right to name a host of public officials. In parliament he chose his advisers, dismissing and replacing them at will. He also held broad veto powers over bills adopted by the legislature. Yet, over the course of the union's first decade, the governor's powers were radically curtailed.

Responsible government came only after dramatic battles. The Colonial Office urged Canada's governors to avoid concessions lest Canada agitate for independence. But pragmatic governors such as Bagot, a diplomat, understood the necessity, in order to govern, of appointing an Executive Council, or cabinet, that would have the support of a majority in the Assembly. Taking into account the growing power of the French bloc, he invited LaFontaine to join his council. When the latter shrewdly demanded that Baldwin, too, have a place, the unhappy Bagot again yielded.

Colonial administrators expressed the strongest regrets—to which Bagot replied that, had he acted otherwise, "Canada would have again become the theatre of a widespread rebellion, and perhaps the ungrateful separatist or the rejected outcast from British dominion." Despite Bagot's apparent recognition of the principle that he could only choose ministers who commanded the support of a majority of the members of the Assembly, no guarantee existed that the governor might not some day replace his advisers if he disagreed with them. Moreover, Bagot's government, consisting of a wide variety of personalities of various political hues, did

Governing in the Canadas Before and After Responsible Government

Before responsible government was introduced, the Legislative Assembly had no effective control over the Executive Council, on whose advice the governor relied. With the coming of responsible government, the Executive Council could remain in office only as long as it had the Legislative Assembly's support.

Source: Adapted from P.G. Cornell, M. Hamelin, F. Ouellet, and M. Trudel, *Canada: Unity in Diversity* (Toronto: Holt, Rinehart and Winston, 1967), p. 143.

not really constitute a ministry. Party government, though undeniably a little closer, had not yet come to the province.

Sir Charles Metcalfe, named governor in 1843, was determined to maintain the British connection. He did not intend to submit to LaFontaine, and he would certainly not commit himself to taking his advice. Not surprisingly, Metcalfe enjoyed little electoral success in Canada East, where LaFontaine had built up an effective political machine.

The moderate regime that governed the colony from 1844 until 1847, led by the eloquent Conservative "Sweet William" Henry Draper as attorney general for Canada West and virtual prime minister, succeeded in adopting several important pieces of legislation. True responsible government still did not exist, however. Although the Executive Council did have the confidence of the Assembly, the governor's powers remained very broad. Moreover, Draper's attempts to build significant French support failed utterly.

Lord Elgin

The pace of events quickened with the arrival of Lord Elgin, the new governor general, in 1847. By this time Britain had moved toward laissez-faire liberalism and free trade, and saw little need to regulate colonies' trade relations. Indeed, the British government was now convinced that only colonial autonomy could hold the empire together, and it instructed Elgin to accept this principle and to behave in a strictly neutral fashion.

The elections of 1848 produced a strong majority for LaFontaine's group in Canada East and a significant majority for Baldwin's Reform movement in Canada West. The Reformers' victory achieved, Lord Elgin called on LaFontaine and Baldwin to form a government. Henceforth, the governor assented to legislation adopted by Parliament, unless he judged it contrary to the interests of Great Britain. Elgin proved as much in 1849 when he agreed to sign, despite personal reservations, the Rebellion Losses Bill, which compensated those who had lost property during the Rebellions of 1837–1838 in Canada East (the question of losses in Canada West had been settled in 1845).

Elgin's action infuriated Montreal's Tories. Denouncing "French domination," a mob invaded Parliament and put it to the torch, then stoned Elgin's carriage, ransacked LaFontaine's house, and rampaged through the town. Canada West experienced considerable unrest, too. The Tories staged protest meetings to denounce the rewarding of "rebels" and "pardoned traitors," and thousands signed petitions demanding Elgin's recall. A Toronto mob burned Baldwin and Lord Elgin in effigy.

In spite of the violence that surrounded its coming, responsible government moved Canada forward along the road to democracy and political autonomy. For that reason, most historians have viewed its coming as a great milestone in Canada's history. The voters, through their elected representatives, would now exercise greater control over government—or at least the property-holding male portion would, for in 1849

This painting by Joseph Légaré depicts the burning of the Canadian parliament building in Montreal on the night of April 25, 1849. It is believed that rioters, protesting the passage of the Rebellion Losses Bill, smashed the gas mains, then set fire to the escaping gas. Earlier that day, crowds of English-speaking protesters had thrown stones and rotten eggs at Lord Elgin's carriage because the governor general had sanctioned the bill. The riots lasted two days. Subsequently, it was decided that Montreal would no longer be the seat of government, and the capital alternated between Quebec City and Toronto.

M11588 *The Burning of the Parliament Building in Montreal* © McCord Museum.

the Reformers amended the election law to exclude women from the franchise. In spite of the common-law prohibition against female suffrage, a few women had voted in the past.

Perhaps more relevant to the politicians' daily preoccupations, responsible government also ensured that the leaders of the governing party would control patronage. Political scientist S.J.R. Noel asserts that the British resisted responsible government in part precisely because they "appreciated the central importance of patronage in the political process."[3] Another consequence of responsible government was to ensure a shift of power and influence away from conservative traditional elites and toward the new commercial and industrial classes. Business and politicians cooperated closely. In fact, a great many politicians were businesspeople who came to politics to advance both their personal interests and those of the business community. In this sense, it would be naive to claim that responsible government actually gave power to the common people. Yet business domination was not to go unchallenged, and elections did bring members of a variety of other groups to Parliament.

In 1851, both Baldwin and LaFontaine, their goal of responsible government achieved, left politics. The achievement of responsible government did not put an end to close cooperation between French- and English-speaking politicians. It did signify the need to build new alliances. In the turbulent early 1850s, when the loosely organized Reform group split into moderate and radical factions, most French-speaking members of the Assembly, representing the moderate Parti bleu, began to cooperate with Conservatives from Canada West to form governments. This coalition, symbolized by the close association of John A. Macdonald and George-Étienne Cartier, carried over into the post-Confederation period.

Three Indian Chiefs and Peter McLeod Presenting a Petition to Lord Elgin, *by Théophile Hamel (1848). On March 12, 1848, three Montagnais (Innu) chiefs from the Saguenay River, with their interpreter, Peter McLeod, met the governor general and presented their grievances. The newcomers had pushed Aboriginal peoples further and further into the interior, from Tadoussac, to Chicoutimi, to Lac St. Jean. In Canada East, unlike Canada West, the government did not conclude treaties with the resident First Nations. The British argued that the Royal Proclamation of 1763 had not designated the valley of the St. Lawrence and surrounding area as "Indian Territory."*

Private collection/Photo courtesy of the owner.

First Nations in the Canadas

The Act of Union (1841) omitted to make provision for "Indians," or even to provide for the payment of annuities for earlier land surrenders. Nor did the coming of responsible government improve the lot of the Aboriginal peoples. After the British government in 1860 transferred all authority over "Indian affairs" to the Canadian legislature, Canadian politicians imposed even tighter control over the First Nations, and Aboriginal people were given little opportunity to administer their remaining lands themselves. The government committed itself to a system of First Nations education, administered by Christian missionaries and based on model farms and industrial or residential schools, in order to bring about the eventual assimilation of the First Nations.

The Advent of British Free Trade and Repercussions for the United Canadas

In 1846, Britain adopted free trade. British factory owners wanted reduced tariffs to enable Britain to compete in a world market. They also sought the repeal of the Corn Laws (protective tariffs on grain), arguing that repeal would mean cheaper food for the industrial working class and hence an opportunity for employers to lower wages. At the same time, Liberal economists increasingly pointed out the costs, economic and military, of keeping colonies.

These free-trade lobbyists convinced Robert Peel's government to repeal the Corn Laws in 1846. Other free-trade measures included the progressive lowering of the timber preference. Then, in 1849, Britain repealed the Navigation Laws, which had restricted trade with the colonies to British or colonial vessels.

The Annexation Movement

Many members of the commercial elites in the Canadas denounced Britain's move toward free trade because it signified an end to the imperial preferences which gave them, as exporters, an advantage in British markets. Britain's new trade policies helped push large sectors of Canadian commerce into depression. Shipping activity at Montreal declined precipitously. Bankruptcies spread. Some Tories did not hesitate to link their loyalty to economic opportunity. Finding none of the much-vaunted benefits of the British connection, they now campaigned for annexation to the United States.

Montreal became the hotbed of annexationist sentiment. In October 1849, the English-language press published the manifesto of the Annexation Association, signed by 325 citizens, many of them notable businesspeople, such as William Molson and John Redpath. Early in 1850 the formation of the Toronto Annexation Association, supposedly embracing "a large number of the most respectable merchants and inhabitants of this city," was announced. For many Tories, annexation was also a means to escape from so-called French domination.

French Canada and Annexation

French Canada also displayed some interest in annexation, though obviously for entirely different reasons. Louis-Joseph Papineau and others admired American democratic institutions and hated the Canadian union. Radical young intellectuals belonging to the Institut canadien, a literary and debating society in Montreal, also took up the annexationist cause. The movement, however, had no popular base, and other elites in French Canada vociferously condemned annexation, as they saw colonial self-rule to be working. George-Étienne Cartier echoed conservative sentiment when he warned that American democracy signified "the will of the masses." The Roman Catholic clergy, for its part, feared that annexation would put an end to the liberty that it enjoyed under British rule.

In Canada West, annexationism, though noisy, made little headway. Opponents now suggested alternatives. In July 1849, Tories gathered at Kingston to launch the British-American League, which advocated tariff protection and a union of the British North American colonies. With the revival of prosperity in the early 1850s, annexationist sentiment waned. The Americans' unresponsiveness to annexationist tendencies north of the border hastened the movement's decline.

From Transatlantic to Transcontinental Trade

Despite the advent of British free trade, the Canadas neither collapsed nor joined the United States. Commerce soon revived as British North America adjusted to new challenges. Trade increased with the United States, assisted by the growth of railways. Just as the waterways had facilitated east–west trade across the continent and ultimately with Britain, railways best linked the Canadas and the United States for north–south trade. The transition from transatlantic to transcontinental trade had begun.

This transition came swiftly and dramatically. Industrialism in the United States led directly to an initial increase in markets for the Canadian staple products—timber and wheat. The rapidly growing cities of the eastern seaboard and of the American Midwest needed lumber to construct houses and commercial buildings, and wheat to feed a growing population. Grain prices tripled. As a result, agriculture surpassed timber as the major staple of all British North American trade in the 1850s.

The 1850s inaugurated what historian A.R.M. Lower described as "the North American assault on the Canadian forest."[4] As demand for Canadian lumber increased, American lumber firms and sawmill owners established themselves in Canadian forest areas, especially the Ottawa valley.

Equally, Canadian timber found a rising market in Canada West, with its growing immigrant population. Saw and planing mills, sash and shingle factories, and cabinet-making firms arose to serve this local market. Yet Britain still remained the most lucrative market for Canadian timber until into the 1860s.

Farmers in Canada West benefited the most from this increased demand for wheat. Good prices, along with high yields, provided them with capital to increase their hectarage and to diversify their farming. In addition to wheat, they exported wool, meat, eggs, butter, and cheese, especially to the United States. Farmers in Canada East did not fare as well. A shortage of good agricultural land, combined with problems of climate and fertility, meant that they produced little wheat for export. They did export other grains such as oats and barley, along with dairy products in limited quantities.

Reciprocity with the United States

To expand its lucrative trade with the United States, the Canadas wanted a reciprocal trade agreement. The British government endorsed the idea, as a means of easing tensions and reducing Canadian dependence on the mother country. At first, strong American protectionist sentiment prevented acceptance of the idea. The slavery issue in the United States was also an obstacle. Some northern senators favoured free trade because they now believed it a prelude to annexing the Canadas, which would lead to a preponderance of free states in the Union. Southern senators opposed it for the same reason, until Governor General Lord Elgin convinced them that a prosperous Canada through free trade would be better able to resist annexation to the United States.

Another roadblock to reciprocity concerned Maritime fisheries. Britain and the United States had different interpretations of the territorial waters in British North America from which American fishers were excluded under the Convention of 1818. Neither side wanted an armed conflict, and Britain was willing to use the fisheries issue as a negotiating tool for free trade of colonial natural products in the United States. In the end, Britain threatened to withdraw its patrol boats (which prevented American encroachment), unless Nova Scotia agreed to the treaty.

The Reciprocity Treaty of 1854, approved by the American senate and ratified by the colonial legislatures, allowed for the free trade of major natural products, such as timber, grain, coal, livestock, and fish, between the British North American colonies and the United States. As well, it gave joint access to coastal fisheries. The agreement ran for a ten-year period commencing in 1855 and was subject to renewal or termination.

Closer economic ties with the United States coincided with the Canadian railway-building era. Increased Canadian–American trade provided the incentive for new rail lines and greater continental economic integration.

The first British North American railway, a 23-km line made of wooden rails that linked Montreal and the Richelieu River, was completed in 1836. But the real era of railway building occurred in the 1850s. By 1856, railways linked all the major urban centres in Canada West. Such expansion came as a result of the combination of popular interest, public and private financial support, and private promotion. One of the negative factors was the environmental impact. As new communities arose, both forests and land came under greater assault. The locomotive contributed greatly to the rapid disappearance of the white pine forests of the Canadas.

Governments eagerly courted railways. These "engines of progress" seemed worth the price even though they required huge expenditures of public funds. Most of the capital for railway building came from Britain and the United States. As the British North American colonies had insufficient credit ratings to borrow vast sums abroad, their governments inevitably became involved in railway financing.

Private companies built four key railway lines in the United Canadas in the 1850s. The St. Lawrence and Atlantic line between Montreal and Portland, Maine, completed in 1853, gave Montreal access to a year-round ice-free port on the Atlantic, and made the city once more competitive with New York in continental trade. The second line, the Great Western Railway, completed in 1855, went from Niagara Falls via Hamilton and London to Windsor. This line sought to capture the trade of the American Midwest by offering a quick route from Chicago through to New York by way of the Canadas. The third major line, the Northern Railway, which ran from Toronto to Collingwood, on Georgian Bay, serviced the rich farmland north of Toronto and opened up the forested area of the Georgian Bay and Muskoka regions. The fourth and most ambitious railway scheme of the decade was the Grand Trunk.

The Grand Trunk Railway

The Grand Trunk Railway was originally to run from Windsor, Canada West, to Halifax, Nova Scotia, thus linking the interior of British North America with an ice-free Atlantic port. When plans to build the Maritime section failed, the company purchased the St. Lawrence and Atlantic line, which ran between Montreal and ice-free Portland, Maine. The scheme proved costly, however, because the track needed major repairs. Equally expensive was the Grand Trunk's decision (taken after it failed in its attempt to purchase the Great Western) to build a competing line through the heart of Canada West from Toronto to Sarnia. As a result, the two railways often ran parallel to each other and serviced the same area.

George-Étienne Cartier, a government minister, proudly guided the Grand Trunk's charter through the Assembly. A prominent member of Montreal's business community, Cartier served as director of a host of banking, insurance, transportation, and mining companies. At the same time, he acted as solicitor for the Grand Trunk Railway and chaired the Legislative Assembly's Railway Committee. Many other politicians were closely linked with the railways and used their positions in government to attempt to assist their companies with tax concessions, loan guarantees, the assumption of bad debts, and outright grants. They exhibited few scruples about combining personal and state interests. None of today's conflict-of-interest legislation existed at that time.

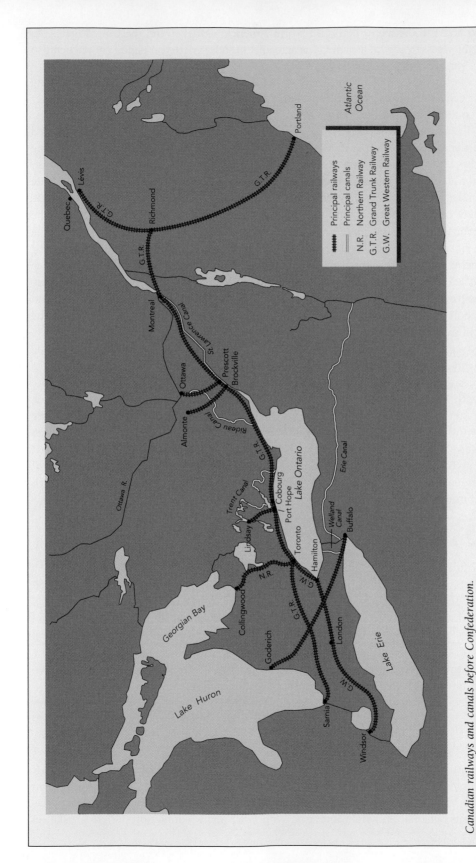

Canadian railways and canals before Confederation.

Source: Adapted from P.G. Cornell, J. Hamelin, F. Ouellet, and M. Trudel, *Canada: Unity in Diversity* (Toronto: Holt, Rinehart and Winston, 1967), p. 239.

In 1859, the Grand Trunk completed the Victoria Bridge, one of the great engineering feats of the century. This 2700 m bridge spanned the St. Lawrence at Montreal. The railway itself, with 1760 km of track, became the longest in the world. This distinction came at great cost to the Canadian public. From the beginning, the company ran into financial trouble, leading its London bankers to approach the provincial government for help. The government agreed to bail it out. To make matters worse, this extravagantly built trunk line had little success in tapping American markets. In the 1850s and 1860s, the Grand Trunk Railway never made a profit.

Railway travel in the mid-nineteenth century could be challenging in the winter. A Grand Trunk Railway locomotive with snow-clearing machine, Lévis, Quebec, February 1869.

Alexander Henderson/Library and Archives Canada/PA-149764.

Moreover, railways in the 1850s and 1860s were unsafe. One accident in 1854 killed 52 people and injured 48. Railway historian G.R. Stevens noted: "Every railway operation seemed to be conducted in a casual and dangerous manner."[5] In a number of derailments the engine drivers had spotted livestock on the line, but instead of slowing down, they speeded up, trying to knock them off the tracks. Signals were ignored, and maintenance of the roadbed was neglected.

Politics in the 1850s and Early 1860s

After 1850, with responsible government a reality, tensions arose between moderate and radical Reformers in Canada West on such divisive issues as political reform, railway policy, financial affairs, and church–state relations. The radical or left-wing Reformers, called "Clear Grits" ("grit" being American slang for firmness of character), denounced Montreal business interests, actively promoted agrarian democracy, and, under journalist George Brown's leadership, became vocal champions of "rep by pop," or representation according to population, the implication being that Canada West, with its larger and rapidly increasing population, deserved a greater number of seats—and, therefore, a preponderant influence over government policy—than did francophone Canada East.

At the same time, in Canada East, the Parti rouge gained ground. The *rouges* tended to be somewhat anticlerical, republican, strongly nationalistic, and—like the Clear Grits in Canada West—highly critical of the close links between government and business. The governing coalition now sought support from conservatives and moderates and as a result, in 1854, the Conservative Party of the future took shape, jointly led by John A. Macdonald and George-Étienne Cartier. George Brown and the Clear Grits of Canada West loosely allied with the rouges, but only once, and just for a two-day period in 1858, did they form a government. Into the early 1860s the Conservatives with precarious majorities ruled. By 1864 the inability of the Province of Canada to produce a stable majority government pushed the colony into a state of political deadlock.

A Capital Is Chosen

In the 1850s, politics often seemed divorced from the everyday concerns of common people. The difficulty of choosing a seat of government or a capital for the united province symbolized this apparent detachment. Political, ethnic, and geographical rivalries transformed the issue into one of the most divisive confronting the union. After 1849, with the burning of the

Parliament building in Montreal, the seat of government shifted between Toronto and Quebec City. Eventually, the Assembly appealed to Queen Victoria to choose a permanent capital. In 1857, it was announced that Ottawa would become the capital.

Urban and Commercial Development

The railways promoted commercial development. They attracted foreign investment, and they employed thousands of workers to lay and maintain track. New railway-related industries sprang up across the province—engine foundries, car shops, rolling mills, and metalwork shops—that all needed skilled and unskilled workers.

Along with canal-building and shipbuilding, railways encouraged the development of a host of secondary industries: flour mills, sawmills, tanneries, boot and shoe factories, textile shops, breweries, distilleries, and wagon and carriage manufacturers. Shipbuilders in Montreal and Quebec City built many of the steamboats that plied the St. Lawrence River and the Great Lakes. Ironworks were established in Hamilton because of the city's easy access to the American coal fields in Pennsylvania. Significant developments in the manufacturing of agricultural implements occurred, especially in Newcastle, Canada West, where Daniel and Hart Massey produced a combined rake, reaper, and mowing machine in 1855, marking the beginning of a lucrative Canadian industry.

This industrial growth led to the creation of a host of towns, especially along the rail lines in Canada West, to service the prosperous agricultural hinterland. Each provided a market centre for local produce and an import centre for manufactured goods. London became the major centre in southwestern Canada West. Hamilton developed as an early industrial city whose port dominated the hinterland to the west and south, extending its influence into the Niagara peninsula.

Toronto enjoyed a central location and good harbour facilities on Lake Ontario. As the railway hub of Canada West, it also serviced a wealthy rural hinterland. Its leading commerce, the import trade, quintupled in value between 1849 and 1856. A new urban mercantile elite appeared in the 1850s. In 1852 the Toronto Stock Exchange opened. By the end of the decade, the city had become the undisputed regional business centre of Canada West.

Montreal remained the largest city and dominant metropolitan centre in British North America. Its location on the St. Lawrence gave it a great advantage over inland Toronto, especially after the canal improvements of the 1840s. The completion of the Grand Trunk Railway provided the city with an ice-free port on the Atlantic at Portland, Maine, and access to the agricultural hinterland of Canada West. Montreal also benefited from the Reciprocity Treaty of 1854, which helped it become a major export centre of Canadian timber and wheat for American markets.

Social Developments

Annually, 25 000 to 40 000 immigrants entered the Canadas, especially the western section, whose population surpassed that of Canada East by 1851. Overall, the population of the Canadas nearly doubled to 2 million between 1841 and 1851.

Many new immigrants came from Ireland, fleeing the famine that resulted from the failure of the potato crop. Recent research by historian Donald Akenson shows that the great majority of Irish immigrants farmed on isolated homesteads in rural areas rather than settling in urban ghettos. Furthermore, most were Protestant.

Harriet Tubman (far left) with some of her "passengers" from the Underground Railway.

The "Underground Railway"

Between 30 000 and 40 000 African Americans also came to the Canadas by 1861. The passage of the Fugitive Slave Act in the United States in 1850 meant that thousands of presumably free African Americans living in the northern states were liable to be captured and sent back into bondage. Instead, many escaped to the Canadas by way of the Underground Railway—a secret, complex network of free blacks, former slaves, and white American and Canadian abolitionists. The largest number of slave fugitives crossed at Amherstburg, situated at the narrowest point of the Detroit River. Other major "terminals" included Windsor, Hamilton, Toronto, and Kingston. One of the most famous "conductors"—as those who helped lead slaves to freedom were termed—was the former slave Harriet Tubman. In all, she made nineteen trips to the South, bringing out at least 300 slaves, and successfully evading all her would-be captors.

COMMUNITY PORTRAIT

The Orange Community in Toronto's Cabbagetown

Formed by Irish Protestants in Ireland in 1795, the Orange Order spread rapidly throughout Ireland and England. In 1830, the Grand Lodge of British North America was organized. By 1870 Canada had more than a thousand Orange Lodges, many in Toronto. Although the Orange Order's membership was spread across all neighbourhoods, Cabbagetown, or East Toronto, an important destination point for Irish Protestant immigrants, boasted the greatest number of Lodges in the city.

The growth of railways and industries in Toronto created large numbers of jobs. In the 1840s, after immigrants spread along both sides of King Street East, they settled on the vacant land to the north. There the newcomers built squatters' shacks and planted vegetable gardens, hence the district's name, "Cabbagetown."

The largely working-class neighbourhood, close to the adjacent factories and packing houses, soon became the home of a vibrant Orange community. Not only Irish immigrants but also English and Scots assisted the spread of the organization. While the bulk of the membership came from the working class, the Toronto Orange community crossed class lines and had a significant middle-class component.

The Orange Lodge celebrated the British Crown and Protestantism. It opposed Catholic schools and the use of the French language outside Quebec. But in the British Protestant fortress of Victorian Toronto, Irish Catholics, not French Canadians, constituted the resident minority group. As John McAree, a prominent Toronto journalist, wrote in *Cabbagetown Store*, his memoir of Cabbagetown: "Catholics were generally spoken of as Dogans, a term of contempt.... They were considered as foreign as if they had been Italians, and were viewed with suspicion." In mid-nineteenth-century Toronto, Protestants outnumbered Catholics by three to one. Clearly religion, not "race," was the focus of opposition of the Order.

Twelfth of July Orange parade along King Street in Toronto, 1874.

Toronto Reference Library/T13222.

The cohesion of Cabbagetown's Orange community came from a system of secret rituals, an internal hierarchy of five "degrees," and the public celebration of July 12, the date of William of Orange's ("King Billy's") victory at the Battle of the Boyne. The Catholics' defeat in 1690 led to the Protestant minority's maintenance of its domination of Ireland. In the nineteenth century, and well into the twentieth, Cabbagetowners, on "the Glorious Twelfth," crammed with thousands of other Torontonians along downtown streets to catch a glimpse of "King Billy" on his white horse in the Orangemen's huge parade, their counterpart to the St. Patrick's Day celebrations.

Some sparring did occur between the Orange community of Cabbagetown and the residents of predominantly Catholic Corktown, located south of Queen Street. In the late 1860s, the militant Orange Young Britons arrived to strengthen the Orange community. John McAree describes this group "made up of husky, strutting young men, mechanics and labourers who were extremely provocative. They would parade frequently and always made it a point of invading a neighbourhood east of Parliament Street and south of Queen Street where there was quite a Roman Catholic settlement. These parades always wound up in fist fights and the throwing of stones."

The Orange community in Cabbagetown assisted its members and their families. It served as a social club, and a mutual aid society, which the lower classes could afford to join. Lodge members helped each other in times of sickness. A primitive insurance system existed to cover burial costs and even to provide lump-sum payments to widows. Orangemen also helped fellow members in the community to find work.

FURTHER READING

J.M.S. Careless, "The Emergence of Cabbagetown in Victorian Toronto," in Robert F. Harney, ed., *Gathering Place: Peoples and Neighbourhoods of Toronto, 1834–1945* (Toronto: Multicultural History Society of Ontario, 1985), pp. 25–45.

Cecil J. Houston and William J. Smyth, *The Sash Canada Wore: A Historical Geography of the Orange Order in Canada* (Toronto: University of Toronto Press, 1980).

Gregory S. Kealey, "The Orange Order in Toronto: Religious Riot and the Working Class," in Michael J. Piva, ed., *A History of Ontario: Selected Readings* (Toronto: Copp Clark Pitman Ltd., 1988), pp. 71–94.

J.V. McAree, *Cabbagetown Store* (Toronto: The Ryerson Press, 1953).

Migrant Mobility in the Canadas

Within Canada West, people moved frequently. In a case study of rural Peel County, just west of Toronto, social historian David Gagan has shown that prior to 1840 the county had ample cheap land and a relatively self-sufficient population of farmers.[6] Two decades later, it had become a major wheat exporting region. Young people moved away from the now overpopulated country areas, to newer farming areas within the province, to the growing towns and cities of Canada West, or even to the American Midwest. Those who remained tended to be better off, with larger farms, a higher standard of living, and better-educated children than those who left. Transiency also characterized urban centres. Individuals of all social groups and classes moved frequently, hoping to improve their living conditions.

In Canada East, continued high birth rates increased the population. By the 1840s, however, existing land was depleted, new agricultural land was scarce, seigneuries were subdivided to the point where the habitants could no longer support their families, and unemployment was high in the urban centres. Large numbers of people began to migrate, in search of industrial jobs in New England or of new farmland in the American Midwest.

The departure of French Canadians for the United States alarmed the Roman Catholic clergy, who feared that migrants would lose their language and their religion. In an effort to stem the exodus, the church urged the colonization of regions further north. These efforts enjoyed some success, but emigration continued. In recognition of this fact the church sent many priests to minister to New England's French-speaking communities.

Urban Structure in Canada West

Within the towns and cities of Canada West, a fairly rigid social structure existed. A growing commercial middle class, consisting of merchants, shopkeepers, and artisans, led society, socially and politically, and was joined by a rising male professional class of clergy, lawyers, doctors, and teachers. Middle-class women were expected to stay at home, where they performed domestic duties and reared children.

Below the professional class stood wage labourers, many of them immigrants. This urban proletariat suffered from poor housing, inadequate sanitation, and seasonal unemployment. Most relied on their own resources to survive. The prevailing ethos held that success came to those who worked hard; frustration and failure were the result of a lack of individual initiative. Canada West thus remained a society modelled on the agrarian values of hardy "yeoman farmers" and robust, self-reliant pioneers. Many working-class families hired out their children for additional family income; other families expected young children to take responsibility at home while older children and the parents worked outside the home.

Urban Development in Quebec

Only two urban centres claimed the title of "city" in Canada East in the 1850s: Montreal and Quebec City. Quebec was the centre of the timber trade. The majority of its commercial elite were English-speaking families associated with that trade. Many of the city's numerous labourers, who inhabited the city's Lower Town, also worked in the timber industry. Here, in overcrowded and dirty conditions, French-Canadian and Irish workers intermingled. In contrast, the Upper Town, where the English lived, was considered "one of the cleanest cities in the world."

Montreal was the largest and the most industrialized city in British North America. As factories were built in the 1840s and 1850s, employment prospects attracted workers from the countryside. By the 1860s, the French-speaking population once again outnumbered the English-speaking in Montreal. These French Canadians, along with the Irish immigrants, provided cheap labour for such industries as footwear manufacturers, furriers, wood-products manufacturers, distilleries, breweries, tobacco factories, brickyards, and sugar refineries.

The eastern end of the city remained overwhelmingly working class and predominantly French Canadian. Poor sanitation resulted in high mortality rates. The city's west end, however, was decidedly bourgeois and British. The English-Canadian commercial entrepreneurs had begun to build luxurious residences on the slopes of Mount Royal. Historian Paul-André

Linteau argues that "social divisions became so visible in Montreal's industrial sector that the city earned the fitting description 'City of wealth and death.' "[7]

Poor working-class families in the city often abandoned their children to the Grey Nuns' Foundling Hospital. Many soon died as a result of their weakened condition upon arrival and the lack of pasteurized milk. The Roman Catholic church also looked after the several thousand Irish orphans whose parents had died on the Atlantic crossing. Raised as French Canadians, they intermarried with that group.

A Working-Class Consciousness

Industrialization stimulated the development of a working-class consciousness in the Canadas, as impersonal working conditions, due to the expansion of the factory system, became the norm. From the 1830s, skilled and semiskilled workers joined together to form local trade unions and self-help organizations to deal with changing conditions. With definite skills to offer employers, they enjoyed far more job security than did labourers. Generally speaking they preferred strikes as a weapon, while unskilled workers had recourse to spontaneous rioting.

Labourers organized two early strikes: one on the Lachine Canal in 1843, and the other on the Welland Canal in 1844–1845. In both cases, they demanded improved working conditions and higher wages. In 1849, during the protests over free trade, shoemakers in Montreal ravaged a shoe factory and destroyed the sewing machines, in the tradition of the British Luddites, who opposed the mechanization of industry. By the 1860s strikes had generally replaced riots as the main form of labour protest, although they, too, were illegal. (Even trade unions were illegal until 1872.) Police or troops often assisted employers in quelling labour unrest.

The Prohibition Movement

The rise of an urban working class had an impact on the prohibition movement throughout British North America. By the 1850s, there was a noticeable shift in emphasis from temperance—abstinence through self-discipline—to outright prohibition. Social historian Graeme Decarie argues that this shift in Canada West came about as a result of a perceived threat to traditional rural Protestant middle-class values from the growing urban working class (often made up of Irish Catholics). Prohibition became a means for some middle-class Protestants to reassert their position of power and prominence.[8] Quebec's great "apostle of temperance" was Charles Chiniquy, a lively and eccentric Roman Catholic priest, who persuaded thousands to take the pledge of abstinence. (Sexual escapades and charges of embezzlement later led to Chiniquy's excommunication from the Roman Catholic church.)

Religion

Religion played an important role in Canadian society. In Canada West, in the 1840s, the Church of England was the declared church affiliation of one-fifth of the population. The Presbyterians and Methodists followed closely, and then the Baptists. Roman Catholics, mainly Irish immigrants, made up 14 percent of the population in 1841.

This shift in focus of churches from rural to urban meant a shift in emphasis from evangelicalism and an emotional approach to religion to an educated clergy and a more rational approach to faith. As well, urban-oriented society required churches to address issues of social reform with regard to such groups as the poor and the sick.

In Canada East, Ignace Bourget, Roman Catholic bishop of Montreal, successfully encouraged French religious orders to come to Quebec to help "Christianize" his diocesans. He also founded new male and female orders that took responsibility for elementary education, the classical colleges, hospitals, and charitable organizations. Bourget was an advocate of ultramontanism, the belief that the state should be linked to and dominated by the church. To this end, he worked to ensure that education remained under the control of the church instead of coming under state control.

Education and Culture

In the mid-nineteenth century, education entered public debate in the Canadas. Schools multiplied to keep pace with the growing population, and the question of separate schools became a contentious issue in Canada West.

Education in Canada West

State-supported schools developed in the union period. In Canada West, legislation created the office of superintendent of education to oversee educational matters and established local boards of education with powers to tax inhabitants to build and maintain schools. Opposition to the bill arose among those who argued that public funds should also be used to support separate schools for Roman Catholics, just as they were to support Protestant schools in Quebec. French-Canadian members of the Assembly from Canada East gave the supporters of separate schools in Canada West the majority they needed to ensure that Catholic schools received state funding.

At the heart of the separate-school controversy lay the question of the role of education. Roman Catholic leaders believed that education should have a religious component and that religious instruction should be in keeping with the teachings and beliefs of the Roman Catholic church. Opponents of separate schools, such as Egerton Ryerson, who served as superintendent of education for Canada West (Ontario) from 1844 to 1876, and George Brown, the influential political reformer and newspaper editor, argued that education should be free, publicly funded, and nonsectarian. They believed that separate schools perpetuated sectarianism and undermined the common-school system. The debate between these two approaches to education continued throughout the nineteenth century.

Separate and common schools proliferated in Canada West in the 1850s and 1860s. A Roman Catholic separate-school system came into being, with tax support from parents, who were exempt from paying common-school taxes. In 1863, a final pre-Confederation education bill allowed separate schools to receive a share of both the provincial and municipal grants, and extended separate schools into rural areas. In return for these concessions, separate schools, like their common-school counterparts, submitted to provincial inspection, centralized control of curriculum and textbooks, and government control of all teacher training. This system remained in effect when Canada West entered Confederation as the province of Ontario in 1867.

Common or public schools also came under greater centralized control as a result of Ryerson's efforts. His Common School Act of 1846 established a board of education responsible for assisting the chief superintendent in establishing provincial standards, founded a normal school to train teachers, and made locally elected school boards responsible for operating the schools in their sections. These schools were expected to teach children good moral values—that is, Christian values—as well as to prepare them for work in an expanding commercial economy. Ryerson believed a centralized and highly regulated system could best achieve these goals. Here lay the foundation of the modern Ontario school system.

A similar process of secularism occurred in higher education. In 1849, the government changed the Anglican-affiliated King's College into the nonsectarian University of Toronto.

Once King's College had been transformed into the "godless" University of Toronto, John Strachan, Anglican Bishop of Toronto, founded Trinity University. (Later Trinity, the Methodists' Victoria University, and St. Michael's, a Roman Catholic college, all became affiliates of the University of Toronto.)

Education in Canada East

In Canada East, the Lower Canadian School Act of 1846 provided for two state-aided school systems, one Catholic and one Protestant. Within each Catholic school in Canada East, the local priest had the right to veto the selection of teachers and textbooks, thus leaving only the task of financing the schools to the provincial authorities.

Later, the legislature established a normal school to educate teachers, and set up the Council of Public Instruction to assist the superintendent in making regulations for the normal school, for the organization and administration of common schools, and for the grading of schools and teachers.

At the university level, the English-language McGill University, chartered in 1821, gave instruction in law, medicine, and the arts. Under the guidance of its able principal, William Dawson, McGill later acquired a distinguished reputation, especially in scientific research and medicine. In 1852, Université Laval was founded, having developed out of the Séminaire de Québec, founded by Bishop Laval in 1663. Steeped in the French Catholic tradition, the first French-Canadian university soon gained a position of respect in Canada East, with its courses in theology, civil law, medicine, and the arts.

Culture in the Canadas

With the growth of towns and the rise of an urban middle class, the range of cultural activities expanded. In Canada East, François-Xavier Garneau wrote a monumental *Histoire du Canada* as a direct response to Lord Durham's denunciation of French Canadians as a "backward people." Octave Crémazie was the greatest French-Canadian poet of the period, popular for his nostalgic references to the glories of New France. Good-quality newspapers existed, and journalists and public figures gave popular lectures on important topics of the day such as education and nationality. In 1843 newspaper editor Ludger Duvernay organized the Société Saint-Jean-Baptiste de Montréal, a patriotic organization established to promote the interests of French Canada.

Literature in English developed slowly. Poetry became popular during the 1860s. William Kirby described the migration of Loyalists to Niagara in his poem *The U.E.L.*, while Charles Sangster captured the beauty of the Canadian landscape in *The St. Lawrence and the Saguenay*. Other writers included Susanna Moodie and her sister Catharine Parr Traill, both of whom obtained publishers, and a readership, in Britain. Amateur historians wrote in praise of early pioneers. However, no significant publishing industry existed until the late nineteenth century.

In 1855 John McMullen, a journalist, produced the first history of Canada in English. McMullen sought to "infuse a spirit of Canadian nationality into the people generally." Newspapers, among them Toronto's *Globe*, helped cultivate a national feeling among English Canadians.

In the mid-nineteenth century, Canada's urban music life expanded, although few Canadian-born professional musicians could support themselves with only their performances and teaching. Growing prosperity also enlarged the market for artists. Well-known painters included Cornelius Krieghoff and Napoléon Bourassa. By 1860, William Notman of Montreal had already established his reputation as a photographer.

Tourism as a Form of Popular Culture

In popular culture, areas of wilderness began to take on special significance as tourist spots, often in juxtaposition to what was meant by their opposite—civilization—in the Victorian mind. As the wilderness began to be "conquered" and thus lost its threatening nature, as Aboriginal people became more "civilized" and declined dramatically in numbers, and as landscape became imbued with a sense of the romantic and sublime, tourism emerged as a "growth industry." Historian Patricia Jasen notes,

> The tourist industry was an ally of many forms of economic development in the nineteenth century, such as the growth of railways and steamer companies, and all of these industries were intimately associated with the gospel of expansionism, whereby the fate of the "unsettled" regions of Canada was identified with the interests of the metropolis.[9]

Tourism was, however, the preserve of the upper and middle classes. Only they had money and leisure time.

Niagara Falls, above all other tourist attractions, became a special place, attracting as many as 40 000 visitors a year by the late 1840s. From the beginning, Niagara Falls became associated with sexual pleasure, especially as "the Honeymoon Capital of the World." Historian Karen Dubinsky has shown how the "purity" of the Falls, its gendered nature as a female icon, evident in such descriptions of the Falls as "the Queen of the Cataracts," and the fact that the observer of such beauty was usually depicted as a male, "enhanced the spectatorial pleasure of 'doing' Niagara."[10] Already in the mid-nineteenth century, tourist agents realized the importance of identifying natural sites as places of pleasure, especially sexual pleasure.

During the 1840s and 1850s, the United Canadas underwent considerable economic and social change. Canadians adjusted to the end of the mercantile system of trade, to the advent of the railway age, and to rapidly changing social conditions in both rural and urban life. This was an age of transition from a British-oriented to an American-oriented economy and from a pioneer to a commercial society. The shift took decades to complete, but it saw its start in the period 1840 to 1860. Culturally, a French-Canadian identity already existed, but beside it an Upper Canadian or English-Canadian collective identity continued to take shape.

Politically, the coming of responsible government represented a significant milestone in the movement toward democracy and autonomy. For the French, in particular, the dire prophecies of assimilation made at the birth of union did not materialize, though ethnic and religious prejudice remained rampant throughout the era. Chronic political instability helped seal the fate of the union. By 1864, the Canadas again prepared for constitutional change.

NOTES

1. S.J.R. Noel, *Patrons, Clients, Brokers: Ontario Society and Politics, 1791–1896* (Toronto: University of Toronto Press, 1990), p. 175.

2. Peter Way, "The Canadian Tory Rebellion of 1849 and the Demise of Street Politics in Toronto," *British Journal of Canadian Studies*, 10 (1995): 10.

3. Noel, *Patrons, Clients, Brokers*, p. 151.

4. See A.R.M. Lower, *The North American Assault on the Canadian Forest* (Toronto: Ryerson Press, 1938).

5. G.R. Stevens, *Canadian National Railways*, vol. 1 (Toronto: Clarke Irwin, 1960), p. 110.

6. David Gagan, *Hopeful Travellers: Families, Land and Social Change in Mid-Victorian Peel County, Canada West* (Toronto: University of Toronto Press, 1981), pp. 20ff.

7. Paul-André Linteau, "Montreal: City of Pride," *Horizon Canada*, 4 (1984): 88.

8. Graeme Decarie, *Prohibition in Canada*, Canada's Visual History Series, vol. 29 (Ottawa: National Museum of Man, ca. 1975), p. 3.

9. Patricia Jasen, *Wild Things: Nature, Culture, and Tourism in Ontario, 1790–1914* (Toronto: University of Toronto Press, 1995), p. 152.

10. Karen Dubinsky, " 'The Pleasure Is Exquisite but Violent': The Imaginary Geography of Niagara Falls in the Nineteenth Century," *Journal of Canadian Studies*, 29, 2 (Summer 1994): 75.

BEYOND THE BOOK

The Reciprocity Treaty, 1854

http://www.collectionscanada.ca/confederation/023001-2996-e.html
A digitized copy of the Reciprocity Treaty of 1854.

Safe Passage: Aids to Navigation on the St. Lawrence

http://www.mccord-museum.qc.ca/en/keys/webtours/VQ_P1_5_EN
The St. Lawrence was the critical transport waterway for economic activity in the Canadas in the nineteenth century. This site details how the St. Lawrence was navigated with documents and drawings of the era.

The Cult of Domesticity

http://www.mccord-museum.qc.ca/en/keys/webtours/VQ_P1_6_EN
Pictures and records of the home life of women in Canada in the mid-1800s. Marriages, family life, and recreation are topics explored.

Pastimes of Yesteryear, 1840–1867

http://www.mccord-museum.qc.ca/en/keys/webtours/VQ_P1_4_EN
A detailed exploration of how leisure time was spent in the Canadas in the mid-1800s, complete with photographs, paintings, and other digitized historical documents.

Roughing It in the Bush

http://www.canadiana.org/ECO/mtq?doc=26276
Roughing It in the Bush was first published in England in 1852. It details Susanna Moodie's experiences as an immigrant homesteading with her family in the woods of Upper Canada.

Union and Responsible Government

http://www.canadiana.org/oitm/themes/constitution/constitution11_e.html
A detailed account of political developments of the era such as the impact of the Durham Report and the process toward responsible government. Also included are links to original primary documents such as the Rebellion Losses Bill of 1849.

Freedom's Land

Canadian Experience—Freedom's Land: Canada and the Underground Railroad (CBC, 2005).

BIBLIOGRAPHY

The union years are examined in J.M.S. Careless, *The Union of the Canadas: The Growth of Canadian Institutions, 1841–1857* (Toronto: McClelland & Stewart, 1967); and W.L. Morton, *The Critical Years: The Union of British North America, 1857–1873* (Toronto: University of Toronto Press, 1964). Economic history is examined in Fernand Ouellet, *Economic and Social History of Quebec, 1760–1850* (Toronto: Macmillan, 1980); and Douglas McCalla, *Planting the Province: The Economic History of Upper Canada, 1784–1870* (Toronto: University of Toronto Press, 1993). Donald G. Creighton develops the Laurentian thesis in *The Empire of the St. Lawrence: A Study in Commerce and Politics* [1937], with new introduction by Christopher Moore (Toronto: University of Toronto Press, 2002).

On agriculture, see John McCallum, *Unequal Beginnings: Agriculture and Economic Development in Quebec and Ontario until 1870* (Toronto: University of Toronto Press, 1980); and Serge Courville and Normand Séguin, *Rural Life in Nineteenth-Century Quebec* (Ottawa: Canadian Historical Association, 1989). A.R.M. Lower reviews the timber trade in *Great Britain's Woodyard: British America and the Timber Trade, 1763–1867* (Montreal/Kingston: McGill-Queen's University Press, 1973). On railway building in the 1850s, see G.P. de T. Glazebrook, *A History of Transportation in Canada*, vol. 1 (Toronto: McClelland & Stewart, 1964).

Urban and commercial development is discussed in Jacob Spelt, *Urban Development in South-Central Ontario* (Toronto: McClelland & Stewart, 1972 [1955]); and G. Tulchinsky, *The River Barons: Montreal Businessmen and the Growth of Industry and Transportation, 1837–1853* (Toronto: University of Toronto Press, 1977). R. Cole Harris and John Warkentin, *Canada before Confederation* (Ottawa: Carleton University Press, 1991 [1974]), provide an overview of social developments in the Province of Canada. A more recent account appears in Cole Harris, *The Reluctant Land. Society, Space, and Environment In Canada before Confederation* (Vancouver: UBC Press, 2008), pp. 231–376. Books on minority groups include Donald H. Akenson, *The Irish in Ontario: A Study in Rural History* (Montreal/Kingston: McGill-Queen's University Press, 1984); and Robin W. Winks, *The Blacks in Canada*, 2nd ed. (Montreal/Kingston: McGill-Queen's University Press, 1997).

Biographies of political figures include Donald G. Creighton, *John A. Macdonald: The Young Politician* (Toronto: Macmillan, 1956) and Richard Gwyn, *John A: The Man Who Made Us: The Life and Times of John A. Macdonald. Volume One: 1815–1867* (Toronto: Random House, 2007); and J.M.S. Careless, *Brown of the Globe*, 2 vols. (Toronto: Macmillan, 1959 and 1963). On the development of the state, see Allan Greer and Ian Radforth, eds., *Colonial Leviathan: State Formation in Mid-Nineteenth-Century Canada* (Toronto: University of Toronto Press, 1992). Works on political culture include Jane Errington, *The Lion, the Eagle, and Upper Canada: A Developing Colonial Ideology* (Montreal/Kingston: McGill-Queen's University Press, 1987); and A.B. McKillop and Paul Romney, eds., *God's Peculiar Peoples: Essays on Political Culture in Nineteenth-Century Canada* (Ottawa: Carleton University Press, 1993). British policy toward Canada is discussed in Phillip Buckner, *The Transition to Responsible Government: British Policy in British North America, 1815–1850* (Westport, CT: Greenwood Press, 1985); and Ged Martin, *Britain and the Origins of Canadian Confederation, 1837–67* (Vancouver: University of British Columbia Press, 1995).

The First Nations' history is reviewed in Daniel Francis, *A History of the Native Peoples of Quebec, 1760–1867* (Ottawa: Department of Indian Affairs and Northern Development, 1983); and Edward S. Rogers and Donald B. Smith, eds., *Aboriginal Ontario: Historical Perspectives on the First Nations* (Toronto: Dundurn Press, 1994). Women's history is covered in Alison Prentice et al., *Canadian Women: A History*, 2nd ed. (Toronto: Harcourt Brace, 1996); and Micheline Dumont et al., *Quebec Women: A History* (Toronto: Women's Press, 1987). On the history of the working class, consult Paul Craven, ed., *Labouring Lives: Work and Workers in Nineteenth-Century Ontario* (Toronto: University of Toronto Press, 1995).

Educational questions are treated in J.D. Wilson, R.M. Stamp, and L.P. Audet, *Canadian Education: A History* (Scarborough, ON: Prentice-Hall, 1970). On religion see John Webster Grant, *A Profusion of Spires: Religion in Nineteenth-Century Ontario* (Toronto: University of Toronto Press, 1988). Jan Noel examines the temperance movement in *Canada Dry: Temperance Crusades before Confederation* (Toronto: University of Toronto Press, 1995).

Portraits of leading individuals in the Canadas appear in the *Dictionary of Canadian Biography*, now available online at www.biographi.ca. Excellent maps of the Canadas may be found in R. Louis Gentilcore, ed., *Historical Atlas of Canada*, vol. 2, *The Land Transformed, 1800–1891* (Toronto: University of Toronto Press, 1993).

INTRODUCTION

After the deportation of the Acadians from Nova Scotia in 1755, a group of New Englanders, known as the Planters settled there. During the American Revolution, it seemed that Nova Scotia might become the fourteenth American colony; instead, it remained neutral.

When Loyalists arrived in the post-revolutionary period, most settled in the Saint John River valley. They appealed to Britain for their own government, free from the control of Halifax. Britain complied by creating the colony of New Brunswick in 1784. Prince Edward Island had been a colony since 1769. Cape Breton became part of Nova Scotia in 1820. Newfoundland became a colony in 1824.

Between 1815 and 1867, distinct British American colonies emerged on the Atlantic coast. In New Brunswick the economy was based on agriculture and lumbering. In Nova Scotia, fishing villages grew along the Bay of Fundy and the Atlantic seaboard, while agriculture predominated in the Annapolis Valley. Newfoundland's economy was heavily dependent on the cod fisheries of the Grand Banks. All of these Atlantic colonies traded with Britain, the United States, and the West Indies.

By the 1850s, the Maritime colonies had achieved responsible government without resorting to rebellion. In Newfoundland, the naval governor had near-dictatorial powers until 1832, when Britain instituted an elected Assembly and an appointed Legislative Council. But only in 1855 was responsible government implemented, thus ending direct British rule.

In the North West, the Red River colony emerged at the confluence of the Red and Assiniboine Rivers, consisting of French Métis (children of French fur traders and First Nations women), the "Country-born" (offspring of British fur traders and First Nations women), and descendants of the Selkirk settlers who arrived from Britain in the early nineteenth century. The colony's economy was based on a mixture of trade in buffalo hides and small-scale agriculture. Tensions arose here in the 1810s when the Hudson's Bay Company and the North West Company vied for dominance over the fur trade. In 1821, the British government forced them to amalgamate. The new Hudson's Bay Company attempted to monopolize the fur trade, but the Métis resisted.

On the north Pacific coast, Britain and the United States jointly controlled Oregon Territory. In 1846, the two countries agreed to divide the territory by extending the boundary along the 49th parallel from the Rockies to the coast, with Britain acquiring all of Vancouver Island. With the discovery of gold in the Fraser River valley in 1858, Britain created a separate colony on the mainland. In 1866, this mainland colony and the colony on Vancouver Island were united into the colony of British Columbia. In the 1860s, British Columbians had three options: remain a British colony, join the United States, or become part of Canada.

To the north, the land remained in Aboriginal control, visited only by a small number of fur traders and by a few explorers searching for the Northwest Passage to Asia.

Chapter Eight

ATLANTIC CANADA, 1760–1864

TIME LINE

1759–1760	The Planters from New England begin arriving in great numbers in Nova Scotia
1767	Saint John's Island, named Prince Edward Island in 1799, is granted by lottery to British proprietors
1784	New Brunswick and Cape Breton (to 1820) are established as separate jurisdictions
1824	Newfoundland is made a regular British colony
1829	The last known surviving Beothuk, Shawnadithit, dies
1848	Responsible government is achieved in Nova Scotia, and later in Prince Edward Island (1851), New Brunswick (1854), and Newfoundland (1855)
1854	The Reciprocity Treaty with the United States is signed
1864	The governments of New Brunswick, Nova Scotia, and Prince Edward Island agree to meet in Charlottetown to discuss Maritime union

After the British conquest of Canada, the Thirteen Colonies moved toward independence. The United States, however, would not include all of British North America. Nova Scotia, the new colony of Saint John's Island (created in 1769 and renamed Prince Edward Island in 1799), Newfoundland, and the former French colony of Quebec remained part of the British empire.

Britain easily maintained control of the small, isolated colony of Saint John's Island, with its settler population of only 1000 recent British arrivals, and Acadians. As for Newfoundland, its Anglo-Irish population looked eastward to Britain rather than southward to the Thirteen Colonies. In contrast, over half of Nova Scotia's approximately 20 000 inhabitants came from New England. They maintained strong economic and cultural ties with their former homeland. Nova Scotia, which then comprised the whole of present-day Nova Scotia and New Brunswick, faced a difficult decision concerning which side to support in the American Revolution. Initially, it looked as if Nova Scotia might become the fourteenth insurgent colony, but it chose to stay in the British empire in 1775–1776, and it did so again in the War of 1812.

In the early nineteenth century the population of Atlantic British North America lived widely scattered in isolated coastline communities and forested valleys, with only a few larger centres, such as St. John's, Saint John, Halifax, and Fredericton. Economically, Newfoundland remained dependent on the fisheries. But the full development of the land-based resources in the Maritimes began in the early nineteenth century. On the eve of Confederation, Nova Scotia, New Brunswick, and Prince Edward Island had healthy economies based on agriculture, fish, forest products, and trade with the West Indies.

The half-century following the Napoleonic Wars also witnessed major political developments. By the 1850s, Nova Scotia, New Brunswick, Prince Edward Island, and Newfoundland had achieved responsible government, with the Executive Council (Cabinet) in each colony drawn from the majority party in the Assembly, and responsible to it. Power now passed to the elective branch of government.

New England's Outpost

With the deportation of the Acadians in 1755 and the capture of Louisbourg in 1758, Americans began moving north. The British authorities wanted to attract loyal Protestant settlers in order to prevent the deported Acadians' return. In crowded, heavily settled southeastern Massachusetts, eastern Connecticut, and Rhode Island, the invitation had great appeal among the poorer farmers. Hundreds of fishers anxious to locate closer to the Grand Banks also came. These New England farmers and fishers became known as the Planters. Between 1759 and 1767, some 8000 Planters from New England settled in Nova Scotia. Most of the immigrants went to the Annapolis valley in peninsular Nova Scotia, to fertile lands previously cleared and diked by the Acadians, and to the area around Cumberland, near present-day Sackville, New Brunswick. A much smaller number entered the Saint John River valley, forming small frontier communities at the mouth of the river and at Maugerville (just south of present-day Fredericton), along the lower Saint John River. On account of the difficult conditions a number of the recent arrivals returned to their homes in New England in the 1760s.

The Planters who remained worked to create a new English-speaking Nova Scotia. But the lack of roads linking the settlements prevented regular communication. As historian George Rawlyk noted, "on the eve of the American Revolution, Nova Scotia was little more than a political expression for a number of widely scattered and isolated communities."[1] Nevertheless, on the eve of the American Revolution, New Englanders constituted about half of Nova Scotia's total population of nearly 20 000.

Americans were still migrating to the forested lands north of the Bay of Fundy when hundreds of Acadians returned. In 1764, the British government permitted them to settle in

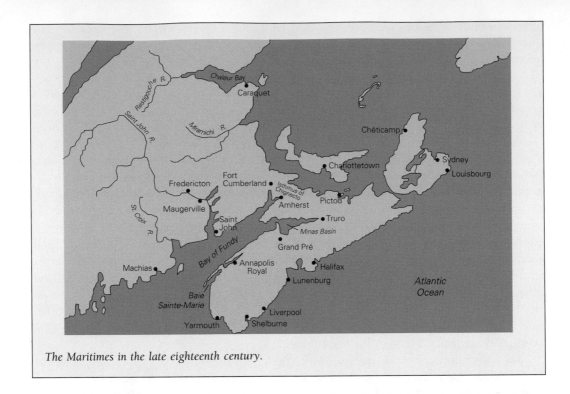

The Maritimes in the late eighteenth century.

Nova Scotia, providing that they dispersed throughout the colony. Many returned not to their farms, which were now occupied by New Englanders, but to the Bay of Chaleur, on the present-day border between Quebec and New Brunswick. The settlement of Caraquet became a focal point for the region. Other Acadians lived on farms along the lower Saint John River.

Several thousand British immigrants came to Nova Scotia in the 1760s and 1770s. They joined the original British residents of Halifax, the 1500 or so Acadians who had returned, and the approximately 1500 "foreign Protestants," largely Germans, who resided south of Halifax in the area around Lunenburg.

Nova Scotia and the American Revolution

Halifax, as Nova Scotia's only urban centre, became the colony's capital. It housed the military establishment and published the province's only newspaper. The upper level of Halifax society, headed by the governor, included his senior officials, and a group of merchants who had grown rich from army and navy contracts. A handful of smaller merchants and professional people also lived in the colony's capital. The rest of the city's population consisted of poor fishers, carpenters, mechanics, and labourers. Nova Scotia obtained an elected assembly in 1758, but few rural members could afford to take their seats as unpaid legislators. As a result, a small clique of Halifax merchants controlled both the Assembly and the Governor's Council.

The rebellion rhetoric in the Thirteen Colonies in 1775–1776 found an audience in rural Nova Scotia. Many New Englanders resented Britain's unfulfilled promises of constitutional rights. At annual town meetings, New England voters elected their officers and decided local issues. But in Nova Scotia in the 1760s, this form of township democracy did not exist; instead, London built a tightly controlled, centralized government structure. The merchant-controlled Assembly in Halifax, which strongly supported the governor, worked to eliminate local township government.

It appointed justices of the peace to administer the local areas and did not allow the election of township officials.

The communities farthest from Halifax showed the greatest enthusiasm for the American cause. The town of Machias, on the vaguely defined border between Nova Scotia and Maine, the Maugerville settlement on the lower Saint John River, and the Chignecto–Cumberland region at the head of the Bay of Fundy became active centres of support for the American Revolution. Jonathan Eddy, a New Englander who farmed in the Chignecto region, took the lead in organizing the revolutionary movement there. His invasion force of about 180 men attacked British-held Fort Cumberland in 1776. But they had no artillery to mount a siege. Few New Englanders on the isthmus openly supported Eddy's small, poorly trained, undisciplined, and badly led army. With the arrival of British reinforcements, Eddy's troops fled in disarray. The British burned the homes and barns of his supporters. The following summer, British naval vessels entered the Bay of Fundy and took control of the area. The Americans' lack of a navy and their failure to win sufficient support among Nova Scotians best explain Britain's success in expelling the revolutionaries.

First Nations and Acadian Responses

The British also obtained the neutrality of most of the thousand or so Mi'kmaqs and Maliseets who held the balance of power north of the Bay of Fundy. By now the British had adopted the French techniques of gift diplomacy, giving their Aboriginal allies presents of food, medicine, and ammunition. In addition, Britain appeared to be the stronger of the two opponents after it extended its control over the Bay of Fundy and captured the coastline of northern Maine from the Americans. Thanks to the First Nations, the upper Saint John River valley remained in the British zone of influence throughout the war. The Acadians, for their part, had no interest in becoming involved in the civil war between the two English-speaking groups.

Growing Antagonism toward the American Revolutionaries

While the American insurgents consolidated their hold on the former Thirteen Colonies, Nova Scotia moved in a different direction. American raids on Nova Scotia made many once-sympathetic Nova Scotians antagonistic to the American revolutionaries. No Nova Scotia port (except Halifax) escaped the raiders, who seized anything they could carry away. These attacks alienated wealthy citizens in Yarmouth, Lunenburg, and Liverpool, and prompted them to launch their own retaliatory attacks against American shipping. By 1781, settlements in the Minas Basin and the Bay of Fundy area, which in 1775–1776 had opposed increased taxes for military defence, now willingly accepted militia service and taxes to meet the cost of defending the colony.

Henry Alline and the New Light Movement

The unwillingness of many New Englanders in Nova Scotia to support the American Revolution can also be explained by a great religious revival in the colony led by a charismatic young man named Henry Alline. In the late 1770s and early 1780s, a religious gospel rather than a political one monopolized the attention of Nova Scotians.

Born and raised in Rhode Island, Alline belonged to the Congregational church, the church to which most New England immigrants in Nova Scotia adhered. In 1760 his family settled in one of the richest farming areas in the colony—the Minas Basin, near present-day Windsor. The 12-year-old received no further schooling, for no school existed in his township. Nor was there a church. Families maintained their religion through family prayer, Bible reading, and religious discussions at home. But Alline came into contact with an evangelical group that emphasized the need for an intensely emotional conversion experience known as the "New Light."

In 1776, at the age of 28, Alline began his career as an itinerant preacher. Convinced that God had selected him to carry His message, he travelled constantly. The evangelist often rode as far as 80 km a day, bringing religion to rural people. His willingness to preach under all conditions struck a responsive chord among the economically impoverished rural Nova Scotians on their frontier farms. They heard Alline and believed him when he told them that Nova Scotia had become the new centre of Christendom.

Alline's religious revival filled the spiritual vacuum in the new settlements far away from the revolutionary struggle. Very effectively, he spread his message that good Christians should work to secure their spiritual salvation rather than fight military battles. He convinced many Nova Scotians that they were performing a special role—bringing the world back to God—and that Christ merited their allegiance, not the British or the revolutionaries. As a result, Nova Scotia's "New Light" communities chose political neutrality and worked instead to perfect their spiritual condition.

Alline died of tuberculosis in early February 1784, leaving behind scores of disciples and hundreds of followers. After his death, his manuscript journals were copied and recopied by hand and circulated among his followers until they were published in 1806. Alline's disciples, popularly referred to as Allinites, later became members of the Baptist church and carried on the teachings of the "Apostle of Nova Scotia."

Throughout the Thirteen Colonies, a substantial number of Americans opposed the American Revolution and wanted to remain loyal to Britain. Historians now estimate that approximately 20 percent of the white American population in 1776 (roughly half a million people) became Loyalists.[2] They were strongest in New York, partly because New York had a strong British aristocracy, and weakest in Connecticut, Massachusetts, and Virginia. Loyalists came from every class, race, occupation, religion, and geographical region. They supported Britain for many diverse reasons, ranging from personal loyalty to the Crown to a fear that the revolution would threaten individual freedoms.

Loyalists who served as colonial office holders had a vested interest in maintaining the status quo. But a high proportion of Loyalists also came from religious and cultural minorities. Not yet having joined mainstream American society, recent immigrants from Europe (Germany, the Netherlands, and the British Isles) and members of religious minorities (such as the French Huguenots, Maryland Roman Catholics, and Quaker pacifists) held on to the British connection for fear that increased American power could result in a loss of their religious freedoms. The First Nations, particularly the Iroquois, looked upon Britain as the lesser of two evils, since Britain wished to slow the advance of the American settlers westward, anxious as it was to avoid the increased expenditures of more wars with the Aboriginal peoples. African Americans saw an opportunity to free themselves as slaves by joining the British and fleeing their owners.

Persecution of the Loyalists

Persecution of the Loyalists began as early as 1774, when it became more and more difficult to maintain neutrality in face of the approaching struggle. With the passing of the Declaration of Independence, the local revolutionary committees stepped up their activities against Loyalists. Various states disenfranchised, put in prison, banished, and fined "Tories" and confiscated their property as well. In Loyalist-controlled areas, outrages were also committed against, and restrictions of civil liberties imposed on, those believed to be supporters of the revolution.

WHERE HISTORIANS DISAGREE

Why Didn't Nova Scotia Join the American Revolution?

On the eve of the American Revolutionary War in 1775–1776, about half of Nova Scotia's 20 000 settlers were New Englanders. The colony appeared to be a northern outpost of New England. Why, then, did it refuse to join the revolution?

Historian Beamish Murdoch offered the first explanation. New England farmers, who had been given land previously owned by the Acadians when they arrived after the Conquest, were, as a result, "full of intense loyalty and affection to the British government."[1] Some 70 years later, in the 1930s, Professor Viola Barnes added an economic motive: Halifax merchants and Governor Francis Legge kept Nova Scotia loyal to the Crown because it was in their best interest to do so. When the Americans boycotted West Indies trade, Halifax merchants saw their opportunity to appropriate the trade themselves. "In short," she wrote, "Nova Scotia remained loyal because the merchant class in control believed the Province profited more than it lost by the connection with the mother country, and because the Governor, with their help, was able to prevent the radicals from stirring the people to revolt."[2]

Other historians now entered the fray. W.B. Kerr challenged Barnes's interpretation. He questioned why Nova Scotia merchants would object to New Englanders carrying a monopoly of their trade, since they were New Englanders themselves. Furthermore, they were free to pursue their own trade if they so desired. Kerr then offered his own explanation, "the almost total want of sympathy among artisans, fishermen, and farmers for the American cause." Furthermore, the Nova Scotia legislature, made up of a majority of New Englanders, expressed their loyalty to the King on the eve of the revolution, acknowledging him to be the "supreme Legislature of the province and it is our indispensable duty to pay a due proportion of the expense of this great Empire."[3] Nova Scotia historian D.C. Harvey added yet another explanation: Nova Scotians "were inclined to submit to the will of the stronger."[4] Simply put, British naval power surpassed that of the rebels.

In 1937, noted historian J.B. Brebner argued that geographical isolation, as well as close economic ties to Britain through mercantile trade, kept Nova Scotia insulated from activities elsewhere on the continent. As he concluded: "Nova Scotia had insulated and neutralized the New England migrants so thoroughly that as Nova Scotians they had henceforth to look eastward to London for direction and help rather than southward to Boston as they had done in the past."[5]

Beginning in the 1940s, historians became interested in religious revivalism as a factor in keeping Nova Scotians neutral. M.W. Armstrong saw the "Great Awakening" (as this revival was called) as "an expression of democratic ideals and spiritual independence" that raised the minds of Nova Scotians above worldly concerns. How could "King George" and the revolution compete with "King Jesus" and redemption, he queried?[6] In 1959, sociologist S.D. Clark applied Frederick Jackson Turner's frontier thesis to an understanding of Nova Scotia's neutrality during the revolution.[7] He saw the New Light religious revival in the outposts of

Nova Scotia as a frontier movement of social protest that strengthened the spirit of local autonomy and resolved their determination to be politically independent of both Britain and its Halifax political agents, and New England.

Professors Gordon Stewart and George Rawlyk introduced their "Missing Decade" thesis. They argued that those New Englanders who migrated to Nova Scotia in the early 1760s missed the rebellious rhetoric that occurred between 1765 and 1775. Therefore they could not identify with their arguments.[8] Rawlyk then went on to explore the role of Henry Alline, the charismatic leader of the religious revival in Nova Scotia, in keeping Nova Scotians neutral. Rawlyk argued that Alline's message to Nova Scotia "Yankees" that they had a divine mission "to lead the world back to God" gave them a purpose above and beyond that of worldly revolution.[9]

More recently, J.M. Bumsted has questioned both the size and the importance of the New England population in Nova Scotia during the American Revolution. He argues that as the war got under way, Nova Scotia "Yankees" who supported the rebel cause returned to New England and therefore played no part in Nova Scotia's decision. As well, the strong British military presence in the colony, and resentment among Nova Scotians at the destructive behaviour of the American rebels within the colony, kept them neutral.[10] The question of why Nova Scotia did not become the fourteenth state continues to intrigue historians.

1. Beamish Murdoch, *History of Nova Scotia or Acadie*, vol. 2 (Halifax: J. Barnes, 1865–67), p. 562.

2. V.F. Barnes, "Francis Legge, Governor of Loyalist Nova Scotia, 1773–1776," *New England Quarterly*, July 1931; quoted in George A. Rawlyk, ed., *Revolution Rejected, 1775–1776* (Scarborough, ON: Prentice-Hall, 1968), pp. 32–33.

3. W.B. Kerr, "The Merchants of Nova Scotia and the American Revolution," *Canadian Historical Review*, 33 (1932): 22.

4. D.C. Harvey, "The Struggle for the New England Form of Township Government in Nova Scotia," *Canadian Historical Association Report*, 1933: 22.

5. John Bartlet Brebner, *The Neutral Yankees of Nova Scotia* (Toronto: McClelland & Stewart, 1969), p. 310.

6. M.W. Armstrong, "Neutrality and Religion in Revolutionary Nova Scotia," *New England Quarterly*, March 1946: 57–58.

7. S.D. Clark, *Movements of Political Protest in Canada, 1640–1840* (Toronto: University of Toronto Press, 1959).

8. Gordon Stewart and George Rawlyk, *A People Highly Favoured of God* (Toronto: Macmillan, 1972).

9. G.A. Rawlyk, *Ravished by the Spirit: Religious Revivals, Baptists, and Henry Alline* (Montreal/Kingston: McGill-Queen's University Press, 1984).

10. J.M. Bumsted, "1763–1783: Resettlement and Rebellion," in P.A. Buckner and J.G. Reid, eds., *The Atlantic Region to Confederation: A History* (Toronto: University of Toronto Press, 1994), pp. 156–83.

The decisive battle of the revolutionary war was fought on October 19, 1781, when Britain's Lord Cornwallis surrendered his army of 7000 at Yorktown, Virginia. As the war now neared its end, the British evacuated southern ports such as Wilmington, Charleston, and Savannah, to which the Loyalists had fled for protection. Persecution reached new levels. Several of the newly independent states subjected the Loyalists to double and triple taxation, and Congress encouraged the states to confiscate their property. Physical violence against Loyalists continued. It became clear that Britain had to do something for them. The British continued to hold New York City and Long Island, and many Loyalists (at one point, 30 000) assembled there, awaiting evacuation.

At the peace negotiations, the American commissioners agreed that no further persecutions of Loyalists would take place. But while Congress urged the states to grant restitution and amnesty, it had no power to enforce its requests. Except in one or two states, every clause in the Treaty of Paris relating to the Loyalists was abrogated. When news of the preliminary peace reached the United States in the spring of 1783, the proscriptions, confiscations, and harassment of Loyalists resumed.

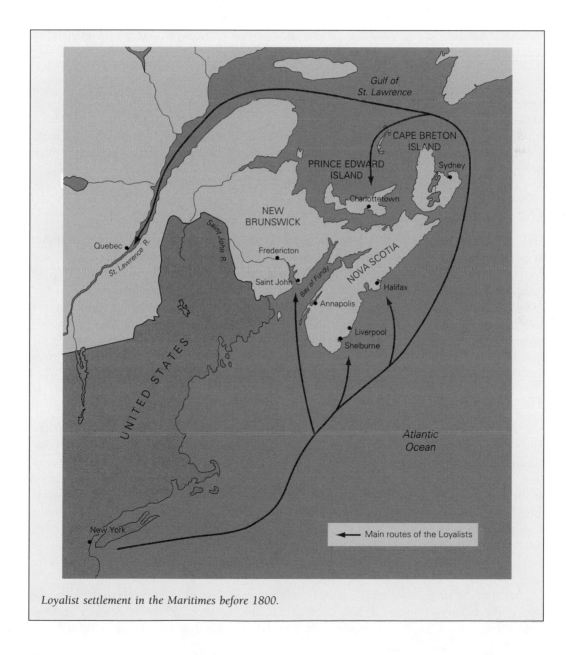

Loyalist settlement in the Maritimes before 1800.

Loyalist Communities in the Maritimes

The exodus of thousands of Loyalists and their families began even before the peace treaty. Traditionally, the number of exiles has been estimated at 100 000, but this figure is probably inflated. Historians Wallace Brown and Hereward Senior believe that British North America received more than 50 000 white, black, and First Nations Loyalists. The British Isles received approximately 10 000, several thousand went to the British West Indies, and a small number (mainly Germans) returned to the Rhine valley. The overwhelming majority of the Loyalists were of European background, as Brown and Senior note, but approximately 6000 African-American Loyalists migrated to the Maritimes, the West Indies, and Sierra Leone in West Africa. Some 2000 Iroquois also left New York. In all, 70 000 people—approximately the population of New France at the time of the conquest—left the United States.[3]

Both during and after the war, the more influential Loyalists, such as royal officials, wealthy merchants, landowners, professionals, and high military officers, sailed directly for England to press their claims for compensation. The humbler element settled in the remaining British North American colonies.

The Loyalists favoured Nova Scotia over Quebec at a ratio of roughly two to one. Nova Scotia's fisheries, its large tracts of empty land, and the potential trade with the West Indies attracted them. Nova Scotia, too, was the shorter trip by sea. Small groups of Loyalists had been finding their way to Halifax since 1775. The evacuation of New York in 1783, though, led to an unanticipated invasion. The arrival of thousands of Loyalists strengthened Atlantic British North America's ties to the Crown.

The Loyalists' First Settlements

About 15 000 Loyalists went to what became New Brunswick in 1784; about the same number to peninsular Nova Scotia, and about a thousand each to Prince Edward Island and Cape Breton, with a few families to Newfoundland. The great migration to the Atlantic colonies more than doubled their population with the arrival of over 30 000 civilian refugees and disbanded soldiers. Arrival proved a mixed blessing. In spite of the British government's promises, the colonists found that few preparations had been made to receive them. At Saint John, for example, no shelter had been prepared, provisions were in short supply, and the land along the river was not surveyed.

The Black Loyalists

For the African-American Loyalists great disappointment also awaited them. Among African Americans' ranks were men and women who had heeded the British proclamation of 1779 that offered freedom to any slaves who left their American masters and rallied to support the Crown. Some blacks had taken part in combat; others had served as spies, guides, nurses, and personal servants. In 1783, some 3000 African-American Loyalists arrived in the Maritimes, having won their freedom during the American Revolution by crossing over to the British lines. The British government promised them freedom, but it did not grant them equality. They were given smaller and less fertile grants than the other Loyalists, and substantially fewer provisions and tools. They could not vote, sit in non-segregated sections of churches, or even fish in the Saint John harbour.

Many of the white Loyalists also found economic conditions in Nova Scotia difficult. In one stroke, the colony's population had doubled and the resources of "Nova Scarcity" proved insufficient to meet the demand. Eventually, over half the Loyalists who came to Nova Scotia went elsewhere. Some moved to Upper Canada, others went to England, a number returned to the United States, and a number of free African-American Loyalists eventually resettled in Sierra Leone in British West Africa.

The Founding of New Brunswick

Shortly after the arrival in what is today New Brunswick, elite Loyalists from the St. John River petitioned London to have the section north of the Bay of Fundy removed from Nova Scotia and made a separate Loyalist province. They argued that the distance of the Saint John settlements from Halifax made it difficult to transact business with the capital. No doubt they also realized that the creation of a new colony would provide administrative offices for themselves. In the summer of 1784, Britain created the new colony of New Brunswick. The following year the major settlement at the mouth of the great river was named Saint John. The new capital, approximately 100 km north of Saint John, received the name of Frederick's Town (the "k," "s," and "w" were dropped shortly thereafter), in honour of Frederick Augustus, Duke of York, the second son of George III.

Building a Loyalist Province

The Loyalists gradually built a new society in the Saint John River valley. It was hard work even for the affluent, for New Brunswick had a severe shortage of labour. Slowly a series of largely self-sufficient agricultural communities developed on favourable coastal locations and in the lowland river valleys. The town of Saint John became the major urban centre, with a population of 3500 in 1785. The Acadians' settlements, formed originally by those who had fled to the Miramichi to escape deportation between 1755 and 1758, were located along the eastern and northern shores of New Brunswick.

Ironically, the First Nations, whose allegiance had been critical in retaining western Nova Scotia for the Crown, suffered the most. The Loyalists encroached on their hunting and fishing territories. They helped themselves to Mi'kmaq and Maliseet land, fish, game, and timber. The British confiscated portions of their territories as Crown land without financial compensation. In the Great Lakes area the Royal Proclamation of 1763 protected First Nations land rights, but the British ruled that the Proclamation did not apply in the Maritime colonies. Britain assumed that the French had already dealt in the Maritime area with the issue of Aboriginal title, but they had not.

The Loyalists in Prince Edward Island

About 800 Loyalists travelled to Saint John's Island, soon to be renamed Prince Edward Island. They formed about one-fifth of the population. In Nova Scotia and New Brunswick, the authorities eventually supplied the Loyalists with free land, government timber, and tools. On Prince Edward Island, however, the hapless newcomers became tenant farmers on land granted to absentee proprietors.

In 1767, the British government had divided the entire island into long belts of land, stretching from north to south. It then proceeded to grant all 67 townships of roughly 8000 ha each to favourites of the Crown. The new landlords had to pay a small annual fee, or quitrent, for their land; they also had to promise to bring over settlers.

To attract Loyalists to their lands, the landowners promised them grants of land with secure titles. But once the settlers cleared their lands, erected buildings, and planted orchards, the proprietors refused to grant land title to those who wanted to become landowners. Many

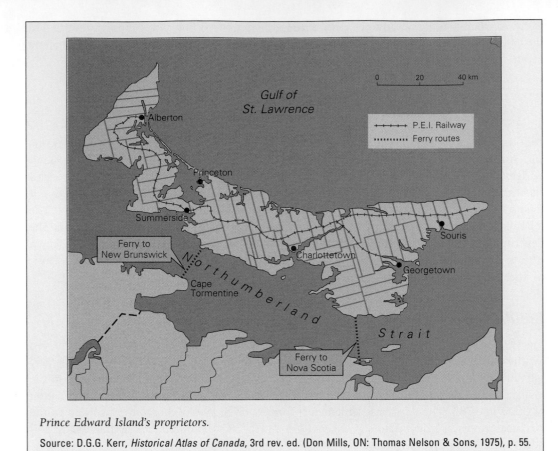

Prince Edward Island's proprietors.

Source: D.G.G. Kerr, *Historical Atlas of Canada*, 3rd rev. ed. (Don Mills, ON: Thomas Nelson & Sons, 1975), p. 55.

settlers obtained no redress and left in disgust. Those who remained fought for 75 years for justice. Only in 1860 would a land commission recommend that free grants be made to those who could prove that their ancestors had been attracted to the island by the original promises made to the Loyalists. A final attempt to resolve the land question was made in 1873, in conjunction with Prince Edward Island's entry into Confederation.

The Loyalists on Cape Breton Island

About a thousand Loyalists came to Cape Breton Island. The British government made the island a separate colony. The new capital was named Sydney after the British colonial secretary. But the British government provided little financial support for the colony. London did not even establish an assembly for the island. In 1820 the colonial office, without any consultation with the inhabitants, decided to rejoin Cape Breton to Nova Scotia.

During the War of 1812 the island was relatively prosperous. Major social and economic development, however, came with the arrival of Scottish immigrants, which began from 1802 onward—Catholic Scots from the Hebrides, the coastal islands off the northwest of Scotland, many of whom spoke only Gaelic. The magnificent hills and seacoast reminded them of their homeland. They became fishers and farmers. By the mid-nineteenth century the Scots had become the dominant community on Cape Breton Island, outnumbering the Mi'kmaqs, Acadians, and Loyalist descendants combined.

The Atlantic Economy from the Revolutionary War to the War of 1812

Real economic growth in the Maritimes began only after the outbreak of war between Britain and France in 1793 and, particularly, after the rise of Napoleon in the late 1790s. The British government now spent lavishly on fortifications in Halifax, constructing public and military buildings. Halifax became the strongest fortress outside Europe and the main supply base for the British West Indies.

After the beginning of the Napoleonic Wars, a flourishing timber industry developed in British North America. Britain required a safe supply of masts and spars for building warships, and it needed timber for construction. The imperial government gave tariff preferences for British American timber. This led to a lumber boom in New Brunswick, the Maritime colony with the greatest timber resources. Wood products would dominate New Brunswick's export economy for the next half-century. Heavily forested New Brunswick, being closer to Britain, was better situated than were the Canadas for this trade.

Inadvertently, the United States also promoted the prosperity of the Maritimes. After France and Britain imposed blockades on each other in 1806, President Thomas Jefferson, in retaliation against both countries' restrictions on neutral trade, prohibited all commerce out of American ports. But the policy backfired, for by closing American ports in 1807, the president ruined New England's trade—and enriched that of the Maritimes.

Since Britain depended on American foodstuffs as much as the United States needed British manufactured goods, Anglo–American trade continued, but now through illegal channels. An active smuggling trade developed, with cargoes being transferred at sea or carried overland across the British–American frontier. In defiance of their government, American ship captains sailed into British ports, making the Maritimes in 1808 into a great clearinghouse for international trade. The Maritime colonies now purchased American produce and goods and then re-exported these materials as if they were their own. Similarly, they sold British manufactured goods to the Americans. This thriving trade continued throughout the War of 1812.

During the entire War of 1812 New England, in effect, was neutral. The legislatures of the New England states openly condemned the war that had ruined their commerce. As Washington lacked the military capacity to impose its will on New England, its trade with Britain and its Maritime colonies continued. Only naval activity on the high seas reminded Maritimers that they still lived in a war theatre. The occupation by the British in 1814 of part of the coast of present-day Maine allowed more opportunities for commercial profit.

The outbreak of the last and longest of the wars between Britain and France, the Napoleonic Wars (1793–1814), also contributed to the new prosperity on Newfoundland. The price of dried fish rose substantially during the later years of the war, because the French had to abandon their Newfoundland fishery. France simply could not protect its fishing fleet in wartime when the country needed to mobilize all of its naval resources to fight England. English vessels also stayed at home. The resident population, and the fisheries, grew. By 1815, residents owned almost the complete fishing fleet and produced the entire yield of saltfish.

During these prosperous years, shipowners, settlers, and St. John's entrepreneurs invested heavily in the fishery, creating a resident Newfoundland fleet. They began sending ships to less crowded parts of the coast, to the northern part of the island, and on to Labrador. Each June, thousands of Newfoundland fishers sailed for Labrador to catch cod. As the Labrador fishery expanded, Britain reattached Labrador to Newfoundland, taking it out of Lower Canada's control in 1809.

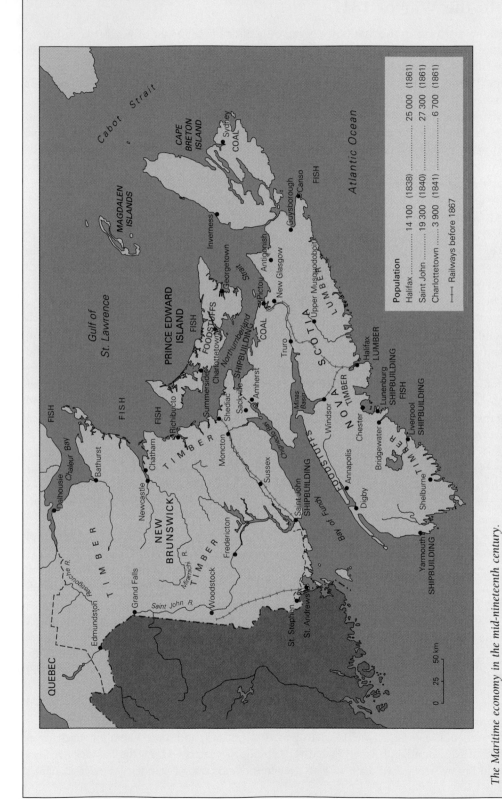

The Maritime economy in the mid-nineteenth century.

Source: Adapted from D.G.G. Kerr, *Historical Atlas of Canada*, 3rd rev. ed. (Don Mills, ON: Thomas Nelson & Sons, 1975), p. 52.

Economic Developments, 1815–1850

The peace treaty of 1783 granted American citizens fishing privileges in the inshore waters of the British North American colonies. However, during the negotiations of the Treaty of Ghent, which ended the War of 1812, the British argued that the Americans had abrogated this right by declaring war. Under the Convention of 1818, the Americans lost the privilege of landing and drying their fish in the three Maritime colonies; they retained the right to do so only on unsettled shores in Newfoundland. This helped the British Atlantic fishery. American vessels continued to enter British American harbours to obtain water, purchase wood, or repair damages; but not until the signing of the Reciprocity Treaty in 1854, which provided for free trade in natural products between British North America and the United States, did Americans regain access to the inshore fisheries.

Newfoundland's maritime economy expanded after the War of 1812. Sailors entered the waters off Newfoundland and Labrador's northern coasts to harvest the seal herds on the ice floes. Mammals and fish provided the bulk of the world's industrial oil in the early nineteenth century, and young seals had an excellent fat, for fine-quality oil. Their skins could also be sold in England. The industry grew rapidly. Between 1831 and 1833, the seal fishery averaged between 30 and 40 percent of Newfoundland's total exports. More than 600 000 seals were harvested in 1831 alone. By the 1850s, 13 000 men were employed annually in the seal hunt. It supplemented the production of salt cod.

Agriculture

After the War of 1812 agriculture remained weak in the Maritime colonies. While farming flourished on Prince Edward Island, in Nova Scotia's Annapolis valley, and in New Brunswick's Saint John River valley, it did not fare as well in other areas. Nova Scotia and New Brunswick as a whole continued to depend on American foodstuffs to feed their populations well into the nineteenth century. Commercial farming remained very limited, with only Prince Edward Island, the "Garden of the Gulf," exporting large amounts of farm produce. In the case of Nova Scotia and New Brunswick, the lack of good roads, a scattered population, and the absence of protection against American imports accounted for the limited agricultural exports. Nevertheless farming, more than either logging or fishing, remained the livelihood of a majority of Maritimers. Even a large number of those employed in logging and fishing worked on a part-time basis in agriculture to support their families.

An increase in immigration after 1815 added to the size of the local market and encouraged greater agricultural production. New Brunswick had roughly 75 000 inhabitants in 1824 and almost 200 000 by 1851. During the same period, Nova Scotia's population rose from approximately 100 000 to 275 000. Prince Edward Island's population increased from 23 000 in 1827 to 72 000 in 1855, making it the most densely inhabited colony in British North America, because of its small size.

The Timber Industry

Forestry became the leading growth industry in the Maritimes after the War of 1812, New Brunswick being known as the "timber colony." As early as 1826, three-quarters of the province's export revenues came from wood products—square timber, lumber, and ships. In the 1840s, New Brunswick survived the gradual reduction of the British preference on colonial timber. British and American demand remained high. By 1865, forest products made up two-thirds of New Brunswick's total exports by value, in contrast to about 10 percent of Nova Scotia's and Prince Edward Island's exports.

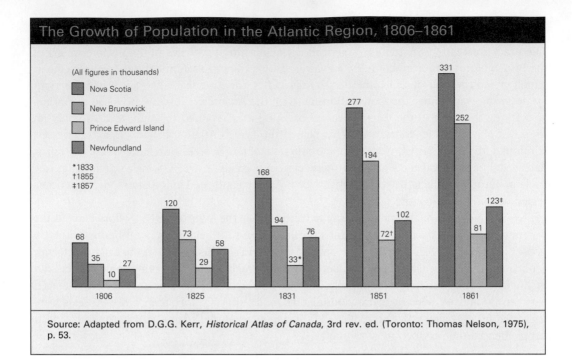

The Growth of Population in the Atlantic Region, 1806–1861

(All figures in thousands)

- Nova Scotia
- New Brunswick
- Prince Edward Island
- Newfoundland

*1833
†1855
‡1857

1806: 68, 35, 10, 27
1825: 120, 73, 29, 58
1831: 168, 94, 33*, 76
1851: 277, 194, 72†, 102
1861: 331, 252, 81, 123‡

Source: Adapted from D.G.G. Kerr, *Historical Atlas of Canada*, 3rd rev. ed. (Toronto: Thomas Nelson, 1975), p. 53.

Shipbuilding

Shipbuilding became a major sideline of the timber industry. Square timber, a bulky commodity, had to be shipped in relatively large vessels, and as Britain could not meet the need for such ships in wartime, so the Maritime shipbuilding industry expanded, making it the first major manufacturing industry in the Maritime region. The Maritimes soon supplied many of the new wooden ships used to ferry timber to Britain.

Generally Maritime shipbuilders built broad-beamed vessels designed to maximize carrying capacity, not speed. They increased sail capacity and improved ships' hulls. They extended the average life of Nova Scotia and New Brunswick vessels from a mere nine years in the 1820s to fifteen years by the end of the century. These shipbuilders also constructed their vessels cheaply. An iron steamer in Britain cost four or five times as much in the 1860s as did a wooden vessel from the Maritimes. The popularity of steamers, however, grew rapidly because of their speed and reliability, leaving only a tiny market for wooden ships by the end of the century.

WHERE HISTORIANS DISAGREE

The Timber Industry in Early New Brunswick: An Environmental Perspective

Environmental history is a relatively new field in Canadian history. In 1989, historian Ramsay Cook lamented the lack of historical interest in the impact of settlement and industry on the natural environment: "Even the no longer so new social history has largely ignored the environment in the rush for class, gender and ethnicity."[1]

In regard to the forests of New Brunswick, however, environmental concerns have long been raised. As early as 1825, for instance, Peter Fisher raised the alarm in his *Sketches of New Brunswick*, the first historical study published in the province:

> The persons principally engaged in shipping the timber have been strangers who have taken no interest in the welfare of the country; but have merely occupied a spot to make what they could in the shortest possible time.... Instead of seeing towns built, farms improved and the country cleared and stocked with the reasonable returns of so great a trade, the forests are stripped and nothing left in prospect, but the gloomy apprehension when the timber is gone, of sinking into insignificance and poverty.[2]

A century later, Arthur R.M. Lower developed this same theme of senseless pillage in three books on Canada's forest industries: *Settlement and the Forest Frontier in Eastern Canada* (1936), *The North American Assault on the Canadian Forest* (1938), and *Great Britain's Woodyard: British America and the Timber Trade* (1973). He concluded his last book with this statement: "The Canadian forests contributed to the prosperity of the British timber importer and the enrichment of the American lumberman.... [But] it must be concluded that the new colonies got the minimum out of the wreck of their forests."[3]

In *Northern Enterprise*, a study of five centuries of Canadian business, Michael Bliss took issue with Arthur Lower:

> The old idea that the rape of the forests was simply a using up of natural wealth with no compensating benefits is a romantic mockery of the realities and difficulties of colonial development.

> When A.R.M. Lower wove that theme into his writing about Canadian forest industries, with particular reference to New Brunswick, he was parroting some of the industry's least-informed critics.

Instead Bliss endorsed and cited a New Brunswick contemporary of Peter Fisher, who stated that the timber trade

> has brought foreign produce and foreign capital into the Province, and has been the chief source of the money by means of which the country has been opened up and improved; by which its roads, bridges and public buildings have been completed; its rivers and harbours made accessible; its natural resources discovered and made available; its Provincial institutions kept up and its functionaries paid.[4]

Graeme Wynn, who studied the question in depth twenty years ago, takes a middle-of-the-road position. The historical geographer underlines that an export staple was needed to give New Brunswick its economic liftoff. That staple was timber. From 1805 to 1850 the heavy exploitation of the colony's forests transformed the colony from "an undeveloped backwater of 25 000 people to a bustling colony of 190 000." At the same time, Wynn notes the waste and destruction. For example, he commented about early-nineteenth-century sawmilling: "Sawdust dumped into the rivers soon became sodden, sank to the bed of the stream, disturbed the river ecology, and obstructed navigation. In suspension it floated downstream, was deposited on banks and intervals, and drastically reduced fish populations." The debris of bark, slabs, edgings, mill rubbish, and sunken logs was also carried over entire river systems, he noted.

In the end Wynn withholds judgment, claiming the need for further research before definitive statements could be made. With regard to Lower's books, he sees them as "reconnaissance surveys rather than final charts ... early interpretations need to be re-examined as more information becomes available."[5]

William Cronon's *Changes in the Land: Colonists and the Ecology of New England*[6] might be a good model for a follow-up study, as it combines a thorough documentary search with in-depth biological knowledge. A good beginning for New Brunswick is Gilbert Allardyce's 1972 article on Alma Parish in Albert County, New Brunswick.[7] In the nineteenth century the parish's forests and fishlife appeared inexhaustible. By 1850,

however, sawmill dams blockaded the rivers and prevented the passage of salmon toward their headwater spawning grounds all along the Fundy coast. Still, lumbering aggressively increased, which meant more sawdust. Timber killed fishing. When the lumber became exhausted in the early twentieth century, Alma Parish was left with nothing to support settlement, as it had little fertile land for farming. Today Alma Parish forms Fundy National Park. In any assessment of the impact of the nineteenth-century timber industry on New Brunswick, both the long-term and the short-term consequences need to be considered.

1. Ramsay Cook, "Review of the Natural History of Canada," *Canadian Historical Review*, 60 (1989): 386.

2. Peter Fisher, *Sketches of New Brunswick* (Saint John: Chubb and Sears, 1825), p. 72; reprinted in Arthur R.M. Lower, *Great Britain's Woodyard: British America and the Timber Trade, 1763–1867* (Montreal/Kingston: McGill-Queen's University Press, 1973), p. 33.

3. Lower, *Great Britain's Woodyard*, p. 250.

4. Michael Bliss, *Northern Enterprise* (Toronto: McClelland & Stewart, 1987), p. 136.

5. Graeme Wynn, *Timber Colony: A Historical Geography of Early Nineteenth Century New Brunswick* (Toronto: University of Toronto Press, 1981), pp. 24, 33, 93, and 174.

6. William Cronon, *Changes in the Land: Indians, Colonists and the Ecology of New England* (New York: Hill and Wang, 1983).

7. Gilbert Allardyce, "'The Vexed Question of Sawdust': River Pollution in Nineteenth Century New Brunswick," *Dalhousie Review*, 52, 2 (Summer 1972): 177–90.

Banking

The financial needs of the merchants involved in the timber industry and shipbuilding led to the rise of banks. In Britain, commercial banks developed in the eighteenth century, and in the 1790s scores of them opened in the United States. The Halifax Banking Company, the first bank in Nova Scotia, began trading in money in 1825. A group of merchants founded the Bank of Nova Scotia in 1832, and by 1840 it had branches throughout Nova Scotia. New Brunswick's first bank, the Bank of New Brunswick, was chartered in Saint John in 1820; the second, the Commercial Bank, in 1834. Prince Edward Island's first bank opened in the mid-1850s. The banks dealt in foreign-exchange transactions, made loans, and circulated bank notes, on the understanding that the paper notes could always be redeemed, on demand, in real coinage. Depending on the risk the bankers were prepared to take, the banks could generally keep two or three times as many notes in circulation as they had gold or silver coins to redeem them. (The issuing of notes in place of coins allowed the banks to double or triple the amount of interest they collected.)

Saint John and Halifax

Strong rivalries existed between the two major regional centres in the Maritimes: Saint John and Halifax. Initially Saint John held the advantage, as the largest city. It controlled the timber trade of the Saint John River valley, had an important shipbuilding industry, and was the natural market for the farmers and fishers on both sides of the Bay of Fundy. Nearly half of the industrial output of New Brunswick was produced in and around Saint John. By the mid-nineteenth century, Saint John had emerged as the Maritimes' major industrial centre, with foundry, clothing, and footwear industries. Together they surpassed shipbuilding in value by the 1860s. But the great merchants of Saint John delayed investing in manufacturing iron and steel. Such financial conservatism held back the development of a viable industrial base in New Brunswick by two decades.

Halifax, the military headquarters for the region, had a large, secure, ice-free harbour, very close to major North Atlantic shipping lanes. It also benefited from the Caribbean trade and from its role as Nova Scotia's banking, judicial, and intellectual centre. In terms of industrial base, it developed a specialization in food-processing industries, such as sugar refining, brewing, and distilling. But it did not have a readily accessible hinterland. Also, unlike Montreal and Saint John, it lacked a major waterway comparable to the St. Lawrence or the Saint John River. Halifax did succeed in bringing Prince Edward Island, Cape Breton Island, and the Miramichi country of eastern New Brunswick into its commercial orbit, but it lost the important Bay of Fundy region to Saint John.

The Maritimes and the United States

Issues of borders and trade dominated Maritime–American relations in the mid-nineteenth century. When Britain adopted free trade in the 1840s, many Maritimers looked to continental reciprocity—the free admission into British North America and the United States of each other's natural resources—as a viable alternative. New Brunswick saw reciprocity as the key to gaining

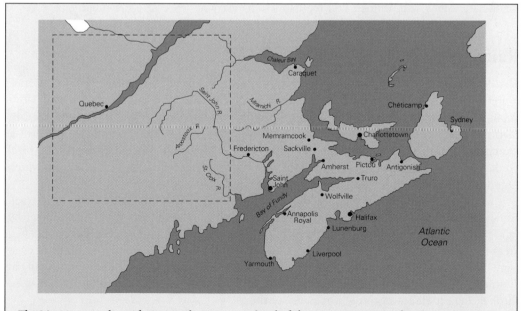

The Maritimes in the mid-nineteenth century. A detail of this map appears on the next page.

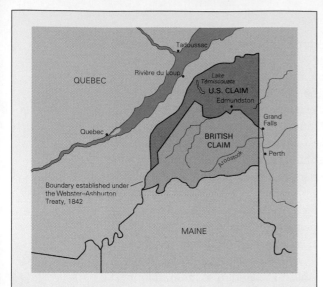

The Anglo–American boundary dispute, settled by the Webster–Ashburton Treaty in 1842.

entry for its timber into the American market of 23 million people. There could be no hope of reciprocity, however, until a border controversy between New Brunswick and Maine was settled. The Webster–Ashburton Treaty of 1842 resolved the controversy. It established the present-day New Brunswick–Maine boundary. The treaty left Maine a wedge of land projecting between New Brunswick and the Canadas, yet it kept intact the vital communication route between Quebec and Fredericton via Lake Témiscouata.

Reciprocity proposals met with a favourable response in Nova Scotia with its fish for export, in New Brunswick with its timber, and in Prince Edward Island with its farm produce. The Americans, for their part, wanted access to the Maritime inshore fisheries from which they had been excluded in 1818. The inclusion of the fisheries led the United States to sign a reciprocity agreement with the British North American colonies in 1854.

The Reciprocity Treaty (1854–1866)

The treaty led to the desired increased trade with the United States. The Maritime colonies now bought one-quarter to one-half of their total imports from the Americans. In return, New Brunswick shipped to the United States increased amounts of lumber; Prince Edward Island shipped more foodstuffs; and Nova Scotia shipped a slightly greater amount of fish. Certainly, the twelve years of the reciprocity treaty proved prosperous, but not solely on account of the treaty. The high demand generated by the American Civil War (1861–1865) led to high prices for the Maritimes' fish, timber, and foodstuffs. The carrying trade also benefited.

Railways

The leading Maritime cities sought to build railways inland to expand their economic hinterlands. Between 1853 and 1866, New Brunswick built 350 km of railways and Nova Scotia constructed 235 km. Maritime promoters envisaged one day linking the ice-free Maritime ports with the St. Lawrence valley and with the grain-producing American Midwest. Merchants in Halifax and Saint John had visions of their respective cities serving as the focal point from which European commerce could be channelled into the continent and from which American and Canadian exports could be sent abroad.

Yet railways proved expensive both to build and to operate. A single kilometre of track could cost as much as a sizable sailing vessel. Moreover, operating costs were much higher by rail than by sea. To make money, the railway company owners needed both densely populated areas to provide local revenue and the shortest possible direct routes; neither Halifax nor even Saint John had such hinterlands. The larger communities in the interior were too distant, in contrast with those neighbouring Boston, New York, or Montreal, and the land routes passed through long stretches of thinly populated territory.

The Population of Atlantic British North America

In the nineteenth century, thousands of Scottish and Irish immigrants crossed the North Atlantic to British North America to escape overcrowding, famine, and poverty. They joined those already-established residents: the Acadians, African Maritimers, First Nations people, and the descendants of the Planters and the white Loyalists, as well as recent English immigrants. The table here reveals the changing ethnic composition of Maritime British North America.

The number of permanent residents in Newfoundland doubled from about 20 000 in 1800, to about 40 000 in 1830. By the 1830s the Irish Catholic population numbered half the island's population. Most of the others were of English background. Mistrusting each other, the Irish and English communities separated themselves geographically.

Women in the Maritimes

The Maritimes, in the mid-nineteenth century, as was the case throughout North America, remained a male-dominated society. Men, for instance, owned almost all property and housing. At best, women had only limited rights under the law to protection and safety. In 1836 Prince Edward Island disenfranchised propertied women, as did New Brunswick in 1843 and Nova Scotia in 1851.

Although deprived of the vote, women could, and did, deliver petitions to their legislatures. They played a major role, for example, in petitioning for prohibition. On the positive side as well, after 1849 New Brunswick finally allowed women to attend the provincial Normal School. They numbered close to one-half of New Brunswick's teachers by the late 1850s. Yet they were only paid the same wage as a domestic servant. And unlike men, who obtained higher wages and could teach the older students, women were still denied entrance to colleges.

In terms of women's rights, Nova Scotia in 1857 became the only British North American province prior to Confederation to allow legal divorce on the grounds of cruelty, such as wife battering. This was indeed an advance, but New Brunswick and Prince Edward Island took no immediate steps to imitate this legislation.

National Origins: Nova Scotia, 1871, New Brunswick, 1871, and Prince Edward Island, 1881

	NORTH AMERICAN INDIAN		ENGLISH AND WELSH		SCOTS		IRISH		FRENCH	
	Number	%	Number	%	Number	%	Number	%	Number	%
Nova Scotia	1 666	0.4	113 520	29.2	130 741	33.7	62 851	16.4	32 833	8.5
New Brunswick	1 403	0.5	83 598	29.2	40 858	14.3	100 643	35.3	44 907	15.7
P.E.I.	281	0.3	21 568	19.8	48 933	44.8	25 415	23.3	10 751	9.9

	GERMAN		DUTCH		AFRICAN		SWISS		TOTAL
	Number	%	Number	%	Number	%	Number	%	Population
Nova Scotia	31 942	8.2	2 868	0.7	6 212	1.6	1 775	0.5	387 800
New Brunswick	4 478	1.6	6 004	2.1	1 701	0.6	64	—	285 594
P.E.I.	1 076	1.0	292	0.3					108 891

Source: R. Cole Harris and John Warkentin, *Canada before Confederation: A Study in Historical Geography* (Ottawa: Carleton University Press, 1991 [1974]), pp. 184–85. Data from Census of Canada.

The First Nations in the Maritimes and Newfoundland

The Maritimers with the longest residency had the greatest difficulty in adjusting to changing conditions in the early and mid-nineteenth century. The British and the Maritime governments held that the Mi'kmaqs' and the Maliseets' title to the land had already been extinguished—first, by the fact that the French had occupied the area and, second, as a result of the Treaty of Utrecht in 1713, which the British claimed gave them sovereign title to Acadia. The New Brunswick government set aside reserves for the Mi'kmaqs and the Maliseets, but the lack of proper legal descriptions and surveys of the reserve lands encouraged settlers to encroach into these areas. A similar situation developed in Nova Scotia. The first reserve was only established on Prince Edward Island in 1870. By the time of Confederation, the First Nations constituted roughly 0.5 percent of the total population of Nova Scotia, New Brunswick, and Prince Edward Island.

The Beothuks, Newfoundland's original inhabitants, did not survive European contact. In the seventeenth century they withdrew from the coastal areas where the European newcomers set up shore stations. They did not, as did the Mi'kmaqs in the Maritimes, trade and interact with the Europeans. Consequently, by staying in the interior to avoid the newcomers, they lost access to the valuable food supplies off the coast. They became greatly weakened by starvation and tuberculosis, which the Europeans had inadvertently introduced. By 1800, the Beothuks had almost totally disappeared.

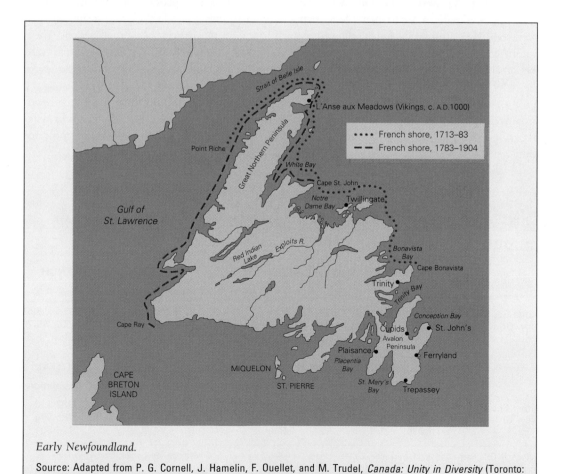

Early Newfoundland.

Source: Adapted from P. G. Cornell, J. Hamelin, F. Ouellet, and M. Trudel, *Canada: Unity in Diversity* (Toronto: Holt, Rinehart and Winston, 1967), p. 111.

The pressure on the Beothuks had grown in the eighteenth century. Several factors contributed to increased European settlement in the Northeast and the interior: a salmon fishery developed near the river mouths of northeastern Newfoundland; settlers began to trap fur-bearing animals in the interior; and the spring seal hunt, which was best operated from the northeastern coast, grew rapidly. When the Beothuks encountered the Europeans on the northeastern coast, violence often erupted. The settlers harassed them and raided their camps. The Beothuks retaliated. According to contemporary reports and oral traditions, they killed about a dozen settlers and wounded nearly as many more between 1750 and 1790. The settlers took their own revenge, killing and wounding Beothuks and destroying their wigwams. The Beothuks' lack of firearms weakened their ability to defend themselves.

Several naval officers and settlers in the late eighteenth and early nineteenth centuries worried about the Beothuks' fate, as it was already obvious that the First Nation was on the point of extinction. Demasduwit, a young woman, was taken captive in 1819 and lived for one year. Then, in 1823, three starving Beothuk women were captured. Both the mother and one of her two daughters died shortly afterward of tuberculosis. But the second daughter, Shawnadithit, called Nancy, a young woman between 16 and 20, survived for six years. She lived at first as a servant in the household of a justice of the peace, but spent the last year of her life in St. John's, informing William Cormack, a champion of the Beothuks, about her people's culture, history, and language. Shawnadithit died in 1829. Apart from two or three Beothuks who may have resided with the Newfoundland Mi'kmaqs, she was the last of the Beothuks.

Political Changes in the Mid-Nineteenth Century

After the American Revolution, the British government imposed, as it did in the Canadas, rigid political structures, controlled from above. Reformers wanted the members of the Executive Council (or Cabinet) responsible to the majority party in the Assembly. If the Council lost a confidence vote in the Assembly, or lost support in a general election, its members had to resign. Secondly, the governor was required to accept the recommendations of the Executive Council, dependent as it was on majority support in the Assembly. This is what they meant by responsible government.

Joseph Howe led the Nova Scotia Reformers. In 1827, Howe purchased the *Novascotian*, a Halifax newspaper, which he remade into the most influential newspaper in the province. In the election of 1847, the Reformers fought on the issue of responsible government, and finally won a majority. On February 2, 1848, the Colonial Office agreed that henceforth the Executive Council had to collectively resign if it lost the Assembly's confidence. Nova Scotia thus became the first British North American colony to obtain responsible government. New Brunswick, Prince Edward Island, and Newfoundland followed. All had responsible government by 1855.

During the American Revolution, Nova Scotia supported Britain and remained within the Empire. It became a place of refuge for the Loyalists after the British defeat. Yet, even with the Loyalist influx, the colonies of Nova Scotia, Prince Edward Island, and the new colony of New Brunswick remained relatively small in population, and weak economically. The War of 1812 proved a prosperous time for the British North Atlantic colonies. The economic upsurge after the war, led by shipbuilding, the timber industry, fishing, and agriculture, added to the region's development. By the mid-nineteenth century, the three Maritime colonies had become recognizable economic and political units.

Population-wise, eight of every nine people in the region had been born there. But the inhabitants were far from homogeneous. Religious, ethnic, and provincial divisions remained, and some groups, such as the Mi'kmaqs and the African Maritimers and, to a lesser extent, the

Acadians, had been pushed to the margins of Maritime society. Women were politically disenfranchised and relegated largely to the domestic sphere. The colonies had become much more consolidated than half a century earlier, but even within their own provincial boundaries, regional loyalties remained strong.

As for Newfoundland in the 1860s, it looked eastward toward Britain, not westward toward the mainland. Newfoundland's patterns of trade and settlement linked it to Europe, the West Indies, and the United States. Newfoundland's geography and distinctive history also placed it very much apart from the Canadas and even from the three Maritime colonies.

NOTES

1. George A. Rawlyk, "The American Revolution and Nova Scotia Reconsidered," *Dalhousie Review*, 43 (1963–1964): 379.

2. Paul H. Smith, "The American Loyalists: Notes on Their Organization and Numerical Strength," *William and Mary Quarterly*, 3rd series, 25 (1968): 269.

3. The estimates of the Loyalists' numbers appear in Wallace Brown and Hereward Senior, *Victorious in Defeat: The Loyalists in Canada* (Toronto: Methuen, 1984).

BEYOND THE BOOK

National Historic Site: Old Town Lunenburg

http://whc.unesco.org/en/list/741
An interactive, 360-degree panography of the Lunenburg National Historic site. Click on "WHTour" in the Links section to view.

Black Loyalists

http://epe.lac-bac.gc.ca/100/200/301/ic/can_digital_collections/blackloyalists/documents/documents.htm
Autobiographical accounts of Black Loyalists who originally immigrated to Nova Scotia in the late eighteenth century. Experiences of the loyalists are broken down by themes such as arrival and religious faith.

Maritime Loyalists

http://www.canadiana.org/citm/themes/pioneers/pioneers4_e.html#maritime
Digitized regulations and governmental acts made in the late 1700s to accommodate the influx of Loyalist immigration.

Cécile Boudreau

http://www.biographi.ca/009004-119.01-e.php?&id_nbr=2283
Cécile Boudreau was an Acadian who escaped the 1755 deportations. Her biography describes her and her family's hiding from the British, and their eventual settling in Nicolet, Québec.

Atlantic Communities

http://www.collectionscanada.ca/05/050408_e.html
Photographs by a French photographer named Paul-Émile Miot of people and communities in Newfoundland and Cape Breton Island in the mid-1800s.

History of Law and the Courts in Newfoundland and Labrador

http://www.heritage.nf.ca/lawfoundation/default.html
This website details the administration of law in Newfoundland and Labrador over the 17th, 18th, and 19th centuries. Acts and charters that form the legal system are digitized and transcribed.

Renaissance of the Island Acadians

Renaissance of the Island Acadians. Directed by Anne-Marie Rocher (National Film Board of Canada and Productions Testa Inc., 2004). This documentary explores a community of Acadians on Prince Edward Island, as they try to revive the language and culture of their ancestors in the face of great challenges.

The Book of Negroes

Lawrence Hill, *The Book of Negroes: A Novel* (Toronto: HarperCollins Publishers Ltd., 2007). Tells the story of slavery through a remarkable woman's life, from her capture from her West African home, to a plantation in the American South, to Nova Scotia, then back to Africa.

His Majesty's Yankees

Thomas H. Raddall, *His Majesty's Yankees* (Toronto: McClelland and Stewart, 1977 [1942]) reviews the tumultuous times of the American Revolution in Nova Scotia.

The Afterlife of George Cartwright

John Steffler, *The Afterlife of George Cartwright* (Toronto: McClelland and Stewart, 1992). A re-creation of an eighteenth-century English gentleman's adventures on the coast of Labrador.

BIBLIOGRAPHY

For a general overview of this period, see Phillip A. Buckner and John G. Reid, eds., *The Atlantic Region to Confederation: A History* (Toronto: University of Toronto Press, 1994), pp. 156–260; Margaret R. Conrad and James K. Hiller, *Atlantic Canada: A Region in the Making* (Toronto: Oxford University Press, 2001); and W.S. MacNutt's *The Atlantic Provinces, 1712–1857* (Toronto: McClelland & Stewart, 1965), pp. 76–102. Cole Harris reviews both New France and Acadia in *The Reluctant Land. Society, Space, and Environment In Canada before Confederation* (Vancouver: UBC Press, 2008), pp. 137–230. For bibliographical guides consult the essays in M. Brook Taylor, ed., *Canadian History: A Reader's Guide*, vol. 1, *Beginnings to Confederation* (Toronto: University of Toronto Press, 1994), by Barry Moody, "Acadia and Old Nova Scotia to 1784," pp. 76–111; Ian Ross Robertson, "The Maritime Colonies, 1784 to Confederation," pp. 237–79; and Olaf Uwe Janzen, "Newfoundland and the International Fishery," pp. 280–324.

For articles on all aspects of British Atlantic Canada, the three editions of Phillip A. Buckner and David Frank, eds., *Atlantic Canada before Confederation*, vol. 1, *The Acadiensis Reader* (Fredericton: Acadiensis Press, 1985, 1988, 1998) are invaluable. Important portraits of Atlantic political, economic, and cultural leaders appear in the volumes of the *Dictionary of Canadian Biography* devoted to the nineteenth century. It is now available online: www.bibliographi.ca.

John Bartlet Brebner reviews Nova Scotia's response to the American Revolution in *The Neutral Yankees of Nova Scotia* (Toronto: McClelland & Stewart, 1969 [1937]). For an introduction to Henry Alline and his New Light movement, see the booklet by D.G. Bell, *Henry Alline and Maritime Religion* (Ottawa: Canadian Historical Association, 1993). Valuable overviews of the Loyalists include Christopher Moore, *The Loyalists: Revolution, Exile, Settlement* (Toronto: Macmillan, 1984); and Wallace Brown and Hereward Senior, *Victorious in Defeat: The Loyalists in Canada* (Toronto: Methuen, 1984).

A review of Halifax's history by three professional historians is Judith Fingard, Janet Guildford, and David Sutherland, *Halifax: The First 250 Years* (Halifax: Formac Publishing, 1999). T.W. Acheson's *Saint John: The Making of a Colonial Urban Community* (Toronto: University of Toronto Press, 1985) studies New Brunswick's largest city. For the history of St. John's, consult Patrick O'Neill, *The Story of St. John's, Newfoundland* (Erin, ON: Boston Mills Press, 1975).

Graeme Wynn, a historical geographer, looks at early New Brunswick in *Timber Colony* (Toronto: University of Toronto Press, 1981). For background on Cape Breton Island, see Stephen J. Hornsby's *Nineteenth Century Cape Breton: A Historical Geography* (Montreal/Kingston. McGill Queen's University Press, 1992). J.M. Bumsted's *Land, Settlement, and Politics on Eighteenth-Century Prince Edward Island* (Montreal/Kingston: McGill-Queen's University Press, 1987) focuses on developments in Prince Edward Island. A lively popular history of the island is Douglas Baldwin's *Land of the Red Soil* (Charlottetown: Ragweed Press, 1990). Frederick W. Rowe's *A History of Newfoundland and Labrador* (Toronto: McGraw-Hill Ryerson, 1980) remains the most complete study of Newfoundland's history.

For background on the Aboriginal peoples in what is now Atlantic Canada, consult F.S. Upton, *Micmacs and Colonists: Indian–White Relations in the Maritimes, 1713–1867* (Vancouver: University of British Columbia Press, 1979); and Harold E.L. Prins, *The Mi'kmaq Resistance: Accommodation and Cultural Survival* (Fort Worth, TX: Harcourt Brace, 1996). In *We Were Not the Savages: First Nation History*, 3rd ed. (Halifax: Fernwood, 2000), Daniel N. Paul provides a Mi'kmaq perspective on the arrival of non-Aboriginals. On the Beothuk the most important study is Ingeborg Marshall, *A History and Ethnography of the Beothuk* (Montreal/Kingston: McGill-Queen's University Press, 1996).

Important maps of Atlantic British North America in the late eighteenth and nineteenth centuries appear in the first two volumes of the *Historical Atlas of Canada*, vol. 1, R. Cole Harris, ed., *From the Beginning to 1800* (Toronto. University of Toronto Press, 1987); and vol. 2, R. Louis Gentilcore, ed., *The Land Transformed, 1800–1891* (Toronto: University of Toronto Press, 1993).

Chapter Nine

THE NORTHWEST TO THE 1860s

TIME LINE

1690	Henry Kelsey, a Hudson's Bay Company employee, sets out on a journey into the interior of North America
1730s	Pierre La Vérendrye establishes French posts around Lakes Winnipeg and Winnipegosis
1761	French traders withdraw from the interior as a result of the French capitulation at Montreal
1780s	Formation of the North West Company
1812	The Selkirk colony is established on the Red River
1818	The 49th parallel becomes the boundary line between American and British claims from Lake Superior west to the Rocky Mountains
1821	Union of the Hudson's Bay Company and the North West Company
1849	Free trade is obtained in the Red River

The Blackfoot-speaking peoples occupied the rich buffalo ranges of present-day southern Alberta and northern Montana in the mid-eighteenth century. The horse, brought to Mexico by the Spanish, reached them about 1730, at about the same time that Cree middlemen brought them guns. Apart from possibly one or two "northern white men," as they later termed the English, the only Europeans that the Blackfoot speakers encountered on the northern plains in the 1740s and 1750s were French traders from Canada, whom they called "real white men."

After the fall of New France in 1760, hundreds of Europeans ventured into the interior from the north, the east, and the south. The best furs came from the North West, and independent fur traders from Montreal came to buy them. In the early 1780s, these Scottish and American fur traders formed the North West Company (whose agents came to be called Nor'Westers) to challenge the Hudson's Bay Company, already more than a century old. Thirty years of competition between the two companies ended with their merger in 1821. Even after the Métis broke the Hudson's Bay Company monopoly in the Red River Colony in 1849, the company remained the leading commercial power in Rupert's Land.

The French and the English in the Interior

The French came west in search of a short route to China. Well into the eighteenth century the French believed in the existence of a gulf that cut deeply into the continent from the Pacific, like Hudson Bay or the Gulf of Mexico. They hoped that somewhere between the 40th and 50th parallels of latitude a navigable strait joined the "Western Sea" to the Pacific Ocean. In 1730, Pierre Gaultier de Varennes et de La Vérendrye, commander of the fur-trading post on Kaministiquia (present-day Thunder Bay), offered to establish a post on Lake Winnipeg. He agreed to conduct explorations for the Western Sea from this base, at no expense to the Crown.

From Kaministiquia, La Vérendrye travelled westward in the 1730s, building fur-trading posts in the Lake of the Woods district and around Lakes Winnipeg and Winnipegosis. The French never found the Western Sea, but they did locate the key to the interior—the Saskatchewan River, whose twin branches flow through the central plains in a huge, wavering Y.

The English established trading posts in the late seventeenth century at the mouths of rivers emptying into Hudson Bay. From these forts they carried on a profitable trade with the Cree and Assiniboine, who, acting as middlemen, brought furs to them and came to dominate the exchange of furs. They charged the First Nations in the interior a considerable markup on the European goods they obtained from the English and, until 1713, from the French.

The Hudson's Bay Company sponsored only two inland expeditions southwest of York Factory, their major post on Hudson Bay. In 1690–91 they sent Henry Kelsey, a young employee, just out of his teens, known to the Hudson's Bay Company's committee in London as (to quote the original document) "a very active lad, delighting much in Indians' compa[ny], being never better pleased than when he is Travelling amongst them,"[1] to explore the interior. He travelled from York Factory with a Cree band and reached the prairies, probably in present-day east-central Saskatchewan.

Indian Greeting White Man, *a painting by the American illustrator Frederic Remington (1861–1909). "Real white men" is what the Blackfoot of Alberta call the French in the Blackfoot language, probably because traders from New France were the first Europeans to make contact with them.*

Frederic Sackrider Remington, *The Parley*, [alternate title, *Indian Greeting White Man*], date unknown, paper print, Collection of Glenbow Museum, Calgary, Canada, 60.2.20.

But upon his return the company decided not to establish costly forts in the interior. As long as the Crees and the Assiniboines brought good furs to them, the English would stay on Hudson Bay.

Then a series of armed clashes occurred on Hudson Bay between the French and the English. By the Treaty of Utrecht in 1713, France recognized England's possession of the coastline of Hudson and James Bay. But the French continued to trade in the interior. So, more than half a century after Kelsey's journey, the English changed their minds. They now felt the effect of strong French competition. In 1754, they sent Anthony Henday inland to convince the First Nations to give up their trade at the French posts and to come to the bay. In the manuscript copies of his report, which is far more precise than Kelsey's, Henday identified the specific groups in the interior and provided notes on their way of life.[2]

The Impact of the Europeans on the First Nations

The arrival of the Europeans greatly altered the First Nations' way of life through the introduction of guns, horses, and new trade patterns. It also led to the rise of a mixed people: the Métis.

The impact of firearms differed for the Woodland peoples such as the Woods Cree and the Woods Assiniboine; and those on the Plains, such as the Blackfoot. The Woodland peoples came to rely on guns much more than those on the Plains, who really only used them in warfare. For the Woodland First Nations, specialists in hunting furs, the gun generally proved more efficient than the bow and arrow, as it eliminated long hours of trapping, waiting for the animal to weaken through loss of blood. Moreover, they had access to the service centres where gunsmiths could repair them; for instance, at York Factory on Hudson Bay, in what is now northeastern Manitoba. Hence, the Woodland groups, despite certain disadvantages—the awkward loading of powder and shot, barrels that were prone to explosion, and the firearms' easy breakage in cold weather—used them a great deal. This reliance on firearms tied them closely to the fur-trading posts.

Distant from service centres, the Plains peoples preferred to use in the buffalo hunt sinew-backed bows with metal-tipped arrows, which did not make a noise that prematurely stampeded a herd. Their experienced hunters could easily reload a bow on horseback. But in battle, the Plains peoples used firearms. Guns had obvious advantages. Bullets went a longer distance than arrows and had greater killing power. Rawhide shields and armour offered little protection against a musket ball. In addition, the gun's loud report gave its user a psychological advantage in battle.

In the early eighteenth century, the Chipewyans, armed with guns, moved further into the woodlands immediately north of the Woodland Crees. Directly supplied by the English at Churchill, the Chipewyans sold European goods to interior nations. Like the Woodland Crees farther south, the Chipewyans became the traders' middlemen. In addition, European guns gave them an advantage in their struggle with the Inuit to the north and the Crees.

Apparently, the Cree already lived along the North Saskatchewan River in the late eighteenth century, but their repeated intrusions ended their initially friendly relations with the Blackfoot or "Prairie People." Individual Cree bands travelled over the plains independently. No single chief coordinated the expansion.

The horse had a greater impact than the gun on the Aboriginal peoples of the prairies. The Blackfoot used horses for hunting buffalo. Horse-mounted warriors replaced those on foot in driving and luring the animals into buffalo pounds or over cliffs (buffalo jumps). Mounted hunters rushed straight into a herd, singled out an animal, rode beside it, and killed it at close range with two or three arrows from their bows. The horse caused a cultural revolution on the Great Plains. It became a symbol of wealth. Some rich individuals owned up to 100 horses. By giving away or even lending horses, individuals enhanced their prestige. Horses were borrowed for hunting and for war parties, with the borrower returning in payment a portion of the game killed or of the goods seized. The horse thus contributed to a class structure among the Aboriginal peoples of the prairies, based on the number of horses owned.

The introduction of the horse had other effects. It intensified warfare between First Nations. Combat on horseback with a bow and arrow, lance, war club, or knife—or a European rifle—led to increased casualties. The horse also enabled the Woodland Assiniboines and many of the Woodland Crees to hunt buffalo on the prairies, thus lessening their dependence on European guns and trade goods. In general, life became very mobile for the First Nations of the Great Plains, particularly for the equestrian Blackfoot-speaking communities.

The Fur Trade after the Fall of New France

After the fall of New France in 1760, the Hudson's Bay Company anticipated a trade monopoly in the North West. But the company soon faced new rivals: aggressive Scottish and American traders operating out of Montreal. In the early 1770s, these traders employed large numbers of French-speaking voyageurs and sent large shipments of goods to the West.

Their arrival on the prairies led to clashes with the First Nations population. In 1779, the Plains Cree attacked a trading post on the North Saskatchewan River, killing two traders. Other incidents occurred, including a battle at a post on the Assiniboine River in 1781, in which three traders and 30 First Nations people died. Only a smallpox epidemic in 1781–1782 saved the traders from large-scale Aboriginal retaliation.

In the early 1780s, the Montreal traders combined their capital to form the North West Company, a decentralized fur-trading operation that soon expanded beyond the French fur trade in the West to include the Peace, Mackenzie, and Columbia River districts.

The Emergence of the North West Company

The North West Company employed experienced French-Canadian, Métis, and Iroquois canoeists. These hardy voyageurs would cross half a continent. As a rule, they were short (long legs were a definite disadvantage in a birchbark canoe), with great strength and endurance. On the journey, they slept only 5 to 6 hours a day. They paddled from 12 to 15, even 18, hours a day if they had to. With their light paddles and rapid strokes, they made 40 to 60 strokes a minute. They regularly portaged loads of 80 kg, sometimes 120 kg, on their backs over rocky trails.

The North West Company underwent great expansion in the 1780s and 1790s. In 1778, fur trader Peter Pond reached the Athabasca and Peace River country (in present-day northern Alberta), rich with fur-bearing animals. In 1789, Alexander Mackenzie journeyed down the Mackenzie River and, in 1793, reached the Pacific Ocean. The company then opened up posts in the Mackenzie Basin and, later, along the Columbia River.

Despite its opponent's great territorial expanse, the Hudson's Bay Company had the advantage of a shorter, hence less expensive, transportation route—Hudson Bay was considerably closer than Montreal to the inland posts. The smaller company could take trade goods to the Athabasca country at about one-half the cost. The Hudson's Bay Company's York boats, although slower and much heavier than a canoe, could carry greater amounts of trade goods in, and more fur bundles out, than could the Nor'Westers' canoes.

A HISTORICAL PORTRAIT

George Nelson

If asked to name the most celebrated fur traders of the late eighteenth and early nineteenth centuries, most historians would immediately mention Samuel Hearne, David Thompson, Alexander Mackenzie, Simon Fraser, Peter Fidler, or Peter Pond. A host of names would follow, but most likely it would be a long while before the name of the lowly, underpaid North West Company clerk George Nelson would surface. He produced no great maps or surveys, made no great voyages of exploration, rose to no great administrative heights. He achieved no fame in his lifetime at all, in contrast to his younger brothers: Wolfred Nelson, a Patriote in the Lower Canadian Rebellion of 1837, and later mayor of Montreal, and Robert Nelson, the Patriotes' leader in 1838, and later a very successful surgeon in the United States.

But for the attention of fur-trade historians Jennifer Brown, Robert Brightman, and Sylvia Van Kirk, George Nelson might still be unknown to students of the Canadian fur trade. His chief distinction, as Brown and Brightman point out in their edited work, *"The Orders of the Dreamed": George Nelson on Cree and Northern Ojibwa Religion and Myth, 1823,*[1] comes from his sensitive recording, in a memoir written nearly two centuries ago, of western Cree and Ojibwa beliefs. He listened to the people and carefully recorded their stories. Sylvia Van Kirk describes his memoir as "one of the finest early ethnographic documents of its kind."[2]

George Nelson (1786–1859) was the son of Loyalists from New York who fled to Quebec to escape the American Revolution. As the son of an English Protestant schoolmaster, George received a good education. From the age of 16, when he entered the fur trade, he lived among First Nations people. From 1802 to 1823 Nelson served as a clerk in present-day Wisconsin, northwestern Ontario, Manitoba, and Saskatchewan. He married Mary Ann, an Ojibwa woman, who was a valuable helpmate in his work. Upon his retirement from the fur trade they settled with their four daughters at Sorel, just east of Montreal.

During his years in the North West, Nelson wrote constantly. Many of his fur-trade journals and his reminiscences (written 10 to 40 years after the events they describe) have survived and are valuable for an understanding of the Aboriginal peoples of the North West. But his memoir of 1823, written in his last year in the fur trade, while Nelson was stationed at Lac la Ronge in northeastern Saskatchewan, is the greatest ethnological treasure because it offers insight into the religion and myth of the Cree and Ojibwa.

In the text, Nelson provided "detail of their private life," including an account of the shaking tent ceremony used by religious leaders to provide a glimpse into the future. Nelson also discussed the importance of dreams to the Aboriginal peoples. Attention is given to the mythical being known as the Windigo: "Suffice it to say that they are of uncommon size—Goliath is an unborn infant to them: and to add to their dread, they are represented as possessing much of the Power of Magicians. Their head reaching to the tops of the highest Poplars (about 70, or 80, feet)."[3]

Nelson's life in Lower Canada after his retirement was not happy. His wife died in 1831. Only one of their children survived into adulthood. Nelson became estranged from his brothers, Wolfred and Robert, on account of their participation in the Rebellions of 1837–1838. He regarded their activities as treason. As a farmer he had little success. Probably his greatest joy after his wife's death came from writing his reminiscences of his days in "Indian country." He died in 1859 at the age of 73.

1. Jennifer S.H. Brown and Robert Brightman, *"The Orders of the Dreamed": George Nelson on Cree and Northern Ojibwa Religion and Myth, 1823* (Winnipeg: University of Manitoba Press, 1988).

2. Sylvia Van Kirk, in collaboration with Jennifer S.H. Brown, "George Nelson," *Dictionary of Canadian Biography*, vol. 8, 1851–1860 (Toronto: University of Toronto Press, 1985), p. 653.

3. Nelson, *"The Orders of the Dreamed,"* p. 86.

Rivalry between the North West Company and the Hudson's Bay Company

Competition from the North West Company forced the Hudson's Bay Company to go farther inland to obtain the best furs. The expansion of the two companies led to the elimination of the Cree and Assiniboine middlemen, as both the Nor'Westers and the Hudson's Bay Company established

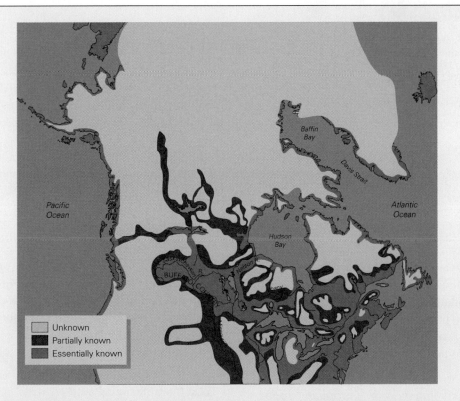

Non-Aboriginals' knowledge of northern North America in 1795.

Source: Adapted from Richard I. Ruggles, *A Country So Interesting: The Hudson's Bay Company and Two Centuries of Mapping, 1670–1870* (Montreal/Kingston: McGill-Queen's University Press, 1991), p. 73.

One of the earliest photographs taken in the Canadian West: a portrait of Susan, a Swampy Cree mixed-blood woman. Photographer Humphrey Lloyd Hime, then 24 years old, took this shot while accompanying the Hind expedition in 1858.

Toronto Reference Library/T14359.

direct contact with the interior hunting bands. The Woodland Assiniboine and the Woodland Cree bands moved out onto the prairie and became provisioners, supplying the two trading companies with pemmican (dried buffalo meat mixed with buffalo fat and berries). Pemmican was easy to transport, kept well, and provided a nutritious, balanced diet. The demands for pemmican were enormous: a voyageur consumed nearly a kilogram a day—the equivalent of approximately three kilograms of fresh meat.

The Rise of the Métis

French fur traders were established in the upper Great Lakes by the 1690s. As they intermarried with Aboriginal women, a group of "mixed-bloods," or Métis, appeared. The number of mixed marriages grew steadily. After a generation or two, Métis settlements extended from the upper Great Lakes west to the Red River and south through the Great Plains to the Arkansas River. Their culture uniquely blended Aboriginal and European customs. They saw themselves as constituting a "new nation."

The Métis at the Red River

In the early nineteenth century, encampments of the French and their mixed-blood descendants developed at the junction of the Red and the Assiniboine rivers (at present-day Winnipeg). The increasing

WHERE HISTORIANS DISAGREE

The First Nations' Role in the Fur Trade

For years, many fur-trade historians argued that the First Nations were passive agents in a trade dominated by more dynamic European traders. In *The Fur Trade and the Northwest to 1857*, for instance, E.E. Rich wrote that

> within a decade of their becoming acquainted with European goods, tribe after tribe became utterly dependent on regular European supplies. The bow and arrow went

> out of use, and the Indian starved if he did not own a serviceable gun, powder, and shot; and in his tribal wars he was even more dependent on European arms.[1]

In the 1970s and early 1980s, Arthur J. Ray, Robin Fisher, Daniel Francis, Toby Morantz, and Paul C. Thistle challenged this interpretation. They underlined the independence of the Aboriginal peoples and their power in the trade.

Historian Olive Dickason summarized the new approach in a review of Paul C. Thistle's *Indian–European Trade Relations in the Lower Saskatchewan River Region to 1840*:

> Common to all of these works is the theme that Amerindians were as aware as Europeans in matters of self-interest, and during the early days of the fur trade at least, were able to manipulate matters to their own advantage. As long as they held the monopoly in fur production, they were also able to dictate the terms by which they were willing to trade. It was only when the exploitative nature of the fur trade began to affect the availability of resources, coupled with the widening technological gap that was a consequence of the Industrial Revolution, that Europeans were able to gain the upper hand.[2]

This led to a recognition of the First Nations' role in the fur trade as partners and initiators, as well as consumers. They became involved by their own choice. As historian Robin Fisher notes, concerning the early West Coast maritime fur trade, "The Indians of the northwest coast exercised a great deal of control over the trading relationship and, as a consequence, remained in control of their culture during this early contact period."[3] He added: "Even in these early years, the Indians were not passive objects of exploitation. Rather, they vigorously grew accustomed to the presence of the Europeans; they also became shrewder in trading with them."[4]

The absence of Aboriginal peoples' narratives remains the great weakness of research into the fur trade. Daniel Francis questions whether this has led historians to overemphasize the importance of the trading exchanges. In his *Battle for the West: Fur Traders and the Birth of Western Canada*, he observed that

> the two groups met briefly at the posts to exchange goods, each receiving from the other things it could not produce for itself. Then they parted, the Indians returning to a world the trader never entered or understood, a world with its own patterns of trade, its own religion and social relations, its own wars and alliances.... [For] the most part traders were peripheral to the real concerns of the Indian people.[5]

Aboriginal-written studies have partially compensated for the absence of earlier First Nations accounts, including George Blondin's *When the World Was New: Stories of the Sahtú Dene* and Edward Ahenakew's *Voices of the Plains Cree*.[6]

---

1. E.E. Rich, *The Fur Trade and the Northwest to 1857* (Toronto: McClelland & Stewart, 1967), pp. 102–103.

2. Olive Dickason, "Review of Indian–European Trade Relations in the Lower Saskatchewan River Region to 1840 by Paul C. Thistle," *Western Canadian Publications Project Newsletter*, 21 (May 1987): 2.

3. Robin Fisher, *Contact and Conflict: Indian–European Relations in British Columbia, 1774–1890* (Vancouver: University of British Columbia Press, 1977), p. 1.

4. Ibid., p. 4.

5. Daniel Francis, *Battle for the West: Fur Traders and the Birth of Western Canada* (Edmonton: Hurtig, 1982), p. 62.

6. George Blondin, *When the World Was New: Stories of the Sahtú Dene* (Yellowknife: Outcrop Books, 1990); and Edward Ahenakew, *Voices of the Plains Cree*, Ruth M. Buck, ed. (Regina: Canadian Plains Research Center, 1995; orig. pub. 1973).

number of intermarriages furthered the growth of the "new nation" of the Métis. Like the mixed-bloods on the upper Great Lakes, the Red River Métis built homes of squared logs covered with bark roofs. They made a special baking-powder biscuit called "bannock," still a staple food in Métis communities today. Although they farmed a little, growing peas and potatoes in small gardens behind their cabins, they lived essentially off the buffalo hunt in the early nineteenth century.

They also introduced European technology to prairie life. For example, they introduced the small wagons used by the French Canadians in Quebec. These "Red River carts," built entirely of wood and tied together with leather, were easy to repair and very efficient. But the carts' constant rubbing of wood against wood made a terrible noise (one observer described it as the sound of a thousand fingernails being drawn across a thousand panes of glass at the same time). As well, the carts stirred up clouds of dust that could be seen several kilometres away. Still, the Red River carts aided the Métis during the buffalo hunt. An ox-drawn cart could carry a load of 400 kg more than 30 km in a day. Several carts could be tied together in a caravan, enabling one driver to handle five oxen and carts. Soon the Red River cart trails rivalled the rivers as transportation routes.

Aboriginal Women in the Fur Trade

By the late eighteenth and early nineteenth centuries, many North West Company and Hudson's Bay Company employees had First Nation wives. Besides providing companionship and emotional support, they offered voyageurs economic benefits too: the daughter of a leading hunter or chief brought to her new husband the trade of his new father-in-law, as well as that of his immediate relations. Aboriginal wives also taught the traders the customs and languages of the First Nations. As well, they acted as guides and interpreters for their husbands. Moreover, they made pemmican, gathered berries, fished, dressed skins, and made moccasins and snowshoes, all essential skills for the fur traders' survival.

By the early 1800s, interracial marriage between Europeans and the First Nations had become so common that about 1000 First Nations women and Métis children lived at North West Company posts. The company encouraged its labourers to marry the mixed-blood daughters of the older employees rather than First Nations women, in an effort to reduce the number of dependants at its posts, and thereby the demands for assistance. Many young Métis women had the ideal background for life as wives at a fur-trading post: they knew both the skills of their First Nations ancestors and the domestic duties required at the post—cleaning, planting, and harvesting.

The Red River Colony

In 1811, Lord Douglas, the Fifth Earl of Selkirk, and a leading shareholder in the Hudson's Bay Company, persuaded the company to establish a European agricultural colony at the forks of the Red and Assiniboine rivers. The colony would provide a home to retire in for Hudson's Bay Company employees and their Aboriginal wives and families. It would also become an agricultural centre to supply provisions for the company's workforce in the interior. As well, the colony could serve as a refuge for evicted Scottish tenant farmers.

The following year, Selkirk recruited the majority of his settlers from Kildonan, Sutherlandshire, in Scotland, where the evictions of the tenant farmers to make sheep runs had been particularly brutal. After his family acquired a controlling interest in the Hudson's Bay Company, Selkirk obtained from the company an enormous land grant of 300 000 km^2 in the Red River valley—five times the size of Scotland—that he named Assiniboia. The location was contentious, because it lay across the North West Company's vital pemmican supply line in the heart of the Red River valley, thus threatening to curtail its availability; however, the North West Company failed to prevent the founding of the colony.

The Establishment of the Selkirk Colony

The advance party of 18 of Selkirk's settlers reached the Red River from Hudson Bay in late August 1812, and another 120 joined them in late October. Miles Macdonell, Selkirk's choice as governor, established the settlers near the junction of the Red and the Assiniboine rivers (now downtown Winnipeg).

The idealistic and impractical Lord Selkirk sent them off without ploughs, with only hoes and spades to use for cultivation. As well, the colony's lifeline of communication stretched back more than 1000 km to a tiny fort on Hudson Bay, visited once a year by ships from Britain. Only the assistance of the local Métis and North West Company traders enabled the Selkirk settlers to survive those first two years.

Then Macdonell unwittingly antagonized the Métis. He issued a "pemmican proclamation" in January 1814 that put an embargo on the export of pemmican from the Red River settlement. This action hurt the North West Company, because it depended on Red River pemmican to

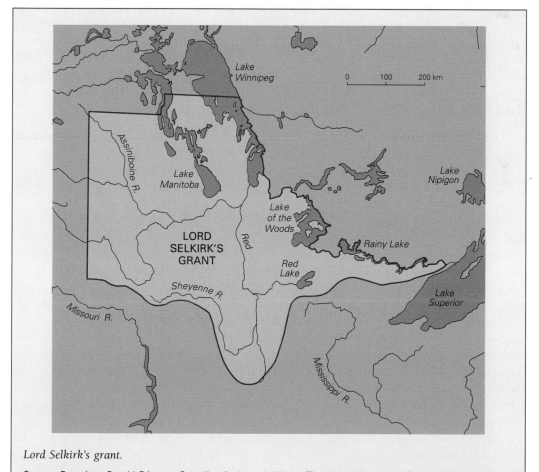

Lord Selkirk's grant.

Source: Based on Gerald Friesen, *Canadian Prairies: A History* (Toronto: University of Toronto Press, 1984), pp. 90–91.

feed its voyageurs in the interior. The proclamation confirmed the Nor'Westers' suspicions that the Hudson's Bay Company had planted the Red River colony to ruin them.

In 1816 the rivalry intensified between the two companies. The Nor'Westers selected young Cuthbert Grant, the son of a Scottish Nor'Wester and a Cree mother, then in his early twenties, and three French-speaking Métis to head a movement of French-speaking Métis to drive out the Selkirk colonists.

Seven Oaks and Its Aftermath

On June 19, 1816, on a field called Seven Oaks, Grant and a party of some 60 or 70 Métis confronted Governor Robert Semple and some 25 settlers and Hudson's Bay Company employees. Fighting broke out, and Semple and 20 of his men lost their lives. Only one of Grant's men was killed.

The victory strengthened Métis unity by reinforcing an identity that had already existed among the French-speaking Métis in the Red River valley. Within hours, Pierre Falcon, the Prairie Métis bard, told the story of the conflict in the "Chanson de la Grenouillère," or "Song of Frog Plain." That song became the French-speaking Métis' national anthem. Their collective memory of the victory gave the French-speaking Métis in the Red River a cohesion and a common identity that the English-speaking mixed-bloods (called the "Country-born") around the Hudson's Bay Company posts to the north lacked.

The violence at Red River prompted the British government to seek a forced solution to the rivalry. It pressured the two financially exhausted companies to unite. In 1821, the Hudson's Bay and North West companies merged. The consolidated company, the Hudson's Bay Company, ended the North West Company's trade route via Montreal and shipped its furs through Hudson Bay. After 1821, only 5 percent of the furs exported from British North America passed through Montreal.

Red River Society in the Mid-Nineteenth Century

The Red River Scottish colonists and mixed-blood farmers faced many environmental challenges throughout the early nineteenth century: grasshoppers, early frosts, and floods. Whenever the Red River overflowed its banks, the water spread quickly over huge areas because of the flatness of the valley. Only by the 1840s did the settlement of some 6000 inhabitants achieve a level of stability and prosperity.

The Métis resided south and west of the forks of the two rivers. They numbered almost half the total population. To the north, down the Red River toward Lake Winnipeg, lived the Country-born, who comprised about a third of the settlement. Their neighbours, the original Selkirk settlers, numbered about a tenth of the Red River population, and the First Nations another tenth.

The Country-born came from the northern Hudson's Bay Company posts. Many of their European ancestors came from the Orkney Islands, northwest of Scotland, a stopping point for the HBC vessels en route to Hudson Bay. Before 1800, the Hudson's Bay Company recruited more than 80 percent of its personnel there. Most of them were under 21 years of age. They worked as contract labourers for three or four years before returning home. Some, however, remained much longer; a few stayed for more than 20 years. These individuals fathered large families. Many used their savings to provide for their "country wives" and Aboriginal children before leaving to retire in the Orkneys or in Scotland. With the establishment of Selkirk's permanent settlement, many retired employees of the company now stayed in the Red River colony with their Aboriginal families. Their children were introduced to farming. Many also joined the Anglican Church, first established in the West by John West in 1820. A few obtained positions in the Hudson's Bay Company.

Although racial bonds and the common use of the Cree or Ojibwa languages united the Country-born and the French-speaking Métis, religion and their place of residence in the Red

River colony divided them. Canadian historian John Foster wrote of the Country-born that a number "moved comfortably among the Métis. Others were more at home with the Indians.... Still others served a leadership role among the Kildonan Scots. Equal diversity could be found in terms of occupation and wealth."[3]

The French-Speaking Métis

The French-speaking Métis created a cohesive community, unified, in particular, by their Roman Catholic faith. The arrival of the first French-speaking priests in the Red River settlement in 1818, followed by the first Oblate missionaries and the first sisters, the Grey Nuns, in the 1840s, strengthened the Métis' Christian faith as well as their knowledge of the language and culture of their French-Canadian ancestors.

Métis Encampment on a Buffalo Hunt, *a painting by Paul Kane. The Upper Canadian painter is one of the best-known early artists of the West.*

912.1.25: *Metis Encampment* (oil on canvas), 1848–1856; Kane, Paul; ROM2003_815_2. With permission of the Royal Ontario Museum © ROM.

The Métis also obtained a sense of community through participation in their expanding buffalo hunt. In the 1840s, they went on two annual hunts from the Red River—in June and in September or October. These expeditions included more than 1000 people. The Métis elected ten captains by vote at a general council, one of whom they named "chief of the hunt," or "governor." Each captain had ten "soldiers" under his command who helped the governor of the hunt maintain order. Rigid discipline prevented the premature stampede of the herds and was essential in the resistance to raids by the Sioux.

The Sayer Trial, 1849

The Métis, the largest group in the Red River colony, came to resent the Hudson's Bay Company's tight control over the settlement. The test case of Métis power came during the trial of Pierre-Guillaume Sayer, a Métis trader arrested in 1849 on a charge of illegally trafficking in furs. The Hudson's Bay Company argued that Sayer violated its monopoly by selling goods to the colonists and trading with the First Nations. The judge, however, imposed no sentence. It would have been difficult to do so, because the Métis hunters constituted the most powerful military force in the colony. When Sayer emerged from the courthouse a free man, the Métis knew that they had broken the Hudson's Bay Company's monopoly. After the trial, the Hudson's Bay Company recognized French as an official language in the Red River colony.

The second test of Métis power came two years later. As the Métis moved farther to the southwest to hunt buffalo, they came into conflict with the Sioux. The Métis–Sioux wars intensified in the 1840s and came to a head in 1851, at the battle of Grand Coteau ("big hillock"), southeast of present-day Minot, North Dakota. The Métis victory at Grand Coteau over a numerically larger party of Sioux demonstrated their growing military supremacy in the Red River and surrounding areas.

The End of the Red River Colony's Isolation

By the 1840s, the Red River Métis had developed a largely self-sufficient economy based on the buffalo hunt, some small-scale farming, and seasonal labour for the Hudson's Bay Company. But it was in the 1850s that the colony's horizons grew enormously, mainly as a result of its more frequent contacts with St. Paul, Minnesota, to the south.

St. Paul gradually replaced York Factory on Hudson Bay as the Red River's major entrepôt. From 1851 to 1869, the number of Red River carts journeying to St. Paul, Minnesota, to sell furs and purchase supplies rose from 100 to 2500. Mail service to the Red River colony came through St. Paul after 1853, rather than by the slower and more cumbersome route through York Factory on Hudson Bay. A railway reached St. Paul in 1855, and within a year the Hudson's Bay Company itself used it to bring in supplies. The establishment of a regular steamboat connection with St. Paul and to the Red River colony in 1859 made the ties with Minnesota (with a population of nearly 200 000 by 1860) all the more binding. Fortunately for British North America the outbreak of the American Civil War in 1861–1865, and the war between the Americans and the Sioux in 1862–1864, prevented Minnesota's annexation of the Red River country in the 1860s.

Many Métis moved farther west in the early 1860s attracted by rising opportunities in the buffalo-hide trade. Those who spent the winter on the prairies to be nearer the herds became known as *hivernants* ("winterers"). The growing Métis involvement in the buffalo-robe trade led them to establish settlements at the forks of the Saskatchewan River, in the North Saskatchewan River valley, in the Cypress Hills area of present-day southwestern Saskatchewan, and at Lac Ste. Anne, about 80 km northwest of Fort Edmonton. Lac Ste. Anne became the largest Métis settlement in the North West outside of the Red River colony until St. Albert (about 15 km northwest of Edmonton) was founded in 1862. By the mid-1860s, the buffalo herds had migrated so far from present-day Manitoba that the Red River–based hunt had almost ended.

In 1871, approximately 2000–4000 mixed-bloods lived along the North Saskatchewan River between the Red River and the Rockies, and about 11 000 at the junction of the Red and the Assiniboine rivers. The Métis and Country-born population of 13 000–15 000 was approximately one-half of the estimated number of Plains First Nations in British North America. The mixed-bloods' increasingly frequent intrusions into the First Nations' hunting grounds in search of buffalo bred resentment.

The Plains First Nations in the Mid-Nineteenth Century

While the Métis and Country-born population doubled in the Red River every 15–20 years, that of the Plains First Nations seriously declined in the mid-nineteenth century. In 1837–1838, smallpox ravaged the Great Plains nations, just as it had a half-century earlier (in 1780–1782). Such diseases tended to be carried along the trade routes—the drainage systems of the Missouri and Saskatchewan rivers. Non-Aboriginal crews usually carried the smallpox viruses. The boat brigades' tight schedules often caused crews to be dispatched while the men were still infectious. They moved into the interior and infected the First Nations who had gathered in their large summer camps. They, in turn, carried the disease farther inland.

Thanks to the efforts of the Hudson's Bay Company traders, many of the Cree around the company's posts were saved. The discovery of a smallpox vaccine in Europe around 1800 checked the spread of the epidemic. The Hudson's Bay Company began an extensive vaccination program among the Aboriginal peoples. The vaccinated population constituted an effective barrier, and the highly contagious disease spread no farther north than the Hudson's Bay Company posts on the northern fringes of the prairies. Saved from smallpox, the Cree became the most numerous First Nations group on the Canadian prairies. After the epidemic ran its course, the Crees could more readily move farther onto the prairies because the strength of the Blackfoot-speaking nations had been so reduced. But smallpox continued to take its toll. In the epidemic of 1870 more than 3500 First Nations, Métis, and Country-born on the Canadian Plains died.

Other infectious killer diseases also ravaged the Aboriginal peoples. In 1864–1865, more than 1000 Blackfoot-speaking people died of an outbreak of scarlet fever. A measles epidemic hit the

Cree. Influenza and whooping cough also spread through their communities. A new disease—tuberculosis—arrived in the 1860s, brought by refugee Sioux from the United States and by Red River people moving west (both groups had already been exposed to the deadly bacterium).

The Arrival of the Whisky Traders

In the mid-1860s, the Blackfoot experienced another assault: that of the American whisky traders. In the 1850s and the early 1860s, the Blackfoot had traded with both the Hudson's Bay Company and the American Fur Company. At Fort Edmonton and Rocky Mountain House they exchanged pemmican and horses, as well as the few beaver furs they trapped, for British trade goods. At Fort Benton, in Montana, they traded bulky buffalo hides and robes (which were difficult for the Hudson's Bay Company to transport profitably in their York boats) for American goods. The hides made excellent coats and robes. They could also be tanned into tough and durable leather suitable for making industrial machinery belts. The American Fur Company bought all that it could, shipping the furs down the Missouri by steamer to St. Louis.

The stability of the Missouri River fur trade suddenly ended, however, in 1864 with the collapse of the American Fur Company. Then, just after the end of the American Civil War in 1865, the discovery of gold brought a flood of prospectors and merchants to the mountains of Montana. With them came a flourishing whisky trade. After U.S. marshals began to enforce laws against the trade, many of the traders moved north to present-day southern Alberta and Saskatchewan to make their fortunes. Their arrival led to great social disruption among groups that had little acquaintance with alcohol and no social controls in place to deal with its consequences.

The North West on the Eve of Canadian Settlement

Until the late 1850s, the fur traders and the early visitors to the North West had all reported that the treeless prairies, which stretched as far as the eye could see, were unsuitable for farming. This perception changed in the late 1850s, and by the 1860s, Canadians had come to covet the North West. The lack of good agricultural land in the United Canadas made the western lands more inviting. In the early 1860s, both the Canadian and the British expeditions to the North West published their findings. Of the two, the British-sponsored expedition led by John Palliser is the best known. Dispatched in 1857, it was commissioned to report on the possibilities for agricultural settlement. In the same year, the Canadians sent out an expedition with Henry Youle Hind, a professor of geology and chemistry at Trinity University in Toronto, as scientific observer. Both expeditions reported on the magnificent possibilities for European agriculture, particularly in the Red River area and in the "fertile belt" of the North Saskatchewan River valley. These findings provided the incentive for the westward expansion of the eastern British North American colonies.

The First Nations remained the dominant group on the Plains until the late nineteenth century. By the 1860s, however, their political power had been reduced by severe population losses through epidemics, the rapidly diminishing buffalo herds, and the rise of a new mixed-blood population who now intruded into their hunting grounds. And, in the Red River area at least, small numbers of Canadians began to arrive.

North of the Prairies

The majority of the North's indigenous peoples, the First Nations and the Inuit, enjoyed uncontested political control of their homelands until the late nineteenth century and, in many more isolated areas, into the twentieth. Arctic explorers, fur traders, and Christian missionaries

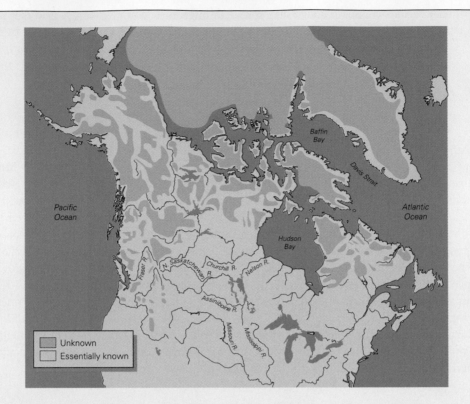

Non-Aboriginals' knowledge of northern North America in 1870.

Source: Adapted from Richard I. Ruggles, *A Country So Interesting: The Hudson's Bay Company and Two Centuries of Mapping, 1670–1870* (Montreal/Kingston: McGill-Queen's University Press, 1991), p. 119.

were the first non-Aboriginal newcomers to come north. A very small number of Christian missionaries, Roman Catholic and Anglican, arrived around 1850, or about half a century after the fur traders. Until the late nineteenth century, however, the number of church workers in the North remained quite small.

A decade or so after Alexander Mackenzie's voyage, in 1789, down the river that now bears his name, the North West Company established its first posts in the Mackenzie River valley. After the merger of the North West and Hudson's Bay Companies in 1821, the revitalized Hudson's Bay Company extended its operations throughout the Mackenzie River valley. By the 1840s, the company was expanding over the Mackenzie Mountains into the Yukon River valley.

As in the south, European epidemics, inadvertently brought north by the fur traders, devastated Aboriginal communities. Anthropologist Shepard Krech III has written that the Gwitch'in (Kutchin) in the northern Yukon and adjacent area, for example, had an estimated population of about 5400 people in the early nineteenth century. By the 1860s, this number had been reduced to an estimated 850 to 900.[4]

In the early nineteenth century, British naval parties resumed the search for the Northwest Passage—not for economic reasons but for the international prestige of locating it. Sir John Franklin became one of the most famous explorers of all time. Sent off, in 1844, with the latest technological assistance, with ships heated by pipes fired from steam boilers, and with a three-year supply of canned food, the expedition seemed guaranteed of success. Yet Franklin, on this, his third Arctic expedition, refused to adapt to indigenous technology. He took no dogs, sleds, pemmican, or Inuit clothing. Within two years, the entire expedition of 129 men perished, as their ships became locked in pack ice near King William Island in the central Arctic. Even their great source of food, the canned provisions, turned out to be a liability, as the seams, soldered with lead, leaked the toxic metal into the food.

Over 30 expeditions searched for Franklin and his missing party between 1847 and 1859: first, unsuccessfully, for survivors; and second, after evidence surfaced of their deaths, for explanations of the expedition's failure. The intensive search resulted in a large part of the Canadian Arctic Archipelago being charted and the northern limits of the North American continent established. Their sailing in and out of Arctic bays and inlets, and their wintering over on Arctic ice, led the English to claim sovereignty over the Inuits' homeland.

The fur trade attracted first the French to the North West, and later the British. Two rival companies in the British period—the Hudson's Bay Company (founded in 1670) and the North West Company (established in the 1780s)—vied for monopoly over the fur trade in the region. In 1821, the British government forced a merger of the two companies under the Hudson's Bay Company name. Settlement grew in the area, first at the junction of the Red and Assiniboine rivers, and later, in the 1860s, farther west, nearer the diminishing buffalo grounds. The intermarriage of fur traders and First Nations had led to the creation of two new peoples, the Métis and the Country-born. By the end of the 1860s, these two mixed-blood groups numbered from 13 000 to 15 000 in the North West, roughly half of the Plains First Nations population, estimated to be 25 000. It was the Métis, with their sense of constituting "a new nation," who would confront the Canadians when they attempted to take control of the region in the late 1860s.

NOTES

1. The HBC Committee in London, quoted in K.G. Davies, "Henry Kelsey," *Dictionary of Canadian Biography*, vol. 2, *1700–1740* (Toronto: University of Toronto Press, 1969), p. 308.

2. Barbara Belyea presents all four surviving versions of Anthony Henday's report on his 1754–1755 journey in *A Year Inland* (Waterloo, ON: Wilfrid Laurier University Press, 2000).

3. John Foster, "The Country-Born in the Red River Settlement (c. 1820–1870)," Ph.D. thesis, University of Alberta, 1973, p. 264.

4. Shepard Krech III, "On the Aboriginal Population of the Kutchin," in Kenneth S. Coates and William R. Morrison, eds., *Interpreting Canada's North: Selected Readings* (Toronto: Copp Clark Pitman, 1989), p. 66.

BEYOND THE BOOK

Champlain Society

http://link.library.utoronto.ca/champlain/search.cfm?lang=eng
The digital collections of the Champlain Society contain several important European accounts of Rupert's Land and the Red River Colony. Browse the database by subject, and select, for example, "Manitoba—History," "Northwest, Canadian—History—Sources," or "Selkirk, Thomas Douglas, Earl of, 1771–1820—Diaries."

Red River Journal

http://www.canadiana.org/ECO/ItemRecord/41912?id=a2008919b6c6abaa
A digitized journal depicting life at the Red River Colony during the years 1820–1823.

Red River Settlement Papers

http://www.nosracines.ca/e/toc.aspx?id=1180
Digitized collection of published letters, dispatches, and other documents from the early Red River Settlement, published in 1819.

Food and the Fur Trade

http://www.whiteoak.org/learning/food.htm
A detailed discussion of how the fur traders obtained and prepared provisions.

Cuthbert Grant

http://www.biographi.ca/009004-119.01-e.php?&id_nbr=3942
Cuthbert Grant was a fur trader and Métis leader in the 1800s. This biography of Grant details his service to the North West Company and his influence among the Métis people as a whole.

In Pursuit of Adventure: The North West Company

http://digital.library.mcgill.ca/nwc/toolbar_1.htm
A database of letters, records, and maps used by the North West Company and other fur-trading companies at the end of the eighteenth and beginning of the nineteenth centuries. Click "Manuscripts" or "Maps/Routes" at the top of the page to search.

The Pathfinders

Canada: A People's History—Episode 6, The Pathfinders. Directed by Michelle Métivier (CBC, 2001).

The Trade

Fred Stenson, *The Trade* (Vancouver: Douglas and McIntyre, 2000). A novel that reviews the years in the North West immediately after the union of the Hudson's Bay Company and the North West Company in 1821.

Isobel Gunn

Audrey Thomas, *Isobel Gunn: A Novel* (Toronto: Penguin Canada, 2000). An historical novel about the first non-Aboriginal woman to live and work around 1806–1807 in what is now known as Manitoba prior to the Selkirk settlement.

RELATED READINGS

Three useful essays on this topic appear in R. Douglas Francis and Donald B. Smith, eds., *Viewpoints: Readings in Canadian History* (Toronto: Thomson Nelson, 2007): Frits Pannekoek, "The Flock Divided: Factions and Feuds at Red River," pp. 152–58; Irene M. Spry, "The Métis and Mixed-Bloods of Rupert's Land before 1870," pp. 159–75; and "The Mitchif Language of the Metis," pp. 175–79.

BIBLIOGRAPHY

Gerald Friesen's *The Canadian Prairies: A History* (Toronto: University of Toronto Press, 1984) provides an excellent overview of the entire period; as does Sarah Carter, *Aboriginal People and Colonizers of Western Canada to 1900* (Toronto: University of Toronto Press, 1999). Cole Harris's chapter, "The Northwestern Interior, 1760–1870," is useful, in his, *The Reluctant Land. Society, Space, and Environment In Canada before Confederation* (Vancouver: UBC Press, 2008), pp. 377–415. Two well-illustrated books are William R. Morrison, *True North: The Yukon and Northwest Territories* (Toronto: Oxford University Press, 1998); and John Herd Thompson, *Forging the Prairie West* (Toronto: Oxford University Press, 1998). For the Mackenzie River basin, see Kerry Abel's *Drum Songs: Glimpses of Dene History* (Montreal/Kingston: McGill-Queen's University Press, 1993). R. Douglas Francis reviews changing perceptions of the Northwest in *Images of the West* (Saskatoon: Western Producer Prairie Books, 1989). Kerry Abel provides a complete bibliographic guide to the historical literature in "The Northwest and the North," in M. Brook Taylor, ed., *Canadian History: A Reader's Guide*, vol. 1, *Beginnings to Confederation* (Toronto: University of Toronto Press, 1994), pp. 325–55.

For information on the First Nations in the eighteenth and nineteenth centuries, consult Arthur Ray, *Indians in the Fur Trade* (Toronto: University of Toronto Press, 1974), and John Ewer's *The Blackfeet* (Norman: University of Oklahoma Press, 1958) and *The Horse in Blackfoot Indian Culture* (Washington, DC: Smithsonian Institution Press, 1955). On cultural change on the northern Plains, an essential work is Theodore Binnema's *Common and Contested Ground: A Human and Environmental History of the Northwestern Plains* (Norman: University of Oklahoma Press, 2001). Barbara Belyea presents the several phases of the fur trade's expansion westward in *Dark Storm Moving Westward* (Calgary: University of Calgary Press, 2007). For background on the impact of disease, see the early section of Maureen K. Lux, *Medicine That Walks: Disease, Medicine, and Canadian Plains Native People, 1880–1940* (Toronto: University of Toronto Press, 2001). Hugh Dempsey's *Firewater: The Impact of the Whiskey Trade on the Blackfoot Nation* (Calgary: Fifth House, 2002) reviews the topic of substance abuse.

Dan Francis provides an overview of the fur trade in *Battle for the West: Fur Traders and the Birth of Western Canada* (Edmonton: Hurtig, 1982). For short sketches of the most important European fur traders, see the essays on Kelsey, La Vérendrye, Henday, Hearne, Thompson, and others in the 14 volumes of the *Dictionary of Canadian Biography* (Toronto: University of Toronto Press, 1966–1998), now available online: www.biographi.ca. The story of Aboriginal women and the fur trade is told by Jennifer S.H. Brown in *Strangers in Blood: Fur Trade Company Families in Indian Country* (Vancouver: University of British Columbia Press, 1980); by Sylvia Van Kirk in *"Many Tender Ties": Women in Fur Trade Society in Western Canada* (Winnipeg: Watson & Dwyer, 1980); and most recently by Susan Sleeper-Smith in *Indian Women and French Men: Rethinking Cultural Encounter in the Western Great Lakes* (Amherst, MA: University of Massachusetts Press, 2001).

The Métis are the subject of many studies. One popular work is D. Bruce Sealey and Antoine S. Lussier, *The Métis: Canada's Forgotten People* (Winnipeg: Manitoba Métis Federation Press, 1975). George Woodcock translated Marcel Giraud's classic *Le Métis Canadien* (Paris: Institut d'ethnologie, Université de Paris, 1945) into English, under the title *The Métis in the Canadian West*, 2 vols. (Edmonton: University of Alberta Press, 1986). Gerhard Ens reviews the movement of the Métis westward in *Homeland to Hinterland: The Changing Worlds of the Red River Métis in the Nineteenth Century* (Toronto: University of Toronto Press, 1996). Jacqueline Peterson and Jennifer S.H. Brown have edited *The New People: Being and Becoming Métis in North America* (Winnipeg: University of Manitoba Press, 1985).

Valuable maps of the Northwest appear in R. Cole Harris, ed., *Historical Atlas of Canada*, vol. 1, *From the Beginning to 1800* (Toronto: University of Toronto Press, 1987); R. Louis Gentilcore, ed., *The Historical Atlas of Canada*, vol. 2, *The Land Transformed, 1800–1891* (Toronto: University of Toronto Press, 1993); and Richard I. Ruggles, *A Country So Interesting: The Hudson's Bay Company and Two Centuries of Mapping, 1670–1870* (Montreal/Kingston: McGill-Queen's University Press, 1991)

Chapter Ten

THE PACIFIC COAST TO THE 1860s

TIME LINE

1774	The Spanish expedition led by Juan Pérez encounters the Haida off the Queen Charlotte Islands
1793	Fur trader Alexander Mackenzie becomes the first European to cross the continent via Lake Athabasca to the Pacific Ocean
1827	Fort Langley is built by the Hudson's Bay Company near the mouth of the Fraser River
1843	The Hudson's Bay Company builds Fort Victoria on Vancouver Island
1846	Under the Oregon Treaty, the 49th parallel becomes the international boundary between British and American claims from the Rocky Mountains to the Pacific
1849	The colony of Vancouver Island is established by the Hudson's Bay Company at the request of the British Crown
1858	The Fraser River gold rush leads to the establishment of the mainland colony of British Columbia, separate from the colony of Vancouver Island
1866	The two colonies of British Columbia and Vancouver Island are united

The First Nations population of present-day British Columbia lived along the major salmon rivers, at scattered village sites along the ocean, and inland along the river systems. Europeans only made first contact with the First Nations of what is now coastal British Columbia in the 1770s, nearly three centuries after large-scale European contact with the First Nations of northeastern North America.

Initially, Spain, Russia, Britain, and the United States competed for control. Eventually, however, only Britain and the United States contested the sector between Russian Alaska and Spanish California. In 1818, they agreed to joint occupancy of the area. Twenty-eight years later, in 1846, the two countries consented to extend the international border along the 49th parallel from the prairies to the Pacific, and to include Vancouver Island in Britain's jurisdiction.

Immigrants first settled at the southern tip of Vancouver Island in the 1840s and then at the mouth of the Fraser River during the gold rush of 1858. In the 1860s, the newcomers claimed ownership of the entire coast and interior of British Columbia, even though well into the nineteenth century, the First Nations outnumbered them.

The First Nations of the Northwest Coast

The First Nations have lived on the Pacific coast for thousands of years. One of the oldest archaeological sites on the North Pacific coast is the Fraser River canyon, which dates back at least 8500 years. The Aboriginal peoples probably arrived in successive waves, for nineteen distinct languages are represented on the British Columbia coast today. Hemmed in by towering mountains, the narrow coastline was heavily populated. It is estimated that nearly half of the total First Nations population of Canada lived in British Columbia at the moment of European contact. For these maritime people, salmon became the main food resource. They used red cedar for the construction of their plank houses, canoes, containers, and carved masks, as well as their most famous creations—totem poles.

Notions of Property

In several respects, the Northwest Coast peoples had a notion of property similar to that of Europeans. A large group of kinspeople, or a lineage—a group of people who had a common ancestor in the real or mythological past—formed the primary unit of their societies. One or several kin groups might occupy the same winter village, and these villages in turn constituted independent units within the larger nation. Local kin groups claimed ownership of the fishing stations, berry patches, cedar groves, and stretches of beach. When they left their permanent winter villages for the salmon fisheries, they went to their own recognized stretches of the rivers. When the Europeans came, the chiefs or leaders of the kin groups made them pay for the wood and even the fresh water they used.

First Nation Impressions of the Europeans

The Squamish of the Capilano reserve at Vancouver tell about the first time their ancestors encountered the newcomers, a century and a half earlier. As Chief Mathias told the story, the warriors hesitated going on board the floating island with cobwebs hanging from the sticks growing on it, until, with great misgivings, the bravest climbed the rope ladder onto the deck. The pale-faced captain, who looked like a corpse, advanced with outstretched hand. Never having heard of the handshake, the chief thought they were being challenged to a First Nation finger-wrestling match. He therefore waved away the man with whom the captain was trying to shake hands and called for the Squamish strongman to accept the challenge. Seeing he was misunderstood, the captain shrugged and approached the chief with outstretched hand. The chief then said to the strongman,

The beautiful seagoing canoes of the Northwest Coast were usually made of a single felled cedar, which was hollowed and shaped to meet specified requirements.

Library and Archives Canada/C-30193.

"He doesn't want you. He thinks you are not strong enough." With that, the chief refused to consider the captain's "challenge." The strangers' gifts also greatly puzzled Mathias's ancestors. It appeared to them that they had received snow in a sack (flour) and buttons (coins).[1]

European Exploration of the Northwest Coast

Although Spain was the first European power to reach the Pacific Ocean, it took the Spanish two-and-a-half centuries to advance northward from Mexico. Crippled by economic depressions, epidemics, and defeats on European battlefields, Spain lost its pioneering spirit. Rival European empires had seized Spanish islands in the West Indies, but luckily for Spain, its European rivals seldom ventured to the Pacific, until Russians arrived in the eighteenth century.

Russian Activity in the North Pacific

Vitus Bering, a Danish navigator in the Russian service, made the first documented Russian voyage to present-day Alaska. In 1728, he sailed along the eastern coast of Siberia until he found the strait that now bears his name. Then, in 1741, he explored an area in present-day southeastern Alaska. His voyage established Russia's claim to the Alaskan Panhandle and led to Russian economic expansion in the Pacific.

Rumours of the Russian activity prompted Spain to advance northward to protect Mexico. They established settlements in California at San Diego, Monterey, and San Francisco, and sponsored expeditions to investigate Russian advances along the Northwest Coast and to assert Spanish sovereignty north of Mexico. Juan Pérez sailed in late January 1774 to Alaska, but bad weather forced him to turn back just north of the Queen Charlotte Islands. Pérez met 150 Haidas off the Queen Charlottes—the first recorded meeting between Europeans and British Columbian First Nations. The meeting was friendly, and the Spaniards traded small shipboard objects for First Nation artifacts.

The Arrival of the British

Instead of the Russians, the British became the Spaniards' greatest rival on the Pacific Northwest Coast. Captain James Cook, already renowned for his discoveries in Australasia and Antarctica, and who had been present at the French surrender of Louisbourg in 1758 and had helped to guide the English armada to Quebec, visited the Northwest Coast on his third expedition to the Pacific in the spring of 1778. Cook's two vessels, *HMS Discovery* and *HMS Resolution*, arrived at Nootka Sound, which had been sighted by Pérez four years earlier. Here, Cook spent a month refitting his ships. Since no other European power knew of the Spaniard's previous visit, Cook (who was killed in January 1779 by Aboriginals in Hawaii) was credited with "discovering" Nootka, and the British claim to the Northwest Coast received international recognition.

The publication, in 1784, of the official account of Cook's third voyage proved a turning point. Captain James King, who had taken command shortly after the death of Cook, recounted in *A*

Voyage to the Pacific Ocean (1784) how sea-otter pelts obtained in trade on the Northwest Coast had brought as much as $120 each at Canton, China. Other mariners saw their opportunity. British and American ships entered the North Pacific sea otter trade.

To strengthen their claim to the Northwest Coast, the Spanish established a colony at Nootka Sound in 1789 that lasted for six years. Spain argued that it had the exclusive right to trade and to control the coast, while Britain claimed that navigation was open to any nation. But, in 1795, Spain agreed to share the northern ports because it badly needed British assistance in its war against France. Thus ended Spain's attempts to exert a Spanish presence north of California.

Imperial Rivalry on the Northwest Coast

The withdrawal of Spain in the mid-1790s left the Northwest Coast open to three contenders: Russia, Britain, and the newly independent United States. North of the present-day Alaskan boundary, the Russians now encountered intense British and American competition for sea-otter pelts. But the Russian traders laboured under several major handicaps. In contrast to both the Americans and the English, they possessed fewer and poorer trade goods and inferior trading vessels. The Russian advance slowed down in the Alaska Panhandle, where they faced strong competition from British and American traders and from Tlingit middlemen, who traded European goods to the interior First Nations in what is now Yukon and northwestern British Columbia.

New tools and pigments became available to the Aboriginal peoples after contact with the fur traders. Carving became more elaborate and colourful. This photo, taken by C.F. Newcombe in 1901, shows the Kwakwaka'wakw village of Blunden Harbour.

Royal British Columbia Museum/PN 258.

Britain strengthened its claim with the dispatch of a three-year expedition under George Vancouver, a naval officer who had served with Cook's expedition in 1778. From 1792 to 1794, Vancouver methodically and painstakingly charted the intricate coastline from Oregon to Alaska.

The outbreak of war between Britain and France in 1793, which lasted until 1815, curtailed British voyages to the Northwest Coast. As Britain withdrew men from its merchant ships for service in the Royal Navy, American entrepreneurs captured Britain's trade in the North Pacific. After the mid-1790s, American traders dominated the coastal trade until the mid-1820s, by which time the sea otter was virtually extinct due to over-hunting.

The First Nations and the Maritime Fur Traders

The Northwest Coast First Nations welcomed the European fur traders with their iron trading goods. They wanted the metal to construct tools. The Spanish discovered that the First Nations coveted iron so much that they even removed the metal strapping from the sides of Spanish ships. Not even the rudder chains were safe. They paid careful attention to the quality of goods they purchased and refused iron that contained flaws or was too brittle. They also bought muskets. In addition to purchasing iron goods, the Aboriginal peoples bought cloth, clothing, and blankets. They also developed an appreciation of rum and another new trade good, molasses.

The coastal First Nations initially exercised considerable control over the early European fur trade, preventing the Europeans from coming into contact with the inland groups. Often the First

Nation traders were middlemen who added a 200–300 percent markup to the furs and goods they traded. Women traders participated actively in the transactions with the newcomers.

Although the linguistic diversity of the Pacific coast exceeded that of Europe, a single trade language called "Chinook" came into use along the West Coast in the 1830s. In its vocabulary of about 300 key words are borrowings from First Nations languages, as well as English and French: "skookum" means powerful or fast, "chuck"—water; "cheechako"—newcomer; "Kinchotsh" (King George Man)—Englishman. It was spoken as well in the inland districts, and the middlemen knew that language. The entry around 1810 of European traders into the interior, however, took away much of the First Nations middlemen's trade. For nearly 40 years, the maritime fur trade prospered, but by 1825 the sea-otter population neared extinction.

The fur trade enriched the coastal peoples' culture. The tools they made from their new supplies of iron allowed them to produce better and more refined headdresses, costumes, and masks for feasts and ceremonies. As well, new dyes and pigments became available through the traders. Although the First Nations carvers favoured the traditional colours, weavers supplemented the original pigments—red and yellow ochres, black and blue-green copper oxide—with the whole spectrum of European trade colours. Wood carving expanded. During these years the totem poles, which displayed individual families' genealogies, underwent much elaboration and reached greater heights.

Although the Northwest Coast peoples enjoyed a higher standard of living after European contact, they also died in large numbers. The absence of accurate statistics makes it difficult to provide even rough estimates of the casualties, but European infectious diseases such as measles, mumps, and, especially, smallpox took their toll, as they did elsewhere in the Americas.

Securing the Inland Fur Trade

After European navigators reached the Northwest Coast by sea, European fur traders arrived by land. Anxious to find a short supply line to the Pacific Ocean, the North West Company searched for a route westward from Lake Athabasca to the Pacific. The Nor'Wester Alexander Mackenzie, the first European to canoe the northern river that now bears his name and to reach the Arctic Ocean, completed the first crossing of North America (north of Mexico) in 1793 by travelling down what is now called the Fraser River, then over to the Bella Coola River, and down to the Pacific. On a seaside rock he simply wrote, "From Canada. By Land." The arduous route proved useless for transporting furs, but the journey made the 24-year-old Mackenzie's reputation as a fearless and daring trader-explorer.

Two other Nor'Westers worked to find a commercial route to the Pacific. In 1808, Simon Fraser, who had first opened up fur-trading posts in the interior of what is now British Columbia, travelled with a small party down the treacherous river named after him. He succeeded, but concluded that the route was unnavigable.

Finally, in 1811, David Thompson, a partner of the North West Company, followed the Columbia River, and thereby connected the North West Company trade route from east of the Rockies to the Pacific Coast. A sea expedition sent by John Jacob Astor's Pacific Fur Company had arrived in late March 1811, just months before Thompson. On the basis of having founded Fort Astoria, the Americans claimed the Oregon country.

The Joint Occupation of the Oregon Territory

As a temporary compromise, Britain and the United States agreed in 1818 to occupy the Columbia country jointly and to decide its fate later. The agreement left commerce open to both British and American traders between latitudes 42° and 54°40′ (from the northern boundary of California to the southern limits of Alaska).

With the merger of the North West Company and the Hudson's Bay Company in 1821, the new Hudson's Bay Company under the management of Sir George Simpson began to exploit the rich fur resources of the Northwest Coast. Having obtained from the British Crown a 21-year lease to the exclusive trade of the "Indian Territory" (the lands between the Rocky Mountains and the Pacific), Simpson located a Pacific depot at Fort Vancouver, in an area of good farmland 150 km up the Columbia River. Other forts followed. The three most important were Fort Langley, near the mouth of the Fraser River, built in 1827; Fort Simpson, on the boundary of the Russian territory to the north, in 1831; and Fort Victoria, strategically located on the southern tip of Vancouver Island, in 1843. The Hudson's Bay Company's energetic commercial activities established a strong British presence on the Pacific coast.

American interest in the Columbia country increased in the early 1840s. Americans began arriving in the 1830s, and by 1843 they numbered about 1000. In the next three years, another 5000 settlers arrived in the Columbia River valley. But thanks to the Hudson's Bay Company's network of posts, inland trails, and shipping routes, Britain dominated north of the Columbia River. Nevertheless, American president James Polk, who won the presidential election in December 1844 with the electoral slogan "54°40′ or fight," demanded all of "Oregon," between latitudes 42° and 54°40′, up to the Russian border.

In his inaugural address in March, President Polk reaffirmed his position that the United States' title to Oregon was "clear and unquestionable." Great popular support existed for his stand. In the summer of 1845, the expansionist newspaper, *The United States Magazine and Democratic Review*, introduced in an editorial the phrase, "manifest destiny." The paper argued that foreign governments were attempting to check "the fulfillment of our manifest destiny to overspread the continent allotted by Providence for the free development of our yearly multiplying millions." Within months, the phrase became common usage throughout the United States.

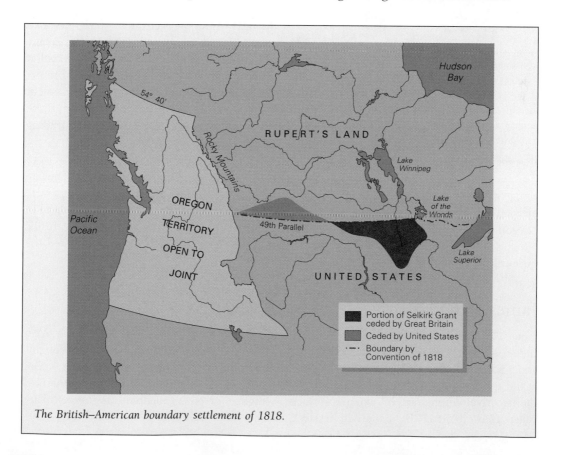

The British–American boundary settlement of 1818.

James Douglas played such an important role in the early history of British Columbia that he is called "the father of British Columbia." He and his wife, Amelia Connolly Douglas, had multiethnic backgrounds—Douglas was of Scottish and African origin, and his wife of Irish, French-Canadian, and First Nations descent.

British Columbia Archives/HP 2656.

Fortunately for Britain's claim, the Americans began a war with Mexico in 1846 over Texas (and later New Mexico and California), and Polk did not want to fight with both Mexico and Britain at the same time. To avoid conflict, Britain retracted its claim to all the land south of the Columbia River. The Anglo–American treaty signed in June 1846 extended the 49th parallel (which had become the international border across the prairies in 1818) from the Rocky Mountains to the Pacific Ocean, and left all of Vancouver Island in British hands.

Anxious to counter the threat of American squatter settlement in its Pacific territory, the British government asked the Hudson's Bay Company to colonize, as well as to manage, Vancouver Island for ten years. A royal grant of 1849 stipulated that the company had to develop the island, make lands available to settlers at reasonable prices, and safeguard Aboriginal rights. By the end of 1849, Fort Victoria served as the company's western headquarters, its shipping depot, and its provisioning centre, as well as the capital of the colony of Vancouver Island. In 1852, the Colonial Office extended the jurisdiction of the governor of Vancouver Island to include the Queen Charlotte Islands.

At the time of the first census in 1855, less than 1000 non-Aboriginal inhabitants lived in the Pacific colony of Vancouver Island. The discovery of coal at Nanaimo on the east coast of the island had led to the founding of a small permanent European settlement there. But until the Fraser River gold rush in 1858, the colony continued primarily as a fur-trading region, with its centre at Fort Victoria.

The fur traders consisted of immigrants from places as diverse as the Orkney Islands and Hawaii, along with French Canadians, Iroquois, and mixed-bloods. Many of the non-Aboriginals were married to First Nations, Country-born, or Métis women. The existence of virtually free land in Oregon and Washington attracted settlers there; on Vancouver Island, land had to be purchased. On Vancouver Island and the mainland, the Aboriginal peoples outnumbered the Europeans by roughly fifty to one.

James Douglas

James Douglas became governor of the colony of Vancouver Island in 1851. A "Scotch West Indian," Douglas was born in British Guiana (now Guyana), the son of "a free coloured woman" and a Scottish merchant. Sent to Scotland for his schooling at age twelve, James later left school at the age of sixteen and joined the North West Company as an apprentice. After the union of the two rival companies, he entered northern "Oregon," or New Caledonia, as the company called it. There, in 1828, he married Amelia Connolly, the daughter of William Connolly, a fur trader from Lower Canada, and his Cree wife. In 1830, the company transferred James to Fort Vancouver, and nine years later he became a chief factor. With his promotion to Fort Victoria in 1849, he became the senior company officer west of the Rocky Mountains.

James Douglas's Aboriginal Policy

Douglas refused to intervene in quarrels among the First Nations, but he did use his power, including Royal Navy gunboats, to settle disputes between them and Europeans. Shortly before he became governor, Douglas wrote that, in all his dealings with First Nations, he had "invariably acted on the principle that it is inexpedient and unjust to hold tribes responsible for the acts of individuals." The governor meted out stern discipline to individuals he perceived as warranting such treatment, but not to their communities. Unlike many of the early settlers on the island, Douglas tried to understand First Nations society. Above all, he did not want the open warfare that had broken out between the American settlers and the Aboriginal peoples in Washington Territory to spill over the border.

To avoid conflict between the First Nations and the settlers, Douglas purchased land from the First Nations before new settlement occurred. Between 1850 and 1854, he made fourteen treaties with groups living in areas that Europeans wanted to settle. In all, he purchased roughly 1000 km^2 of land, or about 3 percent of the total area of Vancouver Island. Douglas allowed the communities to select the land they wanted for their reserves and instructed the surveyors to meet the First Nations peoples' wishes.

In hindsight, Douglas was not overly generous with the amount of land allotted to reserves on Vancouver Island and later on the mainland. Just before he retired as governor of the mainland colony of British Columbia in 1864, he told the legislature, "The areas thus partially defined and set apart, in no case exceed the proportion of ten acres [4 ha] for each family concerned."

Some settlers complained that although Douglas handled First Nations well, he did not handle the colonists properly. They protested that he had not carried out his obligation to settle the island, that he ruled autocratically, and that he relied too heavily on the company's officials for advice. Most of all, they objected to his setting the price of land at £1 for one acre (0.4 ha) when land in the neighbouring American Pacific Northwest went for one-quarter the price. The rising business class in Victoria objected to his "family–Company compact," composed of former Hudson's Bay Company officials and members of his own family.

When settlement on Vancouver Island grew in the late 1850s, Douglas made determined efforts to purchase the First Nations' land and to set aside reserves in the areas into which settlers were moving. But lack of funds made the process more difficult. In 1858, the governor left the Hudson's Bay Company and no longer had access to the company's storehouses. Moreover, the Aboriginal communities wanted larger payments for their land, as they now realized its true value to the newcomers. The Vancouver Island House

At the first elections to the Vancouver Island Assembly in 1856, some 40 voters elected 7 members to North America's smallest legislature. Painting by Charles W. Simpson for a book celebrating the Diamond Jubilee of Confederation in 1927.

Library and Archives Canada/C-013947.

of Assembly, established in 1856, asked Britain to lend it money for First Nations land payments. The Colonial Office refused and replied that the funds should be raised locally. As the colonial legislature considered itself unable to buy out Aboriginal title on Vancouver Island, it gave the First Nations no compensation for their lands after 1859. Without negotiating treaties, the Europeans settled along the Pacific coast. Their settlements were interspersed among small, autonomous Aboriginal villages. The government of Vancouver Island (and later British Columbia) set aside reserves without extinguishing the First Nations' title to the land. (Only a century and a half later, in the 1990s, would the treaty process resume on Vancouver Island and on the coastal mainland.)

Douglas and the Creation of the Colony of British Columbia

After word of a big gold strike on the Fraser River reached California in the spring of 1858, the rush began. The California gold rush of 1849 had lost its momentum, and gold seekers headed north. A tent town arose at Victoria. Many new businesses or branches of American firms, financed by San Francisco capital, were established. One witness counted 225 new commercial buildings in Victoria in 1858.

Once in Victoria, the miners faced the challenge of reaching the gold fields in the interior. They needed boats to cross the Strait of Georgia to the mouth of the Fraser. Lacking the necessary boat-building skills, many launched their own hastily made vessels. Not surprisingly, some swamped, and their owners drowned. Once the would-be prospectors reached the mouth of the Fraser, they faced an additional 250 km journey up the river to the first big strike, just south of Yale, an old trading post. In the last two weeks of May 1858, 10 000 men travelled up the Fraser by canoe, sailboat, and raft. Another 15 000 arrived by the end of the year.

The arrival of thousands of Americans threatened British sovereignty and raised the danger of a war between prospectors and the First Nations. As the senior British official in the area, Douglas claimed the mainland and its minerals for the Crown. He drew up mining regulations, licensed miners, and hired constables. The Colonial Office praised Douglas, even though, strictly speaking, he lacked legal authority on the mainland. The British government remedied the legal shortcoming, and immediately established the colony of British Columbia on the mainland, separate from that of Vancouver Island.

James Douglas served as British Columbia's first governor while still continuing as governor of Vancouver Island (which in 1859 came under the direct control of the Colonial Office, after the royal grant to the Hudson's Bay Company ended). New Westminster, located near the mouth of the Fraser River, became the colony's new capital. Since no assembly was granted on the mainland—the British government did not wish to extend the electoral system to transients who had flocked into the Fraser River gold fields from California and Oregon—James Douglas retained great powers, including the power to legislate by proclamation. Together with Matthew Baillie Begbie, British Columbia's first chief justice, Douglas established a uniform judicial system for the colony. Judge Begbie's circuit court tours established a frontier version of British law in the scattered mining camps.

In 1860, British Columbia's gold rush frontier expanded. About 4000 gold miners (the majority from California and Oregon; the rest from eastern Canada, Britain, Europe, and even China) advanced eastward into potentially rich new gold fields, into the Thompson, Lillooet, and then the southern Cariboo regions. By 1861, with big strikes at Richfield, at Barkerville, and at Lightning on Williams Creek, the Cariboo region became the major mining field. To exploit the gold resources, road links were necessary to the coast. Roads were also needed to guarantee British commercial and military control of the interior. Using public funds, Douglas built the 650 km Cariboo Road, completed in 1863, which connected the gold towns of Yale and Barkerville.

Douglas remained in office as governor of both British Columbia and Vancouver Island until 1864. The settlers long complained about his autocratic ways and his "despotism," but in

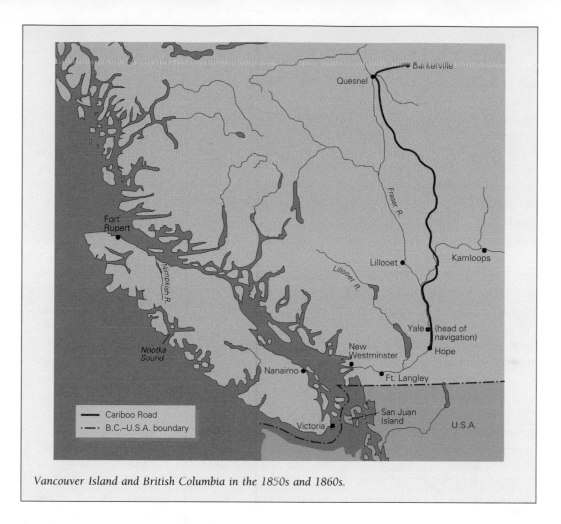

Vancouver Island and British Columbia in the 1850s and 1860s.

their haste to condemn him, they overlooked his accomplishments. On the mainland, he had confronted the Americans and firmly established British institutions. By building the Cariboo Road, he solved the problem of inland communication.

The governor's First Nations policy constituted another achievement. Thanks largely to Douglas, Vancouver Island and British Columbia were spared the fierce wars between First Nations and settlers that raged in the United States. The real test came in the Fraser River valley and the Cariboo country during the gold-rush days in the late 1850s and early 1860s. Apart from an attack in 1864 by Chilcotins on a road-building crew who had entered their territory uninvited, no major acts of First Nations armed resistance occurred.

WHERE HISTORIANS DISAGREE

James Douglas's Contribution to British Columbia

In the historiography of British Columbia, James Douglas is a figure comparable to Champlain in Quebec and to Simcoe in Ontario. Few historians have been more laudatory of his contribution to British Columbia than historian Margaret Ormsby.

In a biographical sketch of Douglas written in 1972, she states: "A man of iron nerve and physical prowess, great force of character, keen intelligence, and unusual resourcefulness, Douglas had had a notable career in the fur trade. As colonial governor his career was even more distinguished. Against overwhelming odds, with indifferent backing from the British government, the aid of a few Royal Navy ships, and a small force of Royal Engineers, he was able to establish British rule on the Pacific Coast and lay the foundation for Canada's extension of the Pacific seaboard. Single-handed in the midst of a gold-rush he had forged policies for land, mining, and water rights which were just and endurable."[1]

Recently, reassessments of Douglas have appeared, and his contribution, while still acknowledged as significant, is now judged more critically. In her study *The West beyond the West: A History of British Columbia*, Jean Barman introduced several criticisms of Douglas's administration. She noted his "overbearing style of governing" and the fact that he readily extended his authority beyond his legitimate power. Moreover, "he alienated newcomers from Ontario and the Maritimes through his haughty demeanour and preference for Britons over Canadians."[2] His feverish road-building program, she added, left the mainland colony of British Columbia burdened by debt.

Douglas's Aboriginal policies have also been questioned. Political scientist Paul Tennant argued that the governor was far less generous to the First Nations than was formerly believed.[3] Earlier commentators such as Robert Cail,[4] Robin Fisher,[5] and Wilson Duff[6] have regarded the governor's Aboriginal policies favourably. Anthropologist Wilson Duff, for instance, wrote in *The Indian History of British Columbia*: "As colonization progressed, his [Douglas's] main concerns, in addition to maintaining law and order, were to purchase the Indian ownership rights to the land and to set aside adequate reserves for their use."[7] Tennant himself does admit that "at a time when aboriginal peoples elsewhere were routinely being forced from their lands and often actively exterminated, Douglas displayed a spirit of tolerance, compassion, and humane understanding."[8] Nonetheless, with the exception of fourteen small treaties signed between 1850 and 1854 on Vancouver Island, Douglas made no further attempts to negotiate the transfer of land title with the First Nations. Moreover, the man who had complete control of the mainland from 1858 to 1864 made no treaties there at all. He, in fact, no longer supported the principle of Aboriginal land title. Instead, he spent large sums of money, principally on roads, to take miners in and out of the interior.

Tennant does acknowledge, however, that at least inadvertently, James Douglas made an enormous contribution to the survival of Aboriginal British Columbia. The governor's decision to set aside reserves for First Nations communities at locations of their own choosing helped to protect these groups from cultural extinction. As Tennant writes, "The surviving members of traditional communities could thus remain resident on preferred sites within their ancestral homelands and so could retain a sense of communal unity and an active connection with historic places and communal memories. Confined to their small reserves, they could nurture a deepening sense of injustice as they witnessed the takeover of their surrounding traditional lands without regard to aboriginal title. Douglas's approach thus facilitated the retention of the communal and tribal group identities that he assumed would vanish."[9]

Recently, after over a century of resistance, British Columbia has begun discussing land claims with Aboriginal groups. This has created much interest in James Douglas's early treaties on Vancouver Island, and, as well, in the reasons for his failure to complete further treaties on the Island and on the mainland of British Columbia. Historical assessment of Douglas's First Nations policies will lead, no doubt, to further discussion of his role in British Columbian history.

1. Margaret Ormsby, "Sir James Douglas," *Dictionary of Canadian Biography*, vol. 10, *1871–1880* (Toronto: University of Toronto Press, 1972), p. 248.

2. Jean Barman, *The West beyond the West: A History of British Columbia* (Toronto: University of Toronto Press, 1991), pp. 80, 97.

3. Paul Tennant, *Aboriginal Peoples and Politics: The Indian Land Question in British Columbia, 1849–1989* (Vancouver: University of British Columbia Press, 1990), p. 29.

4. Robert Cail, *Land, Man and the Law: The Disposal of Crown Lands in British Columbia, 1871–1913* (Vancouver: University of British Columbia Press, 1974).

5. Robin Fisher, *Contact and Conflict: Indian–European Relations in British Columbia, 1774–1890*, 2nd ed. (Vancouver: University of British Columbia Press, 1992 [1977]).

6. Wilson Duff, *The Indian History of British Columbia*, vol. 1, *The Impact of the White Man* (Victoria: Royal British Columbia Museum, 1992 [1965]), p. 61.

7. Ibid., p. 61.

8. Tennant, *Aboriginal Peoples and Politics*, p. 29.

9. Ibid., p. 38.

The First Nations and the Impact of the Gold Rushes

Apart from doing some backpacking and some work at the diggings, the First Nations obtained little economic benefit from the gold rushes. The miners had no intention of sharing British Columbia's rich lands and resources with the original inhabitants. Although James Douglas allowed the First Nations to choose the locations of their reserves, he made no treaties with them on the mainland. They received no compensation for the expropriation of their lands. Moreover, the miners intruded on their village sites, fishing stations, and cultivated areas. The increased number of non-Aboriginals also resulted in the outbreak of disease, such as the smallpox epidemic of 1862 that claimed the lives of many First Nations living both along the coast and in the interior.

British Columbia in the Mid-1860s

British Columbia experienced a post-gold-rush slump in the mid-1860s. Gold production fell, and people left the colony. Still, the region remained rich in natural resources. British Columbia's stands of Douglas fir produced ten times more wood per hectare than New Brunswick's Miramichi or the Canadas' Ottawa valley.[2] But high transportation costs in the 1860s ruled out large-scale exploitation. Beginnings had been made in lumber and fishing as export industries, but coal mining at centres on Vancouver Island, like Nanaimo, remained the most important industry. Some farming had begun, with specialization in wheat in the upper Fraser region, and with dairy and market gardening under way on the island. High American tariffs also reduced both British Columbia's and Vancouver Island's trade with the United States, although Vancouver Island did sell some coal to San Francisco.

In the late 1860s, about 12 000 non-Aboriginals lived in British Columbia and on Vancouver Island, the majority around Victoria and its immediate surrounding area. Between 1000 and 2000 non-Aboriginals resided in the lower Fraser valley. The remainder lived along the routes to the gold fields or at fur-trading posts. Since most Americans had left, at least three-quarters were British or Canadians and, of these, males predominated. In contrast the population of the First Nations, the overwhelming majority in both British Columbia and Vancouver Island, was about 25 000. A small community of African-American settlers from San Francisco, and a few settlers from the Caribbean, resided in Victoria and on the lower mainland. More than 1000 Chinese from California, mostly men, remained to work finds in the Cariboo. As late as 1871 there were only 53 Chinese women in the entire province. Most of the Chinese men came originally from poor rural backgrounds in southeastern China and could not bring over their families. (Other reasons for the small number of females include prejudices in Chinese society against emigration, and the hostile reception often given to Asians in British Columbia.)

Christian Missionaries and the Pacific Coast Peoples

Missionaries sought to convert the First Nations to Christianity in the 1850s. William Duncan began his work at Fort Simpson in 1857 and continued it at neighbouring Metlakatla, where he built a model mission. Other Anglican missionaries followed. Methodists from Canada West also came; Thomas Crosby worked on Vancouver Island and along the northern coastline. In the late 1850s, the Oblate Fathers established Roman Catholic missions along the south coast, in the Okanagan, and in the Fraser valley.

The missionaries tried to convert the First Nations into good European Christians. In their zeal, the missionaries at their Christian mission villages even banned totem poles. In 1900, the annual report of the federal Department of Indian Affairs noted that roughly 80 percent of British Columbia's First Nations were reported to be Christians.

It is difficult to judge the extent to which the First Nations adjusted to the new economic conditions. Independently of both mission and government direction, some First Nations tended potato gardens in the 1850s, and in the decades to follow, they started mixed farming. As early as the mid-1850s, independent Aboriginal loggers delivered logs to sawmills. Many of the Hudson's Bay Company supply ships and several private trading schooners employed First Nations as crew throughout the nineteenth century. First Nations–owned schooners began to appear in the 1870s, some of which they themselves had constructed. From the 1870s on, the First Nations entered the commercial fishing and canning industry. Thus, despite difficult circumstances, a number of them adjusted to the new conditions.

COMMUNITY PORTRAIT

The Black Community of Victoria

Canadians have long congratulated themselves on the improved state of race relations in Canada, and earlier in British North America, in contrast with that in the United States. While it is true that the British Empire abolished slavery in 1833, approximately one-third of a century before the United States, did African British North Americans achieve equality and full participation in their society? The existence of a vibrant, thriving community of people of African descent in Victoria, Vancouver Island, in the late 1850s and 1860s allows for comparisons to be made.

In the 1850s, African Americans faced increasing persecution and denial of civil rights in California. Several members of the African-American community in San Francisco sent a letter of enquiry to the government of the colony of British Columbia. Back came a favourable reply: they would be welcomed. It is interesting to note that James Douglas, the governor of Vancouver Island, had some African ancestry from his West-Indian mother.

The response that African Americans would be welcomed prompted the emigration of approximately 400 people of African background from California to Victoria in 1858 and 1859. Since California was not a slave state, those moving to Vancouver Island were already free. A number came with business experience, and with the advantage of knowing a trade. A few, such as Mifflin Gibbs, brought capital with them. Without a doubt one of the central figures in the migration was Gibbs, a free-born African American, originally from Philadelphia, the son of a Wesleyan Methodist minister. As a young man in his mid-twenties he had moved to San Francisco and, within a year, became a partner in a clothing business. But the discrimination against blacks rankled him. He became one of the first to emigrate northward. Once in the colony, he joined the Victoria Pioneer Rifle Corps, an all-black volunteer militia, known familiarly as the African Rifles, formed to protect the colony against possible American aggression.

In Victoria the newcomers pushed for integration. They sought what was denied to them in the United States: equal access to institutions, services, and the political process. Gibbs himself became a natural-ized British subject, which allowed him to register as a voter. Elected to the Victoria city council in 1866, he served two terms—one as the chair of the important finance committee.

Unfortunately, full equality was not achieved. It soon became apparent that the African-American immigrants still suffered prejudice in their new home. Some churches established segregated sections. Some saloons and other public facilities refused service to them. Theatres made them sit for performances in the balcony seats. These divisions were backed up by physical intimidation. Even the loyal Pioneer Rifle Corps suffered humiliation, as they were barred from parades and public ceremonies. Legal equality prevailed, and some African Americans achieved acceptance, but the colour line remained.

By the late 1860s, a number of African Americans left the colony and returned to the United States. Gibbs himself departed in 1869, and settled in Little Rock, Arkansas. The Civil War had ended, and opportunities surfaced for many in the country of their birth, but the persistence of the colour bar in British North America had also contributed to the exodus. Regrettably, in their new home on Vancouver Island, African Americans had contended with much of the same bigotry that they had tried to escape in pre–Civil War California.

FURTHER READING

Sherry Edmunds-Flett, "Mifflin Wistar Gibbs," *Dictionary of Canadian Biography*, vol. 14, *1911–1920* (Toronto: University of Toronto Press, 1998), pp. 398–399.

Crawford Kilian, *Go Do Some Great Thing: The Black Pioneers of British Columbia* (Vancouver: Douglas and McIntyre, 1978).

James W. St. G. Walker, *Racial Discrimination in Canada: The Black Experience*, Canadian Historical Association Booklet No. 41 (Ottawa: The Canadian Historical Association, 1985).

Britain and the United States over the ownership of the strategic San Juan Island, near Fort Victoria), the black community formed a volunteer militia regiment to protect the colony. In 1872, international arbitration settled the boundary dispute in favour of the Americans, and San Juan Island became part of the United States.

Charles Gentile/Library and Archives Canada/ C-22626.

When American forces threatened Vancouver Island in 1860 (during the dispute between

The Union of the Two Colonies

Major economic problems faced the two settler colonies of British Columbia and Vancouver Island in the mid-1860s. With the end of the gold rush, the economy was depressed and the two governments almost bankrupt. Anxious to save money in administrative costs, Britain promoted union of the two colonies. In 1866, the colonies joined together and New Westminster became the capital. (A vigorous lobby, however, later convinced the governor to move the capital to Victoria in 1868.) Despite the political consolidation of the two colonies, the depression continued. In 1867, a new issue arose: the American purchase of Alaska. This put in doubt the independence of British Columbia.

In 1867, the new united colony of British Columbia, only one year old, was the youngest of Britain's North American colonies. With the exception of a handful of fur traders, none of the approximately 8000 British Columbians of European descent in the colony had lived more than 25 years on Britain's Pacific coast. Thanks to the Hudson's Bay Company, Britain had retained this huge territory against Russian, and particularly against American, advances. But what would be the province's fate?

As the Canadas, New Brunswick, and Nova Scotia completed the final arrangements for their union, British Columbia's settler population debated its future. Non-Aboriginal settlement was so new; the first documented First Nation contact with Europeans had only occurred in 1774. Settlement had only really begun on Vancouver Island in the 1840s, and on the mainland after the Fraser River Gold Rush, less than ten years earlier. Yet, despite their short residence, at no point did the non-Aboriginal settlers consult the resident First Nations population, who, in the mid-1860s, outnumbered them by two to one, about the future of the colony. They proceeded as if the original peoples did not exist. The interior, by in large, did remain under Aboriginal control as well as most of the coastal areas, but the newcomers dominated in, and immediately around, their newly established settlements.

British Columbia was Britain's most recent colonial possession in British North America. Initially Spain, Russia, Britain, and the United States vied for international recognition of their control of the northwest coast, but by the early nineteenth century only Britain and the United States claimed the region. In 1818, the two countries agreed to joint occupancy, and then in 1846 agreed to extend the 49th parallel from the Prairies to the Pacific Ocean with Vancouver Island being solely Britain's possession. The First Nations remained the majority population well into the nineteenth century. The Indigenous people were not consulted about these international agreements concerning the future of their homeland. The colonial government failed to negotiate land treaties with the

Aboriginal population, thus creating a problem that still persists today. The North West Company and the Hudson's Bay Company both traded furs in the region with the Aboriginal population until the two companies merged as the Hudson's Bay Company in 1821. The discovery of gold in the Fraser River valley brought large numbers of gold seekers from California in 1858, which greatly increased the American population in the British Columbia interior, thus threatening British sovereignty in the area. Governor Douglas assumed control of the interior, creating a new British colony on the mainland, which was subsequently amalgamated with the island colony to form the joint colony of British Columbia in 1866. On the eve of Confederation, this new British colony had three choices: remain a British colony, become part of the United States, or join the newly created Dominion of Canada. That the choice would be the third option in 1871 was not immediately evident in the late 1860s.

NOTES

1. Chief Mathias Capilano presents a Squamish version of the Europeans' arrival in "Strangers Appear on English Bay," in *Romance of Vancouver*, vol. 2, compiled by the Native Sons of British Columbia (n.p., 1926), pp. 5–6. A similar version, "How the Squamish Remember George Vancouver," was presented by Chief Philip Joe at the Vancouver Conference on Exploration and Discovery in April 1992; see Robin Fisher and Hugh Johnston, eds., *From Maps to Metaphors: The Pacific World of George Vancouver* (Vancouver: University of British Columbia Press, 1993), pp. 3–5.

2. Donald MacKay, *The Lumberjacks* (Toronto: McGraw-Hill Ryerson, 1978), p. 160.

BEYOND THE BOOK

Beyond the Map: Exploration of the Pacific Northwest

http://beyondthemap.ca/english/index.html
A detailed history of the exploration of the Pacific Northwest, narrated by interviews with leading historians.

1862 Smallpox Epidemic in Victoria

http://web.uvic.ca/vv/student/smallpox
This site details the historical events of the 1862 smallpox epidemic in Victoria, and the reactions of people of First Nations, medical, and governmental backgrounds to it.

Living Landscapes

http://www.livinglandscapes.bc.ca
Details the geographic and ecosystem regions of British Columbia. The geographic features of the province greatly affected travel and settlement.

First Nations Languages

http://www.library.ubc.ca/xwi7xwa/lang.htm
A directory of resources and information about the dozens of First Nations languages spoken in British Columbia, and their history.

National Historic Site: SGang Gwaay

http://whc.unesco.org/en/list/157
SGang Gwaay is a national historic site in the Queen Charlotte Islands (Haida Gwaii) of British Columbia. This site commemorates the culture of the Haida people, and illustrates visual keys to their oral traditions.

Klatsassin and the Chilcotin War

http://www.canadianmysteries.ca/sites/klatsassin/home/indexen.html
In the 1860s armed conflict occurred between the Tsilhqot'in people and European settlers. This website invites you to analyze primary source documents to explore the reasons behind this conflict.

Who Killed William Robinson?

http://www.canadianmysteries.ca/sites/robinson/home/indexen.html
William Robinson was an American of African descent living in British Columbia who was murdered in 1868. Using court documents of the time, revisit this murder trial that found an Aboriginal man hanged for Robinson's death.

Eagle Song

James Houston, *Eagle Song. An Indian Saga Based on True Events* (Toronto: McClelland and Stewart, 1983). This is a fictional account of the captivity of John Jewitt among the Nuu-chah-nulth (Nootka) First Nation of Vancouver Island in the early nineteenth century.

RELATED READINGS

Two articles in R. Douglas Francis and Donald B. Smith, eds., *Viewpoints: Readings in Canadian History* (Toronto: Thomson Nelson, 2007), are useful for this topic: Sylvia Van Kirk, "Tracing the Fortunes of Five Founding Families of Victoria," pp. 184–203; and Adele Perry, "Hardy Backwoodsmen, Wholesome Women, and Steady Families: Immigration and the Construction of a White Society in Colonial British Columbia, 1849–1871," pp. 203–215.

BIBLIOGRAPHY

Good summaries of the history of the two Pacific colonies are Jean Barman's *The West beyond the West: A History of British Columbia* (Toronto: University of Toronto Press, 1991; rev. ed. 1996; 3rd ed. 2007) and Hugh J.M. Johnston, ed., *The Pacific Province: A History of British Columbia* (Vancouver: Douglas & McIntyre, 1996). A wealth of information on British Columbia can be found in Daniel Francis, ed., *Encyclopedia of British Columbia* (Madeira Park: Harbour Publishing, 2000). Tina Loo provides a very useful bibliographical guide in her essay "The Pacific Coast," in M. Brook Taylor, ed., *Canadian History: A Reader's Guide*, vol. 1, *Beginnings to Confederation* (Toronto: University of Toronto Press, 1994), pp. 356–93.

Reviews of British Columbia's Aboriginal past appear in Wilson Duff, *The Indian History of British Columbia*, vol. 1, *The Impact of the White Man* (Victoria: Royal British Columbia Museum, 1997 [1965]); Robin Fisher, *Contact and Conflict: Indian–European Relations in British Columbia, 1774–1890*, 2nd ed. (Vancouver: University of British Columbia Press, 1992 [1977]); John Sutton Lutz's new book, *Makúk: A New History of Aboriginal–White Relations* (Vancouver: University of British Columbia Press, 2008); and two volumes by historical geographer Cole Harris, *The Resettlement of British Columbia: Essays on Colonialism and Geographical Change* (Vancouver: University of British Columbia Press, 1997); and *Making Native Space: Colonialism, Resistance, and Reserves in British Columbia* (Vancouver: University of British Columbia Press, 2002). He provides a chapter on British Columbia in his new book, *The Reluctant Land. Society, Space, and Environment In Canada before Confederation* (Vancouver: UBC Press, 2008), pp. 416–447. Paul Tennant's *Aboriginal Peoples and Politics: The Indian Land Question in British Columbia, 1849–1989* (Vancouver: University of British Columbia Press, 1990) is very useful. Several essays on early Indigenous–European contact on the North Pacific Coast are included in John Sutton Lutz, ed., *Myth and Memory* (Vancouver: University of British Columbia Press, 2007). On the impact on the First Nations of European infectious disease, see Robert Boyd, *The Coming of the Spirit of Pestilence: Introduced Infectious Diseases and Population Decline among Northwest Coast Indians, 1774–1874* (Vancouver: University of British Columbia Press, 1999).

For a survey of European and American activities in the North Pacific, see John Kendrick's *Men with Wooden Feet: The Spanish Exploration of the Pacific Northwest* (Toronto: NC Press, 1985) and James R. Gibson's *Otter Skins, Boston Ships and China Goods: The Maritime Fur Trade of the Northwest Coast, 1785–1841* (Montreal/Kingston: McGill-Queen's University Press, 1992). Barry Gough reviews British contact in *The Northwest Coast: British Navigation, Trade, and Discoveries to 1812* (Vancouver: University of British Columbia Press, 1992) and *Gunboat Frontier: British Maritime Authority and Northwest Coast Indians, 1846–90* (Vancouver: University of British Columbia Press, 1984). *The Dictionary of Canadian Biography*, vol. 4, *1771–1800* (Toronto: University of Toronto Press, 1979) contains sketches of James

Cook by Glyndwr Williams, pp. 162–67, and of George Vancouver by W. Kaye Lamb, pp. 743–48. These are available online at www.bibliographi.ca.

On nineteenth-century political developments, Clarence G. Karr has written an interesting article on Douglas, "James Douglas: The Gold Governor in the Context of His Times," in E. Blanche Norcross, ed., *The Company on the Coast* (Nanaimo, BC: Nanaimo Historical Society, 1983), pp. 56–78. W. Peter Ward and Robert A.J. McDonald, eds., *British Columbia: Historical Readings* (Vancouver: Douglas & McIntyre, 1981) includes James E. Hendrickson's "The Constitutional Development of Colonial Vancouver Island and British Columbia," pp. 245–74. Tina Loo's *Making Law, Order, and Authority in British Columbia, 1821– 1871* (Toronto: University of Toronto Press, 1994) is the first comprehensive legal history of British Columbia in the colonial period. In the field of gender and race history, Adele Perry has written *On the Edge of Empire: Gender, Race, and the Making of British Columbia, 1849–1871* (Toronto: University of Toronto Press, 2001).

For important maps consult the first two volumes of the *Historical Atlas of Canada*: vol. 1, R. Cole Harris, ed., *From the Beginning to 1800* (Toronto: University of Toronto Press, 1987); and vol. 2, R. Louis Gentilcore, ed., *The Land Transformed, 1800–1891* (Toronto: University of Toronto Press, 1993).

Part 4

BUILDING THE NEW DOMINION, 1867–1914

INTRODUCTION

The mid-to-late-nineteenth century saw the formation of European nation states, including Germany in 1866 and Italy in 1871; national consolidation in the United States after the Civil War; and imperial expansion, as in the case of Britain, France, Germany, and the United States. Canada witnessed all three developments in a phenomenally short period of time: the British North American colonies of Nova Scotia, New Brunswick, and the United Canadas came together in 1867 to create the nation state of Canada; within ten years, the country had expanded to include all of the existing British North American colonies with the exception of Newfoundland. The new nation had also undertaken expansion to the Pacific and Arctic Oceans. In the 1870s, Canada made seven treaties with the First Nations in western Canada. The country also became involved in two conflicts with the Aboriginal peoples, first in 1869–1870 in the Red River, and then in 1885 in the North-West Territories, imperial expansion to make the Prairie West "Canada's Empire."

Creating the physical boundaries of a new nation state proved easier than fostering a sense of nationalism. Since the traditional components of cultural nationalism—a common language, cultural tradition, or religion—were absent, national enthusiasts looked to geography and especially to an economic policy of railway building, protective tariffs, and large-scale immigration to promote a feeling of nationalism.

This so-called national policy, as well as the decision of the Fathers of Confederation to create a federal union with political power divided between Ottawa and provincial governments, necessitated the working out of Dominion–provincial relations. This proved acrimonious. Also to be resolved were relations between French-speaking and English-speaking Canadians. A century of bitterness and suspicion preceded Confederation, yet a *modus vivendi* had existed in the union itself. Tension and compromise prevailed from 1867 to 1914. Finally, the new country needed to work out relations with Britain and the United States. Most Canadians favoured continued affiliation with the British empire; union of the colonies of the Canadas, New Brunswick, and Nova Scotia and the granting of Dominion status to the new nation did not mean independence. Equally, Canadians sought trade with the United States, while clearly rejecting any form of political union with it.

The year 1867 and the event of Confederation were not momentous for most Canadians. They continued to identify more with their colonial (now provincial) and local area than with the country as a whole, and their daily lives were unaltered. Still, the very act of union of the three British North American colonies put into place a new structure and dynamic for economic, political, and social change. Part of that new structure was a federal bureaucracy that was insignificant in 1867 but would grow to regulate all aspects of the public and to a significant degree the private life of all Canadians, especially the First Nations people, who became "wards of the state" under the auspices of the federal government.

eleven*Chapter Eleven*

CONFEDERATION

TIME LINE

1857	Queen Victoria chooses Ottawa as the future capital of Canada An economic recession begins
1861	The American Civil War begins
1864	Confederate sympathizers raid St. Alban's, Vermont from British North American territory The "Great Coalition" forms to work toward British North American federation Canadian and Maritime delegates discuss union at the Charlottetown and Quebec conferences
1865	Canadian legislature approves the Quebec Resolutions, but only a narrow majority of French-Canadian members endorse them
1866	The United States government terminates the Reciprocity Treaty of 1854 Leonard Tilley's pro-Confederation party wins the election in New Brunswick Westminster Conference in London, England prepares the passage of the British North America Act through the British Parliament
1867	The British North America Act is passed, creating the Dominion of Canada; it consisted of the colonies of Nova Scotia, New Brunswick, Canada East (Quebec), and Canada West (Ontario) John A. Macdonald becomes Canada's first prime minister

Proposals for the union of the British North American colonies had been considered well before the 1860s, but they never became reality. By the 1860s, however, a number of circumstances came together that made unification possible. Threats of an American takeover as a result of the Civil War; pressure from Britain for unification to lessen British responsibilities for its North American colonies; internal problems in the colonies, such as heavy public debt from extensive railway building; and, in the case of the Canadas, political deadlock, as well as the desire to acquire the North West, led politicians from both the Canadas and the Maritime colonies to consider union. These immediate circumstances, more than a spirit of nationalism, prepared the way for Confederation.

There was no assurance in 1867 that the new experiment in nation-building would succeed. In this respect, Confederation can be seen as but the first step in an ongoing process of nation-building that would continue well into the twentieth century. As well, Confederation set in place a new state with a bureaucratic structure that would grow over time to provide support and guidance for, but also regulate and control, the population under its jurisdiction. Meanwhile, the new nation had a number of immediate issues to work out: Dominion–provincial relations, English–French relations, association with Britain and the United States, and how to keep the new nation united.

The Impact of the American Civil War

The Alabama and Trent Affairs

Fear of an American takeover during the Civil War contributed to British North American unification. Although Britain was officially neutral during the American Civil War, many Britons backed the Confederacy because of their dependence on Southern cotton for the textile industry. The international rules of neutrality prevented the legal construction of Confederate warships in British shipyards, but the South secretly had the C.S.S. *Alabama*, a swift and powerful cruiser, built in a shipyard near Liverpool. During its 22-month rampage on three oceans, the *Alabama* burned or captured 64 Northern merchant vessels and a Union warship before it was sunk in June 1864. The North held Britain responsible for the destruction by the *Alabama* and other British-built Confederate vessels, since, Northern leaders argued, Britain knew the uses to which the South put these ships. As compensation, one Northern proposal included the takeover of all of British North America.

Adding to Anglo–American antagonism was the *Trent* affair. In November 1861, an American warship stopped the British steamer *Trent* and forcibly removed two Confederate envoys on their way to England to secure assistance for the Southern cause. Tempers flared on both sides, with Britain threatening retaliation if the North did not free these Confederate agents, seized in neutral waters, and the North denouncing Britain for aiding the Southern cause. In the end, President Abraham Lincoln released the prisoners on Christmas Day, 1861, to avoid war with Britain.

The St. Alban's Raids

Meanwhile, by 1864, Southern sympathizers planned attacks on the North via Canada. The largest of these attacks occurred at St. Alban's, Vermont on October 19, 1864, during which 26 Confederate supporters terrorized the town, robbed three banks of $200 000, set several fires, wounded two men and killed another, and then fled to Canada. The government of the Canadas arrested them, but a Montreal magistrate released them on a legal technicality. This act of leniency infuriated Northerners. The Canadian government condemned the judge's decision.

As well, the Canadian Assembly passed legislation to deport aliens involved in acts against a friendly foreign state. Nevertheless, Canada still remained suspect among Northerners.

The ensuing tension led Britain to send 14 000 soldiers to British North America to protect her colonies. Many of the troops had to reach their destination by sled, since no rail link existed into the interior of British North America. Britain therefore saw a union of the British North American colonies as a means both to get the colonies to assume responsibility for their own defense, and to achieve a railway link to the Atlantic by providing a larger financial base for railway construction.

Negotiating Confederation

The Great Coalition

In this tense atmosphere, the politicians in the province of Canada addressed the problem of political deadlock in their Assembly. Neither the Conservatives nor the Reformers could form a stable government. Between 1861 and 1864, for example, the province of Canada experienced two elections and three changes of administration. On June 14, 1864, the most recent administration, the Macdonald–Taché coalition, went down to defeat. Governor General Monck urged John A. Macdonald, leader of the coalition, to negotiate with George Brown, leader of the Reform coalition, with the possibility of forming a larger coalition. Despite Brown and Macdonald's hostilities toward each other, the two men agreed to work together to resolve the deadlock. On June 30, a jubilant Assembly heard Brown announce that he and two other Reformers would enter a coalition cabinet to work for federation. Thus was born the "Great Coalition of 1864."

Brown made three demands in return for his support: a federation of all the British North American colonies; representation by population, or "rep by pop," as it became popularly known, by which the number of seats in Parliament from each province would be based on population size; and the incorporation of Rupert's Land into Confederation. Brown's interest in the North West lay in its benefits for the development of Canada West. On January 22, 1863, for example, the Toronto newspaper editor outlined his central Canadian vision of the West:

> If Canada acquires this territory it will rise in a few years from a position of a small and weak province to be the greatest colony any country has ever possessed, able to take its place among the empires of the earth. The wealth of 400,000 square miles of territory will flow through our waters and be gathered by our merchants, manufacturers and agriculturists. Our sons will occupy the chief places of this vast territory, we will form its institutions, supply its rulers, teach its schools, fill its stores, run its mills, navigate its streams.

The Charlottetown Conference

In the early 1860s, the Maritime colonies of Nova Scotia, New Brunswick, and Prince Edward Island considered union among themselves. Despite reservations, the premiers of the three colonies agreed to meet. However, before a date or place had been decided, the government of the Canadas asked permission to attend such a meeting so as to present a proposal for a wider British North American federal union. The Maritimers agreed. The meeting was set for September 1, 1864, in Charlottetown.

At the Charlottetown Conference, the Canadian delegation presented a tour de force. John A. Macdonald and George-Étienne Cartier set out the general terms of the Canadian proposal, particularly those aspects dealing with the division of powers between the central and provincial governments. Alexander Galt, the minister of finance in the Canadas, dealt with economic issues, while George Brown handled constitutional concerns. The main features of their proposal included: continued loyalty to the British Crown through membership in the British empire; a strong central government within a federal union in which the provinces retained control over their own local affairs; and representation in a lower house based on population and an upper house based on regional representation. Thomas D'Arcy McGee, the gifted poet-politician, spoke eloquently in terms of the need for a common British North American vision. Within seven days, the delegates agreed to meet again on October 10 at Quebec City to explore in greater detail the nature of a British North American federation.

The banquet and ball on the final night of the Charlottetown Conference at Province House. The assembly chamber—now decorated with evergreens, flowers, and flags—became the ballroom. Under brilliant gaslight, delegates and their partners danced to the music of two Charlottetown bands from the gallery. At the front and centre of this re-creation by artist Dusan Kadlec appear John A. Macdonald and George-Étienne Cartier.

Province House Ball, 1864 © Dusan Kadlec and Parks Canada

The Quebec Conference

At Quebec, the Canadian delegates presented the general principles set out at Charlottetown in the form of Seventy-Two Resolutions. Within a two-week period, the Resolutions were debated and slightly altered to become the British North American (BNA) Act, the political framework for a union of the British North American colonies.

At the conference Macdonald clearly favoured a legislative union, or a strong central government, believing that the Civil War in the United States resulted from overly powerful state governments. The Maritime delegates feared a loss of their identity in a legislative union and favoured instead a federal union with powerful local governments. George-Étienne Cartier, representing the interests of the French Canadians, also favoured a federal union, with a local government in Quebec strong enough to protect French Canadians' language, civil law, and customs. One Colonial Office official astutely noted the challenge facing the Fathers of Confederation:

> *The great difficulty is to arrange for a real union of the five provinces ... on terms which shall make the central or federal legislation really dominant, so as to make one body politic of the whole, and yet to provide security to French Canadians that this dominacy would not be used to swamp their religion and habits.*

The delegates reached a compromise. They granted powers to the provincial governments, but gave the central government residuary powers (powers not specifically assigned to the provinces). As well, they gave the central government the power "to make laws for the peace, order and good government of Canada." The federal government also gained the right to disallow provincial laws if they went against the national interest.

COMMUNITY PORTRAIT

The Charlottetown Conference as a Political Community

On September 1, 1864, political leaders from the Atlantic colonies and from the United Canadas met in Charlottetown to discuss the possibility of a British North American union. They came together as strangers; so the success of the conference depended on the ability to create a sense of community—for the representatives to come to know and trust each other, and to believe they had something in common. In this respect social events became as important as the political meetings. The wives of the politicians, especially the wives of the Island hosts who organized the social gatherings, made a very important contribution by helping to create this sense of community. As well, the presence of women reminded the politicians that their decisions affected all members of the community, including women and children. As a result, historians have now come to identity these women as the "Mothers of Confederation."

The politicians who met at Charlottetown came with quite different agendas, interests, and hopes. The resulting mistrust, divisiveness, and differences had to be overcome in order to find points of common interest, to cultivate a feeling of community. Luncheons, dinners, banquets, and balls became common occurrences designed to foster the feeling among the politicians that they belonged to a community. In a letter to his wife Anne Nelson, daughter of publisher William Nelson,[1] George Brown from Upper Canada noted the change that came over the delegates as they wined and dined:

Cartier and I made eloquent speeches, and whether as the result of our eloquence or of the goodness of our champagne, the ice became completely broken, the tongues of the delegates wagged merrily, [and] the banns of matrimony between all the provinces of British North America were formally proclaimed.

Brown failed to note in his letter the important role the women played in forging this sense of political community. But at the final banquet, the delegates made the last toast to Mrs. Dundas, wife of the lieutenant governor of Prince Edward Island, and the other ladies present as acknowledgement of their important role in making the Charlottetown Conference a success. The Conference had shaped a political community of the leaders who would go on to forge the new nation of Canada.

FURTHER READING

Moira Dann, *Mothers of Confederation* (CBC transcript) (Toronto: Canadian Broadcasting Corporation, 1989).

Gail Cuthbert Brandt, "National Unity and the Politics of Political History" (presidential address), *Journal of the Canadian Historical Association*, 1992: 3–11.

Christopher Moore, *1867: How the Fathers Made a Deal* (Toronto: McClelland & Stewart, 1997).

J.M.S. Careless, "George Brown and the Mother of Confederation, 1864," *Canadian Historical Association Annual Report*, 1960: 57–73.

The delegates to the Charlottetown Conference, September 1864.
From left to right:

1. Charles Drinkwater, private secretary to John A. Macdonald
2. Hewitt Bernard, secretary to John A. Macdonald
3. Alexander T. Galt, Canada
4. Charles Tupper, Nova Scotia
5. Edward B. Chandler, New Brunswick
6. Hector-Louis Langevin, Canada
7. Edward Palmer, Prince Edward Island
8. John Hamilton Gray, New Brunswick
9. Robert Dickey, Nova Scotia
10. George-Étienne Cartier, Canada
11. Thomas D'Arcy McGee, Canada
12. William A. Henry, Nova Scotia
13. John A. Macdonald, Canada
14. William H. Steeves, New Brunswick
15. John Hamilton Gray, Prince Edward Island
16. John M. Johnson, New Brunswick
17. Samuel L. Tilley, New Brunswick
18. Adams G. Archibald, Nova Scotia
19. Andrew A. Macdonald, Prince Edward Island
20. William Campbell, Canada
21. William MacDougall, Canada
22. George Coles, Prince Edward Island
23. William H. Pope, Prince Edward Island
24. Jonathan McCully, Nova Scotia
25. George Brown, Canada

George P. Roberts/Library and Archives Canada/C-733.

---

1.   Nelson, the publisher of your textbook, is a corporate descendant of William Nelson's publishing firm.

The delegates also agreed on a federal lower house based on representation by population and an upper house based on regional representation, but disagreed on the number of representatives from each region in the upper house—the Senate. The smaller Maritime provinces saw the Senate as a means of strengthening their regional representation to offset their numerical weakness in the lower house. In the end, the delegates agreed that the Maritimes would have 24 seats, the same number given to each of Ontario and Quebec.

The delegates agreed as well, after much debate, that the new federal government would assume the public debt—up to a specified maximum amount—of each province that joined. In addition, the federal government would finance the Intercolonial Railway, linking the Maritimes to the Canadas.

To cover these costs, the federal government was given unlimited taxing powers, including the collection of both direct taxes and indirect taxes, such as customs and excise duties, one of the main sources of revenue at the time. In contrast, the provinces could levy only direct taxes. To compensate the provinces for the cost of education, roads, and other provincial obligations, it was agreed that the federal government pay annual subsidies to the provinces based on 80 cents per head of their population.

The Debate on the Confederation Proposals in the Canadas

After the Quebec Conference, the delegates returned to their respective provinces to secure approval for the resolutions. The Fathers of Confederation had considered submitting the draft constitution for popular approval but later decided to follow the British procedure of ratification by the politicians only. As a result, the Confederation agreement did not at the time (or since) form the basis of a political community with a clear sense of itself and its political rights and constitutional freedoms.

Absent entirely from the constitutional process were the First Nations. To the Fathers of Confederation, the First Nations were wards of the state, upon which sovereignty could be imposed, not people with rights of their own or participants in the political process. As political scientist Peter Russell notes, "Aboriginal peoples were treated as subjects, not citizens, of the new dominion."[1]

In the legislature of the United Canadas, considerable debate ensued. George Brown and his Reformers had some concerns about specific proposals but accepted the agreement reached at Quebec since it was based on "rep by pop." In general, Upper Canadian politicians favoured Confederation, realizing that they had the most to gain from the union.

In Canada East (Quebec), members of the Parti rouge, under the leadership of Antoine-Aimé Dorion, had serious reservations. Dorion argued: "It is not at all a confederation that is proposed to us, but quite simply a Legislative Union disguised under the name of a confederation. How could one accept as a federation a scheme ... that provided for disallowance of local legislation?" Furthermore, he pointed out that in the new House of Commons the English-Canadian representation from Canada West and the Maritimes would greatly outnumber the French-Canadian representation. As well, he denounced the Fathers of Confederation for refusing to put the issue to a vote among the populace.

George-Étienne Cartier countered Dorion's criticisms. He emphasized that in the new federal union, French Canadians would control their own provincial government and legislature, have their own local administration, and retain the Civil Code. Furthermore, the French language would be official in the province of Quebec as well as in the federal administration, and the rights of religious minorities for separate schools would be recognized in all the provinces. On the question of English-Canadian dominance, Cartier pointed out that the "new nationality" would be a "political nationality" only, not a "cultural nationality," and therefore did not require French Canadians to suppress their cultural differences for the sake of some common pan-Canadian nationalism. He also reminded his French-Canadian compatriots of the importance of the British connection to offset the threat of American annexation and the loss of identity that would ensue.

Cartier also presented Confederation to French Canadians as their best hope for cultural survival in a world of limited possibilities. The existing union, crippled by deadlock, could not go on; for French Canadians, union with the United States would be the worst possible fate. The independence of Lower Canada was not feasible. Only a larger federation of British North

American colonies offered French Canadians possibilities beyond their own provincial boundaries at the same time as it protected their affairs within their own province.

Cartier turned to the clergy for support for Confederation, despite his personal concerns about mixing politics and religion. Bishop Ignace Bourget of Montreal, the most powerful French-Canadian bishop, feared for the future of the Roman Catholic church in the new political union with other English-speaking colonies with large Protestant populations. He kept silent about his misgivings, however, since the other Quebec bishops were more favourably disposed, at least in principle. They realized that the alternative to Confederation was support of their arch-enemies, the *rouges*, who were strongly anticlerical.

In the final vote on Confederation in the Legislature of the United Canadas, 91 were in favour and 33 opposed. In the breakdown of votes in the two sections, 54 of the 62 members from Canada West favoured the proposal, as did 37 of the 62 members from Canada East. Of the 48 French-Canadian members present, 27 voted for and 21 against. Overall, Confederation won overwhelmingly, but among French Canadians the victory was narrow, indicating serious reservations on their part.

Opposition to Confederation in Atlantic Canada

In New Brunswick, Samuel Leonard Tilley, who had been premier since 1857 and who had represented the province at both the Charlottetown and Quebec conferences, argued the advantages of Confederation for New Brunswickers: Saint John would be a year-round, ice-free port for the export of Canadian goods to Britain, and a lucrative market would exist in central Canada for Maritime coal and manufactured goods. The promised Intercolonial Railway would make such trade possible.

However, strong opposition to Confederation existed in the province. A.J. Smith, the opposition leader, headed the anti-Confederation forces. He argued that no guarantee existed that the Intercolonial Railway would be constructed and, if it were built, where it would run and thus which area of the province, the north shore or the southern Saint John River valley, would benefit from it. He also pointed out that New Brunswick's economic trade pattern, especially since the Reciprocity Treaty of 1854, had been north–south rather than east–west. Commercial interests in the province had no economic ties with the Canadas. Furthermore, union with the Canadas could lead to a flooding of the New Brunswick market by Canadian imports, and a high tariff structure. In addition, New Brunswickers would be forced to assume a portion of the heavy Canadian debt from canal and railway building. Finally, Smith argued that Confederation would diminish New Brunswick's political power by giving the province representation of only 15 members of parliament in a House of Commons with 194 members. The New Brunswick Roman Catholic clergy also opposed Confederation, believing that a Canada dominated by Protestant "extremists" in Upper Canada could threaten Roman Catholic schools and the church itself.

These issues were debated in the election campaign of early 1865, an election fought chiefly on the question of Confederation. New Brunswickers responded clearly and decisively— Tilley's pro-Confederation government went down to defeat.

In Nova Scotia, Charles Tupper, the pro-Confederation premier, faced a serious challenge from Joseph Howe. Although no longer a member of the Assembly, Howe was still the most powerful political figure in Nova Scotia as the "Father of Responsible Government." Howe argued that Nova Scotia would lose its identity and cease to be an important colony in the great British Empire if it joined Confederation. Furthermore, he pointed out that the province looked eastward to the Atlantic Ocean and Britain, rather than westward to the continent and the Canadas. As he vividly expressed it: "Take a Nova Scotian to Ottawa, away above tide-water, freeze him up for five months, where he cannot view the Atlantic, smell salt water, or see the sail of a ship, and the man will pine and die." He favoured remaining an independent British colony. In the winter of 1866–1867, Howe went to England to present his case for Nova Scotia staying out of Confederation.

In Prince Edward Island, support for Confederation went from modest to nil. At the Charlottetown and Quebec conferences, the island's representatives had driven a hard bargain, pressing for better terms on representation in the Senate and in the House of Commons, and for better economic terms. But when they returned home, their enthusiasm and interest waned when they realized that the islanders themselves opposed Confederation for a number of reasons. One was the problem of absentee landlordism. For over a century, absentee British landlords had controlled island property, much to the resentment of the local population. In 1860, a British commission appointed to investigate the land question issued a report favourable to the islanders, only to have it rejected by the Colonial Office. Thus, when the Colonial Office pressured Prince Edward Islanders to adopt Confederation, they resisted. Also, many islanders saw Confederation as simply replacing one set of distant landlords in Britain with another in Ottawa. In addition, islanders believed that Confederation would give them very little. Union would mean higher taxes to support the enormous costs of the Intercolonial Railway, and higher tariffs to create interprovincial trade—neither of which would greatly benefit Prince Edward Island. They also disliked the proposed form of political representation in the Senate and in the House of Commons, which would give them insignificant political influence in distant Ottawa.

Newfoundland failed to support Confederation out of apathy, not opposition. The Island had not participated in the Charlottetown Conference; it did, however, send two representatives to the Quebec Conference, both of whom endorsed Confederation. These representatives returned to a colony that was initially mildly interested as a result of Newfoundland's declining fishing industry, agriculture, and the timber trade, but who quickly realized that Confederation would not be the solution to their economic ills. For one thing, central Canada was simply too far away to be of benefit to them. R.J. Pinsent, a member of the Legislative Council, summed up the prevailing opinion of Newfoundlanders as follows: "There is little community of interest between Newfoundland and the Canadas. This is not a Continental Colony." Essentially, the island continued to look eastward to Britain rather than westward to Canada for its economic livelihood.

External Pressures

By the end of 1865, public support for British North American Confederation had waned, except in Canada West. All four of the Atlantic colonies opposed it, while Canada East had serious reservations. Two external developments, however, altered the situation: British intervention and an American threat of annexation.

British Support for Confederation

By the mid-1860s Britain wanted to lessen the expense of defending its British North American colonies, and to ease tension in its relations with the United States. Thus, when in the autumn of 1865 a pro-Confederation delegation from the Canadas arrived in London, it was warmly welcomed; an anti-Confederation group from Nova Scotia under Joseph Howe was not. Instead, the British government replaced the anti-Confederation governor of Nova Scotia with one more supportive. The Colonial Office also ordered New Brunswick Governor Arthur Gordon to intervene in his province's politics to ensure the success of Confederation. Finally, the British government agreed to guarantee the loan interest for the proposed Intercolonial Railway if the Maritimes joined Confederation.

The American Contribution to Confederation

While Britain applied direct pressure, the United States did so indirectly. When the Civil War ended in 1865, Northern extremists advocated using the Northern army to annex the British North American colonies. Also, politicians in the American Midwest advocated taking possession of the British North West, as part of the United States' manifest destiny to control the entire North American continent. Influential American politicians, including Hamilton Fish, the secretary of state in Ulysses S. Grant's administration, urged possession of all the British territory in North America.

Amid pressure to annex the British colonies, the American government announced that the Reciprocity Treaty of 1854 would terminate in 1866. American annexationists reasoned that the Treaty's abrogation would cause such economic hardships for the British colonies as to force them to join the United States. Ironically, the announced abrogation of reciprocity had the opposite effect: it encouraged the colonies to consider an alternative commercial union among themselves.

Fenian raids also furthered the cause of Confederation. Fenians were fanatical republican Irishmen in the United States committed to fighting for the independence of Ireland. One scheme they devised was to capture the British North American colonies and use them as ransom to liberate Ireland from British rule. Their marching song explicitly set out their goals:

> *We are the Fenian Brotherhood,*
> *skilled in the art of war,*
> *And we're going to fight for Ireland,*
> *the land that we adore.*
> *Many battles we have won, along with*
> *the boys in blue,*
> *And we'll go and capture Canada for*
> *we've nothing else to do.*

The Fenians expected the support of Irish Catholics in the British colonies, but few supported them. Some prominent Irish individuals, such as Thomas D'Arcy McGee, spoke out strongly against them.

The Fenians posed little military threat until the end of the American Civil War when thousands of Irish-American soldiers, trained, receptive to mobilizing in defence of their native country, and now idle, became available. Furthermore, the Fenians had the implicit support of the American government, which sympathized with their anti-British sentiments. Many American politicians also feared that if they failed to support the Fenians, then they would alienate the large number of American Irish Catholic voters.

The Fenian threat tended to be more psychological than physical. The actual military skirmishes were few and restricted to border areas. The two most important took place in New Brunswick and in the Niagara Peninsula. In April 1866, a small band of Fenians crossed into New Brunswick, where they stole the flag from a customs house before the local militia and British regulars forced them back across the border. Although the raid was insignificant in

In May 1866, the Fenians invaded the Niagara peninsula. Their banners bore the initials "I.R.A." (Irish Republican Army).

Library and Archives Canada/C-18737.

military terms, it helped to turn the tide in favour of Confederation in the New Brunswick election that was taking place at the time. Then in May, 1500 Fenians crossed the Niagara River into Canada West. At Ridgeway on June 2, the Fenians defeated the Canadian militia, but then withdrew, never to return, although they continued to be a threat until 1870.

Turning the Tide in New Brunswick

Finding it difficult to rule with a minority government, the Smith government resigned in April 1866. In the ensuing election campaign, Samuel Leonard Tilley resurrected his earlier arguments for Confederation and added new ones. He pointed out to the people of New Brunswick that in Confederation they could expect lower taxes, the Intercolonial Railway, a fair share in the running of the nation, and a market for their raw materials and manufactured goods—in other words, material progress and modernization.

During the campaign, both parties benefited from external funds. The anti-Confederation forces received money from Nova Scotia and possibly, it has been asserted, from the United States, while the pro-Confederationists obtained financial support from the government of the Canadas. "Give us funds," a desperate Tilley cabled John A. Macdonald. "It will require some $40 000 or $50 000 to do the work in all our counties." Macdonald complied; he did not want Confederation to go down to defeat in New Brunswick simply for lack of money. Direct British intervention and threatened Fenian raids also assisted Tilley's cause. After his resounding electoral victory, Tilley had the New Brunswick legislature immediately endorse Confederation.

Final Negotiations

In the autumn and winter of 1866, delegates from Nova Scotia, New Brunswick, and the United Canadas met in London to prepare the passage of the British North America Act through the British parliament. Although the Maritime delegates pressed for modifications of those aspects of the Seventy-Two Resolutions that provided for a strong central government, in the end the Resolutions were accepted with only a few minor, albeit significant, changes. Subsidies to the provinces would be increased beyond the agreed 80 cents a head by a fixed grant from the federal government. The contentious issue of separate schools was settled by applying the Quebec clause on education, which safeguarded the Protestant separate schools in Quebec, to Catholic schools in other provinces in the union, or to new provinces that had separate schools "by law" at the time they joined Confederation. Furthermore, provisions were included for religious minorities to appeal to the federal government if a provincial government threatened their school systems, as they existed before Confederation.

While the delegates were meeting in London to finalize the terms of Confederation, Joseph Howe continued his opposition to Nova Scotia joining Confederation. He urged British officials to reject union. The British government refused, however, to retract its support. When the British North America Act was signed on March 29, 1867, Howe returned to Nova Scotia cured "of a good deal of loyal enthusiasm" and embittered against the Canadians. He was not alone. Many Nova Scotians saw Confederation as the end, not the beginning, of a vibrant Nova Scotia. Elsewhere, Confederation was accepted, although not with enthusiasm, except in Canada West.

Naming the New Nation

John A. Macdonald wanted to call "the new nation" the "Kingdom of Canada," but the British government objected because it feared that the term would further offend the Americans, implying as it did a more autonomous country. Leonard Tilley had chanced upon an alternative title, as well as an appropriate motto, for the new country—*A Mari Usque ad Mare* (From Sea Even unto Sea)—while reading Psalm 72:

> He shall have dominion also from sea to sea,
> and from the river unto the ends of the earth.

On July 1, 1867, the Dominion of Canada was born. It consisted of the four provinces of Nova Scotia, New Brunswick, Quebec, and Ontario.

Politics

The Conservative Party won the first federal election in November, 1867. John A. Macdonald became Canada's first prime minister. A man with warm personal charm and a sense of humour, he preferred practical politics to philosophical debate. A masterful politician, he remained in the prime minister's office, with the exception of a five-year Liberal interlude in the mid-1870s, from 1867 until his death in 1891. Thus the late nineteenth century is often referred to politically as the Macdonald era.

To win support in Quebec, Macdonald relied on George-Étienne Cartier, particularly as he himself did not speak French. Macdonald once referred to Cartier as "my second self," and indeed he was. From 1867 until his death in 1873, Cartier came second only to Macdonald in the Conservative party.

Sir John A. Macdonald addressing a meeting in Toronto. From the Canadian Illustrated News, *April 31, 1878. "One thinks of those audiences, dead and gone now, the noise, the whisky, the laughter, the tobacco, the smell of unwashed humanity: political meetings were entertainment, the translation of newspapers into life" (P.B. Waite, "Reflections on an Un-Victorian Society," in D. Swainson, ed.,* Oliver Mowat's Ontario *[Toronto: Macmillan, 1972], p. 26). Note all those in attendance are male; women would have to wait over a third of a century before they gained the federal franchise.*

Library and Archives Canada/C-68193.

Establishing Political Conventions

Macdonald and Cartier began a political convention that has often been effectively used in Canadian politics: the cooperation within the governing party of an English-speaking prime minister and a politically powerful French-speaking lieutenant, or vice versa. Such an alliance has ensured the French-Canadian minority an influential voice in federal politics.

Macdonald also established a second political convention. For his first cabinet, he chose individuals from various regions and interest groups—Maritimers, Quebeckers, and Ontarians; Protestants and Roman Catholics; Irish, Scottish, English, and French Canadians; business-people, farmers, fishers, and, occasionally, even working people. The Conservatives also created the first federal bureaucracy. This meant jobs, or rather rewards, for the party faithful. Most of the approximately 500 civil service positions in the first administration went to former bureaucrats from Ontario and Quebec, with only a few token positions going to Maritimers.

The Nature of Confederation

Unity in diversity became the goal of the Fathers of Confederation. They sought to establish domestic peace between English- and French-speaking Canadians, and between Protestants and Roman Catholics, through the creation of a political rather than a cultural nationality. As Cartier noted during the Confederation debates in the United Canadas in 1865: "Now, when we were united together, if union were attained, we would form a political nationality with which neither the national origin, nor the religion of any individual, would interfere."

Despite their laudable intentions, Canada's founders built disunity into the political structure. The new Canadian system, by combining aspects of the American federal and the British parliamentary forms of government, resembled a carriage pulled by two horses moving in different directions.

Debating Dominion–Provincial Relations

For more than a century, historians, political scientists, and legal experts have debated the Fathers of Confederation's true intentions. Those who believe they sought to build a strong central government point out that the BNA Act delegated only precise and very circumscribed powers to the provincial governments. In contrast, the federal government gained the important economic and taxation powers, including the right to grant subsidies to the individual provinces. Ottawa also received the right to make laws for the "peace, order and good government of Canada" in relation to all matters not exclusively assigned to the provincial legislatures. Centralists also contend that the phrase "peace, order and good government of Canada" and the phrase "regulation of trade and commerce" incorporated all powers not exclusively given to the provinces; hence the residuum of powers lay with the federal government. Furthermore, they point out that the lieutenant governors of the provinces, appointees of the Dominion government, could reserve and disallow provincial legislation if it were seen as contrary to national interest.

In contrast, provincial-rights advocates argue that since the colonies established the union, Confederation constituted a compact made among them: a provincial compact. Furthermore, they point to the general phrase "property and civil rights in the province" in section 92 of the BNA Act, which deals with the constitutional rights of the provinces, as proof of the provinces' broad powers. They also note that the provinces received a structure of government parallel to that of the federal government, implying that the provinces' association with the Crown was similar, not subordinate, to the Dominion's. Finally, they direct attention to legal tradition: in the late nineteenth and early twentieth centuries, the Judicial Committee of the Privy Council, the highest court of appeal in the British Empire, consistently interpreted the BNA Act in favour of the provinces.

Canadian–British–American Relations

Nationhood did not mean independence. By law and by desire, Canada in 1867 remained a British colony, with the British parliament controlling Canada's external affairs. In 1867, Canadians, particularly English-speaking Canadians, considered the imperial connection as the best means for Canada to fulfil its destiny. The alternatives were possible annexation by the United States, or existence as an insignificant and isolated nation on the northern half of the North American continent, both of which Canadians considered undesirable choices.

The Economy

More than 80 percent of the Canadian labour force in 1867 worked in the primary industries—farming, fishing, and lumbering—to produce the staple products of trade: wheat, fish, and timber. The Maritimes were the centre of the shipbuilding industry. In 1865 alone, for example, the region built more than 600 vessels. The ports of Saint John, Halifax, and Yarmouth were the major shipbuilding centres in the Maritimes, along with Quebec and Montreal in the Canadas.

But as steel ships replaced wooden ones, and as steam replaced sails as the source of energy, the era of wood, wind, and sails soon declined. Some Maritimers equated the decline of their "golden age" with Confederation, and they resented union.

The vast majority of Canadians in 1867 lived on farms. Agriculture was important in Nova Scotia, especially in the Annapolis valley, while in New Brunswick, farmers made up more than half the labour force. In southern Quebec, dairy farming predominated. Some Quebec farmers, with the encouragement of the Roman Catholic Church and the Quebec government, colonized further north in the Saguenay–Lake St. Jean region, in the Laurentians, or in Témiscamingue in the upper Ottawa valley. These "colonist farmers" had to clear the land of forests before breaking ground. Even then, farming in these northern reaches was marginal because of poor soil, short frost-free periods, and long distances from market centres. As the joke went, northern farmers raised two crops: one stone, the other snow. Probably for every Quebecker who went north to farm, ten went south into the New England states, a movement known as "the Great Hemorrhage," in search of work.

Wheat farming served as "the engine of economic growth"[2] in Ontario, according to the economic historian John McCallum. At the time of Confederation the best agricultural land lay in the province, where 60 percent of the working population farmed. Coarse grain or flour made up half of all exports at mid-century. By the time of Confederation, the peak of wheat production had been reached, with most of the good farmland occupied and some of the older districts becoming exhausted. Fortunately for Ontarians, just as they faced an agricultural crisis, the Canadian government acquired the vast prairie land to the west, which served as an outlet for aspiring young Ontario farmers, as George Brown and the Clear Grits had predicted would happen.

Urbanization

In 1867, only one in five Canadians lived in urban centres, communities with a population over 1000. Canada had only three large cities: Montreal with 105 000 people; Quebec City with 60 000; and Toronto with 50 000. Six other cities had populations greater than 10 000: Saint John and Halifax in the Maritimes, and Hamilton, Ottawa, Kingston, and London in Ontario. A host of smaller towns in the range of 1000–5000 dotted the Canadian landscape. The larger metropolitan centres serviced a hinterland region that went beyond the adjacent rural area, thanks to their extensive rail connections. Montreal's hinterland, for example, included the rural areas of southwestern Quebec as well as eastern Ontario.

The Maritime cities of Saint John and Halifax grew slowly, compared with cities in central Canada. Many of the manufacturers in these two port cities faced hard times because they lacked a large local rural market and faced competition from wealthier entrepreneurs in central Canada. In 1867, industrialists in the Maritimes looked forward to the completion of the Intercolonial Railway, which, they hoped, would make Ontario and Quebec economic hinterlands of Halifax and Saint John.

Canadian cities in 1867 were, with the exception of Montreal, preindustrial. This meant that rich and poor lived in close proximity, with social distinctions marked by the size of one's house, its location on the street, or by the location of a particular street in a district as opposed to distinct districts. In Montreal, however, there already existed predominantly working-class districts in the city core and along the St. Lawrence River and Lachine Canal. Well-to-do families were leaving the inner city to live in the spacious, clean, and airy suburban districts of the west end, with its numerous parks and good public services. Thus, in the case of Montreal, the modern industrial segregated city had made an appearance in 1867. By 1914, such segregated cities would be commonplace throughout the country.

Chief areas of settlement in Canada, 1867.

Source: Based on John Warkentin, *Canada: A Geographical Interpretation* (Toronto: Methuen, 1968), p. 45.

Population

In 1867, the total population of the new Dominion of Canada was 3.5 million. The First Nations numbered approximately 30 000, or roughly 1 percent. The three largest groups were: the Ojibwa (Anishinabeg), in Ontario; the Iroquois, in Ontario and Quebec; and the Mi'kmaq (Micmac), in Nova Scotia and New Brunswick.

Those of French descent made up roughly a third of the total population. More than 85 percent resided in Quebec and had roots in North America extending back two centuries. The Acadians in New Brunswick and Nova Scotia numbered nearly 10 percent of the French-speaking population. Only 3 percent of Canada's francophones lived in Ontario, mainly in the area adjacent to Quebec.

People of British descent accounted for 60 percent of Canada's population in 1867. Some were descendants of Loyalists who had settled on British territory after the American Revolution. Most, however, were British immigrants and their descendants who had arrived in British North America between 1815 and 1860, some 1.3 million in total. In 1867, the Irish made up 25 percent of the total Canadian population, the Scots 16 percent, the English 15 percent, and the Welsh 5 percent.

English-speaking and French-speaking Canadians lived in two separate worlds in 1867. P.-J.-O. Chauveau, the first premier of Quebec after Confederation, compared Canada to the famous staircase of the Château de Chambord in France, built to allow two persons to ascend it without meeting, and even without seeing each other except at intervals. "English and French, we climb by a double flight of stairs toward the destinies reserved for us on this continent, without knowing each other, without meeting each other, except on the landing of politics."

The remaining 8 percent of the Dominion's population consisted of non-British and non-French immigrants and their descendants from Europe and the United States. The majority were from German-speaking states and were welcomed because of the close links between the British monarchy and German principalities. There were, as well, about 65 000 African Canadians. While some were of American Loyalist descent, many had arrived in the mid-1800s, either as freed African Americans, now facing increased discrimination in racially torn America, or as fugitive slaves on the eve of the American Civil War via the Underground Railroad, a loose network of African Americans (sometimes ex-slaves) and white abolitionists who aided slaves. Although slavery had not existed in British North America since the early nineteenth century, racial prejudice existed. Blacks faced discrimination in land grants, schooling, employment, and voting rights.

Ontario and Quebec had nearly four-fifths of the new Dominion's population, with more than 1.5 million in Ontario and about one million in Quebec. The other fifth of Canada's population resided in the Maritime provinces: roughly 400 000 in Nova Scotia and 300 000 in New Brunswick.

Social Life

In 1867, most Canadians lived and worked on their own farms, as close to neighbours, kin, and their own ethnic group as possible. In Quebec, only thirteen years earlier, the seigneurial system had been abolished, which meant individual farmers had acquired title to their lands. Limited financial means made consumer goods a luxury. The village elite generally consisted of the curé, the doctor, the notary, and the local merchants. In Quebec City and Montreal, French Canadians lived amidst a substantial and influential English-speaking population.

Next door in Ontario, most of the population consisted of recent British immigrants or children of immigrants. The majority were freehold farmers who had acquired their land within the last generation. In general, Ontario farmers were better off economically than their Quebec counterparts. They owned larger farms that were newly cultivated and consequently more productive. People lived farther apart, however, and were divided by their different Christian denominational ties.

A HISTORICAL PORTRAIT

Josiah Henson

Josiah Henson was born into slavery on a Maryland plantation in 1789. His earliest recollection at the age of three or four was the day he saw his father return from a terrible beating. As Henson later recalled, "His right ear had been cut off close to his head and he had received a hundred lashes on his back." His "crime"? He struck a white man, the farm overseer, for brutally assaulting Josiah's mother.

Soon afterwards, the Hensons' master split the family up. He sold Josiah's father to a plantation in Alabama and auctioned off Josiah's mother, brothers, sisters, and Josiah himself to separate owners. Fortunately, Josiah was later reunited with his mother.

As slaves, Josiah and his mother lived in appalling conditions, eating corn meal and salted herring. "Our lodging," he recalled, "was in log huts, of a single small room, with no other floor than the trodden earth, in which ten or a dozen persons—men, women, and children—might sleep." By his twenties, the conscientious, hard-working man had so gained his master's respect that he appointed him farm superintendent. When it became clear, however, that his owner had no intention of granting him his freedom, Henson, who had married fifteen or so years earlier and now had a family, escaped with his wife and four children to Canada.

The Hensons spent six difficult weeks following the Underground Railway to Upper Canada. On October 28, 1830, they crossed the Niagara River. Immediately, Henson fell on his knees and gave thanks. In their new home, the Hensons founded an African community named Dawn, near present-day Dresden, Ontario. With the financial assistance of a group of Boston Unitarians, they began the British American Institute for Fugitive Slaves, a school to educate ex-slaves and to teach them a trade.

In the late 1840s, Henson dictated his life story. It was published in Boston as *The Life of Josiah Henson Formerly a Slave Now an Inhabitant of Canada* in 1849. Three years later Harriet Beecher Stowe's novel, *Uncle Tom's Cabin*, appeared. It proved a sensation, the most popular antislavery book published before the outbreak of the American Civil War. The fact that many people identified Josiah Henson as the prototype for the fictional "Uncle Tom" made him famous. Stowe, however, never categorically stated this; people just inferred that it was true. As a result of his fame, Henson made several lecture tours of Britain to raise money for the Dawn settlement.

When the American Civil War ended, many African Americans in Upper Canada returned to the United States, and the community of Dawn died out. In his late eighties, Henson made his final visit to Britain to meet Queen Victoria at Windsor Castle. He died in Dresden in 1883.

Queen Victoria receives Josiah Henson at Windsor Castle, March 5, 1877.

Reproduced courtesy of The American Museum in Britain (Bath, UK).

In the 1860s, Ontarians were on the move. A study of several townships along Lake Ontario near Port Hope revealed that within a five-year span more than half the people were recent occupants or had moved from one place to another within the region. David Gagan's study of Peel County at mid-century confirms this, as does Michael Katz's study of mid-century Hamilton.[3] An increasing number were leaving the country for the cities and towns. Physical mobility, however, did not necessarily mean social mobility, even though the incentive for moving was often to better one's life.

In the Maritimes, people lived predominantly in rural areas or in small towns. Given the sparse populations, poor roads, and a topography that encouraged settlement along the coast, communities were often isolated. In 1867, no major railways yet existed to link communities. In addition, the region's diversified economy of fishing, lumbering, mining, and farming segregated people according to interests and livelihood. As a result, Maritimers in 1867 identified with their particular locale and lacked a provincial and regional consciousness.

Women

Women made up almost half of the population in 1867, yet they lacked basic rights: the right to vote; the right to higher education or professional training; and legal rights. They were not defined as individuals but by their role in the "domestic sphere," as wives and mothers at the service of husbands and children.

Women relinquished their personal property and any wages earned upon marriage. Under British common law, in effect everywhere except in Quebec, husband and wife were legally one. A wife could not sign a contract, be sued in her own name, take her husband to court, or initiate divorce proceedings. Despite such restrictions, over 95 percent of women married. They also bore large families, 7.8 children on average by mid-century. By the end of the century, that number declined to an average of only four children.

Marriage was more a communal than a private affair. Courting occurred in supervised settings, and marriage was a public event. The few surviving women's diaries of this period speak little of love and romance in marriage, and instead emphasize economic security.

In the days before modern conveniences, women's duties lay in the arduous work of keeping a good home. Their daily tasks would consist of cleaning house, cooking, sewing, weaving, and making butter, the rhythm being broken only by church services on Sundays. The change of seasons varied the pattern only slightly, and added garden and field work at harvest time. (A satirical cartoon in *L'Opinion Publique*, an illustrated journal of the day—see here—reveals what many working-class women's sentiments must have been.)

Children were the forgotten group in society, without any legal rights. Those from poorer families usually had to leave school early to help support their families. Most working-class children had little hope of rising above their parents' level and social status.

Trade Unions

The federal government only legally recognized unions in 1872. In the 1860s, the unions that did exist represented skilled workers in a particular locale or a special trade, such as typesetting, shoemaking, and moulding. The first unions for nonskilled workers appeared in shops that introduced modern technology, a development that was beginning to undermine jobs. Increasingly, employers saw workers as employees rather than as apprentices. They brought workers under one roof and paid them according to the quantity, rather than the quality, of their work.

Some workers responded to these changed conditions in the workplace by rioting. By 1867, however, strikes and parades were replacing riots as

"Work," a drawing that appeared in the journal L'Opinion Publique, *November 2, 1871. In the late nineteenth century, gender inequality was as common as class inequality.*

Library and Archives Canada/C-108134.

more acceptable forms of protest, and as a means to demand better wages and working conditions. On June 10, 1867, for example, 10 000 workers paraded in the streets of Montreal as a show of worker solidarity and as an appeal for improved wages and working conditions.

Religion and Education

Religious Denominations

In 1867, almost all Canadians belonged to one of the major denominations. The Roman Catholic Church, the largest in Canada, claimed 40 percent of the country's population (in Quebec, 85 percent) as members. In Quebec the Roman Catholic Church controlled the Catholic education system, supplying both its teachers and its curriculum. Most of the teachers came from the female religious orders. The female orders also administered the hospitals and cared for the sick, the abandoned, and the poor. These female religious communities gave many of their members the opportunity to obtain an excellent education, to occupy responsible administrative positions, and to serve as teachers, nurses, and social assistance workers. They also provided a strong sense of community.

In Protestant Canada, Anglicans slightly outnumbered Presbyterians, who outnumbered Methodists. These Protestant religious groups favoured voluntarism, the legal separation of church and state. They believed that religious instruction should be provided by the church only, in Sunday schools. The Roman Catholic Church, in contrast, maintained that the school system should provide religious, as well as regular, instruction. It therefore opposed the abolition of denominational schools.

Schooling

Schooling had little priority in Canada in the 1860s, although most provinces moved to a form of taxation on property holders to finance state-operated schools. Children fortunate enough to receive formal education might have their classes in the corners of warehouses, blacksmith shops, stores, tanneries, or private homes. Their schooling rarely went beyond the basic "3 Rs"—"reading, 'riting, and 'rithmetic." Very often, teachers had little more education than their students. The most important requisite to teach was simply a willingness to work for low pay and to enforce discipline.

In Ontario, the middle and upper classes paid fees for their children to attend grammar schools (renamed "high schools" in 1871 by the superintendent of education, Egerton Ryerson) and collegiate institutes. In high school, the students learned English, commercial subjects, and natural science, especially agriculture; and in collegiate institutes they also studied the classics in preparation for university. In Quebec, the Roman Catholic Church operated classical colleges, which trained the province's future lawyers, doctors, and priests. Most of the seventeen universities in existence in 1867 were affiliated with a religious denomination, but four exceptions already existed: the University of Toronto, McGill in Montreal, Dalhousie College in Halifax, and the University of New Brunswick in Fredericton. Universities served an elite of only 1500 students in total, mostly sons of the well-to-do (women were not admitted) or a few aspiring members of the upper middle class. Within the university curriculum, the faculties of arts and theology dominated, as teaching and the clergy were the favoured career options after graduation. The arts course was traditional, with an emphasis on classical languages, mathematics, and philosophy. Natural science was assuming greater importance. Engineering courses had not yet been introduced, but law and medicine were taught at some of the larger universities.

COMMUNITY PORTRAIT

The Community of the Sisters of the Congregation of Notre Dame in the Late Nineteenth Century

Founded in 1653 by Marguerite Bourgeoys as a religious community of cloistered women to live and work among the common people, and as a teaching order to provide schooling for the young women of New France, the Congregation of Notre Dame became, by the late nineteenth and early twentieth centuries, the largest and most prestigious religious community of women teachers in Quebec. By 1920, it had over 1600 members and over 150 Roman Catholic schools throughout Quebec, Nova Scotia, New Brunswick, and Ontario.

The Congregation of Notre Dame, like other women's religious orders, provided women with a community in which they could find meaningful work, which, in the case of the Congregation, meant teaching. Many women who entered the Congregation of Notre Dame convents did so on the advice of family members who, in many cases, had preceded them. Thus a strong bond existed between members of the Congregation and their families. Even the terms "sisters" and "mothers" to identify members of women's religious communities, and, in the case of the Congregation of Notre Dame, the epithet "Les Filles de Marguerite Bourgeoys" (Daughters of Marguerite Bourgeoys) reinforced the familial link. Members of the order prayed to Marguerite Bourgeoys, their founder. Within the community, the Golden Rule applied: sisters were expected to be charitable and compassionate to fellow members. The young and healthy, for example, took care of the sick and elderly nuns. At the same time, the community also allowed for a relaxation of the order's rules and regulations to foster camaraderie. At the mother house of the Congregation, for example, sisters were permitted on special occasions to "let loose" by engaging in such communal fun as playing harmless pranks, wearing costumes, or performing imitations of their superiors.

As the Congregation grew, it also became more affluent. Its members enjoyed improved diets of fresh fruits, vegetables, butter, and pastries. The sisters had lighter manual workloads, and thus more time for leisure activities together and for communal prayers. But prosperity also caused strains in the Congregation's communal life. In the 1880s, *les soeurs converses*, or domestic servants, were brought into the community to do the manual work previously done by the sisters themselves. Thus a two-tiered social order emerged, evident in the separation of recreation, clothing habits, and assigned work of the two groups. Furthermore, the Congregation's growth resulted in a more bureaucratic structure that mitigated against its earlier sense of a community of equals. Now a General Superior ruled and administered affairs at the centre, while local and provincial superiors in the Congregation's six "provinces," each corresponding to the regional district of the schools owned by the community, carried out the rulings of the central council and regulated the everyday activities of the sisters. A constitution dictated the rights and responsibilities of each office and outlined the procedure for the appointment of superiors. Nominally, sisters who had been with the community for at least ten years could cast a vote for their leaders, but in reality each chapter selected delegates who made the final decision. And within the community, nuns from upper- and middle-class households wielded greater power than those nuns from working-class or farming backgrounds.

Still, the community of the Congregation of Notre Dame provided its members with a communal and supportive setting in which women lived a religious life while also acquiring a profession and the skills to play a meaningful role in society. In 1908, the Congregation supported the establishment of the first French-language women's college in Quebec: the *École d'enseignment supérieur* (renamed the Collège Marguerite Bourgeoys in 1926). In this way, the Congregation of Notre Dame assisted French-Canadian females to obtain an education equal to their male counterparts.

In 1984, for the first time, the *Constitution and Rules* of the Congregation included some of the inspirational statements of Marguerite Bourgeoys, including the following:

> *Our Foundress invites us to imitate "the life led by the Blessed Virgin throughout her time on earth." Therefore, especially the mystery of the Visitation and in Mary's life among the apostles in the first Christian community, we find spiritual and apostolic inspiration.*

Today, the Congregation of Notre Dame has a worldwide community of approximately 1700 sisters in Canada, the United States, Japan, Central and South America, and Africa.

FURTHER READING

Patricia Simpson, *Marguerite Bourgeoys and the Congregation of Notre Dame, 1665–1700* (Montreal/Kingston: McGill-Queen's University Press, 2005).

Marta Danylewycz, *Taking the Veil: An Alternative to Marriage, Motherhood, and Spinsterhood in Quebec, 1840–1920* (Toronto: McClelland and Stewart, 1987).

Danielle Juteau and Nicole Laurin, *Un métier et une vocation: Le travail des religieuses au Québec de 1901 à 1971* (Montreal: Presses de l'Université de Montréal, 1997).

Nadia Famy-Eid and Micheline Dumont, *Les couventines: L'Éducation des filles au Québec dans les congrégations religieuses enseignantes, 1840–1960* (Montreal: Boréal, 1986).

Congrégation de Notre Dame website, http://www.cnd-m.com, accessed September 6, 2008.

The teachers of Mont Ste-Marie Convent School, 1889.

Centre d'archives, Congrégation de Notre Dame, 2330 ouest, rue Sherbrooke, PQ, H3E 1G8, (514) 931-5891.

This was the Canada of 1867 as the country embarked on its new experiment in nation-building. It was a rural, predominantly farming, society. Social distinctions divided the rural population, and great physical distances isolated communities. In the few towns and cities that existed, social distinctions were evident, but segregation by social districts was only beginning. The Canadian economy remained largely preindustrial and commercial, but manufacturing and industrialization had started in a few large urban centres. Exports included mainly wheat, timber, and fish. Politically, the new nation was about to experiment with a new, two-party system and with a new Constitution that left relationships between the new federal government and the provincial governments to be resolved. The new Dominion also lacked a sense of nationalism. As Prime Minister John A. Macdonald put it: Confederation, "now in the gristle," needed to "harden into bone."

NOTES

1. Peter H. Russell, *Constitutional Odyssey: Can Canadians Become a Sovereign People?*, 2nd ed. (Toronto: University of Toronto Press, 1993), p. 32.

2. John McCallum, *Unequal Beginnings: Agriculture and Economic Development in Quebec and Ontario until 1870* (Toronto: University of Toronto Press, 1980), p. 5.

3. David Gagan, *Hopeful Travellers: Families, Land, and Social Change in Mid-Victorian Peel County, Canada West* (Toronto: University of Toronto Press, 1981); and Michael Katz, *The People of Hamilton, Canada West: Family and Class in a Mid-Nineteenth Century City* (Cambridge, MA: Harvard University Press, 1975).

BEYOND THE BOOK

Sir John A. Macdonald: Canada's Patriot Statesman

http://www.collectionscanada.gc.ca/sir-john-a-macdonald/index-e.html
This website collects thousands of primary source documents such as letters and telegrams regarding Sir John A. Macdonald's personal and political life. Macdonald's political opponents are also featured in this highly detailed, searchable database.

Constructing Parliament Hill

http://www.collectionscanada.gc.ca/structures/parliament/index-e.html
Detailed historical architectural plans and photographs of the construction of Parliament Hill.

Canadian Confederation

http://www.collectionscanada.ca/confederation/index-e.html
Historical documents and images regarding the Confederation of Canada. Biographies of the Fathers of Confederation.

Victoria, BC: November 28, 1867

http://www.ourroots.ca/e/toc.aspx?id=914
Experience life in Victoria, British Columbia in 1867 through this digitized account of a public meeting overseen by the city's mayor.

Photographs of Life in 1867

http://www.mccord-museum.qc.ca/scripts/search_results.php?Lang=1&keywords =1867
Explore the culture of Canada in 1867 through this vast database of photographs taken of individuals and objects in that year.

Immigration Handbook

http://ist.uwaterloo.ca/~marj/genealogy/papers/emguide1864.html
An 1864 handbook for immigrants to Canada.

British North America Act, 1867

http://www.canadiana.org/ECO/mtq?doc=92338
The full text of the 1867 British North America Act, which marked the beginnings of Canada as a nation.

RELATED READINGS

The following articles in R. Douglas Francis and Donald B. Smith, eds., *Viewpoints. Readings in Canadian History* (Toronto: Thomson Nelson, 2007), are relevant to this chapter: Ged Martin, "The Case against Canadian Confederation," pp. 220–41; John A. Rohr, "Current Canadian Constitutionalism and the 1865 Confederation Debates," pp. 241–60; and Paul Romney, "Was Canada Meant to Be a Democracy?," pp. 260–63.

BIBLIOGRAPHY

The three best general texts on Confederation, all written in the 1960s, are Donald Creighton, *The Road to Confederation: The Emergence of Canada, 1863–1867* (Toronto: Macmillan, 1964); W.L. Morton, *The Critical Years: The Union of British North America, 1857–1873* (Toronto: McClelland & Stewart, 1964); and P.B. Waite, *The Life and Times of Confederation, 1864–1867: Politics, Newspapers, and the Union of British North America* (Toronto: University of Toronto Press, 1962). The Canadian Historical Association has published a number of pamphlets on aspects of Confederation by leading scholars in their fields: J.M. Beck, *Joseph Howe: Anti-Confederate* (Ottawa, 1966); J.-C. Bonenfant, *The French Canadians and the Birth of Confederation* (Ottawa, 1966); P.G. Cornell, *The Great Coalition* (Ottawa, 1966); W.L. Morton, *The West and Confederation, 1857–1871* (Ottawa, 1962); P.B. Waite, *The Charlottetown Conference* (Ottawa, 1963); and W.M. Whitelaw, *The Quebec Conference* (Ottawa, 1966). Christopher Moore takes a more recent look at the topic in *1867: How the Fathers Made a Deal* (Toronto: McClelland & Stewart, 1997). A good primary source is P.B. Waite, ed., *The Confederation Debates in the Province of Canada, 1865* (Toronto: McClelland & Stewart, 1963).

On the Maritime provinces and Confederation in 1867, see Phillip A. Buckner, "The 1860s: An End and a Beginning," in Phillip A. Buckner and John G. Reid, eds., *The Atlantic Region to Confederation: A History* (Toronto: University of Toronto Press, 1994), pp. 360–86.

On the American influence on Confederation, consult Robin Winks, *Canada and the United States: The Civil War Years* (Montreal: Harvest House, 1971 [1960]); Greg Marquis, *In Armageddon's Shadow: The Civil War and Canada's Maritime Provinces* (Montreal/Kingston: McGill-Queen's University Press, 1998); Adam Myers, *Dixie and the Dominion: Canada, the Confederacy and the War for the Union* (Toronto: Dundurn Press, 2003); and Claire Hoy, *Canadians in the Civil War* (Toronto: McClelland and Stewart, 2004). Studies of Britain's influence include C.P. Stacey, *Canada and the British Army, 1841–1871*, rev. ed. (Toronto: University of Toronto Press, 1963 [1936]); and Ged Martin, *Britain and the Origins of Canadian Federation, 1837–67* (Vancouver: University of British Columbia Press, 1995).

Portraits of Canada's first prime minister are available in Richard Gwyn, *John A.: The Man Who Made Us: The Life and Times of John A. Macdonald*, vol. 1 (Toronto: Random House Canada, 2007); Donald G. Creighton, *John A. Macdonald: The Old Chieftain* (Toronto: Macmillan, 1955); and P.B. Waite, *Macdonald: His Life and World* (Toronto: McGraw-Hill Ryerson, 1975). For studies of George-Étienne Cartier see Brian Young, *George-Étienne Cartier: Montreal Bourgeois* (Montreal/Kingston: McGill-Queen's University Press, 1981). Gordon T. Stewart discusses the formation of political parties in *The Origins of Canadian Politics: A Comparative Approach* (Vancouver: University of British Columbia Press, 1986).

For a review of the Canadian economy at the time of Confederation, consult Michael Bliss, *Northern Enterprise: Five Centuries of Canadian Business* (Toronto: McClelland & Stewart, 1987); Kenneth Norrie and Douglas Owram, *A History of the Canadian Economy*, 3rd ed. (Toronto: Nelson, 2002); and, in the case of Quebec, P.-A. Linteau, R. Durocher, and J.-C. Robert, *Quebec: A History, 1867–1929* (Toronto: James Lorimer, 1983).

For a study of social life in Montreal, see Bettina Bradbury, *Working Families: Age, Gender, and Daily Survival in Industrializing Montreal* (Toronto: McClelland & Stewart, 1993). Sandra Gwyn provides a glimpse of governing society in Ottawa from 1867 to 1914 in *The Private Capital: Ambition and Love in the Age of Macdonald and Laurier* (Toronto: McClelland & Stewart, 1984). For the story of the Aboriginal peoples, see E.S. Rogers and Donald B. Smith, eds., *Aboriginal Ontario* (Toronto: Dundurn Press, 1994). The best overview of African Canadians remains Robin Winks, *The Blacks in Canada: A History*, 2nd ed. (Montreal/Kingston: McGill-Queen's University Press, 1997).

On women at the time of Confederation, see the relevant sections of Alison Prentice et al., *Canadian Women: A History*, 2nd ed. (Toronto: Harcourt Brace, 1996). For Quebec, see Marta Danylewycz, *Taking the Veil: An Alternative to Marriage, Motherhood, and Spinsterhood in Quebec, 1840–1920* (Toronto: McClelland & Stewart, 1987); for the Maritimes, see Janet Guildford and Suzanne Morton, *Separate Spheres: Women's Worlds in the 19th-Century Maritimes* (Fredericton: Acadiensis Press, 1994).

Craig Heron's *The Canadian Labour Movement: A Short History*, 2nd ed. (Toronto: Lorimer, 1996) surveys Canadian labour history. See, as well, Bryan D. Palmer, *Working-Class Experience: Rethinking the History of Canadian Labour, 1800–1991* (Toronto: McClelland & Stewart, 1992).

For further discussion of religion see John S. Moir, "Religion," in *The Canadians: 1867–1967* (cited earlier), pp. 586–605; and John W. Grant, *A Profusion of Spires: Religion in Nineteenth-Century Ontario* (Toronto: University of Toronto Press, 1988). On education consult Susan E. Houston and Alison Prentice, *Schooling and Scholars in Nineteenth-Century Ontario* (Toronto: University of Toronto Press, 1988); Bruce Curtis, *Building the Educational State: Canada West, 1836–1871* (London: Althouse Press, 1988); and J. Donald Wilson, Robert M. Stamp, and Louis-Philippe Audet, eds., *Canadian Education: A History* (Toronto: Prentice-Hall, 1970).

Chapter Twelve

CONSOLIDATION OF CONFEDERATION

TIME LINE

1868	Nova Scotia attempts to secede from Confederation
1869	Canada purchases Rupert's Land from the Hudson's Bay Company Act for the Temporary Government of Rupert's Land and the North-West Territories is passed Métis resistance breaks out under Louis Riel
1870	Manitoba becomes a province Wolseley expedition sent to the Red River Colony
1871	British Columbia joins Confederation The first of seven treaties signed with the Canadian government covering the territory of present-day northern Ontario
1873	Prince Edward Island joins Confederation
1876	Treaty Six signed with the Canadian government covering the territory of present-day central and northern Saskatchewan and Alberta Indian Act passed
1877	Treaty Seven signed between the Canadian government and the Blackfoot of present-day southern Alberta
1880	Britain transfers jurisdiction over the Arctic Islands to Canada

In his first administration, Prime Minister John A. Macdonald worked to keep the fragile creation called Canada together against the desire of Nova Scotia to secede. He also rounded out the country by purchasing Rupert's Land from the Hudson's Bay Company. From 1867 to 1872, Macdonald's Conservative government brought in Manitoba and British Columbia as provinces and prepared for Prince Edward Island's entry in 1873. Newfoundland, wanting better terms, refused to join. By 1880, Canada would acquire the Arctic region from Britain. Other challenges for the new Canadian government included putting down the resistance of the Métis in the North West, who resented Canadian takeover of the territory without consulting them, and then negotiating a settlement. As well, the government needed to sign treaties with the First Nations in the Prairie West to secure control over their land, and then bring them under federal government jurisdiction through the implementation of the Indian Act. These activities showed the extent to which the Canadian government would go to secure control over the region and its populace and to prevent an American takeover of the area.

The Nova Scotia Repeal Movement

Nova Scotia had opposed union with the Province of the Canadas from the beginning. When Nova Scotians had a chance to vote on Confederation, in September 1867, they elected anti-Confederationists in 18 of the 19 federal seats. Only Charles Tupper won his seat for the confederates, and then by less than a hundred votes. In a provincial election the same year, Nova Scotians elected 36 anti-Confederationists and only 2 pro-Confederationists. In the first meeting of the provincial legislature, the opponents of Confederation presented repeal resolutions to end the "bondage" of Confederation.

The Anti-Confederation League, later patriotically renamed the Nova Scotia Party, was formed in 1866 and led by Joseph Howe. Once again, he headed a committee to London in early 1868 to obtain the Colonial Office's sanction for Nova Scotia's release from Confederation. But the colonial secretary refused to meet Howe. While Howe wanted continued colonial ties with the British, other anti-Confederationists, particularly the business interests in the province, favoured annexation to the United States.

John A. Macdonald saw Canada's opportunity. He knew Howe opposed union with the United States. In return for joining his government, the prime minister promised Howe a cabinet position, control over provincial patronage, and better financial terms for Nova Scotia—an increased debt allowance and a 25 percent increase in the federal subsidy to the province. Although his opponents accused him of betraying Nova Scotia, Howe ran for federal office in a byelection. Assisted by a very generous campaign donation, supplied jointly by the federal Conservative government and central Canadian business interests, Howe won and subsequently joined the federal cabinet.

Howe's "conversion" to Canadian federalism weakened the repeal movement. Only the annexationists remained. In June 1869, the Anti-Confederation League formally changed its name to the Annexation League. The timing could not have been worse for them: their manifesto, advocating closer relations with the United States, coincided with a brief period of prosperity in the province, which undermined their economic grievances. Furthermore, the United States did not appear particularly interested at this time in annexing Nova Scotia.

The final offer of better terms for Nova Scotia won over the moderate anti-Confederationists. In order to weaken opposition to Confederation, Tupper, Howe, and New Brunswick's Charles Tilley successfully pressured Macdonald to give utmost priority to the construction of the Intercolonial Railway. The 800 km publicly funded railway line was completed in 1876 and ran from Rivière-du-Loup in Quebec, along New Brunswick's north shore, to link up with existing lines to Halifax and Saint John.

The Canadian Acquisition of Rupert's Land

Macdonald's Conservative government also faced serious trouble in the North West. American senators and congressmen, particularly from the Midwest, talked openly of annexing the region. In 1864, the United States Congress granted a charter for the construction of the Northern Pacific Railway from St. Paul, Minnesota to Seattle, Washington. It was to be built close to the international border with the intention of capturing more of the trade of the British territory through the building of spur lines.

In 1868, the Canadian government began negotiations in London with the British government and representatives of the Hudson's Bay Company (HBC) to acquire Rupert's Land, roughly defined as all territory whose rivers flowed into Hudson Bay. Thus, unlike the American West, which was won by military conquest, the Canadian West was bought by a government. The agreement reached in 1869–1870 constituted one of the largest real estate deals in history. For an area ten times the size of what was then Canada, the Dominion government agreed to pay the HBC a cash sum of £300 000 (approximately $1.5 million at the time) and to allow the company to retain one-twentieth (roughly 2.8 million ha) of the land of the "fertile belt" (the area along the North Saskatchewan River), as well as the land immediately surrounding its trading posts. The company agreed to transfer the land to the British government, which then turned the territory over to Canada. Historian Chester Martin maintained that the land deal "transformed the original Dominion from a federation of equal provinces ... into a veritable empire in its own right."[1] The Canadian government would rule the region as a colonial possession, suppressing any challenge to its authority, demanding conformity, and dictating to a significant degree the political, economic, and social life of the region's inhabitants.

Administrating the North West

While the negotiations were under way, the Canadian Parliament passed the Act for the Temporary Government of Rupert's Land and the North-West Territory. It provided for a colonial system of government with an appointed governor and council only. Representative

A family of Métis traders in camp, early 1870s. The Red River cart, built without any metal, allowed the Métis to harvest the buffalo herds, which at this point had been greatly depleted on the Canadian side of the border.

Archives of Manitoba: Boundary Commission (1872–1874) 164 (N14100).

and responsible government, and provincehood, would await a larger population. The Canadian government made immediate plans to build a road from the Lake of the Woods to Fort Garry in the Red River colony and dispatched a survey crew to the Red River for an eventual railway to link the North West to the rest of Canada. As well, it appointed William McDougall from Ontario as the first lieutenant governor. McDougall set off by way of St. Paul, Minnesota to take up his administrative duties in the Red River colony. But he never reached his destination. A group of Métis in the Red River colony, led by Louis Riel, a 25-year-old Métis from a well-established Red River family who had been educated in Montreal, forbade McDougall and his entourage to enter Rupert's Land. The Métis also drove out the survey crew.

The mixed-blood population in the Red River area consisted of three groups. About half were French Métis, offspring of the intermarriage of French fur traders and First Nations women. About another third were the "country born," descendants of Scottish and First Nations parents. The remaining group were the descendants of Selkirk's original Scottish settlers and newly arrived immigrants from the Canadas, who together numbered only about 1000 people, less than 10 percent of the total Red River colony's population in 1869.

The Métis Resistance of 1869–1870

The French Métis resented not being consulted over the sale of their homeland. They also disliked the aggressive action and haughty attitude of the small group of Canadian expansionists in the Red River colony working to bring the region into Confederation. In their local newspaper, *The Nor'Wester*, these Canadians ridiculed the Métis and proclaimed Canada's right to take control of the North West as part of the country's "manifest destiny." The Métis reacted by occupying Upper Fort Garry, the seat of government, on November 2, and establishing their own provisional government, thus gaining effective control of the Red River colony.

Prime Minister Macdonald opened negotiations with the Métis. Acting quickly, he dismissed William McDougall and asked the influential Bishop Alexandre Taché of the Red River colony to return from Rome, where he had been attending the Vatican Council, to assist in reaching a settlement. The prime minister also appointed Donald A. Smith of the Hudson's Bay Company to negotiate with the Métis on behalf of the Canadian government.

Riel's provisional government drew up a bill of rights in November 1869, outlining its grievances and demands. That bill became the basis for negotiations. At two public meetings in the Red River colony held in mid-January, Smith promised the Red River colony a better deal, to be decided by a committee of Métis and the Canadian government.

Clash between the Métis and the Canada Party

Meanwhile, the Canadian expansionist party in the Red River colony took action into its own hands. Its members met at the general store owned by John Schultz, a sometime medical doctor and merchant and the leader of the Canada party. Schultz's store became the Canada party's headquarters for its

Louis Riel (seated directly in the centre) with his council, 1870. Riel and his council's resistance to Canada's attempted seizure of the Red River led to the Manitoba Act of 1870, which brought Manitoba into Confederation as the first new province.

Library and Archives Canada/PA12854; Manitoba Museum of Man and Nature/3661.

Thomas Scott, executed March 4, 1870.

Glenbow Archives/NA 576-1.

attacks on Riel's provisional government. The Métis raided the store and imprisoned the Canadians. The Métis agreed to release those prisoners who promised either to leave the colony or to obey the provisional government. A few, like Schultz, refused to comply. He managed to escape from his Métis prison by using a knife, hidden in a pudding by his wife, to cut the ropes on the windows and to lower himself out. He then gathered supporters for an ill-fated attack on Upper Fort Garry. The Métis captured members of the raiding party, including Thomas Scott, a virulent 28-year-old Protestant Irishman and member of the Orange Lodge.

Scott proved a difficult prisoner. He insulted and provoked his Métis guards. Riel decided to hold a Métis court to try Scott for contempt of the Métis provisional government. The court voted to execute the troublemaker. Riel agreed, in order, he claimed, "to make Canada respect us." (Some historians have since argued that Riel complied with the court order so as to maintain his control of the Métis.) On March 4, 1870, a firing squad executed Scott.

Scott's execution turned the Métis resistance from a distant western struggle into a national crisis. Protestant Ontario now had its martyr. When a group of Scott's Red River associates arrived in Toronto to enlist support for their cause, a huge crowd assembled to hear their version of the uprising in the West:

It would be a gross injustice to the loyal inhabitants of Red River, humiliating to our national honour, and contrary to all British traditions for our Government to receive, negotiate or meet with the emissaries of those who have robbed, imprisoned and murdered loyal Canadians, whose only fault was zeal for British institutions, whose only crime was devotion to the old flag.

French Canadians, on the other hand, viewed Riel as the protector of the French-speaking Métis against an aggressive group of Canadianists from Ontario, backed by the Orange Order.

John A. Macdonald proposed a compromise. To appease the Métis and the French Canadians of Quebec, his government passed the Manitoba Act in May 1870, based on the negotiations between the Red River's three-person delegation and the Canadian government. The Red River colony could enter Confederation as a province. To satisfy Ontarians, the prime minister agreed to send an armed force to the Red River colony immediately to secure the region for Canada.

The Manitoba Act

The Manitoba Act created the new province of Manitoba that geographically included only the 35 000 km^2 around the Red River settlement and Portage la Prairie to the west. The rest of the area became the North-West Territories. Manitoba received its own legislative assembly, four federal members of parliament, and two senators. But, unlike the other provinces in Confederation, Ottawa denied Manitoba control over its own public lands and natural resources. The same was true for the North-West Territories. The land and resources of the entire North West remained under the federal government's control, to be used "for the purposes of the Dominion."

The Manitoba Act addressed the issue of linguistic and educational rights of the French-speaking population. In 1867 the Fathers of Confederation had not discussed the rights of

French Canadians outside the province of Quebec. They preferred to address the issue on an ad hoc basis when new provinces joined Confederation. Manitoba became the first new province to join, forcing Macdonald's Conservative government to address the issues of language rights and separate schools. Should French be recognized as an official language? Should separate schools be permitted in provinces with a sizable Roman Catholic population at the time of union with Canada? The Manitoba Act recognized both French and English as official languages. It also established a confessional school system on the Quebec and Ontario models, with separate Protestant and Catholic divisions that would receive government funding.

The Wolseley Expedition

After Manitoba's entry into Confederation, tension continued in the region. In the spring of 1870, Macdonald sent out the promised military force under Lieutenant Colonel Garnet Wolseley. As the troops approached, Riel got word of their arrival and fled. Upon finding Fort Garry abandoned, Wolseley reported in his diary: "Personally, I was glad that Riel did not come out and surrender, as he at one time said he would, for I could not then have hanged him as I might have done had I taken him prisoner when in arms against his sovereign." Riel had left, convinced that he had achieved a great victory for his Métis people. He had won them provincial status, as well as land and cultural rights. Among those land rights was the agreement in the Manitoba Act to set aside a reserve of 600 000 ha for the Métis and their children.

Riel's victory proved transitory, however. Migrants from the rest of Canada, particularly Ontario, quickly moved into Manitoba and took over land once occupied by the Métis. One group of Ontarians seized Métis land on the Rivière aux Îlets de Bois and, in a symbolic gesture of defiance, renamed the river "the Boyne," after William of Orange's decisive victory over the Roman Catholics in Ireland on July 12, 1690. Ontarians soon dominated the political, economic, and social life of the new province. They worked to eliminate the land and cultural rights of the Métis population by introducing amendments to the Manitoba Act that made it difficult for the Métis to prove that they owned the land. Discouraged, many Métis left the province and went farther west either into the North-West Territories or to the Dakotas and Montana to live.

Relations with the First Nations

Treaties

In keeping with British tradition, the federal government negotiated treaties with the First Nations in the North West. Between 1871 and 1877, the government negotiated Treaties 1 to 7, affecting the Aboriginal peoples in the area from northern Ontario to the Rockies.

According to the government's interpretation of the treaties, the First Nations agreed to "cede, release, surrender, and yield up to the Government ... all their rights, titles, and privileges whatsoever" to the lands in question forever in return for certain reserve lands, amenities, and the right to fish and hunt on Crown lands. In the case of Treaty Six with the Cree of present-day Central Saskatchewan and Alberta, the federal government, at the insistence of the Cree, promised assistance in the event of "any pestilence" or "general famine," along with a "medicine chest" to be kept by every Indian agent. First Nations people saw the treaties as their only hope of survival against the rapid encroachment and takeover by white settlers. Canadian officials, on the other hand, saw the treaties and the establishment of Indian reserves as the first step toward the assimilation and ultimate extinction of the First Nations people.

The Indian Act

In 1876, the federal government passed the Indian Act, amended in 1880, to oversee Aboriginal affairs through its newly created Department of Indian Affairs and its Indian agents. It legally viewed the First Nations peoples as minors or special wards of the Crown, without citizenship privileges, such as the right to vote or to own private property. Government officials saw the reserves as training grounds for entrance into the larger society. As John A. Macdonald, the first Minister of the Department of Indian Affairs, pointed out: "The great aim of our legislature has been to do away with the tribal system and assimilate the Indian people in all aspects with the inhabitants of the Dominion, as speedily as they are fit for the change."

Repressive Measures

One way the federal government attempted to assimilate the Aboriginal peoples was by outlawing cultural practices. Particularly offensive from the government's perspective was the *potlatch*, the giving away of gifts in ceremonies, because it reinforced traditional Aboriginal beliefs and practices. The government used various tactics, including making it an offence "to encourage or participate in the potlatch." It instructed Indian agents to collect evidence to use in court cases, played off Christian Aboriginal converts who opposed the potlatch against

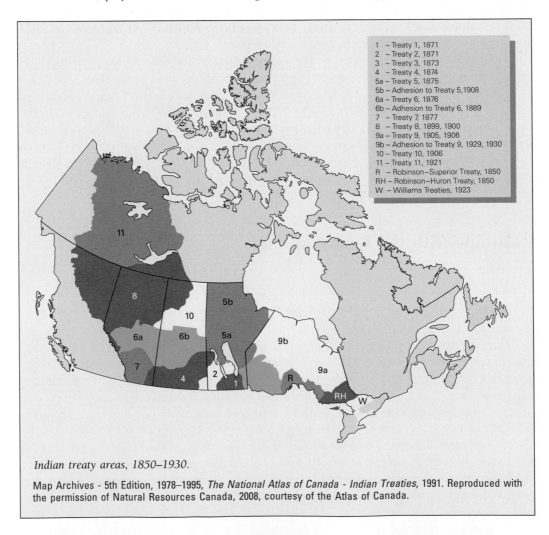

1 – Treaty 1, 1871
2 – Treaty 2, 1871
3 – Treaty 3, 1873
4 – Treaty 4, 1874
5a – Treaty 5, 1875
5b – Adhesion to Treaty 5, 1908
6a – Treaty 6, 1876
6b – Adhesion to Treaty 6, 1889
7 – Treaty 7, 1877
8 – Treaty 8, 1899, 1900
9a – Treaty 9, 1905, 1906
9b – Adhesion to Treaty 9, 1929, 1930
10 – Treaty 10, 1906
11 – Treaty 11, 1921
R – Robinson–Superior Treaty, 1850
RH – Robinson–Huron Treaty, 1850
W – Williams Treaties, 1923

Indian treaty areas, 1850–1930.

Map Archives - 5th Edition, 1978–1995, *The National Atlas of Canada - Indian Treaties*, 1991. Reproduced with the permission of Natural Resources Canada, 2008, courtesy of the Atlas of Canada.

traditionalists, and used extortion to pry ceremonial regalia from West Coast Aboriginal people. In spite of these efforts to end it, the potlatch survived and, in some areas, continued to flourish.

Schools became another of the government's assimilation schemes. Ottawa gave Christian missionaries control of the reserves and residential schools. Among residential schools were industrial schools that taught skills in agriculture and trades for boys and household skills for girls between the ages of 14 and 18. The first three were established in western Canada in 1883–1884: at Qu'Appelle, Dunbow (just east of High River), and Battleford. By the turn of the century, twenty such schools operated in the West.

The schools were intended to teach the Aboriginal children in English or, in many parts of southern Quebec, in French, to become Christians, to denounce their own cultural traditions, and to assimilate into "white" society, especially to become farmers. In the case of the latter objective, First Nations farms consisted of a small parcel of land, not always of good quality, and a few rudimentary implements—what historian Sarah Carter has described as "two acres and a cow."[2]

WHERE HISTORIANS DISAGREE

Interpreting Treaties 1 to 7 in Western Canada

Over the past thirty years the Supreme Court of Canada has upheld the argument that Aboriginal rights exist under Canadian law. Aboriginal rights include those outlined in treaties, possibly the best known of which are the numbered Treaties 1 to 7, signed between 1871 and 1877 in what is now northwestern Ontario and the prairie provinces. According to Canadian judicial interpretation—before the Constitution of 1982—Aboriginal treaties could be amended or altered by federal statute, without the approval of the First Nations who were parties to them. The Constitutional Act of 1982 now entrenches treaty rights. How have historians interpreted the numbered treaties of the 1870s?

Duncan Campbell Scott, deputy superintendent of Indian affairs from 1913 to 1932, wrote the first history of federal Indian administration in 1914. The federal civil servant stressed the honourable and just nature of Indian policy:

As may be surmised from the record of past Indian administration, the government was always anxious to fulfil the obligations which were laid upon it by these treaties. In every point, and adhering closely to the letter of the compact, the government has discharged to the present every promise which was made to the Indians.[1]

No subtleties of interpretation here; the treaties were fair and honourably respected by Ottawa.

George F.C. Stanley became the first university-trained historian to study the western treaties. In *The Birth of Western Canada* (1936), Stanley presents a far more sophisticated and rigorous analysis of the treaties than Scott, yet he reached a similar conclusion: "On the whole, Canada has followed the tradition of the Imperial Government in its relations with native tribes, and has endeavoured to deal fairly with her aboriginal wards."[2] For the next thirty-five years or so, historians essentially accepted the "honourable and just" interpretation of the treaties—or ignored the agreements altogether; in fact no real historical debate about the western treaties emerged until the 1970s.

Much of the new criticism came from First Nations people frustrated that their side of the story had not received attention. In 1969, Harold Cardinal, a young Cree politician and author, published *The Unjust Society*, a fiery indictment of Canadian Indian policy: "The truth of the matter is that Canadian Indians simply got swindled. Our forefathers got taken by slick-talking, fork-tongued cheats."[3] First Nation oral traditions of the treaties also appeared, such as the interviews in the timely book edited by Richard Price, *The Spirit of the Alberta Indian Treaties*.[4] More recently the Treaty Seven Elders and Tribal Council have made available First Nation accounts of Treaty 7 in what is now southern Alberta, in *The True Spirit and Original Intent of Treaty 7*.[5]

Other historians have joined in the debate.[6] Basically, they argue that the First Nations were active agents in the treaty process. The First Nations recognized that it was in their interest to secure the best terms possible in the treaty, that schools and a helping hand to adjust to farming would assist them. Problems arose, however, when the federal government did not fulfil the First Nations' oral understandings of the treaties.

In 1983, George F.G. Stanley reentered the debate. He still dismissed the thought that there were deliberate attempts to deceive the First Nations during the treaty negotiations. Instead he saw the problems as arising from the misunderstandings of treaty terms. "The probability that promises were made to the Indians, which they remember and the Whites have forgotten, seems strong."[7] In short, a historical question that seemed in the early twentieth century to be well understood is now strongly debated. New readings of the old documentary evidence and the availability of Aboriginal oral testimony, as well as a new postcolonial context for discussion, have contributed to this debate.

1. Duncan Campbell Scott, "Indian Affairs, 1867–1912," in Adam Shortt and Arthur G. Doughty, eds., *Canada and Its Provinces* (Toronto: Glasgow, Brook and Co., 1914), p. 600.

2. George F.G. Stanley, *The Birth of Western Canada* (London: Longmans, Green, 1936; Toronto: University of Toronto Press, 1960), p. 214.

3. Harold Cardinal, *The Unjust Society* (Edmonton: Hurtig, 1969), p. 39.

4. Richard Price, ed., *The Spirit of the Alberta Indian Treaties* (Montreal: Institute for Research on Public Policy, 1979; 3rd ed., Edmonton: University of Alberta Press, 1999).

5. Treaty Seven Elders and Tribal Council, *The True Spirit and Original Intent of Treaty 7* (Montreal/Kingston: McGill-Queen's University Press, 1996).

6. To list several of them: John Leonard Taylor, in his essays "Canada's Northwest Indian Policy in the 1870s: Traditional Premises and Necessary Interventions" and "Two Views of Treaties Six and Seven," in Price, ed., *The Spirit*, pp. 3–46; John L. Tobias, "Canada's Subjugation of the Plains Cree, 1879–1885," *Canadian Historical Review*, 64, 4 (1983): 519–48; David Hall, "'A Serene Atmosphere'? Treaty 1 Revisited," *Canadian Journal of Native Studies*, 4, 2 (1984): 321–58; Jean Friesen, "Grant Me Wherewith to Make My Living," in Kerry Abel and Jean Friesen, eds., *Aboriginal Resource Use in Canada: Historical and Legal Aspects* (Winnipeg: University of Manitoba Press, 1991), pp. 141–56.

7. George F.G. Stanley, "As Long as the Sun Shines and Water Flows: An Historical Comment," in Ian A.L. Getty and Antoine S. Lussier, eds., *As Long as the Sun Shines and Water Flows* (Vancouver: University of British Columbia Press, 1983), p. 16.

British Columbia Enters Confederation

With the North West secured, the Canadian government began negotiating with the colony of British Columbia to join Confederation. The colony had three options as to their future destiny: remain a separate British colony, join the United States, or unite with Canada.

Economically, British Columbia was tied closely to the United States. Many of the colony's business firms were branches of American establishments. Much of its trade of raw materials was to the south. In addition, the colony communicated with the outside world via the United States. American vessels, for example, provided the only regular steamship service. Mail required both local and American stamps on letters abroad since it went via San Francisco. When railways made transcontinental travel feasible, it was an American line, the Union Pacific, completed in 1869, that provided British Columbia with connections to the Atlantic seaboard.

British loyalties, however, remained firm. The Royal Navy provided protection. The colonial government followed British parliamentary tradition. The colony also had a predominance of British politicians, from the governor to the majority of representatives in the legislative council. By contrast the Americans, although large in numbers, had relatively few supporters in government.

The weakest link was with Canada. Few Canadians resided in the colony. Nor did any overland route exist to link this West Coast colony to the rest of British North America. Nevertheless, the small Canadian community that did reside in the colony constituted an influential and vocal minority: Amor de Cosmos ("Lover of the Universe," alias William Smith), originally from Nova Scotia, would become premier in 1872, while John Robson, from Ontario, headed the Confederation movement in the colonial assembly. Prime Minister Macdonald corresponded with these pro-Confederation politicians. As well, Macdonald had the British government appoint Anthony Musgrave, previously the governor of Newfoundland and a known supporter of Canadian confederation, as the new governor of British Columbia when Governor Seymour, who had opposed union, died in 1869.

Britain valued British Columbia as an important link in its "all red route to the Orient"—an imperial trading network tying Britain to India and China through British territory. By convincing British Columbia to join Confederation, Britain could achieve both objectives. William Gladstone, Britain's prime minister, argued at the time that Victoria, as "the San Francisco of British North America," could achieve greater commercial and political power as part of Canada than as "the capital of the isolated colony of British Columbia."

Before and after: Propaganda photos used to promote the benefits of Indian residential schools. From Thompson Ferrier, Indian Education in the North West *(Toronto: Department of Missionary Literature of the Methodist Church, 1906), pp. 4–5.*

Library and Archives Canada/C-104585 and C-104586.

Canada's territorial evolution from a nation of four provinces (1867), to five (1870), to seven (1873), and to nine (1905).

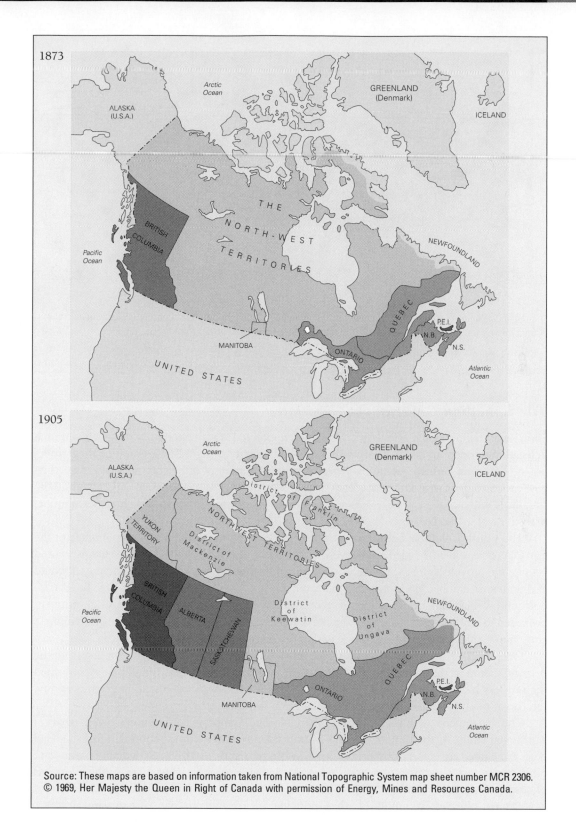

Source: These maps are based on information taken from National Topographic System map sheet number MCR 2306.
© 1969, Her Majesty the Queen in Right of Canada with permission of Energy, Mines and Resources Canada.

British Columbia's settler population was very small in the 1870s. This photo, taken outside the legislative buildings in Victoria, shows the entire British Columbia civil service in 1878.

British Columbia Archives/HP-17826.

The Canadian Government Negotiates

Soon after taking office, Governor Musgrave appointed a three-member British Columbia delegation to open up negotiations with the Canadian government. The committee drew up its list of demands. British Columbia would consider joining Confederation if the Canadian government agreed to assume the colony's $1 million debt, grant responsible government to the province, undertake a public works program, and complete a road to link British Columbia with the rest of the country.

The British Columbia delegation found a receptive audience in Ottawa. A committee of the Canadian government, headed by George-Étienne Cartier, agreed to all the demands. Ottawa would assume the provincial debt, and request that Britain implement responsible government. It would also undertake a public works program that would include the underwriting of a loan to build a dry dock and to maintain a naval station at Esquimalt. Most importantly, the Canadian government promised to build not just a road but a railroad, to be begun within two years of British Columbia's entry into Confederation and completed within ten years—a most ambitious promise.

On July 20, 1871, British Columbia joined Confederation. Canada now stretched from the Atlantic Ocean to the Pacific Ocean. In the same year, Britain and the United States confirmed the borders between Canada and the United States in the Treaty of Washington, thus ending the threat of an American annexation of Canadian territory.

The agreement with British Columbia left one important issue unresolved, that of Aboriginal lands. At the time of British Columbia's entry into Confederation, land treaties had been concluded for only a tiny portion of Vancouver Island. In 1873, the federal government requested British Columbia to acknowledge Aboriginal land title and to increase the allotment of reserve land for a family of five from 10 to 80 acres (4 to 32 ha). The British Columbia government objected, claiming that the Aboriginal peoples already had enough land.

An Unwilling Newfoundland and a Reluctant Prince Edward Island

Opposition to Confederation in Newfoundland

Only the British colonies of Newfoundland and Prince Edward Island remained as potential new provinces. Newfoundland trade had been with Britain and the West Indies, not with the other British North American colonies. Thus the Newfoundland merchants opposed Confederation. So too did Newfoundland's Roman Catholics, because they feared that a wider union would offset their favourable position in the colony. They had their own government-funded schools, which many believed a union with "Protestant Ontario" might threaten. Also, Irish Catholics saw Confederation as comparable to the reviled union of Ireland and England.

Union with Canada became the chief campaign issue in the election of 1869. Charles Fox Bennett, a St. John's merchant, headed the anti-Confederation faction. He pointed out that Confederation would result in the imposition of Canadian taxes on boats and fishing gear, and in exploitive competition from the mainland. He reminded Newfoundlanders of Nova Scotia's opposition to Confederation, while injecting his own strong dose of local Newfoundland nationalism. As one contemporary folk song ran,

> Would you barter the rights that your fathers have won?
> No! Let them descend from father to son,
> For a few thousand dollars Canadian gold,
> Don't let it be said that our birthright was sold.
> Newfoundland's face turns to Britain
> Her back to the Gulf.
> Come near at your peril
> Canadian wolf!

Pro-Confederationists appeared to be on the defensive. They could only present union with Canada as an uncertain alternative to the current depressed economy of Newfoundland rather than as a bold, positive move. Furthermore, an improved sealing and fishing season in 1869 worked against their cause. In the end, Newfoundlanders rejected Confederation, with nineteen seats in the colonial assembly going to anti-Confederationists and only eight to pro-Confederationists. That defeat effectively ended the Confederation debate in Newfoundland for the next 25 years.

Opposition to Confederation in Prince Edward Island

Initially, Prince Edward Island opposed Confederation more strongly than did Newfoundland. If anything, islanders favoured economic union with the United States, seeing it as a possible return to the prosperity that the island had enjoyed during the period of the Reciprocity Treaty (1854–1866). In 1868, American congressman Benjamin Butler visited Charlottetown to negotiate a reciprocal trade agreement.

Fear of American annexation of Prince Edward Island led Prime Minister Macdonald to reopen negotiations. Late in 1869, he extended another invitation to the islanders to join Confederation. He agreed to more generous financial terms than in 1864; guaranteed communication and transportation links with the mainland; and promised islanders assistance in buying off the remaining British absentee landlords who still owned large tracts. At the same time, the Canadian prime minister convinced Britain to block a reciprocal trade agreement between Prince Edward Island and the United States. Still the islanders resisted.

By the early 1870s, however, financial problems on Prince Edward Island made Confederation more appealing. A coalition government headed by J.C. Pope had embarked in 1871 on an ambitious railway-building scheme that threatened to push the island into bankruptcy. In 1872, work on the railway ceased for lack of funds. The Union Bank of Prince Edward Island, which held large numbers of the railway debentures, feared a financial collapse and appealed to Britain for assistance. London financiers replied that the island would be in a better negotiating position if it joined Canada.

This time Charlottetown approached Ottawa. In early 1873, the Canadian government renewed its earlier offer: to assume the island's debt; to pay the annual interest on an $800 000 imperial loan; to provide a special subsidy of $45 000 to buy out the absentee landowners and thus bring all land under provincial control; and to take over the railway guarantee. As well, it promised to establish and maintain an efficient all-year steamer service between the island and the mainland.

In the election of April 1873, the choice became Confederation or the imposition of increased taxes to pay off the debt. In the end, provincial debt and railways were the real "Fathers of Confederation" in Prince Edward Island. On July 1, 1873, Prince Edward Island joined the Dominion of Canada as its seventh province.

Canadian Acquisition of the Arctic Archipelago

The Alert, *a ship in the British expedition led by Captain George Nares, by an ice floe, Dobbin Bay, 1875–1876. The* Alert *was the first vessel to land on the shores of northern Ellesmere Island.*

Library and Archives Canada/C52521.

With the exception of Newfoundland and the Arctic archipelago, Macdonald had now completed the consolidation of British North America. Initially, Canada had no interest in the Arctic archipelago, seeing it only as a frozen wasteland. But in July 1880, the British government transferred title of its Arctic "possessions" to Canada. They did so without bothering to consult the First Nations peoples in the region, believing such consultation was not necessary.

Three oceans, one country—in just thirteen years, Canada had become Britain's largest colony. In the first decade after Confederation, the Dominion of Canada acquired three new provinces and an enormous geographical area. Fear of American encroachment was a factor in its rapid expansion, but internal economic pressures such as the need for more land for agricultural development, the necessity of east–west trade, and a growing railway-building program also contributed. By 1880, Canada had become a transcontinental nation. Now the challenge was to work out new Dominion–provincial relations, reconcile regional differences, and create a Dominion-wide economic policy.

NOTES

1. Chester Martin, *Dominion Lands Policy* (Toronto: McClelland & Stewart, 1973), p. 9.

2. Sarah Carter, "Two Acres and a Cow: 'Peasant' Farming for the Indians of the Northwest, 1889–97," *Canadian Historical Review*, 70, 1 (March 1989): 27.

BEYOND THE BOOK

The British Colonist

http://contentdm.library.uvic.ca:8000/cdm4/browse.php?CISOROOT=%2Fcolonist
The British Colonist (now the *Victoria Times-Colonist*) was the major newspaper of Victoria, British Columbia in the late 19th century. This website contains digitized editions of the newspaper as published at the time of British Columbia joining Confederation.

Newfoundland: The Confederation Debate

http://www.heritage.nf.ca/law/debate.html
An account with digitized newspaper images and photographs of Newfoundland's initial rejection of Confederation.

Canadian Illustrated News and the Red River Resistance

http://www.lac-bac.gc.ca/cin/026019-202-e.html
Articles from 1869 and 1870 in the *Canadian Illustrated News* regarding the Red River resistance.

Numbered Treaties Overview

http://www.canadiana.org/citm/specifique/numtreatyoverview_e.html
Contains digitized texts of all numbered treaties with First Nations.

British Columbia Terms of Union

http://www.canadiana.org/ECO/mtq?display=9_03428+0687
The text of the original document detailing the terms of union under which British Columbia was admitted into Confederation.

The Manitoba Act, 1870

http://www.canadiana.org/ECO/mtq?display=9_03428+0669
The full text of the Manitoba Act of 1870, a compromise between the Canadian government and the Métis on Rupert's Land. This act brought Manitoba into Confederation as the first new province.

From Sea to Sea

Canada: A People's History—Episode 9: From Sea to Sea. Directed by Jim Williamson (CBC, 2001).

BIBLIOGRAPHY

Students interested in the Atlantic region's resistance to Confederation should consult Ged Martin, *Britain and the Origins of Canadian Confederation, 1837–67* (London: Macmillan, 1995), and also his edited collection *The Causes of Canadian Confederation* (Fredericton: Acadiensis, 1990). For Nova Scotia also see George Rawlyk, ed., *The Atlantic Provinces and the Problems of Confederation* (St. John's: Breakwater, 1979); and J. Murray Beck's booklet *Joseph Howe: Anti-Confederate* (Ottawa: Canadian Historical Association, 1965). On Newfoundland's resistance to Confederation, see James Hiller, "Confederation Defeated: The Newfoundland Election of 1869," in *Newfoundland in the Nineteenth and Twentieth Centuries: Essays in Interpretation* (Toronto: University of Toronto Press, 1980), pp. 67–94; and the relevant section in Frederick W. Rowe, *A History of Newfoundland and Labrador* (Toronto: McGraw-Hill Ryerson, 1980). Francis Bolger reviews Prince Edward Island's decision to join Canada in *Prince Edward Island and Confederation* (Charlottetown: St. Dunstan's University Press, 1964). Popular studies include Donald Weale and Harry Baglole, *The Island and Confederation: The End of an Era* (Charlottetown: Williams & Crue, 1973).

Alvin C. Gluek, *Minnesota and the Manifest Destiny of the Canadian Northwest: A Study in Canadian–American Relations* (Toronto: University of Toronto Press, 1965) examines American annexationist sentiments toward the Canadian North West. On the Riel resistance, see W.L. Morton's introduction to *Alexander Begg's Red River Journal* (Toronto: Champlain Society, 1956); see also George F.G. Stanley, *The Birth of Western Canada* (London: Longmans, Green, 1936; rep. Toronto: University of Toronto Press, 1960), and J.M. Bumsted, *The Red River Rebellion* (Winnipeg: Watson & Dwyer, 1996). On Manitoba's entry into Confederation, see W.L. Morton, *Manitoba: A History* (Toronto: University of Toronto Press, 1957). Sarah Carter's *Aboriginal People and Colonizers of Western Canada to 1800* (Toronto: University of Toronto Press, 1999) is a useful summary of developments in the Red River and on the prairies.

Useful surveys of First Nations relations with Canada that cover this period are J.R. Miller, *Skyscrapers Hide the Heavens: A History of Indian–White Relations in Canada*, 3rd ed. (Toronto: University of Toronto Press, 2000); Olive P. Dickason, *Canada's First Nations: A History of Founding Peoples from Earliest Times* (Don Mills, ON: Oxford, 2002); and A.J. Ray, *I Have Lived Here since the World Began* (Toronto: Key Porter, 1996), and his *The Canadian Fur Trade in the Industrial Age* (Toronto: University of Toronto Press, 1990). See as well J.R. Miller, *Canada and the Aboriginal Peoples 1867–1927*, CHA Historical Booklet No. 57 (Ottawa: Canadian Historical Association, 1997).

On the treaties signed after Treaties 1 to 7 on the Plains, see Richard Price, ed., *The Spirit of the Alberta Indian Treaties*, 3rd ed. (Edmonton: University of Alberta Press, 1999). In *Indian Treaty-Making Policy in the United States and Canada, 1867–1877* (Toronto: University of Toronto Press, 2001), Jill St. Germain reviews American and Canadian experiences.

The Canadian government's policy toward First Nations people is reviewed by Brian Titley in the early chapters of his *A Narrow Vision: Duncan Campbell Scott and the Administration of Indian Affairs in Canada* (Vancouver: University of British Columbia Press, 1987). The government's farming policy for the First Nations in Western Canada is outlined in Sarah Carter, *Lost Harvests: Prairie Indian Reserve Farmers and Government Policy* (Montreal/Kingston: McGill-Queen's University Press, 1990). Two historical studies of Indian residential schools are: J.R. Miller, *Shingwauk's Vision: A History of Native Residential Schools* (Toronto: University of Toronto Press, 1996); and John S. Milloy, *A National Crime: The Canadian Government and the Residential School System 1879–1986* (Winnipeg: University of Manitoba Press, 1999).

On British Columbia and Confederation, see Margaret Ormsby, *British Columbia: A History* (Toronto: Macmillan, 1958); Jean Barman, *The West beyond the West: A History of British Columbia*, rev. ed. (Toronto: University of Toronto Press, 1996); and Hugh J.M. Johnston, ed., *The Pacific Province: A History of British Columbia* (Vancouver: Douglas & McIntyre, 1996).

For maps and charts, see L.R. Gentilcore et al., eds., *Historical Atlas of Canada*, vol. 2, *The Land Transformed, 1800–1891* (Toronto: University of Toronto Press, 1993).

Chapter Thirteen

A "NATIONAL POLICY"?

TIME LINE

1868	Canada First movement launched
1872	Dominion Lands Act passed
1873	North-West Mounted Police (NWMP) established Pacific Scandal erupts over the contract for a transcontinental railway Liberal party comes to power under Alexander Mackenzie
1875	Supreme Court of Canada established
1876	Alexander Graham Bell invents the telephone in Brantford, Ontario
1878	Conservatives reelected under John A. Macdonald
1879	The National Policy of high tariff established
1880	Canadian Pacific Railway Company formed
1885	Completion of the Canadian Pacific Railway Head tax imposed on Chinese immigrants
1896	Liberal party comes to power under Wilfrid Laurier Beginning of major wave of immigration
1897	British preferential tariff established as part of the Liberals' national policy

In 1874, Edward Blake, the premier of Ontario and future leader of the federal Liberal party, identified the issue: "The future of Canada depends very much upon the cultivation of a national spirit." The problem was that in the late nineteenth century no agreement even existed on the definition of a Canadian, let alone the nature of a Canadian identity. When French-speakers referred to "*les Canadiens*," they spoke of themselves alone; they called English-speakers "*les Anglais*." British Canadians, in turn, considered themselves the only Canadians and termed those speaking French "French Canadians." The First Nations peoples did not use the term "Canadians" to describe themselves, because they had their own designations for their own nations, such as Dene, Anishinabeg (Ojibwa), or Innu (Montagnais), names that meant "people" or "human beings" in their languages.

Could common economic goals and interests unite Canadians? John A. Macdonald's Conservative government believed so. In 1879, his party proposed a Dominion-wide economic policy of nation building based on a "National Policy" or national tariff to protect Canada's infant industries. Once in place, the Conservatives believed, the tariff would provide the capital to pay the expenses of building the transcontinental railway. The railway, in turn, would link an industrialized East with the soon-to-be-developed agricultural West. The growth of central Canadian industry, the settlement of the West, and the building of the transcontinental railway would create a nation. After 1896, the Liberals under Wilfrid Laurier adopted their own version of the Conservatives' national policy. The shaping of this national policy, which clearly favoured the business interests of central Canada, created social divisions by pitting business interests against farmers and workers, the latter having to pay higher prices for manufactured goods made in Canada than if imported duty free from the United States; the national policy also contributed to central Canada being the heartland of industrialism and the West and the Maritimes being the hinterlands producing the raw materials for industrial growth and purchasing the manufactured goods.

Emerging English-Canadian and French-Canadian Expressions of Nationalism

In the spring of 1868, five young English-speaking Canadian nationalists met in Ottawa to launch the Canada First Movement. Concerned about the lack of myths, symbols, and national spirit surrounding Confederation, they sought to identify and promote a nationalism for the new Dominion of Canada. They believed that Canada's greatness lay in its northern climate and rugged landscape, which combined to create a superior Anglo-Saxon race. They saw English-speaking Canadians as the "Northmen of the New World."

French Canadians and the Aboriginal peoples rejected the Canada First Movement's vision of the new Dominion. In reality, "Canada First" meant "English Canada First." The members showed their true colours through their support of Dr. John Schultz's group of Canadian expansionists in the North West.

While Canada First sought a British and Protestant Canada, many French Canadians envisioned a French-speaking, Roman Catholic nation. In the late nineteenth century, Quebec became more French and Catholic than it had been since before the Conquest. The provincial government cultivated closer ties with France under Napoleon III, especially after the French helped to protect the papal lands in central Italy against Giuseppe Garibaldi's army, which was fighting for the unification of Italy. Five hundred volunteer soldiers, the *Zouaves*, or "mercenaries of the Lord," left Quebec between 1868 and 1870 to serve in the papal army.

Ignace Bourget, the influential bishop of Montreal, and his disciple, Louis-François Laflèche, later named bishop of Trois-Rivières, led the ultramontane movement within the Roman Catholic church. Ultramontanes believed in the subordination of the state to the church. In their view, the pope constituted the supreme authority over religious and civil matters. Bourget reminded his followers in a circular in 1876: "Let us each say in his heart, 'I hear my *curé*, my *curé* hears the bishop, and the bishop hears the Pope, and the Pope hears our Lord Jesus Christ.'" Laflèche set out the basic principles of its nationalism in 1866:

> *A nation is constituted by unity of speech, unity of faith, uniformity of morals, customs, and institutions. The French Canadians possess all these, and constitute a true nation. Each nation has received from Providence a mission to fulfill. The mission of the French Canadian people is to constitute a centre of Catholicism in the New World.*

The ultramontanes began a political movement in 1871. They issued a *Programme catholique*, which proclaimed the church's right to advise Roman Catholics on how to vote. Catholics were expected to vote for the *bleus* (Conservatives), blessed with the colour of heaven, and not for the anticlerical *rouges* (Liberals), damned by the colour of the fires of hell.

Thus, by 1870, extreme and conflicting nationalisms had surfaced in both English- and French-speaking Canada. These movements reflected an attempt on the part of extremists in both linguistic groups to define a nation in cultural, rather than strictly political, terms.

Liberal Rule: 1873–1878

The Conservatives won the federal election of 1872, but just one year later a political scandal broke. It was revealed that Macdonald and Cartier had accepted more than $300 000 in campaign funds from Sir Hugh Allan, president of the Merchants' Bank and owner of the prestigious Allan Steamship Lines, whose newly created Canada Pacific Company was a major contender for the government charter to build the transcontinental railway promised to British Columbia. The major financial backing for Allan's group came from the United States. An American railway tycoon, angry at his exclusion from the consortium, supplied the Liberal opposition with the incriminating evidence of a financial kickback to the Conservatives from Allan and his American backers.

The Liberals accused the Conservatives of immorality and corruption. Macdonald denied involvement: "These hands are clean," he assured the House of Commons. But fearing a want-of-confidence vote, he announced his cabinet's resignation on November 5, 1873. The governor general asked the Liberals to form a government, which they did without an election being held. Two months later, in January 1874, the new prime minister, Alexander Mackenzie, dissolved Parliament and called an election, which the Liberals won.

Alexander Mackenzie, a stonemason, had replaced George Brown as leader of the Liberal Party in 1868. Mackenzie inherited numerous political problems. For one thing, the Liberal party had little internal unity. It was a freewheeling coalition of factions—*rouges*, Clear Grits, and Liberal Reformers—who had come together less out of a sense of common philosophy or a unified party platform than out of a common dislike for the Conservatives and their program. The party also consisted of a number of "prima donnas" who challenged Mackenzie's leadership. George Brown, as the founding leader of the party, loomed large in the background; Richard Cartwright, a Conservative defector who left after Macdonald denied him the post of minister of finance, wanted a senior post; Antoine-Aimé Dorion led the party's *rouge* faction and sought the role of Mackenzie's Quebec lieutenant. Finally, Mackenzie faced the enigmatic Edward Blake, former premier of Ontario (1871–1872) and a brilliant parliamentary debater, who appeared indecisive about whether to stay in the party, yet seemed to aspire to lead it.

Another political problem lay in the fact that the Liberals took office just as Canada entered an economic depression. As trade declined, the federal debt increased sharply. Mackenzie responded by slowing down the railway-building scheme the government had inherited from the Conservatives, thus alienating advocates of the railway and especially British Columbia, which threatened to leave Confederation if the railway was not built as promised.

The Liberals did excel in bringing in a number of constitutional and political reforms. In 1875, they established the Supreme Court of Canada as a national appeal court. While final appeal still rested with the Judicial Committee of the Privy Council in Britain and continued to do so with regards to civil matters until 1949, the Supreme Court became the first Canadian court to review Canadian laws. The Liberals also restricted the powers of the governor general, Britain's representative in Canada, by withdrawing his right to disallow legislation without consulting the Canadian parliament.

Among political reforms, the Liberals introduced the secret ballot and the practice of holding federal elections on the same day in each constituency across the country. They also closed the taverns on election day to reduce the possibility of buying votes for drinks. Controverted elections were transferred out of the hands of parliamentarians and into the courts. Mackenzie and his cabinet extended the federal franchise effectively to all non-Aboriginal males, whether they held property or not. The Liberals also ended the system of dual representation that allowed an individual to hold a federal and a provincial seat simultaneously.

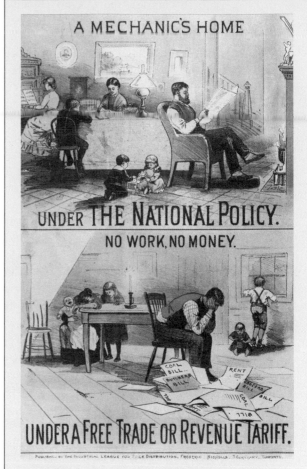

According to the National Policy's supporters, a high tariff meant prosperity (top); free trade meant unemployment and poverty.

Library and Archives Canada/C-95466.

The National Policy of John A. Macdonald

The Mackenzie administration lacked an economic agenda. It had wanted a reciprocity treaty with the United States similar to the one signed in 1854, and had in 1874 successfully drafted such a treaty. But the highly protectionist American Senate defeated the bill, leaving the Liberals without a viable commercial policy.

The Conservatives found an alternative. The Canadian Manufacturers Association convinced John A. Macdonald and the Conservative party that increased import duties, in the form of a tariff, would promote manufacturing in Canada, thus diversifying the economy and lessening the dependency on exports of raw material. Macdonald maintained that the tariff would benefit all regions of the country through economic growth, and thus called the tariff the "National Policy."

Advocates of the National Policy argued that a protective tariff would shift trade from a north–south to an east–west axis. It would provide Canadians with their own national market, thus reducing their dependency on the United States. Furthermore, manufacturers—both Canadian and foreigners building plants in Canada—would ensure more jobs for Canadian workers, technicians, and managers.

In contrast, the Liberals argued that the tariff would erect a fiscal barrier around the country. Furthermore, they maintained that, while the tariff or National Policy was "National" in name, it was regional in interest. It served the needs of central Canadians alone, and more specifically, the needs of the manufacturers and industrialists of the urban centres of Ontario and Quebec who could live off the bounty of the government. Furthermore, it would put the burden of national unity on the hinterland regions, which would become the suppliers of raw materials for the prosperous metropolitan centres of central Canada. In social terms, a corresponding inequality would develop, since workers, farmers, and fishers would have to pay a higher price for consumer goods, whether imported (as a result of the higher tariff) or produced in Canada (as a result of higher production costs).

Despite Liberal opposition to the implementation of the National Policy in 1879, when the Liberal party under Wilfrid Laurier came to power in 1896, it adopted its own version of the National Policy. As the United States still refused to discuss free trade, the Liberals had little choice. In 1897, W.S. Fielding, the Liberal finance minister, introduced a tariff that maintained high duties on imported goods, such as textiles and iron and steel products coming from the United States, and goods from other countries that restricted the entry of Canadian goods. At the same time, the new policy lowered tariffs to any country admitting Canadian goods at a rate equal to the minimum Canadian tariff. As Britain already adhered to such a policy, it became known as the "British tariff."

This tariff—the National Policy (capitals) of high protection that ranged from 10 to 30 percent on imported manufactured goods—became part of a general policy of nation-building, known as the "national policy" (no capitals), that consisted as well of the building of a transcontinental railway (the Canadian Pacific Railway), and settlement of the West. The logic went as follows: the high tariff would foster east–west trade; the transcontinental railway would provide the means for doing so; and settlement in the West would provide the raw materials essential for industrial growth and a market for manufactured goods. It is debatable to what extent the Conservatives actually envisioned an integrated national policy at the time or whether it has been seen as such in hindsight. Nevertheless, the three-part program of the national policy became the basis of the Conservatives' economic policy during the Macdonald era and was adopted by the Liberals during the Laurier era.

Transcontinental Railways

Building the Canadian Pacific Railway

Even before the formulation of the national policy, a transcontinental railway was considered an indispensable part of nation-building. Settlers wishing to go from Toronto to Manitoba via British territory in the 1870s, for example, had to travel via the United States or else by steamboat and wagon. As well, the resources of the West could only be developed for national use with a railway. Furthermore, British Columbia's entry into Confederation depended on the "trail of iron" as the only means to link this isolated colony to central Canada. The United States and Britain also applied pressure. Fear of American takeover of the West meant the need for Canadian control of the region that a railway would provide. Britain encouraged the Canadian government to build a railway as part of its trade route with Asia entirely through British territory, known as "an all red route to the Orient." Finally, a transcontinental railway, it was felt, would permit Canada to compete with the United States as a great North American nation.

Macdonald's Conservative government favoured a private company to undertake the project. Two companies competed for the contract: the Interoceanic Company, headed by Senator David Macpherson of Toronto and backed by British financiers; and the Canada Pacific Company, a Montreal consortium under Sir Hugh Allan, with American financial backing.

WHERE HISTORIANS DISAGREE

The National Policy

The national policy of high tariffs, railway building, and development of the West, first established by the Conservative government in the late nineteenth century, generated considerable debate at the time and much debate since among historians and economists. Historian Donald Creighton spoke for many in the central Canadian nationalist tradition in arguing that the national policy, especially the protective tariff of 1879, was an essential component of Canada's growth as an independent nation. Creighton writes: "In international affairs, the tariff asserted the principle of independence as against both Britain and the United States. In domestic matters, it expressed the hope for a new varied and self sufficient national life."[1] Craig Brown notes the success of the national policy in instilling a feeling of nationalism in Canada when traditional national symbols, such as a common language, a common cultural tradition, or a common religion, were absent.[2]

Historian Ben Forster has noted how other factors—besides or possibly instead of, nationalism—were important in shaping Canada's national policy. He points to a wide range of political and economic factors and interests—including business, industry, agriculture, and government—as all having made a contribution from 1825 to 1879 in shaping the policy.[3]

Economist John Dales has questioned the success of the national policy as a policy of nation-building. Dales argues that the national policy was from the beginning a "dismal failure."[4] Railway building became an expensive undertaking for the Canadian taxpayer through heavy government subsidies to the Canadian Pacific Railway Company, established in 1880 to build the transcontinental line. Second, immigration and the settlement of the West did not occur until well after the national policy was in place and then for reasons independent of the national policy itself. Third, the high tariff placed region against region. It also created an artificial climate for industrial growth that ironically made Canada more, not less, dependent on the United States through a branch-plant economy. Dales also questioned to what extent international economic trends dictated Canadian economic policy.

Historian Michael Bliss agrees that the protective tariff fostered the "Americanization of the Canadian economy," but points out that that was exactly what it was intended to do. "By 1911," he writes, the "concern ... was not to limit what had already been called an American 'invasion' of Canada, but rather to sustain and encourage the branch-plant phenomena."[5]

Some historians in western Canada and the Maritimes have presented the negative impact of the National Policy of tariff protection, especially on their regions. David Bercuson writes: "The ill effects [of the National Policy] abound: high prices for the manufactured products of Central Canada (added to by shipping costs) and the loss to East and West of significant commercial intercourse with New England and the northwestern areas of the United States."[6] It resulted in the growth of industry in central Canada at the expense of the hinterlands.

Economist Kenneth Norrie has countered this viewpoint in reference to western Canada.[7] He argues that the lack of industrial development in the West had nothing to do with the National Policy and everything to do with the West's location—away from the heart of North American development—and its lack of a sufficient population base to make industrialization viable.

The debate on the National Policy received renewed vigour during the national debate over both the Canada–United States and the North American free-trade agreements in the late 1980s and early 1990s. Central to any discussion of the future of Canada, the National Policy will long be a subject of debate.

1. Donald Creighton, *Dominion of the North* (Toronto: Macmillan, 1957), p. 346.

2. Craig Brown, "The Nationalism of the National Policy," in R. Douglas Francis and Donald B. Smith, eds., *Readings in Canadian History: Post-Confederation*, 6th ed. (Toronto: Nelson Thomson Learning, 2002), pp. 3–8.

3. Ben Forster, *A Conjunction of Interests: Business, Politics, and Tariffs, 1825–1879* (Toronto: University of Toronto Press, 1986).

4. John Dales, "Canada's National Policies," in Francis and Smith, eds., *Readings in Canadian History: Post-Confederation* (cited above), pp. 8–17.

5. Michael Bliss, "Canadianizing American Business: The Roots of the Branch Plant," in I. Lumsden, ed., *Close the 49th Parallel etc.: The Americanization of Canada* (Toronto: University of Toronto Press, 1970), p. 29.

6. David Bercuson, ed., *Canada and the Burden of Unity* (Toronto: Macmillan, 1977), pp. 3–4.

7. Kenneth Norrie, "The National Policy and Prairie Economic Discrimination, 1870–1930," in Donald Akenson, ed., *Canadian Papers in Rural History*, vol. 1 (Gananoque, ON: Langdale, 1978).

Macdonald favoured a merger of the two companies, but neither Macpherson nor Allan would agree. In the end, the government awarded the contract to the Canada Pacific Company in return for generous financial contributions on Allan's part to the Conservative campaign fund in the election of 1872. The resulting "Pacific Scandal" forced the Macdonald Conservative government to resign and ended the short-lived Canada Pacific Company.

Mackenzie's Liberal government continued the railway, but only on those sections where settlement warranted construction and only as public money became available, relying on waterways and even American lines to fill the gaps. To move slowly, however, meant reneging on the Conservatives' promise of completing the railway to British Columbia in ten years. An annoyed Edgar Dewdney, an MP for British Columbia, insisted on "The Terms, the Whole Terms and Nothing but the Terms."

When the Conservatives returned to office in 1878, they pursued their goal of a railway once again. A new private company emerged: the Canadian Pacific Railway Company (CPR), made up of a group associated with the Bank of Montreal, headed by George Stephen, R.B. Angus, and Donald Smith. The syndicate agreed to build the railway across northern Ontario from Callander (near North Bay) to Port Arthur and from Winnipeg to Kamloops by May 1, 1891. In return, the government offered $25 million in financing and 25 million acres (10 million ha) of land consisting of alternate sections not already sold in a belt nearly 40 km wide on both sides of the track across the Prairies. Land not "fit for settlement" could be exchanged for better land elsewhere. The company also obtained free of charge the 1200 km of track already completed or under construction, which had an estimated worth of $31 million. The government promised the company the exemption of construction materials from duty. As well, its property and its capital stock would be free from taxation. Its grant of 10 million ha of land remained tax exempt for 20 years or until sold. Finally, the government agreed to a monopoly clause: no competing line could be built south of the main CPR line until 1900.

In Parliament, Liberals and even some Conservative backbenchers questioned the need for such generous terms. The two-month debate that followed proved one of the longest and most acrimonious in the history of Parliament. Yet Macdonald held his party together, and the Conservatives voted down the 25 amendments proposed by the Liberal opposition.

Very early on the new CPR Company altered the route of the railway from that proposed by Sandford Fleming's survey team in the early 1870s along the North Saskatchewan River and through the Yellowhead Pass to a southerly prairie route through Pile O' Bones Creek (Regina), Swift Current, Fort Calgary, and the Kicking Horse Pass. A number of reasons account for this sudden shift. First, the company feared that the American Northern Pacific Railway would siphon off the trade of the southern prairies, bringing the region within the American sphere of influence. Second, Elliott Galt, the son of Alexander Galt, a Father of Confederation, had discovered coal deposits near Lethbridge that could be exploited as a source of fuel for the locomotives on the southern route. Third, John Macoun, a botanist and recent leader of a scientific expedition in the West, reported that the southern prairies held greater agricultural potential then previously believed. Most importantly, the company hoped through the sudden switch to bypass speculators, who had bought up land along the proposed northern route. When speculators attempted to do the same along the southern route—guessing where divisional points and stations might be—the company arbitrarily changed its plans and placed stations and divisional points on property it owned.

Once the government agreed to the route, construction began. In 1881 the syndicate hired William Cornelius Van Horne, an experienced American engineer, as general manager to oversee construction. Van Horne drove his men without mercy. He boasted that his construction gang, which at one time had 5000 workers and 1700 teams of horses, could lay 800 km of prairie track in a year. Already by August of 1883, the line had reached Calgary.

Still ahead lay the difficult mountain terrain. Surveyors had already chosen the Kicking Horse Pass through the Bow River valley, despite its steep incline, as the best route through the Rocky Mountains. However, only late in the summer of 1882 did Major A.B. Rogers, an experienced railway surveyor, locate a pass that allowed the CPR to cross the more westerly Selkirk Mountains. Difficulties abounded: laying track along the sides of mountains, blasting tunnels through rock, bridging swift mountain rivers. The construction of the British Columbia section, particularly that built by Andrew Onderdonk from Port Moody on the coast nearly 400 km into the interior, cost enormous amounts of time and money and took the lives of hundreds of the estimated 15 000 Chinese workers who had been hired as cheap labour to do the difficult and dangerous tasks of tunnelling and handling explosives. Chinese Canadians had a saying that "for every foot of railway through the Fraser Canyon, a Chinese worker died." Onderdonk himself estimated that three Chinese died for every kilometre of track laid.

Construction costs rose. For one thing, Van Horne insisted on the best materials to ensure long-term use. Also, Macdonald insisted on building along the north shore of Lake Superior instead of relying on the inefficient waterway system or on competing American lines. This meant blasting through hundreds of kilometres of Precambrian rock. In addition, the company had to buy up eastern lines to connect the Pacific railway with Toronto and Montreal. When the CPR's construction boss was asked about the prospect of not having sufficient funds to complete the project, he replied: "If we haven't got enough, we'll get more, that's all about it." The money did come—from investors, from the sale of stock, and from bank loans. When these sources proved inadequate, the company turned to the only remaining source, the government.

In the summer of 1883, the syndicate asked the government for an additional $22.5 million, the equivalent of a year's revenue for the federal government. Macdonald was about to turn them

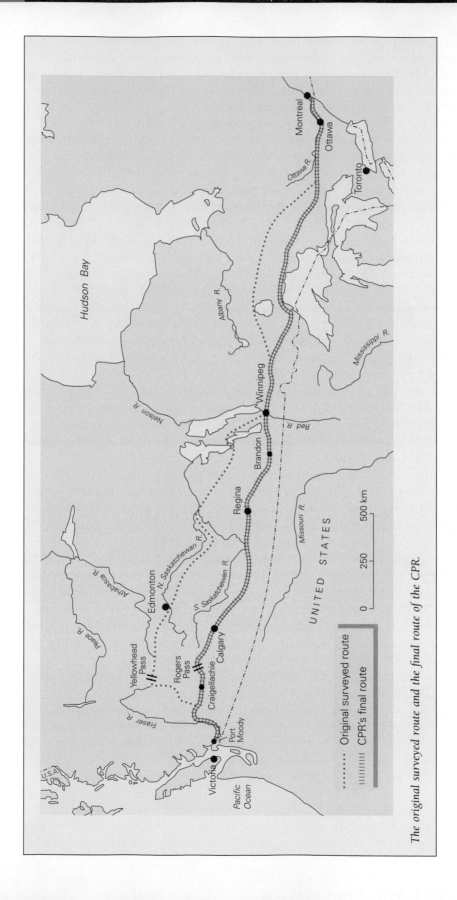

The original surveyed route and the final route of the CPR.

down when J.H. Pope, his secretary, reminded him: "The day the Canadian Pacific bursts, the Conservative party bursts the day after." Macdonald convinced his party to agree to another loan, but only after the CPR agreed to mortgage the entire main line, all the rolling stock, and everything else connected with the railway. The money kept construction going through 1884, but by the end of that year, the company once again plunged toward bankruptcy.

On the evening of March 26, 1885, George Stephen met with Macdonald to appeal for more government money. The prime minister turned him down. Stephen returned home convinced the railway would, after all, go under. Then, in the morning, came the extraordinary news: the Métis had rebelled under Louis Riel, defeating the North-West Mounted Police in a battle near Duck Lake in the North-West Territories. Macdonald's luck had saved him once again. The uprising justified the railway. That day in Parliament, the government voted to send troops out on the railway to fight Riel and the Métis. It also introduced a bill to finance the remaining mountain section of the railway.

On November 7, 1885, Donald Smith drove in the last spike at Craigellachie, a proud moment for all who had been involved in the project. The American-born Van Horne remarked that "to have built that road would have made a Canadian out of the German Emperor." But the cost of such national pride was high. In the end, the Pacific railway cost the Canadian government 10.4 million ha of the best prairie land, an estimated $63.5 million in public funds, and government loans of $35 million. Yet as a private company it did very well, and by 1905 it would have capital of $228 million. Was the project worth the costs to the government? People then and since have debated that question.

The driving of the last spike, November 7, 1885, 9:30 a.m., at Craigellachie, British Columbia. The important CPR financial backer Donald A. Smith (later Lord Strathcona) holds the heavy spike hammer. Behind Smith stands white-bearded Sandford Fleming, former engineer-in-chief; to the left is the burly figure of W.C. Van Horne, CPR general manager.

Glenbow Archives, Calgary, Canada/NA-218-3.

Two New Transcontinental Railways

During the economic boom of the Laurier era (1896–1911), Canada added two new transcontinental railways. The first was the Canadian Northern Railway, begun by Donald Mann and William Mackenzie, two Ontario-born entrepreneurs, who had bought up defunct lines in the West to have substantial holdings by 1901. They applied to the federal government for financial assistance to build from Port Arthur (now Thunder Bay) to Montreal. The Grand Trunk Railway, an eastern-based company, wanted to build a line westward to profit from prairie grain traffic. The logical solution would have been for the two companies to cooperate, but each feared the other would dominate in any joint venture. At the same time, Laurier believed the country could support three transcontinental railways.

The Liberals backed the Grand Trunk, but insisted that in the east the new rail line go through northern Ontario and Quebec to its terminus at Moncton, New Brunswick. The federal government even offered to underwrite the costs of the 2880-km-long eastern section. This section, known as the National Transcontinental, would be leased to the Grand Trunk for fifty years at a modest annual rate of 3 percent on construction costs. The first seven years of operation would be rent-free. A new company, the Grand Trunk Pacific, a subsidiary of the Grand Trunk, would build the western section from Winnipeg to the Pacific. The federal government agreed to guarantee 75 percent of the bond money for its construction.

Meanwhile, Mann and Mackenzie went ahead with their transcontinental line, convinced that Ottawa would, if they encountered difficulties, assist. As a result, in many areas of the West, these competing lines ran parallel to each other and sometimes within sight of one another.

In the meantime, the two companies added 18 000 km of prairie railway—six times more line than the CPR had when completed in 1885. It gave Canada the dubious distinction of having by 1914 more kilometres of rail line per capita than any other country in the world. The new lines also opened up lucrative mining areas in northern Ontario and Quebec, and provided employment for thousands during the construction and operational phases.

The Dominion's Strategy for the North West

Development of the West became a high priority of Macdonald's Conservative government. Without a populated West, no justification existed for a transcontinental railway. Without a railway, east–west trade could not occur. And without internal trade, the National Policy of tariff protection was meaningless.

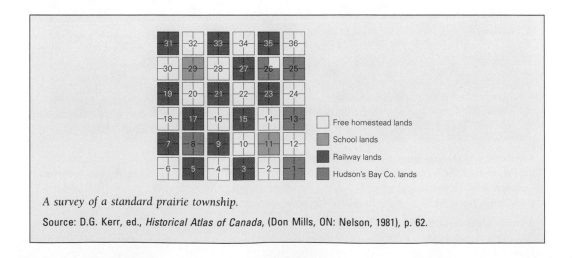

A survey of a standard prairie township.

Source: D.G. Kerr, ed., *Historical Atlas of Canada*, (Don Mills, ON: Nelson, 1981), p. 62.

In preparation for settlement, the Canadian government surveyed the land into townships of 36 square miles (92 km^2) and consisting of 36 sections. Each section, one square mile (2.6 km^2) in size, contained 640 acres (259 ha). Sections were subdivided into more manageable quarter-sections of 160 acres (65 ha).

Not all land was available for settlement. The HBC received "one twentieth of the land of the fertile belt" as part of the sale of Rupert's Land to the Canadian government in 1869. In Manitoba, the Canadian government appropriated, as part of the Manitoba Act of 1870, 1.5 million acres (600 000 ha), or one-seventh of the new province, for the benefit of the Métis. The CPR received 25 million acres (10 million ha), and other railway companies also received land as part of their contracts until the practice ended in 1894. Additional land was set aside for schools. The remaining land belonged to the federal government to sell or to turn over to private land companies to sell. This latter

NWMP Commissioner James Macleod, standing second from right, with his men at Fort Walsh in the Cypress Hills, in what is now southwestern Saskatchewan, in the late 1870s. Macleod treated the Aboriginal peoples with dignity and respect. The Blackfoot called him "Stamixotokan," or "Bull's Head," and welcomed his promise of a new order.

Glenbow Archives, Calgary, Canada/NA-52-1.

scheme proved disastrous. Most of the 26 colonization companies in existence in 1883 were owned by friends of Macdonald's government and held up to 3 million acres (1.2 million ha) of land, most of which remained idle either as a result of failed immigration or speculation on the part of the companies that land prices would rise.

To encourage settlement, the government passed the Dominion Lands Act in 1872. It provided a quarter-section free to each head of family or 21-year-old male if he did the following: paid a $10 registration fee, resided on the land for three years, cultivated 30 acres (12 ha), and built a permanent dwelling.

Women's property rights in the West were seriously curtailed. Married women did not qualify for free land under the Dominion Lands Act, and only a few widowed women succeeded in receiving the 160-acre land grant. In 1886, the North-West Territories government abolished a woman's right to the dower—a one-third interest in her husband's property upon widowhood. Western Canadian women protested the dower legislation for over thirty years before it was rescinded in 1917.

To ensure peaceful settlement, the federal government established territorial courts and created its own police force in 1873, the North-West Mounted Police (NWMP). They established important posts throughout the West: Fort Walsh in the Cypress Hills, Fort Macleod on the Old Man River, and Fort Calgary at the junction of the Bow and Elbow rivers. The NWMP administered Canadian law to the Aboriginal peoples, curtailed the whisky traders, and assisted the early settlers. Their success lay in what they represented: their red tunics and white helmets symbolized British over American law and tradition, a collective as opposed to an individual authority. As the American writer Wallace Stegner pointed out, "One of the most visible aspects of the international border [in the West] was that it was a colour line: blue below, red above, blue for treachery and unkept promises, red for protection and straight tongue."[1]

Immigration and the Settlement of Western Canada

Up until the turn of the century, only a limited number of immigrants entered the North West from outside Canada. They consisted of 7000 Mennonites from southern Russia who were being persecuted under a policy of Russification by the Tsarist government that demanded universal conscription, a policy that went against the pacifist nature of Mennonites. Also, 2000 Icelanders left their homeland, with its limited supply of fertile land and declining fishing industry, to settle on the shores of Lake Winnipeg. Selected groups of Jewish immigrants came in the 1880s. Sir Alexander Galt, Canada's high commissioner in London, joined the archbishop of Canterbury and several titled English gentlemen in aiding victims of Russia's pogroms (massacres of Jews) and offered the Canadian prairies as a refuge. The Canadian government encouraged the new settlers to farm, but many chose instead to become small shopowners, merchants, or labourers in urban centres, particularly Winnipeg.

The Mormons were the largest single American group to arrive in western Canada before 1896. Charles Ora Card, a religious leader, entrepreneur, and colonizer from Utah, led them northward in 1887 to establish farms at Lee's Creek (later renamed Cardston in his honour), Sterling, and Magrath in present-day southern Alberta, where they hoped to avoid the discrimination they had experienced in the United States due to their practice of polygamy, or multiple marriages. The Canadian government encouraged them to settle in the Palliser Triangle area since they had practised dryland farming in Utah.

Most new settlers in the West prior to 1896 were migrants from Ontario, English-speaking Quebec (French-speaking Quebeckers did not move out West in great numbers), and the Maritimes. Being the first to arrive, they became the established commercial and political elite, ensuring that the region became integrated with the rest of the country.

Between 1896 and 1914, more than one million people immigrated to western Canada, ensuring the success of the third component of the "national policy"—settlement of the West. What had changed after 1896 to account for this tremendous influx of immigrants? Both "push" and "pull" factors played a role. The push factors varied as widely as did the migrants themselves but included such elements as limited agricultural land, a desire to escape from the drudgery of working in factories and living in urban slum areas, religious persecution, and simply adventure and the prospect of a better life.

The pull factors were equally varied and related to world conditions in general and the Canadian West's attractions in particular. The rapid growth of international trade after 1896 meant jobs. Prosperity also increased demand for raw materials, especially for food for the growing urban population. Farmers in the West could benefit from a ready market and a high price for Canadian wheat. Increased prosperity also meant declining interest rates and lower freight rates, which in turn resulted in higher profits for exports of Canada's bulky natural resources. Most importantly of all, Canada benefited from the closing of the American frontier after 1890. After the best land—especially well-watered land—in the American West ceased to be available, the Canadian prairies became the "last best West."

Improved farming conditions also made the Canadian West attractive. Better strains of wheat, such as Marquis, that matured earlier than Red Fife, could thus be grown in northern areas of Alberta and Saskatchewan without risk of frost damage. The price of wheat quadrupled between 1901 and 1921. Better machinery such as the chilled-steel plough (introduced from the United States), improved harrows and seed drills, and tractors and threshers also aided western farmers. A steam-thresher could process more in a day than a farmer could by physical labour for an entire season.

Credit also goes to Clifford Sifton, an energetic Manitoba politician with a business background, and Laurier's minister of the interior. He pressured the HBC and the CPR to sell their reserved lands at reasonable rates to prospective settlers. He discontinued the practice of using land grants as incentives to railway promoters. He also simplified the procedure for obtaining a homestead and encouraged settlers to buy up an adjacent section, if available, by allowing them the right to preempt such land by making an interim claim on it and to purchase it at a reduced rate from the government later on.

As well, his department produced numerous pamphlets—such as *The Wondrous West*; *Canada: Land of Opportunity*; *Prosperity Follows Settlement*; and *The Last Best West*—that contained glorified descriptions of conditions in the Canadian West. In 1896 alone, his department printed 65 000 pamphlets; four years later, the figure reached one million. Millions of brochures were sent out to prospective immigrants in the United States and in Europe, in over a dozen languages. As well, he advertised in thousands of newspapers, arranged for lecture tours and promotional trips for potential settlers (particularly Americans), and offered bonuses to steamship agents based on the number of immigrants they brought to Canada.

Immigrant Groups

British immigrants came mostly on their own and at their own expense. There were exceptions. The Barr colonists, a group of Londoners who came together under the aegis of Reverend Isaac Barr at the turn of the century, settled in the Lloydminster area on the border between Saskatchewan and Alberta. Also, some 80 000 "Home Children" came to Canada between 1867 and 1924 to work as agricultural and domestic servants. Despite some known incidences of gross neglect and child abuse, the government supported the movement and deemed it successful. Most British immigrants adjusted relatively easily to Canadian life. They did not have to learn a new language or radically different customs, and many were relatively well off. Those who lacked farming experience, however, had a more difficult time adjusting. But not all British received a warm welcome; some employment ads read, "No English Need Apply." Canadians resented the haughty attitude of upper-class Englishmen in particular, many of whom refused to fit into Canadian society.

American immigrants were high on Sifton's list of desirable settlers. Although not British, the majority of them were of Anglo-Saxon extraction. As they already spoke English, they mixed easily with their Canadian neighbours and participated fully in their new communities. As well, many were experienced farmers. Many ex-Canadians returned. About a third of those coming from the United States were newcomers from Europe, such as Germans and Scandinavians who had initially settled in the American West.

In an age of racial-superiority theories, African Americans were not welcomed. While Canadian agents told white Americans that the climate of the North West was mild and healthy, they informed black Americans of the region's rigorous and severe climate. When a group of well-to-do African Americans from Oklahoma crossed into Canada in 1910, local newspapers, especially the Edmonton *Journal* (Edmonton was reported to be their destination), warned of an "invasion of Negroes." In the end, the effort to restrict black immigrants succeeded. Between 1901 and 1911, fewer than 1500 African Americans came to Canada, as against hundreds of thousands of other Americans.

The Canadian government had little success attracting large numbers of western Europeans. The French government openly discouraged Canadian immigration agents, because it feared a future war with Germany, whose population was almost double that of France. The Scandinavian countries also restricted emigration, fearing the negative result of such migration, especially of skilled workers, on their own economies. Germany prohibited immigration agents within its borders and fined steamship lines for carrying emigrants.

To get around these emigration restrictions, Clifford Sifton allowed W.T.R. Preston, Canada's immigration inspector in London, to set up a clandestine organization, the North Atlantic Trading Company, in 1899 to work with European shipping agents to bring western Europeans to Canada. Each agent received a $5 bonus for every healthy man, woman, or child over twelve who was a bona fide farmer, farm worker, domestic servant, or accompanying family member. This illegal scheme ended in 1905 after public outcry against undue profiteering, but not before the company had succeeded in bringing in 50 000 emigrants from Western Europe.

A HISTORICAL PORTRAIT

Robert, a Barnardo Boy

Robert[1] was a "Home Child," one of some 80 000 British boys and girls sent to Canada between 1868 and 1925 to work as agricultural and domestic servants. He belonged to the Barnardo Homes, the largest of the child care organizations in England, begun by Dr. Thomas Barnardo in 1870 in London's East End, to assist waifs, strays, orphans, and street urchins by providing them with a "home." The original Barnardo Home had a sign out in front that read: "No destitute child ever refused admission." While in operation, the Barnardo Homes took in over 30 000 destitute children.

Robert Francis, as a young boy.

Doug Francis's personal photo collection.

Robert was one of them. He was admitted into the home on November 23, 1921, at the age of 9, along with an older brother, Alfred, and a younger brother, Harold. Another brother, Sidney, was old enough to be on his own. Their mother, Emily, had died from pregnancy complica-

tions in 1920, and their father, Edward, a brewer's labourer, died a year later from pneumonia. A maiden aunt, Annie, took them in for a brief time, but when she was unable to care for them any longer, they were admitted to the home. They were given the familiar Barnardo uniform of a tunic, a pair of red-striped trousers, and a hat like that of a Salvation Army officer.

From the beginning, Dr. Barnardo had arranged to send "his" children overseas to "the colonies," where he believed they had a better chance at a new life than in the slums of London. Robert had a choice of going to either Canada or Australia, and chose Canada. He and his brother Harold left England on the SS *Melita* on September 18, 1924, with the customary "Barnardo trunk" that contained all of their earthly possessions; Alfred stayed in England with Sidney. It was the last time the four brothers would see each other.

Upon arrival in Canada Robert and Harold were sent to the Barnardo's Canadian Office and Distributing Home for Boys in Toronto. From here, they were sent north to Bracebridge to a bush farm in Muskoka, where a widow had requested two boys as farm workers. Like so many Home Children, the boys did not have a good initial experience in Canada. She saw them as indentured labourers. They ate separately from the family and slept in an unheated section of the house. They were underfed, and Robert recalled drinking the cow's milk from the bucket before taking it into the house. They attended school but missed many days when needed around the farm. Robert wrote to the officials in Toronto to complain about the harsh conditions, and an inspector came out, but only after informing the lady of his impending visit. Robert recalled that day as the only time he ate with the family and had a scrumptious meal. When the official left, conditions became even more intolerable.

It was customary for employers of Home Children to pay them a wage when they reached the age of 15. When Robert became 15, the lady let the boys go. They were then sent down to the Niagara Peninsula, where a large number of Barnardo boys were located, to assist on the fruit and vegetable farms. Robert's new "home" was a wonderful contrast to his first; the farm owner, Sidney Wright, had been a Barnardo boy himself. Robert got to be part of the family, enjoying the privileges of regular family members. Unfortunately, he was let go when, during the depression, the family could no longer afford him. He moved to another farm in the area, where once again he was treated as "just a Barnardo boy." He stuck it out until he married a local girl whose parents owned a farm, at which time he took over the family farm. The couple had three children and lived in the community for the remainder of their lives.

1. Robert is Robert Francis, the father of one of the textbook authors.

Sifton encouraged immigrants from Eastern Europe. Ukrainians were particularly targeted because they were considered hardworking and experienced farmers. By World War I, 170 000 Ukrainians had come to Canada from the Austro-Hungarian empire. The first group of 4000 Ukrainians—or Galicians, as the immigration agents called them because they came from the province of Galicia—settled at Star and Josefberg, 65 km east of Edmonton.

Some 7000 Doukhobors (meaning "spirit wrestlers") came from Russia in the late 1890s because of persecution for their pacifist and anti-tsarist beliefs. Leo Tolstoy, the noted Russian novelist, and Peter Kropotkin, a leading Russian anarchist, admired their simple, communal lifestyle and assisted them to emigrate from Russia. James Mavor, a professor of political economy at the University of Toronto and a friend of Kropotkin's, helped settle them in Canada. They founded three colonies, two near Yorkton, Saskatchewan and another near Saskatoon.

All was peaceful until a radical Doukhobor wing calling itself The Sons of Freedom marched toward Winnipeg in search of Christ and a new earthly paradise, and in expectation of the arrival of their leader, Peter Veregin, recently released from captivity in Russia. The group walked naked through the Doukhobor villages in a quest for a state of purity akin to that of Adam and Eve before "the Fall." Public outcry provided an excuse for Frank Oliver, Clifford Sifton's successor as minister of the interior (1905–11), to confiscate half of their Saskatchewan land. In protest, 5000 Doukhobors trekked to the Kootenay district near Grand Forks, British Columbia, where Peter Veregin had purchased private land.

Although he tolerated eastern European immigrants as potentially good farmers, Sifton disdained southern Europeans. He believed them to be migratory labourers who would only settle in the urban centres.

Asian immigration occurred mainly on the west coast. To restrict Asian immigration, as a result of public outcry in British Columbia, the federal government imposed a head tax on Chinese immigrants—$50 in 1885, $100 in 1900, and as high as $500 by 1903. The government would

Doukhobor women pulling a plough. During their first spring in Canada, the Doukhobors had a limited number of beasts of burden. With most of their men away working on railway construction to earn money for the community, the women hitched themselves to the plough.

Saskatchewan Archives Board #SPA R-B 1964(1).

have done the same with Japanese immigrants, but Japan was a military ally of Britain and a major trading partner of Britain and Canada. Instead, the Canadian and Japanese governments agreed to restrict Japanese immigrants to Canada to 400 a year.

A few immigrants came from India. As British subjects, they had a special claim for entry into another country within the British Empire. However, West Coast citizens opposed their entry. In May 1914, the ship *Komagata Maru* brought nearly 400 Punjabis, mostly Sikhs, to Vancouver. For two months, port authorities refused them entry. In the end, the Punjabis were forced back to India, amid cries of "White Canada forever" and the refrain of "Rule Britannia."

Nativist Attitudes

An ethnic hierarchy of preferred immigrants developed among English Canadians. Not surprisingly, the British and Americans, for the most part "Anglo-Saxon" Protestants, stood at the top of the list. Next

The tax certificate for Lau Shong (or Shing), 1912, for $500, the amount required to bring in Chinese immigrants.

Library and Archives Canada/C-96443.

came the northern and western Europeans, particularly Scandinavians, Germans, and Dutch, considered by many English Canadians to have the best qualities of "Anglo-Saxons" and thus welcomed. After the "chosen races" came the central and eastern Europeans, seen as industrious people and good farmers. Less tolerated in this group were Ukrainians and Doukhobors, because of their exclusiveness and "strange" customs. Lowest in the hierarchy of European immigrants came Jews and southern Europeans, both considered difficult to assimilate and regarded as poor farmers. Ranked well below Europeans came those of African background and Asians (Japanese, Chinese, and South Asians)—all believed to be inassimilable. Those that came were denied the franchise, barred from the professions, and subjected to discrimination in housing and in access to public places.

The First Nations people also faced discrimination. Both the Liberal and the Conservative administrations put intense pressure on First Nations communities to surrender reserve land. A number of illegal losses of reserve lands occurred, particularly in the last years of Laurier's administrations. Frank Oliver, as Laurier's minister of Indian affairs and minister of the interior, passed a law in 1908 that allowed the government to remove First Nations people from reserves near towns of more than 8000 residents. Then, in 1911, he amended the Indian Act to allow companies and municipalities to expropriate reserve land for roads, railroads, or other public purposes.

Underlying these racist attitudes was the belief that "foreign" immigrants could only become Canadians by abandoning their own customs and language so as to assimilate. Few English Canadians at this time thought in terms of a culturally pluralistic society. Their only concern was how best to integrate the various ethnic groups into a unified Canada. They looked to the churches and especially to the schools to inculcate British-Canadian customs and one language.

By 1914, the era of nation building was complete with a national economic policy: the National Policy, or high tariff; the completion of the transcontinental Canadian Pacific Railway; and settlement of the West through large-scale immigration. But certain groups, classes, and regions of the country felt alienated or neglected. Their discontent contributed to a new era of protest and a resurgence of regionalism.

NOTE

1. Wallace Stegner, *Wolf Willow: A History, a Story, and a Memory of the Lost Plains Frontier* (New York: Viking, 1966), p. 101.

BEYOND THE BOOK

The National Policy

http://www.mccord-museum.qc.ca/en/keys/webtours/CW_PolitiqueNationale_EN
Explore John A. Macdonald's National Policy through an exhibit of political cartoons of the era.

CPR: The Scottish Connection

http://www.mccord-museum.qc.ca/en/keys/webtours/VQ_P2_18_EN
An exhibit of contributions and connections of Scottish Canadians to the Canadian Pacific Railway.

North-West Mounted Police

http://www.rcmp-grc.gc.ca/history/marchwest_e.htm
Commissioner George Arthur French's diary of the North-West Mounted Police's initial march to western Canada.

Immigrant Voyage Stories

http://ist.uwaterloo.ca/~marj/genealogy/voyages/arcadia.html
An account by Ukrainian Dmytro Romanchych of his voyage across the Atlantic to immigrate to Canada in 1897.

Immigration from Asia

http://www.canadiana.org/citm/specifique/asian_e.html
Digitized versions of the Chinese immigration act over time, and other documents regarding immigration and immigrants from Asia.

Atlas of Alberta: Railways

http://ra.tapor.ualberta.ca/cocoon/atlas
Highly detailed maps that illustrate all railway lines built in Alberta, especially at the turn of the century. Histories for each are provided detailing how they were constructed.

Under the Willow Tree

Under the Willow Tree: Pioneer Chinese Women in Canada. Directed by Dora Nipp (National Film Board of Canada, 1997).

Under the Ribs of Death

John Marlyn, *Under the Ribs of Death* (Toronto: McClelland and Stewart, 1967; first appeared 1957). A novel about the son of Hungarian immigrants who is trying to become an "English" Canadian, in early-twentieth-century Winnipeg.

RELATED READINGS

The following articles in R. Douglas Francis and Donald B. Smith, eds., *Viewpoints: Readings in Canadian History* (Toronto: Thomson Nelson, 2007) are relevant to this chapter: Jean Barman, "Taming Aboriginal Sexuality: Gender, Power, and Race in British Columbia, 1850–1900," pp. 301–320; and Howard Palmer, "Reluctant Hosts: Anglo-Canadian Views of Multiculturalism in the Twentieth Century," pp. 321–34.

BIBLIOGRAPHY

The nationalism of the Canada First movement is discussed in the chapter "The First Fine Careless Rapture" in F.H. Underhill, *The Image of Confederation* (Toronto: Canadian Broadcasting Corporation, 1964); and in David Gagan, "The Relevance of 'Canada First,'" *Journal of Canadian Studies*, 5 (November 1970): 36–44. On the rising French-Canadian nationalism of the 1870s, see Arthur Silver, *The French-Canadian Idea of Confederation, 1864–1900*, 2nd ed. (Toronto: University of Toronto Press, 1997); and Mason Wade, "Growing Pains: 1867–96," in his *The French Canadians: 1760–1945* (London: Macmillan, 1955), pp. 331–92.

Dale Thomson's *Alexander Mackenzie: Clear Grit* (Toronto: Macmillan, 1960) gives a good portrait of Canada's second prime minister. The ideas underlying Canadian liberalism in the 1870s are examined by F.H. Underhill in "The Political Ideas of the Upper Canadian Reformers, 1867–1878", in his *In Search of Canadian Liberalism* (Toronto: Macmillan, 1960), pp. 68–84; and by W.R. Graham in "Liberal Nationalism in the 1870's," *Canadian Historical Association Report*, 1946: 101–19. On the politics of the Laurier era, see R.C. Brown and R. Cook, *Canada, 1896–1921: A Nation Transformed* (Toronto: McClelland & Stewart, 1974). On the national policy, see the endnotes to "Where Historians Disagree: The National Policy" in this chapter.

Pierre Berton's two-volume popular study, *The National Dream: The Great Railway, 1871–1881* (Toronto: McClelland & Stewart, 1970) and *The Last Spike: The Great Railway, 1881–1885* (Toronto: McClelland & Stewart, 1974), describes the building of the Canadian Pacific Railway. For a less nationalistic view of the railway, see A.A. den Otter, "Nationalism and the Pacific Scandal," *Canadian Historical Review*, 69, 3 (September 1986): 315–39. On the Chinese contribution to the building of the CPR, see Paul Yee, *Building the Railway: The Chinese and the CPR* (Toronto: Umbrella Press, 1999).

On railway building during the Laurier era, consult T.D. Regehr, *The Canadian Northern Railway: Pioneer Road of the Northern Prairies, 1895–1918* (Toronto: Macmillan, 1976); and G.R. Stevens, *Canadian National Railways*, 2 vols. (Toronto: Clarke Irwin, 1960). In *The Canadian Pacific Railway and the Development of Western Canada* (Montreal/Kingston: McGill-Queen's University Press, 1989), John A. Eagle examines the CPR's contributions to western Canadian economic growth between 1896 and 1914. Suzanne Zeller's *Inventing Canada: Early Victorian Science and the Idea of a Transcontinental Nation* (Toronto: University of Toronto Press, 1987) and her *Land of Promise, Promised Land: The Culture of Victorian Science in Canada* (Ottawa: Canadian Historical Association, 1996) examine the role of scientists in shaping the idea of a transcontinental nation.

On the development of the Canadian West in the 1870s and 1880s, see Gerald Friesen, *The Canadian Prairies: A History* (Toronto: University of Toronto Press, 1984). On the promotion of the West as a "Promised Land," see R. Douglas Francis and Chris Kitzan, eds., *The Prairie West as Promised Land* (Calgary: University of Calgary Press, 2007). Also useful for primary sources is L.G. Thomas, ed., *The Prairie West to 1905: A Canadian Source Book* (Toronto: Oxford University Press, 1975). For an account of homesteading, see the essays in David C. Jones and Ian Macpherson, eds., *Building beyond the Homestead: Rural History on the Prairies* (Calgary: University of Calgary Press, 1985). A detailed study of settlement in one prairie town is Paul Voisey, *Vulcan: The Making of a Prairie Community* (Toronto: University of Toronto Press, 1988). On the North-West Mounted Police, see R.C. Macleod, *The North-West Mounted Police and Law Enforcement, 1873–1905* (Toronto: University of Toronto Press, 1976), and William Baker, *The Mounted Police and Prairie Society, 1873–1919* (Regina: Canadian Plains Research Center, 1998).

Overviews of immigration to western Canada are available in R.C. Brown and R. Cook's chapter "Opening Up the Land of Opportunity," in *Canada, 1896–1921: A Nation Transformed* (Toronto: McClelland & Stewart, 1974); Pierre Berton's *The Promised Land: Settling the West, 1896–1914* (Toronto: McClelland & Stewart, 1984); and Gerald Friesen's *The Canadian Prairies: A History* (Toronto: University of Toronto Press, 1984). See as well Paul Robert Magocsi, ed., *Encyclopedia of Canada's Peoples* (Toronto: University of Toronto Press for the Multicultural Society of Ontario, 1999).

On immigration to western Canada in the pre-1896 era, see Norman Macdonald, *Canada: Immigration and Colonization, 1841–1903* (Toronto: Macmillan, 1966), and the relevant articles in Franca Iacovetta et al., *A Nation of Immigrants: Women, Workers, and Communities in Canadian History, 1840s–1960s* (Toronto: University of Toronto Press, 1998). Clifford Sifton's role in promoting immigration to the West is examined in D.J. Hall, "Clifford Sifton: Immigration and Settlement Policy, 1896–1905," in Howard Palmer, ed., *The Settlement of the West* (Calgary: University of Calgary Press, 1977), pp. 60–85; and in D.J. Hall's two-volume biography, *Clifford Sifton*, vol. 1, *The Young Napoleon, 1861–1900* (Vancouver: University of British Columbia Press, 1981), and vol. 2, *The Lonely Eminence, 1901–1929* (Vancouver: University of British Columbia Press, 1985).

The immigration of British home children is the subject of Joy Parr's *Labouring Children: British Immigrant Apprentices to Canada, 1869–1924* (Montreal/Kingston: McGill-Queen's University Press, 1980) and Kenneth Bagnell's *The Little Immigrants: The Orphans Who Came to Canada*, rev. ed. (Toronto: Dundurn Press, 2002). On American farmers' immigration to western Canada, see Carl Bicha, *The American Farmer and the Canadian West, 1896–1914* (Lawrence, KS: Coronado Press, 1968); and Harold Troper, *Only Farmers Need Apply* (Toronto: Griffin House, 1972). European immigration is discussed in Donald Avery, *"Dangerous Foreigners": European Immigrant Workers and Labour Radicalism in Canada, 1896–1932* (Toronto: McClelland & Stewart, 1979). George Woodcock and Ivan Avakumovic's *The Doukhobors* (Toronto: McClelland & Stewart, rep. 1977) deals with this important group. The story of Jewish immigration to Canada is told in Irving Abella, *A Coat of Many Colours: Two Centuries of Jewish Life in Canada* (Toronto: Lester & Orpen Dennys, 1990), and Gerald Tulchinsky, *Taking Root: The Origins of the Canadian Jewish Community* (Toronto: Stoddart, 1992).

Black immigration to western Canada is covered in Robin Winks, *The Blacks in Canada: A History*, 2nd ed. (Montreal/Kingston: McGill-Queen's University Press, 1997). On Asian immigration to British Columbia in the pre–World War I era, see Jin Tan and Patricia E. Roy, *The Chinese in Canada* (Ottawa: Canadian Historical Association, 1985); Peter Ward, *White Canada Forever: Popular Attitudes and Public Policy toward Orientals in British Columbia*, 3rd ed. (Montreal/Kingston: McGill-Queen's University Press, 2002); Patricia Roy, *A White Man's Province: British Columbia Politicians and Chinese and Japanese Immigrants, 1885–1914* (Vancouver: University of British Columbia Press, 1989); and Hugh Johnston, *The Voyage of the Komagata Maru: The Sikh Challenge to Canada's Colour Bar* (Delhi: Oxford University Press, 1979). On nativist attitudes see Howard Palmer, *Patterns of Prejudice: A History of Nativism in Alberta* (Toronto: McClelland & Stewart, 1982).

Chapter Fourteen

CONFLICTING VISIONS: 1867–1914

TIME LINE

1872	Oliver Mowat begins the provincial-rights movement
1885	The North-West Rebellion breaks Louis Riel is executed
1886	Parti national is formed in Quebec
1887	First interprovincial premiers' conference held Imperial Federation League forms in Canada
1891	Conservatives win federal election Sir John A. Macdonald dies
1897	Laurier–Greenway compromise is reached on Manitoba Schools Question Queen Victoria celebrates her Diamond Jubilee
1899	The South African War begins
1903	Alaska boundary dispute is settled
1905	Saskatchewan and Alberta become provinces
1910	Naval Service Bill introduced
1911	The Reciprocity Treaty with the United States is rejected in the federal election Conservatives win federal election under Robert Borden

"We have come to a period in the history of this country when premature dissolution seems to be at hand." So wrote Wilfrid Laurier, the official leader of the opposition, in the early 1890s. Canada appeared to be a failure. Bickering between Ottawa and the Dominion's seven provinces had become endemic. A provincial-rights movement flourished in Ontario; secessionist sentiments resurfaced in Nova Scotia; and regional protest arose in the North West. In Quebec, French-Canadian nationalist feeling strengthened in reaction to the execution of Louis Riel, and in the course of the debate concerning the Jesuits' Estates Act, and in relation to denominational schools in Manitoba. As well, a deep economic depression resulted in one million people leaving for the United States in the 1880s. These problems caused some Canadians to doubt the ability of the country to survive as a fully independent country. They disagreed, however, whether Canada's future should lie in closer relations with the United States, in a federated union with Britain, or in formulating its own foreign policy as an autonomous nation within the British Empire. No one seemed to know the solution to Canada's problems; some, like Laurier, questioned whether a solution existed.

The Provincial-Rights Movement in Ontario

Oliver Mowat, Liberal premier of Ontario from 1872 to 1896, can rightfully be considered the "father of provincial rights." He endorsed the concept known as the provincial-compact theory—a belief that Confederation constituted a compact entered into by the provinces of their own volition, and one that could be altered or terminated with their consent. Mowat, as premier, continued the policy of Edward Blake, his predecessor, of making the province dominant within the federation. One opportunity to do so arose over the question of the boundary line between Ontario and Manitoba.

The Ontario Boundary Dispute

The origins of the Ontario–Manitoba boundary dispute dated back to pre-Confederation days. The British had never established a precise boundary line between Rupert's Land and the colony of Upper Canada (Ontario). Mowat argued that Ontario's western boundary should run due north from the source of the Mississippi River, which was slightly west of Lake of the Woods at a place called Rat Portage (present-day Kenora). In contrast, Macdonald and the federal Conservatives wanted to draw the boundary between Ontario and Manitoba near Port Arthur on Lake Superior, so as to restrict Ontario's size.

The issue remained unresolved when in 1881 Macdonald unilaterally awarded the disputed territory—from Lake of the Woods eastward to Thunder Bay—to Manitoba. Since the federal government owned Manitoba's natural resources, it was in a position to control the land and the mineral rights. Ontario continued to dispute the awarded area granted to Manitoba.

After two years of legal chaos, both governments agreed to submit the issue to the Judicial Committee of the Privy Council in London, the supreme legal authority in the British Empire. In 1884 the Judicial Committee fixed the western limits of Ontario at the northwest angle of Lake of the Woods (the present boundary). However, not until 1889 did the federal government finally confirm Ontario's boundaries and the province's right to the natural resources within the disputed territory.

Powers of the Lieutenant Governor and Federal Disallowance

Mowat also won a series of victories in other disputes with the federal government, notably over the powers of the lieutenant governor, and the federal power of disallowance (the right granted to the federal government in the BNA Act to disallow any provincial law considered to conflict

For years, the Canadian, Ontario, and Manitoba governments fought over the boundary line between Ontario and Manitoba. This map of Canada in 1882 shows the contested area.

Based on information taken from National Topographic System map sheet number MCR 2306. © 1969, her Majesty the Queen in Right of Canada with permission of Energy, Mines and Resources Canada.

with federal law). Mowat argued that the lieutenant governor had the same position in the province as the governor general in the federal government, thus making the provinces coordinate sovereignties on a par with the federal government on constitutional matters. The Judicial Committee of the Privy Council upheld Mowat's position. Next Mowat argued that the provinces had certain legal powers before Confederation that they retained after 1867, thus making their jurisdiction independent of that of the federal government rather than subordinate to it. Once again, he won his case. Thus, by 1896 and the end of Conservative rule, Mowat had succeeded in strengthening provincial powers and Ontario's rights, at the expense of the federal government's jurisdiction.

Protest in Atlantic Canada

Mowat had allies in Atlantic Canada in his fight with the federal government. Anti-Confederation sentiments reemerged once again in the 1880s as Maritimers protested their perceived inferior position in the new Dominion.

The Maritimes faced difficult economic times in the 1880s. The Conservatives' high protective tariff of 1879 contributed to regional dissatisfaction. Fish and lobster exports had dropped a staggering 75 percent in the early 1880s when the Americans raised their import duty on Maritime fish in response to the high Canadian tariff. Shipbuilding declined, as iron steamers replaced wooden sailing ships. Yarmouth, for example, once a thriving centre of Nova Scotia's shipbuilding industry, built only six vessels in 1880, four in 1884, and none in 1887. Many Nova Scotians left in search of jobs elsewhere.

Secession Threats in Nova Scotia

From 1878 to 1884, Nova Scotia's Conservative government asked Ottawa for financial assistance. But Macdonald's top priority remained the CPR and the development of the West. The unwillingness of Ottawa to help contributed to the Liberals' provincial victory in 1884 under their leader W.S. Fielding on a wave of anti-Confederation sentiment. Fielding also attempted to extract larger subsidies from Ottawa. When he too failed, he introduced a secessionist resolution in the Nova Scotia legislature in 1886. The premier appealed to the other Maritime provinces to secede as well but they declined. Fielding even found little sustained support in his own province. Once again, the secessionist movement in Nova Scotia died out.

Discontent in the North West

Macdonald faced more serious problems in the North West. In Manitoba, settlers complained that the lack of transportation competition kept freight rates higher in western Canada than those in central Canada. The Manitoba government responded by chartering competitive lines to the American border. When the federal government disallowed these provincial charters on the grounds that they threatened the "national interest," Liberal premier Thomas Greenway threatened to solicit American financial—and, if need be, military—support. The federal government gave in, abandoned its policy of disallowance, and bought out the CPR monopoly.

The First Nations, particularly the Crees in the Treaty Six area, felt betrayed by the federal government's failure to keep its treaty promises of providing food rations in time of scarcity. The Aboriginal people also resented the government's refusal to allow them to choose their own reserve lands, as promised in the treaty.

The western Métis were also angry with Ottawa. After the Red River resistance of 1869–1870, many of the Manitoba Métis moved to the South Saskatchewan River Valley. Once again, their livelihoods appeared threatened as settlers moved in. They appealed to the federal government to recognize their land claims, but Ottawa was slow to respond.

Many of the settlers in the northern region were also discontented. The CPR's decision to reroute the railway through the southern region left them hundreds of kilometres away from a rail link to eastern markets. As well, the more politically active settlers demanded an elected assembly for the North-West Territories and representation in the federal parliament in Ottawa.

In 1884, the Métis, with the support of the "country-born" (English-speaking mixed-bloods) in the Prince Albert area, welcomed Louis Riel, back from exile in the United States, to lead their protest. They believed that Riel could obtain for the North West what he had for Manitoba fifteen years earlier. But the Riel who returned in 1884 was not the same Riel of 1869. During the intervening years, he had been hospitalized in two mental asylums in Quebec and had spent years in exile in the United States. He became convinced that God had chosen him to be the "prophet of the New World," responsible for creating a reformed Roman Catholic state on the prairies. He saw his invited return to the North West as part of God's plan.

The North-West Rebellion of 1885

Initially, Riel and his followers avoided violent action. They petitioned Ottawa on December 16, 1884, to ask for more liberal treatment for the Aboriginal people, a land grant for the mixed-bloods, responsible government for the North-West Territories, western representation in Ottawa, a reduction of the tariff, and the construction of a railway to Hudson Bay as an alternative to the CPR. The federal government acknowledged receipt of the petition and promised to appoint a commission to investigate problems in the North West. But apart from making a list of who was of mixed blood in the region upon which to grant land, it took no action.

In mid-March, Riel established a provisional government with himself as president for the purpose of once again taking up arms against the federal government as he had done in 1869. The situation, however, was different in 1885. A federal police force now existed in the North-West Territories; thousands of settlers had located there; and a railway linked the region to central Canada. Moreover, a significant number of non-Aboriginal settlers in Prince Albert did not support Riel, while the Roman Catholic Church denounced him as a heretic for his unorthodox religious views.

WHERE HISTORIANS DISAGREE

The Causes of the North-West Rebellion of 1885

Earlier generations of English-speaking Canadian historians blamed the North-West Rebellion of 1885 on one man: Louis Riel. The rebel leader, a madman, incited violence. In 1905, R.G. MacBeth wrote that "rebellion was rampant with a madman at its head."[1] In contrast, French-Canadian historians saw Riel as a misguided leader acting out of concern for his Métis people. Both groups of historians saw Riel and the rebellion largely in terms of the continuing controversy of English Canadians versus French Canadians, Protestants versus Catholics.

Canadian historiography took a new turn in the 1930s. Influenced in part by Frederick Jackson's Turner's "frontier" school of thought, already well established in American historiography, several Canadian historians saw the Métis as frontier hunters and nomads who opposed the advancing frontier of a different cultural group. Historian George F.G. Stanley saw the rebellion of 1885 as a clash between "primitive and civilized peoples."[2] French ethnologist Marcel Giraud also subscribed to this cultural-conflict thesis, while American popular writer Joseph Kinsey Howard depicted Riel as the symbolic leader of all North American Aboriginal peoples struggling to free themselves from white domination.[3]

Historian W.L. Morton denied that the Métis were "primitive": they were an advanced society, whose interests and values simply differed from those of other Canadians. Moreover, he argued, the Métis formed part of a larger western Canadian society that felt aggrieved by the indifference of Ottawa to western concerns. The rebellion of 1885 was therefore more than a Métis uprising incited by one man; it was a resistance by the people of the North West as a whole, and in this respect the first of a series of western protest movements against central Canada in general, and the federal government in particular, for their failure to address western complaints.

Thomas Flanagan questions whether the Métis had to rebel to force the Conservative government to act. He argues that "the Métis grievances were at least partly of their own making; that the government was on the verge of resolving them when the Rebellion broke out; that Riel's resort to arms could not be explained by the failure of constitutional agitation." Flanagan does not exonerate Ottawa, but claims that the government's mistakes were "in judgment, not part of a calculated campaign to destroy the Métis or deprive them of their rights."[4] Flanagan argues that Riel acted as much out of self-interest or, at least, private motives, as for his Métis followers.

Historian D.N. Sprague has challenged Flanagan's assertion that the government was playing fair. He argues that Métis grievances over land claims in Manitoba during and after the resistance of 1869–1870 continued to poison Métis–Ottawa relations in Saskatchewan, where so many Métis had fled when the situation in Manitoba became intolerable. Sprague implies that the federal government deliberately provoked Riel into forming a second provisional government so as to accuse him of treason.

Recently, the debate has shifted away from Riel to the Métis themselves. Why did they follow Riel? The shift in perspective has led to the study of Métis society in an effort to explain what conditions prevailed within the community that would have caused its members to follow Riel into rebellion. Diane Payment has examined Métis society in the South Saskatchewan River valley.[5] Noting that not all Métis

supported Riel, historian David Lee examines the reasons why some Métis did and others did not support their leader.[6]

In *Homeland to Hinterland*, Gerhard Ens argues that the economy and society of the Red River Métis underwent dramatic change between 1840 and 1890 from being pre-capitalist and "subsistence" to being a dynamic capitalist market economy, based on the buffalo-robe trade, in the North-West Territories. The result was out-migration from the Red River Colony well before 1870. Ens maintains that migration after 1870 was part of this earlier trend as economic opportunities for the Métis in Manitoba continued to decline, along with the added economic difficulties the Métis experienced as a result of the "intolerant actions and behaviour of the incoming Protestant settlers from Ontario,"[7] rather than as a result of any action by the Canadian government. Furthermore, he argues that the Métis who supported Riel in the uprising of 1869–1870 came from those Métis who believed Manitoba could still be their economic "homeland." Those who did not, simply moved further west in search of better economic opportunities, only to reenact, unfortunately, the same scenario fifteen years later. By this time, however, the West as a whole had become an economic "hinterland" to central Canada.

1. R.G. MacBeth, *The Making of the Canadian West* (Toronto: W. Biggs, 1905), p. 144.

2. George F.G. Stanley, *The Birth of Western Canada* (London: Longmans, Green, 1936), p. vii.

3. Joseph Kinsey Howard, *Strange Empire: The Story of Louis Riel* (Toronto: James Lewis & Samuel, 1952).

4. Thomas Flanagan, *Riel and the Rebellion: 1885 Reconsidered* (Saskatoon: Western Producer Prairie Books, 1983), pp. 146, 147.

5. Diane Payment, *The Free People—Otipemisiwak: Batoche, Saskatchewan, 1870–1930* (Ottawa: National Historic Parks and Sites Canada, 1990).

6. David Lee, "The Métis Militant Rebels of 1885," in R. Douglas Francis and Donald B. Smith, eds., *Readings in Canadian History: Post-Confederation*, 6th ed. (Toronto: Nelson Thomson Learning, 2002), pp. 45–62.

7. Gerhard Ens, *Homeland to Hinterland: The Changing Worlds of the Red River Métis in the Nineteenth Century* (Toronto: University of Toronto Press, 1996), p. 170.

The Military Campaign

Meanwhile, the Métis took matters into their own hands. On March 26, 1885, the Métis militant leader Gabriel Dumont and his followers successfully routed a group of about 100 settler-volunteers and the North-West Mounted Police at Duck Lake, near Batoche. Subsequently, a band of Crees surrounded Battleford, while militant Cree warriors killed nine people near Frog Lake, northwest of Battleford.

Within a month, the federal government dispatched 3000 troops to the North West under the command of Major General Frederick Middleton, to join the 2000 volunteers and Mounties already in the region. Middleton organized the troops in three columns: at Qu'Appelle, Swift Current, and Calgary.

The Métis ambushed Middleton at Fish Creek, south of Batoche, on April 24. Lieutenant Colonel William Otter successfully relieved Battleford, but on May 2, Cree chief Poundmaker defeated Otter's force at Cut Knife Hill. Major General Thomas Bland Strange led the Alberta Field Force from Calgary, by way of Edmonton and the North Saskatchewan River, against another Cree chief, Big Bear, and his band at Frenchman's Butte in late May. As at Fish Creek, the encounter was a draw, with both sides retreating at the same time.

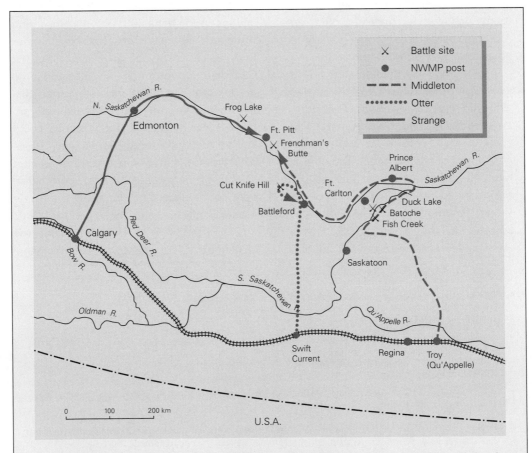

Military operations in the North-West Rebellion, 1885. This map shows the routes of the three military columns: to Batoche, under Major General Middleton; to Battleford, under Lieutenant Colonel Otter; and to the Ft. Pitt area, under Major General Strange.

The main battle took place at Batoche, Riel's headquarters, beginning on May 9. Within three days, Middleton's superior troops forced the Métis to retreat. Riel surrendered on May 15, while Dumont and others fled to the United States. Poundmaker and Big Bear surrendered soon afterward.

Trials

In the trials that followed, the Canadian government prosecuted more than 125 Aboriginal people and hanged eight of them publicly. This mass hanging was intended to send a message to the First Nations community against further opposition. Big Bear and Poundmaker each received prison sentences of three years. They were released before their terms ended, because of poor health; both died within a year of their release.

Big Bear (front row, second from the left) and Poundmaker (front row, far right), shown at their trials, 1885. Father André (back row, second from the right) spent the night before Riel's execution in prayer with him, and walked with him to the scaffold.

Glenbow Archives, Calgary, Canada/NA-3205-11.

A jury of six men, all of British background, tried Louis Riel for treason in a Regina courtroom. Riel pleaded not guilty. Two psychiatrists examined Riel during the trial. Both concluded that Riel was sane, that he could distinguish right from wrong.

Riel's speech in English to the jury eloquently explained his reasons for involvement in the rebellion:

No one can say that the Northwest was not suffering last year ... but what I have done, and risked, and to which I have exposed myself, rested certainly on the conviction I had to do, was

Louis Riel's address to the jury during his trial at Regina, July 1885.
Glenbow Archives, Calgary, Canada/NA-1081-3.

called upon to do something for my country.... I know that through the grace of God I am the founder of Manitoba.... Even if I was going to be sentenced by you, gentlemen of the jury, I have the satisfaction if I die—that if I die I will not be reputed by all men as insane, as a lunatic.... Gentlemen of the jury, my reputation, my liberty, my life are at your discretion.

The jury deliberated for an hour before reaching its verdict: Riel was guilty of treason.

Prime Minister John A. Macdonald twice postponed the execution. Then on November 16, 1885, Riel mounted the gibbet at Regina. The trapdoor was sprung. A Métis, a French-Canadian, and later a western-Canadian martyr was born.

While Riel's execution gained Macdonald support in Ontario, it cost him support in Quebec. In hindsight, it is evident that Riel's execution contributed to the demise of the Conservatives in Quebec in the 1890s and to the rise of the Liberals.

Significance of the North-West Rebellion

The North-West Rebellion of 1885 marked a transition on the Prairies; henceforth the settler society would dominate. Many events symbolized the transition: the execution of Riel and the imprisonment of Big Bear and Poundmaker; the use of the newly completed CPR to transport troops west to suppress the insurgents; and the establishment of an elected territorial assembly a year later, in 1886, in which no Métis were present. Possibly the most poignant, however, was the animus generated over the capture of two Ontario women—Theresa Delaney and Theresa Gowanlock—by a group of Cree during the rebellion. In accounts of the capture, confinement, and ultimate release of these two women, they came to embody the virtues of the "civilizers" from the East and, by contrast, the "barbaric" nature of the Aboriginal population, especially First Nations women. The liberation of these captives at the hands of the supposedly cruel, treacherous "savages" marked the triumph of the forces of "good" over "evil" and provided a rationale for the "necessary" suppression of the minority by the dominant society.

Rising French-Canadian Nationalism

The Riel controversy intensified the nationalist sentiment of some French-Canadian leaders. Honoré Mercier, leader of the Quebec wing of the Liberal party after 1883, expressed this nationalist position at a rally in Montreal: "Riel, our brother, is dead, victim of fanaticism and treason—of the fanaticism of Sir John and some of his friends, of the treason of three of our people who sold their brother to keep their portfolios." He appealed to his fellow Quebeckers to form a Parti national, an exclusively French-Canadian party. His new party won the provincial election of 1886.

In 1887, Wilfrid Laurier became the federal Liberal leader. He proposed a French-Canadian nationalism that was an alternative to Mercier's, one that included French Canadians across the country. It was a nationalism based on compromise between French Canadians and English Canadians. In one of his speeches, Laurier presented a message of tolerance reminiscent of that given by George-Étienne Cartier at the time of Confederation.

We form here, or wish to form, a nation composed of the most heterogeneous elements. Protestants and Catholics, English and French, German, Irish, Scottish, each, let us not forget, with its own traditions and prejudices. In each one of these opposing elements, however, there is a common point of patriotism, and the only veritable politics is that which dominates this common patriotism, and brings these elements toward a unified goal and common aspirations.

The First Interprovincial Conference

In 1887, Mercier called an interprovincial conference, the first of its kind, to challenge the federal government's hegemony. The provincial premiers summed up the provincial-rights position. They argued that Confederation was a contract among the British North American colonies that had agreed to establish a new country. Therefore, the provinces should control the federal government. Among their demands were appeals for larger federal subsidies, abolition of the federal power of disallowance, and senate reform to strengthen provincial power.

Cultural and Religious Feuds

Unfortunately, Laurier's appeal for unity between English and French Canadians and Protestants and Roman Catholics went unheeded in the ethnically and religiously intolerant atmosphere of the late nineteenth century. Two issues—the Jesuits' Estates Act and the Manitoba Schools Question—revealed just how bitter ethnic relations and religious differences had become.

The Jesuits' Estates Controversy

The dispute over the Jesuits' Estates began in 1888 when the Jesuits appealed to the provincial government of Quebec to have their property, which had been confiscated at the time of the conquest, returned or else that they receive financial compensation for their losses. Premier Mercier appealed to the pope to act as arbiter. On the basis of the pope's recommendation, Mercier implemented the Jesuits' Estates Act.

D'Alton McCarthy, an anti-Catholic and a Conservative MP from Ontario, argued that the pope had no right to meddle in Canadian affairs. He moved a resolution in the House of Commons to have the federal government disallow the Jesuits' Estates Act. He considered the Act to be the latest in a series of attempts by the Jesuits and French-speaking Roman Catholics in general to rule Canada. McCarthy failed to get sufficient support in the Conservative Party to disallow the Act, but succeeded, through his actions, in diminishing the support for the Party in Quebec.

The Manitoba Schools Question

Ethnic and religious tensions next focused on the school question in Manitoba. By 1890, the English-speaking Protestant population in Manitoba had increased tenfold, greatly outnumbering the French-speaking population, which had essentially remained static. This imbalance did not appear to cause problems in Manitoba until D'Alton McCarthy delivered an emotional speech at Portage la Prairie in August of 1889 against denominational schools in Manitoba as

Immediately after Riel's execution on November 16, 1885, French Canadians rose in protest against the federal government. In Montreal, demonstrators burned Sir John A. Macdonald in effigy at the base of the statue of Queen Victoria in Victoria Square. From Frank Leslie's Illustrated Newspaper, November 28, 1885.

Saskatchewan Archives Board/R-D1776.

A photo of the first interprovincial conference, called by Honoré Mercier in 1887, to challenge the authority of the federal government. The Quebec premier appears seated second from the left. Ontario's Oliver Mowat, the "Father of Provincial Rights," is seated in the centre. W.S. Fielding, who tried during his premiership to take Nova Scotia out of Confederation, is beside Mowat on the right.

Library and Archives Canada/C-011583.

undermining the future greatness of Canada. A few months earlier, he had helped form an Equal Rights Association, which claimed in its platform to stand for "equal rights of all religious denominations before the law, special privileges for none." He objected that the French-Canadian and Métis Roman Catholics in the West should not, as a minority, have "special privileges." On the same platform as McCarthy sat Joseph Martin, attorney general for the Manitoba government. He pledged his government's support in abolishing the dual school system, as well as French as an official language, in Manitoba.

In 1890, the Manitoba government passed a Schools Act that established a provincial department of education and a system of nonsectarian public schools that alone would receive the provincial grant for education. Denominational schools could still exist, but without government funding. Those contributing to such schools must do so in addition to their public-school taxes. The same session of the legislature abolished French as an official language, contrary to section 23 of the Manitoba Act of 1870.

Manitoba Catholics Fight School Legislation

Discontented Roman Catholics had three options: appeal to the federal government to use its right of disallowance of provincial legislation; take the issue to the courts to have the legislation declared *ultra vires*, or unconstitutional; or appeal to Ottawa to intervene on behalf of the minority through remedial legislation as set out in section 93 of the BNA Act. Eventually, they pursued all three possibilities.

Macdonald resisted using the federal government's right of disallowance, fearing that the Manitoba electorate's disapproval of such an action would strengthen the provincial government's power. He favoured court action and agreed that the federal government would pay the legal costs of the appellant. The case, known as *Barrett v. the City of Winnipeg*, went through the provincial court, which upheld the Manitoba government's position, to the Supreme Court of Canada, which upheld the right of the Roman Catholic minority to have state-supported separate schools. Then, the Judicial Committee of the Privy Council in London reversed this decision in favour of the Manitoba government's position, much to the consternation of Manitoba's Roman Catholics.

One final option remained. The Manitoba Roman Catholics appealed to the federal government for remedial action under section 93 of the BNA Act. The Conservatives introduced the remedial legislation bill in Parliament in January 1896. It provided for a nine-member board to run the separate-school system, to be supported by the Roman Catholics' own tax monies; the schools in this system would share a portion of the provincial educational grant; and, to ensure proper standards, the separate schools would be inspected regularly and funds would be withheld if they were judged inefficient. Clearly, remedial legislation favoured the Roman Catholic position. However, Parliament dissolved on April 23, with the bill still not passed into law. Four days later, Mackenzie Bowell resigned as Conservative leader under pressure from the Orange wing of his party, angered over his handling of the schools question.

The Election of 1896

The Conservatives entered the federal election of 1896 with a new leader, Charles Tupper—the party's fifth leader in five years. The Manitoba Schools Question proved only one of several contentious issues in the election, although an important one. In Quebec, the Conservatives stressed during the election campaign that they had introduced remedial legislation on behalf of the Manitoba Roman Catholics. In English-speaking Canada, Conservative candidates emphasized that the bill was not, and might never become, law.

The Liberals were in an enviable position. As the opposition, they could denounce the Tories without offering concrete alternative policies. On the controversial schools question, Laurier simply promised that the Liberals, if elected, would end the dispute through compromise with the Manitoba Liberal government in a way that would respect provincial rights.

The Liberals narrowly won the election of 1896. Outside Quebec, they tied the Conservatives in the number of seats. But in Quebec they obtained two-thirds of the province's share.

The Laurier–Greenway Controversy

Laurier and Manitoba's premier Greenway struck a compromise: religious instruction would be allowed in the public schools for half an hour at the end of each day. Roman Catholic teachers could be employed in urban schools with 40 Roman Catholic pupils or in rural districts with 25. On the language question it was agreed that, when ten of the pupils in any school system spoke the French language or any language other than English as their native language, the teaching of such pupils would be conducted in English and French or the other language "upon the bilingual system."

The French-Canadian Roman Catholic minority in Manitoba would have obtained more under the Conservatives' remedial legislation. Laurier's compromise allowed religious instruction but led to the abolition of the state-supported separate-school system. French would be retained only when sufficient population warranted it; hence, it lost the status of equality with English that it had had under the Manitoba Act of 1870. Moreover, it became a language like any other in Manitoba, all of which were unofficial except English. (In 1916, at the height of World War I, even the bilingual clause of the Laurier–Greenway compromise was abolished, making English the only language of instruction in the province's schools.) The Roman Catholic hierarchy in

Canada accused Laurier of capitulating to the English-Canadian Protestants but in the end was persuaded to accept "the compromise" as the best that could be hoped for, given the Roman Catholics' minority position.

The Schools Question in Alberta and Saskatchewan

The schools question in the West arose again in 1905, with the creation of the two new provinces of Saskatchewan and Alberta. The original ordinances of the North-West Territories Act of 1875, as amended in 1877, had provided for both Protestant and Roman Catholic schools to receive public funding. As well, both French and English could be used as languages of instruction. In the early 1890s, however, the territorial government made English the official language of instruction in the Roman Catholic school system, restricting French to the primary grades only for French-speaking children. Then, in 1901, the territorial government restricted religious instruction to the last half hour of the school day, as in the case of Manitoba.

When the time came to draw up the autonomy bills to bring Saskatchewan and Alberta into existence, Charles Fitzpatrick, the federal minister of justice and a Quebec Roman Catholic, and Henri Bourassa drafted the educational clause to restore the original system of 1877. The clause permitted the free establishment of Roman Catholic and Protestant schools as well as the use of French in the school system. The powerful Clifford Sifton, who had once been a cabinet minister under Manitoba premier Greenway, opposed the educational clause, claiming it went against the wishes of the government of the North-West Territories. He resigned from the Cabinet in protest.

Laurier intervened and allowed Sifton to redraft the educational clause, although he did not invite him back into the Cabinet. Sifton's revised clause restricted the rights of the French-Canadian Roman Catholic minorities to the limited concessions granted in the ordinance of 1901. Laurier accepted the "honourable compromise," as he described the Sifton amendment. But Bourassa denounced it as a sellout. It infringed on the rights of French Canadians as set out in the original North-West Territories Act. In the end, however, the Sifton amendment became law.

At the same time that the country was facing conflicting visions internally, it was also having to deal with conflicting visions as to its destiny in relation to Great Britain and the United States.

Continentalism

The Liberals favoured stronger continental ties in the 1880s and 1890s. Closer links could take many forms. Some Liberals wanted a restricted reciprocity agreement, which would apply to natural products only. Others favoured unrestricted reciprocity, or free trade, in some manufactured goods as well as in natural resources. Still others proposed commercial union—an integrated economic union with a free interchange of all products, a sharing of internal revenue taxes, and a common tariff policy against other countries. At the extreme end of this spectrum came political union. Goldwin Smith, an outspoken critic, advocated political union with the United States in his book, *Canada and the Canadian Question* (1891).

The Trade Question and the 1891 Election

Laurier, as Liberal leader, favoured commercial union in principle; but he believed it was too extreme a position for a party platform, so he committed the party to unrestricted reciprocity instead in the election of 1891. Macdonald claimed that unrestricted reciprocity threatened Canada's independence, because it would ultimately lead to political union with the United States. He maintained that protectionism was the means to prevent American assimilation and to uphold the British connection. He declared his loyalty to Britain in his popular campaign slogan, "A British subject I was born, and a British subject I will die," and proceeded to drape himself in the British flag.

The Conservatives won the election of 1891, but only by a narrow majority of 27 seats. They lost seats to the Liberals in close votes in the rural areas, which tended to support free trade, but won most of the urban vote in Ontario and Quebec, where protectionism was strong. The election of 1891 ended unrestricted reciprocity as a Liberal policy, and the party moved toward its own version of a national policy, including a high tariff. Two decades would pass before the Liberals would champion "continentalism" once again in the election of 1911.

Imperialism

Many English-speaking Canadians favoured stronger British ties through imperial federation. After 1875, British leaders came to appreciate the importance of colonies in maintaining Britain's military and economic supremacy in the world. In particular, overseas colonies proved important for British hegemony as Germany and Italy became major European powers and as the United States threatened to supplant Britain as the leading English-speaking country in the world. Furthermore, rivalry between imperial countries meant competition for colonial markets and for world trade, thus giving an economic emphasis to the new imperialism. The cry from imperialists that "trade follows the flag" led British manufacturers and many in the working class to support imperialism in the late nineteenth century.

Race Theory and Imperialism

The new imperialism, however, represented for many of its followers much more than trade, tariffs, and guns. It was an intellectual and spiritual force. Imperialists distorted Charles Darwin's theory of evolution in the animal kingdom by applying it to society, in a concept known as Social Darwinism. Race theorists argued that some groups or races were born "superior"—were better fit to survive—than others, and that, in Britain and in colonies settled by whites, the Anglo-Saxon "race" constituted the elite. Imperialists argued that their "race's" superior position made it imperative for "Anglo-Saxons" to spread their "virtues"—their British values and Christian beliefs, the two being considered synonymous—to the less fortunate "infidels" of Asia, Africa, and the Pacific. They believed they must take up this "white man's burden," as the British author Rudyard Kipling expressed it.

Women played an important role in the imperialist movement. Organizations such as the Imperial Order of the Daughters of the Empire (IODE), founded by Margaret Polson Murray, became strong advocates of imperial sentiment. Its motto—"One Flag, One Throne, One Country"—summarized its aspirations. By World War I, it would become one of the largest English-Canadian women's voluntary associations.

British women, however, were much more than advocates of imperialism; they were also symbols, or

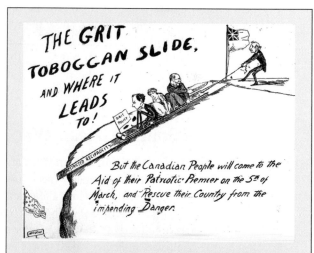

This cartoon shows Liberal leader Wilfrid Laurier and Richard Cartwright, his Liberal financial critic, on a toboggan slipping down the slope of "Unrestricted Reciprocity" with the symbolic Miss Canada between them. With the knife of Reciprocity, Cartwright is cutting the rope that prevents the toboggan from falling into "Annexation." Macdonald, straining to hold the toboggan back, calls for help to save Canada in the forthcoming federal election, March 5, 1891.

By Bengough, Library and Archives Canada, March 5, 1891.

icons, of imperialism, as representatives of the moral, religious, and spiritual components of its ideology. They were the bearers of the finest British civilization and thus the true "empire builders." Their children were the offspring of the dominant race, and thus the means to ensure its survival. English-Canadian imperial literature extolled the virtues of the fairer sex of the empire builders, by contrasting the noble attributes of British women with the degenerate qualities of "coloured women" in the subservient colonial society. As well, protecting this "fairer sex" became a pretext for suppressing and controlling the indigenous population.

Imperialism and Canadian Nationalism

English-Canadian imperialists believed that Canada could offer the British Empire much, economically, militarily, and spiritually. In turn, the empire could advance Canada's national interests. English-Canadian imperialists envisioned imperial federation as a means to free Canada from economic depression, ethnic tension, provincialism, and threatened American annexation, thus enabling it to reach greater heights—"a sense of power"—in the world. In this sense, as historian Carl Berger has written, "imperialism was one form of Canadian nationalism."[1]

Imperialism drew its greatest support in Canada from a small English-speaking social and political elite, mainly Protestant ministers, lawyers, teachers, and politicians. In 1887 they formed a Canadian branch of the Imperial Federation League, an organization begun in Britain three years earlier. Descendants of United Empire Loyalists joined in large numbers, seeing imperialism as the fulfilment of their long-time dream of a "United Empire," which gave the League its greatest support in Ontario and New Brunswick, the two provinces with the largest number of Loyalist descendants.

British imperialism peaked in the 1890s. Joseph Chamberlain, appointed Colonial Secretary in 1895, personified the imperial spirit and spearheaded the movement. Two years later, Queen Victoria celebrated her Diamond Jubilee—60 years as the ruling monarch—in a spectacular celebration to show the world the splendour and the might of the British Empire. Special commemorative stamps were issued, among them a Canadian stamp showing a map of the world splashed with red for all the British possessions. The inscription read: "We hold a vaster empire than has been." A year after Queen Victoria's Diamond Jubilee, several Canadian provinces established Empire Day on May 23—the day before Queen Victoria's birthday.

The South African War

The supreme moment for English-Canadian imperialists came with the outbreak of the South African War in 1899. Britain appealed to the Dominions to assist in fighting the Boers, descendants of European settlers, mainly Protestants from the Netherlands, in South Africa. The English-language newspapers, especially those in Montreal and Toronto, demanded immediate Canadian participation. Lord Minto, the governor general, and Major General Edward Hutton, commander of the Canadian militia, worked out plans for a Canadian contingent, without informing Prime Minister Laurier. A cable from Joseph Chamberlain, the British colonial secretary, thanked Canada for its "offer to serve in South Africa." His thanks were premature, however, since the Canadian government had not yet made an official statement of support.

Meanwhile, anti-imperialistic sentiments toward the South African War arose in Quebec. If French Canadians sympathized with anyone in the struggle, it was with the Boers, whom they regarded as a kindred oppressed minority. Henri Bourassa, a young politician and brilliant orator like his grandfather, the legendary Louis-Joseph Papineau, leader of the Rebellion of 1837 in Lower Canada, opposed Canadian involvement in this distant imperialist war. Bourassa equated imperialism with militarism and commercialism, and thus condemned the British Empire "not because it is British, but because it is Imperial. All empires are hateful. They stand in the way of human liberty, and true progress, intellectual and moral. They serve nothing but brutal instincts and material objects." Bourassa also argued that the sending of Canadian troops to South Africa would establish a "dangerous precedent" for future imperial wars to which Britain would expect Canada to contribute.

For two days, Laurier's cabinet met to find a solution. On October 13, 1899, Laurier devised a compromise. He proposed that the Canadian government equip and transport a volunteer force of 1000 men for service on the British side. Once in South Africa, however, the troops would become the British government's responsibility and would fight as British soldiers. Laurier reminded imperialists and French Canadians alike that this decision to send troops should not be "construed as a precedent for future action." (Eventually Canada sent 7300 men to South Africa, of whom 245 died overseas, more than half from disease.) While Laurier's compromise did not satisfy the extremists on both sides, it did succeed in keeping the Liberal Party and the country together. But Bourassa resigned from the party in protest and ran instead as an independent.

Growing French-Canadian Nationalism

Imperialist sentiments in English-speaking Canada contributed to a parallel French-Canadian nationalism in Quebec. In 1903, a group of young French-Canadian nationalists, inspired by Henri Bourassa, founded the Ligue nationaliste and their own newspaper, *Le Nationaliste*, a year later. The organization had a three-point program: Canadian autonomy within the British Empire; provincial autonomy within a federal state; and the rational development of Canada's resources. Other French-Canadian nationalists founded the Association catholique de la jeunesse canadienne-française (ACJC), or "Catholic Association of French-Canadian Youth," in 1904. This group, under the leadership of Lionel Groulx, a Catholic priest and teacher, recruited new members from the classical colleges. They saw the Roman Catholic church as playing an important role in shaping Quebec nationalism.

The members of the Prince Edward Island Transvaal contingent before their departure for South Africa. In total, some 7300 Canadian volunteers fought in the South African War (1899–1902).

The Patent and Copyright Office Collection/Library and Archives Canada/C-7983.

Jules-Paul Tardivel, a Franco-American born in Kentucky, who came to Quebec in 1868 to study French and then took up the causes of ultramontanism and French-Canadian nationalism, took a more extreme position. In his newspaper, *La Vérité*, and in his futuristic novel, *Pour la patrie* (1895), Tardivel proposed Quebec's separation from Canada to create a Roman Catholic state on the banks of the St. Lawrence River. In an exchange published in 1904, Tardivel and Bourassa outlined their differing conceptions of French Canada at this time. Tardivel distinguished between his exclusive French-Canadian form of nationalism and Bourassa's broader Canadian nationalism. Tardivel wrote: "Our own nationalism is French-Canadian nationalism.... For us our fatherland is—we do not say precisely the Province of Quebec—but French Canada; the nation we wish to see founded at the hour marked by Divine Providence is the French-Canadian nation." Bourassa replied:

> For us the fatherland is all Canada, that is, a federation of distinct races and autonomous provinces. The nation that we wish to see develop is the Canadian nation, composed of French Canadians and English Canadians, that is of two elements separated by language and religion, and by the legal dispositions necessary to the preservation of their respective traditions, but united in a feeling of brotherhood, in a common attachment to the common fatherland.

In this interchange lay the essence of two currents of twentieth-century French-Canadian nationalism: one leading to separatism, the other to a bilingual and bicultural nation.

Relations with the United States

The Alaska Boundary Dispute

At the turn of the century, a new dispute arose between Canada and the United States, this time over the boundary between Alaska and the Yukon Territory. The news that gold had been discovered in the Yukon in 1897 suddenly made the boundary question of utmost importance. The Americans sought a continuous border along the Pacific coast, thus denying Canada's claim to several fiords with access to the Yukon.

The Canadians and the Americans, along with the British, agreed to settle the issue through a six-member tribunal, three from each side, to review the disputed border. Britain appointed a British judge and two Canadian lawyers for its side. In the end, Lord Alverstone, the lone British member of the tribunal, sided with the Americans, who claimed that the boundary line should be around the heads of the inlets, giving the United States territorial control of them. Many Canadians at the time, including the prime minister, considered Alverstone's decision to side with the Americans to be "one of those concessions which have made British diplomacy odious to Canadian people." Such action increased the will of Canadian leaders to gain greater control of their own foreign policy.

Renewed Prospects of Reciprocity

After the contentious Alaska boundary dispute, Canadian–American relations actually improved. On January 26, 1911, the Liberals made a surprise announcement in Parliament that a reciprocal trade agreement had been reached with the Americans that allowed Canadian natural products free entry into American markets in exchange for letting American manufactured goods into Canada at a lower tariff rate. The agreement only required ratification by the American and Canadian governments. The American Congress passed the legislation in July 1911. It remained only for the Canadian parliament to give its approval.

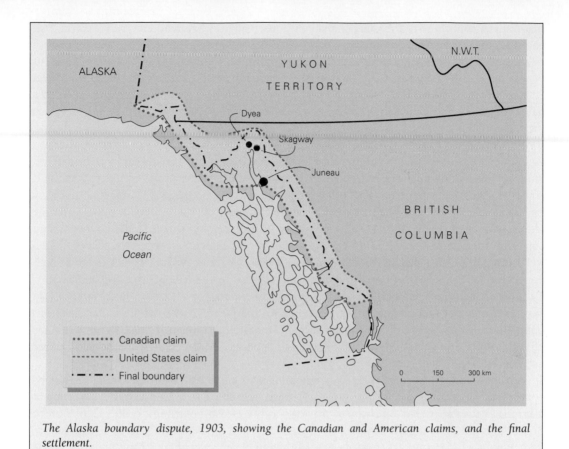

The Alaska boundary dispute, 1903, showing the Canadian and American claims, and the final settlement.

Very quickly, opposition to the reciprocity agreement arose in central Canada. A group of eighteen prominent Toronto manufacturers, industrialists, and financiers petitioned the government against the agreement. The group went on to become the core of a newly created Canadian National League. The league published a pamphlet, *The Road to Washington,* in which it warned that the reciprocity treaty was the first step toward American annexation of Canada.

Inopportune statements by imprudent American politicians aided the league's campaign. Champ Clark, speaker-designate of the House of Representatives, said of the agreement: "I am for it, because I hope to see the day when the American flag will float over every square foot of the British North American possessions clear to the North Pole." President Taft himself noted: "Canada stands at the parting of the ways." By this he meant that Canada had to choose between remaining an isolated protectionist country or trading with the Americans. But anti-American proponents in Canada interpreted the statement to mean that Canada had to choose between Britain and the United States. Emotional arguments about loyalty and nationalism replaced economic ones.

The Naval Crisis

The controversy over reciprocity coincided with the contentious naval question. In 1908, the British press warned of Germany's growing naval strength, which threatened Britain's control of the high seas. The British Conservative opposition demanded that the British government immediately build eight super-battleships, or dreadnoughts. Many English Canadians insisted that Canada contribute to the cause. Canadian Conservatives wanted an emergency direct cash contribution to Britain in the present crisis, while the ruling Liberals favoured the immediate establishment of a Canadian navy under Canadian command, to be used by Britain in the event of war if the Canadian parliament approved. In January 1910, Laurier introduced the Naval Service Bill. It proposed that Canada construct five cruisers and six destroyers and establish a naval college to train Canadian officers. The Canadian government could, "in case of war," place the force under imperial command with the Canadian parliament's approval.

Opposition to the Naval Service Bill arose at both extremes. English-Canadian imperialists denounced this "tin-pot navy," as they described it, as a disgrace to Canada's role in the empire. French-Canadian nationalists, led by Henri Bourassa, opposed the proposed navy, because it could be used to fight imperial wars of no interest to Canada. Bourassa was in favour of a navy for home defence, but not one that would involve Canada in the "whirlpool of militarism." He questioned whether Canada needed a navy at all, since the only threat to the country could come from the United States, with whom Canadians had enjoyed a century of peace.

During the 1911 federal election campaign, Laurier faced vigorous attacks from both imperialists in Ontario, who branded him a continentalist on the reciprocity issue, and French-Canadian nationalists, who called him an imperialist on the naval issue. "I am neither," an exasperated Laurier protested during an election rally in St. Jean, Quebec. "I am a *Canadian.*" His policy, he claimed, was one of "true Canadianism, of moderation, or conciliation." Nevertheless, the Liberals lost the election as a result of the combined opposition of Ontario imperialists and Quebec nationalists.

Robert L. Borden became the new prime minister. One of his government's first decisions concerned the naval issue. Despite strong Quebec opposition, the Conservative government introduced the Naval Aid Bill, which provided a direct cash contribution of $35 million to Britain to build three dreadnoughts. The Liberals attacked the Naval Aid Bill as a sham and as an inadequate alternative to Laurier's naval program. They used their strong majority in the Senate to defeat the bill. Thus, on the eve of World War I, Canada had neither made a contribution to the British navy nor built up a navy of its own.

The period from 1880 to 1914 saw a resurgence of regionalism, and a debate over the future of Canada. Provincial-rightists successfully challenged the power of the central government on a number of constitutional issues, thus making Canada in practice a federal state with a more even division of power between the federal and provincial governments. Regional protests arose in the Maritimes with the attempt by Nova Scotia once again to secede from Confederation, and in the West over the North-West Rebellion of 1885. As well, English- and French-speaking Canadians feuded over Riel's execution, over the Jesuits' Estates Act in Quebec, and over linguistic and religious rights in schools, first in Manitoba and then in Saskatchewan and Alberta.

Canadians also debated the nation's destiny in the world. Most English Canadians favoured some form of association with either Britain, in an imperial federation, or with the United States, in a continental association, over Canadian independence. French-Canadian leaders preferred either an autonomous Canadian nation within the British Empire, or greater autonomy for Quebec within Canada. Few Canadians thought in terms of Canadian independence; most felt that the country was not yet strong enough, or sufficiently united, to be independent.

NOTE

1. Carl Berger, *The Sense of Power: Studies in the Ideas of Canadian Imperialism, 1867–1914* (Toronto: University of Toronto Press, 1970), p. 259.

BEYOND THE BOOK

Alexander Campbell

http://library2.usask.ca/northwest/campbell/campbell.html
Alexander Campbell was a sergeant with the 7th Fusiliers militia of London, Ontario. Campbell kept a sketchbook and journal of his time as he served during the North-West Rebellion of 1885, and his works are digitized here.

The Ontario Boundary Act, 1889

http://www.justice.gc.ca/eng/pi/const/lawreg-loireg/p1t10-1.html
Full text of the Ontario Boundary Act.

Letters of the 1885 North-West Rebellion

http://www.canadianletters.ca/letterlist.php?collectionid=98&docid=2&warid=2
Digitized diary of Walter F. Stewart, Ontario Staff Sergeant who fought in the 1885 rebellion. His diary details the attack on Batoche, the surrender of Poundmaker, and his return to Ontario after the conflict was over.

Quebeckers, the Roman Catholic Church, and the Manitoba Schools Question

http://www2.marianopolis.edu/quebechistory/chronos/manitoba.htm
A descriptive chronology of the developments related to this controversy.

The Laurier–Greenway Compromise

http://www.ola.bc.ca/online/cf/documents/1896ManitobaSchool.html#top
The Laurier–Greenway Compromise, also known as the Manitoba School Act of 1896, attempted to resolve the issue of religion and language in education.

The Program of the Ligue nationaliste

http://www2.marianopolis.edu/quebechistory/docs/nligue/eng.htm
The 1903 document outlining the goals of Quebec's Ligue nationaliste.

The Imperialist

Sara Jeanette Duncan, *The Imperialist* (Toronto: McClelland and Stewart, 1964; first appeared 1904). An account of life in a small Ontario town, a fictionalized Brantford, Ontario, at the end of the nineteenth century.

RELATED READINGS

The following articles from R. Douglas Francis and Donald B. Smith, eds., *Viewpoints: Readings in Canadian History* (Toronto: Thomson Nelson, 2007), examine topics covered in this chapter in greater depth: David Lee, "The Métis Militant Rebels of 1885," pp. 268–84, and A. Blair Stonechild, "The Indian View of the 1885 Uprising," pp. 284–96.

BIBLIOGRAPHY

For an overview of Dominion–provincial relations in the late nineteenth century, see P.B. Waite, *Canada, 1874–1896: Arduous Destiny* (Toronto: McClelland & Stewart, 1971). The provincial-rights movement in Ontario is discussed in Christopher Armstrong, *The Politics of Federalism: Ontario's Relations with the Federal Government, 1867–1942* (Toronto: University of Toronto Press, 1981); and Paul Romney, *Getting It Wrong: How Canadians Forgot Their Past and Imperilled Confederation* (Toronto: University of Toronto Press, 1999). On political protest in Atlantic Canada in the 1880s, see Judith Fingard, "The 1880s: Paradoxes of Progress," in E.R. Forbes and D.A. Muise, eds., *The Atlantic Provinces in Confederation* (Toronto: University of Toronto Press, 1993); T.W. Acheson, "The Maritimes and 'Empire Canada,'" in D.J. Bercuson, ed., *Canada and the Burden of Unity* (Toronto: Macmillan, 1977), pp. 87–114; and George Rawlyk, ed., *The Atlantic Provinces and the Problem of Confederation* (St. John's: Breakwater Books, 1979).

The most authoritative account of the North-West Rebellion is Bob Beal and Rob Macleod, *Prairie Fire: The 1885 North-West Rebellion* (Edmonton: Hurtig, 1984). For the Aboriginal perspective on the 1885 Rebellion, see Blair Stonechild and Bill Waiser, *Loyal till Death: Indians and the North-West Rebellion* (Calgary: Fifth House, 1997). Donald B. Smith's biography, *Honoré Jaxon: Prairie Visionary* (Regina: Coteau Books, 2007), looks at the life of Will Jackson, who became Riel's secretary. For a historical perspective on the Delaney–Gowanlock captivity, see Sarah Carter, *Capturing Women: The Manipulation of Cultural Imagery in Canada's Prairie West* (Montreal/Kingston: McGill-Queen's University Press, 1997). On Louis Riel, see the readings cited for Chapter 12 of this book, as well as the titles listed in "Where Historians Disagree" in this chapter. A historiographical article is J.R. Miller, "From Riel to the Métis," *Canadian Historical Review*, 69, 1 (March 1988): 1–20.

Quebec's views on federal–provincial relations are analyzed in R. Cook, *Provincial Autonomy: Minority Rights and the Compact Theory, 1867–1921* (Ottawa: Queen's Printer, 1969); and Arthur Silver, *The French-Canadian Idea of Confederation, 1864–1900* (Toronto: University of Toronto Press, 1982). J.R. Miller's *Equal Rights: The Jesuits' Estates Act Controversy* (Montreal: McGill-Queen's University Press, 1979) deals with that subject in depth. On the Manitoba Schools Question and its impact on the election of 1896, consult Paul Crunican, *Priests and Politicians: Manitoba Schools and the Election of 1896* (Toronto: University of Toronto Press, 1974). Lovell Clark has compiled a collection of sources in *The Manitoba School Question: Majority Rule or Minority Rights* (Toronto: Copp Clark, 1968). Treatment of the schools question in Alberta and Saskatchewan can be found in Manoly R. Lupul, *The Roman Catholic Church and the North-West School Question: A Study in Church–State Relations in Western Canada* (Toronto: University of Toronto Press, 1974).

The politics of the 1890s are discussed in John T. Saywell's introduction to *The Canadian Journal of Lady Aberdeen, 1893–1898* (Toronto: Champlain Society, 1960); P.B. Waite, *The Man from Halifax: Sir John Thompson, Prime Minister* (Toronto: University of Toronto Press, 1985); and H. Blair Neatby, *Laurier and a Liberal Quebec: A Study in Political Management* (Toronto: McClelland & Stewart, 1973).

The most comprehensive survey of Canada's relations with Britain and the United States remains C.P. Stacey, *Canada and the Age of Conflict: A History of Canadian External Relations*, vol. 1, *1867–1921* (Toronto: Macmillan, 1977). Canadian–American relations in the late nineteenth century are dealt with in John Herd Thompson and Stephen J. Randall, *Canada and the United States: Ambivalent Allies*, 3rd ed. (Montreal/Kingston: McGill-Queen's University Press, 2002); J.L. Granatstein and Norman Hillmer, *For Better or for Worse: Canada and the United States to the 1990s* (Toronto: Copp Clark Pitman, 1991); and C.C. Tansill, *Canadian–American Relations, 1875–1911* (Toronto: The Ryerson Press, 1943).

Norman Penlington's *The Alaska Boundary Dispute: A Critical Appraisal* (Toronto: McGraw-Hill Ryerson, 1972) and John Munro's *The Alaska Boundary Dispute* (Toronto: Copp Clark, 1970) cover that issue.

Carl Berger's *The Sense of Power: Studies in the Ideas of Canadian Imperialism, 1867–1914* (Toronto: University of Toronto Press, 1970), analyzes the beliefs of English-Canadian imperialists. Carman Miller, *Painting the Map Red: Canada and the South African War 1899–1902* (Montreal/Kingston:

Canadian War Museum, McGill-Queen's University Press, 1992), discusses Canadian imperialism in the context of the South African War. On the IODE, see Katie Pickles, *Female Imperialism and National Unity: Imperial Order Daughters of the Empire* (Manchester: Manchester University Press, 2002).

French-Canadian views on imperialism and nationalism during this era can be found in M. Wade, *The French Canadians, 1760–1945* (Toronto: Macmillan, 1955), pp. 447–535; and in Susan Mann, *The Dream of Nation: A Social and Intellectual History of Quebec*, 2nd ed. (Montreal/Kingston: McGill-Queen's University Press, 2002), pp. 167–83. Joseph Levitt's pamphlet *Henri Bourassa, Catholic Critic* (Toronto: Canadian Historical Association, 1976) summarizes the ideas of this French-Canadian thinker.

The issue of reciprocity in the 1911 election is analyzed in L.E. Ellis, *Reciprocity, 1911: A Study in Canadian–American Relations* (Toronto: The Ryerson Press, 1939).

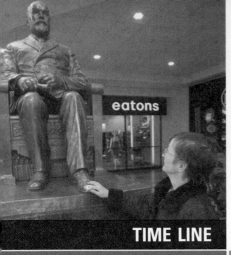

Chapter Fifteen

URBAN AND INDUSTRIAL CANADA

TIME LINE

1869	The T. Eaton Company begins
1872	Trade Union Act is passed
1873	An economic recession begins
1889	Royal Commission on the Relations of Labour and Capital issues its report
1891	An Ontario Bureau of Mines is established
1894	Labour Day established as a national holiday
1897	Herbert Ames publishes *City below the Hill*, a sociological study of Montreal
1900	A federal Department of Labour is established
1902	International Nickel Company of Canada formed
1905	The Industrial Workers of the World (IWW) known as "Wobblies," forms in Canada
1906	Ontario Hydro is created
1908	Henry Ford introduces the Model T The Fishermen's Protective Union is founded in Newfoundland
1910	The Royal Commission on Industrial Training and Technical Education is estabilished
1917	Order of Sleeping Car Porters, the first African-Canadian railway union, is formed

By the turn of the century, a number of factors—worldwide prosperity, the success of the national policy, better world prices for raw materials, a decline in freight rates, and a new attitude toward business—combined to enable Canada to undergo its industrial revolution. Industrialization also spurred urbanization. Not all regions experienced uniform and sustained economic growth. The Maritimes languished, and the West developed as a great agricultural area, while central Canada became the heartland of industrial growth. Even here, industrial growth was uneven. Ontario outperformed Quebec, while in Quebec, the minority Anglophone population greatly predominated over francophones as industrial entrepreneurs. Nor did all classes benefit equally. The upper and middle classes benefited at the expense of the poorer class. But overall, Canada entered an age of general prosperity through industrialization and resource extraction that led Prime Minister Wilfrid Laurier to predict that the twentieth century would be Canada's century.

Industrialization and urbanization transformed the lifestyles of Canadians. Farming became more mechanized and businesslike and required fewer farm hands, thus contributing to rural depopulation as young farm family members moved into the towns and cities to work. First Nations people in all regions, and especially in the North, experienced increased competition from outsiders in jobs they had traditionally done. In the urban centres, working-class districts emerged that were substandard in terms of a healthy environment. The working class also worked long hours in factories which were unclean and unsafe. Workers looked to charitable institutions for assistance, fraternal organizations and clubs for camaraderie and identity, and unions for better wages and working conditions.

Canada's Economic Expansion

By the turn of the century, the national policy finally worked as intended. Growth in the primary industries increased the demand for secondary industry. The CPR and the two new transcontinental railways—the Canadian Northern and Grand Trunk Pacific/National Transcontinental—brought hundreds of thousands of immigrants westward and took away to market the West's natural resources. Equally, a growing rural population in the West required eastern manufactured goods, from agricultural implements to common household items. Stimulated by additional foreign investment, industry and manufacturing expanded to meet the increased demand for consumer goods. This meant jobs for workers. Service industries, as well as governments (national, provincial, and municipal), also became major employers. Indeed, by 1921 as many people worked in service industries as in the primary sector.

Canada became an attractive country for investment. The federal government provided financial assistance to private companies. The governments of Quebec and especially Ontario offered bonuses, subsidies, and guarantees to industrialists to locate new plants within their borders. Banks provided another source of internal revenue. The three largest—the Bank of Montreal, the Royal Bank (also with its headquarters in Montreal), and the Toronto-based Bank of Commerce—centralized their operations, invested in new industries, and provided capital for entrepreneurs. Foreign investment increased as well. British financiers invested chiefly in the form of indirect portfolio investments (loans in the form of bonds). In contrast, American investors preferred ownership to indirect investment through the establishment of branch plants.

Large corporations emerged. In 1902, a handful of consolidated companies existed; by 1912, there were nearly 60. The most noteworthy included: Dominion Canner Limited, which in 1910 amalgamated 34 smaller canning factories; Canada Cement, a consolidation of eleven cement companies in 1909; and Stelco (the Steel Company of Canada), formed in 1910 out of several small Ontario and Quebec iron and steel mills.

Canada's Population, 1861–1921 (thousands)

YEAR	NATURAL INCREASE[*]	IMMIGRATION	EMIGRATION	NET MIGRATION	POPULATION
1861					3230
1861–71	610	260	410	−150	3689
1871–81	690	350	404	−54	4325
1881–91	654	680	826	−146	4833
1891–01	668	250	380	−130	5371
1901–11	1025	1550	740	810	7207
1911–21	1270	1400	1089	311	8788

[*]The number of births minus the number of deaths.

Source: From *Canada: Our Century, Our Story*, Ontario ed., Student text by Fielding/Evans. © 2001. Reprinted with permission of Nelson, a division of Thomson Learning, http://www.thomsonrights.com. Fax 800-730-2215.

Role of Government in the Economy

As the saying of the day went, "Government is best which governs least." Ottawa did nothing to regulate the monopolies, apart from passing the Combines Investigation Act of 1910. The Act allowed government to investigate monopoly price-fixing, but during its nine-year lifespan, the investigation board dealt with only one case. As well, corporations took advantage of the division of powers between the federal, provincial, and municipal governments over regulations to play one government off against the other.

Limited state involvement in the economy did occur, however. In the case of Ontario Hydro, when it seemed likely that a small, privileged business group alone might harness the tremendous energy power of Niagara Falls, business interests rallied behind Adam Beck, a manufacturer of cigar boxes and the Conservative member for London in the Ontario legislature, to urge the Ontario government to create a Crown corporation of the hydroelectric power industry. Under Beck, the Hydro-Electric Power Commission of Ontario became the largest publicly owned power authority in the world.

A Positive Attitude toward Business

In Canada's "gilded age," Canadians honoured business successes. In a poll taken in 1908 by the *Canadian Courier*, a major newspaper, nine out of ten of those named "Canada's Top Ten Biggest Men" were captains of industry or railway magnates. The philosophy of Social Darwinism prevailed: survival belonged to the fittest, the successful believed. Their wealth proved their virtue. Many young English-speaking Canadians accepted the theory of the popular American writer Horatio Alger that anyone could rise from rags to riches through hard work, thrift, and self-discipline.

English-speaking Canadians had numerous role models for success: Herbert Holt, the billion-dollar recluse who founded the Montreal Light, Heat and Power Company in 1902 and became president of the Royal Bank; Henry Pellatt, active in the formation of Canadian General Electric and owner of Toronto's Casa Loma, one of the most palatial residences in North America; Joseph W. Flavelle, president of the William Davies Meat Packaging Plant in Toronto and chair of the Bank of Commerce and the National Trust Company; Francis H. Clergue, founder of the Algoma Steel Company of Sault Ste. Marie, Ontario; Patrick Burns, owner of the Burns Meat Packing Company of Calgary; and Max Aitken (later Lord Beaverbrook), a millionaire by the age of thirty, who used his Royal Securities Corporation as an investment bank to fund his many mergers.

Few Canadian merchants eclipsed the success of Timothy Eaton, who opened his Toronto dry-goods store at the corner of Yonge and Queen Streets in 1869. He introduced two new revolutionary practices to Canadian merchandising. First, he accepted cash only. Second, he promised "money refunded if goods not satisfactory." Eaton also knew the value of advertising and took out full-page ads in the Toronto newspapers. By 1882, his business had grown to such an extent that he transformed his operation into a department store that had three floors, 35 departments, electric lights (the first in a Canadian store), the first elevator, and the first store restaurant-café. By the time of his death in 1907 at age 72, Timothy Eaton employed over 9000 people. His "empire" extended across the country and the world.

Canadian entrepreneurs and other corporate leaders relied on a new, skilled managerial class to run the complex, day-to-day operations of their expanded business: increased production data, costs, personnel, and internal communications. These managers were often trained in "scientific management," a term coined by the American Frederick W. Taylor. "Scientific managers" used workers to complete simple and routine jobs at a proficient speed for a minimum wage. Success was judged only in terms of efficiency. Beneath this managerial class and closely supervised by it came the clerical workers who carried out the daily routine office jobs. Increasingly, women performed the mechanized and highly specialized jobs, but under the supervision of male managerial clerks.

In many ways, schools became training grounds for the workplace. In factory-like institutions, teachers taught young people the values of punctuality, obedience, thrift, and self-discipline—values essential for an industrial society. As well, girls could now study domestic science, and boys either manual training or how to prepare for business.

COMMUNITY PORTRAIT

The T. Eaton Company: A Community Store

Timothy Eaton's ability to create Canada's most successful department store by the early twentieth century was due to a variety of factors, but clearly one of the most important was his ability to create a sense of community among his employees. They proudly identified themselves as "Eatonians," an identity that not only linked them to Timothy Eaton and his family but also to a community of fellow workers who had one thing in common: they were employees—or what Eaton preferred to call "associates"—of the T. Eaton Company.

"The Governor," as he became known, cultivated a close personal relationship with his staff, his "loyal subjects," that engendered respect, cooperation, and enthusiasm on their part. His kindness and generosity to loyal workers who experienced financial difficulties was legendary. Employees absent from work for extended periods of time due to illness continued to receive their pay, often along with an order of coal to keep them warm if the illness occurred in the winter months.

When his Toronto store at the corner of Queen and Yonge became too large for him to supervise his staff by himself, and when other stores opened across the country, Eaton hired managers. He handpicked and trained them himself to ensure that they had the qualities to cultivate a sense of community among employees. "The Governor" personally held meetings in his store at which employees could air grievances and suggest ways to improve good relations (and thus increase sales). To cultivate the sense of community, Eaton provided his "associates" with additional benefits such as a 10 percent discount on merchandise, low-interest loans to those wishing to buy a home, a welfare department, a pension and life insurance plan, and deposit accounts with generous interest rates.

Timothy Eaton cultivated the same strong sense of community among his customers, many of whom also considered themselves "Eatonians." As one store brochure stated: "The Eaton Spirit is the combined faith and enthusiastic loyalty we have for the store and for our fellow employees." With the beginning of the Eaton's catalogue in 1884, the "wider community" of Eatonians stretched across the country. One enthusiastic Westerner proclaimed that "the Eaton catalogue is as much a Western institution as the wheat itself." During World War I, the catalogue even cultivated a sense of community among Canadian soldiers on the front. Among soldiers, it became known as "The Wish Book," since soldiers ordered items they wished to own, such as a wristwatch—and that Eaton's often provided at no cost—or dreamed of having when they returned home.

A woman touching the boot of the statue of Timothy Eaton in the Winnipeg downtown Eaton's store. People rubbed the boot for good luck.

Winnipeg Free Press, October 23, 2002, p. A5. Reprinted with permission.

When Eaton died on January 31, 1907, several thousand of his employees followed the funeral entourage from Timothy Eaton Methodist Church to the Mount Pleasant Cemetery. In 1919, on the occasion of the fiftieth anniversary of the founding of the T. Eaton store, company employees presented a life-size bronze statue of Timothy Eaton for the main store as a gift to the Eaton family. A copy of the statue was also given to the main western Canadian store in Winnipeg. From that day on, passersby would rub the toe of the left shoe to the point of making it shiny, hoping that Eaton's good fortune might rub off on them.

In 1999 the T. Eaton Company filed for bankruptcy. A number of reasons account for its demise, but clearly one was the failure of the company to continue to engender the sense of community loyalty its founder had so successfully cultivated.

FURTHER READING

Joy L. Santink, *Timothy Eaton and the Rise of His Department Store* (Toronto: University of Toronto Press, 1990).

Rod McQueen, *The Eatons: The Rise and Fall of Canada's Royal Family*, rev. ed. (Toronto: Stoddart, 1999).

Patricia Phenix, *Eatonians: The Story of the Family behind the Family* (Toronto: McClelland and Stewart, 2002).

This store at the turn of the century shows the diversity of items available to those who had money to purchase them, including Jell-O, which had just come on the market in 1897.

Provincial Archives of New Brunswick/P18-163.

Economic Development in the East and West

In Atlantic Canada, the resource-based economy lost some of its momentum. In Newfoundland, the economy remained highly dependent on the cod and seal fisheries at a time of serious decline in those industries. In the early 1890s, the Newfoundland government implemented its version of Canada's National Policy, known as "the Policy of Progress." It failed, however, to revitalize the Island's economy. In the Maritimes, the West Indies sugar trade fell dramatically in the 1870s, resulting in a decline in trade between Nova Scotia and the West Indies. In the same decade, Britain's demand for Maritime lumber and wooden ships fell, seriously weakening Nova Scotia's and New Brunswick's economies. An industrial economy did emerge, based largely on the Cape Breton coal fields. In fact, at one point in the early 1880s, thanks in large part to the Intercolonial Railway, the National Policy of tariff protection, and a vigorous iron and steel industry, Nova Scotia's industrial growth on a per capita basis actually outstripped that of Ontario and Quebec.

In the long run, however, the Maritimes' industrial expansion faltered. Some historians have pointed out that the region lacked resources as extensive or diverse as, for example, Ontario's. As well, distance from the large markets of central Canada and the small regional population in Atlantic Canada combined to create a significant obstacle to expansion for factories in the region. Furthermore, Maritime investors, like their Canadian counterparts elsewhere, saw western and central Canadian development as potentially more lucrative. As a result of these circumstances, Maritime cities grew at a slower rate than cities elsewhere across the country. Many of them also became dependants of Montreal and, to a lesser extent, of Toronto.

Growth in the West

British Columbia's economy shifted from its Pacific orientation (southward to California) toward central Canada, thanks to the completion of the CPR. The provincial economy remained still predominantly resource-based: mining, forestry, fisheries, and agriculture. Mining speculation ran at a fever pitch by the turn of the century. Extraction of lode gold and silver began in the Slocan and Boundary districts in the 1890s, but copper, lead, and zinc superseded precious metals after 1900. Coal mining, especially in and around Nanaimo on Vancouver Island, also contributed to the province's economy. Forestry outdistanced mining in terms of both wealth and employment. Logging increased by an astonishing 400 percent between 1900 and 1910. Fisheries, especially the salmon fisheries, expanded and consolidated in a highly competitive business. British Columbia Packers Association emerged as the most powerful salmon packing company after 1902, and the small port of Steveston became known as "the sockeye capital of the world."

Agriculture was slow to get established in British Columbia, but by World War I it ranked second to forestry in terms of output. Fruit farming was the most commercially viable, especially after the introduction of refrigerated rail cars at the turn of the century, since much of the fruit was exported. Manufacturing grew in the late nineteenth century, contributing 5 percent of the country's output by 1890. Still, the province's distance from the centre of the industrial development in central Canada, combined with the high freight rates and the small regional market, prevented the province from becoming a substantial and ongoing secondary-manufacturing base. Rather, British Columbia, like the Maritimes, became another hinterland region to central Canada.

The two urban centres of Victoria and Vancouver vied for dominance in West Coast trade. Vancouver won out by 1914, because of the excellent dock and terminal facilities on Burrard Inlet and its role as the western terminus of the CPR. The completion of the Panama Canal in 1914 enabled Vancouver to surpass Winnipeg as Canada's major western city, by enabling prairie farmers to ship their wheat to European markets via the Pacific.

On the Prairies, wheat was king. Hardier strains of wheat and the world demand for wheat after 1896 opened up areas on the northern fringe and in the arid Palliser Triangle to production, increasing substantially both the wheat lands and yields. In terms of yields, that amounted to a record 208 million bushels in 1911. Such growth justified and necessitated new rail lines, especially to service the new areas of settlement. But the Prairies faced the same problem British Columbia and the Maritimes faced: too small a regional market to foster substantial secondary manufacturing. Thus, as intended by the National Policy, the Prairies became subservient to central Canada in terms of economic growth and dominance.

Urbanization occurred at a rapid rate on the Prairies. In 1870, no urban centres existed in the region; by 1911, there were seventeen incorporated cities and 150 incorporated towns. Five dominant cities emerged by servicing surrounding agricultural hinterlands: Winnipeg, Saskatoon, Regina, Edmonton, and Calgary.

Winnipeg's location as the "gateway to the West" with rail links to the East made the entire Prairie West its hinterland. Thanks to this strategic location, it became the third-largest manufacturing city in pre–World War I Canada. Nicknamed the "Hub City," it stood at the junction of three transcontinental railways. The city employed thousands in its rail yards, the largest in the world by 1904, with as many as 1800 freight cars passing through in a single day. But Toronto and Montreal dominated even Winnipeg. Ultimately, all western rail lines led to central Canada.

Industrialization in Central Canada

At the turn of the century, industrialization occurred largely in Ontario and Quebec. Ontario's growth initially was based on small-scale consumer goods industries in a series of towns and cities throughout southern Ontario that depended chiefly on coal as a source of energy and on iron production. In both cases, Ontario benefited from the province's proximity to the Pennsylvania coal fields and the Minnesota iron ranges, although Ontario created its own iron and steel companies as well. Also, a network of rail lines crisscrossed Ontario, linking the numerous towns and cities to the rural countryside and to other urban centres. These centres produced such goods as engines, farm implements, stoves, furniture, and canned goods. Hamilton, predominantly a steel-producing town, also became the home of large railcar shops. But most of Ontario's largest head offices, financial institutions, factories, and warehouses were located in Toronto.

In Quebec, much of the new industry was small-scale and labour-intensive: shoes, textiles, lumber, and foodstuffs (flour, sugar, dairy products). These industries were also concentrated mainly in two cities: Montreal and Quebec City. Montreal had the advantage over Quebec City, the latter becoming more isolated from the major canals and rail networks without a bridge over the St. Lawrence. Montreal also had the majority of financial institutions to provide capital for businesses in the city.

Beginning in 1911, a second industrial revolution occurred when hydroelectric power replaced steam as the main source of industrial energy. Now pulp and paper, and later minerals, became the new resource products. Initially, the pulp produced by Canadian-based companies went for processing in the United States. But at the turn of the century, the Quebec government, at the urging of Quebec nationalists, placed an embargo on exports of pulp from Crown lands. Subsequently, Quebec pulp mills began producing their own newsprint for export. By 1914, Quebec had become a leading industrial province. More than two-thirds of its population worked in nonagricultural activities, and roughly one-half of its population lived in urban centres.

The Uniqueness of Quebec's Industrial Development

For French Canadians, however, Quebec's industrialization had a unique and disturbing aspect: they had almost no control over it. In 1910, of Canada's entrepreneurs, only one out of 40 was French-speaking. French Canadians were the labourers, not the owners of industry.

French-Canadian theorists began to question why. Was this imbalance due to French Canadians' limited pool of capital? Perhaps in part, but French-speaking Canadians in the Dominion faced a larger obstacle: the language of business was English. Education might also have been a factor. The Roman Catholic Church tended to emphasize a humanistic education, particularly at the classical college level, over science and commerce. The Quebec government tried to correct this imbalance by offering financial support for the establishment of technical schools. In 1907 it created the École des Hautes Études Commerciales (HEC), a university-level business school. Yet, many graduates still faced the need to work in English, at least at the managerial level.

An immigrant woman and her children waiting on a curb in front of the CPR Station in Winnipeg, around 1909. Almost everyone who came west came through this station, built in 1904. In 1992 the Aboriginal Centre of Winnipeg Inc. bought the building. The refurbished Aboriginal Centre is now a modern office space.

The United Church Archives, Toronto/93.049P/3111N.

Untreated waste from Toronto, and virtually every other municipality in the Great Lakes area, in both Canada and the United States, polluted the region's water systems.

City of Toronto Archives Fonds 1244, Item 1122A.

Life in the Industrial City

As a result of industrialization, cities became more socially stratified, with working-class districts physically separated from middle- and upper-class areas. The introduction of the electric streetcar and the automobile enabled the middle and upper classes to leave the inner city for suburban districts away from downtown congestion and pollution. The city centres became ghettoized and undesirable places to live. The Commission of Conservation, established by the federal government in 1909, noted in its *Annual Report* in 1914:

> *Industrial smoke disfigures buildings, impairs the health of the population, renders the city filthy, destroys any beauty with which it may naturally be endowed and tends, therefore, to make it a squalid and undesirable place of residence, and this at a time when economic influences are forcing into cities an ever increasing proportion of our population.*

In Montreal and Toronto, most working-class people rented rooms in either boarding or tenement houses—old wooden cottages or two-storey buildings with little or no yard area. Rent could be as high as $10 or $12 a month for basement rooms, roughly 25 percent of an unskilled worker's wages. Few families had the luxury of owning their own houses, since house prices remained well beyond the means of the ordinary worker. In Montreal, an average working-class family of five typically lived in a one- or two-room flat: damp, unventilated, inadequately lighted, and poorly heated. Overcrowding remained a constant problem. In Toronto, some families lived in hastily constructed shacks, in backyard tents, or even on the street. In summer, a stench rose from the cesspools and outdoor privies.

Wife-beating and the sexual abuse of children were common among all classes. Very often such violence in working-class districts was associated with drinking, unemployment, and destitution. Wives had little legal recourse because male-dominated courts rarely challenged the husband's proprietary right over his wife's person and her sexuality. If anything, judges questioned the woman's character. Because of high legal costs, divorce also remained out of the question for most abused women. Children, particularly those of the working class, enjoyed fewer rights and privileges than did women at the turn of the century. They had to assume family responsibilities at an early age, and to grow up and mature quickly.

Education was at a premium. In Montreal, a maximum Grade 3 education was common for working-class children. They had to enter the workforce as soon as possible (age eleven or twelve being the norm) to supplement the family income. The census of 1871 reveals that 25 percent of boys and 10 percent of girls between the ages of eleven and fifteen held jobs outside the home; these statistics did not include boys hired to do odd jobs or girls working as domestics. Ontario and Quebec passed Factory Acts prohibiting the hiring of boys under twelve and girls under fourteen, but they had little impact due to poor enforcement and the difficulty of taking recalcitrant factory owners to court. Those children unfortunate enough to end up in court were more likely to be penalized than protected, and sent to harsh probationary institutions.

Recent research enables us to make some generalizations about those children most likely to work outside the home and those who stayed home. Young daughters were less likely than young sons to be employed outside the home, since girls, by the age of fifteen or sixteen, made only half to two-thirds of the wages paid to boys of the same age for doing a similar job. Also, patriarchal attitudes militated against daughters working in factories, and girls up to the age of sixteen were required at home to help run the household and tend to younger family members. Still, poorer working-class families had to send their daughters out to work because of economic necessity.

Working in the New Industrial Economy

Working Conditions in Canada's Cities

Industrialization created harsh working conditions. In times of demand the average labourer spent at least ten to twelve hours a day, six days a week, at work. Factories were poorly ventilated, noisy, and dirty. Factory foremen ran the factory ruthlessly to ensure maximum efficiency. They often fined workers for tardiness or for talking to fellow workers on the job. Industrial accidents and deaths occurred frequently.

Job security did not exist. Victims of industrial accidents had no workers' compensation. Layoffs, especially during the slower winter months, occurred regularly. Even in good times, unemployment was common, a byproduct of the capitalist system. Before the federal government introduced unemployment insurance in 1940, layoffs meant months of subsistence without wages.

The cost of living in urban centres rose continually and outpaced workers' wages. The federal Department of Labour issued "typical weekly expenditure" budgets listing those items necessary for a family of five to enjoy a minimum standard of living. Although it allowed for only 0.6 kg of fresh meat per week per person, less than a litre of milk a day for a family of five, and no fresh vegetables or fruit, this minimum was more than the average working-class family could afford. In 1901, the estimated cost of living was $13.38 a week. But, at best, the average male worker could, without layoffs, make $425 a year in 1901, or an average of $8.25 a week. Thus, many working-class families needed at least two incomes to stay above the poverty line.

Health

Frequent illness complicated the normal daily problems of living and working. Montreal in particular remained a most unhealthy city in which to live, especially for children. At the turn of the century, approximately one out of every four infants died before the age of one. This was due to impure water, unpasteurized milk, and the limited use of vaccines for smallpox, diphtheria, and tuberculosis. In 1882, the Ontario government established a Board of Health to carry out preventive measures. Other provinces followed suit by 1909.

Society denounced attempts to limit family size. Limitation of family size, especially among those of British stock, was considered "race suicide." Section 179 of the Criminal Code of Canada, prepared in 1892, made it a criminal offence and liable to two years' imprisonment for anyone who attempted "to sell, advertise, publish an advertisement of or have for sale or disposal any medicine, drug or article intended or represented as a means of preventing conception or causing abortion." Despite such threats, many married women sought birth-control information.

Women in the Workplace

At the turn of the century, women made up about one-seventh of the paid workforce. Usually they worked outside the home only between the ages of 14, the youngest age permissible for girls to work after 1885, and 24, the normal marrying age. The routine of housework—rearing children,

Amherst, Nova Scotia Telephone Exchange, around 1909. Telephone operators belonged to the elite of female clerical workers.

Cumberland County Historical Society, Cumberland County Museum, 184-78-2.

cleaning, cooking, washing, mending, and shopping— meant full and exhausting days in an era before labour-saving devices. Marriage, motherhood, and domesticity remained intertwined in the minds of most women, no matter to which class they belonged. The home was considered women's "proper sphere." Men dominated the "public sphere." Nevertheless, many women supplemented the family income by taking in boarders, doing part-time sewing, or doing laundry.

The most economically pressed mothers had no choice but to work outside the home in female-related jobs, such as in textile factories, as waitresses, or as domestics. Women without familial support had to find work. In these cases, they had to rely on friends, neighbours, relatives, or on working-class associations to assist with children. Sometimes immigrant women could count on the support of ethnic groups to provide mutual aid and, occasionally, on employment agencies. Increasingly, however, there arose a segment of working women who were single, non-immigrant girls, popularly known as "working girls," who performed non-domestic, waged work outside the home. Being single, young, independent, and alone, they became the concern of moral reformers who saw them as a threat to the ideal Canadian society as made up of morally upright, married, and motherly women.

Middle-class women depended on domestic help at the turn of the century. Families were larger then, homes harder to keep clean, and food preparation much more time-consuming. Domestics tended to be young girls from rural areas or immigrant women. Indeed, the demand for domestic servants was so great that they were considered "preferred" immigrants. In 1891, 40 percent of all women working outside the home were employed as domestics.

Women preferred factory work to domestic service because of higher wages and shorter hours. Still, in 1900, most women in factories worked up to 60 hours a week. Textile and shoe factories hired women because they could pay them lower wages (approximately half of what men earned) and because they were better workers for the type of work to be done.

Even more preferable for women were office jobs away from the noise and pressure of the factory. By the turn of the century, women were employed in most of the clerical jobs. Conventional wisdom held that women's "natural" feminine characteristics—sympathy, adaptability, courtesy, and even nimble fingers—made them particularly suitable for clerical work. Women also worked as department-store clerks or telephone operators, two of the most "feminized" occupations at the turn of the century.

After domestic, factory, and office work, teaching was the most important female occupation. Teaching was considered an acceptable occupation for women, and one that allowed for the possibility of some upward social mobility, although it provided little financial security. Women received low salaries and had little chance of advancing to become department heads or principals.

A small number of women worked as nurses. Many gravitated toward the Victorian Order of Nurses (VON), formed in 1897, as a model public-health nursing service. Only a handful of women entered Canadian medical schools. For one thing, few hospitals would provide them with hospital privileges after graduation. Unable to attract enough patients, a number of Canada's early female doctors became medical missionaries overseas instead. In all the professions that women entered in small numbers at the turn of the century, they experienced gender discrimination in the form of lower pay than men, lack of control over their work, and pressure to quit once they married.

Charitable and Social Institutions for the Working Class

At the turn of the century, churches and private philanthropic organizations administered limited charitable help. Since society generally held that, with the exception of the handicapped and the aged, individuals alone remained responsible for their plight, charities provided only temporary relief as a stopgap measure—usually a meal of soup, bread, and tea, and a bath and a bed. Skilled workers looked to fraternal organizations—lodges such as the Orange Lodge, the Masons, the Oddfellows, and the Independent Order of Foresters—for financial and emotional support. Some sporting clubs gave their male members a sense of importance and self-worth and a feeling of camaraderie. Females were forbidden to belong to these fraternal or sporting clubs, but in some instances, such as the Oddfellows, women could belong to a parallel organization, such as the Rebekahs. Some associations had mutual-aid plans to care for sick members and to assist widows and orphans in the event of a member's death. They also gave workers a means to express publicly and collectively their discontent with industrial capitalism by supporting parades through the streets of towns and cities to show both solidarity and defiance. In a study of the mining communities on Vancouver Island in the mid- to late nineteenth century, historian John Belshaw shows how drinking, sports, and fraternal associations provided both camaraderie and a source of working-class identity beyond the workplace.[1]

Unions

Between 1850 and 1890, labour unions took root in Canada. At first, most unions were local, dispersed across the country, and specialized. Initially, the government refused to grant them legal recognition or to accept workers' right to collective bargaining. However, in 1872, Macdonald's Conservative government enacted the Trade Union Act, which recognized the right of unions to exist and to organize without fear of prosecution as illegal associations, so long as they registered with the government. Yet, at the same time, the Criminal Law Amendment Act imposed severe penalties, including a prison sentence, for most forms of picketing and union pressure. In the late nineteenth century, only a minority of Canadian workers belonged to unions, and those who did affiliated with a variety of groups, among which three stand out: the Knights of Labor, the Provincial Workmen's Association, and the American Federation of Labor.

The Knights of Labor, an American organization founded in 1869, enjoyed its greatest success among workers in Ontario and Quebec, although it had branches across the country. The Knights developed a working-class consciousness through the organization of workers by industry rather than by craft. The organization favoured arbitration over strikes, an eight-hour day, an end to child labour, the passage of health and safety legislation, and equal pay for equal work. The Knights took in semiskilled and unskilled workers as well as women and blacks, although not Asians.

Most unions refused to support women, arguing that by improving women's wages they encouraged women to remain at work, where they took jobs away from men. In some industries, women formed their own unions. In the garment industry, for example, a number of women joined locals of the International Ladies' Garment Workers Union. Their success in this particular industry might have come partially from the support of male trade unionists who needed their female counterparts to mount effective strikes. Still, unionized women workers remained more the exception than the rule.

Most unions also refused to support visible minorities such as blacks and Asians, seeing them as cheap labour that would undermine unionization. Since these minorities ended up

Knights of Labor procession, King Street, Hamilton, 1885. Parades were an expression of workers' solidarity and a means to achieve public recognition.

W. Farmer/Library and Archives Canada/PA-103086.

working only part-time or seasonal jobs, it was difficult for them to form their own unions. One exception was the occupation of railroad employees. In 1917, porters formed the Order of Sleeping Car Porters—the first African-Canadian railway union in North America. Although the Canadian Brotherhood of Railway Employees initially refused to accept the union, it did so in 1919, making it the first craft union to lift racial restrictions on membership.

The Provincial Workmen's Association, founded in 1879 by the coal miners of Springfield, Nova Scotia, became the Maritime equivalent of the Knights of Labor, and Canada's first industrial union. In 1909, however, the Scottish immigrant James Bryson McLachlan helped introduce to Cape Breton a more militant union, a branch of the American-based United Mine Workers of America. Ten years later, the miners at last gained the eight-hour day and made important gains in their standard of living.

In Newfoundland, William Ford Coaker, a local fisher, founded the Fishermen's Protective Union (FPU) in 1908 to protect fishers from the vagaries of curing weather, fish migration, and volatile markets. Its motto was "To each his own," believing fishers did not enjoy the benefits of their own labour nor the right to a decent living. Coaker advocated a "national plan" that consisted of free and compulsory education, a night-school system, nondenominational education in small outposts, outpost hospitals, and universal old-age pensions. The FPU turned to politics to attempt to achieve its objectives, and won eight seats in the Newfoundland Legislature in the 1913 election. But even here, it faced an uphill battle.

The Trades and Labor Congress of Canada (TLC), the central labour organization founded in 1883, established strong ties with the American Federation of Labor (AFL), a strictly craft-union organization. The conservative leadership of the AFL believed that the primary purpose of unions should be simply to improve the material benefits of its workers—better wages and hours and safer working conditions—rather than to radically reform the capitalist system.

Unskilled workers looked increasingly to politics or radical unions to achieve their objectives. Some worked to create an independent socialist party, while others supported radical unions, such as the Industrial Workers of the World (IWW), founded in 1905. The "Wobblies," as they became known, attempted to organize all workers, regardless of their trade, skill, or sex, into one large union for the purpose of calling a general strike to bring down the capitalist system. The IWW had little impact in eastern Canada but greater success in western Canada.

In the West, conditions remained poor for workers. Wages were exceptionally low, inflation high, employment sporadic, especially in the primary industries, and working conditions, especially in the mines and railway camps, atrocious.

In Quebec, the Roman Catholic Church formed church-affiliated unions as an alternative to what it considered to be socialist and anticlerical international unions that undermined the church's position among the working class. The largest was the *Confédération des Travailleurs Catholiques du Canada* (CTCC), an exclusively Roman Catholic organization founded in 1921, with a priest, as chaplain, effectively in charge of each local.

Limitations of Unions in the Prewar Era

In general, unions had limited success prior to World War I. As late as 1911, less than one-tenth of the national workforce belonged to unions. Most unskilled workers and virtually all women remained non-unionized. Unions were also divided, and their leaders suspicious of one another. Furthermore, unions had few rights. Employers could still fire union workers at will or demand that workers sign contracts in which they promised not to join a union. As well, employers brought in immigrant labourers on the condition that they work as strikebreakers or for extremely low wages. Nevertheless, unions did organize strikes—1000 disputes were recorded between 1900 and 1911. Many of them erupted into physical violence, with the government calling out the militia to end them. This happened on more than thirty occasions before 1914. Most strikes ended without workers gaining any significant concessions.

Governments clearly favoured business interests over workers. The federal Conservative government did, however, establish the Royal Commission on the Relations of Labour and Capital, which in its report in 1889 documented the negative impact of industrialization in Canada. Few reforms resulted from the report. In 1894, the Conservatives established Labour Day, the first Monday of September, as a national holiday for working people. The Laurier Liberal government created the Department of Labour in 1900 to prevent and settle strikes as well as to enforce a fair wage policy.

Skilled workers tried to gain influence through politics. They set out their own agenda, such as the sixteen-point program of the Trades and Labor Congress passed at its meeting in 1898, in which they demanded free compulsory education, an eight-hour day, a minimum wage, tax reform, public ownership of railways and telegraphs, extension of the franchise, abolition of the Senate, prohibition of prison and contract labour, legislative elimination of child labour, and opposition to Chinese immigration—the Chinese being perceived as a threat to labour's employment opportunities and wages. Then they tried to pressure the two traditional parties to adopt some or all of their recommendations. When this approach failed, they fielded their own labour candidates in federal, provincial, and municipal elections. While a few were elected, most labour politicians had limited success and impact, particularly at the federal and provincial levels. Overall, workers had a weak political voice in the pre–World War I era.

From 1880 to 1914, Canada underwent its industrial revolution as a result of the success of the National Policy, large-scale financial investment from within the country and abroad, and a new, more positive attitude toward business. Manufacturing and large-scale industrial production, and accompanying urban growth, meant increased prosperity and an overall higher standard of living. But not all regions of the country, nor all social classes, benefited equally from the economic expansion. The social costs of rapid change were high, especially for the urban poor. In times of need, they looked to charitable and social institutions, and ultimately to unions, for assistance. By the early twentieth century the injustices had become so noticeable that they gained public attention, especially among a rising group of middle-class social reformers.

NOTE

1. John Douglas Belshaw, *Colonization and Community: The Vancouver Island Coalfield and the Making of the British Columbian Working Class* (Montreal/Kingston: McGill-Queen's University Press, 2002).

BEYOND THE BOOK

Montreal 1850–1896: The Industrial City

http://www.mccord-museum.qc.ca/en/keys/webtours/VQ_P2_14_EN
This photographic exhibit details the visibly changing nature of Montreal during industrialization in the second half of the nineteenth century.

The Lions Gate Bridge

http://www.mccord-museum.qc.ca/en/keys/webtours/GE_P4_3_EN
A virtual exhibit with digitized photographs and artifacts regarding the building of the Lions Gate Bridge in Vancouver, British Columbia in the 1930s.

Winds of Change: Reform and Unions

http://www.mccord-museum.qc.ca/en/keys/webtours/GE_P4_4_EN
This photographic exhibit describes labour and social issues in Canada at the turn of the century, complete with cultural artifacts of the time.

Mackenzie King and Labour

http://www.collectionscanada.ca/king/053201/053201130201_e.html
This article describes Prime Minister Mackenzie King's positions on labour, industry, and social justice.

North of the Colour Line

http://www.historycooperative.org/journals/llt/47/02mathie.html
This article describes the story of African-Canadian workers on Canadian railways and their struggle for job security and unionization.

The Great Transformation

Canada: A People's History—Episode 11: The Great Transformation. Directed by Halya Kuchmij and Andrew Burnstein (CBC, 2001).

RELATED READINGS

The following article from R. Douglas Francis and Donald B. Smith, eds., *Viewpoints: Readings in Canadian History* (Toronto: Thomson Nelson, 2007) examines a topic covered in this chapter in greater depth: Bettina Bradbury, "Gender at Work at Home: Family Decisions, the Labour Market, and Girls' Contributions to the Family Economy," pp. 356–72.

BIBLIOGRAPHY

Michael Bliss's *Northern Enterprise: Five Centuries of Canadian Business* (Toronto: McClelland & Stewart, 1987) provides a comprehensive history of Canadian business. On economic development, consult Kenneth Norrie and Douglas Owram, *A History of the Canadian Economy*, 3rd ed. (Toronto: Nelson, 2002). Also of importance is Christopher Armstrong and H.V. Nelles, *Monopoly's Moment: The*

Organization and Regulation of Canadian Utilities, 1830–1930 (Philadelphia: Temple University Press, 1986). On Quebec consult also Paul-André Linteau, René Durocher, and Jean-Claude Robert, *Quebec: A History, 1867–1929* (Toronto: James Lorimer, 1983). Michael Bliss deals with Canadian business's attitudes in *A Living Profit: Studies in the Social History of Canadian Businessmen, 1883–1914* (Toronto: McClelland & Stewart, 1974).

On industrialization in the Maritimes, see T.W. Acheson, D. Frank, and J. Frost, *Industrialization and the Underdevelopment in the Maritimes, 1880 to 1930* (Toronto: Garamond Press, 1985); and Kris Inwood, *Farm, Factory and Fortune: New Studies in the Economic History of the Maritime Provinces* (Fredericton: Acadiensis Press, 1993). For Newfoundland, see David Alexander, "Economic Growth in the Atlantic Region, 1880–1940," in E. Seager, L. Fisher, and S. Pierson, comp., *Atlantic Canada and Confederation: Essays in Canadian Political Economy* (Toronto: University of Toronto Press, 1983), pp. 51–78. For studies in English of industrialization in Quebec, consult the endnotes for "Where Historians Disagree: Industrial Growth in Quebec" in this chapter. For Ontario's resource development, see H.V. Nelles, *The Politics of Development: Forests, Mines and Hydro-Electric Power in Ontario, 1849–1941* (Toronto: Macmillan, 1970). For a general debate on industrialism in Ontario, consult Ian Drummond, Louis P. Cain, and Marjorie Cohen, "CHR Dialogue: Ontario's Industrial Revolution," *Canadian Historical Review*, 69, 3 (September 1988): 283–314. On British Columbia, see Allen Saeger, "The Resource Economy, 1871–1921," in Hugh J.M. Johnston, ed., *The Pacific Province: A History of British Columbia* (Vancouver: Douglas & McIntyre, 1996), pp. 205–52; and Martin Robin, *The Rush for Spoils: The Company Province, 1871–1913* (Toronto: McClelland & Stewart, 1972).

For the impact of industrialization and urbanization and resource developments on the Aboriginal peoples in Ontario, consult Edward S. Rogers and Donald B. Smith, eds., *Aboriginal Ontario* (Toronto: Dundurn Press, 1994); and for British Columbia, Rolf Knight, *Indians at Work: An Informal History of Native Labour in British Columbia, 1848–1930* (Vancouver: New Star Books, 1996).

On urban trends in Canada, see J.M.S. Careless's booklet *The Rise of Cities in Canada before 1914* (Ottawa: Canadian Historical Association, 1978). For urbanization in the Maritimes, see J.M.S. Careless, "Aspects of Metropolitanism in Atlantic Canada," in M. Wade, ed., *Regionalism in the Canadian Community, 1867–1967* (Toronto: University of Toronto Press, 1969), pp. 117–29. On British Columbia, see Robert A.J. McDonald, *Making Vancouver: Class, Status, and Social Boundaries, 1863–1913* (Vancouver: University of British Columbia Press, 1996). On the Prairies, consult Paul Voisey, "The Urbanization of the Canadian Prairies, 1871–1916," *Histoire Sociale/Social History*, 8 (1975): 77–101; and A.F.J. Artibise, ed., *Town and City: Aspects of Western Canadian Urban Development* (Regina: Canadian Plains Research Center, University of Regina, 1981).

Concerned with the dynamics between rural life and urban and industrial growth are: Daniel Samson, ed., *Contested Countryside: Rural Workers and Modern Society in Atlantic Canada, 1800–1950* (Fredericton: Acadiensis Press, 1994); R.W. Sandwell, ed., *Beyond the City Limits: Rural History in British Columbia* (Vancouver: University of British Columbia Press, 1999); and Kenneth Michael Sylvester, *The Limits of Rural Capitalism: Family, Culture and Markets in Montcalm, Manitoba, 1870–1940* (Toronto: University of Toronto Press, 2001).

For the impact of industrialization and commercialization on the First Nations, see Arthur Ray, *I Have Lived Here since the World Began* (Toronto: Key Porter, 1996).

Working-class life in the major industrial city of Montreal at the turn of the century is discussed in T.J. Copp, *The Anatomy of Poverty: The Condition of the Working Class in Montreal, 1897–1929* (Toronto: McClelland & Stewart, 1974). For family life in Montreal, see Bettina Bradbury, *Working Families: Age, Gender and Daily Survival in Industrializing Montreal* (Toronto: McClelland & Stewart, 1993). For Toronto, see Gregory Kealey, *Toronto Workers Respond to Industrial Capitalism, 1867–1892* (Toronto: University of Toronto Press, 1980); and Michael Piva, *The Conditions of the Working Class in Toronto, 1900–1921* (Ottawa: University of Ottawa Press, 1979).

On women workers, see the relevant sections in Alison Prentice et al., *Canadian Women: A History*, 2nd ed. (Toronto: Harcourt Brace, 1996). For Ontario, see Marjorie Griffin Cohen, *Women's Work: Markets and Economic Development in Nineteenth-Century Ontario* (Toronto: University of Toronto

Press, 1988); and for the Maritimes, see Janet Guildford and Suzanne Morton, *Separate Spheres: Women's Worlds in the 19th-Century Maritimes* (Fredericton: Acadiensis Press, 1994).

On changing notions of sexuality, consult Angus McLaren and Arlene Tigar McLaren, *The Bedroom and the State: The Changing Practices and Politics of Contraception and Abortion in Canada, 1880– 1980* (Toronto: McClelland & Stewart, 1986).

The labour movement is discussed in Craig Heron, *The Canadian Labour Movement: A Short History*, rev. ed. (Toronto: James Lorimer, 1996); and Bryan Palmer, *Working-Class Experience: Rethinking the History of Canadian Labour, 1800–1991* (Toronto: McClelland & Stewart, 1992). On the making of a working-class community in the coalfields of Vancouver Island, see John Douglas Belshaw, *Colonization and Community: The Vancouver Island Coalfield and the Making of the British Columbian Working Class* (Montreal/Kingston: McGill-Queen's University Press, 2002).

Chapter Sixteen

SOCIAL REFORM AND CULTURE: 1867–1914

TIME LINE

Year	Event
1867	The Society of Canadian Artists forms
1874	The Woman's Christian Temperance Union (WCTU) begins
1877	Toronto Women's Literary Club becomes the first Canadian women's suffrage organization
1880	Calixa Lavallée composes "O Canada"
1885	Banff National Park is created
1886	The Amateur Hockey Association of Canada forms
1887	First North American bird sanctuary established at Last Mountain Lake, North-West Territories
1891	James Naismith invents basketball
1893	Algonquin Park established in Ontario Wilfred Grenville begins his mission in Newfoundland and Labrador Lord Stanley donates Stanley Cup
1894	Fred Victor Mission founded in Toronto The Toronto Mendelssohn Choir forms
1895	The Reading Camp Association, the forerunner of Frontier College, begins
1903	*Hiawatha* is the first Canada feature film
1909	Governor General Earl Grey donates Grey Cup

Social reform and cultural developments in the late nineteenth and early twentieth centuries were attempts to create a more just and cultured Canada as the nation expanded territorially and evolved into a predominantly urban and industrial society. Various social reform movements arose to address the social injustices and to solve the social problems that they perceived arising as Canada underwent large-scale industrialization and rapid urbanization. Social gospellers in English-speaking Canada, social action advocates in French-speaking Canada, educational reformers, urban reformers, conservationists, women reformers, and prohibitionists all had their own perspective on what was wrong and offered their unique solutions, but they were united in their hope that the result would be a better, if not an ideal, Canada. Collectively, these reformers made positive changes in Canadian society that assisted the less fortunate and marginalized individuals. However, their ultimate goal of an ideal reformed Canada still eluded them on the eve of World War I.

Cultural enthusiasts looked to improvements in the arts and to the cultivation of popular culture as the best means to create a better, regenerated Canada to offset the growing materialism and debasement that they saw as negative byproducts of urbanization and industrialization. Upper-class Canadians worked for advancements in what today we call the fine arts—music, drama, and the visual arts—along with literature. Middle-class and working-class Canadians were more interested in popular culture. The middle class found enjoyment in such leisure activities as roller skating and dancing, or attending movie theatres and fairs. The working class increasingly enjoyed these same activities, but were more inclined to find enjoyment and camaraderie in taverns, picnics, and festivities. All three groups—upper, middle, and lower—enjoyed sports, although the kinds of sport they participated in and supported varied. By 1914, popular culture had surpassed elite culture, and professional sport prevailed over amateur sport. In both cases—popular culture and professional sport—Canadian culture became more Americanized as a result.

Social Gospel and Catholic Social Action

The Protestant Social Gospel Movement in English Canada

The social gospel movement in English Canada, part of a larger religious revival movement in Britain and the United States, aimed at applying Christianity to solving society's ills so as to create a perfect "Kingdom of God on Earth." The movement developed partially in response to a challenge to religious beliefs from the Darwinian concept of evolution. In *The Origin of Species* (1859) and *The Descent of Man* (1871), Charles Darwin, an English naturalist, advanced his theory that humans had evolved, over millions of years, from earlier forms of life in the animal kingdom. Darwin's arguments challenged the orthodox Christian belief that God created humans in his own likeness and as special beings during the six days of creation.

At the same time that science challenged contemporary Christian theology, a new philosophy of "higher criticism" presented the Bible as a document written by humans, and therefore not the divine and absolute word of God. The Bible may contain moral and religious, but not historical and scientific, truths. In response, a number of church leaders directed their attention away from theological questions to social issues. The new emerging industrialized Canada had a host of social problems that needed to be addressed.

Social gospellers regarded people as inherently good. If individuals erred, they did so not because of any basic weakness or maliciousness of character but because of their social environment. Social gospellers believed in environmental determinism, that environment shaped character. If they could improve social conditions, then people's character would change for the good, which would result in an ideal Christian society.

Social gospellers wanted the church to concern itself with social problems: prostitution, alcoholism, and intolerable living and working conditions, rather than with such "personal sins" as drunkenness, sex, and slovenliness. The Reverend S.D. Chown of the Methodist church summed up the new attitude in a lecture in 1905: "The first duty of a Christian is to be a citizen, or a man amongst men. We are under no obligation to get into heaven, that is a matter entirely of our own option; but we are under obligation to quit sin and to bring heaven down to this earth." Social gospellers strove to create in this world a humane society based on the Christian principles of love, charity, humanity, brotherhood, and democracy.

While united in their aspiration to improve the quality of life, social gospellers were divided on the means to achieve it. As many ways to regenerate and reform society existed as there were regenerators and reformers. But social gospellers can be classified into five broad categories: advocates of direct social assistance; social purists; those who advocated a change of attitude as the means to social change; state interventionists; and socialists.

The "direct social assistance" advocates worked to give immediate aid to society's destitute through the establishment of missions and settlement houses. The most famous of the missions were the St. Andrews Institute, founded by Rev. D.J. Macdonell of the Presbyterian church, and the Fred Victor Mission, begun by the Methodist church with financial assistance from the wealthy Massey family. Both missions were in the slums of downtown Toronto. In Newfoundland, Dr. Wilfred Grenfell established his Grenfell Mission in 1893 to help improve the appalling social conditions he found in northern Newfoundland outposts and along the Labrador coast. Thirteen settlement houses existed across Canada by 1920, offering the basic necessities of food and shelter and, often, a night school and a library. Many provided medical care. Others included gymnasiums, clubrooms, savings banks, and nurseries. The Salvation Army, started by William Booth in England, also established centres in Canada at the turn of the century to help the poor.

A second group, social purists, concerned themselves with issues of sexual vice, such as prostitution (often referred to as "the social evil"), homosexuality, venereal disease, "feeblemindedness" (which they believed resulted from masturbation), and abortion. They sought to eliminate these "evils" by regulating and legislating sexual relations as a means to ensure racial purity and social control.

Initially, sexual control came through the churches, but increasingly came under the control of the state. Cities hired social workers, experts on prisons, and psychiatrists to present the latest "scientific" theories, to educate the public on proper moral standards, and to work with the "sexual deviants" in the jails and mental institutions. Some social theorists, known as "eugenicists," argued for selective breeding by preventing people deemed to have undesirable mental and physical traits from reproducing. All too often the "unfit" and "inferior" were also foreigners, thus adding an ethnic component to the eugenics movement.

The courts assisted the state in regulating morality. In 1892, the Criminal Code itemized offences to "protect" young girls and women by imposing stiff penalties of up to fourteen years on brothel operators and those who enticed women into prostitution. It also legislated against "gross indecency," which referred

A Salvation Army meeting in Calgary, late August 1887. Meetings featured testimony, prayer, music, and song. The Salvation Army, begun by General William Booth in England, came to Canada in 1882.

Library and Archives Canada/C-14426.

to homosexual acts. In Toronto, both juvenile and women's courts were established to deal with issues of promiscuity and "vagrancy."

A third group of social gospellers worked to change people's attitudes. They believed that attitudes of greed, competition, and materialism caused society's problems. Through education, people could learn of the greater benefits of living in a society governed by Christian principles of love, charity, brotherhood, and democracy. In 1918, William Lyon Mackenzie King, about to become the leader of the federal Liberal party, published *Industry and Humanity*, in which he argued that social salvation would come to a society that practised the ethical laws of Christianity. Education, he believed, would teach those ethical laws and inculcate proper moral values.

A fourth group of social reformers believed in state intervention. They argued that the concept of laissez-faire—the belief that governments should not upset the natural laws of the marketplace—had been used by the wealthy in society to exploit the poor. They advocated, instead, state intervention to provide essential social services and welfare assistance for the unemployed and the disabled, and to regulate industry and nationalize key industries to ensure that they served the public good.

For a few social gospellers, such as J.S. Woodsworth—then a Methodist minister, later the founder of the Co-operative Commonwealth Federation (CCF)—innovative reforms and state-regulated social services could only come about through a fundamental restructuring of society. Woodsworth believed that the "ideal Kingdom of Jesus" was a socialist paradise where everyone worked for the well-being of the whole rather than for its individual parts. True social reform meant replacing capitalism with socialism.

By World War I, social reform was shifting from a religious and social gospel to a secular and scientific approach. Reformers were increasingly professionally trained in the social sciences rather than schooled in religion. Social activists were replaced by social workers and sociologists; moral purists replaced by doctors and psychiatrists in the medical profession and by lawyers and judges in the legal profession. These professionals allied themselves with the state to bring about social change, thus contributing to increased government control over the regulation of individuals, even in their private lives.

The Roman Catholic Social Action Movement in Quebec

Social reformers in Quebec worked for reform through the Roman Catholic church. They believed that the family and the church, rather than the state, were the best institutions to deal with social problems. In 1911, the Jesuits founded the Montreal-based École Sociale Populaire (ESP) to develop a social doctrine for the church. The ESP published pamphlets, organized study groups and retreats, and worked to sensitize the clergy to the social needs of their parishioners.

Many priests supported the *caisses populaires*, credit unions founded in 1900 by Alphonse Desjardins, to assist French-Canadian enterprises to get started in hopes of improving the living standards of the working class and of bringing economic liberation to the Quebec people.

Some French-Canadian priests also promoted Catholic unions for Quebec workers. Church leaders feared that workers in secular unions, especially American-controlled ones, would become too materialistic and too socialistic in their outlook.

Educational Reformers

By the turn of the century, a new generation of educational reformers, strongly influenced by Friedrich Froebel, a European philosopher, advocated a child-oriented education that treated children as children, not miniature adults, by providing them with love and by protecting them from the harsh realities of adult life.

To some educational reformers, kindergartens provided the answer. James L. Hughes, a Toronto school inspector, and his future wife, Ada Marean, established the first Canadian public school kindergarten in 1883. Four years later, Ontario formally incorporated kindergartens into the public school system. The Free Kindergarten Association in Winnipeg advocated the same for Manitoba, arguing that "the proper education of children during the first seven years of their lives" did "much to reduce poverty and crime in any community." In Montreal and Quebec City, nuns ran *salles d'asile* or daycare centres for children of working parents. Between 1898 and 1902, more than 10 000 children attended. In addition to these centres, which offered care on a daily basis, orphanages, provincial asylums, and homes for the poor also provided care for children of destitute families.

Other educational reformers pursued temperance education to warn children of the evils of alcohol, while still others demanded social programs in public health and in physical and mental hygiene. All educational reformers appreciated the importance of extended and free schooling. They succeeded by 1905 in getting all provinces except Quebec to legislate free schooling and compulsory attendance for youngsters up to the age of twelve.

The Urban Reform Movement

Urban reformers formed an important part of social reform at the turn of the century. Inspired by the "City Beautiful" movement in the United States and Europe, they believed that reform must include a humane and beautiful urban environment—the physical structure of the city, its aesthetic nature, and the quality of its municipal government.

A host of professionals—engineers, architects, surveyors, medical people, and urban planners—offered advice on how to create the perfect city. Architects emphasized the need for stately buildings, while urban planners stressed parks, treed boulevards, and adequate housing. Medical professionals argued for clean water and air, and campaigned for pasteurized milk as a means to decrease the high rate of infant mortality in Canadian cities, especially Montreal and Toronto.

Wilderness and Wildlife Conservation

The idea of conservation emerged slowly in Canada, cultivated by back-to-nature movements, such as the Alpine Club and Field-Naturalists' Clubs. Woodcraft Clubs, and the Boy Scout and Girl Guides movements, promoted the importance of a wilderness experience for good health, spiritual rejuvenation, and refuge from hectic city life. Schools in British Columbia, Nova Scotia, Ontario, and Alberta initiated nature study classes in the first decade of the twentieth century through the initiative of naturalists' societies, farm organizations, and experimental farms. Novelist Ernest Seton wrote realistic animal stories, such as *Wild Animals I Have Known* (1898), that were popular with Canadian youth.

By the early twentieth century, the overexploitation of the country's wildlife was becoming obvious. The plains bison herds disappeared on the Canadian side of the border as early as 1879. By 1900, the great prairie herds of pronghorn antelope declined to a tiny fraction of their original number. Hunted thoroughly, the passenger pigeon had vanished from Nova Scotia by 1857, from Manitoba by 1898, and from Ontario by 1902. (The last surviving member of this once abundant species died in an Ohio zoo in 1912.) By 1900, trumpeter swans had disappeared from eastern Canada, as had wild turkeys before them. In 1887, the first bird sanctuary in North America opened at Last Mountain Lake, in present-day Saskatchewan.

The federal government responded slowly to the need for conservation. In 1885, it took the first step in the creation of Canada's national parks by reserving more than 26 km^2 of land around the mineral springs near the railway station of Banff. Two years later, it extended the area to 675 km^2 and officially turned the reserve into a national park, Rocky Mountains Park (renamed Banff in 1930). In 1893, the Ontario government established Algonquin Park, south of North Bay, as the province's first wilderness area. Other provinces followed Ontario's example in establishing their own provincial parks. In 1909 the federal government established the Commission of Conservation (1909–1921), which helped to secure the passage in 1917 of the Canada–United States Migratory Birds Convention Treaty, an agreement that was supposed to ensure international protection for migratory bird populations throughout their ranges. In 1919, the Canadian government also convened the first national wildlife conference to discuss with the provinces how best to conserve the country's wildlife.

Later, in the 1930s, the popularity of a man known as Grey Owl assisted the conservation movement. Born Archie Belaney, he took on the identity of an Ojibwa upon coming to Canada from England in 1907. He learned the Aboriginal view of the world, based on a belief that all animals, fowls, fish, trees, and stones were endowed with immortal spirits and possessed supernatural powers. Humans were a part of this animated world, not its master. Through his books, films, and lectures, he presented this perspective, and promoted the protection of Canada's wilderness and wildlife.

Women and Social Reform

By the 1890s, a "new woman" had appeared, demanding an active role in reforming society. Local, provincial, and national women's organizations such as the Woman's Christian Temperance Union, the National Council of Women, the Young Women's Christian Association (YWCA), and the Dominion Women's Enfranchisement Association were a few of the organizations that assisted women in reaching out to society. By 1912 an estimated one out of every eight adult women—the majority of them middle-aged, middle-class, English-speaking Protestants—belonged to a women's group, thus making these organizations influential agents of social reform.

"Rocking the cradle for the world" was how Nellie McClung, an influential reformer, saw women's new role. She wrote:

> Women must be made to feel their responsibilities. All this protective love, their instinctive mother love, must be organized in some way, and made effective. There is enough of it in the world to do away with all the evils which war upon childhood: undernourishment, slum conditions, child labour, drunkenness. Women could abolish all these if they wanted to.

These reform-minded women argued that men had controlled society for ages without making any appreciable improvements; now it was women's turn.

Adelaide (Hunter) Hoodless, another social reformer, offered domestic science or home economics classes through the YWCA as a means to teach young women about nutrition and proper health measures. Later she assisted in having the subject introduced in the schools, and eventually at the Ontario Agricultural College in Guelph and at McGill University in Montreal. In 1897, she started the first Women's Institute near Stoney Creek, south of Hamilton, Ontario as another means to help women increase their knowledge of farm and household management. She also helped found the Victorian Order of Nurses to offer nursing and housekeeping services to impoverished invalids.

The Women's Suffrage Movement

Many women reformers saw the right to vote as the means by which women could obtain the power to reform society. The women's suffrage movement began in Ontario, but had its greatest successes in the prairie provinces. In the newer settler society of the west, women played a more active role, often working alongside their husbands in establishing a homestead and building a farm. They also took the initiative to reform society in an effort to achieve greater gender equality. Early on, they won the support of western farm organizations that also struggled for national recognition and were, therefore, better able to empathize with women's efforts for equality. The prairie farmers' newspaper, the *Grain Growers' Guide*, founded in 1908, added a women's column to its paper in 1911, while the Grain Growers' Association of Manitoba, Saskatchewan, and Alberta endorsed women's suffrage as early as 1912.

The West had several outspoken women actively involved in the struggle for female suffrage, such as Henrietta Edwards, Emily Murphy, Louise McKinney, Nellie McClung, and Irene Parlby. Perhaps Nellie McClung, with her gift for oratory, her energy, and her delightful sense of humour, best epitomized the suffrage movement. Her spirited leadership rallied many others to the cause of women's suffrage. In 1912, she joined the Winnipeg Political Equality League, and then in 1916, on the eve of the Manitoba provincial election in which women's suffrage was an issue, she wrote *In Times Like These*, a witty but powerful social commentary on suffrage. The suffragists made their first breakthrough in that election when the Liberals came to power. The new government introduced a suffrage bill, making Manitoba the first province in Canada to grant women the right to vote.

WHERE HISTORIANS DISAGREE

Women and Reform

Canadian gender history, although a relatively new field of historical study, has already raised a healthy historical debate. One contentious issue has been the primary motive behind the women's reform movement. The first historians to write on the subject in the 1960s and early 1970s argued that women reformers sought only the right to vote—women's suffrage—believing that political equality would bring about an era of societal reform. This narrow focus on the ballot box seemed to explain why the movement for reform died out so rapidly in the 1920s, once women's suffrage had been achieved.

Some historians see women's reform as part of a greater "progressive reform" movement that went well beyond a concern for the enfranchisement of women. In his introduction to a reprint of Catharine L. Cleverdon's classic study, *The Woman Suffrage Movement in Canada*, Ramsay Cook linked women's reform to the larger social gospel movement. "The suffragists were a part of a more general, middle-class reform movement that was concerned to remove a wide range of injustices and evils that afflicted the country."[1]

Other historians question this idealized image of women reformers as being motivated purely by religious zeal. Historian Veronica Strong-Boag argues that power, fame, and influence motivated them, at least those associated with the influential National Council of Women of Canada. She notes that "the female relatives of Canada's powerful men, energized by a changing external environment and by their own recent access to higher education and the professions, had few formal ways of expressing their complementary desires for national leadership and influence."[2] In short, these middle-class women reformers worried more about their own position of power in society than about the disadvantaged.

Carol Bacchi applied the feminist theories of the 1980s to the leaders of the suffrage movement in the 1910s, and found the suffragists wanting.[3] She argued that suffrage leaders were middle-class reformers more than they were feminists, and as such were more conservative than radical in outlook. They succeeded in getting the vote for women, according to Bacchi, only because men in positions of power at the time realized that giving women the right to vote would not upset the status quo. In a review of Bacchi's book,[4] which was based essentially on a study only of women leaders in Montreal, Toronto, and the Prairies, historian Ernest Forbes, relying on his own work on Halifax women reformers, challenged her conclusions. In Halifax, at least, according to Forbes, suffrage leaders were feminists before they were reformers, and used their position to encourage women to get out of the home, and even provided them with opportunities to do so. In this respect, they were "revolutionary" in aspiration. Furthermore, he argued that although Halifax suffragists were from the middle class, they addressed working-class issues. Thus Forbes appealed for more "local studies" to help draw a definitive conclusion about suffragists on a national level.

Historian Margot Iris Dudley took up Forbes's challenge and examined the women's suffrage movement in Newfoundland.[5] She discovered a group of women reformers who crossed class lines and even religious divisions between Catholics and Protestants, and who allied themselves with the International Alliance of Women, based in London, England. Her study called into question the assumption that the women's suffrage movement in Canada was middle-class, Protestant, and narrowly national.

More recently, some women historians have concentrated on the 1920s to see whether the women's reform movement died out after political emancipation as previously believed. Historians Linda Kealey and Joan Sangster have studied a group of "radical women" in the 1920s to show that, for these women, left-wing politics became the means to achieve real change, something that was not possible in the more conservative social reform movement.[6] Nevertheless, these women had to adopt male tactics and abandon the "private sphere" in order to succeed in the traditionally male-dominated "public sphere."

Veronica Strong-Boag has reentered the debate to argue that the real struggle for reform did not take place in politics—in the public sphere—but rather in a highly politicized private sphere. "Theirs was the feminism of the workplace, day-to-day life. It was not for the most part an organized movement as the campaign for enfranchisement had been, but it flowed from a similar awareness of women's oppression and a desire to end it."[7] Strong-Boag's study underlines the need to rethink the categories of political/apolitical, public/private, and male/female.

Linda Kealey appeals for a broader definition of "public" and "political" in dealing with women reformers to include "the home, the neighbourhood, and the community, as well as ... the union, the party, or the workplace."[8] She argues that some socialist women reformers were concerned with women workers as wage earners or working-class wives and mothers, while others advocated a radical transformation of the industrial capitalist system. In either case, they succeeded in bringing working-class women's issues into the public domain, despite opposition from men and even middle-class female reformers.

Janice Newton shows how Canadian women reformers within the socialist movement rejected the middle-class obsession of the suffragists to get the vote and instead worked for equality of working-class women through such organizations as the Canadian Socialists League, the Socialist Party of Canada, and the Social Democratic Party.[9]

Monda Halpern has examined social reform among Ontario farm women. She argues that farm women spoke the language of "social feminism," which she defines as being "informed by domestic community needs and values."[10] Those values were ones of nurturing, cooperation, love, and peace, ones that were closely associated with maternal feminism. By applying these values in the public domain, she argues, farm women succeeded in challenging patriarchy to a greater extent than equity feminists, such as the suffragists.

It is ironic that just as Canadian women obtained a political voice, First Nations women were denied one. Under their traditional system of governance, for example, the women of the Six Nations (Iroquois) Confederacy chose the Confederacy's chiefs, but under the Indian Act of 1880, they did not even have a vote in community decisions. This topic deserves to be studied.

Five Iroquois women of the Grand River community, photo probably taken in the 1870s. The woman holding the book, second from the left, is Ellen Loft, Fred Loft's mother. Fred Loft later founded the League of Indians of Canada, the first pan-Indian Aboriginal organization in Canada.

Courtesy of the late Bernice Loft, granddaughter of Ellen Loft.

Presentation of a petition by the Winnipeg Political Equality League for the Enfranchisement of Women, December 23, 1915. Mrs. Amelia Burritt, then 93 years old, gave the document to the provincial government. In 1916, Manitoba became Canada's first province to grant women the franchise.

Archives of Manitoba/Events 173/3 (N9905).

1. Ramsay Cook, "Introduction" to Catharine L. Cleverdon, *The Woman Suffrage Movement in Canada* (1950). Reprint. (Toronto: University of Toronto Press, 1974), p. xvii.

2. Veronica Strong-Boag, *The Parliament of Women: The National Council of Women of Canada, 1893–1929* (Ottawa: Canadian Museum of Civilization, 1976), p. 410.

3. Carol Bacchi, *Liberation Deferred? The Ideas of the English Canadian Suffragists, 1877–1918* (Toronto: University of Toronto Press, 1983).

4. Ernest Forbes, "The Ideas of Carol Bacchi and the Suffragists of Halifax," *Atlantis*, 10, 2 (Spring 1985): 119–26.

5. Margot Iris Dudley, "The Radius of Her Influence for Good: The Rise and Triumph of the Women's Suffrage Movement in Newfoundland, 1909–1925," in Linda Kealey, ed., *Pursuing Equality: Historical Perspectives on*

Women in Newfoundland and Labrador (St. John's: Institute of Social and Economic Research, Memorial University, 1993).

6. Linda Kealey and Joan Sangster, *Beyond the Vote: Canadian Women and Politics* (Toronto: University of Toronto Press, 1989).

7. Veronica Strong-Boag, "Pulling in Double Harness or Hauling a Double Load: Women, Work and Feminism on the Canadian Prairies," *Journal of Canadian Studies*, 21 (Fall 1986): 34.

8. Linda Kealey, *Enlisting Women for the Cause: Women, Labour, and the Left in Canada, 1890–1920* (Toronto: University of Toronto Press, 1988), p. 10.

9. Janice Newton, *The Feminist Challenge to the Canadian Left, 1900–1918* (Montreal/Kingston: McGill-Queen's University Press, 1995).

10. Monda Halpern, *And on That Farm He Had a Wife: Ontario Farm Women and Feminism, 1900–1970* (Montreal/Kingston: McGill-Queen's University Press, 2001), p. 8.

Women Reformers in Quebec

Women involved in social reform in Quebec had a more difficult battle than their sisters in English-speaking Canada, since the image of women as mothers and guardians of the home was more entrenched in the French-Canadian ethos than it was in English Canada. Nevertheless, the local council in Quebec of the National Council of Women of Canada, founded by Marie Lacoste Gérin-Lajoie, Caroline Béique, and Josephine Dandurand in 1907, became a forum for French-speaking women who advocated women's suffrage. The Fédération nationale Saint-Jean-Baptiste, another reform-minded organization, fought for such causes as the pasteurizing of milk to reduce infant mortality, better working conditions for women, and the elimination of alcoholism and prostitution. It also contributed to better women teachers' pensions, improved working conditions for women in factories and stores, increased home economics courses, and established pure-milk depots.

The Prohibition Movement

Throughout Canada, many women reformers worked for prohibition. Prohibitionists argued that the only way to eradicate drinking was to prohibit it through government legislation. However, the division of jurisdiction over alcohol between the federal and provincial governments complicated the question. The federal government had the power to restrict the manufacture of, and interprovincial trade in, alcoholic beverages, but provincial governments controlled retail sales. Thus, prohibitionists had to apply pressure on both levels of government.

They achieved an initial victory in 1878 with the passage of the Scott Act, which allowed the residents of each municipality or county to decide by a simple majority vote whether their constituency would be "wet" or "dry." Prohibitionists, however, demanded that governments outlaw the liquor trade completely. The federal Conservative government delayed acting on the issue until the mid-1890s, when it established the Royal Commission on the Liquor Traffic. During the election campaign of 1896, Laurier and the Liberals promised a plebiscite on the question of prohibition if they gained office. When they won, the prohibitionists held them to their promise.

The results of Canada's first plebiscite were split. Every province except Quebec voted on the dry side. But voter turnout throughout Canada had been low—only 44 percent. Furthermore, of those who did vote, only a small majority of about 13 000 had favoured prohibition. Laurier used these "indecisive" results to avoid enacting legislation that he feared would divide the nation. The Liberals' refusal to follow through on their promise angered the prohibitionists and gave them even greater resolve to banish alcohol.

The Woman's Christian Temperance Union (WCTU), formed in Ontario in 1874 and quickly becoming a national organization with some 16 000 members by 1914, identified alcoholism as the greatest single cause of domestic violence and divorce. They linked prohibition with women's suffrage. If women had the right to vote, they argued, alcohol abuse would end. As Mrs. Jacob Spence, first superintendent of the Ontario WCTU's Franchise Department, noted: "The liquor sellers are not afraid of our conventions but they are afraid of our ballots." For many prohibitionists, drunkenness became associated with "foreigners." For them, controlling alcohol offered a means of regulating immigrants and of ensuring their conformity in a heterogeneous society.

Despite their efforts, however, prohibitionists remained in the minority before World War I. On the eve of the Great War, only Prince Edward Island had implemented provincial prohibition, while on the national level the federal government had resisted pressure to restrict the production, and interprovincial distribution, of "demon rum" and all liquor in general.

Canadian Culture

Culture refers to activities associated with education and leisure. In the late nineteenth and early twentieth centuries, it was expressed in such traditional areas as music, drama, and the visual arts—along with literature. Interest in cultivating these areas of culture was predominantly the domain of the upper class or the social elite of society. This elite saw culture as a way of transferring and maintaining the values, beliefs, and ideals of British society into Canada; culture, in essence, was one way to ensure a continuity with the mother country and the centre of Western civilization in Europe, thus offsetting the limitations of living in an isolated part of the world where harsh conditions mitigated against cultural sophistication and where living next door to the United States posed a constant threat.

Music

While music was the most widespread of cultural activities in the late nineteenth century in both English-speaking and French-speaking Canada, only a few choral groups or orchestras achieved national fame or performed at the level of comparable groups in European society. The most famous were the James Street Baptist Church Choir in Toronto, consisting of 250 voices, the Toronto Mendelssohn Choir, the Montreal Oratorio Society, the Société musicale des Montagnards Canadiens and Les Orphéonistes de Montréal.

Calixa Lavallée, the composer of "O Canada." Ironically, this work, which has been Canada's national anthem since 1980, was originally composed in 1880 for St. Jean Baptiste Day, now recognized as Quebec's national holiday.

Heritage Canada 5 (2) (May 1979): 13.

Notable Canadian composers included Guillaume Couture, organist and conductor of the Montreal Philharmonic Society, and William Reed, who composed the organ recital *Grand Choeur in D Major*, considered to be one of the finest organ works written by a Canadian. However, by far the most popular was Calixa Lavallée. His fame came from his composition "O Canada" in 1880, first performed at the request of the Société Saint-Jean-Baptiste in Quebec City. It was an immediate hit. The English-Canadian equivalent to "O Canada" was "The Maple Leaf Forever," originally a patriotic poem written for a poetry contest in Montreal, where it won second prize, and then put to music by Alexander Muir, a Toronto school principal.

Local church choruses, bands, and orchestras proliferated in the late nineteenth century. Many of the brass bands formed around militia camps as a form of local entertainment for the troops. But some of the most impressive were in Indian residential schools as a means to impose discipline and order.

Opera had an appeal for the upper class. Tour companies performed a variety of operas from grand to ballad and comic. Most of these tours originated in Europe, and then came to North America. However, by the turn of the twentieth century, the major cities of Montreal, Quebec City, and Toronto had their own local opera companies.

The nineteenth century is often referred to in musical circles as the "age of the virtuoso"—a time when gifted soloists astounded the public with superb performances. Canada's most internationally known virtuoso was Emma Albani. Born Marie Lajeunesse in Chambly, near Montreal, in 1847, she adopted the stage name Emma Albani while on a European tour in the early 1870s. The French-Canadian diva sang at the best opera houses in Europe. She made various visits from her home in England to Canada—in 1883, 1889, and a grand tour from Halifax to Victoria in 1896–1897.

Visual Arts

In 1860, on the occasion of the official opening of the Victoria Bridge, a magnificent structure that spanned the St. Lawrence River from Montreal to Longueuil, the government of the Canadas held a "Great Exhibition" of Canadian art in Montreal. The exhibition contained paintings by Quebec's famed Cornelius Kreighoff, known for his quaint depictions of habitant life, and by Charles Jones Way, a younger artist from England whose majestic paintings of Canadian scenery caught the eye of the Prince of Wales upon his visit to British North America that year. Also on exhibit were photographs by William Notman, a Scot who by 1860 had established a thriving photograph studio in downtown Montreal. In the 1860s and 1870s, the Notmans opened over a dozen branches in Ottawa, Saint John, Halifax, and even several eastern American cities. Many of Canada's aspiring artists of the day began their careers in Notman's Studio.

After the "Great Exhibition," English-speaking artists in the city formed the Art Association of Montreal. It became the nucleus for the Society of Canadian Artists, founded in 1867. The society set an ambitious goal: to foster a pan-Canadian artistic tradition so as to make Canadian artists known both within Canada and abroad. Shortly after the formation of the Montreal society, the Ontario Society of Artists formed in 1872. They promised to do everything in their power to promote Canadian art, including holding annual exhibitions of their works and working toward the building of a permanent public art gallery in Toronto. Out of these two societies, the one in Montreal and the other in Toronto, came the beginnings of the Canadian Academy of the Arts, founded in 1880 with the help of Governor General Lord Lorne. A year later, Queen Victoria officially prefixed "Royal" to its title. Lucius R. O'Brien, famous for his romantic paintings of the Saguenay region of southern Quebec, became its first president, a position he held for ten years. Women countered with their own organization, the Women's Art Association. Established in 1890, it soon spawned branches throughout the country to support women artists.

O'Brien was also the chief Canadian contributor, with almost one-quarter of the 500 illustrations, to the two-volume *Picturesque Canada*, the most ambitious publishing project of the day when launched in 1876. George Munro Grant, principal of Queen's University and a Canadian art enthusiast, wrote the text, in which he overlooked the American visual contributions and instead underscored the importance of the volumes for the growth of a

Lucius R. O'Brien, Sunrise on the Saguenay, *1880. This painting, first exhibited at the opening of the Royal Canadian Academy of the Arts in 1880, won O'Brien much praise and recognition. Sunrise is traditionally considered to have been the first work entered into the collection of the National Gallery of Canada.*

Lucius R. O'Brien *Sunrise on the Saguenay, Cape Trinity,*1880 Photo © National Gallery of Canada National Gallery of Canada, Ottawa Royal Canadian Academy of Arts diploma work, deposited by the artist, Toronto, 1880.

pan-Canadian nationalism. "I believe that a work that would represent its characteristic scenery and the history and life of its people," he wrote, "would not only make us better known to ourselves and to strangers, but would also stimulate national sentiment and contribute to the rightful development of the nation." Grant's text and O'Brien's paintings together reflected the growing national spirit of English-speaking Canadians, who looked to the Canadian landscape for the essence and the soul of Canada. (Individuals like Grant did not, however, look to the First Nations for future strength for Canada. In *Picturesque Canada*, the principal of Queen's University himself contributed the article on "The North-West Manitoba," in which he wrote: "The Indians of Manitoba are gradually disappearing before the stronger races.")

While some Canadian artists were looking for Canada's identity in its landscape, others found it in the country folk. The Quebec artist Wyall Eaton took the Quebec habitant as his subject. Horatio Walker of Ontario did a six-month walking tour along the St. Lawrence River from Montreal to Quebec City in which he painted scenes of French-Canadian farmers and farm life. His colleague, Homer Watson, did the same for Ontario rural folk. Walker and Watson were joined by William Brymner, Paul Peel, and George Reid, other Ontario artists who had studied in Paris, as well as Robert Harris of Prince Edward Island. Peel would become one of Canada's best-known painters in Europe in the late nineteenth century.

Canadian artists got an opportunity for international fame when the British government invited Canada to contribute paintings to a Colonial and Indian Exhibition in London, England in 1886, the year preceding Queen Victoria's Golden Jubilee. The Canadian display included works by such established painters as Adolphe Vogt, William Raphael, John A. Fraser, and O'Brien. But it was the paintings of the younger, Paris-trained group that caught the attention of British art critics.

Canadian Literature

English-Canadian poetry became established in the 1880s. The "Confederation Poets"—the name literary critics have given to the four poets Charles G.D. Roberts, Bliss Carman, Archibald Lampman, and Duncan Campbell Scott—gave a spiritual dimension to Confederation. They sought the essence of Canada in nature—in the physical world of rocks, streams, and woods, and in the country lifestyle of the farmer and lumberjack. They depicted nature in the highly romantic terms of the British Romantic poets who inspired them. They were the literary equivalent of the Canada First movement, and of the Canadian Academy of the Arts, seeking to discover the soul of the new nation.

Isabella Valancy Crawford depicted nature as half-human, as possessing a soul that was very much in tune with the human soul. In her mind, both "souls" struggled with love and death—common themes in her nature poetry. Pauline Johnson became the most famous female poet in the late nineteenth century. Johnson—or Tekahionwake, her Mohawk name—celebrated her Iroquois heritage, at the same time expressing a Canadian, and an imperial, feeling. In her poem "Canadian Born," she expressed her imperialistic fervour:

> *The Dutch may have their Holland, the Spaniard have his Spain,*
> *The Yankee to the south of us must south of us remain;*
> *For not a man dare lift a hand against the men who brag*
> *That they were born in Canada beneath the British flag.*

In Quebec, a generation of poets used François-Xavier Garneau's magisterial *Histoire du Canada*, published between 1845 and 1848, along with folklore, patriotic feeling, and religion, as themes for their poetry.

However, Quebec's poetry came into its own with the École littéraire de Montréal, founded in 1895. The École received acclaim for its poetry, which broke free of the patriotic-romantic verse that then dominated. Its most famous member was Émile Nelligan. This poet of genius produced some 170 poems when he was between the ages of seventeen and twenty. Perhaps his best-known is *"Le Vaisseau d'or"* ("Ship of Gold"). Unfortunately, Nelligan lost his grip on reason in 1899, at the age of twenty-one, and spent the last 11 years of his life in mental institutions.

Notable English-Canadian novelists and short-story writers emerged in the late nineteenth century. The most famous had regional settings. Norman Duncan's *The Way of the Sea* (1903) and Theodore Goodridge Roberts's *The Harbour Master* (1913) were set in Newfoundland. Lucy Maud Montgomery's first novel, *Anne of Green Gables* (1908), captured the spirit of her native province of Prince Edward Island through her beloved orphan character, Anne Shirley. Gilbert Parker's *The Seats of the Mighty* (1898), a historical novel about New France, became an international bestseller. Popular French-Canadian novels of the Quebec rural countryside appeared, one of the most popular being Ernest Choquette's *Claude Paysan* (1899). Stephen Leacock acquired international recognition as one

Pauline Johnson was one of Canada's greatest performers in the late nineteenth and early twentieth centuries. She travelled across the Dominion many times on tour. When one old dowager asked the Mohawk poet if her father really was an Indian, she replied, "Was your father really a white man?"

Library and Archives Canada/C-85125.

Émile Nelligan (1879–1941), the legendary Quebec poet and member of the École littéraire de Montréal. The intense young man was already confined to a mental asylum at the time this photo was taken in 1904.

Library and Archives Canada/C-88566.

of the great humorists writing in the English language. *Sunshine Sketches of a Little Town* (1912), an affectionate satire of small-town Ontario life in the fictitious town of Mariposa, and *Arcadian Adventures of the Idle Rich* (1914), a parody of city life, were the best known of about sixty books that earned Leacock a reputation as the "Mark Twain of the British Empire." In the West, the settlement of the prairies provided a rich subject and inspiration for a generation of prairie novelists. Authors such as Ralph Connor (Charles Gordon), Robert Stead, Nellie McClung, and Janey Canuck (Emily Murphy) wrote of the settlement experience of the Canadian prairies with highly utopian depictions of the West. In British Columbia, Martin Allen Grainger's *Woodsmen of the West* (1908) captured life in the logging industry on the West Coast. Robert Service's verse, published in his *Songs of a Sourdough* (1907), *The Spell of the Yukon* (1907), and *Ballads of a Cheechako* (1909), established his reputation as a writer of humorous ballads.

Canadian Theatre

English-Canadian theatre grew slowly in the period from 1867 to 1914 and was restricted to the major urban centres. Even here, the prevailing mood in the late nineteenth century was of "anti-theatre," according to the theatre historian Murray Edwards. One reason for such a low opinion of acting was its association with "immorality and debauchery" in the mind of church leaders. The stage was regarded "as the gate of Hell,"[1] Edwards notes. While this may have been the perception of leaders of public opinion, it was not always the view of theatregoers. Sarah Bernhardt, the flamboyant French actress, for example, succeeded in "packing the house" no matter where she performed in the country.

By the turn of the century, theatre had become well established, but it remained a foreign phenomenon. American money built most of the new theatres, and American touring companies provided nearly all the English-language entertainment. These companies made no attempt to use local talent, and in fact discouraged the growth of indigenous talent by getting Canadians accustomed to looking beyond Canada's borders for theatrical talent. Only in the interwar years would a respectable Canadian theatre develop, in competition with the new moving-picture industry.

Quebec plays often had a political theme to them. In May 1880, Louis Fréchette's *Papineau* appeared at Montreal's Académie de Musique, and his *Retour de l'exilé* ("The Return of the Exile") played in June of the same year. Both plays concerned the heroes and events of 1837–38 and advocated a reconciliation of French and English, while still holding out hope of the *Canadiens* one day freeing themselves from British rule. At the same time, the Saint-Jean-Baptiste Society organized *soirées de famille* ("family nights") in which young aspiring actors and actresses put on local plays under the guise of "elocution lessons" so as to ward off any interference from the Roman Catholic church.

The Promotion of Canadian Culture

Canada's viceroys played an important role in promoting English-Canadian and French-Canadian culture, seeing it as a component of nation-building. Just as Canadian leaders believed that the Canadian economy needed state intervention in the form of the National Policy to grow, so too they believed that Canadian culture required state assistance to mature free of American and British competition.

Government assistance took a variety of forms. Some Canadian viceroys, for example, bought and displayed Canadian art in their official residency. Lord Dufferin, Canada's third governor general (1872–78), went further. He laid the groundwork for the establishment of the Royal Canadian Academy of the Arts, modelled after the British Royal Academy. Dufferin's successor, the Marquis of Lorne, brought the Academy, along with the National Gallery of Canada, its successor, into existence in the early 1880s.

The prosperity and expansion at the turn of the century led to new government initiatives. Governor General Earl Grey sponsored the Earl Grey Musical and Dramatic Trophy Competition, which held national competitions in different Canadian cities yearly in an effort to promote and elevate the quality of Canadian talent. Grey, a fervent imperialist, also sponsored lecture tours to promote the British empire both within Canada and abroad. To promote the study of Canadian and British history, Grey founded the Historical Landmark Association of Canada, the precursor of the Historical Sites Board of Canada, in 1907, whose mandate was to establish national historic sites.

By the turn of the century, Canadian governors general and the public could rely on a growing business community for some financial support of the arts. The Canadian Pacific Railway Company hired artists in the 1880s to create works of art for their hotels, châteaux, railcars, and offices and to design their promotional posters. Later it gave Dominion Drama Festival finalists a round-trip ticket to Ottawa for the price of a one-way fare to make it possible for the finalists to participate in the annual competitions. For writers and dramatists it often provided free passes to enable authors to read their works across the country and dramatists to stage their plays.

Private family businesses also supported the arts—the wealthy Massey family of Toronto, in particular. As early as the 1870s, the Massey Manufacturing Company established a company band—the Massey Concert Band—a glee club, an employees' orchestra, and even a literary magazine, *Massey's Illustrated*, published between 1882 and 1895. In 1894, Hart Massey built the magnificent Massey Hall, with a seating capacity of 4000, and underwrote the costs of the Toronto Symphony Orchestra and the Toronto Mendelssohn Choir.

Popular Culture

One of the leading historians of popular culture defines it as "culture that is *popular*," that is to say, "culture that is widely accessible and widely accessed; widely disseminated, and widely viewed or heard or read."[2] He also maintains that both the producers and the consumers of popular culture decide what is "popular."

Popular culture developed slowly in Canada, because both its producers and its consumers were in short supply at least until the turn of the twentieth century, if not until the beginning of World War I. At that time, new technology enabled a national and mass culture to emerge. Historian David Sutherland notes that "steam-powered production machinery, cheap newsprint, telegraph communications, a comprehensive rail network, and efficient postal delivery"[3] enabled both mass newspapers and magazines to appear. These mass media differed from earlier newspapers and magazines in being more sensational, focusing on subjects of popular interest such as war and crime, including advertisements from large department stores that catered to the "masses," such as Eaton's, and featuring articles of a personal nature, particularly on the lives of popular individuals.

Canadian Cinema

Developing a Canadian movie industry for the growing number of movie theatres that emerged in Canada at the turn of the century was a constant challenge. The challenge was to carve out a uniquely Canadian perspective in films as compared to that of Hollywood in the United States in the case of English Canada and that of France in the case of Quebec. Early films tended to be of a promotional nature, as a way to attract immigrants, for example, as opposed to entertainment.

Hiawatha, the Messiah of the Ojibway (1903) became the first single-reel film. The producer used Aboriginal performers and filmed on a First Nations reserve in Ontario, but the inspiration for the film was American: based on the renowned American poet Henry Wadsworth Longfellow's *The Song of Hiawatha.*

Four Canadian film companies formed between 1912 and 1914 to produce films on Canadian subjects in an effort to create a Canadian-based fictional narrative, quickly becoming the popular style of film of the day. They produced the following four popular movies: *The Battle of the Long Sault*, about an Iroquois attack on Montreal in 1660; *Madelaine de Verchères*, about a Quebec heroine who defended a fort against the Iroquois; *The War Pigeon*, an account of the War of 1812; and *Evangeline*, based on another of Longfellow's popular poems, by that title, which dealt with the expulsion of the Acadians in 1755. These films were the exception in terms of Canadian films in that they had a wide appeal. In general, Canadian cinema suffered the fate of other forms of popular culture in Canada in the pre–World War I era: insufficient producers and consumers to sustain a uniquely Canadian film industry.

Sport

Amateur sport clubs formed in major urban centres at the time of Confederation onwards in such sports as hunting, curling, golf, lawn tennis, and, in port cities, yachting. They were as much social meeting places for Canada's political, economic, and commercial elites as they were sport centres. Most were male-dominated, and the domain of white Anglo-Saxon Protestant (WASP) groups. Women and ethnic groups were forced to create their own clubs and teams, especially in such popular sports as basketball, ice hockey, and baseball. Most girls, however, pursued athletic interests and team sports in the sanctum of schools and colleges until a more receptive audience for women athletes and more public facilities became available. First Nations and African Canadians formed their own teams and were known to defeat Anglo-Canadian teams in such sports as baseball, lacrosse, and hockey.

Women's Field Hockey Team. Photographed by Walter Gage, between 1900 and 1910.

Photographed by Walter Gage, between 1900–1910, Courtney and District Museum and Archives/ P315-1747.

While many of these amateur teams remained local, some national teams emerged in such sports as football, baseball, lacrosse, and ice hockey. The Amateur Athletic Union of Canada formed in 1909 as the first truly national sport association. By 1912, it already included 1300 clubs and over 100 000 individual members, and regulated all aspects of amateur sport.

As in the case of elite culture, popular culture also benefited from the support of Canadian viceroys. In 1893, Lord Stanley, the governor general of Canada, donated the coveted Stanley Cup in hockey. The Montreal Amateur Association was the first team to win the cup, while the Ottawa Hockey Club, referred to as simply "the Ottawas," then renamed "the Silver Seven," and finally called "the Senators," won it most often between 1893 and 1914. In 1909, Governor General Earl Grey donated the cup that continues to be the highest prize in Canadian football. Such trophies enhanced the popularity of these sports and increased the competition. Both of these sports, as well as baseball, soccer, and basketball, became more Americanized as competition extended across the border with American teams. These popular sports also became more professionalized, which meant that salaries increased and good players could make a living from sport alone. From this point onward, money and victory overrode gentlemanly conduct and pleasure as the objectives of the sport. In essence, sport became a business enterprise, a reflection and byproduct of the competitive industrial society that spurned such popular sports.

Middle-Class Culture

At the turn of the century, the middle class had more time and money for leisure. In the cities, leisure centres arose such as rollerskating rinks, dance halls, amusement parks and theatres, and fairs. The most popular in the Victorian era became Toronto's Industrial Exhibition, the forerunner of the Canadian National Exhibition. Founded in 1879, it entertained a broad segment of the populace of Toronto and its surrounding towns in the last few weeks of summer. Industrial fairs expressed the perspective of the dominant or hegemonic groups in society, usually the industrial and mercantile members of the rising middle class.

Working-Class Culture

A working-class culture fully emerged in both English-speaking and French-speaking Canada in the late nineteenth century through a proliferation of associations, societies, clubs, and lodges. They provided a meeting place where male workers (female workers could not belong) of common background and interest could meet and enjoy each other's company. Taverns served the same purpose in larger urban centres. Joe Beef's Canteen, established in Montreal in the 1860s by Charles McKiernan, an Irish Protestant ex-soldier, became one such place. It offered its working-class clientele food, drink, and accommodation—a blanket and access to a tub, a barber, "medical" advice, and "cures"—all for 10 cents.

By the 1880s, larger working-class associations such as the Knights of Labor assumed the role that Joe Beef's Canteen and other similar establishments, such as Dan Black's Tavern in Hamilton, had played. Through the American-based organization's ritualistic procedure of secret pledges, obedience, and committed charity, working men and women formed a common bond and a sense of pride. Festivals, dinners, picnics, and workers' balls provided social gatherings to "cement the bonds of unity."

Aboriginal Culture

Although many English Canadians and French Canadians in the late nineteenth century had a sentimental regard for the First Nations peoples, it did not extend to a belief that First Nations had a right to keep their ancestral cultures and religions. Canadians, like the rest of the Western world, believed that the First Nations were inferior and therefore had to be assimilated into the "superior" Western European culture. This negative perspective justified suppressing any aspect of Aboriginal culture that might get in the way of achieving assimilation.

Yet, in a peculiar twist of irony, as Canadians believed that the First Nations were about to disappear, they became more fascinated with this "quaint" and disappearing "race." They wanted to include First Nations ceremonies and customs in their country fairs and stampedes. The federal government opposed such trends, since it went against their policy of assimilation.

COMMUNITY PORTRAIT

The Huron Community of Wendake

When the French first visited the Wendake people in the early seventeenth century, they lived on a small peninsula between the Georgian Bay and Lake Simcoe in southern Ontario. The French called them "Huron." By the early 1650s, the Iroquois from present-day New York State drove the Huron from their territory. A small group of them retreated to the region around Quebec City. In 1697, they moved to their new home of Lorette, or Wendake, near the St. Charles River, only fifteen kilometres north of Quebec. They continued to practise their traditional slash-and-burn agriculture and to live in bark longhouses.

Two hundred years later, Léon Gérin, a French Canadian federal civil servant and pioneer sociologist, visited Wendake. He found a community of about 400 people who, in terms of their housing, dress, and religion, appeared to be almost identical with their French-Canadian neighbours. The village consisted of about fifty houses or so, low-roofed wooden buildings, small whitewashed structures in double row, as in the French-Canadian tradition. Some homes had very small gardens beside them, while others were placed so closely together that no room existed for a garden. Encroachments by non-Aboriginal settlers had reduced the village site itself to a very small tract of land. The Hurons also had a reserve for hunting as well as a timber tract, but both were not adjacent to the village site. In terms of dress, only one old Huron woman, in her 90s, dressed in her traditional costume of the last century. The men dressed like the French Canadians around them, but, for special occasions, the chiefs and leading men wore their traditional Aboriginal costumes. Apart from a handful of Protestants, all the Hurons were Roman Catholics; one of them, Prosper Vincent, had become a priest. L'Abbé Vincent could not speak Huron, but he was one of the last members of the community to know a number of Huron dances and songs.

The Hurons at Wendake spoke exactly the same French as the French Canadians around them, with the identical accent and expressions. The use of Huron as a daily language had effectively died out half a century earlier. Other changes had occurred. No longer, for example, were the clans as important as they had once been. In the past, one obtained one's clan identification from one's mother, but now a number of Huron men had married French-Canadian women, thus in essence ending female lineage.

Their immediate locality was not well adapted to agriculture, and as a result, the Huron gradually abandoned their farming activities. Some Huron still practised hunting, trapping, and guiding, but the vast majority worked in the village itself, especially in the manufacturing of moccasins and snowshoes. On an average 10 000 to 15 000 hides were cut annually at Wendake. In 1898, the Hurons made 140 000 pairs of moccasins and about 7000 pairs of snowshoes. The improved transportation system of the late nineteenth century allowed for the expansion of the market for the sale of these items throughout Canada and the United States.

In 1869, the federal "Act for the gradual enfranchisement of Indians," later incorporated into the federal Indian Act of 1876, made rules that further eroded the community's Aboriginal traditions. The Act ruled that when an Indian woman married a non-Indian, or someone that was not under the Indian Act, she automatically lost her Indian status. The same would be true for their children. It did stipulate that when a non-Indian woman married an Indian under the Indian Act, she gained Indian status, as did any future children they might have. But the Indian Department worked to achieve the complete assimilation of the Huron into the surrounding French-Canadian population by encouraging the "enfranchisement" or voluntary giving up of Indian status by adult Huron males. (Under Bill C-31 in 1985, Canada gave up enfranchisement, and amended the Indian Act to permit those who had given up, or lost, their status to regain it.)

Despite such changes, Gérin also found evidence that the Wendake Huron were determined to resist assimilation and to maintain their unique Aboriginal traditions and customs. For example, they still held all of their land communally. They also fought to maintain their traditional hunting rights, and resisted

the leasing of reserve lands in their hunting grounds to sports clubs. Gérin found that the Wendake Huron saw themselves as a culturally separate community, different and distinct from the larger French-speaking community because of their Huron roots and traditions. They refused to abandon their First Nations status, and Wendake.

"Our people are at peace." The Wendake Huron chief Ovide Sioui, at left, accepts the pipe from Six Nations (Iroquois chief) Andrew Staats, in centre. In early August 1921 the Hurons and the Iroquois made peace at the tercentenary commemoration of Champlain's landing at Penetanguishene, on the Georgian Bay in Ontario.

Toronto Reference Library/T 33409.

By the turn of the century, the cultural traditions of other ethnic groups also emerged, as immigrants came in large numbers and brought their customs, ceremonies, and special festivities with them. The fact that many of these customs were frowned upon by the host society did not prevent newly arrived ethnic groups from enjoying their own customs within their own communities.

Social reform movements had accomplished much during the period from Confederation to World War I, but still fell short of their ultimate goal of social regeneration. World War I would spur many of the social reform movements forward, particularly women's suffrage and prohibition.

During the same period, Canadian culture proved to be a delicate but persistent enterprise. Most cultural endeavours began as amateur and local and only slowly evolved into being professional and national. As well, elite culture increasingly gave way to popular culture. However, just as Canada was slow to cultivate a national political culture, so too the country only gradually developed a national popular culture, beginning in the pre–World War I era, gaining strength in the interwar years, but really reaching strength in the post–World War II period, when a critical mass of producers and consumers of popular culture were present.

NOTES

1. Murray D. Edwards, *A Stage in Our Past: English-Language Theatre in Eastern Canada from the 1790s to 1914* (Toronto: University of Toronto Press, 1968), p. 28.

2. Lawrence W. Levine, "The Folklore of Industrial Society: Popular Culture and Its Audiences," *AHR Forum, American Historical Review,* 97, 5 (December 1992), p. 1373.

3. David A. Sutherland, "A Changing Society," in R. Louis Gentilcore et al., eds., *Historical Atlas of Canada,* vol. 2, *The Land Transformed* (Toronto: University of Toronto Press, 1993), p. 133.

BEYOND THE BOOK

The Woman's Christian Temperance Union

http://www.abheritage.ca/famous5/achievements/mckinney_WCTU.html
A detailed history of the Woman's Christian Temperance Union and its role in prohibition in Canada. Includes many digitized historical photographs and WCTU publications.

Pastimes of Yesteryear

http://www.musee-mccord.qc.ca/en/keys/webtours/VQ_P3_5_EN
This photographic exhibit describes the common pastimes of people in Quebec between the years 1896 and 1919. Sports, dances, and other forms of leisure or recreation are explored.

English-Canadian Literature

http://www.canadiana.org/ECO/Browse?brange=collection&Language=en&id=session
This collection contains digitized copies of over 800 works of early Canadian drama, fiction, biography, and exploration accounts written before 1900. Select "English Canadian Literature" to browse the collection, and then "Show Advanced Options" to search by date.

Pauline Johnson

http://www.humanities.mcmaster.ca/~pjohnson/home.html
Digitized materials of the work and life of Pauline Johnson, poet and entertainer at the turn of the century.

Hockey in 1899

http://www.collectionscanada.ca/hockey/index-e.html
Read "Hockey: Canada's Royal Winter Game," Arthur Farrell's 1899 handbook about how to play the sport.

Sheet Music from Canada's Past

http://www.collectionscanada.ca/sheetmusic/index-e.html
This site explores Canada's musical heritage with essays, digitized song albums, and audio files of early Canadian recordings.

The White Dawn

James Houston, *The White Dawn* (New York: The New American Library, 1972), a historical novel about three survivors of a lost whaleboat in an isolated Inuit village, who were allowed to live there.

RELATED READINGS

The following article in R. Douglas Francis and Donald B. Smith, eds., *Viewpoints: Readings in Canadian History* (Toronto: Thomson Nelson, 2007), is relevant to this chapter: Peter DeLottinville, "Joe Beef of Montreal: Working-Class Culture and the Tavern, 1869–1889," pp. 372–92.

BIBLIOGRAPHY

Chapters 15 and 16 in R.C. Brown and R. Cook, *Canada, 1896–1921: A Nation Transformed* (Toronto: McClelland & Stewart, 1974) provide an overview of the social reform movements. Paul-André Linteau, René Durocher, and Jean-Claude Robert, *Quebec: A History, 1867–1929* (Toronto: James Lorimer, 1983), and Susan Mann, *The Dream of Nation: A Social and Intellectual History of Quebec*, 2nd ed. (Montreal/Kingston: McGill-Queen's University Press, 2002), deal with social reform in Quebec.

The social gospel is examined in Richard Allen's *The Social Passion: Religion and Social Reform in Canada, 1914–28* (Toronto: University of Toronto Press, 1971) and Ramsay Cook's *The Regenerators: Social Criticism in Late Victorian English Canada* (Toronto: University of Toronto Press, 1985). On religion and moral reform, consult Mariana Valverde, *The Age of Light, Soap, and Water: Moral Reform in English Canada, 1885–1925* (Toronto: McClelland & Stewart, 1991).

Educational reform in the context of social reform is the subject of Neil Sutherland's *Children in English-Canadian Society* (Toronto: University of Toronto Press, 1976). On higher education, see Paul Axelrod and John Reid, eds., *Youth, University and Canadian Society: Essays in the Social History of Higher Education* (Montreal/Kingston: McGill-Queen's University Press, 1989). Paul Rutherford's "Tomorrow's Metropolis: The Urban Reform Movement in Canada, 1880–1920," *Canadian Historical Association Report*, 1971: 203–24, deals with urban reform. Janet Foster discusses the early conservation movement in *Working for Wildlife: The Beginning of Preservation in Canada* (Toronto: University of Toronto Press, 1978). A valuable collection of essays on Canadian environmental history is Alan MacEachern and William J. Turkel, eds., *Method and Meaning in Canadian Environmental History* (Toronto: Nelson, 2009).

For women and social reform, see "The 'Woman Movement,'" which is chapter 7 in Alison Prentice et al., *Canadian Women: A History*, 2nd ed. (Toronto: Harcourt Brace, 1996); and the endnotes of "Where Historians Disagree: Women and Reform" in this chapter. On the Woman's Christian Temperance Union, see Sharon Anne Cooke, *"Through Sunshine and Shadow": The Woman's Christian Temperance Union, Evangelicalism, and Reform in Ontario 1874–1930* (Montreal/Kingston: McGill-Queen's University Press, 1995).

A synthesis of the arts in Canada has yet to be written. For an overview consult Maria Tippett's *Making Culture: English-Canadian Institutions and the Arts before the Massey Commission* (Toronto: University of Toronto Press, 1990). Music is discussed in Helmut Kallmann, *A History of Music in Canada, 1534–1914* (Toronto: University of Toronto Press, 1960). On the history of painting, consult J. Russell Harper, *Painting in Canada: A History*, 2nd ed. (Toronto: University of Toronto Press, 1966); and Dennis Reid, *A Concise History of Canadian Painting*, 2nd ed. (Toronto: Oxford University Press, 1988). For Quebec see, as well, Guy Viau, *Modern Painting in French Canada* (Quebec: Department of Cultural Affairs, 1967). An analysis of the tercentenary celebration of the founding of Quebec can be found in H.V. Nelles, *The Art of Nation-Building: Pageantry and Spectacle at Quebec's Tercentenary* (Toronto: University of Toronto Press, 1999).

Literary history is well documented in Carl F. Klinck, ed., *Literary History of Canada*, 2nd ed. (Toronto: University of Toronto Press, 1976). For Quebec, see Guy Sylvestre, *Literature in French Canada* (Quebec: Department of Cultural Affairs, 1967). On Pauline Johnson, see Veronica Strong-Boag and Carol Gerson, *Paddling Her Own Canoe: The Times and Texts of E. Pauline Johnson* (Toronto: University of Toronto Press, 2000).

For the history of Canadian theatre in English-speaking Canada, see Murray D. Edwards, *A Stage in Our Past: English-Language Theatre in Eastern Canada from the 1790s to 1914* (Toronto: University of Toronto Press, 1968). For western Canada, consult E. Ross Stuart, *The History of Prairie Theatre: The*

Development of Theatre in Alberta, Manitoba and Saskatchewan 1833–1982 (Toronto: Simon and Pierre, 1984). For Quebec, see Jean Hamelin, *The Theatre in French Canada* (Quebec: Department of Cultural Affairs, 1967).

On popular culture, see Mary Vipond, *The Mass Media in Canada* (Toronto: James Lorimer & Co., 1989); and for cinema George Melnyk, *One Hundred Years of Canada Cinema* (Toronto: University of Toronto Press, 2004).

For sports in Canada, see Alan Metcalfe, *Canada Learns to Play: The Emergence of Organized Sports, 1807–1914* (Toronto: McClelland & Stewart, 1987); and Colin Howell, *Blood, Sweat, and Cheers: Sport in the Making of Modern Canada* (Toronto: University of Toronto Press, 2001). For women and sport, see M. Ann Hall, *The Girl and the Game: A History of Women's Sport in Canada* (Peterborough: Broadview Press, 2002).

For a discussion of an emerging middle-class culture in English-speaking Canada, see Lynne Marks, *Revivals and Roller Rinks: Religion, Leisure, and Identity in Late Nineteenth Century Small-Town Ontario* (Toronto: University of Toronto Press, 1996); and Keith Walden, *Becoming Modern in Toronto: The Industrial Exhibition and the Shaping of a Late Victorian Culture* (Toronto: University of Toronto Press, 1997).

On working-class culture, the best source is Bryan Palmer, *Working-Class Experience: The Rise and Reconstitution of Canadian Labour 1880–1991*, 2nd ed. (Toronto: Butterworths, 1993). An insightful article on taverns and working-class culture is Peter de Lottinville, "Joe Beef of Montreal: Working-Class Culture and the Tavern, 1869–1889," reprinted in R. Douglas Francis and Donald B. Smith, eds., *Readings in Canadian History: Post-Confederation*, 7th ed. (Toronto: Nelson Thomson, 2006), pp. 226–46.

Among the best studies of the impact of the dominant society on the First Nations are Katherine Pettipas, *Severing the Ties That Bind: Government Repression of Indigenous Religious Ceremonies on the Prairies* (Winnipeg: University of Manitoba Press, 1994); and Edward Ahenakew, *Voices of the Plains Cree* (Toronto: McClelland & Stewart, 1973).

Part 5

THE IMPACT OF TWO WORLD WARS AND THE GREAT DEPRESSION, 1914–1945

INTRODUCTION

Like bookends, two world wars enclose the years 1914–1945. Canada felt the impact of the wars in a number of ways, but most of all by sending over 600 000 men into battle in World War I of which more than 60 000 died, and nearly 1 million in World War II with over 40 000 deaths. Canadian soldiers, sailors, and pilots distinguished themselves in both wars, thus advancing Canada's national recognition abroad.

During World War I, insufficient numbers of men were available to work in the factories and munitions plants, thus requiring more women to work outside the home. This helped women to achieve political, although not economic, equality. During the War, the state intervened in the lives of Canadian citizens to a greater extent than ever before: regulating and restricting what people could buy; dictating wages and working conditions; and introducing new forms of taxation. In 1917, Robert Borden's government created a Union party made up of Conservatives and a number of English-Canadian Liberals. Immediately, it implemented conscription, a move that deeply divided English-speaking and French-speaking Canadians. The two traditional parties survived the war, but a new third party, the Progressive party, emerged, beginning a tradition of federal multi-party rule.

In the 1920s, Canada took control over its foreign relations and achieved constitutional autonomy from Great Britain. An economy of pulp and paper, mineral production, and the manufacturing of consumer goods replaced the old wheat economy during this period.

The Great Depression of the 1930s forced all three levels of government—federal, provincial, and municipal—to assume responsibilities for the social welfare of the people under its jurisdiction. Four new political parties emerged—the Reconstruction Party, the Cooperative Commonwealth Federation (CCF) and Social Credit on the Prairies, and the Union Nationale in Quebec—all desperate to find a solution to the economic crisis.

World War II might have ended the depression, but it plunged the country into another war. When Adolph Hitler's army swept through western Europe, even capturing France, the Canadian government was forced to assist the Allies with men—and for the first time women serving at the front—along with warships, aircraft, and financial aid. Prime minister William Lyon Mackenzie King was also forced to implement conscription in 1944, a move that once again deeply divided French Canadians and English Canadians. Internationally, Canada signed the Ogdensburg Agreement with the United States in August 1940 to form a joint Canadian–American defence pact. It proved to be the turning point from an era of British protection to American protection.

While significant changes had occurred in a number of ways in the period from 1914 to 1945, two are to be noted in particular: an increasingly interventionist state internally, and closer military and economic ties with the United States externally.

Chapter Seventeen

CANADA IN THE GREAT WAR

1914	World War I begins Canadian Parliament passes War Measures Act First Division of the Canadian Expeditionary Force leaves for England
1915	John McCrae writes "In Flanders Fields"
1916	Canada fights in the ill-fated Battle of the Somme In the Battle of Beaumont-Hamel, Newfoundland loses three-quarters of its troops Women in the four western provinces are the first to get the right to vote provincially "Bilingual" schools are abolished in Manitoba
1917	Canadian troops are triumphant in the Battle of Vimy Ridge Military Service Act (the conscription bill) becomes law The newly formed Union Party under Robert Borden wins the federal election A massive explosion in Halifax harbour occurs The government-owned Canadian National Railways (CNR) is created
1918	The Department of Soldiers' Civil Re-establishment, the Women's Bureau, and the Food Board are established The Union government imposes national prohibition Canadian soldiers enter Mons Armistice signed ending World War I Women over 21 (except female status Indians and female Asians) get the right to vote The Spanish flu epidemic breaks out, killing over 50 000 Canadians

World War I marked a turning point in Canadian development. Between 1914 and 1918, Canada sent 625 000 men to the war front and several hundred women as nurses to assist—an enormous contribution for a nation of only eight million people. The Canadian Expeditionary Force fought valiantly in a number of key battles, but at great human cost. One in ten of those who fought on the battlefields of Europe died in the service of their country; an even greater number were wounded in deadly trench warfare. The numbers were even higher proportionately for Newfoundlanders; an estimated one out of four died. During the war, the government intervened in the affairs of the state to an unprecedented degree: establishing such institutions as the Canadian National Railways and the Canadian Wheat Board; and financing the war through a federal income tax and the sale of Victory Bonds. Women assisted the war effort through millions of hours of volunteer work, and by filling vacancies in factories and offices left by men who went overseas. The war initially united Canadians, but then divided them. Prime Minister Robert Borden established a Union government for a united war effort, but then immediately implemented conscription that deeply divided French Canadians and English Canadians. Workers and industrialists quarrelled about who contributed the most to the war effort. Social reformers, particularly women suffragists and prohibitionists, used the war as a catalyst for their causes. During the war, Canadian leaders succeeded in bringing the Canadian troops under Canadian command, and insisted on a more active role in deciding imperial war policy.

Canada Joins the War Effort

The murder of Archduke Ferdinand, heir to the Austro-Hungarian throne, by a young Serbian nationalist in June 1914 began a chain of events that led to World War I. Austria attacked Serbia, an ally of Russia. Germany backed Austria, while France came to the defence of Russia. Britain, an ally of France, had promised to defend Belgium's neutrality. When Germany invaded Belgium, Britain declared war (August 4, 1914). As a member of the British Empire, Canada was automatically at war.

Initially, Canadians united behind the war effort. Throughout the country, loyal demonstrations occurred, involving impromptu parades, flag-waving, and, in the streets of Montreal, the singing of "La Marseillaise" and "Rule Britannia." Even the anti-imperialist Henri Bourassa initially supported Canadian participation, seeing the survival of France and Britain as vital to Canada. Many believed that the Allies would achieve a quick victory—by Christmas. Most English-speaking Canadians viewed the war in black-and-white terms: good versus evil; democracy versus tyranny; the Anglo-Saxons versus the "Huns." The dichotomy continued throughout the war years. Newspapers, magazines, and films would report on the war in a way that brought it "home" to the average Canadian citizen, and in such a way as to distance "us" from "them"—the enemy. Such identification was important to create a national consensus to galvanize all Canadians behind the war effort and to help them get through four painful years.

Parliament unanimously passed the War Measures Act in 1914, which gave the Cabinet the right to suspend the civil liberties of anyone suspected of collaborating with the enemy and to regulate any area of society deemed essential for the conduct of the war. Under the Act, Ottawa required all those classified as "enemy aliens"—people who held citizenship in enemy countries, mostly German and Austro-Hungarian immigrants—to carry identity cards and to report once a month to the local police or to the Royal North-West Mounted Police. Ottawa also established 24 internment camps, from Halifax to Nanaimo, and interned those who were considered dangerous, as well as anyone who refused to register. During the war years, the Canadian government imprisoned about 8000 individuals.

The Canadian Expeditionary Force

Canada's permanent army in July 1914 numbered only 3000, with an additional 60 000 in the militia. Its navy consisted of only two antiquated British cruisers, the *Niobe* and the *Rainbow*, and Canada did not have enough sailors even to serve these two. Cadet training had been implemented in schools and some universities in most provinces. Sam Hughes, who had been a "volunteer" since the age of twelve, and had fought in the South African War, served as the minister of militia. He had also worked in his own determined way to build up the volunteer sector of the Canadian militia between 1911 and 1913. It would be the volunteer nature of the Canadian Corps along with the absence of class divisions that would prove to be great assets of the Canadian army in the Great War.

At first, tens of thousands of young men answered the call to serve. Within two months, 30 000 Canadian volunteers were trained at Valcartier, a military camp 25 km northwest of Quebec City. Pleased by the enlistment results and anticipating a short war, Prime Minister Robert Borden promised that he would not implement conscription.

The First Division of the Canadian Expeditionary Force of some 36 000 sailed for England on October 3, 1914, the largest convoy ever to cross the Atlantic until that time. More than 60 percent of those troops, known as "Hughes's Boys" after Sam Hughes, were recent British immigrants, mostly unmarried, frequently unemployed, and emotionally close to Britain. Native-born Canadians of British stock made up 25 percent of the soldiers. The remainder included French Canadians, non-British immigrants, and Aboriginal Canadians. Among the

As subjects of Canada's enemy, the Austro-Hungarian Empire, many "enemy aliens," most of them ethnic Ukrainians, faced internment; these men were interned at Castle Mountain, Banff National Park.

Glenbow Archives/NA-1870-6.

Force were 101 volunteer nurses. After training on Salisbury Plain in southern England, the First Canadian Division joined the British Army under the command of Lieutenant General E.A.H. Alderson for action in Flanders, in northwestern Belgium, and in adjacent France.

A "White Man's War"

From the beginning, the war was considered a "white man's war." As in other allied armies, the Canadian army discouraged visible minorities from enlisting. When fifty African Canadians from Sydney, Nova Scotia attempted to enlist, the recruiting officers told them: "This is not for you fellows, this is a white man's war." They then pressed for a totally African-Canadian battalion. Major General Willoughby Gwatkin, Canada's chief of the General Staff, agreed but only if officered by "white men." Daniel Sutherland, a contractor from Nova Scotia experienced in railway construction, commanded the No. 2 Construction Battalion (Coloured), the only African-Canadian battalion in Canadian military history. Nearly 600 of them went overseas to southern France, but on a separate transport ship so as to avoid "offending the susceptibility of other troops." They joined the Canadian Forestry Corps, where they played an important role in the lumber camps. The battalion engendered pride in the African-Canadian community both at the time and since.

Japanese Canadians also faced discrimination in their effort to enlist. When Canadian military authorities denied them the right to join regular units, the Canadian-Japanese Association of Vancouver raised an exclusively Japanese unit. The 227 enlistees drilled at their own expense but under British veteran and militia captain R.S. Colquhoun. Eventually 185 of them served overseas in different battalions.

First Nations men faced similar obstacles to enlisting. The Canadian Militia Council forbade the enlistment of status Indians on the belief that "Germans might refuse to extend to them the privileges of civilized warfare." Still, they persisted. Sam Hughes permitted them to establish their own units so long as they were under the watchful eye of "white" officers who could cultivate their "natural" talents as fighters and marksmen. The 114th became an all–First Nations unit; but it was broken up upon arrival in England, its members dispersed to various battalions, where many ended up doing mainly labour duty.

By 1917, the Canadian authorities, now desperate for all possible human power, lifted restrictions on the enlistment of visible minorities. By the end of the war, a significant number had enlisted: some 3500 First Nations (registered Indians under the Indian Act), probably several thousand Métis, over 1000 African Canadians, and several hundred Japanese Canadians. Unfortunately, they gained little in return for their service. At war's end, they were still denied respect and equality.

Canadian Patriotic Fund poster. It is ironic that the Canadian Patriotic Fund was using a First Nations representative to solicit war fund donations when First Nations men were facing obstacles to enlisting.

Toronto Reference Library.

The Nature of the Great War

From the outset the Great War was a war of attrition, one designed to kill as many of the enemy as possible. The fundamental concept of war remained Napoleonic. Like the French emperor a century earlier, the belligerent parties tried to destroy the main enemy army. They made no attempt to hit a tactical point, and in fact *blitzkrieg* tactics—short, quick military attacks— would only develop in the last months of the war.

As early as October 1914, deadlock developed on the Western Front. The two opposing sides faced each other across a narrow "No Man's Land," in deep trenches stretching from Switzerland to the North Sea. Four years of trench warfare began for an area no bigger than southern Ontario. From the beginning, the Canadian troops were singled out for their skill at trench raiding. It was the Princess Patricia's Canadian Light Infantry who first used the tactic of surprise attacks on enemy trenches at night, in the first battle of St. Eloi in February 1915, and their success greatly boosted the morale of the Canadian Corps.

On the Western Front, all soldiers faced the same intolerable conditions: mud, vermin, rotten food, and the stench of rotting flesh. The soldiers spent hours digging trenches, tunnels, dugouts, and underground shelters, only to have them washed away by the rain and mud or abandoned in haste. Then there was the noise. As Canadian military historian John Swettenham has written:

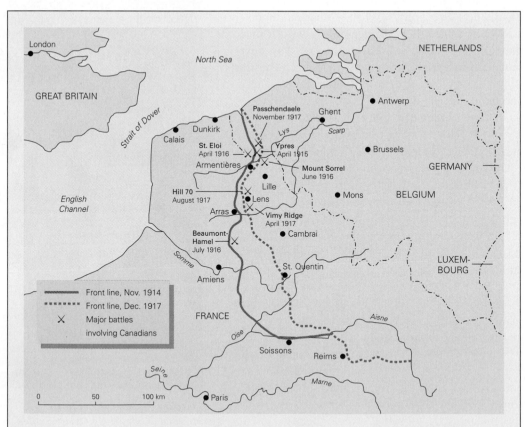

Canada at war, 1914–1917. Minimal advances were made between 1914 and 1917, despite seven major battles involving Canadians.

Source: Based on Elizabeth Abbott, ed., *Chronicle of Canada* (Montreal: Chronicle Publications, 1990), p. 579.

It has been likened to an infernal orchestra made up of ear-splitting crashes from heavy artillery, the deeper roar of mined charges, the flailing crack of field pieces, the higher-pitched note of rifles, the ghastly staccato rattle of machine-guns, the shriek and wail of shells, and the insect zip and whine of bullets, but no words can ever describe it adequately.[1]

Amid these horrors came something worse—chemical warfare. The Germans first used chlorine gas, a greenish substance that caused coughing, choking, and burning eyes and skin, on April 22, 1915, at the Battle of Ypres. One Canadian officer described it vividly:

A great wall of green gas about 15 or 20 feet high was on top of us. Captain McLaren gave an order to get handkerchiefs, soak them and tie them around our mouths and noses.

A British soldier later recalled what he saw when he and his contingent arrived to relieve the Canadians:

We stopped at a ditch at a first-aid clearing station. There were about 200 to 300 men lying in that ditch. Some were clawing their throats. Their brass buttons were green. Their bodies were swelled. Some of them were still alive. Some were still writhing on the ground, their tongues hanging out.

Half of the men in surgeon John McCrae's brigade were killed or wounded. While waiting on the rear step of an ambulance for the wounded to arrive, he wrote "In Flanders Fields," the most popular poem of the Great War. The poem made the poppy flower the enduring symbol of those who died.

At Ypres, the Canadians made their reputation by preventing a German breakthrough in the Allied lines to drive to the English Channel. But nearly 2000 Canadians lay dead, with another 3410 wounded and 775 taken prisoner—out of a total divisional fighting strength of 10 000. After Ypres, historian Daniel Dancocks explains, "there was no more bravado about an early victory over the Hun, no more fears of missing out on 'the fun.'"[2]

In 1915 and 1916, three more Canadian divisions joined the 1st Canadian Division in France. Lieutenant General Sir Julian Byng, a British regular officer, replaced Alderson as commander of the Canadian Corps. There was also a change of equipment. The Canadian-built Ross rifle, insisted upon by Sam Hughes, jammed in trench warfare. In the spring of 1916, the Canadian cabinet overruled Hughes and officially replaced the Ross rifle with the better-built British Lee-Enfield.

The Ross rifle fiasco highlighted the incompetence of Sam Hughes as minister of militia and defence. Accused of corruption, of failure to attend to his departmental duties, and of mishandling the administration of the war, Hughes had his responsibilities reduced by Prime Minister Borden. Then, in November 1916, Borden sacked Hughes, chiefly for openly criticizing the prime minister.

The Interventionist State

The war led Ottawa to intervene in Canada's economic, social, and military affairs to an unprecedented degree. Through the newly created Board of Grain Supervisors (after 1919 the Canadian Wheat Board), the government regulated all aspects of the production and distribution of wheat. Hectarage in wheat doubled, and the price per bushel increased by more than 50 percent. The government also regulated the production, distribution, sale, and consumption of coal, wood, and gas fuels. As well, the government nationalized two new transcontinental railways, the Canadian Northern and the Grand Trunk Pacific. Between 1917 and 1920, the Canadian government incorporated these railways into the publicly owned Canadian National Railways (CNR).

The federal government also got involved in selling Victory Bonds to finance the war. They proved immensely popular—more than one million Canadians purchased the bonds by war's end, thus generating close to $2 million in revenue. The government also introduced another important financial innovation: direct taxation. First it imposed a business-profits tax; then, in 1917, it imposed its first federal income tax. Ottawa promised that the new income tax would only remain for the duration of the war. While these new sources of revenue helped, costs continued to outdistance revenue, thus forcing the government to borrow vast sums at home and abroad at high interest rates. The national debt increased fivefold, from $463 million in 1913 to $2.46 billion by 1918.

Women and the War

Women made major contributions to the war effort. Twenty-five hundred women served as nursing sisters in the Canadian Army Medical Corps, working overseas at station hospitals, on hospital ships, and on ambulance trains. Forty-three died in the service of Canada. Margaret Macdonald, director of the army nursing sisters, received the Royal Red Cross and the Florence Nightingale Medal for her effort, while Matron Ethel Ridley was invested with the Order of the British Empire for her efforts as principal matron in France.

Women also contributed through their work for voluntary organizations, including the Imperial Order of the Daughters of the Empire (IODE), Red Cross clubs, the Great Veterans' Association, the Next-of-Kin Association, the YWCA, and the Women's Patriotic Leagues. They rolled bandages and knitted socks, mitts, sweaters, and scarves for the troops, raised money to send cigarettes and candy overseas, and marshalled support for the cause, not least by persuading wives and mothers to allow their men to enlist. Volunteering was a way to express patriotism, to mediate fear and grief, and to demonstrate worthiness. Women headed the Canadian Patriotic Fund, established in 1914, to assist families of soldiers overseas. They lobbied for mothers' pensions, day nurseries, and health inspection. By 1918, the government established federal agencies, such as the Women's Bureau and the Food Board, to assist women in their effort. Some women also encouraged their children to help by growing "victory gardens" to increase the amount of food available for overseas.

Unmarried women entered the workforce in large numbers, as did some married women, to ease the wartime labour shortage. On farms, in factories, and in offices, women filled positions previously occupied by men. In summertime, the YWCA recruited hundreds of female volunteers in the cities and towns to help on farms. The Women's Canadian Club organized a Women's Emergency Corps to recruit women for the munitions-production industries.

In wartime industries, however, gender discrimination remained: lower wages for women, lack of union support, and inadequate daycare facilities. Nevertheless, a number of women used their new bargaining position to raise social issues such as women's suffrage, child labour, and conditions in jails and asylums.

Fighting on the Battlefields of Europe

On June 1, 1916, the First Division troops, under their new commander Arthur Currie, a Canadian, contributed to the Battle of Sorrel in the Ypres Salient, a small triangular area around the town of Ypres. The Germans began an intense artillery barrage that enabled them to break through the Allied lines to capture Mount Sorrel. By June 13th, the Canadian Corps had recaptured all that had been lost to the Germans, a great victory but at the loss of 8000 men in just 12 days of fighting.

A month later, Canadian and Newfoundland soldiers joined British and French soldiers in the massive but ill-conceived Battle of the Somme against heavily fortified German positions. On July 1, the first day of the Big Push or Grand Assault at Beaumont-Hamel, the Newfoundland Regiment suffered 720 casualties—three-quarters of the unit. It was the greatest single disaster in Newfoundland's history, and the heaviest loss by any army on any single day in the history of the Great War. Britain recognized Newfoundland's efforts by awarding its regiment the title "Royal." At the end of the war, the people of Newfoundland purchased the land at Beaumont-Hamel, and erected a statute of a lone bull caribou, the regiment's emblem. For Newfoundlanders, the battle, commemorated annually on July 1, came to represent what Vimy Ridge would for Canadians.

Canadian soldiers made their major contribution to the Battle of the Somme in the assault on the Regina Trench, a shallow ditch on the outskirts of the town of Courcelette. The Royal 22nd Regiment, the famous "Vandoos," led the attack. Their commanding officer, Lieutenant-Colonel Thomas Tremblay, wrote: "If hell is as bad as what I have seen at Courcelette, I would not wish my worst enemies to go there." After a week of fierce fighting and heavy casualties, the Canadians captured the Regina Trench and the town of Courcelette. This was one of the last battles—and one of the few victories—in the infamous Battle of the Somme in which, during the three-month period, the Canadian Corps lost close to 2500 men.

Canada's finest hour came in the Battle of Vimy Ridge. On Easter Monday, April 9, 1917, some 70 000 Canadian soldiers, under the command of Julian Byng, along with British units, made a major attack against the German-held Vimy Ridge. Earlier in the war, both the British and French armies, with heavy losses, had failed to dislodge the Germans. This time, the Canadians took it. David Lloyd George, the British prime minister, recalled in his memoirs: "The Canadians played a part of such distinction ... that thenceforth they were marked out as storm troops; for the remainder of the war they were brought along to head the assault in one great battle after another." After the battle, Borden appointed Arthur Currie as the first Canadian commander of the entire Canadian Corps.

Canadians and Newfoundlanders also served with distinction in the air and on the sea. Canada did not have an air force of its own, but some 2500 Canadian flyers, trained in Canada by the Royal Flying Corps after 1917, joined the Royal Air Force (RAF). A number became high-scoring "aces," such as British Columbia's Raymond Collishaw, Manitoba's "Billy" Barker, Ontario's Roy Brown (credited with shooting down the notorious Baron von Richthofen—the "Red Baron"—in April 1918), and the legendary Billy Bishop, who was credited with shooting down 72 German fighters,

Canada's Enlistment/Casualty Rate, 1917

MONTH	ENLISTMENTS	CASUALTIES
January	9 194	4 396
February	6 809	1 250
March	6 640	6 161
April	5 530	13 477
May	6 407	13 457
June	6 348	7 931
July	3 882	7 906
August	3 177	13 232
September	3 588	10 990
October	4 884	5 929
November	4 019	30 741
December	3 921	7 476
Total	**64 339**	**122 946**

Source: David Corbett, Canada's Immigration Policy: a Critique. (Toronto, University of Toronto Press, 1957) p. 121.

earning a Victoria Cross. But casualties were high. As the British never issued parachutes in World War I, there were no parachute escapes for Canadians from burning or disabled aircraft. The airplanes, too, were very flimsy; more pilots died in crash landings than in the air. Canadians wanting to serve at sea joined the Royal Canadian Navy, under the command of the British Royal Navy. Some 8800 Canadians and 200 Newfoundlanders joined. Among their duties was the patrolling of Canadian and Newfoundland waters against German U-boats (submarines).

"Invite Us to Your Councils"

As the war progressed, Canadian politicians demanded a greater voice in Britain's war policy. At the outset of the war, the British government treated Canada and the other dominions as colonial subordinates, neglecting to consult with them about war strategy or even to keep them informed of developments on the war front.

When David Lloyd George became prime minister in December 1916, he implemented changes. He invited the Dominion prime ministers to London to meet as an Imperial War Cabinet, a group consisting of the British War Cabinet and Dominion representation. There, in March 1917, for the first time, Borden learned about the Allied position, discussed strategy, and, most importantly, became involved in the decision-making process.

Recruitment

With continuous high casualties in Europe, Ottawa stepped up its recruitment drive. In his New Year's Day address of 1916, Borden announced his "sacred promise" that Canada would send a total of 500 000 to the war front, double the current number. In the first half of the year, it appeared that the government could honour its commitment. By June 1916, the total wartime recruitments numbered over 300 000. Then recruitment dropped off dramatically. In summer, farmers needed young men to help on the farms. Munitions factories were in need of more workers. The government responded by establishing the National Service Board, which had a mandate to "determine whether the services of any man of military age are more valuable to the state in his present occupation than in military duties and either to permit or forbid his enlistment." The government assigned registration cards to every male of military age. It concluded that 475 000 potential recruits existed.

Borden next established the Canadian Defence Force in the spring of 1917. This force was designed to get men who opposed fighting overseas to sign up for home defence. They would replace those already in uniform who were willing to serve on the war front. This last desperate attempt to get more troops without conscription failed. In the first month of operation, fewer than 200 signed up for home defence.

National Disunity

As voluntary enlistment dried up, complaints arose about those groups who appeared reluctant to give their full support to the war effort. Once again, this exposed the geological fault line that divided French and English Canadians. Several reasons can be given for the coolness of French Canadians to the war effort. To them, the war was alien and remote. They had few or no emotional ties to Britain or even to France. Few of the officers at the Royal Military College in Kingston, the training school for military officers, were French-speaking, since English remained the sole language of instruction. In Quebec, an English-speaking elite with little sympathy for, and even less contact with, French Canadians headed the recruitment effort. As well, Sam Hughes, the minister of militia and defence, did little to encourage French-Canadian enlistment. He placed French Canadians in English-speaking units and seldom appointed or promoted French Canadians to the rank of officer. Initially, apart from the one French-language battalion, the "Vandoos" (the Royal 22nd Regiment of Quebec), English ruled as the language of the army.

The Ontario Schools Question

The question of language rights for French Canadians outside Quebec also poisoned relations between French-speaking and English-speaking Canadians during the war years. This time the controversy centred on Ontario. By 1910, French Canadians made up nearly 10 percent of Ontario's population. These Franco-Ontarians appealed to the Ontario government to protect their bilingual schools (or "English–French schools," as they were called) and to promote French-language interests.

These English–French schools came under attack from both the Orange Order and Irish Catholics. The Orange Lodge believed that the use of the French language in schools undermined the unity of Canada and of the British empire. Irish Catholics feared that language concessions to French Catholics would give French Canadians control of the separate-school system. The Irish Catholics favoured Roman Catholic—but not bilingual—schools.

James Whitney, the Ontario premier, appointed a commission to investigate. The commissioners pointed out the inadequate training of many teachers in the English–French schools but stopped short of making any recommendations to solve the problem. In 1912, the Whitney government implemented Instruction 17, or "Regulation 17," which made English the official language of instruction and restricted French to the first two years of elementary school. A year later, Whitney amended Regulation 17 to permit French as a subject of study for only one hour a day.

French-speaking Canadians in Ontario and Quebec reacted. At the Guigues school in Ottawa, an "army" of French-speaking mothers, brandishing long hatpins, stood ready to prevent any entry by authorities to remove the bilingual teachers. In Quebec, Henri Bourassa denounced the Ontario government as more Prussian than the Prussians: French Canadians need not go to Europe to fight the enemy; it resided next door. Bourassa carried his message into Ontario. Everywhere he went in Ontario, he met with hostility from English-speaking Canadians.

The Ontario schools controversy dragged on for years, during which time Franco-Ontarians were deprived of schooling in their own language. Not until 1927 did the Ontario government find a solution: each school designated for bilingual education would be considered on its merits by a departmental committee.

Ethnic Tensions

The wartime hysteria poisoned relations with various ethnic groups. Prior to the war, Germans were considered ideal immigrants, but during the war years they were vilified as "blood-crazed madmen." The Canadian propaganda machine, through newspaper editorials, books, advertisements, movies, songs, and church sermons, ensured that this image of the enemy prevailed. It also presented the counterimage of the Allies, and especially the Canadian soldiers, as brave and noble warriors. Such propaganda played out in various ways. In Berlin, Ontario,

On June 10, 1916, the 102nd Battalion embarked for overseas from Comox, Vancouver Island. The whole Courtenay–Comox community came to the harbour to see them off.

Courtenay and District Museum and Archives/ P215-1141.

An ad placed in The Farmer's Advocate, *December 13, 1917, by the "Citizens' Union Committee." The federal election of December 1917 was one of the most divisive in Canadian history as a result of the implementation of the Military Service Act, or conscription bill, that past summer.*

Courtesy University Archives, Killam Memorial Library, Dalhousie University.

for example, the city government held a plebiscite on whether to change the name of the city. Although over two-thirds of the city's population were of German descent, it was decided, by a narrow vote, to rename the city "Kitchener," after the British military hero who drowned at sea on June 5, 1916.

The Conscription Crisis

In the spring of 1917, Prime Minister Borden visited Canadian soldiers in British hospitals and at the front while attending a meeting of the Imperial War Cabinet in London. The desperate situation and the British pressure on Canada to increase its commitment of men convinced him to break his promise, made at the outset of the war, not to introduce conscription for overseas military service.

He favoured a coalition government of Conservatives and Liberals as the best means to introduce compulsory service, so he approached Wilfrid Laurier, leader of the Liberal Party, about the possibility. While Laurier agreed with the need for a coalition government for the war's duration, he opposed a Union government that would introduce conscription, which neither he nor his Quebec followers favoured. "I oppose this bill," he warned when the Conservatives introduced the Military Service Act in Parliament, "because it has in it the seeds of discord and disunion, because it is an obstacle and bar to that union of heart and soul without which it is impossible to hope that this Confederation will attain the aims and ends that were had in view when Confederation was effected."

Opposition to Conscription

The Military Service Act, the official title of the conscription bill, became law in July 1917. Throughout that summer, anticonscriptionist riots broke out in Montreal. More riots followed in the spring of 1918, after the actual implementation of conscription in January 1918.

Others, besides French Canadians, opposed conscription. Farmers resented their sons' forced departure from the farm, where they contributed to the war effort through food production. Workers saw military conscription as the first step toward compulsory industrial service, forcing them to remain at one job for the war's duration. Both groups demanded the "conscription of wealth"—heavier taxes on the rich and the nationalization of banks and industries—to ensure that financiers and businesspeople made their sacrifice for the war effort.

Some pacifist groups, such as the Quakers and the Mennonites, opposed wars as inherently evil and immoral. Others, not having a religious affiliation, opposed war as a wasteful and destructive means of settling world problems. The Canadian Women's Peace Party, forerunner of the Women's International League for Peace and Freedom, advocated a nonviolent struggle at home rather than war abroad as a means to reform society in order to root out the inherent causes of violence and war.

Union Government and the Election of 1917

Despite Laurier's refusal to join Borden in a coalition government, Borden did convince a number of Liberal members of parliament and provincial Liberal leaders to join his Union government. Then he dissolved Parliament and called an election.

Before dissolving Parliament, the Unionists implemented two bills to strengthen their chances at the polls. The Military Voters Act enfranchised all members of the armed forces, no matter how long or short a time they had lived in Canada. The governing party could use the soldiers' vote in whatever constituency it wished, when a constituency was not identified. The Wartime Elections Act gave the vote to Canadian women who were mothers, wives, sisters, or daughters of servicemen (this did not apply to female relatives of status Indian servicemen), but denied the vote to conscientious objectors and to naturalized Canadians from enemy countries who had settled in Canada after 1902.

Both the Unionists and the Liberals fought the election of 1917 largely along cultural lines. A Unionist election poster claimed that a vote for Laurier was a vote for Bourassa, the Kaiser, and the Germans. A group of Union supporters issued a map of Canada with Quebec in black, the "foul blot" on the country. On the Sunday before the election, an estimated three-quarters of the Protestant ministers across Canada responded to a Unionist circular, appealing for support of the Union party in their sermons.

In Quebec, political leaders painted conscriptionists as a greater danger to the country than the Germans. Bourassa and the *nationalistes* argued that Canada had done enough for the war. "Every Canadian who wishes to combat conscription with an effective logic," he declared, "must have the courage to say and to repeat everywhere: No Conscription! No Enrolment!"

The outcome of the election proved predictable. The Union Party won two-thirds of the constituencies outside of Quebec but only three seats, all in English-speaking ridings, in the province. Ninety percent of the soldiers' vote went to the Union government. The federal government was now literally an English-Canadian government. The Liberals won 62 of the 65 seats in Quebec but only 20 seats in the rest of the country.

The War and Social Reform

The war greatly advanced the cause of social reform. During the war, English-Canadian reformers argued that just as the troops fought for a noble cause on the battlefront, so should those at home—against materialism, alcoholism, and corruption. Social gospellers saw the war as the final struggle for bringing God's kingdom to earth. Others saw it as the beginning of regeneration for a "New Canada" coming out of the carnage of war.

The Success of Women's Suffrage and Prohibition

Women's suffrage and prohibition both gained support during the war. Women reformers argued that men's aggressive nature, often aggravated by alcohol, had caused the worldwide cataclysm. If women had the right to vote and an opportunity to rule, wars would cease. They also pointed out the inconsistency of fighting for democracy abroad while denying women the democratic right to vote at home. In 1916, the four western provinces granted women the right to vote in provincial elections. Ontario followed in 1917, Nova Scotia in 1918, New Brunswick in 1919, Prince Edward Island in 1922, and Quebec in 1940.

Federally, the franchise came in three stages: the Military Voters Act of 1917 awarded the vote to women serving in the armed forces or as nurses in the war; the Wartime Elections Act extended voting privileges to women, aged 21 years and over, whose fathers, husbands, or sons served overseas; and finally, in 1918, all women, recognized as British citizens in Canada, over the age of 21, gained the right to vote federally. Still excluded from the franchise were status Indians, Asians, and conscientious objectors, including Mennonites and Hutterites.

For What? *by Frederick Varley, one of the four war artists who later joined the Group of Seven. Varley's bleak painting of a burial party at work behind the front lines makes a horrible statement on the futility of war.*

F.H. Varley, *For What?* Accession number: 19710261-0770, Catalogue number: 8911, Beaverbrook Collection of War Art © Canadian War Museum (CWM).

The war also helped the cause of prohibition, at least temporarily. Prohibitionists equated their struggle with that of the men at the front. As well, prohibitionists criticized human and material resources being wasted to make liquor at this time of critical shortage. The prohibitionists' first victory came in 1915, when the Saskatchewan Liberal government closed all bars, saloons, and liquor stores. Immediately, this move brought liquor under the control of provincially operated outlets. Alberta went further by endorsing outright provincial prohibition later the same year. Manitoba followed in early 1916. By the end of 1917, every provincial government except Quebec had implemented prohibition legislation. In 1918, the newly elected federal Union government imposed prohibition on Quebec. Within a week of his electoral victory in December 1917, Prime Minister Borden moved to prohibit the manufacture, importation, and transportation of any beverage containing more than 2.5 percent alcohol.

French-Canadian Reformers in the War Years

French-Canadian clerics and laypeople pressed for social, not political, reform during the war period. In 1917, Father Joseph-Papin Archambault, of the Jesuit-inspired École sociale populaire, issued a tract, *La question sociale et nos devoirs de catholiques*, in which he appealed to Roman Catholics to reach out to the working class. In 1920, he began the Semaines sociales, an annual weeklong meeting of clerics and laypeople to discuss social questions.

Final Year of the War

As social reformers fought for victories at home, soldiers continued their efforts on the war front. By 1917, the situation in Europe had deteriorated for the Allies. The Germans' unrestricted submarine warfare in the North Atlantic brought the United States into the war against Germany in April 1917, but American troops would not be mobilized in force in Europe until the summer of 1918. In October and November, the Allies suffered hundreds of thousands of casualties in the last phase of Field-Marshal Haig's Flanders offensive, including 16 000 Canadian deaths in the battle of Passchendaele, an attempt to take an insignificant ridge in a sea of mud. In October 1917, revolution broke out in Russia, and by November, Lenin led the Bolsheviks to power. They immediately made peace with Germany. Now the Germans could concentrate on the Western Front.

In the spring of 1918 came an all-out German counteroffensive. Once again the Allies faced defeat. Only with the Germans' "black day" at Amiens on August 8, 1918, the beginning of the final "Hundred Days" campaign, did the Allies turn the tide. The Canadian Corps under Currie's command played a key role in the final assault. With victories at Drocourt-Quéant, Cambrai, and Valenciennes, the Canadians pushed on to the city of Mons. Mons had been the site of Britain's first defeat at the hands of the Germans in 1914; thus, its recapture on the night of November 10th held symbolic importance. The next morning at 11 a.m., the Germans surrendered and signed the Armistice. The "Great War" was over.

Few Canadian conscripts ever fought on the battlefield in the Great War. While the implementation of conscription put 100 000 more men into the army by the war's end, only one-quarter of them reached the front before the armistice. Overall, some 600 000 Canadians fought in the Great War; 60 000 of them died.

Success of the Canadian Corps

The Canadian Corps proved itself in the Great War. In assessing its success, historians have pointed to its volunteer nature, the absence of class distinctions and of preconceived rules of conduct of military operations (both of which hindered the established European armies), the fact that the Corps stayed together during the war, the rural and small-town roots of many of the soldiers who were used to a rugged lifestyle, and finally the fact that Canadian soldiers had something to prove: a pride in being Canadian.

COMMUNITY PORTRAIT

The Canadian Corps: A Community of Soldiers

The young men who joined the Canadian Expeditionary Force or the Canadian Corps did so for a variety of reasons. Initially, many sought adventure in what they believed would be a short war, over by Christmas. Unemployment led others to enlist. In the initial two years of the war recent immigrants from Britain formed the largest single group. Problematic for French-speaking Canadians was the language of command: English. The transition into a disciplined, hardened, unified fighting force—a community of soldiers—took time to form. But it did happen.

Many of the Canadian-born recruits came from farming backgrounds or small rural hamlets or villages, with a propensity to work together for a common cause. The fact that these young men trained together and, in most cases, fought together at the war front reinforced the feeling of camaraderie and the sense of themselves as a community of soldiers. Uniting them as well was the realization that they faced

death together at the hands of a common enemy. In an open letter to his cousin Henri Bourassa, Talbot Papineau, a member of the Corps, noted how working together and facing death together forged a sense of community. Canadian soldiers, he wrote in 1916, "are being knit together into a new existence, because when men stand side by side and endure a soldier's life and face together a soldier's death, they are united in bonds almost as strong as the closest of blood ties." English-born Greg Neale, a farmer from Lloydminster on the Saskatchewan-Alberta border, recalled how he found a sense of community in the military. "For years, and especially for an impressionable boy, all my relations were there. Your battalion was there, your company was there, your platoon was there. You belonged to them. You were an identifiable person."

The Canadian Corps also had the good fortune of having commanders who reinforced this sense of unity and community. Julian Byng, who took command of the Corps in May 1916, although British, bonded with his men and worked alongside them to the point where they became identified as "the Byng Boys." When Canadian-born Major General Arthur Currie, a former real estate agent from Victoria, replaced Byng in the spring of 1917, an even closer bond of unity and community as Canadian soldiers formed. Currie insisted that the Canadian Corps be kept together as a fighting force under Canadian command for the duration of the war.

At Vimy Ridge on Easter Monday, 1917, all four divisions of the Canadian Corps fought together for the first time. In preparation for that battle, they had trained together down to the minutest detail. They knew that the Corps's success depended on the interconnection and cooperation of the individual soldiers. Harold Innis, later an outstanding social scientist at the University of Toronto, noted the importance of working together as a community of soldiers. Reflecting on his war experience, he recalled that all soldiers realized "other men's lives depended to an important extent on how much work we did." Together, at Vimy, the Canadian Corps captured the all-important Ridge from the Germans. Earlier attempts by both the British and French had failed. For many Canadian soldiers, it was the defining moment. Greg Clark, later a leading columnist for the *Toronto Daily Star*, recalled it best in a CBC radio interview entitled "In Flanders Fields." Although he realized that the losses at Vimy had been horrendous, still for him the Vimy campaign and the war in general had enlarged him in mind and spirit. He attributed his individual survival and the overall success of operations such as Vimy "to the community of men closest to him."

FURTHER READING

Ted Barris, *Victory at Vimy: Canada Comes of Age, April 9–12, 1917* (Toronto: Thomas Allen Publishers, 2007).

Pierre Berton, *Vimy* (Toronto: McClelland and Stewart, 1986).

Terry Copp, "The Military Effort, 1914–1918," in David Mackenzie, ed., *Canada and the First World War: Essays in Honour of Robert Craig Brown* (Toronto: University of Toronto Press, 2005), pp. 35–61.

Sandra Gwyn, *Tapestry of War: A Private View of Canadians in the Great War* (Toronto: HarperCollins Publishers Ltd., 1992).

Jonathan Vance, *Death So Noble: Memory, Meaning, and the First World War* (Vancouver: UBC Press, 1997).

Demobilization

In 1919, the Canadian government faced insurrection among its soldiers stationed in demobilized camps in Britain and Europe, waiting to return home. In early 1918, it had created the Department of Soldiers' Civil Re-establishment in anticipation of this problem. But even its personnel were unprepared for the difficulties involved in arranging for 300 000 troops to return and be integrated back into Canadian society.

The problem of dealing with demobilized soldiers paled in comparison with an even greater domestic crisis in the immediate postwar era: the Spanish influenza epidemic, brought back home almost certainly by returning soldiers. The first major outbreak occurred in September 1918 in Quebec. In some cities, people were ordered to wear gauze masks in public; in others, theatres and schools were closed, public meetings were banned, and church services were cancelled in an effort to check the deadly disease. Labrador was devastated by the influenza, with a third of the Inuit dying between November 1918 and January 1919. In the fall of 1919, the federal government established the Department of Health to deal with the epidemic. In the end, an estimated 50 000 Canadians died from this "silent enemy"—almost as many as had died in the Great War itself.

The wartime rhetoric that the Great War would lead to a better Canada, a glorious nation of peace and prosperity, rang hollow in 1919. The war had strained English- and French-Canadian relations to an unprecedented extent. Equally, the war had taxed the nation's capacity in both industrial production and human resources. The total of all Canadian casualties—killed, missing, prisoners of war, or wounded—reached a quarter of a million people.

Canada had also lost its optimism. Fifteen years earlier, Prime Minister Wilfrid Laurier had predicted that the twentieth century would be Canada's, just as the nineteenth century had been that of the United States. In 1919, Laurier died. His vision had perished before he did, another casualty of the killing fields of Europe.

NOTES

1. John Swettenham, *To Seize the Victory: The Canadian Corps in World War I* (Toronto: Ryerson Press, 1965), p. 106.

2. Daniel Dancocks, *Welcome to Flanders Fields: The First Canadian Battle of the Great War, Ypres, 1915* (Toronto: McClelland & Stewart, 1988), p. 249.

BEYOND THE BOOK

Oral Histories of World War I

http://www.collectionscanada.gc.ca/first-world-war/interviews/index-e.html
Veterans of World War I share their stories in these digitized, fully transcribed audio interviews. Memories of Vimy Ridge, Passchendaele, and more are explored.

Allied Propaganda Art in World War I

http://www.royalalbertamuseum.ca/vexhibit/warpost/english/exhibit.htm
An exhibit containing dozens of scanned Allied propaganda posters used in World War I, and analysis of them.

The First World War: Canada Remembers

http://archives.cbc.ca/war_conflict/first_world_war//topics/2425
Video and radio testimonials of soldiers and their experiences in combat in World War I.

An Echo in My Heart

http://ca.geocities.com/echoinmyheart@rogers.com
Detailed digitized letters written between Evelyn Albright and Frederick Albright. The Albrights were married in Canada in 1914, and Frederick enlisted and was sent overseas in 1917. The letters span 1910 to 1917.

The Call to Duty: Canada's Nursing Sisters

http://www.collectionscanada.gc.ca/nursing-sisters/index-e.html
Digitized letters, diaries, and photographs present the life and experiences of six Canadian nurses in World War I. An essay describing the Canadian nursing profession as a whole during World War I is also available.

The Cobourg World

http://www.canadianletters.ca/CobourgMain.php
A database of digitized letters from Canadian soldiers, as published in wartime in the *Cobourg World*, a local newspaper in Cobourg, Ontario.

Wanted! 500,000 Canadians

http://www.mccord-museum.qc.ca/en/keys/webtours/GE_P3_1_EN
A virtual exhibit detailing Canadian recruitment efforts for the Canadian Expeditionary Force in World War I.

Three Day Road

Joseph Boyden, *Three Day Road* (Toronto: Penguin Canada, 2005). A novel centred on the experiences of two Cree men, soldiers in World War I.

Barometer Rising

Hugh MacLennan, *Barometer Rising* (Toronto: McClelland and Stewart, 1969; first appeared 1941). A historical novel about Halifax during World War I.

The Wars

Timothy Findley, *The Wars* (Markham, ON: Penguin Canada, 1978). An extraordinary historical novel about the horrors of the "Great War."

RELATED READINGS

The following articles in R. Douglas Francis and Donald B. Smith, eds., *Viewpoints: Readings in Canadian History* (Toronto: Thomson Nelson, 2007), relate to topics in this chapter: "Race and Recruitment in World War I: Enlistment of Visible Minorities in the Canadian Expeditionary Force," pp. 334–51; "An Open Letter from Capt. Talbot Papineau to Mr. Henri Bourassa," pp. 397–403; "Mr. Bourassa's Reply to Capt. Talbot Papineau's Letter," pp. 403–8; Will R. Bird, "Ghosts Have Warm Hands," pp. 408–13; and Ronald G. Haycock, "Recruiting, 1914–1916," pp. 414–32.

BIBLIOGRAPHY

For overviews of Canada during World War I, see Desmond Morton and J.L. Granatstein, *Marching to Armageddon: Canada and the Great War, 1914–1919* (Toronto: Lester & Orpen Dennys, 1989); Daniel Dancocks, *Spearhead to Victory: Canada and the Great War* (Edmonton: Hurtig, 1987); and Bill Freeman and Richard Nielson, *Far from Home: Canadians in the First World War* (Toronto: McGraw-Hill Ryerson, 1999). A valuable collection of essays is David Mackenzie, ed., *Canada and the First World War: Essays in Honour of Robert Craig Brown* (Toronto: University of Toronto Press, 2005). On Robert Borden, see R.C. Brown, *Robert Laird Borden: A Biography*, 2 vols. (Toronto: Macmillan, 1975, 1980); and John English, *Borden: His Life and World* (Toronto: McGraw-Hill Ryerson, 1977). For a study of party and politics during the Borden era consult John English, *The Decline of Politics: The Conservatives and the Party System, 1901–1920* (Toronto: University of Toronto Press, 1977).

John Swettenham, *To Seize the Victory* (Toronto: Ryerson Press, 1965), and Robert James Steel, *The Men Who Marched Away: Canada's Infantry in the First World War, 1914–1918* (St. Catharines: Vanwell, 1989), describe Canadian involvement at the front, as does Sandra Gwyn's *Tapestry of War: Politics and Passion: Canada's Coming of Age in the Great War* (Toronto: HarperCollins, 1992). G.W.L. Nicholson, *The Fighting Newfoundlander: A History of the Royal Newfoundland Regiment* (Ottawa: Government of Newfoundland, 1964), recounts Newfoundland's contribution to the Allied army. On Canada's first military commander consult A.M.J. Hyatt, *General Sir Arthur Currie: A Military Biography* (Toronto: University of Toronto Press, 1987). On the Canadian air force, see S.F. Wise, *Canadian Airmen and the First World War* (Toronto: University of Toronto Press, 1980); and for the navy, Michael L. Hadley and Roger Sarty, *Tin-Pots and Pirate Ships: Canadian Naval Forces and German Sea Raiders 1880–1918* (Montreal/Kingston: McGill-Queen's University Press, 1991).

James W. St. G. Walker looks at race relations in the Canadian army in "Race and Recruitment in World War I: Enlistment of Visible Minorities in the Canadian Expeditionary Force," *Canadian Historical Review*, 70, 1 (March 1989): 1–26. On First Nations soldiers, see Fred Gaffen, *Forgotten Soldiers* (Penticton, BC: Theytus Books, 1985); and James Dempsey's *Warriors of the King: Prairie Indians in World War I* (Regina: Canadian Plains Research Center, 1999). On Ukrainian internments, see Frances Swyripa and John Herd Thompson, eds., *Loyalties in Conflict: Ukrainians in Canada during the Great War* (Edmonton: Canadian Institute of Ukrainian Studies, 1983). For information about the nearly 4000 Canadians held in German prison camps in World War I, see Desmond Morton, *Silent Battle: Canadian Prisoners of War in Germany, 1914–1919* (Toronto: Lester, 1992). The role of propaganda on the war effort is examined in Jeffrey A. Keshen, *Propaganda and Censorship during*

Canada's Great War (Edmonton: University of Alberta Press, 1996). On the shaping of the war on the home front, see Robert Rutherdale, *Hometown Horizons: Local Responses to Canada's Great War* (Vancouver: UBC Press, 2006); and Ian Miller, *Our Glory and Our Grief: Torontonians and the Great War* (Toronto: University of Toronto Press, 2002). On voluntary contributions, see Desmond Morton, *Fight or Pay: Soldiers' Families in the Great War* (Vancouver: UBC Press, 2004).

The question of government intervention in the state during the war is discussed in R. Cuff, "Organizing for War: Canada and the United States during World War I," *Canadian Historical Association Report*, 1969: 141–56. For women's contributions to the war effort, see the relevant sections of Alison Prentice et al., *Canadian Women: A History*, 2nd ed. (Toronto: Harcourt Brace, 1996). The Halifax explosion is well documented in Alan D. Ruffman and Colin D. Howell, eds., *Ground Zero: A Reassessment of the 1917 Explosion in Halifax Harbour* (Halifax: Nimbus, 1994).

The conscription crisis is covered in J.L. Granatstein and J.M. Hitsman, *Broken Promises: A History of Conscription in Canada* (Toronto: Copp Clark Pitman, 1985 [1977]). The Canadian peace movement is studied in Thomas Socknat, *Witness against War: Pacifism in Canada, 1900–1945* (Toronto: University of Toronto Press, 1987). Often forgotten are the veterans; consult D. Morton and G. Wright, *Winning the Second Battle: Canadian Veterans and the Return to Civilian Life, 1915–1930* (Toronto: University of Toronto Press, 1987).

For the Ontario schools questions, see Chad Gaffield, *Language, Schooling, and Cultural Conflict: The Origins of the French-Language Controversy in Ontario* (Montreal/Kingston: McGill-Queen's University Press, 1987). For the impact of World War I on social reform, consult John Herd Thompson, *The Harvests of War: The Prairie West, 1914–1919* (Toronto: McClelland & Stewart, 1978). On Canadian imperial and foreign relations during World War I, see R.C. Brown's "Sir Robert Borden, the Great War and Anglo-Canadian Relations," in J.S. Moir, ed., *Character and Circumstance* (Toronto: Macmillan, 1970), pp. 201–24; and C. P. Stacey, *Canada and the Age of Conflict*, vol. 1, *1867–1921* (Toronto: Macmillan, 1977). On the flu epidemic of 1918, see Eileen Pettigrew, *The Silent Enemy* (Saskatoon: Western Producer Prairie Books, 1983). Sandra Gwyn's *Tapestry of War: Politics and Passion: Canada's Coming of Age in the Great War* (Toronto: HarperCollins, 1992) examines the significance of the war for Canada's advancement; while Jonathan F. Vance looks at the construction of a myth within Canada of the Great War in *Death So Noble: Memory, Meaning and the First World War* (Vancouver: UBC Press, 1997).

Chapter Eighteen

THE INTERWAR YEARS

TIME LINE

1919	Canada joins the League of Nations Winnipeg General Strike breaks out
1920	Maritime Rights Movement forms Group of Seven holds their first art exhibition
1921	Liberals elected under W.L. Mackenzie King Newly formed Progressive Party wins 65 seats in the federal election Agnes Macphail becomes the first woman elected in a federal election
1929	The Persons Case recognizes women in Canada as "persons" for legal purposes The New York stock market crashes
1930	Conservatives come to power under R.B. Bennett
1931	Statute of Westminster recognizes Canadian autonomy from Britain
1934	The Dionne quintuplets, the world's first surviving quintuplets, are born
1935	In the On-to-Ottawa Trek unemployed workers head to Ottawa
1936	The Canadian Broadcasting Corporation (CBC) begins
1937	The Royal Commission on Dominion–Provincial Relations is established

The decades from 1919 to 1939 were ones of adjustment. In the period from 1919 to 1929, it was an adjustment to postwar conditions, while in the period from 1929 to 1939, it was an adjustment to the Great Depression, the worst depression in world history. The war was followed in 1919 with the first general strike in Canadian history, occurring in Winnipeg. In the postwar era, both major federal political parties chose new leaders, and regional protest movements surfaced in the Maritimes and in the West. In foreign affairs, Canada continued to move toward autonomy. Economically, Canadians looked increasingly to the United States rather than to Britain for both financial needs and foreign trade. Socially, reform declined, but disadvantaged groups such as women and workers continued their fight for recognition and rights.

The Great Depression dominated the 1930s. The spectacular crash of the New York stock market in October 1929 signalled the crisis. Bank failures, a decline in international trade, plummeting commodities prices, spiralling government debts, and massive unemployment followed.

Canada and the United States experienced the Western world's most severe decline in industrial production and gross national product. Unemployment soared. With no jobs available, thousands of Canadians faced for the first time the degradation of going on public relief. Young, single men "rode the rods" across the country in search of work, and when unable to find work, many ended up in relief camps under intolerable conditions. People looked to government for answers. First the Conservatives under R.B. Bennett attempted to deal with this unprecedented economic disaster when elected to power in 1930. When they failed to satisfy the electorate, they were defeated and the Liberals returned under Mackenzie King. Many Canadians looked to new third parties, and some turned to extreme right- and left-wing organizations for solutions. Farm organizations and trade unions attempted to help their members, but with limited success. Women fared no better; in fact, they lost what gains they had made toward economic equality. Some Canadians looked to religion for answers, and a more conservative religious perspective prevailed. Popular culture—particularly movie-going and sport—thrived as temporary diversions from the depressed conditions of everyday life.

The Depression certainly had an impact on those who lived through it. Some remember those years as the best of times in terms of social bonding as people pulled together to help each other; others remembered them as the worst of times as they had to struggle simply to eke out a living.

The Winnipeg General Strike

Widespread labour unrest followed the armistice. Strikes broke out from Halifax to Vancouver as workers tried to make up for the restraints applied in wartime and to protect themselves in an inflationary economy. At the annual meeting of the Trades and Labor Congress in Quebec City in 1918, the western delegates broke ranks with the conservative eastern members who controlled the meeting. A month later, the Western Labour Conference called for a single industrial union, the One Big Union (OBU), at its meeting in Calgary. But before its organizers could hold the founding convention, new developments broke out in Winnipeg. On May 1, 1919, metalworkers' and

"Bloody Saturday," June 21, 1919, a violent confrontation that occurred between peaceful marchers and the Mounties and special police during the Winnipeg General Strike. Note the burning streetcar.

David Miller Collection/Library and Archives of Canada/C-33392.

builders' unions struck for better wages and improved working conditions. Other Winnipeg union workers, including police officers, firefighters, and telephone and telegraph operators, joined them on May 15, swelling the number of strikers to some 30 000, thus enabling them virtually to close down the city. To provide essential services and to regulate the strike, the organizers created a central strike committee. Business and government officials saw this committee, with its power to dictate what went on in the city, as the beginnings of a "Bolshevik uprising." They countered by creating the Citizens' Committee of 1000, an anti-strike organization.

Fearing that the strike would spread to other centres, the federal government intervened. Arthur Meighen, the minister of justice and minister of the interior, and Gideon Robertson, acting minister of labour, arrived in Winnipeg to assess the situation. They came already convinced that the strike was a conspiracy.

On the night of June 16, Meighen ordered the Royal North-West Mounted Police to arrest ten of the Winnipeg strike leaders, along with labour newspaper editors, including J.S. Woodsworth, and some returned soldiers. In protest, the strikers organized a silent parade on Saturday, June 21. Violence erupted, and the mayor of Winnipeg called in the Mounties to disperse the crowd. The confrontation saw one man killed and another wounded and many others injured. "Bloody Saturday," as it became known, ended with the dispersal of the workers and the establishment of military control of the city. On June 26, the strike committee called off the strike, without the workers having gained any of their objectives.

WHERE HISTORIANS DISAGREE

The Winnipeg General Strike

Canadian labour and working-class historians agree on the importance of the Winnipeg General Strike of 1919, but on little else. Initially, the historiography reflected the opposing ideological perspectives of the two sides at the time: the strike opponents seeing it as a revolution aimed at creating a Soviet-style regime in Canada; its supporters seeing it as a legitimate tool by which workers could obtain collective bargaining to secure better wages and working conditions.

Historian D.C. Masters wrote the first scholarly study of the strike. He emphasized the British background of the strike leaders so as to reinforce the legitimacy of the strike within the British democratic tradition and denied any connection between the strike and the One Big Union

(OBU) (often seen as an attempt to create a working-class solidarity as a prelude to a Bolshevik-style revolution). He also challenged those who saw the strike as a spontaneous uprising, claiming "it came at the end of a series of controversies which had raged in a crescendo since at least 1917." Thus, he concluded that "there was no seditious conspiracy and that the strike was what it purported to be, an effort to secure the principle of collective bargaining."[1]

In contrast, sociologist S.D. Clark emphasized the importance of the One Big Union in his introduction to D.C. Masters's study, which was part of a series under Clark's general editorship. Clark saw the OBU, along with the Progressive Party among western farmers, as "expressions of protest against eastern dominance ... in the tradition of American frontier radicalism."[2] In this respect, Clark concluded, "the movement was revolutionary"—ironically, a direct contradiction to the conclusion that Masters, whose book Clark was introducing, had drawn!

Historian David Bercuson provided a comprehensive study of the general strike in *Confrontation at Winnipeg*. He traced the roots of the strike back to labour unrest in the city in 1906, if not to the turn of the century. The massive influx of immigrants came at a time of major social and industrial changes that turned Winnipeg into a city sharply divided along class lines. Bercuson denied that the strikers were revolutionaries; instead they were striking for legitimate working-class concerns. But, he argued, the fact that they failed to achieve their objectives set back "the cause of labour for at least another generation."[3] Fellow labour historian Irving Abella concurred. "Labour's trauma started at Winnipeg in 1919," he wrote. "With the suppression of the Winnipeg General Strike ... the rapid demise of organized labour in Canada began."[4]

Historian Norman Penner disagreed with this negative assessment of the strike's aftermath:

> [F]or more than a year, the Winnipeg General Strike and the trials of its leaders kept the labour movement in a constant state of agitation and turmoil which succeeded in translating the economic struggle into a political victory.... Hence the Winnipeg General Strike must be seen as part of the cumulative impact of labour on Canadian life, a constant force which accounts for labour's strength and status in Canada today.[5]

Bercuson introduced a new issue into the debate in an article that examined the strike in the context of the larger issue of western labour radicalism.[6] He argued that western workers were more radical than elsewhere in the country because of unique western frontier conditions, including immigrants who came with utopian dreams of a better lifestyle, only to find themselves up against ruthless and repressive industrialists who thwarted their hopes. Failed expectations, Bercuson argued, were a sure cause for radicalism. He concluded that the Canadian western industrial frontier bred class consciousness and radical working-class attitudes rather than equality and harmony.

Labour historian Greg Kealey vehemently disagreed with Bercuson's theory that the West was more radical than the rest of the country. Also, Kealey questioned Bercuson's implication that the Winnipeg General Strike could only have occurred in Winnipeg, the most urban of societies. Kealey pointed out that that year was punctuated by strikes and labour unrest throughout the country; in fact, labour unrest in Canada in 1919 was really part of an international working-class solidarity. He went on to argue as well that the strike was part of "larger structural changes in capitalist organization on both a national and international scale."[7] Seen from this wider perspective, the strike was not a failure, but only a momentary defeat before labour emerged even stronger in the move toward industrial unionism in the 1940s.

Bercuson dismissed Kealey's argument in a historiographical chapter that appeared in a revised edition of *Confrontation at Winnipeg*. He claimed that evidence of numerous strikes and/or revolts across the country did not constitute proof of working-class revolt. Few of these strikes were "politically motivated and those that were—the Vancouver general strike, for example—were dismal failures." Nor had Kealey proven that the strikers were consciously trying to overthrow capitalism. Kealey's essay, he claimed, was "little more than pamphleteering. He is rallying the revolutionary troops; he is certainly not advancing scholarship." Then Bercuson criticized Marxist history in general as reading back into the past the present dreams of workers. In the case of the Winnipeg General Strike, there was no evidence of any connection whatever between the strike and the rise of industrial unionism in the 1940s, and "only the most slender thread connecting the strike to the rise of the CCF."[8] As for the significance of the Winnipeg General Strike in Canadian history, it lay in "its unique occurrence that took place for particular reasons and which had specific consequences" and not for some "hidden inner meaning" found only in the minds of historians.

Bryan Palmer entered the debate to argue that the significance of the strike lay in the fact that it reflected both "the continuity of class struggle and the changes that had taken place as a consequence of the twentieth-century conditions of monopoly capital, state intervention, and labour market segmentation."[9] Craig Heron agreed with those labour historians who saw the strike as only one of a series of strikes between 1917 and 1925 in industrial centres across the country, where "workers formed their own organizations, marched off the job in record numbers, engaged in defiant acts of solidarity, and made bold new demands."[10] He urged labour historians to study the ethnic and gender component of workers' revolts.

The debate on what happened in Winnipeg in 1919 and its consequences continues. Clearly, though, the strike remains the best-known example of a general strike in Canadian history.

1. D.C. Masters, *The Winnipeg General Strike* (Toronto: University of Toronto Press, 1950), pp. 127, 134.

2. S.D. Clark, "Introduction" to Masters, p. viii.

3. David Bercuson, *Confrontation at Winnipeg* (Montreal/Kingston: McGill-Queen's University Press, 1974), p. 176.

4. Irving Abella, "Introduction," in Irving Abella, ed., *On Strike: Six Key Labour Struggles in Canada, 1919–1949* (Toronto: James Lewis & Samuel Publishers, 1974), p. xii.

5. Norman Penner, *Winnipeg 1919: The Strikers' Own History of the Winnipeg General Strike*, 2nd ed. (Toronto: James Lorimer, 1975), pp. xxiii, vii–viii.

6. D.J. Bercuson, "Labour Radicalism and the Western Industrial Frontier: 1897–1919," *Canadian Historical Review*, LVIII, 2 (June 1977): 154–75.

7. Gregory Kealey, "1919: The Canadian Labour Revolt," *Labour/Le Travail*, 13 (Spring 1984): 15.

8. Bercuson, *Confrontation at Winnipeg*, rev. ed. (Montreal/Kingston: McGill-Queen's University Press, 1990), pp. 202, 205.

9. Bryan Palmer, *Working-Class Experience: Rethinking the History of Canadian Labour, 1880–1991* (Toronto: McClelland & Stewart, 1993), p. 180.

10. Craig Heron, "Introduction," in Craig Heron, ed., *The Workers' Revolt in Canada, 1917–1925* (Toronto: University of Toronto Press, 1998), p. 4.

New Postwar Political Leaders

As the 1920s began, William Lyon Mackenzie King succeeded Laurier as Liberal leader, while Arthur Meighen succeeded Robert Borden. These two new leaders had completely opposite approaches to politics. King sought compromise. To him, right answers did not exist in politics, only answers that seemed better because they offended fewer people. As a result he often spoke in ambiguities and in generalities. Meighen, by contrast, stated his position clearly and unequivocally. He upheld principles over compromise and believed that Canadians should be made to see the truth as he saw it. To him, every problem had a solution, and he clearly articulated solutions often without regard for the possible political repercussions.

Regional Protest

The Maritime Rights Movement

Regional protest movements arose in both eastern and western Canada. In the Maritimes, the Maritime Rights movement fought for a greater Maritime voice in national politics. By the 1920s, the number of seats from the Maritimes in the House of Commons had fallen by one-quarter (to 31) and even more in proportion to other areas of the country where the population was expanding, as a result of depopulation, as thousands left the region in search of work. Economically, manufacturing companies in the region reestablished themselves in the larger markets of central Canada. A decline in demand for Cape Breton coal and steel hurt that regional industry. Shipbuilding also went into decline as Canada competed with Britain and the United States for international sales.

The Maritimes also suffered from tariff reductions throughout the 1920s that had formerly protected its industries from international competition. A rise in freight rates of 200 percent or more on the Intercolonial Railway also hurt the region's economy. As well, when the Canadian government nationalized the Intercolonial Railway as part of the Canadian National Railways (CNR), it moved the Intercolonial's head office from Moncton to Montreal, and thus the railway ceased to promote regional interests.

A.P. Paterson, a grocer from Saint John, New Brunswick, led a group of influential business and professional people in the region to launch the Maritime Rights movement. The group demanded increased federal subsidies for the Maritime provinces, more national and international trade through the ports of Halifax and Saint John, and improved tariff protection to strengthen the region's steel and coal industries.

In the federal election of 1921, the movement pressed Maritime Liberal candidates to swear "to advocate and stand by Maritime rights first, last and all the time." The Liberals won all but six of the Maritime constituencies. However, the Maritime members of parliament could not keep their promises, since Mackenzie King's Liberal minority government depended too much on Prairie support to be able to cater to Maritime needs, and especially to raise the tariff.

Disillusioned, Maritime voters switched to the Conservatives in the 1925 federal election, giving the party all but three of the 31 seats. Unfortunately for Maritimers, the Liberals returned to power in 1926. King established a royal commission to investigate the group's complaints. But before it reported, the Maritime Rights movement had disbanded.

The Progressive Movement

In the West, farmers had been demanding for some time reduced freight rates, an end to the monopoly of eastern-owned grain-elevator companies, an increase in the CPR's boxcar allotment for grain trade, a railway to Hudson Bay to rival the CPR, and most of all, a reduction in the tariff. With the election of a "nonpartisan" Union government in 1917, farmers hoped that it would remove the

Arch Dales' cartoon in the Grain Growers' Guide *in 1915 conveys western farmers' views of Canada's political and economic reality.*

Glenbow Archives, Calgary, Canada/NA 3055-24.

tariff. When it failed to do so, Thomas Crerar, the minister of agriculture from Manitoba in the Union government, resigned from the Cabinet in 1919. Nine other western Unionist MPs followed. They formed the nucleus of a new National Progressive Party.

The party won an amazing 65 seats in the federal election of 1921. They won 39 of the 56 seats in the West, and gained a significant 24 in Ontario. But the party had no seats in Quebec and just one in the Maritimes. The party was also weakened by an internal split between a Manitoba-based wing under Crerar and an Alberta-based wing under Henry Wise Wood, an American populist farmer who came to Alberta in 1905 and became president of the United Farmers of Alberta (UFA) in 1916. Crerar wanted the Progressives to act as a pressure group to force the minority Liberal government to implement policies favourable to farmers. Wood saw political parties as inherently evil, and favoured replacing them with "group government" made up of all occupational groups in society.

Unable to resolve their differences, the party proved politically ineffective. They declined the role of official opposition. Then, in 1922, Crerar resigned as leader. His successor, Robert Forke, had no better luck uniting the party. The party lost political strength throughout the 1920s, and was, by the election of 1930, a spent force.

Advances to Nationhood

Prime Minister Robert Borden emerged from World War I determined to ensure that Canada benefited from its major contribution to the war through enhanced national status. First he pressed for Dominion representation in the British Empire delegation at the Paris Peace Conference, which met in 1919 to settle the war. He won representation for Canada at the Conference not only as a power in its own right, but also as a member of the British Empire delegation.

Borden also insisted on Canada's right to membership in the League of Nations' General Assembly as well as eligibility for membership in the governing council of the new international body. Once in the League of Nations, however, Canada wanted to limit its commitment. It opposed Article 10 of the League's charter, which bound members to come to the aid of other league members in times of attack. Borden feared that this agreement would commit Canadians to involvement in world disputes that were of no interest to them. (In the end, Article 10 remained in place.) Clearly, by the end of the war and in the immediate postwar period, Canada had taken the first few important steps along the road from colony to nation. The sense of nationalism these events reflected was one of the enduring legacies of the Great War for Canadians. As Jonathan Vance has shown in *Death So Noble*, the pride in Canada's soldiers infused the memories, stories, and myths of the Great War.[1]

From Colony to Nation

In the 1920s, King's Liberal government made further advances towards Canadian autonomy. In 1922, King refused to automatically come to Britain's defence when British troops were threatened by Turkish nationalists while maintaining the neutrality of the Dardanelles, the straits that linked the Black Sea to the Mediterranean Sea. When pressured by British leaders, King replied that only the Canadian parliament could decide Canadian participation, and King was in no hurry to call Parliament. By the time it did meet, the crisis had passed. A year later, the Canadian government signed the Halibut Treaty, a Canadian–American agreement relating to fishing rights on the Pacific coast, without acquiring British parliamentary approval, the first time that Britain had been bypassed in signing international agreements affecting Canada.

The next step toward Canadian autonomy came with the signing of the Balfour Declaration at the Imperial Conference of 1926. It recognized the dominions as "autonomous communities within the British empire, equal in status, in no way subordinate to one another in any respect of their domestic or external affairs, though united by a common allegiance to the Crown, and freely associated as members of the British Commonwealth of Nations."

The final step to securing full Canadian autonomy occurred in 1931 with the signing of the Statute of Westminster. This act prohibited the British parliament from declaring any law passed by the Canadian parliament as being *ultra vires*, or unconstitutional, except for laws amending the British North America Act. Canada insisted on continued British approval for these latter laws because of the failure of the federal and provincial governments to agree on an amending formula.

The Economics of Adjustment

In the 1920s, the Canadian economy shifted from the old staple economy of fish, timber, and wheat to a new resource economy of pulp and paper, mining, and the production of consumer goods. The new economy made Canada more dependent on the United States as its major trading partner. In 1923, for the first time, Canadians exported more to the United States than to Britain. Pulp and paper became Canada's leading new export. At the beginning of the 1920s, paper mills in Canada produced 938 million tons (1 ton = about 0.907 tonnes) of newsprint; by the end of the decade, this production increased more than threefold to 2981 million tons— enough to print 40 billion newspapers a year. Mining followed a similar pattern. After a sluggish period in the early 1920s, it revived as a result of an American demand for Canadian-based metals to produce such consumer goods as automobiles, radios, and electrical appliances.

Whole new areas opened up across the country, but particularly in the Laurentian Shield area of northern Ontario and Quebec, with the discovery of new lodes of copper, zinc, lead, and precious metals. Hydroelectric production quadrupled in the mid-1920s, providing power for the pulp and paper industry and for the refineries.

A Revolution in Transportation and Communication

Growth in the primary sector multiplied markets in the secondary sector. The most spectacular secondary growth occurred in the automotive industry. Next to the United States, Canada became in the 1920s "the most motorized country on the globe."

Initially, Canada produced its own cars. At one time as many as seventy small companies manufactured, assembled, or sold automobiles in Canada. But Canadian companies failed to keep pace with their automated American counterparts, and eventually sold out to the American giants. By the end of the decade, the American "big three" manufactured three-quarters of the cars purchased in Canada.

Aviation expanded greatly in the 1920s. Veteran World War I flying aces assisted in opening up the North by flying geologists and prospectors into remote areas of the Canadian Shield and providing service to isolated northern settlements. In 1924, Laurentide Air Services began Canada's first regular air-mail service, into the Quebec gold fields at Rouyn–Noranda. Other companies followed, and for several years the Canadian government permitted each company to print and issue its own postage stamps.

Important communications inventions became popular in the 1920s. The telephone became a standard household item. Radios, the great communications invention of the 1920s, helped to end isolation and loneliness. The first scheduled broadcast in North America took place in Montreal in May 1920, when station XWA (later CFCF) relayed a musical program to a Royal Society of Canada meeting in Ottawa.

Disillusionment and the Decline of Reform

Idealism and reform declined by the mid-1920s. In part, this was due to the success of each of the reform movements in achieving their goals. By 1921, workers had a higher standard of living and had achieved better recognition from employers. Women had the franchise federally and in most provinces. Prohibitionists had succeeded in eliminating legalized drinking. Educational reformers' achievements included better schools, children staying in school longer, and better-qualified teachers. Yet, in a sense, all these groups had failed in their ultimate objective: a new, regenerated, harmonious, and ideal Canada.

In some instances, a reaction to reform set in. Prohibitionists, for example, saw the provincial temperance acts removed one by one. By the end of the decade, government-regulated outlets sold liquor in every province except Prince Edward Island.

Social gospellers within the mainstream churches retreated during the prosperous 1920s, as churchgoers became more concerned with personal prosperity and individual salvation than with social regeneration. Church reformers within the Methodist, Presbyterian, and Congregationalist churches did succeed in 1925 in creating the United Church of Canada. They hoped that this new church would rejuvenate the reformers' zeal and challenge the secularization of Canadian society. But when the new church challenged society, it appeared to some as too radical and reform-minded. Many members left and joined fundamentalist churches that upheld more traditional values and beliefs, or they became members of conservative sects and cults.

In Quebec, the Roman Catholic community reacted to the growing secularization of society. Abbé Lionel Groulx, the editor of *L'Action française*, saw the onslaught of urban and industrial society as anathema to everything French Canadians believed in: the land, the church, the family, and the French-Canadian nation. In his journal, he launched an all-out attack—*l'action française*—on those forces that he believed were contributing to the anglicization and Americanization of Quebec.

Women in the 1920s

Women made only modest gains in the 1920s. The women's suffrage movement had obtained the vote, but the electorate returned few women to either federal or provincial governments. Agnes Macphail was the only woman elected in the federal election of 1921, making her Canada's first woman member of parliament. Provincially, women did better at entering politics, although the results remained far short of their expectations. As late as 1940, only nine women sat in provincial legislatures, all of them in the four western provinces.

Women still faced discrimination. For example, not until 1929 in the famous "Persons Case" were women considered "persons" and thus eligible for membership in all Canadian legislative bodies. Five Alberta women reformers—Emily Murphy, Irene Parlby, Nellie McClung, Henrietta Edwards, and Louise McKinney—fought the court case up to the highest court of appeal, the Judicial Committee of the Privy Council in England.

Few women had the opportunity for a secondary education; in 1929, only a quarter of the national secondary-school student body were women. Of the few who entered the professions, most became teachers or nurses, while only a handful became physicians, lawyers, or professors, and a very tiny number engineers.

Women who worked outside the home in industry or business—20 percent of the labour force in 1929—held traditional female jobs as secretaries, sales clerks in department stores, and domestics. Others worked on assembly lines in textile or tobacco factories, canneries, or fish plants. In these jobs, women earned considerably less than men doing the same job. Economic equality remained an elusive goal for women.

Unions did little to organize working women, even in the female-dominated industries. Seldom did they support women on strike. Agreements with employers commonly included lower female wage scales. In some cases, male-dominated unions demanded equal pay for women and men—not to combat discrimination against women but rather to ensure that employers would have no financial reason to replace male employees with females.

Although many farms were becoming more mechanized in the 1920s, the farmhouses remained basic. Prairie farm wives were also expected to help outside the house at critical times of the year, while they continued caring for the children, cooking, cleaning, laundering, and sewing. Rural reform leaders advocated household-science courses, cooperation, and the use of more household appliances as ways of alleviating the burden.

Urban middle-class women enjoyed a higher standard of living than their rural counterparts. Many benefited from modern labour-saving devices such as refrigerators, electric stoves, and vacuum cleaners, and from such luxuries as electricity and running water. Ironically, however, these "conveniences" increased the amount of time women spent in the home.

The Aboriginal Peoples

The experience of the First Nations peoples in the 1920s varied across Canada. In the northern forested areas, the First Nations and Métis suffered greatly when boom prices for furs led to an influx of non-Aboriginal trappers. As well, intensive trapping resulted in a serious depletion in the numbers of beaver. Some First Nations and Métis people worked as tourist guides, in commercial fishing, and as miners, railway workers, and loggers. In the South, farming on the reserves declined as heavy expenditures became necessary for the new farm machinery. Among the Iroquois, high-steel rigging, although dangerous work, was popular and lucrative. On the Pacific coast, First Nations people could obtain jobs in logging and commercial fishing. A number of independent First Nations operators owned and operated gas-powered gillnetters, trollers, and seine boats.

Labour in the 1920s

Labour unions faced difficult times in the 1920s, as wage cuts, industrial consolidation, improved technology, and managerial efficiency all weakened the labour movement. Workers retaliated by staging strikes. Most strikes failed to improve wages or working conditions, and many ended in physical violence. Union membership plummeted by more than one-third by mid-decade, reaching a low of 260 000 members.

Unions were also divided. The conservative Trades and Labor Congress (TLC) continued to favour craft unions and to advocate advancement only through conciliation and government intervention. In 1927, a new, militant All-Canadian Congress of Labour (ACCL) union was established. It favoured industry-wide unions and strike action. In Quebec, some workers and farmers joined Roman Catholic unions, guided by priests and sanctioned by the Church. These unions attempted to isolate their members from the more secular and often socialistic "foreign"—American or English-Canadian—unions. Throughout the 1920s, unions in Quebec never succeeded, however, in attracting much more than one-quarter of the total Quebec union membership.

Cultural Developments

Art

Cultural life flourished in the 1920s. In English-speaking Canada, the Group of Seven dominated contemporary art. Their first exhibition was held in May 1920. The exhibition catalogue claimed that art must reflect "the spirit of a nation's growth." The Group of Seven believed that "spirit" could best be found in the land—in the trees, rocks, and lakes of the Ontario northland. They depicted the land in brilliant mosaics of bright colours. For the Group of Seven, the Ontario northland symbolized the nation in the same way that the West did in the American tradition—a mythical land that became a metaphor for the Canadian people. As well, the "North" represented a counterforce to the "South," especially the United States, where urbanization, industrialism, and materialism threatened to undermine the Canadian spirit.

In British Columbia, Emily Carr had begun in 1908 to visit First Nations communities and to paint scenes of their villages, buildings, and totem poles. In 1932, at age 57, Carr launched into the most productive period of her artistic career. At the start, she emphasized nature themes and was beginning to focus on First Nations subjects in her paintings.

Members of the Group of Seven at a 1920 luncheon at the Arts and Letters Club. Left to right: A.Y. Jackson, Fred Varley, and Lawren Harris; Barker Fairley, a strong supporter of the Group but not a member; Frank Johnston, Arthur Lismer, and J.E.H. MacDonald. Absent was Frank Carmichael.

Arthur Gross, The Arts and Letters Club, Toronto.

On the Prairies, Lionel LeMoine FitzGerald, of Winnipeg, and Illingworth Kerr, from Lumsden, Saskatchewan, captured the region's uniqueness on canvas. In the Maritimes, a group of local artists arranged for their own exhibition and issued their own magazine, *Maritime Art*, which by 1940 had become Canada's first full-fledged art magazine. This Maritime group assisted Jack Humphrey and Miller Brittain, both born and raised in Saint John, New Brunswick, where they spent most of their lives, in becoming internationally recognized Maritime artists.

Literature

A new literary culture emerged in the 1920s. In English-speaking Canada, two new journals captured and epitomized the cultural renaissance: the *Canadian Forum* and the *Canadian Historical Review*. The Canadian Authors' Association (CAA), founded in 1921 for the purpose of using literature "to articulate a national identity and to foster a sense of community within the country," aided young English-Canadian writers in publishing their works.

In poetry, E.J. (Ned) Pratt of Newfoundland used familiar Canadian historical events as the subjects for his poems and elevated them to mythical proportions. Some of his most famous were *Brébeuf and His Brethern*, about the heroic seventeenth-century French Canadian martyr, and *Towards the Last Spike*, about the building of the Canadian Pacific Railway.

At McGill University, a group of young, rebellious poets known as the "Montreal group"— F.R. Scott, A.J.M. Smith, A.M. Klein, and Leo Kennedy—endorsed the modernist movement. They wrote in free verse, discarded the norms of punctuation, and chose their subject material in the modern city. They began two small literary journals, the *McGill Fortnightly Review* (1925–1927) and the *Canadian Mercury* (1928–1929), as vehicles for their works.

In French-speaking Quebec, a group of young poets challenged the establishment in the pages of *Le Nigog*, the first arts magazine in Quebec, and founded by architect Fernand Préfontaine, writer Robert de Roquebrune, and musician Léo-Paul Morin. Ironically, although this group and the "Montreal group" resided in the same city, they worked in isolation from one another.

While most novels continued to be romantic and escapist, three prairie novels stood out for their realism: Frederick Philip Grove's *Settlers of the Marsh* (1925), in which Grove explored the inner psychic tension of a Norwegian settler on the Prairies; Martha Ostenso's *Wild Geese* (1925), about the tyrannical patriarch Caleb Gare, who aims to dominate both his land and his family and in the process destroys himself; and R.J.C. Stead's *Grain* (1926), which describes the tensions that farm boy Gander Stake faces in having to choose between life on the farm and in the city.

Popular Culture

English-speaking Canadian popular culture became more Americanized in the 1920s. Canadians who had never set eyes on the *Canadian Forum* or even the mass-circulation *Maclean's* knew about such popular American magazines as *Ladies' Home Journal*, *McCall's*, and *Saturday Evening Post*. Canadian newspapers also adopted an "American" style: glossy, plenty of advertising, sensational headlines and stories, comic strips, substantial sports sections, and a heavy reliance on American wire services for international coverage.

Radio made great advancements in the 1920s. By the end of the decade, some sixty Canadian stations existed across the country, consisting mainly of news, lectures, or recorded music. But most of them carried American material. As a result, in 1928, the Canadian government established the Aird Commission to review public broadcasting. The Aird Report recommended that broadcasting become a public monopoly, without competitors and with limited commercial content.

Movies contributed to the Americanization of Canadian culture in the 1920s. Initially, it did not appear that this would be the case; between 1919 and 1923, Canada had a thriving domestic feature film industry that used Canadian settings, casts, and crews. But thereafter, what Canadian companies existed succumbed to the American "Big Five" studios—Paramount, MGM, Warner Brothers, Fox, and RKO.

Sports

The professionalization and Americanization of Canadian sports accelerated in the 1920s. At the beginning of the 1920s, professional hockey was solely Canadian. Then the National Hockey League expanded into the lucrative urban market of the United States. By 1930, only two of the NHL teams were Canadian: the Toronto Maple Leafs and the Montreal Canadiens, although almost all the players were Canadians.

In other sports, a number of Canadian amateurs won international recognition. Track-and-field athletes Percy Williams and Ethel Catherwood won gold medals at the 1928 Olympics. George Young made a name for Canada in swimming by winning the 32 km race from the California mainland to Catalina Island. In the Maritimes, Captain Angus Walters sailed the *Bluenose* to three successive wins in the International Fisherman's Trophy—in 1921, 1922, and 1923. The famous Edmonton Grads women's basketball team, formed from students and graduates of an Edmonton high school, set a world record by winning 502 games and losing only 20 during its entire career from 1915 to 1940.

As the 1920s ended, Canada appeared to be entering a new era of prosperity, comparable to that at the turn of the twentieth century. While not all Canadians benefited from the prosperity and some groups, such as women and labourers, still struggled to achieve recognition and equality, hope abounded that progress would continue. Few Canadians predicted that the end of 1929 would inaugurate the worst depression in world history.

The Advent of the Great Depression

On October 29, 1929—"Black Tuesday"—the crash of the New York stock market precipitated stock market crashes around the world. International trade declined as nations imposed high tariffs on foreign trade in an effort to protect industries and workers in their own countries from foreign competition. Worldwide overproduction of commodities such as wheat, newsprint, and metals—all important Canadian exports—saw prices plummet.

The Great Depression affected the entire Western world. It hit Canada severely, because the national economy had expanded so rapidly and so extensively in the first three decades of the twentieth century. In essence, having risen so high, it had further to fall. Industrial production fell by over one-third between 1929 and 1932. During the same period, Canada's gross national product sank two-fifths in current dollars. Imports declined in volume by about 55 percent and exports by 25 percent. The unemployment rate soared.

Within Canada, the Prairie West and British Columbia probably suffered most because of the dependence of these regions on primary industries, especially wheat production, and their overexpansion in the previous decades. As well, the Prairie West suffered from a climatic disaster: ten years of exceptional and persistent drought, extreme summer and winter temperatures, unusual weather patterns, and grasshopper infestations. The topsoil turned to dust and blew away. British Columbia had to contend with high numbers of transients; Vancouver became known as "the Mecca for the unemployed."

From 1928 to 1932 wheat prices fell from $1.29 to 34 cents a bushel for No. 1 Hard, the best wheat on the market. Prices for lesser grades were considerably lower. Also, farmers themselves paid for the cost of shipping the grain to the lakehead, eroding profit even further. Some western farmers found it cost less to burn their crops than to harvest them. The wheat pools went bankrupt.

Similar dramatic conditions prevailed in other primary resource sectors. Mines closed down for lack of business and thousands of investors lost everything. The pulp and paper industry had over-expanded in the 1920s. When the Depression hit, the newsprint market collapsed, and, along with it, the pulp and paper industry.

Money markets followed. Banks and other financial institutions had generously approved loans in the 1920s. In the Depression, they recalled loans and demanded mortgage payments. But the average Canadian investors could not retrieve their money or cover their debts. Many people abandoned their homes and farms, leaving banks with property that no one could afford and hence had little monetary value.

Dust storm near Lethbridge, Alberta—a familiar sight in Prairie Canada during the "Dirty Thirties."

Glenbow Archives, Calgary, Canada/NA-1831-1.

Companies and factories cut back on wages and on employees. By 1933, over 20 percent of the entire Canadian labour force remained unemployed. In some regions of the country, the figures rose as high as 35 percent and even 50 percent.

The R.B. Bennett Government's Response to the Depression

The Conservatives under R.B. Bennett won the election of 1930 on the promise that they would solve the problems of the Depression. Bennett introduced a high-tariff policy on manufactured goods as one solution; unfortunately, the high tariff hurt Canadian trade, especially with the United States, which retaliated with their own high tariff.

Bennett also introduced the Unemployment Relief Act, which provided $20 million of assistance to the poor. But he soon discovered that much more was needed. Between 1930 and 1938, Ottawa would provide nearly $350 million in relief for the jobless and for destitute farmers, while municipal and provincial governments added another $650 million. Still, the problem of destitution persisted.

Relief

For the first time, thousands of Canadians faced the personal degradation of going on relief— the "pogey," as it was called. In a society built on a philosophy of self-help, relief was an admission that one could no longer fend for oneself. Many people lost their sense of self-worth.

Those on relief faced the further humiliation of having to acknowledge their failure publicly. They lined up in a church basement or firehall waiting for relief. When their turn came, they had to proclaim their destitution by swearing that they did not own a car, a radio, or a telephone and that they were in arrears in rent payments, and had received notice of discontinuation of electricity and water service, as well as impending eviction. Then the authorities gave them food vouchers to purchase the minimum necessities at local stores—a further reminder of their impoverished condition.

To give those on relief the illusion of working for their relief payments, governments created makeshift jobs known as "boon-doggling." The town of New Toronto, Ontario, for example, required relief workers to haul large stones to vacant lots, where they were smashed and used for road construction. Winnipeg men on relief sawed wood, pulled weeds along city boulevards, and swept the city streets. Rumours abounded of some municipalities that had "relief men" dig holes one day and fill them in the next, simply to keep them occupied.

To avoid drifters coming into town for assistance, most municipalities had lengthy residence requirements to qualify for relief. This hurt immigrants in particular. The Immigrant Act allowed for the deportation of immigrants on relief. Between 1930 and 1935, Ottawa returned an unprecedented 30 000 immigrants to Europe.

Relief Camps and the On-to-Ottawa Trek

By 1932, more than 1.5 million Canadians (15 percent of the nation's population) depended on relief. The country seemed ripe for rebellion. Of particular concern were unemployed single men, many of whom "rode the rods" across Canada in search of work, begged for food and clothing, camped in shantytowns on the outskirts of cities, and lined up at soup kitchens and hostels for food and shelter. To deal with these transient unemployed single men, the Bennett government established relief camps across the country. During the four-year period that they existed, an estimated 20 000 single, homeless male "volunteers" lived in intolerable conditions and worked long hours at menial jobs designed simply to keep them busy for a meagre 20 cents a day.

In the spring of 1935, men in British Columbia work camps jumped the trains en route to Ottawa to protest conditions. They picked up other camp men and unemployed workers along the way. By the time they reached Regina they were over 2000 strong. The federal government ordered the RCMP to break up the march. The ensuing confrontation, on Dominion Day, 1935, left one plainclothes policeman dead and numerous strikers and police officers injured. The police arrested 120 of the trekkers and convicted eight of them. Only strike leader Arthur Evans and a few others were permitted to continue to Ottawa, where Bennett denounced them as "red" agitators and dissidents.

Canada's millionaire prime minister came to represent the callous indifference of the rich to the suffering of the unemployed and destitute. In fairness to Bennett, beneath his cold exterior existed a warm generosity. Thousands of Canadians wrote personal letters to him expressing their hardships and appealing for help. Very often he sent them money from his own pocket.

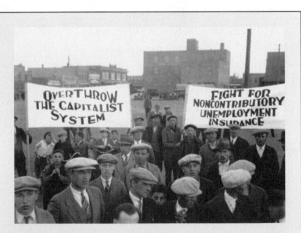

A demonstration of strikers at Market Square on the eve of the Regina Riot on Dominion Day, 1935. During the riot, one plainclothes policeman was killed and numerous strikers and police officers were injured.

Dick and Ada Bird Collection/Saskatchewan Archives Board/ R-A27560-1.

Bennett's New Deal

Bennett enacted a number of measures that, over time, strengthened Canada's economy. He established the Bank of Canada, to "promote the economic and financial welfare of the Dominion." His government passed the Natural Products and Marketing Act, which set up a federal marketing board with authority over all "natural products of agriculture and of the forest, sea, lake or river." The Conservatives also introduced the Canada Grain Board Act, which gave Ottawa control of the marketing of coarse grains, including wheat. In 1934, Bennett also appointed the Royal Commission on Price Spreads to investigate the buying practices of major department stores and the labour conditions in certain industries. Out of that commission came legislation to institute unemployment insurance and to regulate wages and working hours. Unfortunately both bills were struck down by the Judicial Committee of the Privy Council as unconstitutional.

Despite these measures, Bennett's Conservatives were defeated in the election of 1935, and the Liberals under Mackenzie King returned to power. But in the popular vote in that election, more than 25 percent of Canadians voted for one of the new parties that entered the election.

Third Parties

The CCF

Two of those new parties began on the Prairies. The Co-operative Commonwealth Federation (CCF) drew together dissident groups of farmers, labourers, socialists, academics, and disenchanted Liberals. At the party's first convention in Calgary in August of 1932, it chose Labour MP J.S. Woodsworth, a prominent social gospeller and one of those arrested for supporting the Winnipeg General Strike of 1919, as their leader.

From the beginning, the CCF distanced itself from the two mainline parties by having a clear socialist program, the "Regina Manifesto," to deal with the Great Depression. The CCF favoured government control of the economy through the nationalization of the means of production, distribution, and exchange. It also worked for a more equitable distribution of wealth, the creation of a welfare state, and the pursuit of international peace through the League of Nations.

The CCF entered the federal election in 1935 with high hopes of becoming a major party. It did acquire the reputation of being "the conscience of the House of Commons." But the party won only seven seats, all from the West.

Social Credit

In Alberta, the Social Credit Party began in 1935. It blamed the Depression on the financial institutions that hoarded money, thus preventing consumers from buying the abundant goods that the capitalist system produced. The party's solution was for the government to inject money into the economy by giving each adult a monthly "national dividend" of $25. To people without sufficient money to buy even the necessities of life, the theory proved appealing.

Social Credit found a popular leader in the charismatic William "Bible Bill" Aberhart. He used his popularity as a lay preacher on the radio to attract financial contributions from his listeners to build his Prophetic Bible Institute in Calgary, which he used to distribute Social Credit material after he had "converted" to Social Credit in the summer of 1932. However, only on the eve of the 1935 provincial election did he form his Social Credit Party. Despite its late launch, the party swept Alberta, winning 56 of the 63 seats.

The federal CCF caucus meets with its secretary J.S. Woodsworth, who is standing in the centre. On the extreme left sits Tommy Douglas, later Premier of Saskatchewan, and the first federal leader when the CCF changed its name to the New Democratic Party.

Library and Archives Canada/PA 167544.

Union Nationale

In Quebec, a new party, named the Union Nationale, under conservative leader Maurice Duplessis, emerged and won power by allying with a dissident left-wing group within the Liberal Party called Action libérale nationale, headed by Paul Gouin. After the election, the right-wing Duplessis purged his government of the Gouin faction.

Duplessis attacked a number of dissident groups in the province, including socialists, communists, and trade unionists. In 1937 he introduced the "Padlock Law," which made it illegal for any group to use a house or hall "to propagate communism or bolshevism" or to publish or distribute literature "tending to propagate communism." Duplessis used the law to lock premises suspected of being used for communist activities, to ban publications, and, on a couple of occasions, to arrest dissidents.

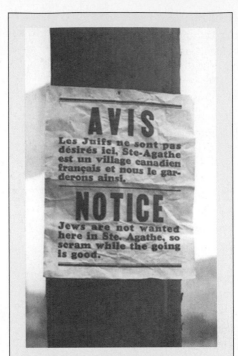

An anti-Semitic poster at Sainte-Agathe, a resort area in the Laurentians north of Montreal, 1939.

Library and Archives Canada/PA-107943. Reprinted with permission of The Gazette, Montreal.

Communists and Fascists

Extreme left- and right-wing political movements, such as the Communist Party and fascist groups, grew during the interwar years. The Communist Party of Canada, founded in 1921 in Guelph, Ontario, thrived in the economic-crisis conditions of the Depression, especially among immigrants threatened with deportation. From the party's inception, the federal government attempted to repress it by invoking section 98 of the Criminal Code, which made it illegal to advocate "governmental, industrial or economic change within Canada by the use of force, violence or physical injury to persons or property, or by threats of such injury." On the eve of World War II, the Communist Party had 16 000 members; however, when the Soviet Union signed a non-aggression pact with Adolf Hitler that summer, many quit in protest. In June 1940, the Canadian government declared the Communist Party illegal.

Fascists proved less numerous than communists. The Deutscher Bund Canada, founded in 1934 and led by German Canadians, never had more than 2000 members, while the Canadian Nationalist Party, founded by right-wing militants, and the allied Swastika clubs, added a few thousand more. In Quebec, Adrien Arcand's National Social Christian Party, modelled on the Nazi Party, claimed to represent the last stand of Roman Catholicism against communists and other "atheist" groups. While Arcand remained a marginal and eccentric character, anti-Semitism found support among nationalist movements in the province, such as the Jeune-Canada and the Ligue d'Action nationale. It also remained strong, in a more hidden way, in English-speaking Canada. Not surprisingly, thousands of persecuted Jews fleeing Nazi Germany found Canada's doors firmly closed. A leading member of the immigration department summarized the department's viewpoint toward Jewish immigrants with the comment "None is too many."

Labour in the Great Depression

Workers became more militant in the desperate conditions of the Great Depression. "Red" trade unions grew, and some affiliated with the Communist Party of Canada. For example, the Workers' Unity League (WUL) was born out of a directive from Moscow that communist-led unions should separate from "reformist" unions, and prepare for the coming world revolution.

Communist demonstration in Toronto, late February 1931, at the corner of Spadina and Dundas.
City of Toronto Archives, Fonds 1266, Item 23267.

At its peak in 1932, the WUL had an estimated 40 000 members. It claimed leadership of most of the strikes across the country in the early 1930s.

In 1935 a new union, the American-based Congress of Industrial Organizations (CIO), emerged in Canada to "organize the unorganized." The Canadian CIO's greatest success occurred in 1937, when the CIO-inspired United Auto Workers led the strike at the General Motors factory in Oshawa, Ontario. The CIO also organized Montreal's female garment workers, as well as coal miners in Nova Scotia. But elsewhere in the country, the CIO made little headway in the 1930s.

Women in the 1930s

Initially, the Depression benefited women who wanted to work because they could be hired at half a man's wages. Soon, however, a backlash occurred. Women were accused of taking jobs away from unemployed men who had wives and families to support. Women also faced difficulties getting relief even if they were eligible for it. Authorities reasoned that single unemployed women posed no threat to society, as did single unemployed men. Furthermore, they assumed that these women would be cared for by their families. As well, authorities feared that relief to women would contribute to the breakdown of the family.

Birth control was seldom an option women could consider, although by 1937 birth-control clinics existed in Toronto, Hamilton, and Windsor. Also available was A.H. Tyrer's popular book, *Sex, Marriage and Birth Control* (1936). The popular belief of the day was expressed by Dr. Helen McMurchy, director of the Dominion Division of Child Welfare, who described birth control among those of British background as "race suicide." French-Canadian nationalists used the same argument in Quebec. Still, a few doctors provided birth-control information and devices, but they did so at the risk of losing their medical licence. For some women, self-induced miscarriages seemed to be the only alternative to unwanted children or children they simply could not afford.

Mackenzie King's Government's Response to the Depression

Once back in power after the federal election of 1935, Mackenzie King's Liberals continued some of the Conservatives' policies to cope with the Depression and added some of their own. The Liberals, for instance, supported the Bank of Canada and made its governor responsible to Parliament for monetary policy. But the Liberals abolished the Conservatives' high-tariff policy by negotiating low-tariff agreements with both Britain and the United States.

Prairie Farm Rehabilitation Program

The Liberals continued the Conservatives' policy of aid to the drought-stricken farmers of western Canada and extended it further by implementing the Prairie Farm Rehabilitation Act (PFRA). The Act provided money to the experimental farms in the dry-belt area of the Palliser Triangle to apply the latest scientific knowledge to attempt to get the soil to regain its productivity. Two innovations followed: first, the Noble plough, invented by Charles Noble of Nobleford, Alberta, which cut the roots of weeds without turning over the topsoil to expose it to sun and wind; second, "trash farming"—instead of ploughing and harrowing their fields to make them look neat and clean, farmers were encouraged to leave the dead plants and grain stubble on the field to prevent wind erosion. The PFRA's program also provided money to build dugouts for spring runoff water for cattle, helped reseed vacant and pasture land, and, in the case of destitute farm families in the Palliser Triangle area, assisted relocation to better farming areas to the north.

The CBC, TCA, and NHA

The Liberals created two innovative national institutions and introduced two important social security measures in the 1930s. In 1936, they reorganized the Canadian Radio Broadcasting Commission into the Canadian Broadcasting Corporation (CBC). The CBC's mandate was to regulate private broadcasting and to develop its own network across the country with Canadian content in both official languages. In 1937, the Liberals also established Trans-Canada Air Lines (TCA), the forerunner of Air Canada, as a Crown corporation.

Two other federal initiatives proved successful: the Municipal Improvements Assistance Act, which authorized $30 million in federal loans at 2 percent interest for special municipal public-works projects, and the National Housing Act (NHA), which made federally backed mortgages easier to obtain. The NHA provided $30 million worth of mortgages for low-income tenants. It also allowed potential homeowners to borrow at least 60 percent of value for up to 20 to 25 years, and repayment of both interest and principal under a system of blended payments. This arrangement allowed more people to buy a home, if they could afford one.

The King government discontinued Bennett's relief camps, and instead established the National Employment Commission to reexamine and restructure the administration of direct relief. The commission made two important recommendations: first, that the federal government take over unemployment payments because this was too big and expensive an undertaking for municipal or provincial governments; and second, that the government adopt, a policy of deficit financing to provide additional relief and stimulate economic growth.

Royal Commission on Dominion–Provincial Relations

Before moving on either issue, King created the Royal Commission on Dominion–Provincial Relations to explore all aspects of relations between these two levels of government in light of the current economic crisis. The Commission recommended a stronger federal government economic presence. But its report did not appear until 1940. In the meantime, Parliament imposed the War Measures Act, which gave the government licence to impose many aspects of the report's centralist agenda without consulting the provinces, at least for the duration of World War II.

Religion

The trend in the 1930s was to move away from radical religion, with its emphasis on social reform, to a more conservative faith, with its emphasis on personal salvation and the importance of tradition. Nevertheless, a few radical groups gained some support during the Depression. The Fellowship for a Christian Social Order, founded by members of the United Church, argued for an overthrow of the capitalist system and replacing it with socialism as their answer to the economic crisis. The Student Christian Movement (SCM) provided study groups on most Canadian university campuses in the 1930s to discuss social issues and advocate social change.

Conservative and fundamentalist groups flourished in the decade. Disciples of the British Oxford Movement toured Canada, delivering a message of "revelation, not revolution" to overflow audiences. In Quebec, many in the Roman Catholic Church supported a back-to-the-land movement as the best means to combat both unemployment and "moral decrepitude."

Still others, particularly in the Maritimes, looked to cooperatives as the answer. Moses Coady, director of the extension department at St. Francis Xavier University in Antigonish, Nova Scotia, and Jimmy Tompkins, a fellow priest, worked to improve the lives of poor farmers, miners, fishers, and their families through cooperatives. The cooperatives might be credit unions, or perhaps centres for selling fish or farm produce.

Culture in the 1930s

During the 1930s, entertainment often became a means of escape from the realities of the Depression. Owners of radio sets in English-speaking Canada listened to the American comedy show *Amos 'n Andy*, the most popular program of the decade, and *Hockey Night in Canada* with announcer Foster Hewitt. Recording artists such as Willie Eckstein, Percy Faith, Guy Lombardo and his Royal Canadians, and Don Messer got their start on Canadian radio. French Canadians enjoyed the successful serials written specifically for radio, such as *Le Curé de Village* and *La Pension Velder*.

Mass magazines, both Canadian and American, featured stories of wealth and glamour, while films from Hollywood portrayed romance and fantasy. Walt Disney's *Snow White and the Seven Dwarfs* became a box-office hit. While English Canada was looking to Hollywood for its feature films, French Canada was excelling in documentaries. Albert Tessier and Maurice Proulx, two Catholic priests who took an amateur interest in documentaries, made films that glorified Quebec's natural landscape and the life of its rural inhabitants as their contribution to the back-to-the-land movement in the province.

The birth of the Dionne quintuplets near Callander, Ontario in May 1934 attracted worldwide attention and brought over three million people to see a glimpse of them at a special hospital set up to care for them under the auspices of the Ontario government, which quickly appreciated the profit to be made from this "tourist attraction." Even this real-life event was a form of escape for many.

Art

In 1933, the Canadian Group of Painters (CGP) formed as a loose-knit association that provided moral support for artists who were affiliated with it. Art education became one of their goals. French-Canadian painters in the 1930s showed a fascination with the land. Marc-Aurèle Fortin, for example, painted scenes of the village of Sainte-Rose and along the north shore of Montreal Island. Religious subjects appeared in the early paintings of Jean-Paul Lemieux. He chose colourful Fête-Dieu processions in Quebec streets and other religious events as subjects for his paintings. They too, like Fortin's, were noted for their quiet nostalgia and gentle lyricism.

Literature

In literature, Morley Callaghan's three novels—*Such Is My Beloved* (1934), *They Shall Inherit the Earth* (1935), and *More Joy in Heaven* (1937)—stood out as good examples of realistic novels, a reaction to the sentimental and romantic literature of an earlier generation. Irene Baird's *Waste Heritage* (1939) dealt with labour unrest and unemployment in Vancouver during the Depression. The most outstanding French-Canadian novel in the 1930s was Ringuet's (Philippe Panneton's) *Trente Arpents*, translated into English as *Thirty Acres*, a realistic novel that follows the fall of its central character, Euchariste Moisan, from initial prosperity on his farm to a broken man in a New England factory town.

Theatre

During the 1930s in Quebec, several of the best-known French-Canadian playwrights, such as Gratien Gélinas, made a living by writing scripts for radio productions, especially for the Canadian Broadcasting Corporation (CBC). Although the Roman Catholic Church opposed public theatre for entertainment purposes, the clergy did support amateur theatre for educational purposes. In English Canada, professional theatre languished, to be replaced by amateur theatre groups. Governor General Lord Bessborough assisted amateur theatre by founding in 1932 the Dominion Drama Festival, an annual competition. The best provincial productions went on to national finals, held each year in a different major city.

Working-class political theatre was popular during the Depression, especially the *agitprop* (a combination of the words "agitation" and "propaganda") theatre used by communist sympathizers to advance class struggle. The Workers' Experimental Theatre became the first agitprop troupe in Canada. It held its first performance on May 6, 1932, at the Ukrainian Labour Temple, followed in the summer of 1933 by three tours through southern Ontario. Its greatest success occurred in December 1933, when the group staged *Eight Men Speak*, a mock trial drama of the arrest two years earlier in 1931 and attempted assassination at the Kingston Penitentiary of Tim Buck, leader of the Communist Party, to an audience of 1500 at the Standard Theatre in Toronto. Many of the actors themselves risked arrest (and in some cases deportation) for taking part in the play, while theatre owners were threatened with revocation of their licences should they permit the play to be staged.

Sport

Sport became another form of popular entertainment and a distraction during the Depression. In winter, hockey dominated. Hockey stars became household names among sports-minded families: the Toronto Maple Leafs' famous "Kid Line" of Charlie Conacher, Joe Primeau, and Busher Jackson; the legendary Eddie Shore of the Boston Bruins, known for his speed and scoring flair; Francis "King" Clancy of the Toronto Maple Leafs, who once played every position on the ice in a single game; and Howie Morenz of the Montreal Canadiens, who with his speed and flashy stick handling was easily the greatest hockey superstar of the 1930s. In summer, baseball continued to be Canada's most popular sport. Every community had a local team, and the larger towns and cities enjoyed franchises in minor professional leagues.

The decades from 1919 to 1939 in general were ones of boom and bust. In that sense, this period appeared no different than earlier eras in Canadian history. However, significant differences were evident. The Canadian economy shifted to a new resource economy of pulp and paper, mining, and the production of consumer goods that made the country even more dependent on the United States. During the 1930s, unemployment rose to higher rates than ever before, forcing governments to implement social welfare and social security measures that would become standard fare in the post–World War II era. Regional protest grew while new regionally-based third parties became permanent fixtures in national politics. Social, gender, and ethnic groups intensified their struggles for equality. In these respects, the interwar years were ones of adjustment to a different Canada.

NOTE

1. Jonathan F. Vance, *Death So Noble: Memory, Meaning and the First World War* (Vancouver: UBC Press, 1997).

BEYOND THE BOOK

William Lyon Mackenzie King Diaries

http://king.collectionscanada.ca/EN/default.asp
Digitized, fully searchable diaries of the Prime Minister of Canada William Lyon Mackenzie King spanning six decades.

Indian Affairs Annual Reports: The 1920s

http://www.collectionscanada.gc.ca/databases/indianaffairs/index-e.html
Digitized copies of the annual reports of the federal Department of Indian Affairs during the 1920s. The annual reports from 1864 to 1990 are available as well on this site.

The Famous 5

http://epe.lac-bac.gc.ca/100/206/301/lac-bac/famous_five-ef
Digitized letters by the Famous 5, an account of the "Persons Case," and further resources about Henrietta Muir Edwards, Emily Murphy, Louise McKinney, Irene Parlby, and Nellie McClung.

The Dirty Thirties

http://www.mccord-museum.qc.ca/en/keys/webtours/GE_P4_1_EN
A virtual exhibit of life in the Great Depression in Canada, with digitized photographs and analysis.

United Farm Women of Alberta: Monthly Bulletins

http://asalive.archivesalberta.org:8080/access/asa/documents/display/GLEN-247
Digitized monthly bulletins of the United Farm Women of Alberta, covering economic, social welfare, and other topics.

The Inkameep Indian Day School

http://www.virtualmuseum.ca/Exhibitions/Inkameep/english/index.php
This website digitizes art created by First Nations children of the school between 1932 and 1942. The students expressed their mixed culture through the arts, and many paintings demonstrate this duality.

The Skin of a Lion

Michael Ondaatje, *In The Skin of a Lion* (Toronto: McClelland and Stewart, 1987). This novel details the lives of immigrants in Toronto in the 1920s and 1930s and the changing nature of the city.

Clara Callan

Richard B. Wright, *Clara Callan* (Toronto: HarperCollins Publishers Canada, 2002). This novel, set in the Great Depression, explores the lives of two sisters, one of whom lives in a small Ontario town and the other in New York. Diary entries and letters tell their stories.

As for Me and My House

Sinclair Ross, *As for Me and My House* (New York: Reynal & Hitchcock, 1941; numerous reprintings). The arrival of a couple at Horizon, Saskatchewan during the Great Depression, and the challenges they face socially and physically.

BIBLIOGRAPHY

For an overview of the interwar years, consult John Herd Thompson with Allen Seager, *Canada, 1922–1939: Decades of Discord* (Toronto: McClelland & Stewart, 1985). On the 1930s, see Michiel Horn's booklet *The Great Depression of the 1930s in Canada* (Ottawa: Canadian Historical Association, 1984).

On the Winnipeg General Strike, see the references listed at the end of "Where Historians Disagree: The Winnipeg General Strike" in this chapter.

On politics in the interwar years, see H.B. Neatby, *The Lonely Heights*, vol. 2, *1924–1932*, and *The Prism of Unity*, vol. 3, *1932–1939* (Toronto: University of Toronto Press, 1970, 1976), for Mackenzie King. Roger Graham's *Arthur Meighen* (Ottawa: Canadian Historical Association, 1965) deals with King's political rival in the 1920s, and Richard Wilbur's booklet *The Bennett Administration* (Ottawa: Canadian Historical Association, 1969) deals with King's rival in the 1930s. H. Blair Neatby provides an overview of politics in the 1930s in *The Politics of Chaos: Canada in the Thirties* (Toronto: Macmillan, 1972).

Maritime protest in the 1920s is discussed in E.R. Forbes, *The Maritime Rights Movement, 1919–27: A Study in Canadian Regionalism* (Montreal/Kingston: McGill-Queen's University Press, 1979). On the Progressive movement, see W.L. Morton, *The Progressive Party in Canada* (Toronto: University of Toronto Press, 1950). On the CCF in the 1930s, see Walter Young, *The Anatomy of a Party: The National CCF* (Toronto: University of Toronto Press, 1969). On Social Credit, see David R. Elliott and Iris Miller, *Bible Bill: A Biography of William Aberhart* (Edmonton: Reidmore Books, 1987); and Alvin Finkel, *The Social Credit Phenomenon in Alberta* (Toronto: University of Toronto Press, 1989). On the Union Nationale in Quebec, see Richard Jones's booklet *Duplessis and the Union Nationale Administration* (Ottawa: Canadian Historical Association, 1983); and H.F. Quinn, *The Union Nationale*, rev. ed. (Toronto: University of Toronto Press, 1979). For the Communist Party, see Norman Penner, *Canadian Communism: The Stalin Years and Beyond* (Toronto: Methuen Publications, 1988). Extreme right-wing movements are examined in Martin Robin, *Shades of Right: Nativist and Fascist Politics in Canada, 1920 to 1940* (Toronto: University of Toronto Press, 1991). Irving Abella and Harold Troper, *None Is Too Many: Canada and the Jews of Europe, 1933–1948*, 3rd ed. (Toronto: Lester, 1991), is a poignant account of Canada's treatment of Jewish refugees.

On the economics of the interwar years, see Michael Bliss, *Northern Enterprise: Five Centuries of Canadian Business* (Toronto: McClelland & Stewart, 1987); and Kenneth Norrie and Douglas Owram, *A History of the Canadian Economy*, 2nd ed. (Toronto: Harcourt Brace, 1996).

How Canada dealt with jobless or "radical" immigrants is discussed in Barbara Roberts, *Whence They Came: Deportation from Canada, 1900–1935* (Ottawa: University of Ottawa Press, 1988). James Struthers has studied the relief question in *No Fault of Their Own: Unemployment and the Canadian Welfare State, 1914–1941* (Toronto: University of Toronto Press, 1983). On the On-to-Ottawa Trek, see Bill Waiser, *All Hell Can't Stop Us: The On-to-Ottawa Trek and the Regina Riot* (Calgary: Fifth House, 2003).

On women in the interwar years, consult the relevant chapters in Alison Prentice et al., *Canadian Women: A History*, 2nd ed. (Toronto: Harcourt Brace, 1996); and Veronica Strong-Boag, *The New Day Recalled: Lives of Girls and Women in English Canada, 1919–1939* (Toronto: Copp Clark Pitman, 1988). The equivalent study for Quebec women is Andrée Lévesque, *Making and Breaking the Rules: Women in Quebec, 1919–1939* (Toronto: McClelland & Stewart, 1994).

Birth control is the subject of Angus McLaren and Arlene Tigar McLaren's *The Bedroom and the State: The Changing Practices and Politics of Contraception and Abortion in Canada, 1890–1980* (Toronto:

McClelland & Stewart, 1986). On the Dionne quintuplets, see the special issue of the *Journal of Canadian Studies*, 29, 4 (Winter 1995).

Labour in the interwar years is discussed in Bryan D. Palmer, *Working-Class Experience: Rethinking the History of Canadian Labour, 1800–1991* (Toronto: McClelland & Stewart, 1992); and Irving M. Abella, *Nationalism, Communism and Canadian Labour: The CIO, the Communist Party and the Canadian Congress of Labour, 1935–1956* (Toronto: University of Toronto Press, 1973). On labour in Quebec in the 1930s, see Evelyn Dumas, *The Bitter Thirties in Quebec* (Montreal: Black Rose Books, 1975).

Canadian culture is dealt with in "The Conundrum of Culture," in *Canada, 1922–1939* (as cited earlier), pp. 158–92. On cultural nationalism, see Mary Vipond, *The Mass Media in Canada* (Toronto: James Lorimer, 1992). On the Group of Seven, consult Peter Mellen, *The Group of Seven* (Toronto: McClelland & Stewart, 1970); and Charles C. Hill, *The Group of Seven: Art for a Nation* (Ottawa: National Gallery of Canada, 1995). On working-class theatre, see Richard Wright and Robin Endres, eds., *Eight Men Speak and Other Plays from the Canadian Workers' Theatre* (Toronto: New Hogtown Press, 1976); and Toby Gordon Ryan, *Stage Left: Canadian Theatre in the Thirties* (Toronto: CTR Publications, 1981). University education in the 1930s is the subject of Paul Axelrod's *Making a Middle Class: Student Life in English Canada during the Thirties* (Montreal/Kingston: McGill-Queen's University Press, 1990). Radio is discussed in Mary Vipond, *Listening In: The First Decade of Canadian Broadcasting, 1922–1932* (Montreal/Kingston: McGill-Queen's University Press, 1992). For Canadian sport, see Colin Howell, *Blood, Sweat, and Cheers: Sport in the Making of Modern Canada* (Toronto: University of Toronto Press, 2001); and for women and sport, M. Ann Hall, *The Girl and the Game: History of Women Sport in Canada* (Peterborough: Broadview Press, 2002).

Important reviews of First Nations history in the interwar years include Arthur Ray, *The Canadian Fur Trade in the Industrial Age* (Toronto: University of Toronto Press, 1990); and John Leonard Taylor, *Canadian Indian Policy during the Inter-War Years, 1918–1939* (Ottawa: Indian and Northern Affairs Canada, 1984). John S. Lutz reviews twentieth-century developments on the Pacific coast in *Makúk: A New History of Aboriginal-White Relations* (Vancouver: UBC Press, 2008).

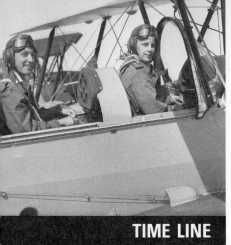

Chapter Nineteen

CANADA IN WORLD WAR II

TIME LINE

1939	World War II begins
1940	Ottawa sets up a federal unemployment insurance scheme Canada and the United States sign the Ogdensburg Agreement
1941	The Canadian Women's Army Corps is established
1942	A plebiscite on conscription is held in April; Canadians outside Quebec say "yes", a large majority of Quebeckers vote "no" Canadian troops participate in an ill-fated raid on the French port of Dieppe
1943	Canadian troops join Allied forces in the invasion of Italy
1944	The Family Allowance Act, Canada's first universal social welfare program, takes effect Canadian troops participate in the invasion of Normandy Ottawa decrees conscription
1945	World War II ends Workers stage a lengthy strike at the Ford motor plant in Windsor, Ontario to obtain recognition of collective bargaining rights Canada joins the United Nations

On September 1, 1939, the German army invaded Poland. Two days later, Britain and France declared war on Germany. Canada's own declaration of war followed on September 9. Surely few people imagined at this moment that the world would have to endure fully six years of untold destruction and death.

The war and its immediate aftermath forced Canadians to reflect upon their international responsibilities. To what degree and in what manner should they participate in the war effort? And how should Canada contribute to maintaining the peace that finally returned in 1945? These questions often provoked bitter controversy.

The development of a huge war industry brought a rapid end to the depression that had gripped Canada during the 1930s. In response to citizens' demands, the federal government also began to set up social programs to alleviate economic hardship. The role of women changed, as women left the home to work in industry, partly to replace men who had joined the armed forces. Union membership climbed rapidly, as unemployment fell to low levels. In federal–provincial relations, the war effort brought Ottawa to centralize power at the expense of the provinces. In international affairs, Canada shifted its focus from Britain to the United States as its major ally and trading partner. Indeed, the war transformed Canada in many ways.

Neutrality and Appeasement in the 1930s

In the 1930s, Canada used its newly won autonomy in foreign affairs to avoid military entanglements overseas. When, for example, Italian dictator Benito Mussolini invaded the independent African kingdom of Abyssinia (Ethiopia) in 1935, Prime Minister Mackenzie King made it clear that Canada should not become involved. He disavowed the Canadian representative at the League of Nations who had spoken in favour of imposing severe sanctions upon Italy. Britain and France saved Canada from further embarrassment when, in exchange for peace, they offered Mussolini the territory he had already overrun.

Adolf Hitler, who became chancellor of Germany in 1933, posed the greatest threat to world peace. Systematically, he set out to increase Germany's power. First, he reoccupied the hitherto demilitarized zone of the Rhineland in 1936, in violation of the Treaty of Versailles. Then, in 1938, he annexed Austria. Next, he seized the western part of Czechoslovakia, a conquest that Britain and France accepted, in the hope of avoiding war. Finally, in March 1939, the German leader annexed what remained of Czechoslovakia. Throughout all these acts of aggression, Canada supported Britain and France's policy of appeasement, of making concession after concession.

Many supporters of appeasement in Canada saw Hitler and Mussolini as bulwarks against the spread of communism, as defenders of order in an era of chaotic revolution. Yet other explanations exist for Canada's support of appeasement. King and his foremost advisers favoured it out of fear that British policies might undermine Canadian autonomy and again draw the country into imperial conflicts. With his sure political instincts, King also knew that another war, just like World War I, risked dividing Canadians in a bitter internal conflict that might destroy national unity as well as his government and the Liberal party.

Furthermore, isolationist sentiment ran deep in Canada, as it did in the United States, which had never even joined the League of Nations. Historian Frank Underhill said it more bluntly than most: "All these European troubles are not worth the bones of a Toronto grenadier."

In any case, many Canadians wondered, what impact could Canada have upon events? In 1938–1939, the country's total budget for the armed forces was a trifling $35 million. The navy had fewer than a dozen fighting ships, and the air force, only 50 modern military aircraft. The professional army had just 4000 troops; the navy, 3000; and the air force, only 1000. Twenty years of neglect had gravely weakened Canada's defences. Clearly, the nation could not even defend its own coasts, let alone dispatch fully equipped and trained forces to Europe.

Trainee pilots at No. 5 Elementary Flying Training School, Kenyon Field, Lethbridge, August 1940.

Glenbow Archives, *Calgary Herald*, NA-2864-3445.

Canada and the War against the Axis

When Britain declared war on Germany, Canada's support was not in doubt. Theoretically, Canada could have remained neutral, as the United States did until the Japanese attack on Pearl Harbor in December 1941. But Canada's strong emotional ties with the mother country made this option impossible.

Thanks to the "phoney war," as that period of relative quiet in the early months of the conflict was called, the Canadian government was able to postpone making wrenching decisions concerning the nature of Canada's participation. Nevertheless, during this period one vitally important part of Canada's contribution to the war got under way: the British Commonwealth Air Training Plan (BCATP), which was conducted in, and heavily funded by, Canada.

Negotiations with Britain to establish the terms of Canada's involvement proved arduous, even rancorous. As historian Desmond Morton observes, "King's attachment to England did not always extend to Englishmen."[1] The final plan gave control of the schools to the Royal Canadian Air Force (RCAF), which the federal government had organized immediately after World War I. By the end of the war, the BCATP had trained 130 000 aviators, nearly half the Commonwealth's air crews. The project also gave a tremendous boost to the aeronautics industry and, thanks to the more than $2 billion spent, to the Canadian economy in general.

The War Effort, 1940–1942

The Nazis' invasion of Western Europe in the spring of 1940 transformed the war. The rapid German advance led to the near-capture of the entire British Expeditionary Force at Dunkirk. After France fell in June, Britain and its dominions stood alone against Germany. Overnight, Canada became Britain's chief ally. Until the German invasion of the Soviet Union in June 1941, it remained so. During these dark months, Britain's surrender seemed highly possible.

To assist Britain and combat the Nazis, Canada built up a much larger army, constructed dozens of warships and hundreds of aircraft, and converted the entire economy to war production. In response to Britain's wartime financial needs, Canada lent, and then gave, huge sums of money through mutual-aid agreements, with no strings attached, although most of the money was spent in Canada on war materials destined for Britain.

Combat action for Canadian troops came first in the Pacific theatre. In hindsight, the federal government had foolishly agreed to reinforce British troops in Hong Kong. The colony fell to the Japanese on Christmas Day, 1941. More than 550 Canadians perished either in the attack or afterwards in the harsh conditions of Japanese slave labour camps. Later, Canada played a relatively minor role in the war in the Pacific. Plans to increase Canada's air and sea participation in summer 1945 were cancelled after the Americans dropped atomic bombs on two Japanese cities.

Canadians in Europe experienced their baptism of fire in August 1942, in the ill-conceived major Allied raid on the French coast at Dieppe. In a few terrible hours, more than 60 percent of the 5000 Canadian participants were killed or captured. For long months after that tragedy, Canadian troops continued garrison duty in Britain. They were not completely inactive: indeed,

A HISTORICAL PORTRAIT

Sir Frederick Banting and Pilot Joseph Mackey

Sir Frederick Banting is well known as the discoverer, with Charles Best, of insulin, used in the treatment of diabetes. Joseph Mackey was an American pilot, one of several hundred pilots and crew who worked for Ferry Command, an enterprise set up by the British and responsible for flying more than 9000 planes across the Atlantic for delivery in Great Britain.

The first flights began in February 1941. Banting, wanting to go to England, sought space on an aircraft as a passenger. He was assigned to the Lockheed Hudson piloted by Mackey. After bad weather finally cleared, five planes, including Mackey's, took off from Gander airport in Newfoundland. Shortly after takeoff, the left engine of Mackey's plane failed. The pilot turned back. Then the right engine lost power and the plane crashed. Mackey was injured, but not seriously. The other two crew members were killed. Banting suffered a concussion and internal bleeding. He died a few hours later despite Mackey's efforts to save his life. Three days later, Mackey was spotted by a plane and rescued. He later sold his story to a Toronto newspaper and then donated the proceeds to the children of his deceased radio officer.

More than 500 airmen lost their lives while working for Ferry Command, often in crashes of large Liberator bombers used to bring the crews home. About 50 passengers were killed, too. Banting was the first.

Source: Carl A. Christie, *Ocean Bridge: The History of RAF Ferry Command* (Toronto: University of Toronto Press, 1995), pp. 62–72.

thousands of marriages between Canadian servicemen and British women took place. One Montreal journalist commented that the Canadian army was "the first formation in the history of war" in which the birth rate exceeded the death rate!

Canadian–American Wartime Relations

War inevitably drew Canada closer to the United States. In August 1940, King and the American president, Franklin D. Roosevelt, signed the Ogdensburg Agreement, which created the Permanent Joint Board on Defence (PJBD), responsible for discussing military questions of mutual interest. As early as 1938, the two countries had begun to exchange military information. In the summer of 1940, King himself pushed for talks on common defence planning. Most Canadians approved of the continental defence tie, as they believed Canada could not rely on its own (then virtually nonexistent) defences or on Britain's. Thus, when Roosevelt proposed the PJBD, King was delighted, although he apparently had some doubts about making the board permanent.

Historians differ in their interpretations of this rapprochement. Donald Creighton, always alert to the imperial designs of Canada's southern neighbour, saw the Ogdensburg Agreement as a major step toward the Liberals' surrender of Canadian autonomy."[2] In contrast, J.L. Granatstein and Norman Hillmer have argued that King "wanted to protect Canada and to help Great Britain as much as possible, and he understood and accepted that this obliged him to seek even closer relations with Roosevelt's America."[3] Indeed, during the early months of war, Canada seems to have enjoyed some influence in the United States, notably through King's use of quiet diplomacy with the president.

The Hyde Park Declaration

King and Roosevelt signed a second agreement, the Hyde Park Declaration, in April 1941. It proved an even more important milestone in Canadian–American relations than the Ogdensburg Agreement.

Canada's wartime economic relations with both Britain and the United States led to this understanding. Since 1939 Britain had ordered ever-increasing amounts of war supplies from Canada and the United States, but it lacked the dollars to pay for them. Meanwhile Canada had accumulated huge deficits in its American trade, largely because of its enormous purchases of equipment destined for Britain. When in 1941 the United States passed the Lend-Lease Act, which exempted Britain from making cash payments on its orders for war materials, Canada worried that it would now lose British business.

King nevertheless managed to get a reasonably satisfactory agreement with the Americans: the United States promised to increase its defence purchases in Canada substantially, enabling Canada to make its own purchases of war equipment in the United States. Britain could continue buying Canadian goods and Canada could even get relief, through Lend-Lease, for its American purchases of war supplies to be sent via Canada to Britain. The agreement ended Canada's dollar shortage by 1942. Some scholars see the Hyde Park Declaration as another blow to Canadian independence. In view of Canada's precarious situation, however, the country probably could not have obtained better financial terms.

After Hyde Park, Canada's influence with the United States waned. The American entry into the war in December 1941 substantially changed American perspectives. Relinquishing its isolationism, the United States became more concerned with global rather than hemispheric issues. Canada lost its special status and became a junior partner in the Anglo–American–Russian alliance to defeat the Axis powers from 1942 to 1945. Even at the two wartime conferences held in Quebec City that brought together the British and the American war leaders, Winston Churchill and Franklin D. Roosevelt, Canada acted merely as host. King's presence was largely confined to the official photos.

Fitting the guns on a 28-ton (25-tonne) tank at Montreal Locomotive Works, Montreal, around 1942.

Photograph Collection and Library Services Canada/Science and Technology Museum, Image CN 001876.

The Wartime Economy

On the eve of war, 20 percent of Canadian workers lacked jobs. Barely a year later, full employment was within sight. The wartime emergency led to large-scale federal economic intervention. Soon Canada produced 4000 airplanes a year, as well as ships, tanks, and huge quantities of shells and guns. Investment in industry doubled between 1939 and 1943. War materials had priority over civilian goods, whose production was severely curtailed.

Just as during World War I, the burgeoning economy generated inflationary pressures. Prices spiralled upward. In response, Ottawa implemented drastic wage and price controls. The government also resorted to so-called voluntary measures. It exhorted homemakers to put their savings into Victory Bonds and urged merchants to offer customers their change in war savings stamps. The government used the revenue from the bonds and stamps to purchase arms and build bombs. And that—as one patriotic poster proclaimed—was how homemaker "Mrs. Morin bombarded Berlin"! Women also established branches of the Consumers Service that, among other activities, denounced merchants who violated the law. Such measures succeeded in curtailing inflation.

Rationing

The relative scarcity of various consumer goods led to rationing. The government issued books of coupons and recruited thousands of female volunteers to distribute them to shoppers. Sugar became the first product to be rationed. Later, Ottawa added tea, coffee, butter, meat, and gasoline to the list. Occasionally, shortages provoked an outcry. When brewers could not supply enough beer, Ontario workers threatened to boycott the sale of Victory Bonds. "No beer, no bonds!" was their warning.

The lack of automobiles and of the gasoline to make them run explains, together with full employment, an enormous increase in the use of urban public transport. During the war, buses and trams were often severely overcrowded. Mothers shopping for food had to compete with commuters for space. The media urged shoppers to avoid travelling at peak hours. Women frequently faced sexual harassment as men complained about "feminine intrusion into their cultural privacy and social space," particularly "their" smoking section at the rear of the bus.[4]

Business leaders improved their public image, tarnished during the Depression years, by helping the federal government organize the country's war production. Proud to be called "Howe's boys," many went to work, often for a symbolic annual salary of one dollar, for the powerful C.D. Howe, minister of munitions and supply, the department in charge of all war procurement. Howe set up numerous Crown corporations and adopted the techniques of private enterprise. He also avoided the accusations of graft and profiteering that had so plagued Robert Borden's government during World War I.

Women and the War Effort

According to traditional Canadian beliefs and practices, married women belonged in the home. Yet many women, particularly unmarried women, had worked outside the home long before the war, generally in low-paying occupations such as teaching, office work, retail sales, factory labour in textile and clothing mills, and as domestics. Now, in response to the general labour shortage created by the war, many more women entered the civilian work force. Department of Labour advertisements urged women to "roll up [their] sleeves for victory"; the men overseas needed support and women had to "back them up—to bring them back."

Women often did what was traditionally men's work. When a plywood factory opened in Port Alberni on Vancouver Island in 1942 to supply plywood for ammunition boxes, 80 percent of the workers hired were women. Many of these affectionately nicknamed "plywood girls" had brothers who were in the armed forces.

To attract women to factories from small towns and rural areas, employers offered women relatively attractive wages, particularly in war industries; indeed, women's wages increased faster than men's wages during the war years, although they remained substantially lower. Ottawa, for its part,

Women war workers return home after shift change, Edmonton, 1943.

Library and Archives Canada/National Film Board of Canada/ PA-116122.

temporarily amended the income tax laws to make it possible for husbands to continue to enjoy a full married exemption while their wives earned wages. Then, in mid-war, when a chronic lack of "manpower" made it essential to recruit mothers, the provinces of Ontario and Quebec set up a modest number of government-funded nurseries. Most women, however, had to leave their children in the care of relatives and friends.

Patriotic appeals drew thousands of women into volunteer work. They recuperated and recycled such items as paper, metal, fat, bones, rags, rubber, and glass. They also collected clothes for free distribution and prepared parcels to be sent overseas. Together with their unpaid labour in the home, women's voluntary efforts constituted, in the words of historian Ruth Roach Pierson, "far and away the largest contribution made by Canadian women to the war effort."[5]

Women in the Armed Services

For the first time, women served in the armed services. By the end of the war, 50 000 women had enrolled, but these "Jill Canucks" were not "pistol-packing Mommas" and they did not hurl grenades.[6] The armed services assigned them positions considered proper to their sex and always paid them less than males. They remained subordinate to men of the same rank, and they commanded only other women. Such auxiliary women's units as the Canadian Women's Army Corps, created in 1941, supplied female support staff to release men for combat training and other duties.

Efforts to achieve fairness and equality did not permeate all aspects of life in the services. Male dominance of the military meant a double standard on sexual morality; literature on venereal disease, for example, warned servicemen to beware of "diseased, predatory females," but women received no similar advice regarding "loose men." Pregnancy was cause for an immediate discharge on medical grounds.

The War and National Unity

The Canadian government worked to keep support high for the war effort. The National Film Board (NFB), founded in 1939, produced "progressive film propaganda" designed to enhance Canadians' faith in their country. In the same year, Ottawa set up the Bureau of Public Information to promote patriotism and "Canadianism" among all ethnic groups in English-speaking Canada. The bureau published hundreds of pamphlets, arranged for news stories, magazine articles, and radio broadcasts, and subsidized "loyal" segments of the foreign-language press.

Wartime Treatment of Minority Ethnic Groups

The federal government also took measures to combat widespread anti-immigrant attitudes during the war. Ironically, while attempting to unite Canadians, the government meted out harsh treatment to members of ethnic groups whose homelands were at war with Canada,

Japanese Canadians being "relocated" to camps in the interior of British Columbia. More than 20 000 Japanese and Japanese Canadians were relocated, and their property confiscated and auctioned off, after the Japanese attack on Pearl Harbor in December 1941.

Tak Toyota/Library and Archives Canada/C-46350.

believing that they constituted a danger to the state. Under the War Measures Act, the federal government interned hundreds of German Canadians, although the RCMP found no evidence of domestic subversion. Upon Italy's entry into the war, the RCMP began to fingerprint and photograph thousands of Italian Canadians, and arrested some 700. Businessman James Franceschini was one of those interned; he saw his businesses placed in the hands of the Custodian of Alien Property and the equipment sold off at fire-sale prices to his Montreal competitors. A few members of the clergy and university professors questioned the arrests. Most Canadians appeared, by their silence, to acquiesce.

More than any other group, Japanese Canadians felt the brunt of Canadians' animosity. After the Japanese surprise raid on Pearl Harbor in December 1941, which brought fears of an invasion of the Pacific coast, the federal government evacuated the more than 20 000 Japanese and Japanese Canadians living in coastal British Columbia. Most evacuees were transported to camps in the interior of the province, but several hundred males deemed "dangerous" were placed under armed guard at a camp in the Lake Superior bush country. Those interned saw their property confiscated and auctioned off. After the war, Ottawa resettled the Japanese Canadians across Canada and even attempted to deport thousands—many of whom were Canadian citizens—to Japan.

Most historians view wartime government policy toward the Japanese in Canada as the result of longstanding racial hostility toward this group. "The threat of Japanese subversion was created by the union of traditional racial attitudes and perceptions shaped by the fears and anxieties conjured up by war," historian Peter Ward contends.[7] A hostile public easily convinced federal politicians to act. Historians Patricia Roy and others, however, have argued that Ottawa carried out the evacuation of the Japanese "as much for their own protection, and, by implication, the protection of Canadians in Japanese hands."[8] Forty years later, the federal government apologized to Japanese Canadians for their wartime treatment and offered financial compensation.

French Canada and the War

French Canada posed a special challenge. Although French Canadians generally accepted participation, as in World War I they remained adamantly opposed to compulsory military service for overseas operations. The stringent Defence of Canada Regulations, which provided for the censorship of antiwar sentiment in the media, attempted to curb opposition to government war policy in Quebec. The CBC also acted as a "propaganda vehicle" in favour of the war effort.

Several reasons help to explain French Canada's lack of enthusiasm for the war. During the 1930s many French-Canadian intellectuals showed sympathy for the fascist leaders of southern Europe, whom they viewed as stalwart opponents of communism. Traditionalists predicted that the war would cause the breakup of families because it brought women into the factories. For their part, the defenders of provincial autonomy attacked Ottawa's wartime intrusion into the provincial government's jurisdiction. Furthermore, nationalists denounced the danger of linguistic assimilation by a Canadian army in which the French language was often proscribed.

French Canada opposed military conscription for overseas service. This photo shows a demonstration against conscription in Montreal.

Library and Archives Canada/*The Gazette* (Montreal)/PA-107910.

Most French Canadians, however, simply did not feel immediately concerned by a war in Europe. Having been estranged from France politically, culturally, and demographically for nearly two centuries, they had few ties with that country. They certainly felt no strong loyalty to England. Most, however, agreed to Canada's involvement on the condition that enlistment be voluntary.

Plebiscite of 1942

As the war dragged on and military leaders demanded reinforcements, many English-speaking Canadians called for conscription. They interpreted King's refusal to consider conscription as putting political advantage, especially his solid support in Quebec, ahead of the war effort. King certainly moved cautiously. In mid-1940, his government decreed compulsory military training but for home service only. When recruiting for overseas service lagged in 1941, the government decided to retain the home-defence conscripts for the duration of the war, in the hope that many would volunteer to serve overseas. When few signed up, and pressure mounted for King to send more troops, King decided to ask Canadians, by plebiscite, to release his government from its anti-conscriptionist commitments. In Quebec, nationalists accused the prime minister of betraying his sacred promises, and urged French Canadians to vote "non." The results of the vote, held in April 1942, revealed the deep division between Quebec and the rest of Canada. While 72 percent of Quebeckers answered "no," 80 percent of the electorate of the other provinces responded "yes."

Still Mackenzie King delayed. When asked if the time had come to implement conscription, he replied evasively: "Conscription if necessary, but not necessarily conscription." Remembering the disastrous consequences of the conscription crisis of 1917 for national unity and for both major political parties, King hoped that conscription would never be necessary. Until late 1944, Canada continued to rely on voluntary enlistments, although some of the volunteers were home-defence conscripts, "convinced" by moral pressure and even physical abuse to "go active."

Canada Intensifies Its War Effort

On the Atlantic Ocean, the Royal Canadian Navy (RCN), which enlisted a total of 100 000 men and 6500 women during the war, took on the responsibility of defending the convoys that transported troops and supplies to Britain. The job was dangerous. Moreover, living conditions on the escorting corvettes were often dreadful, as seawater penetrated continually during bad weather. "The smell just got worse and worse," one sailor remembered. "The ship was a floating pigpen of stink. You couldn't get away from it...."

In the first years of the war, Allied naval losses were staggering; shipyards were unable to build replacements fast enough. Initially, the Canadian navy had few successes in the antisubmarine war. But once properly trained and equipped, it played a significant role in the Battle of the Atlantic by sinking, or helping to sink, many German U-boats.

On land, Canadian troops saw sustained combat from July 1943. In the mistaken hope that casualties

Members of the Fusiliers Mont-Royal Regiment in Falaise, France, just after the Normandy invasion. A Canadian Sherman tank offers the tired infantrymen protection, in the narrow streets of this Norman town, August 1944.

Library and Archives Canada/PA-115568.

would be light, King pressured the British to allow Canadian forces to join in the Allied invasion of Sicily. Nearly 100 000 Canadian troops took part in the lengthy Italian campaign that followed. Some 6000 Canadian soldiers lost their lives, and another 20 000 were wounded. The fierce battle to capture the strategic town of Ortona alone cost the Canadians 700 dead: they fought from doorway to doorway, from rooftop to rooftop, sometimes even moving from house to house without going outside, through a technique of breaking through the walls between houses known as "mouse-holing." Although they faced Germans who often were better armed, the Canadians relentlessly pushed north, breaching the imposing German fortifications of the Gothic Line in September 1944.

Canadians also played a significant role in the Normandy invasion of June 6, 1944. Assisted by the RCN, Canadian troops took an entire German-held beach. The Canadian division suffered greater casualties than the British formations, but it also advanced further inland than any other Allied division on D-Day. Over the next few weeks, the Canadian army's progress across Normandy was slowed by several costly failures. In possibly the Canadians' worst reversal, a complete battalion, the Canadian Black Watch, was virtually annihilated on July 25 in an unsuccessful attempt to take Verrières Ridge, south of Caen.

Allied bombing errors resulted in substantial Canadian casualties. Moreover, at least 150 Canadian deaths were in reality coldblooded murders by German soldiers, well behind the lines. In one notorious incident, a group of Canadian prisoners was marched to the Abbaye d'Ardennes, where they were shot in the garden after interrogation. The German commander held responsible later served some time in prison before being released to a hero's welcome in Germany.

The Canadians also organized the bloody sieges of Boulogne, Calais, and Le Havre. Then, in autumn 1944, in dreadful conditions of cold and mud, Canadian troops played a major role in the fight to secure the approaches to the Belgian port city of Antwerp. One effort involved an attempt to dislodge the Germans on Walcheren Island, at the mouth of the Scheldt delta. The approach by land was over a long rock-and-earth causeway that became a veritable hell for Canadian attackers raked by intense enemy bombardment. After heavy losses, the Canadians managed to establish a bridgehead on the island; then the British modified their strategy and decided to attack elsewhere.

Conscription and the End of the War

By late 1944, after several months of fighting in France and in the face of an important German counteroffensive, Canadian officers overseas were demanding reinforcements, particularly the well-trained home-defence conscripts. The Conservatives, in opposition, urged the government to decree conscription. Within the Cabinet, Colonel J.L. Ralston, the minister of national defence, also pushed for compulsory military service. King, still not ready, replaced Ralston with General McNaughton, who failed to recruit the necessary volunteers. On November 22, just as several of his English-speaking cabinet ministers prepared to resign, King yielded. Canada would again have conscription.

Few Canadian conscripts ever served overseas, however, and conscription ultimately had no effect on winning the war. In spite of the criticism from both supporters and opponents of conscription, and perhaps because the criticism came from both ends of the spectrum, King was able to portray himself as a moderate. He and his Liberal party managed to survive the crisis. To their credit, they had limited the ethnic bitterness that occurred in the conscription crisis in 1917.

WHERE HISTORIANS DISAGREE

Canadian Participation in the Land War in Northwestern Europe

Throughout the early 1990s, the media extensively marked the fiftieth anniversary of the events of World War II. Canadian historians also showed new interest in that conflict and, in particular, in the role Canadians played in combat in northwestern Europe.

The tragedy at Dieppe in August 1942 has been the subject of several studies. In *Unauthorized Action: Mountbatten and the Dieppe Raid*, Brian Loring Villa assigns British Chief of Combined Operations Lord Louis Mountbatten responsibility for having ordered the raid. Villa quotes Canadian newspaper magnate Lord Beaverbrook, who bitterly accused Mountbatten of having the blood of "thousands of my countrymen on your hands."[1] But Villa also notes that General A.G.L. McNaughton, commander of Canadian forces in Britain, had delivered numerous bellicose statements. When, at last, an opportunity to use Canadian troops presented itself, McNaughton could scarcely decline the offer. Even the cautious Prime Minister King had to take into account the rising criticism of Canadians who wanted to see their country's troops take a more active part in the struggle.

For J.L. Granatstein, General H.D.G. Crerar, who commanded the 1st Canadian Corps, shares responsibility. Crerar, he says, "had come to England convinced that the army had to see action soon, both for its own morale and for domestic Canadian consumption."[2] After Dieppe, Crerar's approach was to rationalize the raid by speaking of lessons learned, an approach that Granatstein says "may even be right." Peter Henshaw also believes that the Canadian commanders were primarily responsible for the Dieppe fiasco: "Their struggle for autonomy, and for a leading Canadian role in raids, interacted with British interservice rivalries in a way that was decisive for the progress of the planned raid."[3]

Denis and Sheilagh Whitaker, the former a captain at Dieppe, blame British Prime Minister Winston Churchill, who needed to prove to Soviet dictator Joseph Stalin that it was impossible in 1942 to open a second front against the Germans. They argue that Churchill's strategy "was successful, no matter how high the costs."[4] Moreover, the Allies gained essential experience at Dieppe in preparation for D-Day. The lessons learned, they say, "saved countless lives as a result of their far-reaching influence on the success of future operations."[5] W.A.B. Douglas and Brereton Greenhouse agree. Because of Dieppe, the Allies realized that "objectives must be more realistic, tactics more sophisticated, and training more rigorous. Communications must be more comprehensive, equipment more appropriate, and, most of all, fire support by sea and air must be overwhelming."[6] In a study of how Dieppe was presented to the public, Timothy Balzer notes that allied authorities planned in advance to portray any failure as success and to manipulate the press to further this claim. For example, communiqués were to stress the lessons learned before any lessons were learned.[7]

Canadians participated actively in the lengthy campaign in northwestern Europe that followed the invasion of Normandy. Casualties were high. Indeed, in John A. English's view, "the lives of many soldiers were unnecessarily cast away." Who should be blamed? English responds, "those who left them exposed in open wheatfields to be harvested like so many sheaves.... The responsibility must rest with the high command."[8] English argues that senior officers had little idea of how to direct a modern army in field operations, while many officers at the divisional and brigade levels were of doubtful professional competence.

The Valour and the Horror, a television series on Canada's role in World War II broadcast by the CBC and Radio-Canada in January 1992, provoked bitter controversy. War veterans and several historians accused the writer-producers, Brian and Terence McKenna, of distorting history and of unduly maligning military commanders. A Senate subcommittee held hearings on the series— a gesture that the media attacked as a threat to freedom of expression.

In a review commissioned by the CBC, historians S.F Wise and David J. Bercuson both found the series to be "bad history."[9] Wise, for example, refuted the film's portrayal of poor Canadian generalship. Bercuson, while affirming a general belief that "the Canadian Army as a whole did not acquit itself well in the Normandy fighting," decried the "failure" to put events in Normandy into a broader context.[10] In a report partly based on the reviews done by Wise and Bercuson, the CBC ombudsman concluded that the series failed to "measure up to the CBC's demanding policies and standards."[11] The McKennas responded that the ombudsman's choice of historical advisers was "prejudicial" to them and that his judgments were "almost entirely unsubstantiated in fact."[12]

Clearly the controversies that have developed concerning Canada's participation in the war illustrate the problems of interpreting history and defining the "truth."

1. Brian Loring Villa, *Unauthorized Action: Mountbatten and the Dieppe Raid*, 2nd ed. (Toronto: Oxford University Press, 1994), p. 18.

2. J.L. Granatstein, *The Generals: The Canadian Army's Senior Commanders in the Second World War* (Toronto: Stoddart, 1993), p. 102.

3. Peter Henshaw, "The Dieppe Raid: A Product of Misplaced Canadian Nationalism?," *Canadian Historical Review*, 77 (1996): 252.

4. Denis and Sheilagh Whitaker, *Dieppe: Tragedy to Triumph* (Toronto: McGraw-Hill Ryerson, 1992), p. 290.

5. Ibid., p. 304.

6. W.A.B. Douglas and Brereton Greenhous, *Out of the Shadows: Canada in the Second World War*, rev. ed. (Toronto: Dundurn Press, 1995), p. 128.

7. Timothy Balzer, "'In Case the Raid Is Unsuccessful ...': Selling Dieppe to Canadians," *Canadian Historical Review*, 87 (2006): 409–30.

8. John A. English, *The Canadian Army and the Normandy Campaign: A Study of Failure in High Command* (New York: Praeger, 1991), p. 256.

9. S.F Wise and David J. Bercuson, *The Valour and the Horror Revisited* (Montreal/Kingston: McGill-Queen's University Press, 1994), p. 10.

10. Ibid., p. 51.

11. Ibid., p. 72.

12. Ibid., p. 88.

An Evaluation of Canadian Participation

During the last months of the war, in early 1945, Canadian troops participated in the liberation of the Netherlands and in the final offensive against Germany. By the war's end, 250 000 troops had served in the Canadian army in northwestern Europe; more than 11 000 of them died. In addition, from 1942, Canadian aviators conducted thousands of perilous night-bombing missions that destroyed most of Germany's large cities; Canadians eventually made up about a quarter of Bomber Command's crews. More than 17 000 of the nearly quarter-million Canadians who served in the RCAF lost their lives. All told, more than 1 million Canadians out of a total population of 11.5 million saw military service in Canada and overseas during World War II. About 42 000 were killed, and nearly 55 000 were wounded; many of these would never recover.

Over 3000 status Indians enlisted, mostly in the army; indeed, until 1943, Navy regulations required that enlistees be "British born subjects, of a white race." Some 200 died in service. These figures do not include the Métis, Inuit, or non–status Indians, for whom no information is available.

Private Huron Eldon Brant, member of the Tyendinaga Mohawk community, receives the Military Medal for bravery at Grammichele, Sicily, 1943, from General Bernard Montgomery. One year later he was killed during an attack near Rimini.

Captain Frank Royal/Library and Archives Canada/PA-130065.

The war caused innumerable personal tragedies, as thousands of Canadians lost a loved one. Sometimes the sad announcement came brutally. One Canadian girl wrote to her soldier boyfriend in France, and after a few weeks the letter came back stamped "Killed in action." The soldiers' return, in some cases after five years of absence, provoked poignant emotions: time brought change, and lengthy absences had often altered perceptions of relationships. The divorce rate rose substantially.

Was Canada's role essential to the Allied victory over the Axis powers? Canada's military strength certainly paled in comparison with the resources that its huge southern neighbour was able to mobilize. Yet, for a small country, Canada's contribution was enormous. In the war in Italy and in northwestern Europe, Canadian forces made a decisive contribution. It is safe to say that, without their aid, the war, and the terrible suffering that it wrought, would have dragged on even longer.

Organized Labour during the War

Organized labour made significant gains in the war years. Thanks to the war, the labour surplus of the 1930s became a shortage in the early 1940s. As employment rose, so, too, did union membership, particularly in the new industrial unions, which combined all workers in a particular industry in a single union. Between 1940 and 1945, union membership doubled to more than 700 000.

Although the war brought jobs and, in general, higher wages, grievances remained. Employers fiercely resisted union attempts to impose collective bargaining. The federal government intervened constantly to prevent strikes that could hurt war production. It applied wage controls that labour denounced as inequitable. Moreover, as historian Laurel Sefton MacDowell has shown, it sought particularly "to conciliate business, its wartime ally in developing the war economy."[9] For example, business representatives sat on government policy boards; labour did not.

Industrial Conflicts

Workers' growing resentment contributed to a wave of industrial conflicts that peaked in 1943. That year, one union member in three went out on strike. The government responded to the unrest with new rules which recognized the right of workers in industries under federal jurisdiction to join unions and to bargain collectively. It established certification procedures, set out penalties for unfair labour practices by which employers commonly interfered with workers' attempts to set up unions, and established a labour-relations board to administer the law. After the war most provinces adopted comparable rules.

A bitter strike at the Ford motor plant in Windsor, Ontario in 1945 concerned labour security, among other issues. The union wanted an agreement specifying that all employees had to belong to the union and that the company had to deduct union dues from wage cheques—"union shop and checkoff" was the workers' demand. Ford adamantly refused. To ensure a tight picket line, militant strikers set up a massive automobile blockade in the streets around the plant. Federal and provincial authorities as well as the Canadian Congress of Labour itself intervened, without success.

Finally, the two sides agreed to accept binding arbitration. Justice Ivan Rand of the Supreme Court of Canada proposed what became known as the Rand Formula: since all employees benefited from union activities, all should pay union dues, to be collected by the company and remitted to the union. Workers need not join the union, however. Rand also recommended heavy penalties for unauthorized, or "wildcat," strikes. Although he admitted that a strike was not a "tea party," he strongly condemned the workers' motor blockade.

The late 1940s saw more dramatic confrontations between labour and management, often in provinces whose governments sided openly with employers. Still, unions felt more secure as the war years ended. The relative labour peace of the 1950s resulted, in part, from these wartime gains.

The State's New Role

Though the war eliminated unemployment and restored a degree of prosperity, it exacted heavy financial sacrifices from people. By 1943, as war fatigue set in and increasing Allied success pointed the way to final victory, Canadians reflected on the postwar society they wanted to build. In particular, many wanted governments to introduce measures that would help those in need and establish greater equality within society.

Social Welfare Measures

In 1940, after obtaining the consent of the provinces to amend the British North America Act, the federal government adopted an unemployment insurance plan. Then, in 1943, the government's Committee on Reconstruction urged the immediate creation of a full welfare state, with a national health insurance scheme, old-age pensions, and children's allowances. Fearful of the costs involved, Ottawa adopted a cautious and piecemeal approach. In 1944, it introduced a family allowance program providing monthly payments to help Canadian mothers support their children. King, worried about the left-wing CCF's high ratings in the polls, hoped that the measure would boost support for the Liberals. Certain Conservatives denounced the project as a "baby bonus" designed to benefit Quebec with its alleged big families, while nationalists in Quebec condemned it as an infringement upon provincial autonomy. Business reacted favourably; it hoped that the allowances would diminish pressure to raise wages. Undoubtedly, King's cautious, reformist approach to social problems helped ensure the Liberals' reelection in 1945, as CCF support weakened.

Housing became a serious problem for increasing numbers of urban Canadians during the war years. As migrants flocked to cities to work in war-related industries, many families lived in garages, empty warehouses, shacks, chicken coops, "and indeed, in anything that will hold a bed," as one report put it. As the war ended, Canada's rental-controls administrator estimated that at least 200 000 Canadian households were now living "doubled up" or even "tripled up." Ottawa ignored pleas for public intervention to provide low-rental housing; instead, it acted to reduce down payments and to guarantee mortgages in order to stimulate the building of new homes and enable families with moderate incomes to purchase property.

Women in Postwar Canada

In the middle of the war, Ottawa established a special subcommittee to study the role of women in postwar Canada. The members, all women, assumed that many female workers would return to the home. For those who remained employed outside the home, the subcommittee's report recommended expanded employment opportunities, equal pay, better working conditions, and the granting of children's allowances.

These proposals stirred up substantial opposition. Government planners wanted women out of the workforce to make room for returning soldiers and workers in shut-down war industries. Unions did not want to see women competing for scarce jobs with men. Polls showed that most Canadians—women as well as men—wanted women back in the home after the war. The war experience was the exception, not the rule. In this climate, as historian Gail Cuthbert Brandt wrote, the subcommittee's report was "pigeon-holed and forgotten."[10]

Things appeared to return to "normal" at the end of the war. Many of the barriers blocking women from the workforce went back up again. Historian Susanne Klausen recounts that the "plywood girls" of the Port Alberni plywood factory now became "plywood bags," a derogatory term often used by other women who wished to express their disapproval of young female workers who were occupying jobs that, in their view, should rightfully be given to returning veterans.[11] The proportion of women working outside the home plummeted. Although women slowly began to return to the workforce in the early 1950s, not until the 1960s would the proportion of female workers return to what it had been in 1944—27 percent.

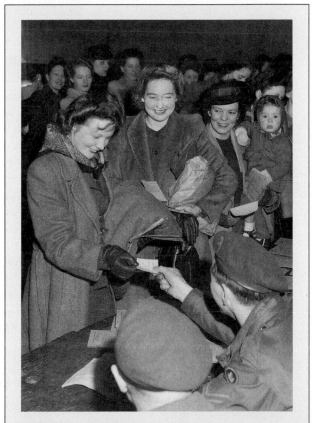

After the war, the number of women in Canada jumped by 40 000, as the war brides (mainly British) joined their Canadian husbands in their new land. They brought with them their 20 000 children, most under the age of three. This photo shows customs and immigration officials checking the papers of British war brides.

Library and Archives Canada/ PA-112368.

Federal–Provincial Relations: Toward Federal Supremacy

The Depression had restricted the autonomy of the provinces, forcing them to rely increasingly on Ottawa for financial assistance. The war created conditions that furthered centralization, as the federal government now took the dominant role in organizing the Canadian economy.

The Rowell–Sirois Report

The Rowell–Sirois Commission on Dominion–Provincial Relations, set up by the King government in 1937, made public its report in 1940. With the objective of stabilizing provincial finances and giving equal services to all Canadians, the commissioners recommended that Ottawa collect all income taxes and, in return, make unconditional grants to the provinces. Disadvantaged provinces should receive special subsidies to enable them to offer social and educational services equivalent to those of other Canadian provinces. The federal government should also assume all provincial debts.

Provincial autonomists condemned the report as a veritable centralizer's "Bible." They argued that its recommendations would place provincial treasuries at Ottawa's mercy and that the federal government would determine provincial activities by what it was willing to pay out. For their part, federal ministers and bureaucrats endorsed the recommendations strongly, particularly those relating to money. Ottawa wanted to ensure control over fiscal policy to pay for the war as well as to diminish inflationary pressures. It thus urged the provinces to "rent" their tax fields to the federal government, at least for the duration of the war, and it proposed to compensate the provinces more generously. All the provinces yielded, although some did so reluctantly.

After 1943, the economic planners in Ottawa set forth their designs for the immediate postwar era. The federal government, they urged, should act as the "balance wheel" of the economy. If it kept its hand firmly on taxation, it could combat cyclical tendencies, either deflationary busts or inflationary booms; it could maintain high and stable employment; and it could offer costly social security measures to all citizens, thus supporting consumer buying power. For these civil servants, economic, political, and humanitarian objectives dictated that the federal government continue to take charge.

As the war ended, King sought to convince the provinces to continue to allow Ottawa to levy all income taxes in return for increased provincial grants, with no strings attached. The federal government also offered to pay part of the cost of a comprehensive health insurance plan and of old-age pensions, and to expand the coverage of federal unemployment insurance. Ottawa eventually managed to reach agreement on the tax proposals with all but Ontario and Quebec. The federalism of the next decade thus remained highly centralized.

The Provinces in the War Years

The war and the aftereffects of the Depression fostered the uneven development of regional economies and thus contributed to the growth of regionalism in Canada. The war had diversified Canada's manufacturing capacity, as well as further promoting its resource-based industries. Quebec, British Columbia, and especially Ontario made dramatic advances. In Quebec, industries such as chemical products and aluminum refining expanded rapidly. In Ontario, factory employment increased greatly. On the Pacific coast, the port of Vancouver prospered. Its shipyards and those of Victoria employed 30 000 workers at their peak. In spite of the war, tourism continued to contribute to Vancouver's development, and wartime promotion ensured that the sector would be poised for rapid postwar expansion.

The North

In 1942, the United States Army Corps of Engineers coordinated the construction teams that built, for defence purposes, a 2500 km highway from Dawson Creek in northeastern British Columbia to Fairbanks, Alaska. This rough American military road, built largely on Canadian soil, was then transformed into a permanent civilian highway. The attack on Pearl Harbor also led American defence planners to worry about the threat to energy supplies in the North West; oil tankers now appeared vulnerable to Japanese submarine attack. As a result, the Canadian Oil (Canol) project was begun to pipe oil from the Imperial Oil Company's field at Norman Wells, on the Mackenzie River.

Changes in the Central Provinces

In Quebec the wartime Liberal government of Adélard Godbout initiated important reforms. In 1940, women in Quebec finally obtained the right to vote, despite the vigorous objections of the church and conservative groups. The government also created Hydro-Québec, a publicly owned hydroelectric utility in the Montreal region. To boost educational levels, it made school attendance obligatory until age fourteen, a measure hitherto opposed by the Roman Catholic clergy. In the area of labour–management relations, it set out the rules intended to force companies to negotiate with their unionized employees.

In Ontario, the Conservatives regained power in 1943. They denounced the supposed threat posed by the socialists of the provincial CCF party, but they also energetically pursued reform policies, notably in health, education, and housing. Provincial planning became important in areas such as forest conservation, industrial development, and water use. By 1945, the CCF was in decline, the Conservatives easily won a majority, and Ontario settled into what would become more than 40 years of Conservative government.

The Maritimes and Newfoundland

The war brought fewer economic benefits to Canadians in the three Maritime provinces, although war spending did boost the regional economy. By 1943, some 75 000 men and women were building and repairing vessels in Maritime shipyards, even at night under floodlights. Halifax became Canada's major port for shipping munitions and other supplies to Western Europe.

Yet, according to historian Ernest Forbes, the impact of Ottawa's war policies on the Maritimes was "largely negative. While the government did generate economic activity, it created relatively little new industry in the region."[12] According to Forbes, C.D. Howe believed it was more efficient to develop industry along the St. Lawrence and in the Great Lakes region, a conviction reinforced by his regional prejudices.

Economic weakness meant that governments lacked funds for investment in health and education. In 1945, Prince Edward Island had only half the number of doctors needed to meet national standards. New Brunswick had Canada's highest infant and maternal death rate, and Nova Scotia followed closely. Teachers in the region were often poorly qualified, and salaries were low. New Brunswick had Canada's highest illiteracy rate, affecting particularly the province's French-speaking Acadian population, who also suffered linguistic discrimination.

In Newfoundland, low fish prices and uncertain markets left the population of the outports in appalling poverty. Eventually, though, the war created a temporary boom in employment through the construction and maintenance of huge American defence projects. As the war came to a close, Britain came to an understanding with the Canadian government to encourage the island's eventual incorporation into Canada.

The family of Private Louis Zarowny welcomes him home, at Mewata Stadium in Calgary, in July 1945. Wounded twice, Zarowny served with the Loyal Edmonton Regiment in Italy and Northwestern Europe.

Glenbow Archives, Calgary, Canada/Herald Collection/NA-2864-3448.

The West

The Prairie provinces, hard hit by the Depression of the 1930s, recovered slowly. Farmers did increase their incomes, thanks to higher prices and to improved harvests. Yet most rural homes still had no indoor plumbing or electricity, and farm villages enjoyed few services.

The war boosted crude-oil production in Alberta, at least until the Turner Valley field near Calgary went into decline after 1942. Coal mines prospered, too, and in Prairie cities the construction industry flourished. But the war did not create the diversified economy that many residents felt the region needed.

Politically, third parties on the Prairies grew stronger, although they tended to moderate their ideology. Social Credit leaders in Alberta denounced socialism and centralization, promised able, business-like administration, and gently laid Social Credit doctrine to rest. The CCF scored its first victory in Saskatchewan in 1944. Its ambitious program promised public ownership of natural resources, security of land tenure for farmers, collective bargaining for workers, and a universal socialized health plan. Once in power, the CCF launched major reforms, but financial and other factors soon forced it to make pragmatic policy adjustments. In British Columbia, the old political order also changed, as Liberals and Conservatives formed a coalition to counter the CCF's growing popularity.

Toward a New Internationalism

The war in Europe ended when Germany capitulated in May 1945. By September, Japan also surrendered. Peace brought with it new problems and, in particular, the difficult question of how to maintain it. In contrast to its position after World War I, Canada was ready to accept responsibility in world affairs. Canada thus participated in the founding conference of the United Nations at San Francisco in April 1945, where it worked to ensure that both the United States and the Soviet Union became members.

Canada also pushed for world economic and social cooperation. Canadian diplomat Lester Pearson chaired the founding meeting of the United Nations Food and Agriculture Organization in Quebec City. As a member of the United Nations Relief and Rehabilitation Administration, Canada became a major supplier of aid to war-torn countries. Canada also joined the International Monetary Fund, as well as the International Civil Aviation Organization, whose headquarters came to Montreal. Canada willingly recognized that its influence was less than that of the United States, but at the same time it attempted, with some success, to get recognition from the Great Powers for states like itself.

World War II changed Canada profoundly, in the country's relations with the world and at home as well. It effectively ended the isolation of the 1930s. Involvement in world affairs brought benefits but carried a price. Despite Canada's attempts to estabish relationships with multilateral associations of states, it also developed closer ties to the United States. For supporters of the rapprochement, the closer links brought security and economic prosperity through trade and investment. For critics, the triumphant move toward nationhood in the interwar years appeared to have abruptly ended, with Canada being relegated once more to colonial status—this time, as a colony of the United States.

At home, the war created an economic boom that instilled hopes among Canadians for a better life. Trade-union organizations made notable gains, as governments enacted legislation establishing a new framework for the conduct of industrial relations. The entry of large numbers of women into the workforce announced a substantial change in their role. New federal social programs meant that Canadians took a significant step in the direction of the welfare state. In federal–provincial relations, Ottawa reasserted a preeminence that endured for two decades. Voters in several provinces elected new governments that stayed in office for lengthy periods. In Ottawa, however, Canadians continued to support King, perhaps because he was, in historian Frank Underhill's words, the leader "who divides us least."[13]

NOTES

1. Desmond Morton, *Canada and War: A Military and Political History* (Toronto: Butterworths, 1981), p. 106.

2. Donald Creighton, *The Forked Road: Canada, 1939–1957* (Toronto: McClelland & Stewart, 1976), p. 43.

3. J.L. Granatstein and Norman Hillmer, *For Better or for Worse: Canada and the United States to the 1990s* (Mississauga, ON: Copp Clark Pitman, 1991), p. 144.

4. Donald F. Davis and Barbara Lorenzkowski, "A Platform for Gender Tensions: Women Working and Riding on Canadian Urban Public Transit in the 1940s," *Canadian Historical Review*, 79 (1998): 442–43.

5. Ruth Roach Pierson, *"They're Still Women after All": The Second World War and Canadian Womanhood* (Toronto: McClelland & Stewart, 1986), p. 33.

6. Ruth Roach Pierson, "'Jill Canuck': CWAC of All Trades, But No 'Pistol Packing Momma,'" *Historical Papers/Communications historiques* (1978): 106–33.

7. W. Peter Ward, *White Canada Forever: Popular Attitudes and Public Policy toward Orientals in British Columbia* (Montreal: McGill-Queen's University Press, 1978), p. 146.

8. Patricia Roy et al., *Mutual Hostages: Canadians and Japanese during the Second World War* (Toronto: University of Toronto Press, 1990), p. 215.

9. Laurel Sefton MacDowell, "The Formation of the Canadian Industrial Relations System during World War Two," *Labour/Le Travailleur*, 3 (1978): 186.

10. Gail Cuthbert Brandt, "'Pigeon-Holed and Forgotten': The Work of the Subcommittee on the Post-War Problems of Women, 1943," *Histoire sociale/Social History*, 15 (1983): 239–59.

11. Susanne Klausen, "The Plywood Girls: Women and Gender Ideology at the Port Alberni Plywood Plant, 1942–1991," *Labour/Le Travail*, 41 (1998): 199–235.

12. Ernest R. Forbes, *Challenging the Regional Stereotype: Essays on the 20th Century Maritimes* (Fredericton: Acadiensis Press, 1989), p. 195.

13. Frank Underhill, "The End of the King Era," *Canadian Forum*, September 1948; reprinted in F.H. Underhill, *In Search of Canadian Liberalism* (Toronto: Macmillan, 1960), p. 127.

BEYOND THE BOOK

Life during the War at McGill University

http://www.archives.mcgill.ca/public/hist_scevents/war/homefront.htm
Digitized pictures and documents detailing student life and war support efforts during World War II.

Enemy Alien

http://asalive.archivesalberta.org:8080/access/asa/documents/display/GLEN-113
Scanned correspondence and records between the federal government and Angelina Rebaudengo regarding her husband's internment as an enemy alien during World War II.

Canadian Letters and Images: World War II

http://www.canadianletters.ca/collections.php?warid=4
A vast database of the letters and photographs of dozens of Canadians who served in World War II.

Political Cartoons in World War II

http://www.mccord-museum.qc.ca/en/keys/webtours/GE_P4_5_EN
An exhibit of digitized political cartoons published in Canadian newspapers in World War II, with a guide to each.

A Soldier's War

http://archives.cbc.ca/war_conflict/second_world_war/topics/103
Digitized radio broadcasts from World War II, and accounts from soldiers of their experiences.

Love and War: Canadian War Brides

http://archives.cbc.ca/war_conflict/second_world_war/topics/1542
Twenty audio and video clips from the CBC's archives detail the arrival of war brides in Canada, and what their new lives and families were like. See also http://www.canadianwarbrides.com/stories.asp for personal biographies of Canadian war brides.

Obasan

Joy Kogawa, *Obasan* (New York: Anchor Books, 1993). A young woman's childhood memories of internment camps during World War II and forced separation from her parents return to her in later life.

Bonheur d'occasion

Gabrielle Roy, *Bonheur d'occasion* (1947), translated as *The Tin Flute* by Hannah Josephson (Toronto: McClelland and Stewart, 1969). A novel that describes the poverty of a Montreal working-class family at the end of the Depression, and the beginning of World War II.

RELATED READINGS

The following articles from R. Douglas Francis and Donald B. Smith, eds., *Viewpoints: Readings in Canadian History* (Toronto: Thomson Nelson, 2007), concern topics dealing with material in this chapter: J. Terry Copp, "Battle Exhaustion and the Canadian Soldier in Normandy," pp. 436–45; and Jack Granatstein, "Staring into the Abyss," pp. 445–57.

BIBLIOGRAPHY

Surveys of Canadian foreign policy from 1930 to 1945 include James Eayrs, *In Defence of Canada*, vol. 2, *Appeasement and Rearmament* (Toronto: University of Toronto Press, 1965); and C.P. Stacey, *Canada and the Age of Conflict: A History of Canadian External Policies*, vol. 2, *1921–1948: The Mackenzie King Era* (Toronto: University of Toronto Press, 1981). Both foreign and domestic policy issues are examined in J.L. Granatstein, *Canada's War: The Politics of the Mackenzie King Government, 1939–1945* (Toronto: University of Toronto Press, 1975, 1990); and in Desmond Morton, *Canada and War: A Military and Political History* (Toronto: Butterworths, 1981).

Among the numerous works discussing Canada's participation in the war, see W.A.B. Douglas and Brereton Greenhous, *Out of the Shadows: Canada in the Second World War*, rev. ed. (Toronto: Dundurn Press, 1995); David J. Bercuson, *Maple Leaf against the Axis: Canada's Second World War* (Toronto: Stoddart, 1995); and appropriate chapters in J.L. Granatstein, *Canada's Army: Waging War and Keeping the Peace* (Toronto: University of Toronto Press, 2002). The Hong Kong debacle is described in Oliver Lindsay, *The Battle for Hong Kong, 1941–1945: Hostage to Fortune* (Montreal/ Kingston: McGill-Queen's University Press, 2006). Mark Zuehlke recounts the Italian campaign in *The Gothic Line: Canada's Month of Hell in World War II Italy* (Vancouver: Douglas and McIntyre, 2003).

Canada's military leaders are studied in Bernd Horn and Stephen Harris, eds., *Warrior Chiefs: Perspectives on Senior Canadian Military Leaders* (Toronto: Dundurn Press, 2001). Other useful works include Terry Copp and Bill McAndrew, *Battle Exhaustion: Soldiers and Psychiatrists in the Canadian Army, 1939–1945* (Montreal/Kingston: McGill-Queen's University Press, 1990); Jonathan Vance, *Objects of Concern: Canadian Prisoners of War through the Twentieth Century* (Vancouver: University of British Columbia Press, 1994); and Peter Nearby and J.L. Granatstein, eds., *The Veterans Charter and Post–World War II Canada* (Montreal/Kingston: McGill-Queen's University Press, 1998).

For writings on naval and air force history see Marc Milner, *Canada's Navy: The First Century* (Toronto: University of Toronto Press, 1999); the same author's *The U-Boat Hunters: The Royal Canadian Navy and the Offensive against Germany's Submarines* (Toronto: University of Toronto Press, 1994); Brereton Greenhous, Stephen J. Harris, William C. Johnston, and William G.P. Rawling, *The Crucible of War, 1939–1945: The Official History of the Royal Canadian Air Force*, vol. III (Toronto: University of Toronto Press, 1994); and Spencer Dunmore, *Wings for Victory: The Remarkable Story of the British Air Training Plan in Canada* (Toronto: McClelland & Stewart, 1994). The story of the child evacuees from England bound for Canada is told in Tom Nagorski, *Miracles on the Water: The Heroic Survivors of a World War II U-Boat Attack* (New York: Hyperion, 2006). Tim Cook describes the work of Canadian historians who chronicled the story of the war in *Clio's Warriors: Canadian Historians and the Writing of the World Wars* (Vancouver: UBC Press, 2006).

Government mobilization policies are looked at in J.L. Granatstein and J.M. Hitsman, *Broken Promises: A History of Conscription in Canada*, rev. ed. (Toronto: Copp Clark Pitman, 1985); and Michael D. Stevenson, *Canada's Greatest Wartime Muddle: National Selective Service and the Mobilization of Human Resources during World War II* (Montreal/Kingston: McGill-Queen's University Press, 2001). Larry Hannant, *The Infernal Machine: Investigating the Loyalty of Canada's Citizens* (Toronto: University of Toronto Press, 1995), deals with questions of internal security and civil liberties. On the wartime treatment of Japanese Canadians, see Peter Ward, *White Canada Forever: Popular Attitudes and Public Policy toward Orientals in British Columbia*, 2nd ed. (Montreal/Kingston: McGill-Queen's University Press, 1990). Jeffrey A. Keshen analyzes the war's negative social ramifications in *Saints, Sinners, and Soldiers: Canada's Second World War* (Vancouver: UBC Press, 2004).

Nancy Christie studies social issues in *Engendering the State: Family, Work and Welfare in Canada* (Toronto: University of Toronto Press, 2000). See also Doug Owram, *The Government Generation: Canadian Intellectuals and the State, 1900–1945* (Toronto: University of Toronto Press, 1986). On women during World War II, see Ruth Roach Pierson, *"They're Still Women after All": The Second World War and Canadian Womanhood* (Toronto: McClelland & Stewart, 1986); Carolyn Gossage, *Greatcoats and Glamour Boots: Canadian Women at War, 1939–1945*, rev. ed. (Toronto: Dundurn Press, 2001); and Alison Prentice et al., *Canadian Women: A History*, 2nd ed. (Toronto: Harcourt Brace, 1996), chap. 12. Maria Tippett examines wartime culture in *Making Culture: English-Canadian Institutions and the Arts before the Massey Commission* (Toronto: University of Toronto Press, 1990). Union activity is described in Desmond Morton with Terry Copp, *Working People: An Illustrated History of the Canadian Labour Movement*, 3rd ed. (Toronto: Summerhill Press, 1990).

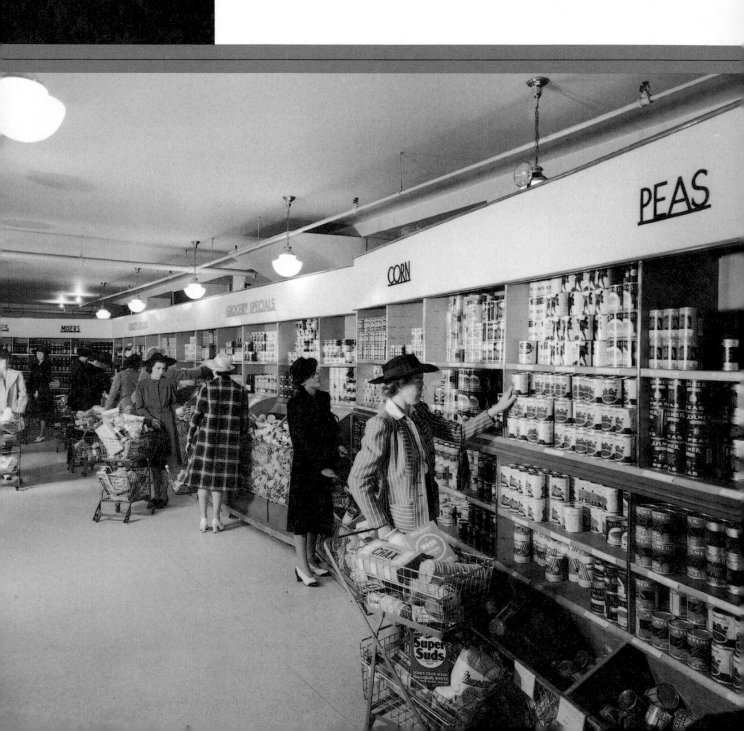

INTRODUCTION

Canada emerged in the last half of the twentieth century as an important industrial nation and a respected secondary world power. Such achievements brought both benefits and problems. Overall, Canadians have enjoyed one of the world's highest standards of living, although certain groups within Canadian society as well as certain regions of the country remain less favoured than others. How to ensure that all Canadians, regardless of ethnic origin, class, gender, or place of dwelling, have equal opportunities continues to be one of the challenges facing Canadian leaders. Canadians have also had to learn to live in a global economy, where they have less control over their economic destiny than ever before. Finally, as the world and Canada face the very serious threats of environmental degradation and declining resources, Canadians are having to consider the consequences of decisions relating to economic development and personal lifestyles.

Internationally, Canada emerged from World War II prepared to play a more active role on the world stage. Caught in the middle of the Cold War between the United States and the Soviet Union, the country chose to play the role of middle power, a role well suited to the country's historic position as the mediator between Britain and the United States. To offset American dominance in the North American defence program, of which Canadians found themselves a part, Canadians have taken an active role in such international organizations as the United Nations, the British Commonwealth of Nations, and the North Atlantic Treaty Organization (NATO). Still, some foreign analysts have criticized Canada for becoming too closely allied to the United States, thus limiting the country's ability to help mediate international disputes and to play a leading role in the debate over the vital issues that confront today's world.

Politically, the Liberal Party's resilience at adapting to change enabled it to govern Canada during most of the period since 1945. The other traditional party, the Conservatives (formerly the Progressive Conservatives), took power when fatigue with the governing Liberals set in and when it succeeded in moderating its own image. Third parties have also played a significant role in what has become at times a multiparty system, as a constant reminder that no party has enjoyed complete support from all regions and all groups within the country. Regional parties have been particularly strong in the West and in Quebec, challenging political leaders to find consensus.

As Canada has modernized, it has become more of a consumer society. Culturally, too, it has taken on the attributes of a mass culture, in which the emphasis is on a popular, mass audience. Both of these trends have moved the country, particularly English-speaking Canada, socially and culturally into the American orbit, making it difficult to maintain a distinctive Canadian identity. Yet, at the same time, national, regional, and local cultural differences have continued to challenge these universal homogenizing trends.

Chapter Twenty

TOWARD A MORE AFFLUENT SOCIETY: 1945–1960

TIME LINE

1947	The Leduc oil field in Alberta begins operation
1949	Newfoundland enters Confederation Canada joins the North Atlantic Treaty Organization
1950	War breaks out in Korea
1952	Canada's first television station begins broadcasting in Montreal
1954	Construction begins on the St. Lawrence Seaway
1956	The Canadian Labour Congress is founded
1957	Lester Pearson wins the Nobel Peace Prize The North American Air Defence Command (NORAD) comes into being A public hospital-insurance program is established The Liberals are defeated by John Diefenbaker's Progressive Conservatives in the federal election The Canada Council is founded to support culture and the arts
1958	The Progressive Conservatives win a huge majority of seats in the federal election
1959	Loggers go out on strike in Newfoundland

After a decade of economic depression and six years of war, Canadians wanted to make up for lost time, forget a bleak past, and look toward the future. Workers sought stable jobs and better wages. Consumers wanted cars, household appliances, adequate housing, and more leisure. Yet modest family budgets, limited availability of goods, particularly in the immediate postwar years, and fears that prosperity would not continue, forced them to be patient and prudent. In addition, the insecurity of the recent past made Canadians look increasingly to governments to provide an array of health, educational, and social services as a safety net against misfortune. In regard to the world outside, they took pride in Canada's prestigious role in international organizations, and in the welcome their country extended to immigrants from war-torn and economically ravaged Europe.

Attitudes remained basically conservative. Traditional values and beliefs continued to govern the behaviour of a majority of Canadians. Although more women worked outside the home, long-held notions concerning the role of women in society loosened only gradually. By the late 1950s, however, attitudes were changing. Slower growth with rising unemployment disrupted the postwar boom. People tired of unimaginative politicians who boasted of past successes and talked in platitudinous generalities. They were now ready to welcome new leaders who would put forth new ideas and propose new solutions.

Economic Nirvana in Canada?

Postwar Canada prospered. Construction boomed. Total industrial output rose by half in the 1950s, and productivity soared thanks to technological innovation. The lighting of the flame on Leduc No. 1 oil well in a farmer's field near Edmonton on a cold February day in 1947 signalled large-scale job creation and rapid population growth in Alberta. The discovery of large deposits of base metals in northern New Brunswick raised hopes for significant job creation in that province. In Ontario, demand for a wide array of goods stimulated industrial expansion. The government-owned Polymer Corporation, in Sarnia, Ontario, produced fully 10 percent of the world's synthetic rubber, widely used by the rapidly expanding automobile industry.[1] By 1951, 10 percent of the Canadian labour force had jobs related to motor vehicles, mostly in southern Ontario.

The average worker had reason to feel satisfied. Rapid economic growth meant that unemploy-ment rates remained very low. Pay packets for factory workers doubled between 1945 and 1956. In spite of significant increases in the prices of food and consumer goods, workers saw their living standards improve. They also worked less, as the 40-hour week became the norm. In addition, federal transfer payments, like family allowances and old-age pensions, put more money into consumers' pockets.

The Age of the Consumer

The era of the consumer introduced a new lifestyle. In towns, people discarded their iceboxes and equipped their kitchens with electric refrigerators. Coal merchants' sales tumbled as homeowners bought electric ranges and switched to cleaner and more efficient gas and oil heat. Families acquired a variety of new appliances intended to reduce the drudgery of housework. Sales of new automobiles mounted in the 1950s as Canadians bought sleek American Fords and Chevrolets, or slim British Morrises and Austins.

Subdivisions proliferated around major cities. In historian Doug Owram's words, "the rise and triumph of low-density residentially-oriented communities was the single most significant urban event of the postwar decades."[2] A million new homes were built between 1945 and 1960. Proud new homeowners hurried to vary the colour of the trim or to plant shrubs in order to distinguish their dwelling from the identical constructions on all sides. Roofs acquired an important new use—as supports for forests of television antennas. Shopping centres sprang up, the first appearing in a Toronto suburb in 1946.

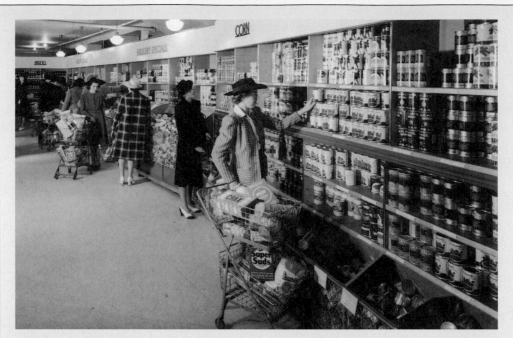

Supermarkets became a symbol of postwar prosperity. Woodward's department store, Vancouver, was one of the first in Canada. It included in-store home economists and baby seats in the shopping carts.

Vancouver Public Library/25644.

The Environment

More prosperous Canadians posed new threats to the environment as well as having an increased interest in protecting it. In search of new outdoor recreational opportunities, more mobile urban dwellers invaded provincial parks. Existing parks quickly became saturated. In response to this demand, Ontario, for example, embarked upon a major program of park expansion. By the late 1950s, however, conservationists worried that increased outdoor recreation threatened the survival of natural areas, and they called for the establishment of nature preserves.

Conservation practices had not yet influenced the methods of the forest industry. Resources still appeared endless. Harvesting aimed at maximum profits. Clearcutting, facilitated by the mechanization of the industry, was the primary method employed because it permitted lower labour costs while hugely increasing logging volumes.

The Less Advantaged

Yet Canadians were often unhappy when they compared themselves, as they did obsessively, with better-off Americans. Canadians complained that refrigerators costing $400 at home could be had for only $275 in the United States. Journalist Blair Fraser remarked that, for Europeans still rebuilding their war-torn economies, second-place Canadians must have seemed like the impoverished tycoon who was down to his last million. Nevertheless, many people of talent, especially entertainers, researchers, and engineers, migrated south, while those who remained behind bemoaned the "brain drain."

Many Canadians saw no boom at all. Few men and far fewer women held the university diplomas that guaranteed good jobs. Salaries were often low, especially for non-unionized

A Historical Portrait

Betty, Ruby, and the Others

At the conclusion of World War II, most working women left the workforce and became homemakers for their breadwinner husbands, and full-time mothers of the two, three, or often more children who quickly made their appearance. The gendered division of labour seemed normal and natural. The happiest women were supposedly those whose husbands were able to purchase a modest bungalow on a small lot in one of the new suburbs.

Do the life stories of these ordinary women confirm the myths of contentment in the home in suburbia? Betty's husband bought a bungalow in Cooksville, Ontario, a west Toronto suburb. Betty, who had a B.A. in music and had worked until her marriage, now settled in as a full-time homemaker. Some modern appliances supposedly made her work easier. In 1950, she already had an automatic washer. Historian Joy Parr shows that, in this regard, Betty, an American immigrant, was not typical of her Canadian neighbours, the majority of whom used labour-intensive wringer washers until the mid-1960s. Such washers cost much less, they consumed far less water, and they enabled users to assert more control over the washing process; the wringers, however, did pose some dangers to children's hands![1]

Betty's husband, Dick, commuted to work in downtown Toronto. He did not just have a job, he had a "vocation." The distinction signified that Dick viewed his work as "socially important" and that he had to devote virtually all his time to it. Betty was thus often home alone with the children because Dick was away on business. She was convinced that she was doing what was expected of her. "A woman's place is in the home," she repeated. Dick agreed. He was sure that women working outside the home were an important cause of divorce and of juvenile delinquency.

One day Betty decided to begin giving piano lessons at home. Perhaps she merely wanted some extra spending money of her own; perhaps she felt that her musical talents were being wasted; perhaps she was simply bored and lonely. Earnings from the job were modest; indeed, Dick often belittled his wife's efforts. At the same time he did not hesitate, over Betty's protests, to delve into the piano money box when he needed some spare change.

Mrs. Hugh Hawkins of Ottawa doing the washing with a traditional labour-intensive wringer washer, 1947. Today young people have heard the expression "through the wringer" but do not know its origin. In this photo, Mrs. Hawkins is putting her laundry through the wringer in order to squeeze out the excess water. Modern automatic washers were as yet rarely seen in Canadian homes.

Library and Archives Canada/PA-115254.

Ruby was another Ontario homemaker in the 1950s. Her sister, Edna Staebler, has edited the letters that Ruby wrote to members of her family. Ruby worried about her appearance—she constantly complained about being overweight. She talked a lot about her children. She also got a job outside the home. In a touching letter to sister Kay, she expounded upon her decision:

I'm so thrilled and so nervous I don't know what to do. You know I've been talking about getting a job for so long because [husband] Fred wasn't earning enough and I guess he got sick of hearing about it.... I'm to go to Musser's store on Monday afternoon and start selling gloves. I'm so scared. I'll have to make change and fit people and be on my feet all those hours— and what will Fred say when he comes home tonite and I tell him?

Gosh, why did I do it? I could be so comfortable here just watching TV and working on my rug and I wouldn't need many clothes.... If I work ... I'll always be in a rush with my housework and have to make dinner at noon. And I won't be home when the kids get home from school.... [But] it would be good training. And I could use the extra money for so many things we need around here ...[2]

"Home dreams" did not fully meet the aspirations of all Canadian women after 1945, as historian Veronica Strong-Boag concludes.[3] Yet much work still needs to be done to reconstitute the life experiences of ordinary women in this period and to reexamine traditional interpretations.

1. Joy Parr, *Domestic Goods: The Material, the Moral, and the Economic in Postwar Years* (Toronto: University of Toronto Press, 1999), ch. 10.

2. Edna Staebler, ed., *Haven't Any News: Ruby's Letters from the Fifties* (Waterloo, ON: Wilfrid Laurier Press, 1995), p. 58.

3. Veronica Strong-Boag, "Home Dreams: Women and the Suburban Experiment in Canada, 1945–1960," *Canadian Historical Review*, 72 (1991): 504.

workers, immigrants, and women. In the immediate postwar years, most people, like the Montrealers whom historian Magda Fahrni has studied, probably limited themselves to the "cautious consumption of necessities."[3] In rural Canada before 1950, only a minority of households even had electricity. The 1951 census revealed that half of Canadian families still did not own an electric refrigerator or a vacuum cleaner; 60 percent had no car; 40 percent had no telephone; and 25 percent did not have an electric washing machine. Indeed, one dwelling in three did not have hot and cold running water. Thousands of small farmers, incapable of earning a living, abandoned their land. Incomes of residents of the Atlantic provinces remained nearly 40 percent below the Canadian average. Large numbers of Montrealers with incomes below the poverty line lived in the tenements of St. Henri, which were portrayed poignantly by Gabrielle Roy in her novel *Bonheur d'occasion* (*The Tin Flute* in English). Many First Nations people began to flee poverty and unemployment on the reserves, in search of better opportunities in urban centres. Disadvantaged provinces offered social services of inferior quality. Throughout Canada, the underprivileged, whether unemployed or sick, handicapped or elderly, could not count on the array of social welfare benefits that, in spite of recent cutbacks, still exist today.

Canada had many second-class citizens, too. French-speakers suffered a linguistic disadvantage, even within Quebec. Women did not enjoy the same employment opportunities as men. Discrimination also afflicted African Canadians, recent immigrants, and Jews. In 1948, Pierre Berton, a young reporter for *Maclean's*, set out to investigate anti-Semitism. When, for example, he attempted to reserve a room at summer resorts north of Toronto, he had much more success using the name "Marshall" than when he identified himself as "Rosenberg." To help combat such discrimination through education, the newly founded Canadian Council of Christians and Jews instituted Brotherhood Week, a major program, in 1948.

Society in this era emphasized family and reproductive heterosexuality, and psychologists warned that overprotective mothers and absent fathers risked provoking homosexual tendencies in their sons. Most homosexuals hid their sexual orientation except perhaps from a few persons close to them. Those who did not faced social stigma as "perverts" and "sex deviates," as well as job discrimination. Gay men were often viewed as potential child molesters and, in the climate of the Cold War, as security risks to be purged from government service. Yet gay and lesbian networks expanded in Canadian cities. Gay men met in bars, baths, parks, and theatres; indeed, newspapers reported frequent arrests in such places. Lesbians socialized at bars that women could frequent and at house parties.

The inequalities suffered by many Canadians engendered increasing discontent. Not clearly articulated in the 1950s, dissatisfaction provoked far-reaching change beginning in the 1960s.

Prosperity and Trade

After demobilization, the federal government worked to convert the Canadian economy back to a free-enterprise system and to avoid a repetition of the severe recession that followed World War I. To achieve this objective, C.D. Howe, now in charge of the country's postwar reconstruction, sold war plants for a fraction of their cost, on condition that they reopen for business. He also wanted to liberalize international trade: only if markets abroad were open, he believed, could a country like Canada, with its economy largely based on exports, prosper. He also wanted the government to use tax policy to promote investment and create jobs.

Canada's trade did expand, albeit unevenly. From the late 1940s, the country had a persistently negative trade balance as imports rose faster than exports. Most Canadian-made manufactured products could not compete in international markets. Canadian production costs remained high because Canadian companies manufactured a wide variety of products in small quantities, and they often relied heavily on imported American components.

After World War II, Canada moved to establish closer economic ties with the United States. Indeed, by 1947, as imports from the United States increased sharply and British regulations made it impossible for Canada to convert into dollars the pounds it earned in trade with Britain, Canada experienced a severe shortage of American dollars. King succeeded in convincing the Americans to permit European countries receiving American aid through the Marshall Plan to use a portion of it to buy Canadian goods, thus resolving the dollar crisis. Ottawa also placed much hope in the General Agreement on Tariffs and Trade (GATT), a multilateral trade agreement, signed in Geneva in 1947, which aimed at stimulating world trade by reducing tariffs.

An Investment Boom

Continental economic integration proceeded apace. Foreign capital poured into Canada, particularly during the Korean War, which lasted from 1950 until 1953. The Americans sought Canada's resources as production of some important minerals declined in the United States. Moreover, to gain access to the Canadian market, protected by high tariffs, American multinational corporations established, especially in central Canada, numerous branch plants that manufactured consumer products and industrial goods.

Most provinces, in their quest for jobs, actively encouraged the entry of foreign capital by keeping taxes and labour costs down. Nevertheless, some observers worried about the "complacency" with which Canadians sold out their country's resources. In particular, the Royal Commission on Canada's Economic Prospects recommended in 1956 that Canada move to control foreign investment. Howe disagreed strongly: Canada needed American enterprise and capital to assure rapid growth.

For the moment, then, there would be no controls. Investment, both Canadian and foreign, financed several important development projects. Pipelines carried oil and gas from Alberta to markets in Ontario and the United States; a railway nearly 600 km long, running north from Sept-Îles, Quebec, opened up ore-rich Labrador; and the construction of the St. Lawrence Seaway and the Trans-Canada Highway began.

Then the boom ended. By 1958, slow growth raised unemployment to nearly 10 percent. Automation eliminated some jobs. When railways switched to diesel engines, for example, they needed fewer machinists, blacksmiths, and firemen. The high-valued Canadian dollar, which brought a premium when exchanged for an American dollar, hurt exports.

A Government of Efficient Administrators

In the postwar years, voters wanted politicians who would manage the country efficiently and achieve greater prosperity. They also called upon the state to protect them from the risks of unemployment, illness, and poverty. The Liberal government of businessmen and administrators largely fulfilled this need. It was a regime that reflected an era.

When William Lyon Mackenzie King finally retired in 1948, he had led the Liberal party for nearly 30 years and could boast of having been the longest-serving prime minister in the history of the British empire. Jurist Frank Scott, who objected indignantly to King's being given credit for everything but putting the oil under Alberta, attributed King's success to his blandness: "He will be remembered wherever men honour ingenuity, ambiguity, inactivity, and political longevity."

Yet many observers of Canadian politics admired King for his accomplishments, even though they disliked him personally and found him uninspiring. Like Macdonald and Laurier before him, he had held the country together effectively through difficult times. His government had also taken the first steps toward establishing a welfare state in Canada.

Louis St. Laurent (left) and Prime Minister Mackenzie King (centre), at the national Liberal convention of 1948 at which St. Laurent was chosen to succeed King as Liberal leader and prime minister. In the background is a portrait of former Liberal leader and prime minister Wilfrid Laurier.

William Lyon Mackenzie King Collection/Library and Archives Canada/CV-23278.

The St. Laurent Government

Louis St. Laurent, chosen as King's successor in 1948, was a former corporation lawyer from Quebec City and the second French-speaking, though fluently bilingual, prime minister. Denounced in his home province during the war for his approval of military conscription, he was clearly no Quebec nationalist. On constitutional questions he opposed the provincial autonomists in Quebec and elsewhere. In foreign affairs, he appeared more internationalist than most Canadians.

The new prime minister followed his predecessor's "accommodative" approach, acting only after general agreement had been reached. Under his leadership, the Liberals continued to occupy the centre of the political spectrum and thus established the consensus so necessary to govern Canada. Prosperity facilitated their task.

Newfoundland Enters Confederation

In 1949, Newfoundland became Canada's tenth province. Confederation had been preceded by months of bitter struggle. Joey Smallwood, leader of the confederate forces, campaigned tirelessly to prove that Newfoundlanders "would be better off in pocket, in stomach, and in health" within Canada. Anti-confederationists denounced those who would "lure Newfoundland into the Canadian mousetrap."

The referendum held in June 1948 allowed Newfoundlanders to choose among three options: Confederation, favoured by both Britain and Canada; responsible government or dominion status; and the unpopular existing system, by which a commission of British-appointed officials governed Newfoundland. Responsible government won; Confederation placed second. Since no clear majority had emerged, a second referendum was held in July in an atmosphere of sectarian bitterness. Most Roman Catholics, fearing loss of their denominational schools, spoke against Confederation, while many Protestants favoured it. In addition, the urban commercial classes generally opposed Confederation, fearing the competition of the big Canadian mail-order companies. The confederates won narrowly this time, with a majority of 52 percent. Canadians and Newfoundlanders now set about negotiating the final terms of union.

Historian David Alexander argues that the decline of the fishing economy, which fell victim to tumbling prices and oversupply, "led Newfoundlanders reluctantly into Confederation."[4] Poverty was endemic. Canada's "safety net" of social programs looked inviting. In addition, Britain clearly desired to quit Newfoundland. For its part, Canada wanted Newfoundland, having discovered the island's strategic and economic importance during World War II. Canadians also worried that the United States might seek to strengthen its ties with the island.

Newfoundland's integration into Canada proceeded rapidly. Immediately upon confederation, family allowances and other federal social programs were ready to function. Income levels improved. Yet the federal government did little to favour the province's economic development, and the province simply "shifted its dependence from London to Ottawa."[5]

Federal–Provincial Tensions

The Liberal government's preoccupation with maintaining a buoyant economy had serious implications for Canadian federalism. Ottawa sought to maintain and even strengthen the fiscal and legislative preeminence that it had acquired during the wartime emergency. But several provinces objected to the federal government's aggressive centralization. Nova Scotia premier Angus L. Macdonald complained that federal subsidies transformed the provinces into "mere annuitants of Ottawa." Ontario insisted on its right to formulate its own economic priorities and programs. In Quebec, the Duplessis government feuded continuously with Ottawa over federal tax and spending policies.

Toward a Welfare State

Neither federal–provincial tensions nor the Liberals' moderate conservatism halted Canada's movement toward a welfare state. In 1951, after all the provinces had agreed to the requisite constitutional amendment, federal legislation authorized sending monthly old-age-security cheques to all Canadians over the age of 70 and to needy Canadians over 65. Family allowances, also a universal program covering all children, now took second place. For the government, the allowances, instituted in 1944, had served their purpose: workers' wages had increased, there had been no postwar depression, and the socialist CCF no longer posed a threat. The government thus chose not to increase allowances to compensate for higher living costs.

Ottawa also adopted other measures concerning health and welfare. In 1948, it enacted the National Health Program, which provided for federal grants to each province in the fields of hygiene and health. In 1956, after a national publicity campaign by the Canadian Welfare Council, Parliament adopted the Unemployment Assistance Act, a shared-cost program designed to assist employable persons on welfare. Provinces also spent significantly more on welfare as case numbers increased. Yet such aid failed to take into account increased housing and clothing costs. For historian James Struthers, in Ontario, at least, "the poor went hungry to pay the rent."[6]

Canadians who became seriously ill in the 1950s knew the prohibitive cost of health care. Increasingly, they called for a national health plan. Several provincial premiers, especially those from the western provinces, most of which had already established hospital insurance, pressured Ottawa into acting. Finally, in 1957, Parliament adopted the Hospital Insurance and Diagnostic Services Act, which provided federal financial assistance to provinces willing to set up a publicly administered hospital insurance program with universal coverage.

The Golden Age of Canadian Diplomacy

After 1945, Canada had to adapt to a new world power structure. It could no longer rely on a permanently weakened Britain as a counterweight to American influence. To offset growing American power, Canada worked to build strong multilateral institutions. At the same time, it did not want world organizations to interfere in its relations with the United States, which it believed it could conduct better alone.

Canada in the Cold War Era

Disappointments were rife in these years, as the postwar era rapidly gave way to the Cold War. As relations between the United States and the Soviet Union soured, Canadian foreign-affairs officials feared that the often bellicose attitude of the United States would only make matters worse. However, events soon shook Canadians' faith in the West's capacity to reach some kind of reasonable entente with the Soviet Union. In late 1945 Igor Gouzenko, a cipher clerk at the Soviet embassy in Ottawa, defected. He revealed the existence of a Soviet espionage network in Canada that reached into several government agencies.

The intensification of the Cold War led Canada into ever-closer relations with the United States. Britain's own decline left Canada little choice. "London's impotence," historian Jack Granatstein argues, compelled Canadian governments to seek "shelter within Uncle Sam's all-encompassing embrace."[7]

As people lost hope that the United Nations could assure world peace through collective security, the Canadian government pushed for an Atlantic alliance for mutual self-defence. After arduous negotiations, the North Atlantic Treaty Organization (NATO) came into existence in April 1949. Canada had hoped that NATO would contribute to the economic and social development of the member nations, but rising East–West tensions, especially the outbreak of war in Korea in 1950, turned the organization into an almost exclusively military alliance. Canada's influence declined as its defence spending fell and its priorities became continental.

New Interest in the North

The Cold War made the Canadian North an area of vital strategic interest to both Canada and the United States. Acting together, the two countries worked to provide a warning system in the event of a Soviet nuclear attack on Canadian and American cities. A chain of more than 40 Distant Early Warning (DEW Line) stations was built in the 1950s across the Arctic. The system remained in full operation for nearly a decade, until intercontinental ballistic missiles largely replaced the bomber threat. Defence relations between Canada and the United States became even closer in 1957 when the two countries signed the North American Air Defence Agreement (NORAD), which formally coordinated their air forces.

The DEW Line and other American proposals revived fears about Canada's sovereignty in the Arctic. Recognizing that one of the surest grounds for Canada's claim would be "effective occupation," the federal government in 1953 arranged for several Inuit families from northern Quebec and Baffin Island to relocate nearly 2000 km away, on Cornwallis and Ellesmere islands in the high Arctic. The migrants lost contact with their communities and, the government's promises aside, found themselves in a much more inhospitable environment than the one they had left behind.

The Commonwealth

In keeping with its desire to balance closer links to the United States with an increased international participation, Canada looked with hope to the evolving British Commonwealth of Nations. The Commonwealth was rapidly changing and becoming more diversified, with the addition of new members such as India, Pakistan, and Sri Lanka (then Ceylon). Canada helped move the Commonwealth in directions that made it an acceptable organization for these new states. It also supported and contributed to the Colombo Plan, which was set up at a meeting of Commonwealth foreign ministers in 1950 to promote economic development in Commonwealth countries in Asia.

Peacekeeping

Canada's early attempts at peacekeeping produced some positive results. In 1950, when communist North Korea invaded South Korea and the United Nations Security Council denounced this act of aggression, Canada contributed a brigade to fight alongside mostly American troops in the name of collective security.

As the war moved toward a stalemate, Lester B. Pearson, Canada's minister of external affairs, helped to restrain the "overzealous" Americans from actions that risked bringing China and the Soviet Union into the war.

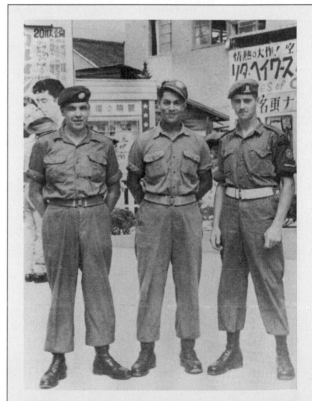

Aboriginal people participated in Canada's armed forces in the Korean War in the early 1950s. The photo shows (left to right) Bill McCauley, Cree; Rene Espaniel, Ojibwa; and Sid Sawyer, non-Aboriginal; in late July 1952, in Kure, Japan. All three men came from Biscotasing, Northern Ontario.

Photo courtesy of Rene Espaniel.

Then, in 1956, came what many considered to be Canada's greatest contribution internationally. In October, despite strong American opposition, Israel, together with Britain and France, invaded Egypt, in response to Egypt's nationalization of the Suez Canal. Wary of the dangerous split developing in the western alliance, Pearson proposed the creation of a multinational United Nations emergency peacekeeping force in the region. He then lobbied tirelessly to have the plan accepted by the General Assembly. For his efforts, he won the Nobel Peace Prize in 1957. According to biographer John English, Pearson's initiative "strengthened the United Nations, moderated the tensions between Washington and London, and helped to maintain both the Commonwealth and NATO."[8]

Yearning for Political Change

The Progressive Conservatives' narrow victory under John Diefenbaker at the polls in 1957 surprised most observers. Certainly the Liberals had boasted during the election campaign that voters would not "shoot Santa Claus." Yet not all Canadians were prosperous. Residents of the Prairies and the Maritimes complained of their regions' underdevelopment. Many senior citizens endorsed Conservative assertions that unindexed old-age pensions were scandalously insufficient. Other voters agreed with the new Conservative leader's denunciations of the "dictatorial" tactics employed by the Liberals in 1956 as they pushed a bill through the House of Commons that arranged for an important loan to a private pipeline company. But most of all, many Canadians simply wanted a change from what appeared increasingly to be cold, insensitive, uncreative leadership by an aging Liberal gerontocracy.

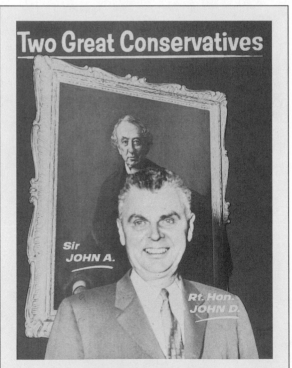

A campaign poster shows John Diefenbaker with his hero, Sir John A. Macdonald.

Diefenbaker Centre poster collection, Diefenbaker Centre, University of Saskatchewan.

The "Diefenbaker Party"

John Diefenbaker surely played a significant role in the success of what became known as the "Diefenbaker party." Diefenbaker sought to change voters' traditionally negative image of the Tories. He wrested control of the party from the Toronto business elite and gave it to "outsiders," many of whom came from western Canada. His oratorical talents, which he used to proclaim Canadians' "appointment with destiny," far outshone anything the Liberals could muster.

The new government barely had time to adopt a few popular measures designed to assist the unemployed, Prairie farmers, and Maritimers before Diefenbaker, anxious to form a majority government, called a new election in March 1958. The prime minister then presented his "vision of opportunity" for Canada, a vision based on the development of resources and of the North. New Liberal leader Lester B. Pearson vainly attempted to brush off what he termed the "oracular fervour and circus parades." The result was a Diefenbaker landslide, with the Progressive Conservatives winning what was proportionally the greatest majority in Canadian electoral history: 208 of the 265 seats in the House of Commons, including 50 seats from Quebec.

From the start, the Conservatives had difficulty governing. Ministers lacked experience and distrusted civil servants inherited from the Liberals; Diefenbaker, a unilingual Anglophone from Saskatchewan, knew little about Quebec and entrusted no senior cabinet portfolios to Quebeckers, and his vision of northern development did not capture the imagination of southern Canadians. The Conservative government's major problem, however, arose from the country's deteriorating economic situation. It responded to rising unemployment with subsidies and increased welfare benefits. Budgetary deficits grew and the business community complained of financial mismanagement.

Labour Relations in Prosperous Times

Postwar economic growth gave a powerful boost to the unions. In 1950, union membership passed the one million mark, or 30 percent of the work force. "Elite" unions in sectors such as heavy manufacturing enjoyed strong bargaining power and succeeded in negotiating high wages. They had frequent recourse to strikes, aimed at forcing employers to recognize union rights, improve working conditions, and increase salaries. In retaliation, companies frequently hired strikebreakers, and violent confrontations sometimes ensued. Provincial governments supported employers directly through anti-union legislation and the use of the police and the courts.

Industrial Unrest

Although most workers signed contracts without going on strike and although sickness resulted in far more loss of work time than did strike activity, certain sensational confrontations earned a place in the annals of Canadian working-class history. In one dramatic encounter in 1946, Steel Company of Canada (Stelco) management used airplanes and boats to avoid picket lines and to transport food and supplies to strikebreakers inside its plant at Hamilton, Ontario. In the same year, textile workers, many of them women, struck in Valleyfield, Quebec. Led by Madeleine Parent and Kent Rowley, the strikers obtained recognition for their union only after bloody skirmishes with police. Parent was then convicted of seditious conspiracy. In 1949, 5000 Quebec asbestos workers struck for five months to improve wages and working conditions. The Duplessis government defended the companies, decertified the union, and sent in special police squads. Some members of the clergy, including Archbishop Joseph Charbonneau of Montreal, defied the government and sided openly with the strikers, one of whose supporters was a young Montreal lawyer, Pierre Elliott Trudeau. Though the settlement gave workers no significant material gains, the strike itself took on great symbolic value: Quebec sociologist Jean-Charles Falardeau even viewed it as a "quasi-revolution."[9]

Conflict continued into the 1950s, as major strikes occurred among loggers, fishers, government employees, and longshoremen in British Columbia, building-trades workers in Halifax and Vancouver, gold miners in Ontario and Quebec, and automobile workers and employees of the International Nickel Company (Inco) in Ontario. In August 1950, 130 000 employees of Canada's two major railways left their jobs, but the government, declaring that "the country cannot afford a railway strike," ordered the workers back. Copper workers at Murdochville, Quebec, struck for seven months in 1957 in a violent but vain confrontation. In 1959, Newfoundland loggers, members of the International Woodworkers of America (IWA), went on strike. Violence broke out when the company recruited fishers to replace strikers. In an effort to break the IWA, Premier Joseph Smallwood set up a union and had the legislature outlaw the IWA in the province. The federal government refused to send the RCMP reinforcements that Smallwood demanded, but the strike nonetheless failed.

Workers versus Workers

Workers not only fought management and governments, they also feuded with one another for political and personal reasons. On the left, communists and democratic socialists battled each other furiously. Both clashed with conservative unionists, who viewed all political links as dangerous for the labour movement.

Anticommunists in the Canadian Congress of Labour (CCL) insisted that, to fight the bosses, "we must get rid of the communists." The communist-led Canadian Seamen's Union (CSU) was crushed when the Canadian and American governments combined with the shippers and Trades and Labor Congress (TLC) officers to replace the CSU with a rival union. However, some Canadian unionists thought that the battle against communists merely permitted American unions to reinforce their hold in Canada.

Greater labour unity came in 1956, when the TLC and the CCL formed the Canadian Labour Congress (CLC), with one million members. This union followed the merger in 1955 of the American labour congresses, the AFL and the CIO. The costly raids by TLC and CCL unions on each other, with no total gain in membership, then ended. Many of the CLC unions were affiliated with the AFL-CIO, and they remained subject to American influence. Indeed, most Canadian workers who were employed by American branch companies found nothing unusual in belonging to American-dominated unions.

Although unions made major gains in the postwar period, much work remained. Collective agreements generally left managers with complete authority over the work process on the shop floor. Vast numbers of workers, particularly in the service sector, remained outside unions. The increasing bureaucratization of the union movement, fostered by what labour historian Peter McInnis has termed the "excessively legalistic and rigid framework" that came to characterize industrial relations, tended to exclude the rank and file from decisions.[10] Labour legislation in several provinces was unsympathetic to unions. Automation made job security an increasingly serious issue. Worker safety also caused grave concern. When fire killed five Italian labourers laying a water main in the Hogg's Hollow district of Toronto, the coroner denounced management's "callous attitude" toward worker safety and noted that almost all the safety regulations had been violated.

The Status of Women

After World War II, most women workers, especially married women, left the paid workforce. Women who continued in paid employment outside the home still had to perform all the domestic and family chores. Cultural stereotypes reinforced the "traditional" role of women: school textbooks depicted men in interesting careers while portraying women as staying at home, cooking meals, and scolding children. Women's magazines such as *Chatelaine* and the *Canadian Home Journal* wrote about sewing, homemaking, gardening, and fashion.

Women in the Workforce

Slowly, however, female participation in the workforce increased. Mothers began to rejoin the workforce after their youngest children enrolled in school. Most women worked as secretaries, nurses, sales personnel, and clerks; only a handful were professionals.

For female workers, inequality abounded. Men generally received higher wages than women for performing the same tasks. Ontario adopted the Female Employees Fair Remuneration Act in 1951, but historian Shirley Tillotson's research shows that it had little tangible effect.[11] Nor did women have equal opportunity for promotions, even in female-dominated sectors such as teaching. Minimum wage rates, fixed by governments, were usually lower for women than for men.

WHERE HISTORIANS DISAGREE

Women and Unions in Postwar Canada

Most working women in 1960 were employed in non-unionized sectors of activity, such as clerical and domestic work. Women made up only about one-sixth of the unionized workforce. Did these women see themselves simply as workers who, like men, wanted to improve wages and working conditions? Or did they see themselves primarily as women with objectives that were different from, and at times contradictory to, those of men? And how did men react to the entry of women into "their" workplace?

Labour historians, preoccupied with labour's battles against employers, did not at first ask these questions. Bryan Palmer, for example, notes that women made up one-quarter of the membership of the militant United Electrical, Radio and Machine Workers' Union (UE), but he does not view their struggle as other than a workers' struggle against the bosses.[1] Craig Heron, for his part, does state that industrial unions of these years had difficulty eliminating the segregation of women into low-wage job ghettos, but he then comments, revealingly, that "even if the male unionists' pride had allowed more equity, most men still assumed that women should be at home, supported by a male wage."[2]

In her study of working women in Peterborough, Ontario, Joan Sangster shows how unions have been arenas of both gender conflict and class solidarity.[3] Looking at the UE, she notes that union leadership endorsed gender equality, partly in order to gain women workers' support for the UE's struggle against a rival union. The UE also tried to focus on grievances that could unite men and women, such as more equal pay rates, because men feared the substitution of female for male labour. While the union itself gave preeminence to class rather than to gender, separate organizations for women within unions eventually provided an innovative means for women to demand better working conditions and wages.

Julie Guard has also studied the experience of women within the UE. Like Sangster, she shows that the union was interested primarily in the class struggle, not in women's rights. It made slow progress in endorsing equal pay for women, in spite of women's attempts to prove that low pay for women put a brake on male wages. She too observes that few women participated in union leadership, a fact that men attributed to personal choice rather than to the "inherent gender bias of union structure and culture."[4]

Joy Parr has examined the effect of gender on strike action against a textile company in Paris, Ontario in 1949. About one-half of the workers were women and, although women were less inclined to join the union than were men, female militancy on the picket line was considerable. Yet, whereas the union itself whipped up male strikers' militancy, female militancy was "forged and sustained in family and neighbourhood relationships" rather than through union organization.[5]

In her study of the United Auto Workers in Canada, Pam Sugiman argues that the traditional view of the UAW as a progressive union that gave vocal support to women's rights is only partly true; the UAW also showed persistent gender bias and allowed blatant inequalities to persist in the working environment. Male union officials were reluctant to view the special concerns of female dues-paying members as legitimate union issues. In the immediate postwar years, women did not generally challenge gender ideologies, separate seniority lists, and large pay differentials. Even in the 1950s, women still did not "openly contest their subordination as a sex" although they did develop "a stronger self-identification as wage earners and as unionists."[6] Thanks to improving economic conditions, women became bolder and made use of grievance procedures to try to improve working conditions.

Interest in the situation of women within postwar unions is relatively recent. Many other case studies will have to be carried out on different aspects of the question before it will be possible to reach general conclusions.

1. Bryan Palmer, *Working Class Experience: Rethinking the History of Canadian Labour, 1800–1991*, 2nd ed. (Toronto: McClelland & Stewart, 1992), p. 287.

2. Craig Heron, *The Canadian Labour Movement: A Short History*, 2nd ed. (Toronto: James Lorimer, 1996), p. 78.

3. Joan Sangster, *Earning Respect: The Lives of Working Women in Small-Town Ontario, 1920–1960* (Toronto: University of Toronto Press, 1995), p. 167.

4. Julie Guard, "Fair Play or Fair Pay? Gender Relations, Class Consciousness, and Union Solidarity in the Canadian UE," *Labour/Le Travail*, 37 (1996): 176.

5. Joy Parr, *The Gender of Breadwinners: Women, Men, and Change in Two Industrial Towns, 1880–1950* (Toronto: University of Toronto Press, 1990), p. 108.

6. Pam Sugiman, *Labour's Dilemma: The Gender Politics of Auto Workers in Canada, 1937–1979* (Toronto: University of Toronto Press, 1994), p. 99.

Churches such as the United Church of Canada which accepted women as ministers nevertheless placed numerous obstacles in the paths of those seeking ordination. United Church moderator James Mutchmor gave Lois Wilson, a minister's wife, reasons for objecting to her ordination: Who would "wear the pants" in the family? Who would have priority in the use of the car? Wilson succeeded in gaining ordination because prominent men supported her. She later became the United Church's first woman moderator.

Only a few women held positions of influence in business or politics in the 1950s. Between 1930 and 1960, the federal government named only seven women senators, while more than 250 men received the coveted lifetime appointment. Few women ran in elections. Only in 1957 did a prime minister, John Diefenbaker, appoint a woman to a federal cabinet post—Ellen Fairclough, from Hamilton, Ontario. Many observers saw this nomination as only a modest beginning. Charlotte Whitton, Ottawa's feisty mayor, clairvoyantly predicted that women were growing so impatient with "the man-made messes of a man-made world" that they would soon insist on a much larger voice in public affairs.

The Baby Boom

With good times, a higher proportion of young adults married. They also married earlier. As Mary Louise Adams explains, "Marriage was a legitimate avenue of sexual expression for those men and women who felt caught between the incitement to sex in the culture at large and the proscriptions against their own engagement in it. Early marriage was one way to bring changes in sexual behaviour into line with the established moral order."[12]

As North American women began, on an impressive scale, to have children, a veritable "baby boom" set in. By 1947, the birth rate in Canada had increased to nearly 29 per 1000, and the average family had three or four children. This relatively large contingent of youth has had enormous repercussions on Canadian society. The precise nature of the impact would alter with time, as the baby boomers went through childhood, adolescence, young adulthood, and middle age. The baby boom led to a rapid increase in Canada's population. Including immigration, the annual growth rate exceeded 3 percent, equivalent to that experienced by many developing countries today.

Higher Education

Few Canadians attended colleges or universities in the 1950s. In 1951, Canada's institutions of higher learning had only 60 000 students, barely 4 percent of the eligible age group. Only about one university student in four was a woman. Most female students enrolled in programs in education or the liberal arts; few entered the sciences or the professional schools. In Quebec, until 1960, the provincial government

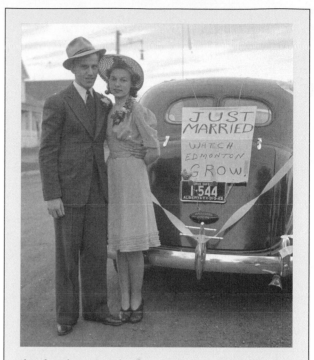

This shot shows an Edmonton couple by a 1940s car with a handwritten sign on the car, "Just Married, Watch Edmonton Grow!" A perfect photo to make the point about the post–World War II baby boom—or is it? This "perfect photo" apparently predates the baby boom: the expiry date on the licence plate reads March 31, 1942.

City of Edmonton Archives/EA-160-898.

denied classical colleges for women the state funds that were made available to all-male colleges. In Toronto, the elite University of Toronto Schools (whose graduates almost all went on to university) admitted no women, even though it was largely state-supported.

In 1951, the Royal Commission on National Development in the Arts, Letters and Sciences, chaired by Vincent Massey and hence better known as the Massey Commission, recommended direct federal financial support for universities. The Soviet launching of *Sputnik*, the first space satellite, in 1957, proved an unforeseen boon to Canadian universities. The fear of Soviet scientific superiority convinced many Canadians that governments should invest much more in higher education. Provincial authorities loosened the purse strings and the federal government instituted a system of grants. Several new universities came into being in the late 1950s.

Culture: Canadian versus American

In the postwar era, Canadian nationalists increasingly felt the dangers of dependence upon American culture. Reduced funding for the Canadian Broadcasting Corporation (CBC) threatened to undermine public broadcasting. Private broadcasters, who wished to offer more American-produced commercial programming, resented the CBC's regulatory role. The federal government also reduced the National Film Board's budget after the war, and private filmmakers sought to obtain its work. Institutions such as the Public Archives of Canada and

Zoologist William Rowan lecturing at the University of Alberta, Edmonton, before 1957. Beginning in the 1960s, class sizes would expand to the bursting point with the arrival of the baby boomers at universities.

University of Alberta Archives/Acc. 82-29-37.

the National Museum of Canada suffered from lack of coordination, while the country still had no national library.

Cultural associations that enjoyed strong Cabinet support brought the government to establish the Massey Commission. In 1951, the commission recommended the establishment of a national arts-funding body, one free of partisan and bureaucratic control. Finally, in 1957, the Liberals founded the Canada Council. It used its endowment to help a multitude of arts organizations, among them ballet companies, theatre troupes (including the Stratford Shakespearean Festival), and orchestras. The council also gave grants to writers and scholarships to graduate students.

Popular Culture

Prosperity enabled many Canadians to spend money on entertainment. They purchased new long-playing records, often of poor quality and relatively costly. They flocked to the movie theatres that proliferated, to watch mostly American-made films. Censorship in all provinces regulated the movies Canadians saw. The British Columbia Moving Pictures Act, for example, outlawed films "considered injurious to morals or against public welfare, or which may offer evil suggestions to the minds of children." Alberta's censors watched carefully for "any materialistic, undemocratic, un-Christian propaganda disguised as entertainment."

The real revolution in the entertainment industry, however, came in the early 1950s with television. At first, television sets were a status symbol because of their relatively high cost. By 1952, Canada's own television broadcasting began in Toronto and Montreal, then quickly expanded to other cities. The CBC and the French-language Radio Canada aired many news programs, and also presented numerous cultural programs, which attracted a small, but influential, audience.

Although the CBC presented Canadian variety shows such as *Showtime*, which featured dance, song, music, and comedy, it also imported popular American variety shows to boost its ratings and increase its commercial revenues. On Sunday evenings, millions of Canadians loyally watched the most famous and longest-lasting of these, *The Ed Sullivan Show*. Sullivan introduced Elvis Presley and his hip gyrations to Canadians in September 1956. He also boosted the fortunes of Canadian comedians Johnny Wayne and Frank Shuster. Both CBC and private television imported popular American comedies such as *I Love Lucy* and *The Jackie Gleason Show*, and presented

The Schiefners, a farm family living outside of Milestone, Saskatchewan, on a Saturday evening in 1956. Hockey Night in Canada: Toronto versus Detroit would be broadcast at 9 p.m.

Library and Archives Canada/ Richard Harrington/National Film Board of Canada coll./Accession 1971-271 NPC/PA-111390.

contemporary American singers like Perry Como and Dinah Shore. Baby-boom children watched Roy Rogers, Lassie, Walt Disney programs, and the popular American puppet show *Howdy Doody*. (The author of these lines was spared a potential lethal blow during an after school fight when he reminded his bulky aggressor, seated on top of him, that it was 5:30, "Howdy Doody Time.")

French-language television had more local content. While it beamed a French-speaking Hopalong Cassidy and many other programs dubbed in French into Quebec living rooms and kitchens, it also carried original productions, such as a series adapted from novelist Roger Lemelin's *La famille Plouffe*. Children watched a captivating Quebec-made puppet show called *Pépino*. The CBC's very successful variety show, *Music Hall*, produced in Montreal, featured French stars such as Edith Piaf, Maurice Chevalier, and Charles Aznavour. By 1957, television production in Montreal, historian Susan Mann writes, was "third in the world to New York and Hollywood and second to none in French."[13]

The advent of television increased popular interest in sport. Armchair spectators marvelled at the exploits of the Edmonton Eskimos' football dynasty. Watching *La Soirée du hockey*, or *Hockey Night in Canada*, became a popular pastime on Saturday night. Fans avidly discussed the feats of Syl Apps, Maurice "The Rocket" Richard, and Gordie Howe, and celebrated the Stanley Cup triumphs of the Toronto Maple Leafs in the late 1940s and of the Montreal Canadiens in the late 1950s.

English-speaking Canadians enjoyed newspaper supplements like the *Star Weekly* and *Weekend*, while French Canadians read a variety of tabloid newspapers. By the end of the 1950s, however, American mass-circulation magazines, among them *Time*, *Reader's Digest*, and its French edition, *Sélection du Reader's Digest*, accounted for 75 percent of the Canadian general-interest magazine market.

Literature

Canadian literature in both languages came into its own in the post–World War II era. In Montreal, Hugh MacLennan published his celebrated novel *Two Solitudes*, with its theme that Canada's two major linguistic communities needed to demonstrate more mutual tolerance. In *The Mountain and the Valley*, Maritimer Ernest Buckler examined the dilemma faced by a brilliant and ambitious Nova Scotia boy who found his creativity stifled by his deep attachment to rural life. W.O. Mitchell, in *Who Has Seen the Wind*, interpreted the struggles of a small-town Saskatchewan boy at the time of the Depression. Throughout the 1950s, Mitchell produced his highly successful "Jake and the Kid" stories for magazine and radio.

Mordecai Richler's *The Apprenticeship of Duddy Kravitz*, a portrait of a young Montreal Jewish entrepreneur, established the Montreal author as a successful novelist. Adele Wiseman's first novel, *The Sacrifice*, was strongly influenced by the experiences of her Russian-Jewish parents. Robertson Davies gained early recognition as an essayist and brilliant novelist. Poet Dorothy Livesay won Governor General's awards for *Day and Night*, in 1944, and *Poems for Peace*, in 1947, while the versatile and flamboyant Irving Layton produced numerous volumes of love poems and prose.

At the same time, an "aesthetic thaw" came slowly to Quebec. In *Refus global*, a manifesto written in 1948, Paul-Émile Borduas condemned what he called Quebec's asphyxiating orthodoxy. The artist's cry for the right to total freedom of expression led to his departure from Quebec. Novelists cast aside traditional themes of religion and rurality. Some, such as Roger Lemelin in *Au pied de la pente douce*, used urban working-class settings. Others, such as Anne Hébert in *Le Torrent* and André Langevin in *Poussière sur la ville*, forcefully portrayed personal dramas. Yves Thériault won international fame with *Agaguk*, a novel about the Inuit. Professional theatre troupes proliferated, with some of their repertories supplied by Quebec playwrights. The play *Tit-Coq*, by Gratien Gélinas, as well as the film that followed, encountered spectacular success. Quebec culture seemed to have attained new vibrancy, despite the province's small market.

Religion

Religion "stands out as one of the great gulfs" separating the 1950s from today, writes historian Doug Owram.[14] The majority of Canadians still attended church or the synagogue regularly. Religion was present in most schools across the country, even in so-called public schools. Nevertheless, the influence of religion often appeared superficial. Possibly, religious practice was linked more to socialization than to faith. The *United Church Observer* frequently bemoaned the limited commitment of many adherents. Presumably churchgoing Quebeckers bought a million copies each weekend of sex-and-crime tabloids like *Allo Police*, which flourished in spite of—and possibly because of—the opposition of the Roman Catholic church.

The quiet Sundays of English-speaking Canada also came under attack. It was said that in Toronto one could harmlessly fire a cannonball down Yonge Street on a Sunday, and the local press editorialized in favour of the maintenance of Toronto's "typically Canadian" Sunday. Then the citizens of "Toronto the Good" voted in favour of Sunday sports in a plebiscite and, in 1951, elected as their mayor a churchgoer who had pledged to make it possible to watch double-headers on Sundays at Maple Leaf Stadium. Across English-speaking Canada, provincial drinking restrictions that determined who could drink, where they could drink, and under what conditions, were increasingly challenged as attitudes changed. In British Columbia, for example, citizens voted in 1952 to authorize the sale of liquor and wine by the glass in respectable cocktail lounges. The beer parlours, often viewed as indecent working-class centres of excess, continued to exist, however, with separate sections for men, and for ladies and escorts.

In the late 1940s and the 1950s, Canadian consumers had more money to spend and new products to spend it on. Workers in most regions of the country easily found jobs, and pay scales increased substantially. Governments went about the task of managing economic growth. For a time, Canada's postwar prosperity camouflaged the poverty and inequalities that remained the lot of many Canadians, in spite of the appearance of several new social programs. When, by the late 1950s, the postwar boom appeared to have run its course, new tensions emerged in society. Canadians now seemed to believe that it was time for a change.

NOTES

1. Matthew J. Bellamy, *Profiting the Crown: Canada's Polymer Corporation, 1942–1990* (Montreal/Kingston: McGill-Queen's University Press, 2005), p. 89.

2. Doug Owram, "Canadian Domesticity in the Postwar Era," in Peter Neary and J.L. Granatstein, eds., *The Veterans Charter and Post–World War II Canada* (Montreal/Kingston: McGill-Queen's University Press, 1998), p. 213.

3. Magda Fahrni, *Household Politics: Montreal Families and Postwar Reconstruction* (Toronto: University of Toronto Press, 2005), p. 11.

4. David G. Alexander, *Atlantic Canada and Confederation: Essays in Canadian Political Economy* (Toronto: University of Toronto Press, 1983), p. 32.

5. Raymond Blake, *Canadians at Last: Canada Integrates Newfoundland as a Province* (Toronto: University of Toronto Press, 1994), p. 6.

6. James Struthers, *The Limits of Affluence: Welfare in Ontario, 1920–1970* (Toronto: University of Toronto Press, 1994), p. 180.

7. J.L. Granatstein, *How Britain's Weakness Forced Canada into the Arms of the United States* (Toronto: University of Toronto Press, 1989), p. 3.

8. John English, *The Worldly Years: The Life of Lester Pearson*, vol. II, *1949–1972* (Toronto: Knopf Canada, 1992), p. 145.

9. J.-C. Falardeau, *Bulletin des relations industrielles*, 4 (1949); quoted in Fraser Isbester, "Asbestos 1949," in Irving Abella, ed., *On Strike: Six Key Labour Struggles in Canada, 1919–1949* (Toronto: James, Lewis & Samuel Publishers, 1974), p. 163.

10. Peter S. McInnis, *Harnessing Labour Confrontation: Shaping the Postwar Settlement in Canada, 1943–1950* (Toronto: University of Toronto Press, 2002), p. 13.

11. Shirley Tillotson, "Human Rights Law as Prism: Women's Organizations, Unions, and Ontario's Female Employees Fair Remuneration Act, 1951," *Canadian Historical Review*, 72 (1991): 532–57.

12. Mary Louise Adams, *The Trouble with Normal: Postwar Youth and the Making of Heterosexuality* (Toronto: University of Toronto Press, 1997), pp. 105–6.

13. Susan Mann, *The Dream of Nation: A Social and Intellectual History of Quebec* (Montreal/Kingston: McGill-Queen's University Press, 1982, 2002), p. 284.

14. Doug Owram, *Born at the Right Time: A History of the Baby-Boom Generation* (Toronto: University of Toronto Press, 1996), p. 103.

BEYOND THE BOOK

Life in Postwar Canada

http://archives.cbc.ca/society/youth/topics/1798
Radio clips detailing life for soldiers in postwar Canada, and their families. Details education issues for veterans, women in the workforce, and the "baby bonus."

Has Confederation Been Good for Newfoundland?

http://archives.cbc.ca/politics/elections/topics/564
This archive of television and radio footage explores Newfoundland's entry into Confederation in 1949, and how it has fared since.

Canada and NATO

http://www.civilization.ca/cwm/nato/nato01_e.html
A history of Canada's involvement in the North Atlantic Treaty Organization, beginning in 1949.

Madeleine Parent

http://www.histori.ca/minutes/minute.do?id=14861
A "Historica Minute" regarding Madeleine Parent and the 1946 textile workers strike in Valleyfield, Quebec.

Massey Commission

http://www.collectionscanada.ca/2/5/index-e.html
The full text of the report of the Royal Commission on National Development in the Arts, Letters, and Sciences (the Massey Commission).

Print Advertising on the Prairies

http://scaa.usask.ca/gallery/persuasion/main.html
A database of print advertising published to audiences in the Canadian prairies. View vivid political, social, and economic ads for the postwar era and other decades.

The Colony of Unrequited Dreams

Wayne Johnston, *The Colony of Unrequited Dreams* (Toronto: Vintage Canada, 1999). A story of the life of future Newfoundland premier Joey Smallwood is narrated from his perspective in this historical novel.

The Rocket

The Rocket. Directed by Charles Binamé (Cinémaginaire inc, 2006). The life of Maurice "Rocket" Richard.

RELATED READINGS

Three readings are included in R. Douglas Francis and Donald B. Smith, eds., *Viewpoints: Readings in Canadian History* (Toronto: Thomson Nelson, 2007), that deal with this topic: Veronica Strong-Boag, "Home Dreams: Women and the Suburban Experiment in Canada, 1945–1960," pp. 463–82; Robert Rutherdale, "Fatherhood, Masculinity, and the Good Life during Canada's Baby Boom, 1945–1965," pp. 483–99; and José Igartua, "The Quieter Revolution: Evolving Representations of National Identity in English Canada, 1941–1960," pp. 506–24.

BIBLIOGRAPHY

Useful general works on this period include Robert Bothwell, Ian Drummond, and John English, *Canada since 1945: Power, Politics, and Provincialism*, rev. ed. (Toronto: University of Toronto Press, 1989); Doug Owram, *Born at the Right Time: A History of the Baby-Boom Generation* (Toronto: University of Toronto Press, 1996); and Kenneth Norrie and Douglas Owram, *A History of the Canadian Economy*, 3rd ed. (Toronto: Nelson Thomson, 2002).

Joy Parr offers a critical study of consumerism in *Domestic Goods: The Material, the Moral, and the Economic in the Postwar Years* (Toronto: University of Toronto Press, 1999). Among works on social history, see Alvin Finkel, *Our Lives: Canada after 1945* (Toronto: James Lorimer, 1997); James Struthers, *The Limits of Affluence: Welfare in Ontario, 1920–1970* (Toronto: University of Toronto Press,

1994); and Jacqueline S. Ismael, ed., *The Canadian Welfare State: Evolution and Transition* (Edmonton: University of Alberta Press, 1987). Housing is studied in Richard Harris, *Creeping Conformity: How Canada Became Suburban, 1900–1960* (Toronto: University of Toronto Press, 2004).

Aspects of environmental history are examined in George M. Warecki, *Protecting Ontario's Wilderness: A History of Changing Ideas and Preservation Politics, 1927–1973* (New York: Peter Lang, 2000); Alan MacEachern, *Natural Selections: National Parks in Atlantic Canada, 1935–1970* (Montreal/ Kingston: McGill-Queen's University Press, 2001); and Richard A. Rajala, *Clearcutting the Pacific Rain Forest: Production, Science and Regulation* (Vancouver: UBC Press, 1998).

The numerous studies available on politicians and politics include Dale C. Thomson, *Louis St. Laurent, Canadian* (Toronto: Macmillan, 1967); Denis Smith, *Rogue Tory: The Life and Legend of John G. Diefenbaker* (Toronto: Macfarlane Walter & Ross, 1995); and Reginald Whitaker, *The Government Party: Organizing and Financing the Liberal Party of Canada, 1930–1958* (Toronto: University of Toronto Press, 1977). On Newfoundland's entry into Confederation, see Raymond B. Blake, *Canadians at Last: Canada Integrates Newfoundland as a Province* (Toronto: University of Toronto Press, 1994).

On Canadian foreign policy of the late 1940s and 1950s, see Robert Bothwell, *Alliance and Illusion: Canada and the World, 1945–1984* (Vancouver: UBC Press, 2007); Adam Chapnick's myth-debunking *The Middle Power Project: Canada and the Founding of the United Nations* (Vancouver: UBC Press, 2005); and Reg Whitaker and Steve Hewitt, *Canada and the Cold War* (Toronto: James Lorimer, 2003). Canadian participation in the Korean War is studied in William Johnston, *A War of Patrols: Canadian Army Operations in Korea* (Vancouver: UBC Press, 2003); and in David Bercuson, *Blood on the Hills: The Canadian Army in the Korean War* (Toronto: University of Toronto Press, 1999). Postwar trade issues are discussed in Michael Hart, *A Trading Nation: Canadian Trade Policy from Colonialism to Globalization* (Vancouver: UBC Press, 2002).

For Canadian–American relations in the defence sector, see Joseph T. Jockel, *No Boundaries Upstairs: Canada, the United States and the Origins of North American Air Defence, 1945–1958* (Vancouver: University of British Columbia Press, 1987). The history of Canada's atomic energy program is discussed in Brian Buckley, *Canada's Early Nuclear Policy: Fate, Chance, and Character* (Montreal/Kingston: McGill-Queen's University Press, 2000). Issues linked to internal security are examined in Amy Knight, *How the Cold War Began: The Gouzenko Affair and the Hunt for Soviet Spies* (Toronto: McClelland & Stewart, 2005); and in Reg Whitaker and Gary Marcuse, *Cold War Canada: The Making of a National Insecurity State, 1945–1957* (Toronto: University of Toronto Press, 1994). On human rights campaigns, see Ross Lambertson, *Repression and Resistance: Canadian Human Rights Activists, 1930–1960* (Toronto: University of Toronto Press, 2005).

Labour has been much studied for this period. Consult Bryan D. Palmer, *Working-Class Experience: Rethinking the History of Canadian Labour, 1800–1991*, 2nd ed. (Toronto: McClelland & Stewart, 1992); Peter S. McInnis, *Harnessing Labour Confrontation: Shaping the Postwar Settlement in Canada, 1943–1950* (Toronto: University of Toronto Press, 2002); and Charlotte Yates, *From Plant to Politics: The Autoworkers Union in Postwar Canada* (Philadelphia: Temple University Press, 1993). Two excellent general syntheses of women's history are Micheline Dumont et al., *Quebec Women: A History* (Toronto: Women's Press, 1987); and Alison Prentice et al., *Canadian Women: A History*, 2nd ed. (Toronto: Harcourt Brace, 1996).

Works on cultural history include Paul Litt, *The Muses, the Masses, and the Massey Commission* (Toronto: University of Toronto Press, 1992); and Paul Rutherford, *When Television Was Young: Primetime Canada 1952–1967* (Toronto: University of Toronto Press, 1990). On heterosexuality and homosexuality, see Richard Cavell, ed., *Love, Hate, and Fear in Canada's Cold War* (Toronto: University of Toronto Press, 2004); and Gary Kinsman, *The Regulation of Desire: Homo and Hetero Sexualities*, 2nd ed. (Montreal: Black Rose Books, 1996).

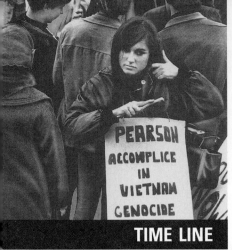

PEARSON
ACCOMPLICE
IN
VIETNAM
GENOCIDE

TIME LINE

Chapter Twenty-One

PROTEST AND
REFORM: THE 1960s

1960	Newly founded York University in Toronto admits its first students The Diefenbaker government adopts a Bill of Rights to protect religious and political liberties
1961	The New Democratic Party (NDP) is launched
1962	Medicare is introduced in Saskatchewan
1963	The Royal Commission on Bilingualism and Biculturalism begins hearings
1964	The Beatles tour Canada in September
1965	The Maple Leaf flag replaces the Red Ensign as Canada's national flag The Canada Pension Plan is set up
1966	Ottawa begins making grants to provinces for postsecondary education
1967	Canada celebrates its centennial Expo 67 (Universal and International Exhibition), held in Montreal, welcomes 50 million visitors The Royal Commission on the Status of Women is appointed The National Health Insurance Program (medicare) comes into being
1968	Pierre Elliott Trudeau becomes prime minister of Canada
1969	Parliament adopts the Official Languages Act

Canada experienced profound social, cultural and political upheavals in the 1960s. Young people, in particular, challenged authority. The universities became centres of protest as demonstrations erupted on campuses. Youth began to reject traditional social and cultural values, and sexual taboos weakened.

Other groups as well wanted to be heard. Women questioned the inequalities of their condition. So did gays and lesbians. Labour became more militant in its attacks on the business "establishment." French-speaking Canadians sought linguistic rights that would put them on an equal footing with English-speaking Canadians. An important minority in Quebec believed that only independence could ensure real equality. English-speaking Canadian nationalists denounced the powerful American presence in most aspects of Canadian life. An Aboriginal resurgence began in reaction to fears of assimilation and an end to special status. A host of new interest groups, with varying agendas, now entered the political forum. No longer could a small group of middle-aged and elderly men, primarily of British origin and speaking only English, govern Canada. For many observers, diversity had triumphed over unity within Canada.

The economic stability of the postwar years was shaken in the 1960s. As the decade opened, Canada faced the highest unemployment levels since the Great Depression. Although prosperity returned, rapidly rising prices soon became a worry. Economic difficulties led to social problems, and rising popular discontent brought an end to political stability; indeed, in Ottawa, minority governments ruled for much of the decade. Several of the provinces also saw political change. Canadians sought new leaders with new visions.

Traditional Churches Questioned

Canadian society in the 1960s became more secular. In Quebec, the influence of the Roman Catholic church waned as that institution largely abandoned to the state its historic role in education and in social institutions. The modernization of certain religious practices by the Vatican II council failed to stem the decline in church attendance. Many clergy left the religious orders, and new recruitment fell rapidly.

Elsewhere in Canada, the major Protestant denominations also lost ground. (Many Protestants who felt that the traditional denominations had become too liberal joined conservative fundamentalist groups, which grew prodigiously.) Sunday school attendance fell sharply. In a controversial book, author Pierre Berton attacked the churches for their lack of relevance, as they vainly attempted to combat the supporters of beer parlours, Sunday movies, and Sunday sports. Rev. James Mutchmor, the head of the United Church's board of evangelism and social service and later moderator of the church, outspokenly denounced the new trends. The "voice against vice" became the most-quoted cleric in Canada in the mid-1960s. Mutchmor's critics mocked: "Let's have much less of Mutchmor!"

Youth Protest

Much of the revolt against established social and cultural patterns was superficial. High school boys put away their hair oil and deserted barber shops, while their mothers remonstrated with them in vain. "Flower children" dressed in fringes and beads and displayed psychedelic colours. Blue jeans became the uniform of a generation. College students and non-students began to sport moustaches, sideburns, and beards.

Sexual experimentation flourished, too, as did a drug culture. Student associations called for the legalization of certain "recreational" drugs such as marijuana. Medical opinion was divided over the issue. As historian Marcel Martel has shown, groups such as the police forces had more success than others in shaping public debate and in imposing their choice of policy, which was to keep the status quo.[1]

"Peace and Love"

Young English-speaking Canadians empathized with the peace-and-love message of such American folk singers as Bob Dylan and Joan Baez. But Canadian folk singers, including Ian and Sylvia Tyson, Gordon Lightfoot, and Joni Mitchell, also achieved an international reputation. The Tysons became popular in the United States at the start of the folk revival in the 1960s, paving the way for other Canadian performers at a time of limited recording opportunities in Canada. Orillia-born Lightfoot began his career in coffee houses and bars; as composer of such pieces as "Early Morning Rain" and "For Lovin' Me," he soon drew crowds to his performances at the Mariposa folk festival and elsewhere.

In French Canada, young people flocked to listen to the *chansonniers* who sang, accompanied only by their guitars or the piano, in the *boîtes à chansons* that sprang up across Quebec in the early 1960s. At first, the lyrics dwelt on apolitical themes such as love and nature. Later, as a powerful nationalist current surged through the province, new themes bearing on the historical experience of Quebec's people and their identity dominated singers' repertories. Gilles Vigneault became one of the most well known singer-songwriters of the era—and his "Mon pays" became the anthem of nationalist youth. The *chansonniers* soon gave way to popular singers, among whom figured a strong feminine contingent, including Ginette Reno, Renée Claude, Pauline Julien, and Monique Leyrac. Robert Charlebois's audacious creativity, evident in his recording of "Lindberg" in 1968, made him one of the most popular male performers of the era.

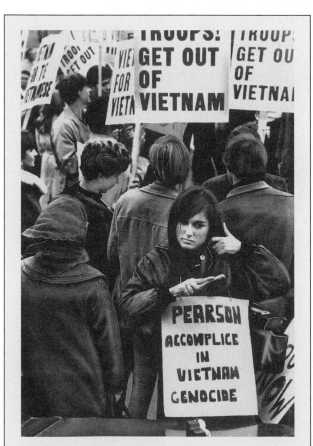

Protest against the war in Vietnam.

R. Olsen/Toronto Star

Many young Canadians listened avidly to rock music during the 1960s. Enthusiastically they fell victim to Beatlemania, especially during the shaggy-haired foursome's tour of Canada in September 1964. On September 8, the *Toronto Star* headlined: "200 Girls Swoon in Battle of the Beatles." Vancouver's Empire Stadium saw even greater hysteria, during a concert by the "Fab Four," as 2000 fans rushed the stage and screams drowned out the singing. As the decade advanced, literally thousands of Canadian rock bands sprang up, usually modelled on British and American groups. Canadian singers received a substantial boost in 1970, when the Canadian Radio-television and Telecommunications Commission (CRTC) established Canadian-content rules for broadcasters.

Student Revolt

For historian Doug Owram, the 1960s constituted "the moment in history that forever defined the baby boom as a distinct generation."[2] The boomers' centres of activity were the university campuses (although the majority of boomers never went to university). Canadian students, like American and Western youth in general, picketed against the increasingly bloody war in Vietnam, where the United States had greatly expanded its military campaign in an effort to prevent Communist-dominated North Vietnam from dislodging the pro-American regime in South Vietnam. Nationalist protest took root and flourished, often tended closely by university professors. Political scientists and economists prepared research studies to show the extent to which Canada had become an American colony, and proposed measures for buying or taking it back. In Quebec's universities, equal fervour was applied to proving that Quebec was a Canadian colony and to devising plans for liberating it.

University protest had political repercussions. In Quebec, where most intellectuals were strong nationalists, it contributed to bringing the language question to the floor of the National Assembly and assisted the rise of the Parti Québécois. In Canada as a whole, it helped Pierre Trudeau, who appeared to challenge the establishment and who brought new ideas to the fore, to win the Liberal leadership and the federal election of 1968. In addition, the nationalist outcry from many English-Canadian universities, particularly in Ontario, caused the Liberals to question the continentalism they had espoused in the 1950s.

Students abandoned classes and occupied administrative offices, demanding more active participation in the university community and the recognition of students' rights. At the University of Toronto, for example, they protested against recruiting on campus by a manufacturer of napalm used by the American military during the Vietnam War. Such protests were all the more visible, in part, because students were now far more numerous. University enrolments doubled during the 1950s, then tripled during the 1960s and 1970s. The parents of baby boomers, many of whom had never finished high school, preached the virtues of a university degree as the key to a bright future.

Higher Education Expands

Provincial governments, convinced that higher education would bring enormous economic benefits to society, dramatically increased spending on universities and established a host of new institutions. One of these was Simon Fraser University, situated atop Burnaby Mountain, near Vancouver, which opened in 1965 with 2500 students. (The main building was well-known architect Arthur Erickson's first major commission. Some critics later blamed Erickson for student unrest because his design of the campus encouraged student interaction.) In Ontario, York University admitted its first 75 students in 1960; a year later the province gave York 500 acres in northwest Toronto for the building of a campus. Laurentian, Trent, Brock, and Lakehead Universities were also set up. Quebec established the public Université du Québec in Montreal with several regional affiliates. The University of Alberta, Calgary branch, became the separate University of Calgary in 1966. New Brunswick's francophones obtained their own university at Moncton. Regional and community colleges began operations in several provinces. The federal government, which had been making grants directly to the universities since 1951, began in 1966 to make contributions to provincial governments for the financing of postsecondary education. In all, government spending on universities increased sevenfold during the 1960s.

As a result of their rapid growth, universities faced serious shortages of trained staff. English-speaking universities recruited heavily on American campuses. Critics accused universities of ignoring Canadian university graduates in their hiring policies, and called for the Canadianization of faculties.

The magnificent University of Lethbridge, main building, designed by famed architect Arthur Erickson. Construction was completed in 1971.

Source: Courtesy of the University of Lethbridge.

A HISTORICAL PORTRAIT

The Student Radicals at Sir George Williams University

The late 1960s saw frequent protests against virtually all aspects of the established order. Students militated for a wide variety of causes, some of which concerned the universities themselves, while others were concerned with the wider society, such as the ban-the-bomb protests. Preferred methods were strikes, sit-ins, teach-ins, and occupations of buildings.

Some militants were ready to take extreme measures in defence of causes that appeared increasingly imprecise. The events of February 11, 1969, at Sir George Williams University (today Concordia University) in Montreal appeared to mark a watershed.

"Police Rout SGWU Militants; $1 Million Computer Centre Wrecked." Thus read the *Montreal Star*'s headline that day. The damage figure was revised upward the next day to $2 million, or approximately $10 million in today's dollars.

In December 1968, some students had levelled charges of racism against a biology professor at the university. In early February 1969, they occupied the Faculty Club in the nine-storey Henry Hall Building in support of their cause. At first they succeeded in generating considerable sympathy. Over time, however, the militant group, thanks to new additions, became more radical, and moderates tended to distance themselves. One prominent mili-

tant proclaimed that he didn't really care about the charges of racism against the professor. "All we want to do is burn down the university. We want the police to come, we want violence."

Militants then broke into the cafeteria on the seventh floor and hurled chairs and tables down escalators, stairwells, and elevator shafts. As police moved against the crowd, occupants turned the fire hoses on against them, then retreated to the computer centre on the ninth floor. When police attempted to evict them from the centre, militants threw computers, punchcards, tapes, and furniture onto the street, and then set fire to the centre.

Police made 90 arrests; those arrested included 42 non-nationals, mainly from the Caribbean and from England. Thirty of those arrested were not students at Sir George Williams.

The events at Sir George Williams provoked a sharp backlash and a demand for a return to order. The *Montreal Star* denounced what it termed "an indefensible act by student anarchists." Acts of intimidation, disruption, and even violence were occurring at the same time on other campuses. But for historian Doug Owram, the SGWU episode, because of the degree of violence and destruction, "foreshadowed the end of the 1960s era."[1]

---

1. Doug Owram, *Born at the Right Time: A History of the Baby-Boom Generation* (Toronto: University of Toronto Press, 1996), p. 286.

Many Canadians dreamed of owning a house in the suburbs. This photo shows the first houses built in Ajax, a small community located between Toronto and Oshawa, around 1948.

Courtesy of the Ajax Archives.

An Interventionist State

Although university teachers and students were among the loudest voices calling for change, Canadians in general endorsed increased state intervention, at all levels, as a necessary tool for reform. They pressured municipal governments to improve the quality of life in cities by controlling the heights of buildings, curtailing expressway expansion, promoting urban transit, fighting urban blight, and improving parks and libraries. They demanded that governments take measures to protect society's weaker elements, and that they act to protect consumers, promote the equality of women, and combat discrimination against minority groups. The cultural lobby requested financial aid to assist Canadian cultural development, while sport organizations urged Ottawa to fund amateur sport and to work to improve Canadian athletes' performances in international competitions.

Governments also intervened modestly to supply disadvantaged Canadians with low-income housing. The 1960s saw the construction of large apartment buildings in central urban areas, often with little public space, a situation that gave rise to a variety of social problems. Toronto's Cabbagetown district, Vancouver's Strathcona area, Halifax's Uniacke Square, and Montreal's Jeanne Mance Park saw such developments.

Most Canadians dreamed of owning a house in the suburbs. Federal government programs made low-cost mortgages available, provincial governments built roads, and local authorities installed services. The Don Mills community of Toronto, built in 1952–1962, served as the prototype of a planned corporate suburb. Around a core area containing a shopping centre and a high school at the intersection of two arterial roads, developers built small apartment buildings and townhouses. Beyond them were four low-density neighbourhood units. Edmonton had its own planned suburb, Mill Woods. Developers made plans for a population of 100 000, which was to live in 23 neighbourhoods that were focused on a town-centre complex containing the necessary services. All large Canadian cities saw these suburbs mushroom in the 1960s.

Population Trends

Demographic upheaval also characterized the 1960s as the baby boom of the late 1940s and 1950s fizzled into a "baby bust." In one decade, the rate of growth of Canada's population dropped by nearly half. The two-child family—the minimum to maintain the current size of the population—briefly became the norm in Canada. Then single-child or childless families became increasingly numerous.

Demographers and sociologists had difficulty explaining the demographic revolution, which other industrialized countries also experienced. Many observers emphasized the availability of better contraceptive methods, particularly the birth-control pill, which became available in Canada in 1966. Contraception and birth-control methods did indeed gain much more exposure and publicity. Only in 1969, however, did Parliament amend Canada's Criminal Code to permit the distribution of birth-control information and devices.

Obviously, Canadians wanted fewer children, and they wanted them later in life. A century earlier, large families had been a necessity—on farms, for example, children meant additional workers and, in general, the extended family cared for its elderly members. In Canada's modern social welfare state, the aged relied less on adult children for financial assistance. As well, the ever-increasing costs of raising and educating them made children appear as financial liabilities. Children could also be perceived as a brake on career development.

Changing Family Patterns

A general revolution in family patterns began in the 1960s. Conservative-minded Canadians had long looked askance at the frequency of marriage breakdown in the United States, symbolized by the rapidly moving love lives of glamorous Hollywood stars. After 1968, when Parliament modified Canadian laws, divorce became frequent in Canada, too.

Traditional sexual taboos gradually became more relaxed as society became more tolerant. Gay and lesbian themes began to feature in films and literary works, among them American-born writer Jane Rule's first novel, *Desert of the Heart*, and Quebec author Michel Tremblay's plays. Same-sex relationships became more open after the government, promising to stay out of the nation's bedrooms, legalized homosexual practices between consenting adults in private in 1969. Many opposition parliamentarians denounced the changes on religious and moral grounds. In spite of their apparent victory, gays and lesbians worried that their concerns had now been reduced to narrow issues of criminal-law reform. A coalition of gay and lesbian liberation groups stated that, in spite of the reform, "we are still confronted with discrimination, police harassment, exploitation and pressures to conform which deny our sexuality."

Young people in general began to experiment with different types of living arrangements. For a time, communes were in fashion, although few lasted long. "Living together," or common-law marriage, hitherto frowned upon socially, gained popularity. Some women favoured living together because they opposed marriage in principle as a form of economic servitude—women working without pay—disguised by the myth of romantic love. In most cases, for both women and men, convenience was probably a compelling factor in favour of such unions.

Women: The Long Road toward Equality

The desire for smaller families symbolized a more general wish by women for a change in their condition. A half-century earlier, women had struggled to obtain the right to vote. Now, in an age of protest, women's groups began to demand that governments intervene to promote equality. Thus began the "second wave" of the women's movement.

Women disagreed strongly over the nature of the "ideal woman." Historian Valerie Korinek describes a contest created by *Chatelaine*, Canada's only mass-market women's magazine. The goal of the contest was to discover Canada's foremost homemaker, "Mrs. Chatelaine," a stay-at-home wife and mother who also did volunteer work and could serve as a role model for readers of the magazine. Some women, however, proposed other models. One suggested setting up a "Mrs. Slob contest," and named herself as winner. She admitted that she did not always serve nourishing meals, she liked fish and chips, she "entertained" only when her neighbours came in to gab, and she didn't

Voice of Women in a demonstration for peace, 1960s.
Voice of Women.

find time to do much volunteer work. She offered her philosophy: "Be happy, don't worry. You do what you can with what you've got when you feel like it."[3]

As the 1960s began, many women felt ready to speak out about the affairs of the country. When journalist Lotta Dempsey lamented what appeared to be the increasing danger of nuclear war and wondered where the voice of women was, she hit a raw nerve: hundreds of women turned out for a public meeting at Massey Hall in Toronto. Thus was born the Voice of Women, whose membership grew to 10 000 in less than a year. Many of its participants later became activists in other women's associations.

Convinced that much more needed to be done, Laura Sabia, president of the Canadian Federation of University Women, promoted the establishment, in 1966, of a new group, the Committee for the Equality of Women in Canada. The coalition pressed Ottawa to create a royal commission on the status of women. Thérèse Casgrain and other members of the Fédération des femmes du Québec also attended in order to demonstrate that francophone women were making the same demands as their anglophone sisters. The federal government agreed to set up a commission, but only after the committee threatened to organize a huge march on Ottawa.

The Royal Commission on the Status of Women, chaired by professional broadcaster Florence Bird, held hearings across Canada and received nearly 500 briefs. Issued in September 1970, the "Bird Report," which one journalist called "a bomb, already primed and ticking," called for a societal change of attitude toward women. It proposed dozens of recommendations concerning women in the workplace, in political life, in education, and in family life.

Women in the Paid Workforce

Male-dominated legislatures did adopt some laws that improved the lot of women. They made divorce simpler and maternity benefits more generous, and they granted tax deductions for child care expenses. Ontario adopted the Women's Equal Employment Opportunity Act in 1970. In spite of many loopholes, the law provided for legal unpaid maternity leave and banned the firing of women upon marriage. Business complained that maternity leaves would eventually lead to paid leaves, a kind of "reward for pregnancy."

Women's major demands for change—and, indeed, the changes themselves—occurred in the workplace. In 1961, only one married woman in five was in the labour force, often in part-time employment. Public attitudes still strongly disapproved of married mothers taking paid employment. By 1971, however, as increasing numbers of married women sought jobs outside the home, the proportion had risen to one in three. By 1981, it reached one in two. Women who worked outside the home needed to find some type of day care for their small children. It would be necessary to wait until the 1970s, however, before even modest state subsidies for provincial daycare centres became available.

Sex segregation in the workplace, resulting in "pink-collar ghettos," still remained the norm. Many women found jobs as salesclerks in the retail stores that proliferated. The expansion of health care and education also created traditional employment for women. In the late 1960s, the federal government became the largest employer of women in Canada: most female employees worked in office or administrative-support jobs, while men dominated in the higher-level, better-paying managerial positions.

Women disagreed over the means to effect necessary changes and, indeed, over the changes that they should seek. Some shared the liberal view that legislative reform would give women more equal opportunities. Other younger, more radical feminists believed that only a fundamental transformation of the economic and social structures that perpetuated the dominance of men would end female oppression. This group regarded the Bird Report as far too conservative. From the late 1960s, these women waged a militant campaign for women's liberation, often on university campuses, through newsworthy demonstrations and rallies, in innumerable organized discussions, and in newspapers.

Labour

In the 1960s, radicals in the universities, in the churches, and in the media joined economic nationalists and reformist political parties such as the Parti Québécois, with its initial pro-worker bias, and the New Democratic Party, the beneficiary of considerable union support, to criticize the large multinational corporations. They castigated business in general for its unquenchable thirst for profits and for its failure to display any social or environmental conscience. They flayed developers for destroying old urban neighbourhoods to build highrise luxury apartment buildings and office towers. Finally, in this age of rising inflation and of concern for consumers' rights, they denounced companies for "gouging" consumers by endlessly raising prices.

The major organized assault on business, however, came from unions. Canadian workers, particularly younger ones from the first cohorts of baby boomers, became increasingly restive during the 1960s. Many of these new workers had high expectations, which they hoped to realize quickly. As well, in the late 1960s, rising consumer prices made it imperative for workers to obtain generous wage settlements.

The union rank and file vigorously attacked authority. Militant workers frequently rebelled against their conservative leaders by launching wildcat strikes (illegal work stoppages), some of which paid handsome dividends. A lengthy wildcat strike by Inco workers at Sudbury, for example, brought miners the highest wages in North America. Another clash at the Stelco plant in Hamilton, with much violence and destruction of property, enabled steelworkers to obtain very substantial wage increases.

Many unionized workers were women. In contrast with the 1950s, when women often hesitated in their resistance to discriminatory practices in the workplace, they now began to wage "a more concerted and organized campaign for gender equality." Results came slowly. In 1968, women employees of General Motors with six years' seniority were being laid off while the company continued to hire new men. One woman vented her frustration with a poem in the newspaper of the local United Auto Workers to which she belonged:

> I read that whole darn paper and never make the grade;
> Do they just count the females when union dues are paid?
> We wait on recognition and it better show up soon,
> I feel more isolated than the men that walked the Moon.
> So all you fancy journalists, here's one thing to remember:
> I'm classed as just a female, but I'm still a union member.[4]

Workers, often women, in the rapidly growing public sector—teachers, hospital workers, civil servants, municipal employees, and others—also sought to improve salaries and working conditions. They successfully lobbied governments to place them on an equal footing with workers in the private sector, to recognize their right to form unions and, in many cases, to strike. Public sector unions soon became the largest in Canada and among the most militant. Lengthy work stoppages in the post office, for example, became notorious.

A Cultural Renaissance

Both English-language and French-language cultural expression underwent a renaissance in the 1960s. Universal education increased the potential market for cultural products, and higher disposable incomes and more leisure time made it possible for people to enjoy them. Federal and provincial grant agencies gave considerable assistance to a wide variety of cultural endeavours.

Literature

The 1960s saw the rapid growth of a vibrant and diverse literature in both English and French, due in part to government support programs. By 1970, most universities in English-speaking Canada offered courses in Canadian literature in English, as did Quebec universities on French-Canadian literature. New literary periodicals were established to publish and critique Canadian writing. Several new publishing houses also appeared.

Many of the most popular writers of the decade were women. Margaret Laurence, who spent her early life in Neepawa, Manitoba, published *The Stone Angel* and *A Jest of God*, two novels set in the fictitious town of Manawaka, which bore a close resemblance to Neepawa. In some of her short stories set in Ontario's Huron County, Alice Munro wrote about the difficulties experienced by an adolescent girl in coming to terms with her family and with life in a small town. Margaret Atwood's first novel, *The Edible Woman*, examined the theme of women's alienation in modern consumer society.

A sense of place and of identity was important for many novelists. Ernest Buckler situated his *Ox Bells and Fireflies* in Nova Scotia. Robert Kroetsch, who grew up in rural Alberta, published an "Out West" series of novels before moving mainly into poetry. Rudy Wiebe, a Mennonite from the prairies, set out to explore the tensions between pacifism and war in *Peace Shall Destroy Many*.

The revolution in poetry brought youth to the fore. Indeed, a volume on Canada's fifteen most outstanding poets in 1970 featured only three who were well known before 1960. Irving Layton, a Romanian Jew whose family settled in an impoverished immigrant district in Montreal, filled his poems with his early impressions and experiences. Gwendolyn MacEwen demonstrated her grasp of the poetic dimensions of history, while Al Purdy chronicled the geographical and historical complexities of Canada in such volumes as *The Cariboo Horses*, which he wrote after a trip to Baffin Island. Milton Acorn's populist poetry featured left-wing causes popular in this era. Leonard Cohen of Montreal achieved renown, both as a poet and as a singer and songwriter. Raymond Souster continued to influence the direction of Canadian poetry by editing the volumes of many poets. A number of Canadian poets, including Souster, gave public readings at the Bohemian Embassy, a Toronto coffee house established in 1960. (Bell Canada, not yet "in," listed this establishment in its Yellow Pages under the general heading "Embassies and Consulates.")

Some Quebec authors found their inspiration in the turbulent nationalism of the Quiet Revolution. Poet Fernand Ouellette dwelt upon the alienation and oppression of the Québécois in *Le Soleil sous la mort*, while Jacques Ferron's short stories dealt with the problems of maintaining Quebec's cultural identity. Hubert Aquin wrote *Prochain épisode* while being held in a Montreal psychiatric clinic pending trial on a weapons charge; the novel's narrator, also confined to a psychiatric hospital, awaits trial on charges related to his underground activities as a revolutionary separatist.

Nationalism formed only part of the general theme of liberation being experienced in Quebec during these years. Many novelists examined the emancipation of the person in relation to society. *Une saison dans la vie d'Emmanuel*, which presented a sombre portrait of a Quebec family dominated by a tyrannical father, brought novelist Marie-Claire Blais a wide international audience. Feminist preoccupations permeated Françoise Loranger's *Encore cinq minutes*, while themes of war, sexual repression, and exploitation of the weak were central to Roch Carrier's highly acclaimed work *La guerre, yes sir!*

A deep concern for Aboriginal rights inspired much of the work of Quebec novelist Yves Thériault. In his *Ashini*, the hero, a Montagnais or Innu, commits suicide in the hope that his death will awaken his people from their apathy and bring them to claim their ancestral lands.

Playwrights Marcel Dubé and Michel Tremblay made major contributions to French-language theatre; Tremblay's *Les belles-soeurs* violated traditional codes by being the first play to be written entirely in *joual*, or working-class slang.

Filmmaking

Canada's film industry in both languages underwent substantial development in the 1960s. Through its diverse activities, the National Film Board made Canadians more conscious of their history and culture. In English, producers worked mainly on documentaries. *Memorandum*, whose subject was Hitler's "final solution" to the "Jewish question," helped build an enviable reputation for producer Donald Brittain, who had previously directed *Fields of Sacrifice*, a memorial to Canadians killed in action during World War II. Canada's centennial year, 1967, saw other noteworthy productions, including *Labyrinth*, which used the Greek myth of Theseus, who entered a labyrinth to find and kill the Minotaur, to symbolize the universality of a person's journey throughout the world. The lavish film, seen by 1.3 million people at Expo 67 in Montreal, attracted much positive press reaction internationally.

French-language filmmakers experimented with subjects linked to French Canada's social ferment. Denys Arcand's *On est au coton* was a film about the textile industry and workers' fears of unemployment because of factory closures. Pierre Perrault's *L'Acadie! L'Acadie!* featured the struggle by Acadian students at the Université de Moncton for the recognition of language rights. Quebec filmmakers also set about making what one magazine called "maple leaf porno." Denis Héroux produced *Valérie* in 1969, asserting the need to "undress the Quebec female." One-third of Quebec's population went to the movies in 1970 to see Claude Fournier's *Deux femmes en or*, a similar production.

Politics in the Age of Mass Media

Canada's political life in the 1960s also felt the winds of change. Since Confederation, Canadian politics has focused increasingly on personalities. Political scientists have attempted to explain this tendency by suggesting that the major political parties have come to differ less and less on questions of basic principle. Leadership has been either a significant asset or a grave liability for parties.

The advent of television increased this focus on the leader. Through the news and televised events such as election campaign debates, it has brought politicians into the homes of Canadians. At the same time, as political scientist Frederick J. Fletcher has pointed out, television has inhibited the thoughtful exposition of policies and promoted "simple and flashy promises and one-line put-downs of the opposition."[5] The media have stressed conflict and confrontation in their coverage, emphasizing sensational and exciting occurrences. Prime Minister Lester Pearson once complained that "when we do discuss policies seriously ... reporters do not even appear to listen, until we say something controversial or personal, charged with what they regard as news value." In spite of television's particular deficiencies, it began to play a major role in moulding the images—favourable and unfavourable—of politicians.

Politics in Disarray

Politics in the early 1960s promoted cynicism among many voters. The country faced grave problems with, at the beginning of the decade, more Canadians out of work than at any time since the Great Depression. The increasing cost of living provoked costly demands from some unions. Relations with the provinces were strained, while growing discord also characterized ties with the United States. Yet neither Progressive Conservative leader John Diefenbaker nor Liberal leader Lester B. Pearson appeared to have a vision or long-term plan for what might be done.

In the early 1960s these two knights in tarnished armour faced each other on the electoral battlefield three times; each time, neither won enough seats in the House of Commons to form a majority government. Each made numerous—and costly—promises in attempts to rally more voter support. Some of their techniques, borrowed from Madison Avenue, elicited mockery and disdain. The Liberals, for example, published colouring books portraying Diefenbaker riding backwards on a rocking horse. They also formed a short-lived "truth squad" to pursue the Conservatives relentlessly across the country to make sure they told the truth. Once elected, Canada's parliamentarians devoted themselves to discussing a seemingly endless succession of alleged scandals. In his memoirs, Pearson gave the title "Politics in Disrepute" to a chapter on the years 1964 and 1965.

John Diefenbaker looks on, as Lester Pearson attempts to uncoil the cord of a translation earpiece. Canada's two French-speaking prime ministers before this period, Wilfrid Laurier and Louis St. Laurent, were both fluently bilingual. After the 1960s, it became much more important for federal anglophone politicians to be able to speak French.

© Estate of John McNeill

The Diefenbaker Government (1957–1963)

The 1960s opened with the Progressive Conservatives led by John Diefenbaker in office in Ottawa. Diefenbaker had first come to power in 1957 with a minority government; then, in elections called in 1958, he won a landslide victory. At first, "Dief the Chief" benefited from a remarkably positive image. Different from many previous Conservative leaders in that he was not closely linked to Toronto's financial establishment, Diefenbaker promised to champion the rights of ordinary Canadians. He was also a fiery orator, able to captivate audiences. Yet by 1960, he had acquired a very negative image. In elections held in 1962, he barely managed to retain power with a minority government. A year later the Diefenbaker government was defeated and the Conservatives returned to the opposition benches.

Diefenbaker's Economic Policies

To some extent, the controversial prime minister became a victim of circumstances. After 22 years in opposition, the Conservatives had no experience with the art of governing. Moreover, the severe recession of 1960–1961, Canada's most serious since the Great Depression of the 1930s, undermined Diefenbaker's popularity. Industry encountered increased difficulty in selling goods to foreign markets, and laid off thousands of workers. Worldwide over-production and declining prices of agricultural products hit Prairie farmers particularly hard.

Diefenbaker finally found markets—in the People's Republic of China, the Soviet Union, and Eastern Europe—for most of Canada's surplus grain. Farm income on the Prairies rose significantly, and Conservative popularity in that region remained strong. Attempts to reduce unemployment were less successful. The government increased spending in the hope of stimulating the economy, but the ensuing budget deficits irked the business and financial community. The minister of finance even had to resort to austerity measures and to arrange emergency credits with the International Monetary Fund.

Even more controversially, in 1962, shortly after announcing why it was inappropriate to peg the Canadian dollar, the government devalued the Canadian dollar, fixing it at a relatively low 92.5 cents (U.S.). This measure provoked both outright condemnation by importers and enthusiastic approval by exporters. The Liberals protested noisily that devaluation would mean higher prices for consumers. They printed thousands of so-called "Diefenbucks"—92.5-cent dollars adorned with the prime minister's likeness—which they used effectively during the election campaign of June 1962. Diefenbaker lost his majority in Parliament that year. Then, in 1963, he lost power to the Liberals, led by Lester B. Pearson. As a former Secretary of State for External Affairs and winner of the prestigious Nobel Peace Prize in 1957, Pearson assuredly had experience in foreign policy and international acclaim. He was less familiar with domestic issues. Moreover, he lacked charisma and had difficulty enthusing voters and generating confidence.

Strained Canadian–American Relations

Diefenbaker worried about Canada's increasing economic dependence upon the United States but he lacked the power or the will to effect fundamental changes in economic relationships. Although he promised to divert trade from the United States to Great Britain, he failed to recognize Britain's need to boost trade links with Europe and thus to distance itself from the Commonwealth. Indeed the renewal in 1959 of Canada's defence production treaty with the United States had the effect of stimulating trade, especially in arms, with that country. Diefenbaker also hoped to reduce American investment in Canada, but the measures he took had little effect.

Issues linked to continental defence embittered relations with the United States. Shortly after the 1957 election, Diefenbaker had personally committed Canada to the North American Air Defence Command (NORAD), the continental air-defence alliance headed by a U.S. Air Force general. Then, in 1962–1963, in a reversal of his original position, he refused to accept the nuclear warheads that the Americans wanted installed in their antiaircraft missiles on Canadian soil. Moreover, he intensely disliked President John F. Kennedy, a feeling the American president reciprocated.

In these years of renascent Canadian nationalism, Canadians began to agonize over the kind of relationship they wanted with their southern neighbour. Diefenbaker's attempts to reorient Canadian policy reflected the will of part of the electorate, but they also provoked the disgruntlement of many other Canadians, including several of his own cabinet ministers. In addition, as historians John Herd Thompson and Stephen Randall point out, Canadian and American priorities moved increasingly apart. While the United States was determined to confront the Soviet threat and was turning into a warfare state, Canada in the 1960s gave greater priority to advancing the welfare state.[6]

The Conservatives and Quebec

In part, Diefenbaker's downfall arose from the Conservatives' weak base of support, notably in Quebec, where the party's organization had long been deficient. Moreover, Diefenbaker understood little of Quebec's awakening in the early 1960s. Conservatives also quickly found that they could not easily reconcile the interests of urban and rural voters, or those of central Canadians and Canadians living in other provinces. The government also seemed disorganized and rife with dissension. Most to blame, in journalist Peter Newman's opinion, was Diefenbaker himself, a "renegade in power" who disillusioned Canadians by giving them a leadership cult, without leadership.[7]

Some voters in Quebec showed their dissatisfaction with both the Conservatives and the Liberals by supporting Social Credit, a fringe group founded in the 1930s. To the surprise and even stupefaction of most observers, Social Credit won one-third of the province's seats in the election of 1962. Leader Réal Caouette, an automobile salesman from Rouyn, in northern Quebec, appealed to Quebeckers' obvious desire for change. Promising a national dividend to all citizens to raise consumers' buying power, as well as help for the aged, the unemployed, and large families, Caouette carried his crusade through rural and small-town Quebec as well as to weekly television audiences.

Less spectacular was the reconstitution of the national CCF. In 1961, in an effort to broaden its support in Canada, the CCF cooperated with the Canadian Labour Congress and with various left-wing organizations to launch the New Democratic Party. The party's reformist program called for jobs, health insurance, free education, and a policy of "co-operative federalism" in federal–provincial relations. Yet electoral results during the 1960s at both the federal and provincial levels proved disappointing. In particular, even most union members failed to support the NDP, which in turn feared becoming too closely identified with unions.

The Pearson Years (1963–1968)

As the Pearson government took office in 1963, economic recovery seemed well under way. Unemployment dropped to about 5 percent as sales increased and companies began hiring more employees. By 1966, however, a new, worrisome trend became evident: prices were moving up more quickly.

Canadians battled rising prices in various ways. Angry shoppers boycotted supermarkets, accusing them of price gouging. The members of strong unions in key sectors of the economy, such as transportation, sought, and often obtained, massive pay increases. These large increases added to inflationary pressures. In 1967, while inflation showed no signs of abating, the economy slowed down noticeably. Economists coined a new word—*stagflation*—to describe the phenomenon of inflation at a time of slow economic growth. First-year economics textbooks insisted that this combination could not occur—but it did, in Canada and throughout much of the world.

Liberal Economic Policies

The Liberals proved incapable of controlling inflation. To little avail, the government urged companies to restrain price increases. It also raised some taxes in an effort to dampen consumer demand. The Conservative opposition's financial critic boldly compared the Liberal minibudget to then-fashionable miniskirts: "Taxes are getting higher and higher and covering less and less." Most Canadians strongly disagreed with the economists' explanation that inflation was caused by the fact that consumers had too much money to spend.

During the Pearson years, Canadian–American trade relations intensified. The Automotive Products Agreement, signed in 1965, provided for free trade among automobile manufacturers, who could rationalize production. Canadian plants now specialized in producing relatively few models. Most economists agree that the "Auto Pact," accompanied by a lower Canadian dollar, brought increased prosperity to southern Ontario, where all of Canada's automobile plants and most of its automotive parts industry are concentrated.

Prime Minister Lester B. Pearson visits President John F. Kennedy, spring 1963.

Library and Archives Canada/C-90482.

Canadians passionately debated the issue of American ownership of Canadian industries in the 1960s. In 1966, Walter Gordon, formerly minister of finance in the Pearson government, published *A Choice for Canada*, in which he argued that the country would have to choose between political and economic independence or colonial status in the American empire. He also set up a task force on the structure of Canadian industry to study "the significance—both political and economic—of foreign investment."

At this time, however, the Liberal government contained very few economic nationalists. Mitchell Sharp, named minister of finance in 1965, did not even want to publish the task force report, while trade and commerce minister Robert Winters assured a San Francisco audience that "Canada welcomes foreign capital regardless of doubt-provoking remarks to the contrary from time to time." Canadians had decidedly not yet reached a consensus on the issue.

The Welfare State

In other areas, Parliament adopted important and popular legislation in this period. The new laws contributed greatly to entrenching the Canadian welfare state by which Canadians acquired new rights for which all residents, through the state, now became collectively responsible. The Diefenbaker government had already increased old-age pensions; now Ottawa moved to improve its social security programs for the poor. The year 1966 saw the adoption of the Canada Assistance Act, a coordination of largely existing provincial measures designed to aid persons who were unable to work or were ineligible for unemployment insurance. The Pearson government also made low-income pensioners eligible for a guaranteed income supplement.

The most important programs launched by the Liberals concerned pensions and medical care. In 1965, Ottawa established the Canada Pension Plan, a compulsory and completely portable contributory plan paid for by workers and employers. Negotiations with the provinces proved arduous: indeed Quebec chose to set up its own provincial plan, respecting the principles edicted by the federal government; money deposited in the fund was then reinvested.

Canadians increasingly called for the state to provide universal medical care. The Liberals had introduced hospital insurance in 1957 and, by 1961, the Diefenbaker government helped finance provincial plans across Canada. With regard to insuring the costs of medical services, Saskatchewan led the way by establishing a health insurance plan in 1962. Strongly opposed to medicare, the province's doctors staged a three-week strike before finally capitulating. Debate over constitutional issues and lack of agreement within the federal government slowed action on a Canada-wide program. Only in 1968 did Ottawa enact into law a national health scheme that provided for financial contributions to provincial medicare plans, all of which had to be universal, comprehensive, portable, and publicly administered. Social and health programs proved costly: health expenses alone nearly doubled from $3.3 billion in 1965 to $6 billion in 1970. Ottawa registered what would be its last budgetary surplus for nearly 30 years in 1969–1970, a year after Pearson's departure from office.

Pearson's Legacy

In addition to his government's landmark social and health legislation, Lester B. Pearson attempted to find solutions to other problems. He sought to conciliate the provinces and initiated a series of federal–provincial conferences on the Canadian constitution. In answer to French Canadians' claims for linguistic equality, he set up the Royal Commission on

Bilingualism and Biculturalism to study the issue and make recommendations. Also, after weeks of debate in the House of Commons, the Pearson government gave Canadians a national flag.

Pearson's numerous critics reproached the Liberal prime minister for his failure to give the country firm and sure leadership (in the direction they wished). Business considered his election promises irresponsibly costly and blamed him for surrendering too easily to the unions. Labour portrayed itself as the victim, not the cause, of inflation. Canadian nationalists accused him of doing little to counter the cultural Americanization of Canada; they also faulted him for authorizing the United States to place nuclear warheads on its missiles in Canada. Canadians hotly debated the issue of American ownership of the Canadian economy, but the Pearson government did little to control American investments.

Quebec nationalists thought that Pearson was resisting their province's legitimate demands, while strong centralists declared that his concessions to Quebec and the other provinces were balkanizing the country and whetting the appetites of separatists. Monarchists censured him for tolerating creeping republicanism, while French Canadians and new Canadians favoured a loosening of Canada's ties with the British crown. Unhappy residents of the Atlantic provinces thought he was doing little to alleviate regional disparities, and westerners judged him ill attuned to their region's interests. In sum, Pearson endeared himself to virtually none of the regions or major interest groups.

Perhaps Pearson and his Liberal administration should not have been expected to build a consensus on the major questions of the day when Canadians themselves disagreed so strongly on the answers. The 1960s were a time of increasing polarization. In that climate, Pearson manoeuvred with some skill. The policy of "co-operative federalism," by which Ottawa showed greater sensitivity to provincial concerns, was perhaps the best that could be hoped for in a climate of confrontation between Ottawa and the provinces, particularly Quebec. In regard to French–English relations, the establishment of a royal commission, though hardly a solution, appeared a logical step to take. As for the economy and the growing problem of inflation, no obvious long-term solutions existed. Indeed the Canadian government did not have the power to control many of the root causes of inflation, such as the sharp rises in the cost of many products in international markets as well as the huge expenditures associated with the American war in Vietnam. Also, even though the Pearson government did have more than its share of scandals, the prime minister's own conduct remained above suspicion.

Finally, concerning Canada's relations with the United States, Canadians first had to debate options before they could make decisions. Growing American military involvement in Vietnam certainly poisoned relations between the North American neighbours.

Canada's own participation in the Vietnamese conflict dated from 1954 when, after war in then French Indochina resulted in the division of Vietnam into the Communist North and the pro-Western South, Canada participated in a tripartite commission to supervise the truce. Then, as the Communist presence within South Vietnam intensified, the United States exerted greater pressure on Canada to defend Western and American interests on the commission. As North Vietnam continued its incursions, the United States began to bombard North Vietnam and to boost substantially its military presence in the South. Public opposition to the war mounted in Canada (and in the United States). Pearson then made a speech in Philadelphia in 1965 urging the United States to stop bombing North Vietnam. U.S. President Lyndon B. Johnson was infuriated by this speech delivered in Johnson's own "backyard." As the war escalated, so did Canadian criticism of American actions in Vietnam, but strong domestic opposition to the war now preoccupied the Johnson government far more than foreign criticism.

A Changing Economy

In addition to the ills of unemployment and inflation that Canadians urged their governments to remedy, the country's economy underwent major structural changes during the 1960s. It entered what might be termed a postindustrial era, in which services, such as those provided by governments, schools, hospitals, the communications industry, retail trade, and financial institutions, constituted the largest sector of employment. Manufacturing placed second. Primary industries, including agriculture, came last—a complete reversal of the Canada of 1867.

Such sectors as transportation and communications developed spectacularly as a result of new technologies. Often they had difficulty finding the highly trained personnel they needed. In several other sectors, workers faced painful adjustments in the wake of job losses. Though employees in traditional "soft" industries such as footwear and textiles, hard hit by lost markets and cheap imports, suffered particularly, other industries also faced problems. Shipbuilders, for example, laid off thousands of workers as the federal government reduced subsidies and Canadian shipyards remained internationally uncompetitive.

Declining prices for their products and fierce competition from abroad led Canada's important natural resource industries to modernize in order to reduce costs. Technological change and market forces created new challenges in agriculture. Large farms, with the equipment necessary to work more land and boost yields, became the norm. Many small farmers, who lacked the means to make the necessary adjustments, were forced to abandon the land that their families had farmed for generations.

Unequal Growth

Some regions of Canada—southern Ontario and parts of western Canada—prospered during the 1960s. Others, including the Atlantic provinces, much of Quebec, and parts of the Prairies, saw increased unemployment and poverty.

Prosperity in Ontario

The 1950s and 1960s were especially good for Ontario. Demand for a wide variety of goods stimulated industrial expansion, especially in the south. Services—banking, merchandising, education, health, and government—multiplied. The construction industry flourished thanks to strong demand for housing. Governments at all levels invested heavily in building highways and urban expressways. They also promoted urban transit, sponsored electric power projects, including nuclear power plants, and completed work on the St. Lawrence Seaway. This intense activity explains why the province's unemployment rate generally stayed below 4 percent from 1945 until 1970. Economist Kenneth Rea calls these the "prosperous years."[8] Rea adds that while the Ontario government might take credit for permitting growth to occur and even, on occasion, stimulating it, the motor pushing Ontario's growth was in fact the private sector.

Western Canada

In the West, the development of natural resources continued apace during the 1960s. Manitoba's government invested heavily in northern development, where it favoured hydroelectric projects, such as the huge installations on the Nelson River, and it attempted to attract private capital through loans and other concessions. Saskatchewan worked to attract private capital to develop its natural resources, including potash and pulp and paper. Alberta's oil production increased when, in 1961, the Diefenbaker government acted to prevent Montreal

On the 56th floor of the Toronto-Dominion Centre, Toronto, April 1966. Constructed from 1963 to 1969, this building was designed by the German-American architect Mies van der Rohe, and reflected the International style of architecture. Skyscrapers like this one came to dominate cityscapes from the 1960s.

The Globe and Mail/66104-38. Reprinted with permission from The Globe and Mail.

refineries, using less expensive crude oil from Venezuela, from entering the Ontario market. This policy forced Ontario to buy slightly more costly oil from the West.

In British Columbia, a conservative Social Credit government led by W.A.C. Bennett assisted large corporations in consolidating their control of the resource sector by offering them tax concessions, low stumpage rates for timber, and cheap hydroelectricity. It improved highway, maritime, and rail transportation. It extended, at heavy cost, a railway that linked the northern interior to the rest of the province. It nationalized the giant B.C. Electric Company and undertook hydroelectric projects. One of these, the enormous Peace River Dam, built across the Rocky Mountain Trench, created Williston Lake, the province's largest body of water.

The Atlantic Provinces

Economic growth was slow in the Atlantic region; indeed, during the period 1951–1971, 15 percent of Atlantic Canada's inhabitants left home in search of work elsewhere. In Prince Edward Island, for example, the traditional "island way of life" increasingly became a myth as many small farmers, unable to compete because of low potato prices, abandoned farming.

Ottawa began to pay heed to the complaints of the inhabitants of the Atlantic provinces, who saw themselves as the major victim's of Canada's regional disparities. In 1962, John Diefenbaker's government set up the Atlantic Development Board to fund projects and improve the region's infrastructure. This initiative, together with equalization grants and other subsidies, facilitated the creation of jobs, albeit often temporary ones, and ensured that the area could offer its citizens services reasonably similar to those provided by wealthier provinces. Then, in 1969, the newly established federal Department of Regional Economic Expansion (DREE)

New Brunswick Premier Louis Robichaud, the province's first elected Acadian premier. His administration in the 1960s built many hospitals, schools, and public buildings.

Provincial Archives of New Brunswick/P57-15.

began to offer incentives to encourage companies to locate in less-favoured areas of the country, such as the Atlantic provinces. The department spent money on highway construction, schools, and municipal services, and attracted some new industry.

Provincial governments also sought to stimulate economic growth. Nova Scotia's Conservative government created Industrial Estates Limited, with well-known businessman Frank Sobey as its first president, to invest in local enterprises; serious losses, however, notably in stereo equipment and heavy water, followed the investment company's initial successes. For its part, New Brunswick's Liberal government led by Louis Robichaud, the first elected Acadian premier, intervened actively in resource development. When pulp and paper companies failed to use Crown lands they held under long-term lease, the government cancelled their licences and awarded them to other companies. When an American mining company reduced operations in its lead and zinc mine near Bathurst, Robichaud engineered a buyout by Canadian investors, including native son K.C. Irving, who set about building a huge smelter complex.

The Irving family's business interests included 3000 gas stations, trucking and bus lines, shipbuilding, huge forest reserves, paper- and sawmills, radio and television stations, and the province's English-language newspapers; these companies employed roughly 25 000 people in New Brunswick. Irving's biographer claimed that "surely no individual in any single Canadian province ... ever held so much raw economic power."[9]

Irving's local roots and power gave him considerable bargaining clout with the provincial government, which he exploited to win concessions. Historian James Kenny concludes that New Brunswick may have escaped dependence on foreign capital, but with Irving it entered into a "new and perhaps more dependent relationship."[10] Irving hired his own companies to perform the construction work on the smelter complex, but delays and ballooning costs finally brought the provincial government to allow a takeover by Noranda. Although the value of the mineral industry increased spectacularly in the 1960s, the industry did not have the desired transforming effects on provincial and local economies.

The Robichaud government also created the Equal Opportunity Program aimed at improving the lot of the province's poorer citizens, often French-speaking Acadians who lived in rural areas in the north and east; in particular, the government greatly expanded health, social, and educational services. These measures generated fierce opposition among anglophones in the south, who regarded them as proof of a costly Liberal plot to "rob Peter to pay Pierre." A cartoon in one of K.C. Irving's newspapers pictured a despotic Robichaud as a modern Louis XIV, with wild eyes, crown askew, and hand clutching a sword threatening his foes. In spite of opposition from English-speakers, the Robichaud government then moved to adopt the Official Languages Act that aimed, over time, to give greater linguistic equality to the province's francophones.

Newfoundland and Labrador

After Newfoundland entered Confederation in 1949, the federal government failed to take the necessary steps to restructure the fishing industry, especially the inshore fishery. What Ottawa did do, in the relatively prosperous 1950s, was to extend unemployment insurance coverage to seasonal fishers, a measure that helped increase the number of fishers at a time when the continued health of the industry necessitated significant downsizing.

Joey Smallwood, premier from 1949 until 1972, hoped to carry out an industrial revolution to create thousands of new jobs, stem emigration, and drag the province "kicking and screaming into the twentieth century." He encouraged foreign investment and sponsored projects to develop the province's natural resources, such as iron and pulpwood, as well as Labrador's vast hydroelectric potential at Churchill Falls. There were some successes, but many costly failures.

Environmental Concerns

Although most Canadians still took a healthy environment for granted in the 1960s, an increasingly vocal minority did begin to realize that industrial development often had deleterious effects upon air and water quality. Critics pointed to pulp and paper companies and smelters in particular as major polluters. They urged governments to force such companies to bear some of the huge costs of cleaning up the production process.

In Ontario, environmentalists focused their attention on water quality in heavily industrialized areas of the province, such as Hamilton harbour. They also denounced detergent manufacturers, who vied with each other to create the longest-lasting suds for washing machines and dishwashers. As these phosphate-laden suds piled up on the shores of lakes and rivers, algae proliferated, depleting oxygen levels and killing multitudes of fish. At the University of Toronto, antipollution campaigners founded Pollution Probe, staging such events as a mock funeral for Toronto's "dead" Don River. After 1970, governments agreed to take steps to cut phosphate use dramatically in an effort to improve water quality.

Beginning of the Trudeau Era

Many Canadians viewed the Diefenbaker-Pearson years as the culminating point of a bygone and increasingly repugnant brand of politics. The public longed for a new style, a new type of leadership, an imaginative and refreshing approach to the complex issues of the day. In 1968, as the Liberals searched for a successor to Pearson, many believed that they had found all this in Pierre Elliott Trudeau.

Trudeau's Background

Trudeau had been elected for the first time in 1965, when Pearson had convinced him to enter the House of Commons to help renew Quebec's presence in Ottawa. During the Duplessis years in Quebec, Trudeau had been a bitter critic of the Union Nationale regime and had helped establish a small-circulation magazine called *Cité libre* to give a voice to liberal-minded Quebeckers. He had also studied at Harvard and the London School of Economics, and travelled widely. Yet Quebec nationalists had no liking for this intellectual who incessantly stigmatized nationalism. Nor did business have confidence in a candidate who lacked experience in the corporate world.

Nevertheless, Trudeau's style and background intrigued delegates at the Ottawa leadership conven-

The election of Pierre Elliott Trudeau as Liberal Party leader, spring 1968.

© Library and Archives Canada. Reproduced with the permission of Library and Archives Canada. Source: Library and Archives Canada/Credit: Duncan Cameron/Duncan Cameron fonds/PA-111214 tion. His image was of a wealthy bachelor surrounded by beautiful women. He was athletic, drove a Mercedes-Benz sports car, and often dressed flamboyantly. As *The Globe and Mail* put it: "He is the man we all would like to be: charming, rich, talented, successful." This image was certainly at the base of the wave of "Trudeaumania" that broke out during the Liberal leadership race and reached its zenith during the June 1968 federal election, which the Liberals won easily.

Trudeau's Program

In marked contrast to Pearson and Diefenbaker, Trudeau made few specific promises designed to buy blocs of voters with their own money. Rather, he expressed a number of general priorities. He spoke of building a "just society" in which personal and political liberties were ensured by a charter of rights, a society in which minorities would be sheltered from the caprices of majorities, in which regions and social groups who had not participated fully in the country's material abundance would have greater opportunities. He wanted to discuss with Canadians their country's future. This emphasis on participatory democracy appealed to and attracted many electors.

Trudeau had much to say on the constitutional question as well. When he asked for a strong mandate to oppose the Quebec government's ambitions to play a role in international affairs, Toronto newspapers congratulated him for his "firmness." For advocates of a strong central government, here was someone who would stand up to the provinces, which they viewed as continually encroaching upon Ottawa's authority. Trudeau could also promise

Expo 67, Montreal 1967—an exciting celebration of Canada's centennial year. Montreal put forward its very best and invited the world. Some 50 million attended.

© Government of Canada. Reproduced with the permission of the Minister of Public Works and Government Services Canada (2008). Source: Library and Archives Canada/C-018536

Quebec that he would promote bilingualism in Canada, notably in the federal civil service, and that he would give Quebec and French Canada a major role to play in federal politics. Trudeau's triumphant victory in the 1968 election suggested that he might succeed in building a new consensus among Canadians if he could overcome the Liberals' weakness in the West.

The Canadian Centennial, 1967

The 1960s were a time of celebration as well as confrontation. In 1967, the year of the Canadian centennial, provinces and municipalities organized various festivities to mark the event. Typically subdued Canadians gave vent to few of the effusions of American-style patriotism, and many wondered whether the country was going to succeed in holding itself together.

One centennial activity was not restrained: Expo 67, staged on an island in the St. Lawrence River at Montreal. The showpiece event brought together more than 60 nations to celebrate the theme "Man and His World." Fifty million visitors passed through the turnstiles, and governments, both federal and provincial, spared no expense, perhaps unfortunately for the taxpayer.

The Canada of 1970 differed greatly from the country that had timidly embarked on an era of change a decade earlier. Materially, most Canadians were now better off; they were also better educated and certainly more liberal in their views. Such minority groups as Aboriginal peoples, French-speaking Canadians, and new Canadians of neither French nor British heritage sought to defend their interests more vigorously and found that society was at least somewhat more attentive to their claims.

Many Canadians, particularly older Canadians, found it difficult to accept the rapid pace of change. They criticized what they saw as a general decline in respect for authority and particularly the many excesses that accompanied social transformation. Others felt that the heightened individualism of the era was incompatible with the need to preserve the nation's unity. For the moment, however, these voices of caution had little impact. Indeed, the 1970s would bring more change against a background of increasing economic difficulties and political disunity.

NOTES

1. Marcel Martel, *Not This Time: Canadians, Public Policy, and the Marijuana Question, 1961–1975* (Toronto: University of Toronto Press, 2006), pp. 198–208.

2. Doug Owram, *Born at the Right Time: A History of the Baby-Boom Generation* (Toronto: University of Toronto Press, 1996), p. 159.

3. Valerie J. Korinek, "'Mrs. Chatelaine' vs. 'Mrs. Slob': Contestants, Correspondents and the Chatelaine Community in Action, 1961–1969," *Journal of the Canadian Historical Association/Revue de la Société historique du Canada*, 7 (1996): 266.

4. Pamela Sugiman, *Labour's Dilemma: The Gender Politics of Auto Workers in Canada, 1937–1979* (Toronto: University of Toronto Press, 1994), p. 136.

5. Frederick J. Fletcher, "Playing the Game: The Mass Media and the 1979 Campaign," in Howard R. Penniman, ed., *Canada at the Polls, 1979 and 1980: A Study of the General Elections* (Washington, DC: American Enterprise Institute of Public Policy Research, 1980), p. 319.

6. John Herd Thompson and Steven Randall, *Canada and the United States: Ambivalent Allies*, 3rd ed. (Montreal/Kingston: McGill-Queen's University Press, 2002), p. 243.

7. Peter C. Newman, *Renegade in Power: The Diefenbaker Years*, rev. ed. (Toronto: McClelland & Stewart, 1989), p. xi.

8. K.J. Rea, *The Prosperous Years: The Economic History of Ontario, 1939–75* (Toronto: University of Toronto Press, 1985).

9. J.E. Belliveau, *Little Louis and the Giant K.C.*, quoted in Rand Dyck, *Provincial Politics in Canada* (Scarborough, ON: Prentice-Hall, 1986), p. 171.

10. James L. Kenny, "A New Dependency: State, Local Capital, and the Development of New Brunswick's Base Metal Industry, 1960–1970," *Canadian Historical Review*, 78 (1977): 38.

BEYOND THE BOOK

CBC: The 1960s

http://archives.cbc.ca/society/youth/topics/1587
Twenty-eight video clips from the CBC's archives describe Canada in the 1960s. Politics, culture, and the economy are all issues explored in this historical footage.

Expo 67: A Virtual Experience

http://www.collectionscanada.ca/expo/index-e.html
Explore digitized mementos and documents from the 1967 centennial exposition in Montreal.

The Birth-Control Pill

http://archives.cbc.ca/health/reproductive_issues/topics/572
A history of the birth-control pill in Canada, which came to market in the 1960s.

The Martlet: 1960s

http://library.uvic.ca/site/archives/featured_collections/uvic_newspapers/martlet_1960/1960.html
Explore student life in the 1960s through this digitized collection of the student newspaper of Victoria College (now the University of Victoria) in British Columbia.

Royal Commission on the Status of Women in Canada

http://www.thecanadianencyclopedia.com/index.cfm?PgNm=TCE&Params=
A1ARTA0007674
A detailed history of the Royal Commission on the Status of Women in Canada.

Pierre Trudeau

http://www.primeministers.ca/trudeau/bio_3.php
Audio interviews and text accounts of Pierre Elliott Trudeau's life and political career.

Trudeau

Trudeau: The Man, the Myth, the Movie (CBC, 2002) delves into Trudeau's life from the late 1960s to 1982.

Expo 67

The impact of Expo 67 on a generation of Canadians is explored in *Canadian Experience —Expo 67: Back to the Future* (CBC, 2004).

RELATED READINGS

In R. Douglas Francis and Donald B. Smith, eds., *Viewpoints: Readings in Canadian History* (Toronto: Thomson Nelson, 2007), the article by Robert Rutherdale, "Fatherhood, Masculinity, and the Good Life during Canada's Baby Boom, 1945–1965," pp. 483–99, deals with the first half of the 1960s.

BIBLIOGRAPHY

Books on the evolution of Canada's welfare state include Penny E. Bryden, *Planners and Politicians: The Liberal Party and Social Policy, 1957–1968* (Montreal/Kingston: McGill-Queen's University Press, 1997); and Alvin Finkel, *Social Policy and Practice in Canada: A History* (Waterloo, ON: Wilfrid University Press, 2006). On housing see John R. Miron, ed., *House, Home, and Community: Progress in Housing Canadians, 1945–1986* (Montreal/Kingston: McGill-Queen's University Press, 1993). A study of Canada's centennial, a highlight of the 1960s, is Gary Miedema, *For Canada's Sake: Public Religion, Centennial Celebrations, and the Remaking of Canada in the 1960s* (Montreal/Kingston: McGill-Queen's University Press, 2005).

On higher education, consult Paul Axelrod and John G. Reid, eds., *Youth, University and Canadian Society: Essays in the Social History of Higher Education* (Montreal/Kingston: McGill-Queen's University Press, 1989). Books on cultural policy include Gary Evans, *In the National Interest: A Chronicle of the National Film Board of Canada from 1949 to 1989* (Toronto: University of Toronto Press, 1991); Michael Dorland, *So Close to the State/s: The Emergence of Canadian Feature Film Policy* (Toronto: University of Toronto Press, 1998); Andrew Stewart and William H.N. Hull, *Canadian Television Policy and the Board of Broadcast Governors, 1958–1968* (Edmonton: University of Alberta Press, 1994); and Ted Magder, *Canada's Hollywood: The Canadian State and Feature Films* (Toronto: University of Toronto Press, 1993). Sport history is discussed in Colin Howell, *Blood, Sweat, and Cheers: Sport and the Making of Modern Canada* (Toronto: University of Toronto Press, 2001).

On the role of women in politics, see Sydney Sharpe, *The Gilded Ghetto: Women and Political Power in Canada* (Toronto: HarperCollins, 1994); and Sylvia Bashevkin, *Toeing the Lines: Women and Party Politics in English Canada*, 2nd ed. (Toronto: Oxford University Press, 1993). How the media responded to the feminist movement is discussed in Barbara Freeman, *The Satellite Sex: The Media and Women's Issues in English Canada, 1966–1971* (Waterloo, ON: Wilfrid Laurier University Press, 2001). On birth control consult Angus McLaren and Arlene Tigar McLaren, *The Bedroom and the State: The*

Changing Practices and Politics of Contraception and Abortion in Canada, 1880–1980 (Toronto: McClelland & Stewart, 1986). Legal aspects of homosexuality are studied in Bruce MacDougall, *Queer Judgments: Homosexuality, Expression, and the Courts in Canada* (Toronto: University of Toronto Press, 2000). Steve Hewitt describes the secret activities of the RCMP on university campuses in *Spying 101: The RCMP's Secret Activities at Canadian Universities, 1917–1997* (Toronto: University of Toronto Press, 2002). Marcel Martel examines drug policy in *Not This Time: Canadians, Public Policy, and the Marijuana Question, 1961–1975* (Toronto: University of Toronto Press, 2006).

Among syntheses of labour history containing material on the 1960s are Desmond Morton with Terry Copp, *Working People: An Illustrated History of the Canadian Labour Movement*, 3rd ed. (Toronto: Summerhill Press, 1990); and Craig Heron, *The Canadian Labour Movement: A Short History*, rev. ed. (Toronto: James Lorimer, 1996). Politics in the 1960s is examined in J.L. Granatstein, *Canada, 1957–1967: The Years of Uncertainty and Innovation* (Toronto: McClelland & Stewart, 1986). Studies of prime ministers include Garrett Wilson and Kevin Wilson, *Diefenbaker for the Defence* (Toronto: James Lorimer, 1988); John English, *The Worldly Years: The Life of Lester Pearson*, vol. 2, *1949–1972* (Toronto: Knopf Canada, 1992); Norman Hilmer, ed., *Pearson: The Unlikely Gladiator* (Montreal/ Kingston: McGill-Queen's University Press, 1999); and Stephen Clarkson and Christina McCall Newman, *Trudeau and Our Times*, vol. 1, *The Magnificent Obsession* (Toronto: McClelland & Stewart, 1990). English Canada's changing identity is discussed in Philip Buckner, ed., *Canada and the End of Empire* (Vancouver: UBC Press, 2005); and in José E. Igartua, *The Other Quiet Revolution: National Identities in English Canada, 1945–1971* (Vancouver: UBC Press, 2006).

On aspects of Canada's international relations, see Robert Bothwell, *Alliance and Illusion: Canada and the World, 1945–1984* (Vancouver: UBC Press, 2007); and John English and Norman Hillmer, eds., *Making a Difference? Canada's Foreign Policy in a Changing World Order* (Toronto: Lester, 1992). Studies of Canadian–American relations include J.L. Granatstein and Norman Hillmer, *For Better or for Worse: Canada and the United States to the 1990s* (Toronto: Copp Clark Pitman, 1991); John Herd Thompson and Steven Randall, *Canada and the United States: Ambivalent Allies*, 3rd ed. (Montreal/Kingston: McGill-Queen's University Press, 2002); and, for economic issues, Bruce Muirhead, *Dancing around the Elephant: Creating a Prosperous Canada in an Era of American Dominance, 1957–1973* (Toronto: University of Toronto Press, 2005).

The best overview of the Atlantic provinces is E.R. Forbes and D.A. Muise, eds., *The Atlantic Provinces in Confederation* (Toronto: University of Toronto Press, 1993). A general survey of Ontario is available in Randall White: *Ontario, 1610–1985: A Political and Economic History* (Toronto: Dundurn Press, 1985); the province's economy is studied in K.J. Rea, *The Prosperous Years: The Economic History of Ontario, 1939–1975* (Toronto: University of Toronto Press, 1985). Overviews of western Canada include Gerald Friesen, *The Canadian Prairies: A History* (Toronto: University of Toronto Press, 1984); John Thompson, *Forging the Prairie West: The Illustrated History of Canada* (Don Mills, ON: Oxford University Press, 1998); and John F. Conway, *The West: The History of a Region in Confederation*, 3rd ed. (Toronto: James Lorimer, 2006). Alberta and British Columbia are studied in Howard and Tamara Palmer, *Alberta: A New History* (Edmonton: Hurtig, 1990); and Jean Barman, *The West beyond the West: A History of British Columbia*, 3rd ed. (Toronto: University of Toronto Press, 2007), respectively.

Chapter Twenty-Two

ABORIGINAL CANADA: WORLD WAR II TO THE PRESENT

TIME LINE

1951	Parliament passes the new Indian Act
1960	First Nations individuals obtain the right to vote in federal elections
1969	The Liberal government introduces its "White Paper" on Indian Affairs
1973	The Supreme Court rules that Aboriginal title exists in Canadian law
1974	Ottawa establishes the Office of Native Land Claims to settle First Nations land claims
1982	The Constitutional Act affirms the existence of Aboriginal and treaty rights
1985	Parliament amends the Indian Act, restoring Indian status to persons who had lost it
1996	The Royal Commission on Aboriginal Peoples issues its report
1999	Nunavut, in the eastern Arctic, becomes a separate territory
2005	Paul Martin's Liberal government signs the Kelowna Accord with Aboriginal representatives, the succeeding Conservative administration of Stephen Harper refuses to implement it

Since the 1950s the Aboriginal peoples have been the fastest-growing population in Canada. The birth rate among the Inuit and status Indians—those registered under the federal Indian Act—is twice the national average. Improved nutrition and hygiene, as well as continued progress in the prevention and therapy of infectious disease, have reduced mortality. Urban migration has increased Aboriginal visibility. What a contrast to the situation immediately after Confederation in 1867, when the First Nations population declined as a result of tuberculosis and other communicable diseases introduced by Europeans. As late as 1932, Diamond Jenness, the distinguished Canadian anthropologist, prophesied: "Doubtless all the tribes will disappear. Some will endure only a few years longer, others, like the Eskimos, may last several centuries."[1]

The growing perception in the dominant society after World War II that the Aboriginal peoples were not "vanishing" led to the development of a more positive attitude. Just as importantly, from the 1930s onward, a new group of politically conscious Aboriginal leaders, with knowledge of the larger society and an ability to articulate their demands, made their voices heard and heightened public awareness of Aboriginal issues. The Indian resistance to the federal government's assimilationist "White Paper" of 1969 led to its withdrawal. In recent decades, the dominant society's attitude toward Aboriginal Canada has greatly changed. In contrast with the mid-twentieth century, the Canadian public now appears more open to diverse heritages, in particular those of the First Peoples.

Land claims began in the mid-1970s for over half of Canada. Successful political lobbying contributed to the inclusion of the Aboriginal peoples—Indians, Inuit, and Métis—in Canada's new constitution in 1982. Widespread recognition of the concept of Aboriginal rights, including self-government, followed in the late 1980s and early 1990s. In 1999 the federal government created Nunavut, a separate political jurisdiction in the eastern Arctic, which the Inuit control because of their numerical dominance. The First Ministers Conference on Aboriginal Affairs in Kelowna in late November 2005, in the last days of the Liberal administration of Paul Martin, resulted in a five-year, $5 billion plan to improve education, housing, economic development, health, and water supplies of the First Nations, Métis, and Inuit peoples.

The Yale–Toronto Conference on the North American Indian

The University of Toronto and Yale Conference on the North American Indian that met in Toronto in 1939 symbolized the transition from the old to the new Canada on Aboriginal issues. The conference was designed "to reveal the conditions today of the white man's Indian wards, and in a scientific, objective and sympathetic spirit, plan with them for their future." Over 70 Canadian and American government officials, missionaries, and academics attended. More importantly, thirteen invited Aboriginal people participated. It was the first conference ever held to discuss First Nations welfare and the first scholarly meeting to include Aboriginal delegates.

For nearly two weeks, the conference delegates discussed North American Aboriginal cultures, reserve economics, health, and education. Perhaps the most revealing information about Aboriginal peoples in Canada came from federal government officials, who pointed out that, beginning in the mid-1930s, Canada's status Indian population had reversed its previous decline and was increasing annually by 1 percent, thanks to both an increase in the birth rate and a decline in the death rate. On the last day of the conference, delegates passed resolutions urging greater attention to "the psychological, social, and economic maladjustments of the Indian populations of the United States and Canada."

Then a dramatic event occurred. The Aboriginal delegates broke from the main group and met separately to pass their own resolutions. They objected to government officials, missionaries, and non-Aboriginal sympathizers speaking for them.

The delegates to the Yale–Toronto Conference on the North American Indian, Toronto, September 1939. This was the first conference held in Canada to discuss Aboriginal welfare and the first scholarly conference to include First Nations delegates.

Pringle and Booth/Courtesy of Ken Kidd, a delegate at the conference.

> *We hereby go on record as hoping that the need for an All Indian Conference on Indian Affairs will be felt by Indian tribes, the delegates to such a conference be limited to bona fide Indian leaders actually living among the Indian people of the reservations and reserves, and further, that such a conference remain free of political, anthropological, missionary, administrative, or other domination.*

This appeal went largely unheard by a Canadian public totally preoccupied by the entry of Canada into World War II, but in retrospect the conference was a turning point.

The Aboriginal Peoples in Wartime

During the war, Canada's status Indian population experienced increased oppression. Acting against verbal promises at several treaty negotiations in western Canada, the federal government initially tried to include status Indians among those eligible for overseas military conscription. Other arbitrary wartime measures included the seizure of reserve lands, the transfer of reserve populations, and the revision of band membership lists. When, for example, the federal government decided in 1942 that it needed a military training facility on Lake Huron, it invoked the War Measures Act to appropriate Ontario's Stoney Point Reserve to establish Camp Ipperwash.

Financial exigency during the war also contributed to First Nations resentment. To save money and promote self-sufficiency, the Indian Affairs Branch unilaterally proposed a centralization plan designed to remove status Mi'kmaq (Micmac) in Nova Scotia from nineteen small reserves to two large inland ones. The abandoned reserves were to be sold. Only mounting First Nations opposition led to the cancellation of the proposal. Then, in northern Alberta, an Indian Affairs Branch official created havoc when he revised the membership lists in the Lesser Slave Lake agency to eliminate 700 individuals whom he claimed were not "true Indians." First Nations reacted by working to strengthen their already existing political organization, the Indian Association of Alberta.

Such actions undermined the Indian Affairs Branch's credibility among the First Nations, as did the fact that the branch's 65 members included only two Aboriginal persons in 1944. Indeed, the war years proved demoralizing for the First Nations. Many enlisted in armed services during the war, but were denied benefits given to the other veterans. Furthermore they continued to be "wards of the state" without the right to vote. Still, the period contributed to fostering a greater political consciousness among the First Nations.

The Aboriginal Peoples of the North

In the interwar years, First Nations people in sparsely populated areas in the North had escaped the full weight of the Indian Act. The federal government had paid little attention to such groups as the Dene in the Mackenzie River valley and the Cree in the James Bay area. During the war, however, the isolation ended for the northern First Nations, Métis, and Inuit. Thousands of armed-service personnel and civilians established military airstrips and radio stations in the North. Small communities arose around these posts. Furthermore, in the late 1940s, with the collapse of the fur market and the failure to meet the migrating caribou herds, starving Inuit depended on the federal government for help. Ottawa responded by flying hungry families to fur trading posts, where food supplies existed. The federal government also brought in nurses and doctors to look after Inuit refugees, and it built hospitals and schools, as well as living quarters. As soon as these non-Aboriginal medical personnel, administrators, and teachers arrived, even on a semi-permanent basis, the federal government built permanent installations, such as power plants, water and sewer systems, and roads. The small non-Aboriginal bureaucracy that administered the social assistance programs gained enormous control over the Inuit.

For those Inuit who had tuberculosis or other communicable diseases, the government provided medical assistance, such as X-rays and immunization. Those patients requiring immediate hospitalization were sent south by plane or boat. By the 1950s, hundreds had obtained hospital care and the Department of Health and Welfare had succeeded in lowering substantially the high mortality rate among the Inuit.

Ottawa now saw its task as bringing the Mackenzie valley First Nations to a level comparable to that of the Inuit in the eastern Arctic. In the Mackenzie valley, the Aboriginal peoples had not experienced the same economic collapse as the Inuit had after World War II. Moreover, they already lived in semi-permanent camps around Hudson's Bay Company posts and Christian missions. Ottawa replaced the mission schools with public schools and provided the same medical services and administrative help as in the eastern Arctic. The government clashed, however, with local chiefs and elders, who resented its intrusion into their communities. Up to this time the First Nations in the Mackenzie valley had run their own affairs.

A New Postwar Attitude toward the Aboriginal Peoples

After World War II, Canadians developed a more positive attitude toward Aboriginal peoples. Several reasons explain this change. First, social scientists discredited earlier pseudoscientific race theories that had held certain "races" to be inherently inferior to others. Second, many Canadians learned through the media of the impoverished living conditions of the northern First Nations and Inuit. Improvements in water and especially air transportation brought even the most remote regions of the Arctic into the southern Canadian consciousness. Third, the expansion of the natural-resource frontier took southern Canadians into Aboriginal territory (a situation that brought First Nations land claims throughout northern Canada to the public's attention). Fourth, the decolonization movement in Asia and Africa and later the civil rights movement in the United States in the 1950s and early 1960s contributed to a new consciousness of injustices to minorities, including the Aboriginal peoples. Most importantly, Aboriginal leaders now made their demands known. A number of demobilized First Nations veterans, for example, sought freedom from tutelage, and recognition of their civil rights. By the end of the twentieth century a new leadership, able to communicate in English or, in parts of southern Quebec, in French, and skilled in legal argument and media manipulation, had emerged to make the First Nations a political force.

The Indian Association of Alberta campaigned after World War II to have Parliament review the Indian Act. Some veterans' organizations and church groups assisted Aboriginal political leaders in pressuring Ottawa to relax the powerful controls it exercised over the reserves. For the first time, Parliament listened. Several provincial Indian organizations participated in the hearings of the Joint Committee of the House of Commons and the Senate on the Indian Act, held from 1946 to 1948. Out of these deliberations came a new revision of the Indian Act in 1951.

The new Indian Act allowed band councils more authority. Women also gained the vote in band council elections. The Act lifted bans on the potlatch and on the Sun Dance, an important religious ceremony. Compulsory enfranchisement, by which male First Nations people relinquished Indian status in return for full citizenship privileges, was abandoned. Yet, the new Indian Act's underlying goal remained the assimilation of the status Indian, seen as both inevitable and desirable. The Act made it easier for individuals to give up their Indian status. It included new provisions to allow the placement of First Nations children in integrated provincial schools. It also gave provincial authorities responsibility for the welfare of Indian children. In the 1960s the provinces became very aggressive in taking First Nations children from their families, from their communities, and placing them in protective care. Thousands of children were removed and settled into foster and adopted homes.

By the 1970s, Ottawa had phased out most of the residential schools and had integrated First Nations children into provincially controlled programs. But integrated schooling did not prove entirely successful. Its shortcomings led a number of bands in the early 1970s to call for community control of their schools. Blue Quills, near St. Paul, Alberta, became the first band-controlled school in 1970. Others followed, and in 1973 the federal government endorsed First Nations–controlled schools.

Gradually the federal government allowed greater local band government. In 1960, for example, the Walpole Island band council in southwestern Ontario assumed responsibility for road improvements and other public works on the reserve. Later, the same band council gained control over the administration of its own local affairs. Many bands in Ontario began to run their own welfare services. Other bands created their own police forces, as Walpole Island did in 1967.

During the 1950s and early 1960s, the dominant society showed a greater sensitivity to some Aboriginal issues. Gradually the provinces granted the provincial franchise to status Indians. In 1960, Ottawa extended the right to vote in federal elections to all status Indians, without requiring that they give up their Indian status. A federally appointed commission reported in the mid-1960s that the First

Prime Minister John Diefenbaker with Plains Cree at Maple Creek, Saskatchewan, during his reelection campaign, October 1965.

© Government of Canada. Reproduced with the permission of the Minister of Public Works and Government Services Canada (2008). Source: Library and Archives Canada/Credit: Bill Cadzow/ National Film Board of Canada/PA-154863

Nations occupied the lowest economic rung on Canada's economic ladder. The commission concluded that "in addition to the normal rights and duties of citizenship, Indians possess certain rights as charter members of the Canadian community." After the publication of the report, Prime Minister Lester Pearson committed his government to revising the Indian Act.

The federal government, which now adopted a more supportive role toward the Aboriginal peoples, helped to build a pavilion for the First Nations at Montreal's Expo 67. First Nations organizers used the building to tell the story of Aboriginal Canada. At the entrance, a message greeted visitors: "The Indian people's destiny will be determined by them and our country, Canada, will be better for it." Inside, visitors saw, in bold script, statements such as "Give us the right to manage our own affairs" and "Help us preserve the moral values, the meaningful way of life, the inheritance of our forefathers." These anti-assimilationist messages announced the First Nations' political agenda for the remainder of the century.

Since the 1970s, increased attention has been paid to the distinctive needs of Aboriginal people, and to their participation in the justice system, but admittedly great challenges remain. Horror stories include that of Donald Marshall, Jr., a Mi'kmaq teenager who was wrongly convicted and imprisoned for murder in 1972. Marshall spent eleven years in prison until a reexamination of the case led to his acquittal in 1983. A judicial inquiry after his release showed that anti-Aboriginal prejudice permeated the justice system.

From the "White Paper" of 1969 to the Constitution of 1982

In 1969 the recently elected Liberal government of Pierre Trudeau inadvertently contributed to the Aboriginal resurgence. Trudeau's predecessor, Lester Pearson, had promised that the Indian Act would be revised only after prior consultation with Indian people. But, without any meaningful consultation, the Trudeau administration published a "White Paper" on Indian policy that announced an end to the Indian Act and the dismantlement of the reserves. Many of the federal government's responsibilities for Indian affairs were to be transferred to the provinces. The elected band councils would evolve into municipal-type institutions. The objective of the new policy was to bring First Nations people immediately into the mainstream society. Trudeau also announced that his government would refuse to negotiate land settlements for the roughly one-half of the country that was not under treaty.

Without delay, young, educated First Nations leaders joined ranks with Aboriginal elders to oppose the government's position paper. It might be said that the White Paper did for the First Nations what Lord Durham's report of 1839 had for French Canadians, in recommending their eventual assimilation. The First Nations rallied to oppose the threat to their continued existence, as had the French Canadians in the 1840s. Although unsatisfied with the colonial relationship imposed by the Indian Act, the First Nations leaders realized that the legislation did at least recognize their special constitutional status. Without the Act, they risked being absorbed into the dominant non-Aboriginal Canadian society. The fact that the federal government began to provide core funding for First Nations political organizations in 1970 encouraged them. It was in Ottawa's interest to do so, as the existence of strong Indian organizations in Canada helped to keep out militant United States Indian groups like the American Indian Movement. A united front of First Nations organizations succeeded in convincing the Liberal government to withdraw the White Paper in March 1971. The provincial and territorial Aboriginal political associations representing status Indians in Canada and the National Indian Brotherhood (founded in 1968, and reorganized in 1982 as the Assembly of First Nations) now worked to secure the constitutional entrenchment of Aboriginal and treaty rights.

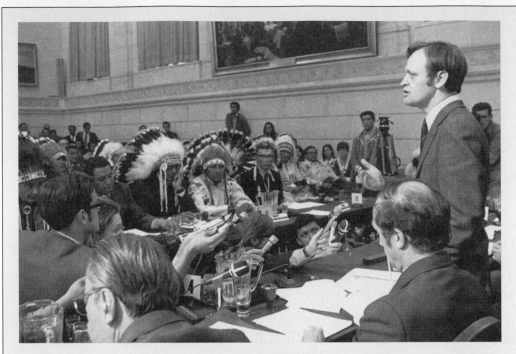

Jean Chrétien, Minister of Indian Affairs, meeting with a delegation from the Indian Association of Alberta and other First Nations groups in Ottawa, June 1970. Prime Minister Pierre Trudeau is seated beside Jean Chrétien. The First Nations representatives have just presented the "Red Paper," their response to the government's controversial White Paper.

© Library and Archives Canada. Reproduced with the permission of Library and Archives Canada. Source: Library and Archives Canada/Credit: Duncan Cameron/Duncan Cameron fonds/PA-170161

Assisting the Aboriginal activists in their cause was the decision of the Supreme Court of Canada in the Nisga'a case of 1973. Although the decision went against the Nisga'a First Nations on a legal technicality, the Supreme Court did agree that the First Nations held Aboriginal title to their lands. Thus, the federal government was pressured into accepting comprehensive claims in the areas of Canada where treaties had not been signed, and accepting specific claims elsewhere. More limited than comprehensive land claims, specific claims usually relate to demands for compensation or the restitution of land or money on the basis of the unfulfilled terms of an existing treaty, or formal legal agreement with the government. In 1974, Ottawa established an Office of Native Claims to rule on Aboriginal land claims.

The first comprehensive land claim was the James Bay and Northern Quebec Agreement, signed in 1975 soon after the enactment of the new federal policy. By this treaty, the Cree and Inuit surrendered their Aboriginal rights to a huge area of 1 000 000 km^2 of land. In return, they gained ownership, in and around their communities, of over 14 000 km^2, as well as exclusive hunting, fishing, and trapping rights over 150 000 km^2. Both they and the general public would obtain equal access to the rest of the land. The Cree and the Inuit were also awarded $225 million over a period of 25 years. In 2002, the Grand Council of the Cree and the Quebec government reached an understanding to extend the original agreement. In exchange for permitting further hydroelectric development on the Rupert and Eastmain Rivers, the Cree will obtain payments valued at $3.5 billion over a fifty-year period. They also received important commitments relating to employment, land, and co-management of the region's resources. In 2007 the 10 000 Inuit of northern Quebec signed an agreement with the Quebec government in 2007 that gave them control over most matters within a huge territory called Nunavik.

The early and mid-1970s were marked by Aboriginal activism. In the United States the rise of the "Red Power" movement led to a series of confrontations. Canada also saw heightened unrest. In late 1971, Alberta First Nations began a six-month sit-in at the Department of Indian Affairs offices in Edmonton to protest the inferior conditions at reserve schools. Ojibwa (Anishinabeg) occupied Anicinibe Park in Kenora, northwestern Ontario, in the summer of 1974, in a land-claim dispute. An Aboriginal caravan from Vancouver reached Parliament Hill in September 1974 to protest poor housing and social services on reserves, as well as land-claim issues.

The emergence of constitutional issues after the election of the Parti Québécois in Quebec in 1976 provided Canada's Aboriginal peoples with an opportunity for constitutional advancement. Among the Aboriginal political organizations that entered the constitutional debate were the National Indian Brotherhood, the first permanent national organization for Status Indians; the recently formed Native Council of Canada (now the Congress of Aboriginal Peoples), which represented Métis and off-reserve and non-status Indians; and the Inuit Tapirisat of Canada, the Inuit political organization. A strong campaign by Aboriginal groups led to the inclusion of section 35(2) in the Constitution of 1982, which gave constitutional protection for the first time to the "existing Aboriginal and treaty rights of the Aboriginal peoples of Canada." The new constitution also, for the first time, identified the Métis, along with the Indians and Inuit, as an Aboriginal people.

First Nations Political Demands from the 1980s to the Present

The definition of Aboriginal rights and the issue of self-government became the major constitutional questions for Aboriginal people in the 1980s and early 1990s. In the course of a series of four conferences held between 1983 and 1987, Canada's first ministers and Aboriginal representatives failed to reach agreement either on the meaning of the phrase "Aboriginal rights" or on a definition of Aboriginal self-government. These meetings did, however, give Aboriginal issues a very high public profile. In 1983, the House of Commons Committee on Indian Self-Government endorsed the concept of full Aboriginal control over matters such as education, child welfare, health care, and band membership. For the first time in a federal document, the term "First Nation" was used.

With the end of the constitutional conferences on Aboriginal rights in 1987, the battleground between Aboriginal groups and the federal government shifted back to the courts. Since the mid-1980s, Supreme Court rulings have provided an expanding interpretation of Aboriginal and treaty rights. Already, by 1984, the court had established the concept of a trust-like, or "fiduciary," relationship between the Crown and the Aboriginal peoples. The federal government had a trust-like duty to act in the best interests of the First Nations it represented. The following year, in another case, judges ruled that Indian treaties must be given a "fair, large and liberal interpretation." Then, in the Sparrow case (1990), the Supreme Court drew on the Constitutional Act of 1982 to establish rules restricting to a minimum government's infringement of Aboriginal and treaty rights.

At four First Ministers' conferences on Aboriginal issues in the mid-1980s, the question of an Aboriginal right to self-government was debated. The federal government argued that First Nations self-government would be a right delegated from the Crown. The First Nations contended that it was an inherent right that they possessed from their historical occupation of what was now Canada. It took until 1995 for the federal government to accept the inherent right of self-government as a matter of policy. The government then began negotiations with a number of First Nations to implement Aboriginal self-government after joint consultation between the existing federal and provincial jurisdictions.

A Cana...
face in ...
summer...

CP Photo...

schools performed well. "Despite its short-comings, the residential school evidently met a need."[2]

According to historian Scott Trevithick, participants in the debate over residential schools "do not fit conveniently into two distinct and opposing camps, but rather find themselves spread out at various places across the playing field."[3] Another early contributor to the discussion in the 1980s was historian Celia Haig-Brown. From her study, rich in oral testimony, of the Kamloops Indian Residential School in central British Columbia, one gains a fuller understanding of the schools. Reflecting her interviewees' vivid and painful memories she emphasizes "the injustice of the system which attempted to control and to transform them."[4] Yet she points out: "Even with the controls already described well in place, the students found time and space to express themselves and to produce a separate culture of their own within the school."[5]

By 1990 the subject of residential schools began to enter the general public's consciousness. The statement by Phil Fontaine, then chief of the Assembly of

Cree children attending an Anglican Church school, Lac La Ronge, Saskatchewan, March 1945.

Library and Archives Canada, Photo by Bud Glunz, PA-124110.

Manitoba Chiefs, that he had suffered sexual abuse as a student at a Manitoba residential school, broke other former students' silence. A number came forward to reveal their own stories of physical, sexual, and emotional abuse. The hearings of the Royal Commission on Aboriginal Peoples also helped publicize the Indian residential school system's weaknesses. Then, in 1996, J.R. Miller published an important study in which he noted that, at the high point of the Indian residential school system, in the early twentieth century, probably about one-third of the eligible Inuit and status Indians of school age attended.[6] He concluded: "It seems clear that the schools performed inadequately in most respects, and in a few areas, wrought profoundly destructive effects on many of their students."[7] For his part, historian John S. Milloy, who wrote a report for the Commission on residential schools, strongly criticized the church–state partnership for its assault on the well-being of the First Nations. "In thought and in deed the establishment of this school system was an act of profound cruelty rooted in non-Aboriginal pride and intolerance and in the certitude and insularity of purported cultural superiority."[8]

Much of the challenge of this topic for academic historians resides in the lack of consensus in the oral evidence. As J.R. Miller wrote: "The existence of former students who hold positive memories of residential school and many others who recall it as a living hell seriously complicates a later age's ability to reach a firm, overall assessment of the problem of abuse in these institutions." He concludes: "In a pathetic sense, that emotional confrontation is also a form of abuse perpetuated indirectly by the residential school system."[9]

1. John Webster Grant, *Moon of Wintertime: Missionaries and the Indians of Canada in Encounter since 1534* (Toronto: University of Toronto Press, 1984), p. 179.

2. Ibid., p. 100.

3. Scott Trevithick, "Native Residential Schooling in Canada: A Review of Literature," *The Canadian Journal of Native Studies*, 18, 1 (1998): 53.

4. Celia Haig-Brown, *Resistance and Renewal: Surviving the Indian Residential School* (Vancouver: Tillacum Library, 1988), p. 115.

5. Ibid., p. 88.

6. J.R. Miller, *Shingwauk's Vision: A History of Native Residential Schools* (Toronto: University of Toronto Press, 1996), p. 142.

7. Ibid., p. 418.

8. John S. Milloy, *'A National Crime': The Canadian Government and the Residential School System, 1879 to 1986* (Winnipeg: University of Manitoba Press, 1999), p. 302.

9. Miller, pp. 341–42.

On June 11, 2008, the federal government made a Statement of Apology to the Aboriginal Peoples for Residential Schools, and for the policy of assimilation. Prime Minister Harper underlined the "profoundly negative" Indian residential schools. He termed former students "survivors," and described the "policy of assimilation" as "wrong." A survey by Innovative Research Group immediately after the issuing of the apology, between June 11 and 13, found that the government had not only obtained near-universal awareness among Canadians but also had very broad support.

Aboriginal Rights

The mid-1990s marked the beginning of a treaty process in British Columbia. From the time of its entry into Confederation in 1871, the province had refused to acknowledge that the Aboriginal peoples had any treaty rights or ancestral claims over traditional lands. In 1990 British Columbia made a historic change of policy, and agreed to enter into treaty negotiations with First Nations groups. In 1993 the province established the British Columbia Treaty Commission. In the 1997 Delgamuukw case concerning British Columbia, the Supreme Court enlarged and clarified the definition of Aboriginal title in Canada. It recognized that Aboriginal title might extend over large areas of traditional lands. This landmark decision also accepted the validity of using Aboriginal oral history and testimony from elders in cases involving Aboriginal title.

In 1999, the federal parliament ratified the Nisga'a Treaty, the first comprehensive claim to be settled south of the Yukon and North West Territories

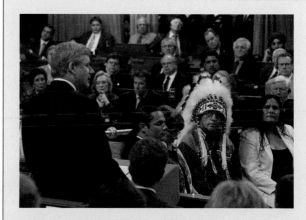

Assembly of First Nations Chief Phil Fontaine, in headdress, watches as Prime Minister Stephen Harper officially apologizes for more than a century of abuse and cultural loss involving residential schools.

CP Photo (Tom Hanson).

since the James Bay Agreement in 1975. The Nisga'a obtained control over 2000 km² of their territory, as well as nearly $120 million in compensation for their lost lands in northwest British Columbia. Currently, approximately fifty First Nations groups in the province are involved in negotiations to make similar agreements. If successful, the First Nations in British Columbia might obtain firm title to about 5 percent of the province's land mass. Recently, however, progress has been slow in treaty negotiations in British Columbia. Indeed, in late 2006, both the federal and provincial auditors general warned that talks were in danger of being overrun by "the changing legal, economic and political environments".[2]

First Nations land issues have advanced in Saskatchewan, where about 15 percent of the population, including nearly one-quarter of the province's children, is Aboriginal. (Throughout all of Canada the total percentage of First Nations and Métis people, as reported in the census of 2006, was about 3 percent.) In 1992, the Saskatchewan Treaty Land Entitlement Framework Agreement provided for compensation for illegal losses of reservation lands in the province. Ottawa negotiated a $450 million settlement in the province for treaty land entitlement. The settlement will compensate for illegal losses of reservation lands in the province. Saskatchewan has also led the way in the creation of urban reserves, providing urban locations for Aboriginal businesses.

Another confirmation of the growing legal and political recognition of Aboriginal rights came in 1999 with the Supreme Court's Marshall decision, concerning the Mi'kmaq. The Supreme Court concluded that the peace and friendship treaties made in 1760–61 between the Mi'kmaq and the British gave the Mi'kmaq a treaty right to a "moderate livelihood" in the Atlantic commercial fishery. Ottawa's continued attempt to try to regulate the Mi'kmaq fishery resulted in sporadic violence in the 2000 and 2001 fishing seasons, particularly at the Mi'kmaq community of Burnt Church, on New Brunswick's Miramichi Bay. The issue is still unresolved.

The danger of violence over unresolved land-claims issues remains very real, as Oka showed in 1990. In 1995, a land-claim dispute in Ontario over an Aboriginal burial site at Ipperwash Provincial Park led to an incident in which an Ojibwa protester was killed. In 2004, a provincial commission of inquiry made several recommendations in an attempt to avoid a similar tragedy in the future. Another confrontation occurred in central British Columbia, also in 1995, at Gustafsen Lake, where First Nations militants claimed the private ranch land they occupied was a sacred site. During a police operation that followed, shots were exchanged and arrests were made, but fortunately there were no casualties.

Numerous other unresolved Aboriginal issues remain. In northern Alberta the Cree of Lubicon Lake argue that they have unextinguished Aboriginal title, and consequently a comprehensive claim. The federal government sees the claim only as an unfulfilled treaty entitlement, a specific claim. The community's distance from major southern urban centres has ensured that the claim has not received as much visibility as claims of First Nations in southern Canada. The Cree of Lubicon Lake seek a modern-day treaty similar to that of the James Bay Cree or the Nisga'a in British Columbia.

Land-claims issues remain contentious. First Nations groups contend that the whole federal claims-resolution process is unfair. Ottawa sets the rules and controls the agenda. Under the existing system, Aboriginal communities lacking sufficient economic resources must obtain research and legal funds from the same government that will decide whether to accept their claim for negotiation. Exasperated by lengthy delays, for instance, a group of Six Nations protestors occupied, in 2006, a disputed tract of land near Caledonia, Ontario, beside the Grand River Territory. In 2007, Ottawa promised a new land-claims policy, one that would grant a federal commission the power to order redress for historic treaty violations. The Caledonia dispute remains unresolved.

Economic and Social Issues for Aboriginal Canada since the 1980s

The findings of the Royal Commission on Aboriginal Peoples in the mid-1990s confirmed the continuing economic and social inequality of the First Nations in Canada. For nearly one-half of the registered Indians living off the reserves, the quality of life remains substantially below that of the average non-Aboriginal Canadian.

Before World War II, nearly all First Nations people lived in rural areas. Then, large numbers migrated to cities in search of industrial jobs. Many experienced discrimination, from the refusal of accommodation to unfair hiring practices. Those who lacked academic and vocational credentials experienced the greatest difficulties. Although Aboriginal friendship centres did help individuals adjust to urban life, they could not alter economic conditions.

The Indian and Metis Friendship Centre in Winnipeg, 1960.
Archives of Manitoba, Nan Shipley Collection 74.

Another issue in urban areas is Aboriginal language retention. Maintaining Aboriginal languages is difficult when few speak their First Nations language fluently, and there are different Aboriginal languages, or dialects of the same tongue. In urban areas only a tiny minority of Aboriginal children speak their Aboriginal languages at home.

Grave social problems continue to plague Aboriginal Canada. The life expectancy of a registered Indian remains about six years less than for the general Canadian population. High suicide rates illustrate the intensity of despair. Poverty is a major issue, as well as the lack of access to quality health care. Tuberculosis and other diseases as well as drug abuse continue to ravage many First Nations communities. Equally worrisome, as Marianne O. Nielsen points out, is the fact that Canada's Aboriginal population is "seriously and tragically overrepresented among the inmates incarcerated in federal and provincial correctional institutions."[3] James S. Frideres and Rene R. Gadacz point out:

> The legal philosophy, the offences, and the court procedures are often the root of the problem, and this is compounded when Aboriginals find themselves in an urban context. In addition, language difficulties, ignorance of the law, poverty (particularly the inability to pay fines), and lack of education add to the disadvantage of Aboriginal people when facing the justice system.[4]

Child welfare services on reserves are often underfunded. In 2007, some 27 000 Aboriginal children lived in foster homes, a figure much higher than the total number of students in Indian residential schools at the high point of their existence in the mid-twentieth century. One out of ten Aboriginal children was in foster care, as against one in two hundred for non-Aboriginal children.[5]

Yet positive trends are evident. The number of individuals identifying themselves as Aboriginal increased sharply between 1996 and 2001. According to the 2001 census, there were approximately 610 000 Indians, 290 000 Métis and non-status Indians, and 45 000 Inuit in Canada, an increase of nearly 20 percent in five years. Natural increase alone cannot explain such rapid growth. It appears that many more individuals now identify with their Aboriginal ancestry, indicating an increased pride in their heritage.

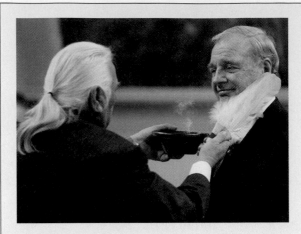

Aboriginal elder Elmer Courchene performs a "cleansing ceremony" at Prime Minister Paul Martin's swearing-in, December 2003.

CP Photo (Jonathan Hayward).

Education is another area in which advances have occurred. In 1995 the federal government published data that showed that almost three-quarters of status Indian students reached Grade 12, compared to only one-fifth in 1970. Similarly the number of status Indians and Inuit in postsecondary education jumped from 4500 in 1970 to 27 000 in 2001. The gap between First Nations and the larger Canadian population has narrowed significantly. As well, First Nations individuals who have obtained postsecondary education means now serve as role models to First Nations youth, creating additional interest in postsecondary institutions as a way of opening up new career options.

Since the 1970s, numerous Aboriginal authors, artists, and performers have emerged. Writers such as Maria Campbell, Thomson Highway, and Basil Johnston have achieved prominence. They join a growing number of Aboriginal artists, such as Robert Davidson, Norval Morrisseau, Daphne Odjig, Bill Reid, and Allen Sapp, who have used art to strengthen and affirm their Aboriginal identity. Several Inuit artists enjoy a worldwide reputation. The musical group Kashtin and Inuit singer Susan Aglukark gained fame in popular music. Tom Jackson achieved a prominent role in both music and acting. Architect Douglas Cardinal won numerous international awards for his work. He designed the Canadian Museum of Civilization in Hull, Quebec and the National Museum of the American Indian in Washington, D.C. Advancement has occurred on other fronts as well. Over the past decade Aboriginal people have served in many important administrative posts, including the CBC board of directors (John Kim Bell), the ombudsman of Ontario (Roberta Jamieson), the lieutenant governor of Ontario (James Bartleman), and the chancellor of Trent University (Mary Simon). Annually the National Aboriginal Achievement Awards have recognized the successes of Aboriginal people in Canada.

Significant progress has also been made in communications. Indeed, Canada has taken a leading role in Aboriginal broadcasting. The Canadian government assisted with the launching of the Aboriginal Peoples Television Network in 1999. Northern and southern Aboriginal communities can now hear their own languages and see their own programming. Lorna Roth, the author of a recent study on First Peoples television broadcasting in Canada, credits this success to the persistent efforts of the Aboriginal peoples to take control of their own media sources, as well as to the support of federal government institutions.

A number of First Nations communities have recently seen substantial economic progress. Some First Nations and Inuit people have gained ownership over vast tracts of land where resource companies have made enormous investments. Oil and gas have provided supplementary income as well as jobs in some communities, such as the Mikisew Cree in northeastern Alberta, who operate a small airline, a construction firm, and an energy service company that provides workers and service contracts to the oil sands industry. The creation of Aboriginal banking institutions and the development of tourism and small business have also helped. An entrepreneurial class is emerging. Some communities, such as the Mnjikning First Nation near Orillia, Ontario, have obtained a measure of economic self-sufficiency from running casinos. But gaming has a negative side as well. A recent study shows that the host community faces increased gambling addiction as well as higher crime levels.[6]

Great challenges remain. Large numbers of status Indians have left their reserves to escape depressed economic conditions. Many of the over 2350 reserves (and many rural communities of non-status Indians and Métis) are very small, scattered, and distant from large urban areas, and they lack the resources and the necessary infrastructure to sustain their populations.

Since the mid-1980s the number of status Indians particularly in urban areas has increased substantially on account of the passage of Bill C-31 in 1985. It restored Indian status to all Aboriginal women who requested it after having married non-Indians and subsequently lost their status under the Indian Act. It also gave status to their immediate descendants, thus increasing the number of registered Indians by 115 000 from 1985 to 2001.

Reinstatement as a status Indian entitles the individual to receive limited medical care, subsidies for higher education, and exemption from all federal and provincial taxation on monies earned on any reserve. Those gaining membership in a specific Indian band (many bands now control their own individual membership) obtain a share of the band's assets, the right to reside on the band's reserve, all hunting and fishing rights, eligibility for federal loans and grants to establish reserve businesses, and free schooling on the reserve. Many band chiefs complain that the legislation has serious economic and social consequences as assets will have to be shared among many more individuals; the federal government has replied that it is necessary to bring the Indian Act into conformity with the antidiscriminatory provisions of the new Canadian Charter of Rights and Freedoms.

Women play a very prominent role in today's First Nations communities. Of the 625 communities represented by the Assembly of First Nations, over one hundred are led by female Aboriginal chiefs. Women are also very prominent in their communities as band councillors. In the non-political sector many women work as teachers and social workers in their communities.

The Métis, the Inuit, and the Federal Government

The position of the Métis differs from that of status Indians. The federal government has maintained that Canada's obligations to the Métis ended once it had dealt with their land claim under the Manitoba Act and issued land allowances (or the money equivalent) to the Métis in the North-West Territories in 1885 and in 1899–1900. The federal government contends that the provinces have responsibility for the Métis. A high point of the Métis's political struggle for recognition came when they succeeded in achieving identification in the Constitution Act of 1982 as an Aboriginal people.

One of the difficulties that remains is to resolve what that identification means in terms of legal rights. A victory came in September 2003 with a Supreme Court decision that recognized that their status as a distinct Aboriginal group granted certain Métis the right to hunt for food. The Powley decision established tests for determining which Métis communities possessed Aboriginal rights to hunt for food. The question of what other Aboriginal rights the Métis might be entitled to, or should negotiate, on a wide range of issues from natural resources to health services and taxation, remains unresolved.

Hunter Steve Powley and his lawyer, Jean Teillet, celebrate after an Ontario court in 1998 for the first time recognized the Métis as a distinct Aboriginal people with protected constitutional rights. Jean Teillet is the great-grandniece of Louis Riel.

CP Photo/Sault Star (Keith Stephen).

Of the three Aboriginal groups, the Inuit have the best chance of retaining control of their lands, because they constitute over three-quarters of the population in the eastern Arctic. Due to the remoteness of the area and, from a southerner's perspective, the severity of its climate, the Inuit will probably always be the majority on the treeless northern tundra. Nunavut (meaning "our land" in Inuktitut), created in 1999, now joins the Yukon and the North West Territories as the third territory in Canada.

The Aboriginal North since the 1970s

The northern First Nations and Inuit have contributed greatly to the placing of Aboriginal issues on the public policy agenda. First Nations political awareness arose in the Yukon in the late 1960s when Chief Elijah Smith urged his people to start looking for guarantees of their rights to their homeland. In the Yukon, and indeed throughout Canada, a new generation of bilingual First Nations leaders came forward to fight for Aboriginal land claims and for an end to the federal government's assimilationist policies. In 1973, the Yukon Native Brotherhood began formal talks with the federal government about unsurrendered Aboriginal rights in the Yukon.

Aboriginal demands for political control in the neighbouring North West Territories date back to the late 1960s, when the first territorial Aboriginal organization, the Indian Brotherhood of the North West Territories, later called the Dene Nation, was formed. In 1970, the Committee for the Original Peoples' Entitlement (COPE) was founded in Inuvik to protect the interests of the Inuit (or the Inuvialuit, as the Inuit of the western Arctic refer to themselves) in the Mackenzie. The following year, an Inuit organizing committee formed the Inuit Tapirisat of Canada, a pan-Inuit organization with a mandate to address questions of northern development and to work to preserve Inuit culture. Later, the Inuit of the eastern and central Arctic established the Tungavik Federation of Nunavut to represent their specific regional concerns. Then, in 1973, the Métis in the region formed their own association, the Métis Association of the North West Territories, which eventually allied with the Dene Nation to submit a joint land claim.

The Berger Inquiry, headed by Judge Thomas Berger in the mid-1970s, brought public notice to First Nations and Inuit concerns. In 1972, the building of a Canadian pipeline to carry American oil and gas from the vast Prudhoe Bay field on the northeastern coast of Alaska south through the Mackenzie valley seemed a certainty—until a commission was set up to investigate its feasibility. Berger undertook a comprehensive environmental, social, and cultural impact study, holding community hearings in settlements potentially affected by the pipeline. His report called for the prior settlement of Aboriginal land claims and a ten-year delay on the development of the Mackenzie valley pipeline. The report eloquently conveyed the Aboriginal peoples' conviction that the North was their own distinct homeland, and not simply a resource frontier for southern Canada. The National Energy Board, the national regulatory body, also rejected the proposed development. Only in the early 1980s was a pipeline built, and then only halfway up the valley, to Norman Wells. Today market conditions favour a full northern gas pipeline. With most Aboriginal land claims now settled, many Aboriginal people no longer oppose the project. Aboriginal people have also welcomed the recent development of diamond mines, which have brought jobs and resource revenue.

Nunavut and Denendeh

In 1979, the Aboriginal majority in the legislative assembly of the North West Territories endorsed the proposed division of the territories. The government of the North West Territories held a plebiscite on the issue in 1982, in which 56 percent of the votes cast favoured division. An Inuit constitutional forum representing Nunavut and a second forum representing the western district, or Denendeh, a northern Athapaskan word meaning "land of the people," were created to discuss how the territorial division might be accomplished. A major stumbling block became the proposed border between the two jurisdictions. To which one would the Inuvialuit, the Inuit of the western Arctic, adhere?

Despite blood ties with their fellow Inuit in the East, the Inuvialuit decided to keep their economic links with the West. The adherence of the western Arctic, rich in newly discovered oil and gas potential, to Denendeh greatly pleased the Dene and the Métis. The addition of the 2500 Inuvialuit helped raise the Aboriginal population of Denendeh in 1982 to near-equality (15 000) with that of the non-Aboriginal population (17 000). In 1987, leaders of the two constitutional forums confirmed in Iqaluit the decision to divide the North West Territories. Subsequently the North West Territories legislative assembly and the federal government approved the territorial division, which occurred on April 1, 1999.

The population of the North West Territories consisted in the late 1990s of approximately 50 000 people, split almost equally into three groups: Inuit and Inuvialuit, First Nations and Métis, and non-Aboriginals. Aboriginal people have rapidly taken control of political structures, and also fill many senior administrative posts. Aboriginal self-government, the goal of the

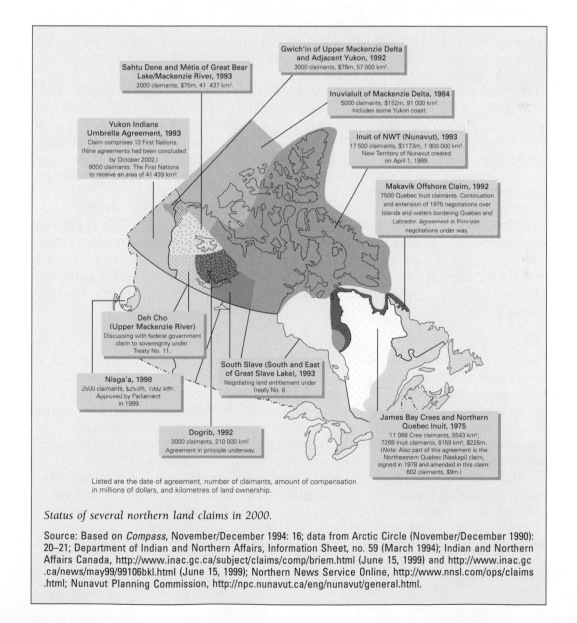

Listed are the date of agreement, number of claimants, amount of compensation in millions of dollars, and kilometres of land ownership.

Status of several northern land claims in 2000.

Source: Based on *Compass*, November/December 1994: 16; data from Arctic Circle (November/December 1990): 20–21; Department of Indian and Northern Affairs, Information Sheet, no. 59 (March 1994); Indian and Northern Affairs Canada, http://www.inac.gc.ca/subject/claims/comp/briem.html (June 15, 1999) and http://www.inac.gc.ca/news/may99/99106bkl.html (June 15, 1999); Northern News Service Online, http://www.nnsl.com/ops/claims.html; Nunavut Planning Commission, http://npc.nunavut.ca/eng/nunavut/general.html.

southern Aboriginal people, is at least partially a reality in the North West Territories, and now in Nunavut as well.

Nunavut strengthens Canada's sovereignty in the Arctic, as Canadian claims to the North West Passage are based largely on the Inuit's use and occupancy of the area. The voyages through the waters of the Arctic Archipelago by an American oil tanker in 1969, and by an American icebreaker in 1985, awakened Canadians to the uncertain status of their northern waters. The rapid advance of global warming has led to suggestions that the thinning of the ice cover in the North West Passage, if it continues, will in the near future make the Passage a viable commercial shipping route. For the Inuit, global warming in the North has already led to doubts about the continuation of such traditional activities as hunting.

In the western Arctic in 1984, COPE, the political organization of the Inuvialuit, signed the first comprehensive settlement with the federal government in the Yukon and the North West Territories. In return for surrendering their claim to the title of approximately 345 000 km^2 of land, the Inuvialuit obtained title to about 90 000 km^2 (an area larger than New Brunswick), including subsurface mineral rights for 13 000 km^2 of this area. They also received financial compensation. In the Yukon Territory, a tentative agreement between the federal government and the Council of Yukon Indians reached in 1994 provided that the Yukon's First Nations bands would retain nearly 9 percent of the territory's land mass, and would also receive $250 million in cash over a fifteen-year period.

In 1990, the First Nations and Métis of the Mackenzie valley area signed a tentative land-claim agreement. Had both Aboriginal groups ratified the agreement, they would have received surface title to an area one-third the size of Alberta and $500 million in cash. However, three of the five regional First Nations groups believed that the clause required them to give up all treaty and Aboriginal rights, and they consequently refused to ratify the agreement. Ottawa then sought to negotiate new claims with each region separately. By 2003, Parliament had settled three of the five regions' land claims.

In the eastern and central Arctic, the Tungavik Federation of Nunavut and the federal government reached an agreement-in-principle in 1990. Three years later, they signed a land-claim settlement that gave the Inuit absolute ownership of lands totalling approximately 350 000 km^2. They also received $580 million for relinquishing their Aboriginal claim to 2 000 000 km^2, an area twice the size of the province of Ontario. In 1993, Parliament passed the Nunavut Land Claims Agreement, which, in conjunction with the act to create the territory of Nunavut, redrew the map of Canada in April 1999.

In 1950 Aboriginal issues rarely entered the consciousness of non-Aboriginal Canadians. Few Aboriginal people lived in cities. Government showed scant interest in natural resource expansion into northern Aboriginal-dominated areas of Canada. Treaty rights were ignored. Canadian history texts began only with the Europeans' arrival in North America.

Now, while social and economic inequalities persist for many Aboriginal people, improvements have been made. Aboriginal and treaty rights gained protection in the Constitution of 1982. The Aboriginal population has ceased declining and is now growing at about twice the overall Canadian rate. At universities and colleges the number of Aboriginal students has soared.

Aboriginal people have gained a new political consciousness, while the attitudes of many non-Aboriginal Canadians toward them have changed markedly. In its report, the Royal Commission on Aboriginal Peoples nicely summarized what happened from the early 1970s to the mid-1990s: "Within a span of 25 years, Aboriginal peoples and their rights have emerged from the shadows, to the sidelines, to occupy centre stage."[7] The resolution of many of the issues involved in the settlement of Indian residential school claims in 2005 and 2006, and in particular the prime minister's apology on June 11, 2008, testify to a new willingness to rectify past injustices.

NOTES

1. Diamond Jenness, *The Indians of Canada* (Ottawa: King's Printer, 1932), p. 264.

2. As reported in Patrick Brethour, "Band to Withdraw from Treaty Talks," *Globe and Mail*, March 31, 2007.

3. Marianne O. Nielsen, "Introduction," in Robert A. Silverman and Marianne O. Nielsen, eds., *Aboriginal Peoples and Canadian Criminal Justice* (Toronto: Harcourt Brace, 1994), p. 3.

4. James S. Frideres and René R. Gadacz, *Aboriginal Peoples in Canada: Contemporary Conflicts*, 7th ed. (Toronto: Pearson Prentice-Hall, 2005), p. 136.

5. Campbell Clark, "Natives to Hit Ottawa with Rights Complaint," *Globe and Mail*, February 5, 2007.

6. Yale D. Belanger, *Gambling with the Future: The Evolution of Aboriginal Gaming in Canada* (Saskatoon: Purich Publishing, 2006), p. 100.

7. Canada, *Report of the Royal Commission on Aboriginal Peoples*, vol. 1, *Looking Forward, Looking Back* (Ottawa: Canada Communication Group Publishing, 1996), p. 216; quoted in Alan C. Cairns, *Citizens Plus: Aboriginal Peoples and the Canadian State* (Vancouver: UBC Press, 2000), p. 3.

BEYOND THE BOOK

Aboriginal Canada Portal

http://www.aboriginalcanada.gc.ca
A vast portal to information about Aboriginal peoples in Canada. Includes community profiles, government programs, and cultural information.

James Bay Project and the Cree

http://archives.cbc.ca/society/native_issues/topics/94
A video and audio history of the controversial James Bay hydroelectric project and the Cree people.

Delgamuukw—A Community Struggle for Aboriginal Title

http://www.upperskeena.ca/vmc/english/index.htm
This site records the legal process the Gitxsan people have pursued for greater self-governance from 1977 to 2002. Video interviews across this time period with community members and chiefs are also made available.

Native Soldiers, Foreign Battlefields

http://www.vac-acc.gc.ca/remembers/sub.cfm?source=history/other/native
A site by Veterans Affairs Canada detailing the history of participation by Aboriginal peoples in the Canadian military.

First Nations and Inuit Health

http://www.hc-sc.gc.ca/fniah-spnia/index-eng.php
Describes the health status of First Nations and Inuit peoples, as well as federal health programs focused on this population.

Residential Schools

http://www.wherearethechildren.ca/en/home.html
This site contains a 3D tour of a residential school, transcripts of interviews with individuals who lived in them, and historical photographs and other resources.

Dreamers and the Land

http://www.virtualmuseum.ca/Exhibitions/Danewajich/english/index.html
Oral histories, songs, and photos of the Doig River First Nation in the Peace River area of northeastern British Columbia.

Cree Spoken Here

Cree Spoken Here. Directed by Ernest Webb and Neil Diamond (Rezolution Pictures, 2001). A documentary about the growing resurgence of the Cree language in Northern Quebec.

Silent Words

Ruby Slipperjack, *Silent Words* (Saskatoon: Fifth House, 1992). A novel about a young Aboriginal boy in northwestern Ontario in the 1960s, and his journey of self-discovery.

RELATED READINGS

R. Douglas Francis and Donald B. Smith, eds., *Viewpoints: Readings in Canadian History* (Toronto: Thomson Nelson, 2007) contains the following articles relevant to this chapter: Alan C. Cairns, "Aboriginal Peoples in the Twenty-First Century: A Plea for Realism," pp. 545–71; and Rob Huebert, "Climate Change and Canadian Sovereignty in the North West Passage," pp. 571–81.

BIBLIOGRAPHY

Recent surveys of the history of Aboriginal Canada include Olive Patricia Dickason, with David T. McNab, *Canada's First Nations: A History of Founding Peoples from Earliest Times*, 4th ed. (Toronto: Oxford University Press, 2002), and her *A Concise History of Canada's First Nations*, adapted by Moira Calder (Toronto: Oxford University Press, 2009); and Arthur J. Ray, *I Have Lived Here since the World Began: An Illustrated History of Canada's Native People*, rev. ed. (Toronto: Key Porter, 2005). Edward S. Rogers and Donald B. Smith, eds., *Aboriginal Ontario* (Toronto: Dundurn Press, 1994), looks at the history of the First Nations in Ontario. John Sutton Lutz's *Makúk: A New History of Aboriginal-White Relations* (Vancouver: UBC Press, 2008) focuses on the Aboriginal history of British Columbia.

Studies of Canadian Indian policy include E. Brian Titley, *A Narrow Vision: Duncan Campbell Scott and the Administration of Indian Affairs in Canada* (Vancouver: University of British Columbia Press, 1986); and J.R. Miller, *Skyscrapers Hide the Heavens: A History of Indian–White Relations in Canada*, 3rd ed. (Toronto: University of Toronto Press, 2000). Harold Cardinal, *The Unjust Society: The Tragedy of Canada's Indians* (Edmonton: Hurtig, 1969; Vancouver: Douglas and McIntyre, 1999), is a Cree's indictment of Canadian Indian policy.

Three recent studies provide overviews of contemporary conditions for Aboriginal people in Canada: James S. Frideres and René R. Gadacz, *Aboriginal Peoples in Canada: Contemporary Conflicts*, 7th ed. (Toronto: Pearson Prentice-Hall, 2005); John Steckley and Bryan D. Cummins, eds., *Full Circle: Canada's First Nations*, 2nd ed. (Toronto: Pearson Prentice Hall, 2007); and J.R. Miller, *Legal Legacy: Current Native Controversies in Canada* (Toronto: McClelland and Stewart, 2004).

Analyses of contemporary Aboriginal and non-Aboriginal relations in Canada include Alan C. Cairns, *Citizens Plus: Aboriginal Peoples and the Canadian State* (Vancouver: UBC Press, 2000); and Tom

Flanagan, *First Nations? Second Thoughts* (Montreal/Kingston: McGill-Queen's University Press, 2000). Dale Turner, a First Nations academic, provides an interesting critique of both books in *This Is Not a Peace Pipe: Towards a Critical Indigenous Philosophy* (Toronto: University of Toronto Press, 2006). For books on the question of Indian residential schools, see this chapter's "Where Historians Disagree: The Debate over Indian Residential Schools, 1879–1986."

On the Métis, see Donald Purich's short survey, *The Métis* (Toronto: James Lorimer, 1988). Ethnographic background of the Aboriginal peoples of the Yukon and the North West Territories is provided in the following volumes of the *Handbook of North American Indians*: vol. 5, *The Arctic*, ed. David Damas (Washington: Smithsonian Institute, 1984), introduces the Inuit; and vol. 6, *The Subarctic*, ed. June Helm (Washington: Smithsonian Institute, 1984), introduces the Dene of the North West Territories. For discussions of Nunavut, see Donald Purich, *The Inuit and Their Land: The Story of Nunavut* (Toronto: James Lorimer, 1992); Mark Dickerson, *Whose North: Political Change, Political Development and Self-Government in the North West Territories* (Vancouver: University of British Columbia Press, 1992); and R. Quinn Duffy, *The Road to Nunavut* (Montreal/Kingston: McGill-Queen's University Press, 1988).

Overviews of the history of the North include Morris Zaslow, *The Northward Expansion of Canada, 1914–1967* (Toronto: McClelland & Stewart, 1988); and William R. Morrison, *True North: The Yukon and North West Territories* (Toronto: Oxford University Press, 1998). Georges Blondin provides an interesting Dene view of the First Nations' history in the Mackenzie valley in *When the World Was New: Stories of the Sahtu Dene* (Yellowknife: Outcrop, 1990). Post–World War II developments are reviewed in John David Hamilton, *Arctic Revolution: Social Change in the North West Territories, 1935–1994* (Toronto: Dundurn Press, 1994).

Students interested in Aboriginal politics in the past forty years are encouraged to consult as a starting point Sally M. Weaver, *Making Canadian Indian Policy: The Hidden Agenda, 1968–1970* (Toronto: University of Toronto Press, 1981). Material on Aboriginal self-government is available in John Bird, Lorraine Land, and Murray Macadam, eds., *Nation to Nation: Aboriginal Sovereignty and the Future of Canada* (Toronto: Irwin, 2002). For land issues, see Ken Coates, ed., *Aboriginal Land Claims in Canada: A Regional Perspective* (Toronto: Copp Clark Pitman, 1992). On the importance of the Supreme Court of Canada's Marshall decision in 1999, see Ken S. Coates, *The Marshall Decision and Native Rights* (Montreal/Kingston: McGill-Queen's University Press, 2000). British Columbia's Nisga'a Treaty is discussed in *The World Is Our Witness: The Historic Journey of the Nisga'a into Canada* (Calgary: Fifth House, 2000). The most complete account of the confrontation at Oka is Geoffrey York and Loreen Pindera, *People of the Pines: The Warriors and the Legacy of Oka* (Toronto: Little, Brown, 1992).

Important new publications on Aboriginal history and contemporary issues include: Blair Stonechild, *The New Buffalo: The Struggle for Aboriginal Post-Secondary Education in Canada* (Winnipeg: University of Manitoba Press, 2006); Yale D. Belanger, *Gambling with the Future: The Evolution of Aboriginal Gaming in Canada* (Saskatoon: Purich Publishing, 2006); Lorna Roth, *Something New in the Air: The Story of First Peoples Television Broadcasting in Canada* (Montreal and Kingston: McGill-Queen's University Press, 2005); *Urban Reserves: Forging New Relationships in Saskatchewan*, F. Laurie Barron and Joseph Garcea, eds. (Saskatoon: Purich Publishing Ltd., 1999); and Cora Voyageur, *Fire-Keepers of the Twenty-First Century: First Nations Women Chiefs* (Montreal: McGill-Queen's Press, 2008).

Chapter Twenty-Three

THE MAKING OF MODERN QUEBEC

TIME LINE

Year	Event
1960	The Quiet Revolution begins
1963	The Royal Commission on Education presents its report
1966	The Montreal metro (subway) system begins service
1970	The "October Crisis" shakes Quebec; Ottawa invokes the War Measures Act
1976	The Parti Québécois takes power
1977	Bill 101, the charter of the French language, is adopted
1980	A referendum is held on sovereignty-association
1990	The Meech Lake Accord dies in Manitoba's Legislative Assembly
1995	In a referendum on sovereignty, 49.4 percent of Quebeckers vote yes, 50.6 percent vote no
2003	The Quebec Liberal party defeats the Parti Québécois in provincial elections
2007	Quebec singer and international star Céline Dion ends a five-year engagement in Las Vegas
2008	Quebec City celebrates the 400th anniversary of its founding with a year-long party

Quebec underwent an era of rapid change in the years after 1960, as the province evolved into a modern, dynamic, secular society. In many ways, Quebec seemed to become more like other regions of North America. Yet, at the same time, most French speaking Quebeckers thought it important that their society reinforce its unique linguistic and cultural character.

Most historians argue that the processes of modernization and secularization began well before 1960, during World War II and even earlier. What changed in 1960 was that a new government showed a readiness to make important reforms. An increasingly interventionist Quebec state became a catalyst for change in nearly all sectors of activity, from the economy and education to health and culture. At the same time, just as was the case elsewhere in the Western world, many Quebeckers demanded and welcomed change.

What undoubtedly attracted outside attention to Quebec after 1960 was the powerful resurgence of nationalism in the province and the profound implications it had for the rest of Canada. When francophones in Quebec complained of being second-class citizens and sought increased recognition for the French language within the federal government and for the French-speaking minorities outside Quebec, English-speaking Canadians had to respond. When various political movements and parties vied with one another in claiming greater political autonomy for Quebec—and, in some cases, even sought outright independence— Canada's future appeared to be in doubt. In this regard, the aspirations of many Quebeckers appeared threatening.

Quebec after World War II

During the period 1945–1960, Quebec changed in many respects. Quebec's population, like Canada's, increased rapidly, partly because of an influx of immigrants, but most of all due to a sharply increased birth rate. The province also underwent rapid economic growth as investment—much of it foreign—accelerated. The United States not only provided a market, it also supplied development capital for resource industries such as mining. Employment in the principal manufacturing industries rose significantly, but the major gains in jobs came in the service industries. Thanks to the booming economy, Quebeckers who, like other Canadians, had endured the sacrifices of depression and war now enjoyed greater prosperity.

Traditional ideas and values began to give way. Religious practice declined, particularly in Montreal. Radio and, especially, television introduced new ideas, new norms. As historian Susan Mann explains, "Television brought the world, no longer filtered by press, priest, or politician, into Quebec's kitchens and living rooms."[1] It was incontestably a subversive influence.

Amid these changes, the very conservative Union Nationale government of Maurice Duplessis, supported by traditional elites, emphasized the importance of religious values and of respect for the established order. The Duplessis government, which began an unbroken sixteen-year reign in 1944, favoured private enterprise, encouraged the entry of foreign (largely American) capital, and kept taxes low. It built roads and bridges, especially in election years, and aided small-scale farmers, from whom it derived its firmest electoral support.

Duplessis's policies alienated Quebeckers who were committed to social change. The premier opposed militant union activity because he believed it deterred investment and brought social disorder. As a result, his government designed labour legislation to limit strikes, and even occasionally used the provincial police to protect strikebreakers or break up demonstrations. It set a low minimum wage for non-unionized workers, which affected large numbers of working women and immigrants.

Premier Maurice Duplessis, third from left at the front, at the dedication of Ste-Thérèse Bridge, August 18, 1946. To the right, the Most Rev. Joseph Charbonneau, archbishop of Montreal. Church and state cooperated to mutual benefit.

Library and Archives Canada/*The Gazette*/C-53641.

Opposition to Duplessis

In the 1950s, Duplessis's opponents became increasingly vocal. They included political foes, union leaders, a few members of the clergy, and the newspaper *Le Devoir*, as well as intellectuals such as Pierre Elliott Trudeau. Although all wanted a more liberal, modern Quebec, these critics differed considerably in their views on nationalism. Some, like Trudeau, viewed nationalism as conservative and reactionary, resulting only in ethnic conflict. Others, among them journalist André Laurendeau, later co-chair of the Royal Commission on Bilingualism and Biculturalism, saw nationalism as a potentially progressive force.

Duplessis's adversaries also attacked the Union Nationale's corrupt political and electoral behaviour. They showed how the party machine shamelessly extorted money from commercial establishments and entrepreneurs throughout the province, and then used it to buy political support so as to ensure reelection. Election day witnessed such abuses as stuffed ballot boxes and police intervention in favour of government candidates.

Progressive elements inside and outside the Roman Catholic church grew restive as the church hierarchy uncritically supported Duplessis in return for subsidies for church schools, hospitals, and social agencies. As well, critics censured the government for "reactionary" attitudes in labour relations, education, and health. Some also claimed that the government's economic-development policies resulted in a virtual giveaway of the province's natural resources to foreigners. Others blamed Duplessis for his obstinate refusal to accept federal money to finance necessary social and educational programs. They also decried the Union Nationale's neglect of urban Quebec, a failure made possible by the government's refusal to revise an outdated electoral map that blatantly favoured rural areas. And they deplored *le chef*'s attacks on the civil liberties of such groups as Jehovah's Witnesses, who were fined and imprisoned for distributing their brochures on the streets.

A Reevaluation of the Duplessis Era

In their generally harsh assessment of the Duplessis record, critics often ignored what might be considered mitigating circumstances. Patronage, although rife in the Duplessis regime, had been endemic in Canadian political life at all levels of government from the country's birth. The premier's refusal of federal funds for roads, universities, and other programs appeared negative, but how else could he fight Ottawa's intrusions into areas of provincial jurisdiction? Even Pierre Trudeau supported Duplessis's refusal to accept federal grants for higher education. Duplessis did welcome foreign capital, just as his Liberal predecessors had done. But such investment provided jobs and opened up new areas of the province for development. The government's spending policies were admittedly conservative, but they made it possible to keep taxes and debts low.

Even more telling is the fact that the Union Nationale enjoyed very substantial public support, winning four consecutive elections between 1944 and 1956. Even in 1960, a tiny shift of votes would have assured the Union Nationale's reelection. Yet by this time Duplessis, who died in 1959, and Paul Sauvé, his popular, reform-minded successor, who died after scarcely three months in office, were gone, and the once-powerful party appeared a spent force compared with the Liberals, who offered a capable new leader, a dynamic team, and a revitalized program. Perhaps many of those who, in the midst of the Quiet Revolution, viewed the Duplessis era as Quebec's *grande noirceur*, or "Dark Ages," tended to accentuate the sombre realities of the Union Nationale years in order to lend greater credence to their own heady visions and ambitious aspirations.

The Quiet Revolution

The term "Quiet Revolution" is often used to describe the years 1960–1966, during which Liberal Premier Jean Lesage and his *équipe du tonnerre* brought rapid but nonviolent change to Quebec. Nevertheless, some observers with a mind to historical continuity point out that the Union Nationale, when it returned to power in 1966, continued the reforms, as did the Liberals under Robert Bourassa after 1970. The Parti Québécois also had an agenda of reform that it implemented in 1976–1980. Thus, it might be said that the Quiet Revolution, in spite of pauses, lasted for two decades.

Liberal Reforms

Once in power, the Liberals acted to end electoral corruption. They also cleaned up much of the petty patronage practised by preceding governments. Early in its mandate, the government set up a royal commission to examine Quebec's educational system. Then it established a provincial ministry of education, thus asserting state control over a sector in which the church had hitherto played such a powerful role. Paul Gérin-Lajoie, the minister, reorganized the province's hundreds of school commissions into 55 regional districts. The government built large, "polyvalent" (comprehensive) secondary schools, improved teacher training, revised curricula, and broadened access to educational facilities. The church retreated. In fact, it had little choice, since it simply did not possess the huge financial and human resources that had to be devoted to schooling in the wake of Quebec's postwar population explosion.

Although educational reforms constituted a very important part of the Quiet Revolution, change pervaded all sectors of Quebec society. In 1962, after heated cabinet debate, René Lévesque convinced Lesage to nationalize the province's private electrical power companies and to merge them with the Crown corporation Hydro-Québec. The giant utility company contributed enormously to the province's development over the next two decades. The government also undertook a series of initiatives to promote a more dynamic francophone presence in an economy dominated by capital from outside the province. In the important sector of labour relations, it revised the labour code and, significantly, granted most employees in the public sector the right to strike. Progressive but costly measures in the field of health care included the establishment of a provincial hospitalization insurance plan, one of the Liberals' major electoral promises in 1960. Henceforth Quebeckers could receive hospital care without regard to ability to pay.

Quebec–Ottawa Relations

In his dealings with Ottawa, Lesage adopted a firm autonomist stance. He sought to end conditional subsidies, by which the federal government paid for part of the cost of a program in return for setting its conditions. He also insisted that Ottawa turn over more tax money to Quebec in view of the province's "prior needs." After the Pearson government in Ottawa unveiled its proposals for the Canada Pension Plan in 1963, Lesage successfully responded with a separate plan for Quebec—one that allowed the province to invest the enormous sums of money generated by such a scheme as it saw fit. The Caisse de dépôt et placement du Québec, set up to administer these funds, became Canada's largest investment fund.

The Quiet Revolution altered the face of Quebec dramatically. Sociologist Guy Rocher saw these years as a "cultural transformation," signifying that, beyond the structural reforms, Quebeckers' basic attitudes and values changed significantly.[2] The changes announced the end of what remained of traditional clerical society as the influence of the Roman Catholic church rapidly waned. Talented authors, musicians, and other artists captured the new spirit in their works.

Francophones also acquired a new confidence in themselves that encouraged them to challenge the inequalities they faced. They strongly criticized a Canada in which the federal bureaucracy spoke only English, in which French enjoyed no official recognition in nine provinces, and in which, even in Quebec, French-speakers carried little economic weight. Here indeed were the makings of a new nationalism.

Revolution and Reaction

Perceptions of the Quiet Revolution have varied considerably. Many in the urban middle class have viewed it as the birth of a modern Quebec, thanks to major reforms carried out in the important sectors of education, political life, the social services, and the economy. A more modern Quebec offered obvious advantages to this group.

By 2000, however, analyses had become more critical, and the almost mythical status given the Quiet Revolution by baby boomers was now contested. Perhaps institutions not linked to the state had suffered too much erosion. Perhaps citizens had become too dependent on an interventionist government. Perhaps the origins of many of the problems which Quebec faced in 2000 could be linked to the failures of the reforms that had been implemented. For example, education had been democratized, but its quality was often judged to be doubtful. The government had intervened vigorously in the economy, but failures had been numerous and costly.

Certainly, in the 1960s, the breathless pace of change upset many more conservative Quebeckers. Disadvantaged citizens in urban areas felt bypassed by the major thrust of the Quiet Revolution, as large-scale spending on education and the rapid growth of the civil service did little for them. In rural Quebec, where hundreds of small schools had been closed and children were being transported long distances by bus to large, impersonal institutions, discontent was rife. After his defeat in 1966, Lesage complained that "education beat us." His biographer, Dale C. Thomson, confirmed that change in this sector "generated more discontent than satisfaction."[3]

The Quiet Revolution engendered big government and bureaucracy, often insensitive to the needs of the individual. Higher spending brought increased taxes. Militant public-sector labour unions made use of their newly acquired right to strike. A small but vocal minority on the left also attacked Lesage, doubting the government's continuing commitment to reform. Radical nationalists viewed Lesage's objective of greater autonomy for the province as insufficient. They favoured separation, with the creation of an independent, more interventionist, French-speaking state.

Return of the Union Nationale to Power

Led by Daniel Johnson, the Union Nationale regained power in 1966, thanks to strong support in rural Quebec and to Lesage's failure to redraw the electoral map. Surprisingly, perhaps, Johnson did not attempt to undo the Liberals' reforms. In the field of education, he applied the recommendations of the royal commission on education and established the Collèges d'enseignement général et professionnel (called CEGEPs), the junior colleges that allowed Quebec students to enrol in occupational programs or to prepare for entrance into the universities. The government also established a fourth French-language university, the public Université du Quebec, which opened campuses in regional centres throughout Quebec.

During the late 1960s, the polarization of Quebec society between left and right over issues such as labour–management relations increased. Strike activity, notably in the public sector, grew dramatically, and, as elsewhere in the Western world at this time, protests shook colleges and universities.

The protest movements in Quebec took on a distinct national and cultural hue. Johnson wanted more than linguistic equality for French Canadians. In keeping with Quebec's time-honoured political tradition, he also sought greater autonomy for the province. Pointing out that Quebec, the home of more than 80 percent of French-speaking Canadians, represented one of Canada's two major ethnic communities or "nations," Johnson argued that a new Constitution should recognize this fact through an appropriate division of powers. Ottawa and most of the other provinces appeared willing, though not enthusiastic, to discuss the constitutional issue, but Pierre Trudeau, Canada's prime minister after 1968, opposed any reduction of federal authority. To Trudeau, the federal government represented all Canadians—not just English-speaking Canadians—and he believed Ottawa could, and should, act to further linguistic equality across the country.

The Debate over Language

The Quiet Revolution made conflict over language inevitable in Quebec. Many French-speaking Quebeckers felt that their language did not occupy the position it deserved in the province. While elsewhere in Canada most francophones learned English, the language of the majority, most English-speaking Quebeckers knew little French. The powerful Montreal business establishment included few French Canadians. Many stores in downtown Montreal failed to offer service to customers in French. Commercial signs in Montreal were often only in English.

Quebec's English-speaking community possessed its own institutions, including schools, newspapers, hospitals, churches, and municipal councils. Quebec was the only province where the linguistic minority—in this case, English-speaking—could function entirely in its own language. Moreover, census statistics confirmed that French Canadians in most regions outside Quebec were losing their battle against assimilation. Only in certain areas could French-speakers be assured of getting at least part of their education in French. In addition, the language of the workplace was almost always English.

Since Confederation, Quebec residents had enjoyed the right or privilege of choosing whether their children would be educated in French or English. In practice, however, the great majority of immigrants to Quebec since World War II saw little reason to learn French, and they had enrolled their children in English-language schools to assure their integration into the English-speaking community. Demographers warned that if current trends continued, Montreal would soon have an English-speaking majority. For French-speaking Quebeckers concerned about the survival of their language, "free choice" of the language of education represented a serious threat.

Many French-speakers wished the government to act in order to ensure that children of non-English origin enrolled in French schools. For its part, the English-speaking community sought the maintenance of free choice of the language of education. The government's legislation, Bill 63, recognized the right of all Quebeckers to enrol their children in

English-language schools. The law pleased the non-French population, but it unleashed storms of protest among French-speaking Quebeckers. Language thus became a full-blown political issue.

A Polarized Quebec

The 1970s were a difficult period for Quebeckers. Issues such as language, Quebec's future political status, inflation and other economic problems, union unrest, and generational conflict divided the province. In 1970, in the midst of an economic downturn, the Liberals, led by youthful economist Robert Bourassa, regained power.

The "October Crisis"

The new government soon found itself stumbling from crisis to crisis. Shortly after assuming office, it was confronted with the "October Crisis," as members of a revolutionary fringe group, the Front de libération du Québec (FLQ), kidnapped James Richard Cross, a British trade representative in Montreal, and, five days later, Pierre Laporte, a Quebec cabinet minister. (Laporte was subsequently found murdered.) Refusing to negotiate with the terrorists, Ottawa intervened: first, it dispatched 8000 heavily armed soldiers to Quebec, to guard public buildings and well-known personalities; then it invoked, for the first time in peacetime, the War Measures Act, which enabled police to arrest more than 500 "suspects" on the mere suspicion of their being sympathetic to the revolutionaries. Nearly all those arrested were eventually released, with no charges being laid against them.

Bourassa appeared equally hesitant in 1971 when, after lengthy discussions on the Constitution, he finally said no to the Victoria Charter, a package of constitutional proposals assembled by the federal government, which included an amending formula and a bill of rights. Hopes for a renewed federalism then dissipated. At the same time, Quebec Liberals faced growing animosity from public-sector unions, whose leaders spoke ominously of their desire to overthrow the government and to replace the capitalist system with socialism. Contract negotiations with the unions led to unruly public service strikes and even, in 1973, to the arrest and imprisonment of three major union leaders.

Bill 22

Nor could Bourassa avoid dealing with the complex language question. With regard to the language of education, his solution, Bill 22, gave access to English-language schools to children whose mother tongue was English and to those of non-French origin who could pass a language test. It also created enrolment quotas for English-language schools in each school district. In the end, Bill 22 pleased no one. Nationalists complained (rightly, as statistics later showed) that the law would do little to bring immigrants into French-language schools. The English-language community and ethnic groups bitterly denounced the measure as arbitrary and even totalitarian. The issue cost Bourassa support in the election of 1976, which he lost to the Parti Québécois.

Perhaps historians will judge the first Bourassa regime (1970–1976) more kindly than did contemporary observers. Bourassa appeared constantly vacillating, but Quebeckers were so sharply polarized on so many issues that major decisions risked alienating large sectors of the electorate. Defenders of the multibillion-dollar James Bay hydroelectric project have argued that its economic advantages have outweighed damage caused to the northern environment. Others point to the provincial medicare program, financed in part by federal monies, or the Quebec Charter of Rights and Freedoms, designed to combat discrimination.

The Growth of Nationalism

Quebec nationalism had been intensifying since the late 1960s, with calls for constitutional reform, stricter language legislation, and an increased francophone presence in Quebec's economy. Some English-language journalists blamed provincial politicians for undermining Quebeckers' loyalty through their aggressive stance in relations with Ottawa. They also censured French President Charles de Gaulle for the support he appeared to give the cause of independence in his celebrated cry of "Vive le Québec libre!" during a brief speech at Montreal's city hall in 1967.

While some politicians may have adopted nationalist slogans to gain votes in elections, the real roots of protest went much deeper. Nationalism has been a force in Quebec since at least the early nineteenth century; although its themes varied over time, it was not a new phenomenon in the 1960s.

"Vive la France! Vive le Québec! Vive le Québec libre!" The crowd roared with approval when French President Charles de Gaulle made his famous remark at Montreal's City Hall, July 24, 1967, in support of an independent Quebec.

CP Photo

Contemporary nationalists, however, tended to be members of the new middle class, including teachers, civil servants, and journalists. Critics have pointed out that these groups had a vested interest in nationalist causes. A bilingual civil service in Ottawa, for example, would create job openings for francophones. But these nationalists also resented the inferior position that French-speakers occupied in Canada and, to a certain extent, in Quebec itself. Events elsewhere in the world, such as the movements of national liberation in Africa and Asia, reminded many French Canadians of what they perceived to be their own condition. In one poignant autobiographical account, Nègres blancs d'Amérique (White Niggers of America in English translation), journalist and FLQ theorist Pierre Vallières portrayed French-Canadian workers as cheap labour, as exploited second-class citizens who had no control over their own society and economy.

The Rise of the Parti Québécois

In 1967, René Lévesque, dissatisfied with the Liberals' constitutional policies, quit the party; the following year, he founded the Parti Québécois (PQ), which sought to achieve independence for Quebec. Lévesque had the prestige and stature needed to rally the great majority of nationalists.

The rise of the PQ was striking, as party leaders successfully linked nationalism to a variety of social causes, thus enabling the party to build a relatively broad coalition of supporters. Unions, increasingly hostile to the Bourassa government, now came to see a sovereign Quebec as one in which workers would be better treated. Many radical feminists, for their part, saw an independent socialist republic as the key to the liberation of women. This strategy helped the Parti Québécois win an election in 1976 contested by three major parties.

In the heady enthusiasm of the moment, many péquistes saw their victory as a vote for independence. Other observers, however, viewed the PQ success largely as a vote for good government and against the scandal-ridden Bourassa regime. The PQ had, after all, promised that it would not try to separate Quebec from Canada until the decision was approved in a referendum. Most voters therefore believed that they had voted only for a change in government.

Quebec under the Parti Québécois

The new government adopted numerous reformist measures. In order to democratize Quebec politics and prevent powerful interests from "buying" favourable legislation, it overhauled the electoral law to prohibit corporate contributions to political parties. The government also introduced a no-fault system of automobile insurance, covering all personal injuries sustained. It brought in agricultural zoning legislation designed to protect increasingly scarce good farm land, much of which had disappeared as a result of urban sprawl. It also supported unions through an anti-strikebreaking law, a move that management bitterly opposed. In 1977 it amended the provincial Charter of Rights to make Quebec the first province to protect gays and lesbians from discrimination.

Bill 101

In contrast to Bourassa's vacillation on the language question, the Parti Québécois's stance seemed clear. In 1977, the National Assembly adopted Bill 101, a charter of the French language, which was intended to make Quebec as overwhelmingly French as Ontario was English. This controversial legislation opened English-language schools only to children who had at least one parent educated in English in Quebec. That "objective" criterion was used because of the impossibility of verifying a child's mother tongue, one of the conditions used by Bourassa's Bill 22, to determine admission. French, with a few exceptions, was to become the language of the workplace. Most signs were to be posted in French only. In short, the Parti

WHERE SOCIAL SCIENTISTS DISAGREE

The Origins and Effects of Quebec's Language Legislation

In 1969, the Quebec government began to adopt laws intended to increase the use of French in the province. These laws, the most important aspects of which have affected education, the workplace, and public signage, have provoked passionate debate and intense conflict.

Many social scientists have viewed the linguistic revolution as the result of the realization by the French-speaking majority of its economic inferiority in Quebec. Geographer Eric Waddell points out that, traditionally, French-speaking Quebeckers who wished to function in the world of business had to achieve fluency in English, while most anglophones remained unilingual. Quebec's language laws should thus be seen as attempts to come to terms with

the "asymmetrical" nature of French–English relations in Canada. The Canadian and North American context places the French language at a heavy disadvantage in regard to English. Even in Quebec, the English language enjoys a visibility that French does not possess outside Quebec.[1] In marked contrast to Waddell's reasoning, the federal Official Languages Act places all minorities on a theoretically equal footing.

Political scientist Richard Handler also asserts that language laws were "aimed at redressing the economic balance of power within Quebec."[2] Likewise, in a study covering a portion of the 1980s, Marc V. Levine notes the extent of the francophone reconquest of

Montreal's economy and concludes that Quebec's language legislation made an important contribution to this dramatic change.[3]

The new and obviously less powerful status of Quebec's anglophones has been the subject of several studies. Many anglophones left Quebec in the 1970s, presumably motivated by political and linguistic fears. In a controversial study, however, sociologist Uli Locher concludes that, even after the adoption of Bill 101 in 1977, anglophones were leaving Quebec primarily because of the lure of greater prosperity in Toronto and the West.[4] Most observers judge that anglophones remaining in Quebec still enjoy far greater rights and privileges than most francophones do elsewhere in Canada. But political scientist Garth Stevenson cautions that Quebec's more generous treatment of its minority cannot be explained solely by the goodwill of the majority. Rather, it is a logical consequence of the demographic balance in Canada and in North America as well as of the vast economic power that anglophones wielded in Quebec until recent times.[5]

Philosopher Charles Taylor attempts to define the basis for the divergent views of anglophones and francophones on the language question. He sees most anglophones, like Americans, putting forth a liberal view of society in which individual rights must take precedence over collective goals. Provisions for bilingualism in federal law can be justified in terms of individual rights: francophones across Canada, at least theoretically, can obtain federal government services in French. Francophones tend to espouse a collective goal: to ensure that there will still be francophones in the next generation. Taylor believes that Quebeckers also share liberal values but that, in order to retain their identity, they distinguish between fundamental liberties, which should never be infringed, and privileges, which are only important.[6]

Many English-speakers decry the very existence of Quebec's language legislation. At the same time, francophones will always feel culturally insecure because of the enormous pressures of the continent's English environment. For example, the publication in 2007 of census statistics showing that fewer than 50 percent of Montrealers had French as their mother tongue brought new worries about the long-term future of the language. The census also showed a continued decline of French-language minorities outside Quebec. Because of the emotional nature of the question, it will remain a subject of passionate discussion and an important challenge for Quebec and Canadian society.

1. Eric Waddell, "State, Language and Society: The Vicissitudes of French in Quebec and Canada," in Alan C. Cairns and Cynthia Williams, eds., *The Politics of Gender, Ethnicity, and Language in Canada* (Toronto: University of Toronto Press, 1986), p. 88.

2. Richard Handler, *Nationalism and the Politics of Culture in Quebec* (Madison: University of Wisconsin Press, 1988), p. 170.

3. Marc V. Levine, *The Reconquest of Montreal: Language Policy and Social Change in a Bilingual City* (Philadelphia: Temple University Press, 1990).

4. Uli Locher, *Les anglophones de Montréal: émigration et évolution des attitudes, 1978–1983* (Québec: Conseil de la langue française, 1988).

5. Garth Stevenson, *Unfulfilled Union: Canadian Federalism and National Unity*, 3rd ed. (Toronto: Gage, 1989).

6. Charles Taylor, "Shared and Divergent Values," in Ronald L. Watts and Douglas M. Brown, eds., *Options for a New Canada* (Toronto: University of Toronto Press, 1991), pp. 53–76.

Québécois hoped to obtain by law for French in Quebec what the "free market" and "free choice" assured English elsewhere in Canada.

The new minority status of Quebec anglophones necessitated often-painful adjustments. Anglophones launched successful legal challenges to certain clauses of Bill 101, which weakened the legislation substantially. Many Anglo-Quebeckers, including a large proportion of young adults convinced that they could have a better future elsewhere, left the province. At the same time, a large number of corporate head offices in Montreal, complaining of the language legislation, high taxes, the dangers of separatism, and poor relations with unions, decided to move westward, mainly to Toronto.

Among the English-speakers who chose to stay in Quebec, bilingualism increased significantly. (Bilingualism outside Quebec, among English-speakers, grew slowly but remained largely an elitist phenomenon.) At the same time, Quebec's "Frenchness" was attenuated by the fact that nearly 40 percent of the majority French-language group reported that they could also speak English. Many Quebeckers whose mother tongue was neither French nor English reported that they were trilingual. In response, *The Globe and Mail* suggested that Trudeau's dream of a bilingual Canada might endure only in Quebec.

The Referendum Debate, 1980

Of even greater interest to Canadians than the language question was Quebec's referendum on political sovereignty, which would decide Quebec's—and Canada's—future. In a shrewdly worded question, which implicitly recognized Quebeckers' divided loyalties, the PQ government asked voters for a mandate to negotiate political sovereignty within an economic association with the rest of Canada. In the hope of obtaining majority support, the government appealed both to Quebeckers' desire for change and, by asking voters to give it only the right to negotiate, to their more conservative instincts. No unilateral declaration of independence would follow a positive vote. The campaign debate was fierce, dividing families and friends. Claude Ryan, Robert Bourassa's successor as the Quebec Liberal leader, led the *non* forces. Prime Minister Trudeau intervened late in the campaign, promising unspecified constitutional change if Quebeckers said no.

On May 20, 1980, Quebeckers defeated the referendum proposal by a 60–40 margin. While almost all non-French-speaking Quebeckers voted no, the French-speaking population split virtually in half. Analyses of the vote showed that the older age groups, the economically disadvantaged, and those with relatively little education tended to vote *non*. Those in the younger age groups and people with more education and higher incomes more often answered *oui*.

The 1980s: The Wheel Turns

The mood of the early 1980s in Quebec was pessimistic. The 1981–1982 recession dramatically cut employment in the resource and manufacturing industries. Unions suffered membership losses as well as rising unpopularity among a public weary of strikes and agitation. Universities condemned the government's stringent cutbacks in financing.

Nor did the outcome of the constitutional debate cause much rejoicing in Quebec. The federal government's proposals gave Quebec none of the powers that its provincial governments had consistently claimed since 1960. Moreover, Ottawa managed to isolate Quebec by playing it off against the other nine provinces. The proposals became law despite Quebec's objections when Queen Elizabeth II proclaimed the new constitution on April 17, 1982. Quebec was legally bound by the terms of the document but it lacked moral legitimacy in the province.

A severe budget crisis, exacerbated by the harsh recession of the early 1980s, forced the Quebec government to reduce services and to increase taxes. Its draconian measures to recover part of the salary increases that had been granted to public service workers alienated the unions. Moreover, the era of large-scale spending and government interventionism had passed as budget deficits increased and a new conservative mood gained strength throughout the Western world, including Quebec. Individualism was celebrated as the new cult, and business leaders became its high priests.

Nationalism in Decline

Younger Quebeckers now worried more about finding jobs than about championing political causes. As nationalist sentiment weakened, Premier René Lévesque decided to put aside, at least for the foreseeable future, the issue of sovereignty-association, a decision that provoked a dramatic revolt within the party and, in 1985, Lévesque's own resignation. In the elections held shortly afterwards, the party lost power to the Liberals under their resurrected leader, Robert Bourassa. Rapid economic growth now made Quebec a leader among Canada's provinces. Reassured by the new political stability, investment accelerated and business flourished.

While the Bourassa government prided itself on offering competent administration, it failed to exercise leadership with regard to environmental issues. Paper mills, aluminum manufacturing plants, and other industries continued to foul the water and air with chemical pollutants, often in flagrant violation of existing regulations. Agricultural wastes, fertilizers, and pesticides polluted the province's rivers. Several incidents involving fires deliberately set in toxic waste and tire dumps dramatized both the dangers of pollution and the government's neglect.

The Revival of Nationalism

Those who had proclaimed nationalism's demise in the early 1980s proved poor prophets. By the end of the decade, both the language issue and Quebec's future links with Canada again became important public topics. The language issue emerged with renewed force in late 1988 over the relatively minor issue of public signs. When the Supreme Court of Canada found Quebec's sign law (which required French-only signs) to be in violation of the freedom of expression provisions of both the federal and the Quebec charters of rights, Bourassa had to act. The Supreme Court had admitted that signs solely in English could be prohibited and that the government could require "the predominant display of the French language." Supporters of French-only signs argued that Quebec needed a French "face" in order to persuade new immigrants to integrate into the francophone community. Bourassa's new law still required French-only signs outdoors, while authorizing bilingual signs within certain stores. Quebec's, and Canada's, anglophones protested vehemently. Passions cooled over time and, in 1993, the Bourassa government adopted more liberal legislation.

Assessing the overall impact of Quebec's controversial language legislation since the early 1970s is a difficult task. Certainly by the 1990s, Montreal "looked" much more French than it had in 1970. Also, almost all immigrant children were enrolled in French schools, but, in many of these, they constituted an overwhelming majority and had little contact with Quebeckers whose mother tongue was French. Thanks in part to the exodus of many anglophones, more francophones now held upper-level positions in business. More workers earned their living in French, but language legislation did not cover small enterprises, many of whose employees were obliged to work in English. Adversaries of Bill 101 warned that language legislation would hurt economic development and tarnish Quebec's reputation, since English-language media gave abundant publicity to anglophone complaints. But what other solution would have made it possible to promote the use of French energetically without undermining the important, even dominant, role of English in Quebec, particularly in the province's economy?

Meech Lake

The constitutional issue followed the linguistic debate. In 1986, the provincial premiers agreed to undertake a "Quebec round" of negotiations, to bring about "Quebec's full and active participation in the Canadian federation" before moving on to other concerns. Quebec put forth five conditions, which included the recognition of the province as a "distinct society" and greater powers with regard to immigration. In June 1987, Prime Minister Brian Mulroney and the ten provincial premiers met in Ottawa and, after arduous all-night negotiations, gave unanimous assent to an accord. Robert Bourassa proclaimed that Quebec could now adhere to the Constitution "with dignity and honour."

In the months that followed, the federal government and eight provinces, beginning with Quebec, ratified the proposals. Then the accord began to unravel as newly elected premiers in the two remaining provinces, New Brunswick and Manitoba, arguing that they were not bound by their predecessors' signatures, demanded substantial modifications. Subsequently, Newfoundland rescinded its approval. Groups representing women, Aboriginal peoples, and ethnic associations objected that their own concerns had not been addressed. Many Anglo-Canadians, ignoring the often unenviable fate of francophone minorities throughout Canada, said they wanted no part of a "distinct society" that would be free to "oppress" its anglophone minority. Other critics, including former prime minister Pierre Trudeau, argued that the Meech Lake Accord would seriously weaken federal authority.

Protracted negotiations among the premiers did produce an add-on agreement that satisfied some critics. Then, however, a dramatic event took place in the Manitoba legislature: a Cree NDP member, with the support of Aboriginal leaders from across Canada, denounced the accord for ignoring the rights of Canada's Aboriginal peoples and signalled his intention to use the rules of parliamentary procedure to kill it. On June 23, 1990, as the deadline for approval expired, the Meech Lake Accord died.

Most Canadians outside Quebec felt relief at the demise of the accord. In Quebec, however, nationalists, including many federalists, perceived the failure of the agreement as signifying English Canada's refusal to accommodate even the province's minimal concerns. Independence now seemed the only possible choice for those who could not accept the status quo. Several federal members of parliament from Quebec quit their parties to join a new group, the Bloc Québécois, which favoured Quebec's secession from Canada. To deflect criticism of his government, Robert Bourassa set up a commission to study Quebec's constitutional future, and promised to hold a referendum. Political scientist Vincent Lemieux has argued that Bourassa wished to use the "threat of independence" to elicit new propositions for a reform of Canadian federalism, and thus make it possible to "avoid independence."[4]

Constitutional Impasse

The federal government did indeed decide to reopen the constitutional issue. This time, Aboriginal peoples, among other groups, played a far more important role in the discussions. Quebec, however, refused to participate in the talks until the final round of negotiations, held in Charlottetown. Quebeckers reacted without enthusiasm to the ensuing agreement. In a referendum held in October 1992, voters in six provinces, including Quebec, rejected the Charlottetown agreement and constitutional negotiations ceased. Sociologist Maurice Pinard pointed out that polls showed a strong majority of Quebeckers felt that the accord offered too little to Quebec; in English Canada, nearly 60 percent of voters felt it gave Quebec too much.[5]

The Referendum of 1995

The seeming impossibility of reaching any constitutional agreement with the rest of Canada favoured an increase in nationalist sentiment in Quebec. More importantly, Jean Chrétien, who became Canada's prime minister in 1993, was perceived by even moderate nationalists as rigidly opposed to Quebec's claims for greater autonomy. In the election of 1993, the nationalist Bloc Québécois proved far more popular than Chrétien's Liberals within the province. The return to power of the Parti Québécois in 1994 made a new referendum certain.

In this referendum, held on October 30, 1995, the provincial government asked electors if they wished Quebec to become "sovereign," after having formally offered Canada a new economic and political partnership. The federalist *non* won a razor-thin victory, with only 50.6 percent of the valid ballots cast, in a consultation in which fully 93 percent of eligible voters participated. Well over 60 percent of French-speakers favoured the *oui* option. Anglophones, allophones, and members of First Nations communities—groups which shared none of the discontent or the aspirations of the francophones—voted no with near-unanimity.

About 200 000 people marched in Montreal's St. Jean Baptiste Day parade, June 24, 1994. The lead banner proclaims, "Next year—My country."

CP Photo (Ryan Remiorz)

Ottawa's Strategy toward Quebec

The "love" shown toward Quebec by large numbers of English-speaking Canadians, who invaded Montreal just before the referendum for an enthusiastic pro-Canada demonstration, evaporated rapidly after the vote. Many reacted with bitterness to the outcome of the

referendum, feeling that separation was now inevitable and that it was time to prepare to drive a hard bargain with a seceding Quebec that would deprive the province of important parts of its territory. In Ottawa, the Chrétien government sought legal means to block secession. In 1998, in an advisory opinion suffused with Solomon-like wisdom, the Supreme Court of Canada affirmed unanimously that no province enjoyed a legal right to secede unilaterally. If, however, Quebeckers repudiated the existing constitutional order unambiguously in regard to the question asked and to the support received, then all parties had an obligation to negotiate constitutional change in good faith.[6] The Court thus recognized that Quebec's constitutional future was a political question. The Chrétien government then adopted, in 1999, legislation to give Ottawa the right to determine unilaterally the conditions under which it would recognize the result of any future referendum.

Relations were sour between Quebec Premier Lucien Bouchard and Canadian Prime Minister Jean Chrétien after the close referendum result in October 1995.

Shaun Best/Reuters

Ottawa also sought to increase the federal government's visibility in Quebec. Lucrative contracts went to advertising agencies which were generous donors to the Liberal Party. While the RCMP launched an investigation into allegations of political favouritism and mismanagement of public funds, Prime Minister Chrétien dismissed evidence of impropriety with an appeal to patriotism: maintaining Canadian unity was well worth "the theft of a few million dollars." Later, when a federal commission inquired into the so-called "sponsorship scandal," detailed revelations of money laundering and false accounting tarnished the entire Liberal party and led to a collapse of its support among Quebec francophones. In elections held in 2006, the Liberals, now headed by former finance minister Paul Martin, placed third, after the first-place Bloc Québécois, which promoted sovereignty for Quebec, and Stephen Harper's resurgent Conservatives.

Contemporary Politics

Yet the fervour for independence was clearly diminishing. Sociologists Simon Langlois and Gilles Gagné found an explanation for the decline in the apparent demobilization of the most ardent sovereigntists—middle-class francophones, 70 percent of whom had supported independence in 1995.[7] As the birth of an independent Quebec seemed to recede into a distant future, this group found little reason to support the Parti Québécois. Support for the PQ weakened as voters blamed the government for mismanaging health care, for forcing the amalgamation of cities and their suburbs (Montreal expanded to comprise the entire island of Montreal in 2002), and for the stagnation of certain regions of the province. In 2003, wanting change, they gave a majority of seats to the federalist Liberals, led by Jean Charest, who promised to improve health care, authorize the secession of suburbs from the new cities, reduce taxes, and decrease state intervention.

Four years later, in 2007, a strong majority of voters now expressed dissatisfaction with the Charest government. They criticized the government for its failure to honour its promises to lower taxes substantially. Most Montreal suburbs, especially the wealthier, majority English-speaking towns, did secede from the city but the Charest government did not give them the autonomy they had previously enjoyed; a new layer of supra-municipal government, put in place by the Liberals to coordinate island-wide services, functioned to no one's liking. In spite of increased spending on health care, Quebeckers generally felt that services had not improved. Plans to reform and streamline the provincial civil service were abandoned after resistance by unions. When the forest sector needed help, Charest acquiesced, but government assistance could not counter the severe crisis faced by the industry.

Dissatisfaction with Charest did not boost the fortunes of the Parti Québécois. Most Quebeckers did not want a new referendum on independence, a major promise of the PQ; they saw immediate concerns, particularly health care, as more important. More socially conservative francophones, feeling that neither the Liberals nor the Parti Québécois represented them, now preferred a third party, the Action démocratique du Québec (ADQ), with its populist anti-elite electoral platform. On constitutional issues, the ADQ took a vaguely autonomist stance, supporting neither independence nor unconditional federalism. Charest did win reelection in 2007, but with only a minority of seats in the National Assembly. The ADQ formed the official opposition, seeing itself as a government in waiting. The Parti Québécois placed third; its members then selected, as new leader, Pauline Marois, who had occupied an array of cabinet portfolios, in the hope that she would breathe new life into the party. By 2008, as the Liberal government successfully avoided controversial issues, Charest's popularity rose while polls showed the ADQ now in third place.

Quebec's Economy since 1990

Economic recession after 1991 provoked a substantial rise in unemployment. Many jobs in inefficient, formerly tariff-protected industries such as textiles and furniture disappeared in the face of competition from imports.

Then, in the mid-1990s, the provincial economy rebounded. Free trade stimulated exports strongly. The provincial government, for its part, actively sought investments. The disastrous ice storm of January 1998, which deprived three million Quebeckers of electricity, some for lengthy periods of time, triggered a period of particularly rapid growth linked to the restoration and upgrading of the provincial electricity grid. By 1999, increased revenues and cuts in services made it possible for the government to eliminate the province's budget deficit and even to lower taxes, thereby earning the approval of bond rating agencies, the business establishment, and undoubtedly taxpayers, but displeasing those who found services less accessible.

After 2000, Montreal underwent exceptional economic expansion, stimulated by growth in such sectors as aeronautics, biotechnology, information technology, pharmaceuticals, and telecommunications. Unemployment levels fell, and Quebeckers' per capita incomes came closer to Ontario levels. According to economist Pierre Fortin, the increasing productivity of the Quebec workforce, due to improved technology, research and development, and educational advances, explained the province's improved performance.[8] At the same time, General Motors closed its huge plant in Boisbriand, north of Montreal, the only automobile plant in the province. After 2005, the rising Canadian dollar (which went from 62 cents in American currency in 2002 to a high of US $1.10 in late 2007) hurt manufacturing exports. The forest industry was hit especially hard, and several regions suffered substantial out-migration. Bright spots in the economy have included new hydroelectric projects in the north, government spending on public transportation and roads, the construction of methane gas port facilities on the St. Lawrence River, and, in Montreal, the creation of many new jobs in information technologies and video games publishing.

Population

Recent demographic trends increased concern for Quebec's future. The 2006 census showed that Quebec was still growing, though at a much slower rate than Ontario, Alberta, and British Columbia. As in other provinces, birth rates remained well below levels necessary for population replacement. Governments attempted to encourage couples to have more children by offering baby bonuses, tax-supported daycare services, and generous parental leave. As well, migration within Canada hurt Quebec, as more people left the province than entered it. Quebec did put considerable effort into attracting immigrants from abroad, but as a French-speaking province in English-speaking North America, it suffered inevitably from a competitive disadvantage with regard to neighbouring Ontario.

Language and Culture in Quebec Today

Three decades after the adoption of Bill 101, the French language charter, most francophones agreed that the situation of French within Quebec remained precarious. Increased trade relations with the United States meant that English assumed rising importance for francophones; indeed, large numbers used mainly English at work. While the children of new immigrants to Quebec normally attended French-language primary and secondary schools, as required by Bill 101, they tended to frequent English-language institutions of higher education. For a large number, English remained the language of social mobility. Many francophones agreed. Enrolment in

English-language primary and secondary schools increased after 1992, as francophone children of mixed marriages entered them. Reports showed that many French-speaking high school graduates had poor mastery of the language. Decidedly, the survival of the French language, even in Quebec, would always be in question.

Culture in an Era of Globalization

What effects did globalization, with its disappearing frontiers, have on Quebec culture? Well beyond the borders of Quebec, stage director and playwright Robert Lepage, lyricist Luc Plamondon, film-writer Denys Arcand (who won an Oscar in 2004), and the Cirque du Soleil, a troupe of acrobats and other entertainers, gained fame. So did such popular singers as Lynda Lemay, Pierre Lapointe, Pierre Garand, better known by his stage name, Garou, and especially Céline Dion. Although American cultural products, such as the film *Titanic*, attracted Quebeckers quite as much as they fascinated other Canadians, in Quebec the hockey film *Les Boys* ran neck-and-neck with it. For some, globalization was perhaps a threat to Quebec's distinct culture; for others, it obviously presented new opportunities.

At the same time, in modern Quebec's pluralistic society, allophone novelists made important cultural contributions. Not surprisingly, they often emphasized themes linked to the

Canada's francophone population, 2006. Note the French-speaking community's strong majority position in Quebec, but minority status (less than 5 percent of the total population) in all other provinces and territories, with the exception of New Brunswick.

Source: Statistics Canada, "Mother Tongue: Canada, Provinces, Territories," 2006 Census.

A HISTORICAL PORTRAIT

Céline Dion and the Global Village

In the 1960s and 1970s, stars such as Gilles Vigneault, Jean-Pierre Ferland, and Pauline Julien, many of them ardent nationalists, rose to fame in Quebec, although on occasion they performed abroad. Since the 1980s, however, many of Quebec's most talented artists have quite literally gone global, working in Montreal, Toronto, Los Angeles, Paris, London, and elsewhere. Céline Dion epitomized this new tendency.

Dion became a child star in Quebec in the 1980s. In 1984, she sang for Pope John Paul II at Olympic Stadium in Montreal. In 1988, she won first place at the annual Eurovision competition, Europe's Olympics-of-song contest, held at Dublin and viewed by 600 million telespectators. In 1993, she won Juno awards in Toronto, singing in recently learned English and, in the words of gushing critics, bridging the cultural gap between Canada's "two solitudes." In 1997, she performed two songs for the Academy Awards to an audience that reportedly numbered one billion people. She also picked up two Grammy Awards in New York City. In her acceptance speech, she addressed Quebeckers in French, a gesture that one *Globe and Mail* columnist thought worth more than "a trillion distinct society clauses."

By 2007, Dion, whom *Time* magazine proclaimed a "global diva," had sold more than 200 million albums, featuring dozens of megahits. Biographer Barry Grills saw her as building cultural bridges from Quebec to the rest of the planet: she occupied "a huge international territory, while still maintaining a direct connection to the culture

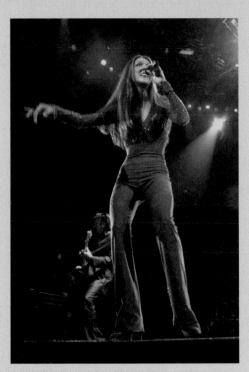

By 1983 Quebec singer Céline Dion was already winning awards. She would go on to become an international diva.

CP Photo/AP Photo/Express News (Kevin Geil)

where, for her, it all began."[1] Yet Dion asserted, in an interview, "I am very much Americanized." In this regard, she seemed to voice the attraction to the American Dream many Quebeckers have felt throughout their history. In 2002, "Canada's biggest cultural export," as *The Globe and Mail* styled Dion, came out of retirement and released a new English-language album, *A New Day Has Come*; thanks in part to lavish publicity, it immediately became a top hit. A *New York Times* critic hypothesized that Dion's success came from her never being specific: the more general and abstract her message, the more people were able to relate what was said to the particularities of their own experience. Here undoubtedly was globalization in action. In 2003, Dion settled in Las Vegas, where, until the end of 2007, she gave more than 700 shows to three million spectators, performing in an enormous replica of the Colosseum specially constructed for her in Caesar's Palace.

1. Barry Grills, *Falling into You: The Story of Céline Dion* (Kingston, ON: Quarry Press, 1997), pp. 9–10.

pain of exile and the hopes for a better life in the new land. Italian-born Marco Micone told Quebeckers in a poem, *Speak What*: "We are a hundred peoples come from afar to share your dreams and your winters." Haitian-born Dany Laferrière, Sergio Kokis, born in Brazil, and Abla Farhoud, from Lebanon, are among the voices "from afar" who have enriched contemporary francophone literature.

The Environment

Through the 1990s, air pollution, much of it originating from industries and coal-fired electric power stations in Ontario and in the American Midwest, continued to degrade Quebec's lakes and forests, and worsened the problem of urban smog. Agricultural pollution of water remained a grave problem, but governments feared that new regulations on farm practices would alienate rural voters. Industrial fouling of the St. Lawrence River and its tributaries also continued, but polluting industries were also important employers. The survival of hundreds of lakes in southern Quebec was jeopardized by lawn fertilizers, wastewater, and sediment from erosion which washed into the water. South of the St. Lawrence River, farmers cut down large swathes of remaining forest to make more fields to produce more corn to feed more pigs or to obtain land for spreading manure from huge pig farms. The power of the so-called "pig barons" was portrayed in 2001 in a film, *Bacon*.

By 2000, the pendulum began to swing toward greater concern for environmental degradation. Environmentalists warned that the province's northern forests were being cut down at a rate substantially in excess of their capacity to regenerate. Well-known pop singer Richard Desjardins even produced a film, *L'Erreur boréale*, denouncing what he saw as the collusion between timber companies and the government that allowed clearcutting of enormous tracts of land with no concern for the survival of forest ecosystems. Finally, after a government-commissioned report called for a substantial reduction of logging quotas, the provincial government did impose lower limits but had to face substantial opposition from companies and workers who blamed government policy and environmentalists rather than a declining resource and a high dollar for their plight.

Like people elsewhere, Quebeckers discussed climate change and ways to reduce the production of greenhouse gases. The Liberal government of Jean Charest launched a plan, financed largely with federal money, whose objective was to enable Quebec to respect the objectives fixed by the Kyoto Protocol. Quebec's contribution to gas emissions was already far below the Canadian average since the province had no oil or gas industry and depended almost entirely on hydroelectricity. Although the government invested in public transport to encourage commuters to leave their cars home, it promised, at the same time, to build more expressways as well as a new highway bridge across the river from Montreal to Laval. Quebec also encouraged the establishment of wind-power farms, although some citizens complained that the huge turbines might have a negative impact on the spectacular scenery that attracted so many tourists.

In the name of conserving biodiversity, the government promised to create new protected areas from which logging and mining operations would be excluded, mostly in northern forests, but it delayed acting in the face of strong opposition from industrial lobbies. Environmentalists also urged Quebec to act to protect the province's remaining wetlands, which performed enormous services as filters and sponges for water. Nearly three-quarters of the wetlands of southern Quebec had been destroyed since 1975. Yet governments, particularly municipal, tended to heed the wishes of developers, interested in draining and building, in view of the additional tax monies that new housing, shopping centres, and industrial parks would procure. Environmental organizations themselves were frequently accused of attempting to block important development projects that could create jobs and wealth.

Although Quebec will remain predominantly French-speaking at least in the foreseeable future, continued assimilation means that French-speakers outside the province will form an ever more tiny minority. Canada's commitment to bilingualism and to equal status for its francophone citizens risks being called into question. Yet regardless of the province's constitutional and linguistic evolution, Quebeckers, like other Canadians, will have to find solutions to the problems posed by living in an increasingly pluralistic society. Quebeckers, again like other Canadians, must continue to work for an accommodation with the Aboriginal peoples to settle long-standing grievances. Recent steps in this direction include the "Paix des Braves," a new accord signed in 2002 with the northern Cree, as well as an agreement signed in 2007 to give the Innu control over a vast region in northern Quebec called Nunavik. Moreover, as the hearings of a government commission on "accommodation practices related to cultural differences" have demonstrated, much energy will have to be directed to integrating new immigrants into the fabric of francophone society. In addition, all Quebeckers, regardless of language or origin, will have to meet the challenges and pay the price of creating and preserving an environment in which human life can continue to flourish.

NOTES

1. Susan Mann, *The Dream of Nation: A Social and Intellectual History of Quebec* (Montreal/Kingston: McGill-Queen's University Press, 2002 [1982]), p. 284.

2. Guy Rocher, *Le Québec en mutation* (Montreal: Hurtubise, 1973), p. 18.

3. Dale C. Thomson, *Jean Lesage and the Quiet Revolution* (Toronto: Macmillan, 1984), p. 309.

4. Vincent Lemieux, "Les partis et l'idée de souveraineté," in Maurice Pinard, Robert Bernier, and Vincent Lemieux, *Un combat inachevé* (Ste-Foy, QC: Presses de l'Université du Québec, 1997), p. 18.

5. Maurice Pinard, "Les fluctuations du mouvement indépendantiste depuis 1980," in Maurice Pinard et al., *Un combat inachevé* (Ste-Foy, QC: Presses de l'Université du Québec, 1997), p. 97.

6. John T. Saywell, *The Lawmakers: Judicial Power and the Shaping of Canadian Federalism* (Toronto: University of Toronto Press, 2002), p. 306.

7. Gilles Gagné and Simon Langlois, *Les raisons fortes: nature et signification de l'appui à la souveraineté du Québec* (Montreal: Presses de l'Université de Montréal, 2002).

8. Pierre Fortin, "L'évolution de l'économie depuis 1960: le Québec a comblé la moitié de son retard sur l'Ontario," *Le Devoir*, March 27, 2000.

BEYOND THE BOOK

First Nations Lands History in Quebec

http://www.lsd.nrcan.gc.ca/english/fh_e.asp
A history of First Nations territorial lands in Quebec. Complete with detailed maps reflecting changes over time, and descriptions of historical changes to territory.

Quebec Elections: 1960–2007

http://archives.cbc.ca/politics/elections/topics/651
Digitized television and radio archives describe the history of elections in Quebec from 1960 to 2007.

1995 Quebec Referendum

http://archives.cbc.ca/politics/federal_politics/topics/1891
A video retrospective of the events of the 1995 Quebec Referendum.

Hydro-Québec

http://www.canadianeconomy.gc.ca/english/economy/1962HydroQuebec.html
A detailed history of Hydro-Québec, a major economic entity in the province.

Bill 101

http://www.cbc.ca/news/background/bill101
An historical backgrounder describing events leading to Bill 101, and a look back since.

Medical Services and the 1998 Ice Storm

http://www.cmaj.ca/cgi/reprint/158/4/520.pdf
An account in the *Canadian Medical Association Journal* of the health effects of the 1998 "ice storm of the century," and its impact on the availability of medical services to citizens.

Breaking Point

The documentary *Breaking Point: Canada/Quebec — The 1995 Referendum* (CBC, 2005) tells the story of the 1995 Quebec referendum from the perspective of the people who lived it.

René Lévesque

René Lévesque: The Miniseries (CBC, 2006); a dramatization of the life of Lévesque.

October 1970

The miniseries *October 1970* (CBC, 2006) tells the story of the October Crisis.

RELATED READINGS

In R. Douglas Francis and Donald B. Smith, eds., *Viewpoints: Readings in Canadian History* (Toronto: Thomson Nelson, 2007), the article by Alain-G. Gagnon, "Québec-Canada's Constitutional Dossier," pp. 525–40, covers political aspects of this topic.

BIBLIOGRAPHY

Although considerable scholarly material on Quebec exists in English, students wishing to study Quebec society need a reading knowledge of French. General syntheses include Susan Mann, *The Dream of Nation: A Social and Intellectual History of Quebec* (Montreal/Kingston: McGill-Queen's University Press, 2002 [1982]); John Dickinson and Brian Young, *A Short History of Quebec*, 4th ed. (Montreal/Kingston: McGill-Queen's University Press, 2008); and Paul-André Linteau et al., *Quebec since 1930* (Toronto: James Lorimer, 1991). A dispassionate interpretation is available in Kenneth McRoberts, *Quebec: Social Change and Political Crisis*, 3rd ed. with a postscript (Toronto: Oxford University Press, 1999). Ronald Rudin proposes a provocative analysis of Quebec historiography in *Making History in Twentieth-Century Quebec* (Toronto: University of Toronto Press, 1997).

Successive political figures are examined in Conrad Black, *Render Unto Caesar: The Life and Legacy of Maurice Duplessis* (Toronto: Key Porter, 1998); Richard Jones, *Duplessis and the Union Nationale Administration* (Ottawa: Canadian Historical Association, 1983); Dale C. Thomson, *Jean Lesage and the Quiet Revolution* (Toronto: Macmillan, 1984); L. Ian MacDonald, *From Bourassa to Bourassa: Wilderness to Restoration*, 2nd ed. (Montreal/Kingston: McGill-Queen's University Press, 2002); and Graham Fraser, *René Lévesque and the Parti Québécois in Power*, 2nd ed. (Montreal/Kingston: McGill-Queen's University Press, 2002). Studies of constitutional issues include Guy Laforest, *Trudeau and the End of a Canadian Dream* (Montreal/Kingston: McGill-Queen's University Press, 1995); and Alan Cairns, *Charter versus Federalism: The Dilemmas of Constitutional Reform* (Montreal/Kingston: McGill-Queen's University Press, 1992). See also Alain-G. Gagnon, *Québec: State and Society*, 3rd ed. (Peterborough, ON: Broadview Press, 2004).

Innumerable works exist on the subject of Quebec's independence. For contrasting viewpoints, see for example Christian Dufour, *A Canadian Challenge: Le défi québécois* (Lantzville, BC: Oolichan Books, 1990); and Robert A. Young, *The Secession of Quebec and the Future of Canada*, rev. ed. (Montreal/Kingston: McGill-Queen's University Press, 1998). In *Misconceiving Canada: The Struggle for National Unity* (Toronto: Oxford University Press, 1997), Kenneth McRoberts is highly critical of Pierre Trudeau's policies for national unity. Analyses of the language question include Graham Fraser, *Sorry, I Don't Speak French: Confronting the Canadian Crisis That Won't Go Away* (Toronto: McClelland & Stewart, 2006); and Garth Stevenson, *Community Besieged: The Anglophone Minority and the Politics of Quebec* (Montreal/Kingston: McGill-Queen's University Press, 1999).

The experience of women in Quebec is covered in Micheline Dumont et al., *Quebec Women: A History* (Toronto: Women's Press, 1987). Cultural development is examined in Richard Handler, *Nationalism and the Politics of Culture in Quebec* (Madison: University of Wisconsin Press, 1988). On Quebec society see Simon Langlois et al., *Recent Social Trends in Quebec, 1960–1990* (Montreal/Kingston: McGill-Queen's University Press, 1992).

Chapter Twenty-Four

IMMIGRATION AND MULTICULTURALISM

TIME LINE

1946	The first group of postwar European refugees arrives in Canada
1947	Parliament repeals the Chinese Exclusion Act
1956	Thousands of Hungarian refugees, fleeing Soviet repression, enter Canada as immigrants
1962	Racial discrimination is officially ended in Canada's immigration regulations
1966	The Department of Manpower and Immigration is established
1971	Ottawa adopts a multiculturalism policy
1982	The Charter of Rights and Freedoms accords constitutional protection to multiculturalism
1986	The Employment Equity Act comes into effect
1988	The Mulroney government acts to stem illegal immigration
1993	Parliament adopts new legislation on immigration to attract more highly educated newcomers
2006	Census statistics show that fully 19.8 percent of Canada's population are immigrants
2007	Ottawa increases its annual immigration target to between 240 000 and 265 000, the highest level in 25 years

The history of Canada's immigrants and ethnic minority groups since 1945 involves three closely intertwined elements: the Canadian government's changing immigration policy; Canadians' response to recent newcomers who have made Canada their new home; and the experience of the immigrants themselves. Discussion of the immigrants' experience gives rise to several more specific questions: Where have the immigrants come from, and why? How have they reacted and adapted to their new environment? And what impact have they had on Canadian society?

Members of Canada's non-French, non-British ethnic minorities began to question their place in Canadian society, particularly after the mid-1960s, a time when so many other components of Canada's population were also challenging the perceived inequalities of their own status. They naturally expressed serious reservations about the then-popular concept of two nations, or two founding peoples, which, while it ignored the existence of the Aboriginal peoples, appeared to give special treatment to Canadians of French and British origins. The federal government's multiculturalism policy, announced in 1971, accorded minority ethnic groups an official status they had not enjoyed in the past. It served as recognition of how Canada, in one century, had become a pluralistic society, one in which people of backgrounds other than English or French made up about one-third of the total population.

Postwar European Immigration, 1945–1957

In 1946, millions of destitute refugees from war-torn areas of Europe remained crowded in camps, awaiting a permanent haven. Canada felt little responsibility for them. Most Canadians, tired of being told to "do their part," probably agreed that the country had other, more urgent, priorities to attend to. Canada had its own children, as well as its injured soldiers and veterans, to look after. Furthermore, economists worried that the war's end would bring on another depression, as it had immediately after World War I. A wave of new arrivals risked swelling the ranks of the unemployed.

European Refugees

Prime Minister William Lyon Mackenzie King sensed Canadians' hesitancy about immigration. He saw little electoral advantage to be gained by opening the country's doors to Europe's homeless. At the same time, he faced mounting pressure from certain religious groups and ethnic associations as well as a few mainly CCF politicians who insisted that Canada had humanitarian obligations toward the unfortunates of Europe.

The Canadian government moved cautiously. The first refugees to arrive in 1946 were some 4000 Polish veterans who had fought with British military units in the war. Hugh Keenleyside, deputy minister of mines and resources (the department that had responsibility for immigration), felt that Canada should admit a few thousand displaced persons immediately. By acting quickly, Canada could obtain the best candidates, improve the country's international image, and encourage other nations to follow suit. In a critical view, John Holmes, an external affairs officer, later claimed that Canada selected refugees "like good beef cattle, with a preference for strong young men who could do manual labour and would not be encumbered by aging relatives."[1] By the fall of 1948, 40 000 refugees had reached Canadian shores. Although the numbers then began to decrease, about 165 000 refugees had come to Canada by 1953. Many of them, after arrival, applied to bring in their close relatives.

A number of refugees were well-educated professionals or highly skilled workers. Often, they concealed their training in order to better their chances with Canadian officials, who

A HISTORICAL PORTRAIT

The Immigrant Experience

One of these postwar refugees was Ann Kazimirski, a Jew born in eastern Poland. After the German invasion of her region in June 1941, the Nazis murdered most of her family. In 1942 she married a local dentist and, because dentists were needed to treat German troops, the couple were allowed to live outside the Jewish ghetto. As Nazi killings of Jews increased, a friend of the Kazimirskis agreed to hide the couple in an attic. One night troops rounded up most of the town's Jewish population of 18 000, took them away in trucks to the outskirts of town, and shot them. Shortly afterwards Ann's mother was captured and murdered before her daughter's eyes. The Kazimirskis escaped through the town's sewers, and hid in the surrounding countryside. In 1949 they reached Canada. Ann later testified in Germany during the trial for war crimes of the Nazi district administrator, identified by Ann as the person in charge of the killings; he was acquitted. Kazimirski returned to Canada and founded a choir group in Montreal, convinced that, while there was much to cry about, there was even more to sing about. She also told her story in a book, *Witness to Horror*.[1]

Another refugee was Maria Redekop Wall, age 47, who reached Canada with her six children and her meagre belongings in September 1948. Wall was part of a group of 8000 Mennonites, a majority of whom were women, who immigrated to Canada in the years 1947–1952. Wall had lived in a Mennonite village in the Ukraine. In 1938,

her husband, like numerous other Mennonite men, was arrested by Soviet police and disappeared. In 1941, Hitler's armies occupied the Ukraine. When the Germans were forced to retreat in September 1943, Wall and her co-religionists, as ethnic Germans, had no choice but to follow. After an arduous four-month trek in horse-drawn vehicles, they reached Poland, where the remaining men were conscripted into the German army. With the Soviet advance into Poland in 1944, the Mennonites were again uprooted. Most were taken prisoner by the Soviets; rape and suicides were common. Wall managed to reach a refugee camp in West Germany but spent many anxious months fearing she would be sent back to the USSR. Indeed, at the end of the war, the Red Army did forcibly repatriate thousands of Eastern Europeans behind the "iron curtain," often condemning them to prison, persecution, and even death. After spending three years in the camp, Wall was finally chosen to go to Canada. She settled in the Fraser Valley in British Columbia, where she bought a berry farm. Adaptation to the new society was not without problems, however, and even within the Mennonite community divergent lifestyles and experiences often strained relations between more conservative Canadian Mennonites and women who had long been forced by extraordinary, and often tragic, circumstances to make decisions and compromises.[2]

---

1.   M. J. Stone, "Ann Kazimirski, Music Teacher 1922–2006," *The Globe and Mail*, November 3, 2006.

2.   Marlene Epp, *Women without Men: Mennonite Refugees of the Second World War* (Toronto: University of Toronto Press, 2000).

sought manual labourers. Industries in need of unskilled labour sponsored many of the refugee immigrants, who readily accepted almost any job, salary, and working conditions. Once in Canada, they fulfilled their contractual obligations on farms, in lumber camps, in mines, and often, in the case of women, in domestic service, before moving on to more suitable occupations.

Immigrant Labour

Employers frequently exploited new immigrants. One notorious scheme involved Ludger Dionne, an MP and owner of the Dionne Spinning Mill Company at Saint-Georges-de-Beauce, south of Quebec City. In 1947, Dionne obtained government authorization to recruit 100 Polish women for his mill. *Time* reported that he paid them 20 cents an hour; after deductions of $6 a week for board, they were left with $3.60 weekly. Dionne assured parliamentarians that young women from Quebec City did not want to work in the small towns and that his working conditions were better than those in Toronto. For good measure, he also accused his detractors of being propagandists for communism.

Economically, many immigrants progressed rapidly. By 1971, Latvians and Estonians, for example, had incomes that were 25 percent higher than the Canadian average. Political scientist Karl Aun explains this evolution in part by the fact that such groups included unusually large numbers of educational, community, cultural, and political leaders.[2] Yet stories abound like the one about the poor Estonian fisherman who, after settling in southern Ontario, saved as much as possible from the earnings of all family members. Then, with the help of a loan from the Estonian Credit Union, he bought a house with several apartments, continued saving and purchased a second apartment house, moved into the best unit, and eventually sent his children to university.

Historian Franca Iacovetta examined the personal histories of several women refugees.[3] Every story was unique. Eighteen-year-old Elena Krotz was recruited by Canadian officials in a displaced-persons camp in West Germany. She had fled her native Czechoslovakia when communist authorities sought to arrest her after she participated in a student protest. After staying for a few weeks at a government hostel, Krotz was sent to the home of a farm couple in southwestern Ontario, to work as a servant. She arrived with all her worldly belongings in two tiny bags: a blanket and one change of clothes. A drive to succeed, the encouragement and mutual support of the community, and the relative youth of the newcomers combined to help these immigrants adjust to their new environment.

Postwar Federal Immigration Policy

Since most prospective immigrants to Canada were not refugees, the country needed a general immigration policy. In a much-discussed speech to the House of Commons on May 1, 1947, Prime Minister King attempted to satisfy both supporters and opponents of immigration. He said that Canada would benefit by boosting its population and that immigration would make the country more prosperous and secure. At the same time he put forth the nebulous notion of Canada's "absorptive capacity," promising that the government would "ensure the careful selection and permanent settlement" of only as many immigrants as could "advantageously be absorbed in our national economy." The number admitted could vary from year to year, in an alternating open-door/closed-door approach.

King's comments also reveal Canadian attitudes of the era. Responding to those who denounced racial distinctions in immigration policy, the prime minister asserted Canada's right to choose its future citizens. The government did repeal the blatantly discriminatory Chinese exclusion law of 1923. Nevertheless, it continued to apply severe restrictions on Asian immigration since, in King's words, the "massive immigration of Orientals would alter the fundamental composition of the Canadian population" and "give rise to social and economic problems."

Canadian Responses to Postwar Immigration

Canadians could not agree on how many immigrants the country needed and who should be admitted. Business and financial leaders lobbied for substantial immigration. They argued that a larger population would benefit the economy and yield per capita savings in areas such as transportation and administration. Ethnic associations and several religious groups also favoured increased immigration.

Many Canadians appeared reluctant to receive any sizable influx of immigrants. Many Canadians of British origin feared that immigration would weaken the British element in Canada. Workers often viewed immigrants as competitors willing to work for lower wages. Unions wanted immigrants to be carefully selected and preferably to occupy unattractive jobs in remote regions that Canadians did not want. As the economy began to slow in the late 1950s, most Canadians felt the country was accepting too many immigrants. Senator David Croll, who had been an enthusiastic advocate of higher immigration a decade before, now joked: "If you put pants on a penguin, it could be admitted to this country." After 1957, the new Progressive Conservative government substantially reduced immigration levels.

French-Speaking Immigrants

As late as 1947, it appeared that if the birth rate of French Canadians remained high, they might one day constitute the largest part of Canada's population. Yet large-scale immigration of non-French-speakers risked undermining the demographic situation of Canada's French-speaking minority. Even in Quebec, francophones often perceived immigrants as a threat because most joined the ranks of the English-speaking minority.

In 1948 the federal government, in hopes of satisfying French-Canadian public opinion, placed French nationals on an equal legal footing with British subjects and American citizens for purposes of entry into Canada. Civil servants, however, immediately subverted the new policy for "security" reasons, arguing that a large proportion of would-be French immigrants might be either communists or former Nazi collaborators. Although the French authorities did not encourage emigration, prospective immigrants literally besieged Canadian consular offices in Paris. While the Canadian consul in Paris made urgent requests for more staff and more office space, Hugh Keenleyside advised the deputy minister of labour to channel "all efforts in the same direction, that is to say, the encouragement of British immigration to Canada." Few French immigrants were admitted.

Clearly, during this period, the Canadian government preferred British immigrants over all others. In 1955, J.W. Pickersgill, minister of citizenship and immigration, asserted that it was only natural that Canada favour British immigration since it was easier to transplant individuals into "similar soil." Although he viewed the massive influx of new arrivals in 1956–1957, 40 percent of whom were British, as "too big for Canada to digest," he added candidly that any attempt to stem the tide of British immigration "would be the finish of the Liberal party in many Anglo-Saxon constituencies."

In the years 1945–1980, between one-half and two-thirds of immigrants to Canada were English-speaking, whereas French-speakers numbered only about 3 percent, and bilinguals 4 percent. The remainder, speaking other languages, soon learned English. By 2000, although

Canada's major sources of immigrants were no longer European, more than half of new immigrants still spoke English, whereas fewer than 10 percent knew French. The census of 2006 showed that immigration was the primary factor in explaining the relative decline of Quebec's population in regard to Canada's total population. Immigration also explained, together with assimilation, why the proportion of francophones in the English-speaking provinces also continued to decline.

An Evaluation of Postwar Immigration Policy

This first wave of postwar immigration, which brought 1.7 million immigrants to Canada, ended in the late 1950s, as unemployment levels rose. The year 1957, however, proved a sort of boom before the bust, with 282 000 arrivals—a figure that still paled in comparison with the 400 000 immigrants who came in 1913, when Canada's population was much smaller. Some 37 000 of these new arrivals were mainly young and often highly skilled Hungarians who fled their homeland in 1956 as Soviet armies crushed the Hungarian revolution. In general, the resettlement of the Hungarian refugees proceeded smoothly.

Such major movements of people gave rise to myths and half-truths. In theory, humanitarian ideals and a sense of international responsibility guided Canadian immigration policy. Canadians believed themselves to be generously offering liberty and opportunity to victims of persecution. In practice, economics usually dictated how many and which immigrants came to Canada. Ottawa sought immigrants possessing certain skills, and initiated bulk labour schemes. Federal authorities directed many immigrants, once in Canada, to farms and to unattractive jobs in remote resource regions. Once they fulfilled their contracts, however, many immigrants soon left for the cities.

Racial bias explains why few immigrants gained entrance from outside Europe and the United States. The introduction of tiny quotas, which remained in effect until 1967, also limited immigration from the Indian subcontinent. In addition, the location of immigration offices and the nature of government promotional literature ensured that the great majority of immigrants came from Britain and the European continent, as well as from the United States.

Jack Pickersgill (right), the federal minister responsible for immigration in the St. Laurent government, greets the dean of the faculty of forestry engineering of the University of Sopron, Hungary in Montreal, 1957. Some 37 000 young and highly skilled Hungarians, including the entire faculty and student body of this faculty, arrived in Canada after the Hungarian uprising of 1956.

Champlain Marcil/Library and Archives Canada/PA-147725
Copyright: Champlain Marcil

This 1955 poster questions the colour code applied to potential immigrants from within the British Commonwealth.

Library and Archives Canada/Marcel Ray/PA-139579

Emigration

During the economic downturn of the late 1950s and early 1960s, immigrants experienced the obverse side of immigration. Disappointed with the lack of opportunities in Canada and embittered by what they considered false promises on Canada's part, many thousands, particularly British, returned home. There they contributed to tarnishing Canada's image, if only temporarily. From the early 1950s to the early 1970s, one in every three or four immigrants to Canada either returned home or moved to the United States.

Even more worrisome to many Canadians was the movement southward of 800 000 native-born Canadians in the period 1952–1971. Perhaps one-tenth of this group consisted of professionals or managers—the much-publicized "brain drain." After a temporary reversal of the movement in the 1960s and early 1970s, at the time of the Vietnam War and race riots in the United States, emigration southward resumed in the late 1970s and 1980s. The problem worsened in the 1990s and early 2000s. In certain years, the number of nurses and physicians who emigrated represented the equivalent of about one-half of the number of graduates from Canada's nursing and medical schools. Many engineers, scientists, teachers, and managerial workers also joined the trek south, attracted to the United States by the prospect of better working conditions and higher salaries and, perhaps, by southern sunshine. The cost to Canada was substantial, as emigrants took with them skills they had developed in largely publicly financed postsecondary schools.

The Immigrant Experience in the 1960s and 1970s

Due to an economic slowdown, the Diefenbaker years (1957–1963) witnessed a slump in immigration. Unions expressed fears that immigrants risked taking Canadian workers' jobs. Most MPs were at best indifferent. Even Diefenbaker, despite favourable public pronouncements in speeches aimed at ethnic groups and despite his own non-French, non-British origins, appeared to have little interest in the question.

Sometimes immigration made sensational headlines. The press reported numerous cases of foreign seamen who jumped ship in Canadian waters and then hurriedly married Canadian women in order to remain in Canada. Large-scale illegal Chinese immigration also appeared to overwhelm the government. Ottawa promised to grant amnesty to most illegals who would come forth and declare themselves (many thousands did), but illegal immigration rings continued to operate.

Toward a Colour-Blind Immigration Policy

The Conservatives introduced new regulations in 1962 that ended the use of race and national origin as reasons for exclusion from Canada. The old discriminatory provisions appeared unacceptable in an era that discredited racism. In 1960, Diefenbaker had proudly presented the Canadian Bill of Rights, which rejected discrimination by reason of race, national origin, colour, religion, or sex. Economic factors also contributed to the reversal of the former policy: Canada could no longer obtain the labour it needed from the "old countries." For a time, southern Europe supplanted Britain and northern Europe as the area of origin of most immigrants to Canada. Then, immigration diminished from these countries, too, and Canada turned its attention toward Asia and the Caribbean.

A New Wave of Immigrants

Assisted by the return of economic prosperity in the early 1960s, the Pearson government (1963–1968) instituted structural changes designed to increase immigration. In 1966, it established the Department of Manpower and Immigration to relate immigration to the needs of the labour market, while the Department of the Secretary of State obtained responsibility for the integration of immigrants into Canadian society.

New immigration regulations set up a points system for selecting independent immigrants. Criteria included education and training, personal qualities, occupational demand, and age and linguistic capacity. Sponsored dependants and, particularly, non-dependent relatives now found it more difficult to gain admittance. The government also set up the independent Immigration Appeal Board, which was almost immediately overwhelmed with appeals from alleged "visitors" who had applied to stay but had been refused and ordered deported.

The gradual elimination of racial discrimination from Canada's immigration policy, the decline of European sources of immigrants, and the expansion of the network of immigration offices around the world transformed the face of Canadian immigration. In 1966, for example, 87 percent of immigrants were of European origin; only four years later, 50 percent came from other regions. The West Indies, Haiti, Guyana, India, Hong Kong, the Philippines, and Indochina all figured among the major suppliers of immigrants in the 1970s.

Immigrant Settlement

Newcomers to Canada did not spread out evenly across the country. Since 1945, about 60 percent of all immigrants have settled in Ontario, especially southern Ontario. Good employment opportunities and the region's prosperous image attracted them, as did well-established ethnic communities with religious centres, clubs, welfare organizations, newspapers, and other services. Quebec, with one-quarter of Canada's population, has usually received fewer than 15 percent of new arrivals—about the same proportion as British Columbia. Alberta, especially during oil booms, also attracted many immigrants. The Atlantic provinces, for their part, experienced little immigration.

In all regions, immigrants settled mainly in major metropolitan areas. As many as one-half chose Toronto, making it North America's most ethnically diverse city and possibly the world's. Vancouver and Montreal also attracted large numbers of immigrants. Big-city Canada thus became much more cosmopolitan.

Immigration in Recent Years

The deep recession of the early 1980s again caused immigration to decline. Economic problems contributed to an anti-immigrant backlash, as many Canadians saw immigrants as competitors for scarce jobs or believed they were crowding the welfare rolls.

Most studies of the relationship between immigration and employment tend to demonstrate that immigrants do not increase unemployment among indigenous workers but rather help to create a larger, more flexible, and more adaptable labour force. Immigrants often work at jobs that Canadians cannot or will not do. Moreover, through their need for housing, food, clothing, and other consumer goods, immigrants increase the size of the domestic market and thereby assist in boosting growth. Other studies have shown that most immigrants have been able to obtain jobs soon after arrival, although Third World immigrants in the independent immigrant category often work in jobs for which they were overqualified.

Regardless of the conclusions of sociological studies, the image of immigrants lined up outside employment offices in times of recession has probably influenced public opinion far more. Thus, during the severe downturn of the early 1980s, the government felt it necessary to revise each year's quotas downward, according to its vague predictions of what the economy could bear. Immigration fell to its lowest levels in more than two decades. After 1986, the government did, however, facilitate the entry into Canada of several thousand "business-class" immigrants—wealthy entrepreneurs, especially from Hong Kong. These individuals agreed to invest their capital in Canada, set up businesses, and, hopefully, create jobs for Canadians.

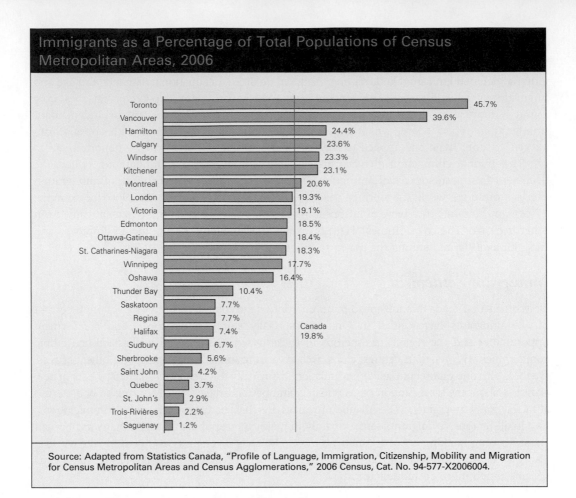

Immigrants as a Percentage of Total Populations of Census Metropolitan Areas, 2006

Toronto	45.7%
Vancouver	39.6%
Hamilton	24.4%
Calgary	23.6%
Windsor	23.3%
Kitchener	23.1%
Montreal	20.6%
London	19.3%
Victoria	19.1%
Edmonton	18.5%
Ottawa-Gatineau	18.4%
St. Catharines-Niagara	18.3%
Winnipeg	17.7%
Oshawa	16.4%
Thunder Bay	10.4%
Saskatoon	7.7%
Regina	7.7%
Halifax	7.4%
Sudbury	6.7%
Sherbrooke	5.6%
Saint John	4.2%
Quebec	3.7%
St. John's	2.9%
Trois-Rivières	2.2%
Saguenay	1.2%

Canada
19.8%

Source: Adapted from Statistics Canada, "Profile of Language, Immigration, Citizenship, Mobility and Migration for Census Metropolitan Areas and Census Agglomerations," 2006 Census, Cat. No. 94-577-X2006004.

How Many Immigrants and from Where?

In the late 1980s, Ottawa gradually raised the ceiling on immigration from 100 000 to 200 000. Then, in 1990, the federal government announced further increases—a politically risky decision as the economy slowed again and as certain groups, such as the Reform Party, based in western Canada, attacked immigration and multiculturalism policies. An average of nearly 220 000 immigrants were nonetheless admitted to Canada each year during the period 1992–1999.

By the 1990s, Sri Lanka and Taiwan had replaced the Caribbean nations as major homelands of arriving immigrants. In the years immediately preceding Hong Kong's cession to China in 1997, the former British colony was Canada's major source of immigrants. Some 200 000 of this group returned to Hong Kong after obtaining Canadian citizenship following three years of residence in Canada. From 2000, annual arrivals fluctuated between 225 000 and 250 000. More than one-quarter of newcomers to Canada now came from just two countries: China and India. The Philippines, Pakistan, Iran, and the Republic of Korea were also major source countries. Outside Asia, immigrants came from the United States and the United Kingdom (although many people from Britain were of Indian origin), as well as Colombia, France, Romania, and Russia.

Thanks to Caribbean and then to Asian immigration, so-called "visible minorities" became an important part of Canada's social fabric. While only 12 000 West Indians lived in Canada in 1961, the figure climbed to 225 000 in 1986. The number of Canadians of Chinese origin increased from 60 000 to nearly 350 000 in the same period, and then to 1 million by 2001. In

Leading Source Countries of Immigrants, Selected Years

1960	1976	1984	1997	2006
Italy	Britain	Vietnam	Hong Kong	China
Britain	United States	Hong Kong	India	India
United States	Hong Kong	United States	China	Philippines
Germany	Jamaica	India	Taiwan	Pakistan
Netherlands	Lebanon	Britain	Pakistan	United States
Portugal	India	Poland	Philippines	Iran
Greece	Philippines	Philippines	Iran	Britain
France	Portugal	El Salvador	Sri Lanka	Korea
Poland	Italy	Jamaica	United States	Colombia
Austria	Guyana	China	Britain	France

Source: Citizenship and Immigration Canada, "Immigration Statistics," various years.

2001, such minorities made up 13 percent of the country's population and more than 35 percent of the populations of Vancouver and Toronto. Projections show that these two cities will become "majority-minority" cities by 2017, in other words, that more than one-half of their inhabitants will belong to visible minorities.

Immigrants and Canada's Economy

In the early 1990s, fewer than 40 percent of immigrants belonged to the so-called "economic class" in which one family member, the principal applicant, was seen as a potential investor in the Canadian economy or assessed for skills deemed in demand in Canada. Most immigrants now belonged to the other two categories of "family class" (that is, close relatives of Canadian residents) and refugees. In response to critics who urged the government to link immigration more closely to economic needs, Ottawa adjusted its rules in 1993 and again in 2002 to favour educated applicants with work experience and confirmed job offers, people judged to be adaptable and to have "flexible and transferable skills" for the "knowledge economy."

Still Canada's immigration system showed signs of strain. In its search for highly educated and well-trained immigrants, Canada had to compete with other countries. Construction companies begged the government to admit the skilled tradespeople they needed and to regularize the status of the thousands of undocumented immigrants it allegedly employed, often for less than the minimum wage; Ottawa, in 2006, refused an amnesty that risked encouraging more illegal immigration.

Business, with its demands for more skilled workers to alleviate worrying labour shortages, was not alone in seeking high numbers of immigrants. Policy analysts including demographers warned that, because of current low fertility rates—Canadian women were expected to have on average 1.5 children—the country's population would begin to contract in the medium term, even at present levels of immigration. Some middle-aged Canadians began to worry about who would pay for their old-age pensions and future health care, and urged the government to bring in more immigrant taxpayers.

Adaptation

Most immigrants from developing countries found their new life in Canada a considerable material improvement over the past. In any case, political conditions prevented many immigrants from returning home, even if they so desired. Provincial governments and community associations have attempted to assist the new arrivals. Mutual aid and support among families have also been important. Still, it has often been difficult to find jobs to match past occupational experience, especially in times of economic slowdown. Moreover, many

Sod-turning for Edmonton's Hindu Centre, 1976.

The Edmonton Journal. Courtesy of the Provincial Archives of Alberta, J. 2621.

workers selected because of their high qualifications had difficulty having their foreign credentials recognized in Canada. As one Toronto newspaper commented, "Foreign-trained engineers may make wonderful taxi drivers, but they also deserve a chance, if their credentials stand up to scrutiny, to be wonderful engineers." Unsurprisingly, a Statistics Canada survey showed that poverty rates among immigrants, despite their high levels of education, remained high. Worse, 40 percent of economic immigrants left Canada within ten years.

The clash between contemporary Canadian values and mores and accepted values and attitudes in the country of origin has frequently caused painful problems for immigrants. Today's immigrants face a much greater cultural shock than did earlier British and European arrivals. For example, the close interaction of the extended family, common in many cultures and providing an extensive support system, is much less present in North America, where the functional unit is now the nuclear family. The role of women in the family, particularly in southern European and South Asian cultures, has generally been defined very rigidly; male authority generally goes unchallenged, and male financial supremacy backs up that authority.

A study of South Asians (people from India, Pakistan, Bangladesh, and Sri Lanka) showed that "only a small proportion" of homeland cultural practices survive the settlement process.[4] Culinary habits and cultural celebrations tend to be maintained in those cities where immigrant groups are sufficiently numerous, but it is more difficult to retain religious practices: Hindu parents, for example, often find that children know far more about Christianity than they do about Hinduism. Historian Hugh Johnson recorded the story of Tara Singh Bains, a Punjabi who arrived in Vancouver in 1953. The now-elderly Bains, a man of strong religious convictions, told Johnson he deplored what he saw as the erosion of spiritual values among members of his community. Bains testified, "Materialism has created so many doorways to attract human thinking towards luxury, enjoyment, and selfishness...."[5]

Unsurprisingly, contact with Canadian mores has provoked much conflict within immigrant families. Parental authority has also weakened in the context of Canada's much more permissive society. The generation gap between immigrant parents and their children has often deepened into a gulf as children become Canadianized through the schools, television, and contacts with friends.

Discrimination

Many immigrants, especially members of visible minorities, suffered discrimination in Canada. In the 1970s and 1980s, the media gave wide publicity to numerous instances in which Sikhs were attacked and their turbans forcibly removed. Blacks were frequently harassed or physically assaulted. In Montreal, a taxi company fired its Haitian drivers, claiming that it was losing business to companies that employed only white drivers. (Haitians responded by buying the city's second-largest taxi company.) Incidents of police shootings of young black people in Montreal and Toronto sparked widespread demands for inquiries into alleged racism in police forces.

Historian Stanley Barrett's research on a suburban Toronto community in the early 1990s showed the existence of widespread racism in regard to visible minorities. He suggested that South Asians saw racism as inevitable, and sought to defend themselves by fostering strong links with their own ethnic communities. African Canadians, more in contact with the "white" community, often felt bitterness and anger in the face of what they perceived as rejection by their neighbours. Barrett also found strong negative attitudes toward French Canadians, who were seen as "intent on taking over and ruining the country."[6]

Most complaints about discrimination have concerned employment and housing. One survey showed that three-quarters of West Indians judged employment discrimination in Toronto to be "very serious." Surveys in eleven other Canadian cities repeated the same finding. Recent census figures showed that income gaps between immigrants and other Canadians were widening; the Canadian Labour Congress cited racism as a major factor. Although provincial human rights commissions did receive numerous complaints of discrimination, many victims failed to report incidents, believing that nothing would be done or, worse, fearing retaliation. Human rights defence groups have criticized the courts for their slowness and their leniency, and have denounced existing laws for their lack of severity.

Reactions to Immigration

"Established" Canadians have had mixed reactions to the new arrivals from the developing nations. Religious and civic groups have strongly urged the admission of refugees, such as the Indochinese "boat people" in the late 1970s and refugees from Kosovo in 1999. Yet the general population has shown substantial opposition to increased immigration in general, and to immigration from developing countries in particular. Various studies have shown that many Canadians dislike immigrants' speaking their home languages in public or wearing traditional dress. They tend to see immigrants as ignorant of Canadian cultural practices and unwilling to "act like Canadians," and they have expressed discomfort with the changes in Canadian society that have been brought about by immigration. Critics also accused Ottawa of not sufficiently screening new immigrants, thus permitting the entry into the country of militants who favoured the use of violence to promote the causes they espoused.

The arrival in Canada, particularly in Vancouver, of a relatively large number of wealthy Chinese immigrants from Hong Kong in the late 1980s brought considerable reaction. Government and business leaders appreciated the large financial investments a number of newcomers made. But some Canadian residents criticized what they perceived as ostentatious displays of wealth, such as the construction of "monster homes." Reacting to a number of unpleasant incidents, Vancouver's first Chinese-Canadian city councillor complained, "The Chinese are damned if they're poor and damned if they're rich." British Columbia's lieutenant governor, Chinese-Canadian David Lam, attempted to calm tensions, recommending that newcomers become more involved in the community and that older residents turn a blind eye to pretentious houses.

The extent to which Canadian society must adapt in order to welcome and integrate newcomers to the country has provoked increasing controversy. Ontarians discussed whether Muslims could establish religious courts to decide issues of family law; the Ontario government decided they could not. During a provincial election campaign in 2007, they also debated whether the state should support all religious schools. The party proposing such assistance was defeated at the polls. Quebeckers examined the meaning of "reasonable accommodation" of religious and other differences. Canadians in general attempted to define so-called "Canadian values" that, they said, should not be compromised and included democracy, tolerance, and equality between men and women.

Refugees

Much of the recent criticism directed at federal immigration policy has concerned refugees. Across the world, millions of human beings became refugees, fleeing war and persecution in their own lands. Canada could not be unaffected by such mass movements. Humanitarian and refugee-advocacy groups as well as ethnic communities favouring more immigration from their home countries judged Canada's refugee quotas to be unreasonably low. They also denounced the government's cumbersome procedures for studying the cases of refugee-status claimants, resulting in backlogs which grew larger each year.

Public opinion gradually became less sympathetic to the cause of refugees. Many critics were undoubtedly influenced by the large numbers of would-be immigrants who entered Canada illegally—so-called "queue jumpers"—and who claimed refugee status, but whose reasons for emigrating from their countries of origin seemed to be primarily economic. Indeed, the "hearing" that virtually all refugee-status claimants now requested—an unforeseen consequence of earlier legislation—became, according to historian Gerald Dirks, "a routine channel for evading the normal admission requirements and getting easy access to Canada."[7] In 1986, the dramatic arrival of a large group of Tamil immigrants from Sri Lanka on the shores of Newfoundland and, the following year, of a group of Sikhs from India on the coast of Nova Scotia, was sufficient proof for many Canadians that Ottawa had lost control over entry into the country.

Public pressure led the Mulroney government to act against illegal immigration in 1988, by which time government efforts to clear the huge backlog of refugee-status claimants had become hopelessly bogged down. The number of new claimants declined. New legislation in 1993 limited the right of rejected applicants to appeal, resulting in a further drop in the number of claimants arriving in Canada. Through the 1990s, the acceptance rate of refugee claimants fell from about 75 percent to about 50 percent. Refugee lawyers blamed "compassion fatigue": panel members, they said, were becoming hardened to stories of abuse and persecution. Religious and ethnic groups feared that the measures also discouraged true political refugees. Government spokespersons countered that Canada still remained far more open to refugees than did other Western countries.

The terrorist attacks of September 11, 2001, in the United States brought new and tighter immigration rules, which took effect in 2003. In response to American accusations that Canada admitted too many refugees without proper security vetting, Canada decided to turn back claimants arriving at Canadian land borders and invited them to seek asylum in the United States, whose rules were reputedly more restrictive. Critics maintained that henceforth more refugees would seek to enter Canada illegally, in order to make their claim from inside Canada. In 2006 Canada began a new system for processing certain refugee applications. The change provided for the acceptance en masse of large groups of displaced people including Sudanese, Somalis, and Afghans.

Multiculturalism

Canadians have often taken pride in the image of their country as a "cultural mosaic" (or a "tossed salad," in one writer's words), rather than as an American-style "melting pot." Official policy no longer favours rapid assimilation, and social scientists prefer to speak instead of integration or of acculturation. In the 1960s, observers began to speak of the emergence of a "third force," consisting of Canadians of neither French nor British descent.

In October 1971, Prime Minister Trudeau told the House of Commons that the government "accepts the contention of other cultural communities that they, too, are essential elements in Canada and deserve government assistance in order to contribute to regional and national life in ways that derive from their heritages." Multiculturalism—but not multilingualism—was to be encouraged. The Constitution of 1982 gave additional, though somewhat vague, protection to multiculturalism. Then, in 1988, a revised Multiculturalism Act provided new funds for promoting cultures and reducing discrimination.

Politicians understood the potential electoral benefits of recognizing the contributions of ethnic groups. Also, the Trudeau government hoped that recognition of multiculturalism would attenuate existing hostility toward bilingualism and biculturalism and that it would appeal to English-Canadian nationalists who wanted a distinct Canadian identity. Yet probably most Canadians, including the British, the French, and the "lukewarm white ethnics" from northern and western Europe, found multiculturalism meaningless. As time went on, impatience with the whole concept grew, especially when governments agreed to provide funding.

By the mid-1980s, the federal government was investing modestly in multiculturalism, funding ethnic daycare centres, heritage-language classes, cultural festivals, and conferences and providing grants for the preparation of histories of the major Canadian ethnic groups.

The 2000 graduating class of Jarvis Collegiate Institute, Toronto. Immigration has made Toronto possibly the most ethnically and culturally diverse of the world's large cities.

Canadian Geographic, January/February 2001, pp. 40–41. Photo courtesy of David Trattles.

Money was made available to revitalize Vancouver's Chinatown and to transform this ethnic neighbourhood into a shining symbol of Canada's new multicultural nature and, at the same time, a valuable tourist attraction. (By 2000, however, Vancouver's Chinatown was in decline; it had also lost its exclusiveness as new Chinatowns grew up in suburbs such as Richmond.)

Several provincial governments also contributed financially to support multicultural policy. The Ontario government, for example, used its Wintario lottery funding program to create a research institute, the Multicultural History Society of Ontario. Many school boards set up courses in nonofficial languages. In Edmonton, for example, immersion schooling could be had in Arabic, Chinese, Hebrew, Ukrainian, and German. Such policies have practical relevance: already by the late 1980s, English was not the mother tongue of 50 percent of the children enrolled in Toronto public schools nor of 40 percent of those enrolled in Vancouver schools.

WHERE SOCIAL SCIENTISTS DISAGREE

Evaluating Canada's Multicultural Policy

The arrival in Canada of large numbers of immigrants, first from Europe and, since the late 1960s, from the Caribbean, Latin America, Asia, and Africa, has immensely diversified Canada's population. Until the 1950s, governments espoused a policy of rapid assimilation of newcomers into the "Canadian mainstream." As interest in the rights of minorities grew throughout the Western world during the 1960s, immigrant groups sought government intervention to help them conserve at least part of their ethnic heritage. In response, Ottawa elaborated, in 1971, a somewhat vague multicultural policy. Since then, governments and public agencies at all levels have launched programs favouring the retention of national cultures.

Official federal policy views multiculturalism as "a powerful bonding agent" that "helps unite us and identify us, while at the same time allowing every element of our society to retain its own characteristics and cultural heritage."[1] Observers have generally been somewhat suspicious of these stated intentions. In 1988, for example, Howard Palmer described federal policy as, at least in part, an attempt to win the ethnic vote in urban Ontario and to temper western Canada's rising opposition to the policy of bilingualism.[2]

Regardless of the inevitable political considerations underlying the policy, has multiculturalism been worth pursuing? Yes, thinks Norman Buchignani, who feels that federal policy has helped groups such as the South Asians feel "comfortable about being South Asian and Canadian at the same time."[3] He also views multicultural policy as heightening awareness among native-born Canadians of the new communities that have recently established themselves in their midst. More critically, Lance W. Roberts and Rodney A. Clifton argue that the policy at least has symbolic value, permitting members of ethnic groups to "participate and benefit as members of a complex industrial society while retaining the sense that they belong to a smaller, more intimate community."[4]

Other observers express doubt. C. Michael Lanphier and Anthony H. Richmond argue that it is probably impossible to reconcile equality of opportunity and integration with "the maintenance of separate identities and cultural pluralism."[5] Gilles Paquet agrees. He sees multiculturalism as having heightened the belief among "other" Canadians that they do not have to adapt their mores while, at the same time, the "dominant cultures" have remained dominant: "The gap between expectations and realities has generated much ... frustration."[6] Peter S. Li and B. Singh Bolaria hold a similar opinion. For them, multiculturalism is "the failure of an illusion, not of a policy."[7] The illusion is that a cultural solution, such as multiculturalism, could solve problems such as ethnic inequality and racial discrimination, whose roots are political and economic. (Perhaps such criticisms explain why, in the 1980s, government multicultural programs broadened their involvement in race relations.) For his part, novelist Neil Bissoondath, who refuses the role of "ethnic" which would have him labelled an "East Indian-Trinidadian-Canadian-Quebecker," argues in a controversial book that the policy of official multiculturalism, by encouraging immigrants to focus on "There," the ancestral homeland, rather than on "Here," the new homeland, actually highlights the differences that divide Canadians rather than the similarities that unite them.[8]

Regardless of the disagreements, Robert A. Harney, a student of the Italian community in particular, saw merit in simply pursuing the debate. Multiculturalism, he said, was part of Canada's eternal search to define itself. "Survival lies in traveling toward an identity, and we will all be better served if that traveling itself remains our identity."[9]

1. *Multiculturalism ... Being Canadian* (Ottawa: Secretary of State for Multiculturalism, 1987), p. 9.

2. Jean R. Burnet with Howard Palmer, *"Coming Canadians": An Introduction to a History of Canada's Peoples* (Toronto: McClelland & Stewart, 1988), p. 176.

3. Norman Buchignani and Doreen M. Indra with Sam Srivastiva, *Continuous Journey: A Social History of South Asians in Canada* (Toronto: McClelland & Stewart, 1985), p. 227.

4. Lance W. Roberts and Rodney Clifton, "Multiculturalism in Canada: A Sociological Perspective," in Peter S. Li, ed., *Race and Ethnic Relations in Canada* (Toronto: Oxford University Press, 1990), p. 133.

5. C. Michael Lanphier and Anthony H. Richmond, "Multiculturalism and Identity in 'Canada outside Quebec,'" in Kenneth McRoberts, ed., *Beyond Quebec: Taking Stock of Canada* (Montreal/Kingston: McGill-Queen's University Press, 1995), p. 314.

6. Gilles Paquet, "Political Philosophy of Multiculturalism," in J.W. Berry and J.A. Laponce, eds., *Ethnicity and Culture in Canada: The Research Landscape* (Toronto: University of Toronto Press, 1994), p. 63.

7. Peter S. Li and B. Singh Bolaria, "Introduction" to *Racial Minorities in Multicultural Canada* (Toronto: Garamond Press, 1983).

8. Neil Bissoondath, *Selling Illusions: The Cult of Multiculturalism in Canada*, rev. ed. (Toronto: Penguin Canada, 2002), p. 222.

9. Robert A. Harney, "'So Great a Heritage as Ours': Immigration and the Survival of Canadian Policy," *Daedelus*, 117 (Fall 1988), p. 93.

The federal government's support of ethnic diversity has given rise to the question of who really speaks for the ethnic communities and, thus, of which associations the government ought to support. Twenty organizations, for example, now represent Edmontonians of various Asian origins. In Vancouver, the well-established Chinese Benevolent Association has on occasion feuded with newer, more activist organizations, such as the Chinese Cultural Centre, over various local issues, in particular a plan to build a freeway through Chinatown. In Toronto, West Indians have a multitude of often-competing organizations whose membership is determined by island of origin.

Increasingly, observers of multiculturalism have expressed fears that the official emphasis on maintaining cultural diversity has impeded the integration of newcomers. For example, they cite the rising tendency of immigrant groups, particularly South Asians and Chinese, to live in self-segregated, often middle class, "ethnic enclaves." In such communities, contacts with the host society are greatly reduced. Market researcher Allan Gregg commented, "In Canada, we may live in a multicultural society, but the evidence suggests that fewer and fewer of us are living in multicultural neighbourhoods."[8] Did such ghettos explain the disturbing conclusion in a report published by Statistics Canada in 2007 that second-generation immigrants belonging to minorities felt less Canadian than children of European immigrants? Were discrimination and exclusion also major factors? Was there a risk that marginalized immigrant communities would lead to social upheavals as in several European countries? There were no sure answers to these questions.

Nonofficial Languages

Heritage-language programs emphasize retention of the mother tongue and are seen to have moral and psychological value. However, immigrants and their offspring, in order to integrate into Canadian society, have had to learn English or, in Quebec, to a lesser degree, French. Although such groups as the Portuguese, the Greeks, and the Chinese have had considerable success in retaining the language of the country of origin, assimilative trends generally become more pronounced over time and the retention of nonofficial languages diminishes sharply. As ethnolinguist Joshua Fishman put it, "for 95 percent of the third generation, the language of the cradle is the language of the streets."[9] Indeed, the 2006 census revealed that one Canadian in five had a mother tongue other than English or French; yet about one-third of this group rarely or never spoke their mother tongue and had adopted an official language, generally English.

Barely 15 percent of Ukrainian Canadians, for example, speak Ukrainian as a home language, and intermarriage has hastened the pace of assimilation. Of Toronto's half-million-strong Italian community, historian Robert Harney estimated in 1984 that only a minority (belonging generally to the original immigrant generation) were "active in Italian institutions."[10] In his opinion, large numbers of Italians have deliberately broken their ethnic links and taken refuge in "Anglo conformity" because of the prejudice they have faced. Studies suggest strongly that linguistic assimilation leads to destruction of the cohesive ethnic community. While the prognosis for linguistic survival appears bleak for older ethnic communities from Europe, the number of Canadians speaking such languages as Chinese, Spanish, Punjabi, Tagalog, and Arabic is increasing rapidly as immigration rejuvenates these groups.

The Impact of Immigration

Immigrants have had an immeasurable impact on Canada's economic, political, social, and cultural life. The contributions of entrepreneurs such as the Reichmann brothers (born in Austria and Hungary), Thomas Bata and Stephen Roman (both born in the former Czechoslovakia), David Lam (from Hong Kong), Montreal publisher Alain Stanké (born in Lithuania), and journalists Adrienne Clarkson and Michaëlle Jean (born in Hong Kong and in Haiti, respectively, and both of whom became governors general of Canada) are noteworthy. Film director Atom Egoyan was born in Cairo, Egypt of Armenian refugee parents, who settled in Victoria, British Columbia in 1963. The young Egoyan at first renounced his ethnic roots; but later, as a university student, he sought to reconnect with them, as his film *Ararat*, bearing on the Turkish massacre and deportation of as many as one million Armenians in 1915, attests.

Top Ten Countries of Birth for Recent Immigrants and All Immigrants, 2006

RECENT IMMIGRANTS[1]	NUMBER	%
1. P.R. of China	155 105	14.0
2. India	129 140	11.6
3. Philippines	77 880	7.0
4. Pakistan	57 630	5.2
5. USA	38 770	3.5
6. Rep of Korea	35 450	3.2
7. Romania	28 080	2.5
8. Iran	27 600	2.5
9. Colombia	25 305	2.3
10. Sri Lanka	22 305	2.0
Subtotal	597 265	53.8
All other countries[2]	512 715	46.2
Total	**1 109 980**	**100.0**

ALL IMMIGRANTS[3]	NUMBER	%
1. United Kingdom	579 620	9.4
2. P.R. of China	466 940	7.5
3. India	443 690	7.2
4. Philippines	303 195	4.9
5. Italy	296 850	4.8
6. United States	250 535	4.0
7. Hong Kong	215 430	3.5
8. Germany	171 405	2.8
9. Poland	170 490	2.8
10. Vietnam	160 170	2.6
Subtotal	2 807 790	45.4
All other countries[4]	3 379 160	54.6
Total	**6 186 950**	**100.0**

[1] Immigrants counted in 2006 and who came to Canada between 2001 and 2006.
[2] Major "other" countries include Russia, France, Mexico, Ukraine, Afghanistan, and Algeria.
[3] All people counted in 2006 not born in Canada.
[4] Major "other" countries include Portugal, Pakistan, Jamaica, Netherlands, Sri Lanka, and Republic of Korea.

Source: Adapted from Statistics Canada, "Immigration and Citizenship Highlight Tables," 2006 Census, Cat. No. 97-557-XWE200602.

Since the late 1970s the number of non-British, non-French writers in Canada has grown substantially, and Canadian literature has become increasing diversified. Indeed, Canada became part of the literary global village as many novels written by new Canadians featured settings that often had little to do with Canada. Austin Clarke, born in Barbados, set *The Polished Hoe*, his ninth novel, a poignant account of injustice, on an imaginary West Indian island in the 1950s. Indian-born Rohinton Mistry used Bombay as his setting for *Such a Long Journey* and *Family Matters*, while Michael Ondaatje, from Sri Lanka, set his fifth novel, *Divisadero* (which earned him a fifth Governor General's Literary Award in 2007) in California and France. In business, in the arts, in politics, indeed in virtually all spheres of activity, the Canada of 2000 reflected the increasing presence of the Asians, Latin Americans, West Indians, Europeans, and other immigrants who had settled in the country in earlier years.

Immigrants have brought new political questions to the fore in such areas as education and social policy, and the ethnic vote has become significant in many constituencies. Immigration has also enabled urban Canada to acquire a much more diverse and vibrant cultural life. Demographically, immigration has boosted Canada's population significantly: from 1981 to 1986, net immigration represented one-fifth of the country's population growth; from 1991 to 1996, more than one-half; and from 1996 to 2006, fully two-thirds. With immigration, the importance of both the British and the French components of the population has declined, while, from a linguistic point of view, the fact that the great majority of immigrants eventually adopt English as their new language has contributed to weakening the relative position of Canada's francophone population and increasing that community's fears for survival.

Immigration brought much of the blue-collar labour that Canada needed for large-scale industrial and resource development in the 1950s. It also provided many of the country's skilled workers and professionals. In the 1960s, for example, hundreds of American university professors entered the country, permitting the rapid expansion of the Canadian university system but also setting the stage for the nationalist outcry against American domination in the early 1970s. Bringing in educated immigrants helped ease the pressure on Canada's already overburdened educational system. Ironically, for a country that has often complained of suffering a brain drain to the United States, Canada has been criticized by some developing countries for attracting the highly qualified people that those developing nations so desperately need to keep at home.

Immigration will surely remain a much-discussed issue. There is little prospect that Canadians can ever agree on how many immigrants the country needs, how many refugees it should welcome, where immigrants should come from, and what role they should play in Canadian society. The integration of immigrants will in some instances be painful, and relations between new arrivals and the host society will raise controversial issues. Nevertheless, there can be no doubt that, because of immigration, the Canada of the early twenty-first century is a much more diverse land than the country that emerged from World War II.

NOTES

1. John W. Holmes, *The Shaping of Peace: Canada and the Search for World Order 1943–1957*, vol. 1 (Toronto: University of Toronto Press, 1979), p. 101.

2. Karl Aun, *The Political Refugees: A History of the Estonians in Canada* (Toronto: McClelland & Stewart, 1985).

3. Franca Iacovetta, "Remaking Their Lives," in Joy Parr, ed., *A Diversity of Women: Ontario, 1945–1980* (Toronto: University of Toronto Press, 1995), pp. 135–67.

4. Norman Buchignani and Doreen M. Indra with Ram Srivastiva, *Continuous Journey: A Social History of South Asians in Canada* (Toronto: McClelland & Stewart, 1985), p. 163.

5. Hugh Johnson, *The Four Quarters of the Night: The Life Journey of an Emigrant Sikh* (Montreal/Kingston: McGill-Queen's University Press, 1995), p. 227.

6. Stanley R. Barrett, *Paradise: Class, Commuters, and Ethnicity in Rural Ontario* (Toronto: University of Toronto Press, 1994), p. 235.

7. Gerald E. Dirks, *Controversy and Complexity: Canadian Immigration Policy during the 1980s* (Montreal/Kingston: McGill-Queen's University Press, 1995), pp. 79–80.

8. Quoted in Marina Jimenez, "Do Ethnic Enclaves Impede Immigration?," *The Globe and Mail*, February 8, 2007, p. 8.

9. Quoted in Robert Harney, "'So Great a Heritage as Ours': Immigration and the Survival of the Canadian Polity," *Daedelus*, 117 (Fall 1988): 83.

10. Quoted in Margot Gibb-Clark, "'Italian Community's a Myth,' Historian Says," *The Globe and Mail*, October 20, 1984, p. 14.

BEYOND THE BOOK

William Lyon MacKenzie King

http://www.abheritage.ca/albertans/speeches/king_1.html
A digitized speech by Prime Minister William Lyon Mackenzie King given in the House of Commons, 1947, detailing Canada's postwar immigration policy.

Auswanderer to Canadians

http://www.virtualmuseum.ca/Exhibitions/Migrations/english/avh/p1.html
Interviews with postwar German immigrants to Canada.

Portraits of Canadian Women of African Descent

http://www.civilization.ca/cultur/citoyennes/citoyennese.html
Interviews and digitized mementos of immigrant Canadian women of African descent.

Seeking Sanctuary

http://archives.cbc.ca/war_conflict/vietnam_war/topics/348
Video and radio material detailing the challenges faced by American immigrants to Canada who left in opposition to the Vietnam War.

Healthy Living for Immigrant Women

http://www.cmaj.ca/cgi/reprint/159/4/385.pdf

Description of a community-level health education program designed for immigrant women to Canada.

Seven Stories: Calgary

http://www.glenbow.org/sevenstories/seven_stories_popup.html

Richly illustrated, seven different Calgarians originally from Southeast Asia describe their different paths as immigrants to Canada, and how their lives have developed here.

Citizenship and Immigration Canada

http://www.cic.gc.ca/english/index.asp

Official website of the Canadian federal ministry of Citizenship and Immigration Canada. Details the process, rules, and statistics of immigration to the country.

Itsuka

Joy Kogawa, *Itsuka* (New York: Anchor Books, 1993). This novel's title means "someday"; it tells the story of the Japanese-Canadian community's struggle to achieve compensation for federal policies during World War II such as internment.

RELATED READINGS

R. Douglas Francis and Donald B. Smith, eds., *Viewpoints: Readings in Canadian History* (Toronto: Thomson Nelson, 2007), contains the following article relevant to this chapter: Will Kymlicka's "The Merits of Multiculturalism," pp. 562–71.

BIBLIOGRAPHY

For comprehensive overviews of Canada's immigration policy, see Ninette Kelley and Michael Trebilcock, *The Making of the Mosaic: A History of Canadian Immigration Policy* (Toronto: University of Toronto Press, 1998); and Donald H. Avery, *Reluctant Host: Canada's Response to Immigrant Workers, 1896–1994* (Toronto: McClelland & Stewart, 1995). Controversial questions are examined in Peter S. Li, *Destination Canada: Immigration Debates and Issues* (Toronto: Oxford University Press, 2003); Daniel Stoffman, *Who Gets In: What's Wrong with Canada's Immigration Policy—and How to Fix It* (Toronto: Macfarlane Walter & Ross, 2002); and Reg Whitaker, *Double Standard: The Secret History of Canadian Immigration* (Toronto: Lester & Orpen Dennys, 1987). Immigrant adjustment is studied in Shiva S. Halli and Leo Driedger, eds., *Immigrant Canada: Demographic, Economic, and Social Challenges* (Toronto: University of Toronto Press, 1999). The scholarly review *Canadian Ethnic Studies* contains a wealth of material on the various facets of the immigrant experience.

Among the many publications on ethnicity, see Augie Fleras and Jean Leonard Elliott, *Unequal Relations: An Introduction to Race, Ethnic, and Aboriginal Dynamics in Canada*, 5th ed. (Toronto: Pearson Prentice Hall, 2007); and Peter S. Li, ed., *Race and Ethnic Relations in Canada*, 2nd ed. (Toronto: Oxford University Press, 1999). Informative essays on all immigrant groups may be found in Paul Robert Magocsi, ed., *Encyclopedia of Canada's Peoples* (Toronto: Multicultural History Society of Ontario and University of Toronto Press, 1999). Norman Hillmer and J.L. Granatstein present an anthology of immigrant testimonies in *The Land Newly Found: Eyewitness Accounts of the Canadian Immigrant Experience* (Toronto: Thomas Allen Publishers, 2006). An ongoing series, "Canada's Ethnic Groups," published by the Canadian Historical Association with the support of the Canadian government's multiculturalism program, provides useful syntheses of immigrant experience in Canada.

The "Generations: A History of Canada's Peoples" series, published by McClelland and Stewart in conjunction with the Multiculturalism Directorate, contains book-length studies of many immigrant groups. The introductory volume to the series is Jean R. Burnet with Howard Palmer, *"Coming Canadians": An Introduction to a History of Canada's Peoples* (Toronto: McClelland & Stewart, 1988).

The Chinese experience in Canada is examined in Peter S. Li, *The Chinese in Canada*, 2nd ed. (Toronto: Oxford University Press, 1998). Studies of Italian immigrants include Nicholas DeMaria Harney, *Eh Paesan!: Being Italian in Toronto* (Toronto: University of Toronto Press, 1998); and Franca Iacovetta, *Such Hardworking People: Italian Immigrants in Postwar Toronto* (Montreal/Kingston: McGill-Queen's University Press, 1992). On Portuguese immigrants, see Carlos Teixeira and Victor M.P. Da Rosa, eds., *The Portuguese in Canada* (Toronto: University of Toronto Press, 2000). Scholarly works on the Jewish community include Robert J. Brym, William Shaffir, and Morton Weinfeld, eds., *The Jews in Canada* (Toronto: Oxford University Press, 1993); and Alan T. Davies, *Antisemitism in Canada: History and Interpretation* (Waterloo, ON: Wilfrid Laurier University Press, 1992).

On multiculturalism, see Richard J.F. Day, *Multiculturalism and the History of Canadian Diversity* (Toronto: University of Toronto Press, 2000); Augie Fleras and Jean Leonard Elliott, *Engaging Diversity: Multiculturalism in Canada*, 2nd ed. (Toronto: Nelson Thomson Learning, 2002); Janice Gross Stein et al., *Uneasy Partners: Multiculturalism and Rights in Canada* (Waterloo, ON: Wilfrid Laurier University Press, 2007); and, for comparative purposes, Will Kymlicka, *Multicultural Odysseys: Navigating the New International Politics of Diversity* (Oxford: Oxford University Press, 2007). Michael Adams presents Canadians' generally favourable attitudes to immigration and multiculturalism in *Unlikely Utopia: The Surprising Triumph of Canadian Pluralism* (Toronto: Viking Canada, 2007). Vigorous critiques of this policy may be found in Reginald Bibby, *Mosaic Madness: The Poverty and Potential of Life in Canada* (Toronto: Stoddart, 1990); and Neil Bissoondath, *Selling Illusions: The Cult of Multiculturalism in Canada*, rev. ed. (Toronto: Penguin Canada, 2002). Studies on racism and discrimination include Frances Henry et al., *The Colour of Democracy: Racism in Canadian Society*, 3rd ed. (Toronto: Thomson/Nelson, 2006); Evelyn Kallen, *Ethnicity and Human Rights in Canada: A Human Rights Perspective on Ethnicity, Racism and Systemic Inequality*, 3rd ed. (Toronto: Oxford University Press, 2003); and Leo Driedger and Shiva S. Halli, *Race and Racism: Canada's Challenge* (Montreal/Kingston: McGill-Queen's University Press, 2000).

[chapter title in cursive script]

Chapter Twenty-Five

CANADA IN THE 1970s AND 1980s: CONSTITUTION AND FREE TRADE

TIME LINE

1970	The environmental movement Greenpeace is founded in Vancouver
1971	Quebec rejects the Victoria Charter, containing Trudeau's proposals for constitutional reform and repatriation
1972	Team Canada vanquishes the Soviet hockey team The National Action Committee on the Status of Women is established
1976	Montreal hosts the 21st Olympic Games
1980	Trudeau launches the National Energy Program
1981	Terry Fox dies of cancer after running halfway across Canada
1982	The Canadian Constitution and the Charter of Rights and Freedoms are proclaimed
1984	Brian Mulroney's Progressive Conservatives take office in Ottawa
1986	Expo 86 is held in Vancouver
1988	The Free Trade Agreement is signed between Canada and the United States
1989	14 women students are slain at l'École Polytechnique in Montreal

The 1970s and 1980s brought continued change to Canada and to the lives of Canadians. Two major political figures dominated public life: Pierre Elliott Trudeau and Brian Mulroney. Trudeau had been chosen leader of the Liberal Party in 1968. Progressive Conservatives chose Mulroney to head their party in 1983. Both leaders succeeded in convincing Canadians to give them strong mandates in the House of Commons, but both soon found it difficult to maintain a workable political consensus in the face of rising discontent. Questions concerning the economy and public finances, relations between the provinces and Ottawa, trade and other links with the United States, and social issues divided Canadians. Regional imbalances within Canada compounded the difficulties. Yet each leader made changes that were to have a profound impact upon Canada's society and economy. Pierre Trudeau repatriated the Canadian constitution from Britain and in particular inserted within it a Charter of Rights and Freedoms. Brian Mulroney negotiated the Free Trade Agreement with the United States, signed in 1988.

During this period women, Aboriginals, francophones, gays and lesbians, ethnic groups, and other minorities brought governments to revise laws and policies in their favour. Public opinion gradually accepted these changes that were transforming Canadian society. Environmental groups also gained increased visibility, showing that more Canadians were coming to appreciate the harmful effects of unregulated economic growth and consumption on their environment.

Immense technological change came to the world, and to Canada, in these years. Memory chips, microprocessors, and floppy disks made their appearance in the early 1970s, and the first hobby computers came on the market later in that decade. In 1981, IBM released its revolutionary personal computer, instantly known as the PC. Bundled together with an optional monochrome display, a dot-matrix printer, up to 256K of user memory, two floppy disk drives, and appropriate software, the package cost a consumer well over $10 000 in today's currency. Proud owners could run database systems, do word processing, or play games. After a few short years, as new and more powerful machines appeared, the earliest models became museum pieces, or more likely headed for landfill sites.

Yet in some ways, more conservative attitudes and values asserted themselves. Economic difficulties, including a deep recession in the early 1980s, contributed to fostering more individualistic preoccupations. The transition proved painful. Increased state intervention in most aspects of life in the 1960s and 1970s had made citizens more dependent on governments and thus more demanding of them. Governments taxed more, but they also borrowed heavily to finance new social programs and address new challenges. Then, particularly after 1980, overstrained public finances dictated cuts in expenditures and rising taxes. In such circumstances there was little money for new programs.

The Trudeau Government

Although Canadians had given Trudeau a solid majority in the elections of 1968, they soon began to blame him for economic mismanagement as the country faced inflation as well as bouts of high unemployment. After 1970, rising prices became a serious and constant worry for consumers. Food and housing costs in particular went up steeply. Rapidly increasing prices of houses pushed younger Canadians out of the housing market. Low-income families, who had to spend three-quarters of their income on food and housing, were hardest hit because the prices of these two components of the cost of living index increased the fastest.

Politicians blamed outside forces for these substantial price increases. After all, inflation plagued most other countries, particularly the United States, where it was fed by the war in Vietnam. Moreover, world food prices moved sharply upward in response to greater demand. The Organization of Petroleum Exporting Countries (OPEC) increased oil prices substantially too, in 1973 and again in 1979.

Nevertheless, domestic causes of inflation also existed. Unions were accused of making unrealistically high wage demands that forced companies to raise their prices. In turn, labour blamed rising prices on excessive corporate profits. Inflation conditioned individuals to expect more inflation and to demand bigger wage increases. This behaviour, though understandable, ensured that the problem persisted.

Trudeau's Critics

The government's apparent inability to handle economic and social issues—not only inflation, but also unemployment, welfare, strikes, and high taxes—provoked voters' discontent. Questions of policy influenced electors as well. Trudeau attempted to give French Canada a larger stake in government by making it easier for francophones to use French in federal institutions and by recruiting more French-speaking politicians and civil servants. Francophones naturally approved of such initiatives, but some anglophones warned darkly that Quebec risked taking over Canada. In addition, by 1972, Trudeau's personality attracted less. The wave of Trudeaumania on which he had ridden to power in 1968 was now transformed into a swelling tide of Trudeauphobia, as the seemingly modest politician of 1968, who had said that he wanted to "dialogue" with Canadians and promote a "just society," became arrogant, remote, and temperamental.

Following the election of 1972, which the Liberals nearly lost, the Trudeau government worked to win back voter approval. It greatly increased public spending on social programs and indexed income-tax brackets and exemptions to the cost of living in order to protect taxpayers from inflation—measures that soon had catastrophic effects on government finances. It liberalized unemployment insurance access rules. To win support in populous central Canada, the government promised to keep oil prices (then increasing rapidly) at levels substantially below world levels—a policy that naturally infuriated the oil-producing provinces of western Canada. When opposition leader Robert Stanfield promised a wage and price freeze in 1974, Trudeau declared his opposition to such a freeze. "Zap! You're frozen!" he mocked in one notorious repartee. Then, after their resounding election victory, the Liberals reversed themselves and adopted a three-year wage and price freeze. The rate of increase in prices did slow, but it took more than controls and guidelines to defeat inflation.

The Rise and Fall of Economic Nationalism

By 1970, many Canadians, particularly in industrialized southern Ontario, were expressing concern for the high degree of foreign (especially American) ownership of the Canadian economy. Some urged large-scale nationalization of foreign-owned businesses and resources, or at least a gradual buying back of large enterprises. Others believed that actual ownership mattered little if Ottawa exercised stronger control over giant foreign-owned corporations operating in the country. Although the Trudeau government set up an agency to screen takeovers, American investment in Canada did not noticeably decline.

Change within Western Canada

The 1970s were years of rapid political, economic, and social change in Canada's western provinces. In spite of important distinctions among the provinces themselves, the region as a whole acquired greater power within Canada and now spoke with a louder voice.

In British Columbia, disenchantment with the long-governing Social Credit government of W.A.C. Bennett favoured the election of the New Democratic Party (NDP), which promised greater economic and social equality. Under combative leader Dave Barrett, it initiated many controversial reforms—its opponents accused it of "legislating by thunderbolt"—including public automobile insurance, a new innovative labour code, and an attempt to preserve agricultural land. Barrett's reforms, high spending, and new taxes led conservative forces to unite in reaction. An economic downturn assisted this new coalition in bringing the populist Social Credit Party back to power in 1975.

In neighbouring Alberta, Calgary lawyer Peter Lougheed revived the provincial Progressive Conservative Party, infusing it with the promise both of change and of continuity with conservative traditions. Strongly supported by urban Alberta, the Conservatives won power in 1971 and established a new political dynasty, sweeping away Social Credit, which had governed the province for 36 years. The immense amounts of oil money flowing into the provincial treasury allowed Albertans to enjoy high-quality social services while paying the country's lowest provincial income taxes and no provincial sales tax.

Saskatchewan's booming economy in the 1970s also generated increasing revenues that enabled the province's NDP government to pursue an agenda of "province-building." It nationalized a large American-owned potash company, and launched a vigorous exploration and development program in uranium. It established an enterprise that served as a holding company for the province's state-owned companies such as Sask Tel, Sask Power, and Saskoil, and that also bought large blocks of shares in private companies.

Agriculture, the province's largest industry, remained subject to violent swings, depending on world wheat prices, export markets, and weather conditions. Low prices for grain and the high costs of technological innovation forced smaller and less efficient farmers to sell their land to larger operators and to migrate elsewhere in search of work. Disused grain elevators, abandoned rail lines, and closed hospitals symbolized the sad breakdown of small-town Saskatchewan.

The left-wing NDP also governed Manitoba for much of the 1970s. In these years of relative prosperity, the province spent heavily on public housing and adopted major tax and social reforms. It also launched a second huge hydroelectric development project in the north. As in British Columbia and Saskatchewan, critics on the right denounced increased state intervention under the NDP, warning that the province was moving toward socialism.

Continuing Dissatisfaction

Between 1974 and 1979, the polls showed support for the federal Liberals fluctuating wildly. By 1979, with Canada again in a severe inflationary crisis, the business community in particular worried about the foundering economy and the rapidly rising federal deficit, which the government financed by borrowing heavily, even at historically high interest rates.

Regional discontent increased, too. Westerners, in particular, complained that Trudeau paid little heed to their concerns. Alberta and Saskatchewan feuded with Ottawa over the pricing and taxing of natural resources. Frustrated wheat farmers, hurt by mounting world surpluses of wheat and sagging prices, exhorted the federal government to act, while

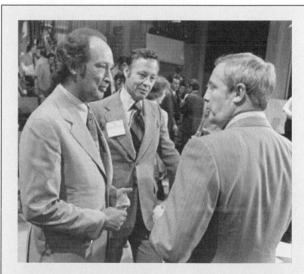

Prime Minister Pierre Trudeau and Alberta premier Peter Lougheed, 1973, at the Western Economic Opportunities Conference in Calgary. Appearances can be deceiving— despite the cordiality evident in this photograph, animosity existed between the two leaders over the federal government's pricing of Alberta oil and gas.

Herald Collection/Glenbow Archives, Calgary, Canada/ NA-2864-23502.

an equally frustrated Prime Minister Trudeau asked rhetorically: "Why should I sell your wheat?" With the notable exception of Quebec, the Trudeau consensus largely broke apart, with the result that the Progressive Conservatives, under their new leader, Joe Clark, a federal MP from Alberta, won a fragile mandate in the election of May 1979.

Conservative Interlude

The energy question precipitated the collapse of Clark's brief minority government and a return to power of the Liberals in 1980. Promoting a policy of "short-term pain for long-term gain," the Conservatives proposed a 4-cent-per-litre excise tax on gasoline designed to bring billions of dollars into the federal treasury in order to attack the rising deficit. When Clark's budget proposals were defeated in the House of Commons, the government was forced to resign. During the ensuing election campaign, Trudeau promised to revoke the immensely unpopular tax. After regaining power, he in turn soon imposed new gasoline taxes.

National Energy Program

Trudeau's final mandate began with a bitter crisis in relations between the federal government and Alberta. Strongly influenced by Ontario's demands to have oil and gas considered "national commodities, belonging to all Canadians," the Trudeau government established the National Energy Program (NEP), with a "made-in-Canada" oil price that allowed Canadian consumers to pay prices lower than the world price. The producing provinces denounced federal price controls, which deprived them of billions of dollars. Ottawa responded that too great a transfer of wealth to one province risked upsetting the equilibrium of Confederation.

Reacting to Ottawa's measures the Alberta government reduced the flow of crude oil to the East, and some Alberta automobile bumpers sported stickers belligerently inviting easterners to "freeze in the dark." Western anger grew, and suddenly respectable separatist parties urged westerners "to take to the lifeboat of independence before it's too late."

Another objective of NEP was to Canadianize the petroleum industry by reducing the role of American oil companies in Canada. The Alberta government also opposed this aspect of federal policy, blaming it for the decline in investment in the oil fields. Likewise western Canada's business community denounced Ottawa's intervention, while the U.S. trade representative complained about the consequences of discrimination against American firms.

The Trudeau government's initiative proved ill timed. Just as it spent billions of dollars purchasing foreign oil companies and assisting exploration by Canadian companies, oil prices crashed dramatically. Ironically, heavily indebted Dome Petroleum, a creation of Liberal energy policies, was sold to an American oil company in 1988.

Recession struck the Canadian economy in 1981–1982. It resulted in part from government monetary policy, particularly high interest rates, designed to dampen inflationary pressures. (Indeed, there appeared to be no solution that would enable governments to combat inflation and unemployment simultaneously.) Recession also stemmed from worldwide overproduction in the resource industries, in agriculture, and in secondary manufacturing. The daily press offered a sombre litany of factory closings, layoffs, and cutbacks

In the West, in particular, the recession undermined the heady confidence that people had felt during the prosperous 1970s. The decline in demand for oil, followed by sharply lower oil prices in 1986, checked Alberta's growth and clearly showed the basic fragility of its resource-based economy. Work on construction projects ceased. The province's jobless rate matched eastern Canadian levels. Real estate values fell sharply. The oil industry called upon both Edmonton and Ottawa for assistance; after having denounced Ottawa's attempts to impose a ceiling on oil prices in 1980, it now urged the federal government to apply a floor price to provide some stability to the industry. At the same time, agriculture faced serious difficulties, as drought afflicted farmers in the province's southern region and declining world prices and increased costs wiped out profit margins.

The Constitution of 1982

Trudeau had more success with his plan to "patriate" the Constitution, and particularly to insert within it a Charter of Rights and Freedoms and an amending formula by which the United Kingdom's formal consent would no longer be necessary for constitutional changes. Although most Canadians outside Quebec approved of Trudeau's initiative, Quebec refused to sign the agreement, which had been negotiated in its absence during what that province's delegates termed "the night of the long knives." Thus, the province that since 1960 had been most insistent on the need for constitutional change was not a party to the reformed Constitution.

The signing of the Canadian constitution by Her Majesty Queen Elizabeth II, April 1982. Prime Minister Trudeau looks on. The new constitution ended the British parliament's power to amend the British North America (BNA) Act, and also included a Charter of Rights and Freedoms.

CP Images (Ron Polling)

Women's groups won the inclusion in the Charter of an article affirming the equality of male and female persons. The Aboriginal peoples' associations succeeded in their efforts to entrench Aboriginal and treaty rights. The Métis also achieved constitutional recognition as an Aboriginal people. But the Charter recognized only existing rights, and left these undefined.

Trudeau's Record

In the immediate term, however, most Canadians were more interested in bread-and-butter issues than in constitutional changes. Finally, the constantly unfavourable polls resulting from Canadians' dissatisfaction with the Liberals' management of the economy and the selection by the Conservatives of businessman Brian Mulroney to replace Joe Clark as party leader convinced Trudeau that he should resign.

The Trudeau years were replete with paradoxes. Trudeau championed the trusty Liberal theme of national unity at each election. Yet, during his term in office, the country faced the most serious threats to its existence that it had ever confronted, from the western provinces and especially from Quebec, which held a referendum on its future links with Canada in 1980 (see Chapter 23). Trudeau had also pushed for the inclusion of the Charter of Rights and Freedoms in the Constitution, insisting on the need to defend Canadians' political liberties. Yet, during the FLQ crisis of October 1970, his government had invoked the War Measures Act and thereby effectively suspended civil liberties, enabling the police to arrest hundreds of individuals and to hold them incommunicado for several days, without ever laying charges against most of them.

Trudeau frequently denounced the dangers of nationalism, especially French-Canadian and Quebec nationalism, but his legislation controlling foreign investment, as well as his National Energy Program of 1980, convinced Americans that he was a strident nationalist. Furthermore, Trudeau had promised to battle regional imbalances. Although measures such as increased equalization payments and other transfers helped reduce disparities, they had "little effect," as economist Paul Phillips has pointed out, "on their root causes."[1]

Trudeau had long spoken of the need to build a "just society," but what role were women to play in bringing such a society about? During the first Trudeau mandate (1968–1972), the House of Commons had only one female member. Feminists complained that parties showed no interest in working to recruit promising female candidates. Although society's changing attitudes brought a slow improvement, by 1980 only 15 women representing three parties won seats in the House. A decade later, although more women were involved in the various phases of party activity, most continued, in political scientist Sylvia Bashevkin's words, to "toe the lines" and to fill "conventional maintenance roles."[2]

In foreign affairs, Trudeau rejected Canada's traditional role as a "helpful fixer" in favour of a policy based on national self-interest. Certainly the sale of arms to military dictatorships during his tenure showed the precedence commercial interests took over human rights. Nonetheless, Canada did significantly increase its developmental assistance to Third World nations. In the early 1970s Trudeau cut defence spending, thereby incurring the wrath of Canada's NATO allies. But Canada ultimately retained all of its alliance commitments, and defence spending increased thereafter.

The Charter and Bilingualism

By the time of Trudeau's death in 2000, Canadians believed the Charter of Rights and Freedoms to be his greatest legacy, a defining element of the Canadian identity. People said they trusted judges more than politicians to defend their rights. Certainly Charter decisions changed the face of Canada, by upholding minority and individual rights. Conservatives accused judges of acting too often as social engineers who usurped the power of elected legislators or who were too lenient on crime. From the early 1990s, however, the courts assumed a more deferential stance toward parliamentarians and law enforcement.

Trudeau's dream of a bilingual Canada at first enthused many Canadians, particularly French-speakers who aspired to linguistic equality. His government adopted the Official Languages Act in 1969 in an effort to make government services more widely available in French. While slow progress made French Canadians despair of ever attaining genuine equality, many English-speaking Canadians complained that they were now the victims of unfair treatment.

At Trudeau's death, French immersion programs remained popular, although questions were raised about their effectiveness. But while English-language study was mandatory in Quebec (and now begins in Grade 1), second-language instruction remained optional in several English-speaking provinces. The federal official languages commissioner blamed the federal government for failing to show leadership in promoting bilingualism. Outside Quebec, many federal offices designated as bilingual were unable to offer service in French. Air Canada consistently flouted language laws with impunity. The census of 2006 showed that, while the number of French-speaking Quebeckers able to converse in English increased to well over 40 percent, English-speaking Canadians outside Quebec became even less bilingual.

Francophone minorities outside Quebec also turned to provincial governments in their attempts to obtain recognition of linguistic rights. In 1968, New Brunswick adopted the Official Languages Act, which gave official recognition to bilingualism. Then, through the 1970s and 1980s, the province's government cautiously proclaimed and applied the law's various clauses. In the early 1970s, Acadians confronted Moncton's mayor, Leonard Jones, an adamant opponent of bilingual municipal services. Jones's obstinacy—which students from the Université de Moncton underlined by depositing a severed pig's head on the mayor's doorstep—probably served as a catalyst for the Acadians' struggle.

In one instance in particular, the battle for rights reached epic proportions. In 1985, the Supreme Court of Canada found that Manitoba had violated the Constitution when it abolished official bilingualism nearly a century earlier. When the court ordered that thousands of public documents be translated into French, francophones proposed a compromise involving far less translation in exchange for new, more useful French-language services. The government agreed but the provincial Conservative party, then in opposition, appealed to what historian Raymond Hébert described as the "underlying virulent racism" of anti-francophone populist groups and adamantly opposed any new "concessions."[3] The NDP government retreated. Yet the crisis in Manitoba eventually helped Franco-Manitobans obtain new rights, primarily the right to administer their own schools, by forcing them to return before the courts.

New rights in the provinces as well as federal assistance to French-language minorities did not stem the decline through rapid assimilation of most French-speaking minorities outside Quebec. Census statistics from 1991 to 2006 showed clearly that, except in Quebec and New Brunswick, the promise of a bilingual Canada was floundering beneath the overwhelming weight of English.

The Progressive Conservatives in Power

Trudeau left John Turner, his successor as Liberal Party leader and prime minister, to justify his failures. In 1984, Canadians reacted by voting for what appeared to be real change: they gave Brian Mulroney and his Conservative party a resounding electoral victory, including a majority of Quebec's ridings. Though women still held fewer than 10 percent of the seats in the House, they made up one-fifth of Mulroney's first cabinet.

The Canada of the mid-1980s differed greatly from that of the 1970s. As in the United States, a more conservative mood prevailed. For many Canadians, Liberal support of increased state intervention and of the federal government's strategic role in the economy now signified unacceptably high levels of government spending, rising taxes, and government interference. The Conservatives' praise for free enterprise and their vision of a more decentralized Canada, a "community of communities," appeared more appropriate.

The Rise and Fall of Corporate Giants

As a sign of the times, a new group of entrepreneurs kindled popular interest. Among them were the Bronfmans, whose companies boasted assets of $120 billion in 1988; Albert and Paul Reichmann, who built a vast real-estate and resource empire, much of which crashed down with the collapse of property values after 1990; Conrad Black of the Toronto-based Argus Corporation, whom journalist Peter Newman presented rather heroically as the new prince of the Canadian establishment—Black would soon be given a seat in the British House of Lords; Galen Weston, who succeeded in the 1980s and 1990s in making the seemingly moribund Loblaws supermarket chain into the industry leader; and Pierre Péladeau, of Quebecor in Montreal, whose holdings grew from a tiny periodical, bought in 1950, to a $450 million newspaper and printing empire. Canadians also watched in alarmed fascination as big multinational businesses became even bigger through mergers frequently worth billions of dollars.

The First Mulroney Government

Although business welcomed the new Conservative government, Mulroney's appeal was much wider. He had promised an "era of national reconciliation," notably in federal–provincial relations. Mulroney appeased the West by dismantling the National Energy Program, and he pleased Quebec by promising to negotiate that province's acceptance of the Constitution of 1982.

Prime Minister Brian Mulroney greets American president Ronald Reagan on his arrival for the "Shamrock Summit" at Quebec City, 1985, during which both leaders made much of their Irish origins. Mulroney hailed the summit as the inauguration of a new positive era in Canadian–American relations.

CP Photo (Paul Chiasson)

Mulroney also satisfied Nova Scotia and Newfoundland by yielding them control of offshore mineral resources. The discovery of gas and oil off the Atlantic coast raised hopes for an economic boom in the region. Mulroney also set up the Atlantic Canada Opportunities Agency, which, like earlier programs, offered grants to businesses operating in the Atlantic provinces. All told, federal grants in the region under Trudeau and Mulroney totalled more than $5 billion between 1970 and 1995, but they produced "no appreciable closing of the gap between have and have-not provinces as measured by per capita income or unemployment rates."[4] Direct money transfers from Ottawa to individuals, in the form of unemployment insurance, welfare, and other payments, did help to boost household incomes.

The Conservatives had also blamed the Liberals for Canada's uneasy relations with the United States. Announcing that Canada was again "open for business," the Mulroney government worked to encourage foreign investment. In the course of Mulroney's two mandates, Canada–U.S. relations underwent, as historian John Herd Thompson put it, "a revolutionary shift toward ideological and political convergence and a remarkable accommodation on a wide range of divisive issues,"[5] particularly those concerning trade, commerce, and energy policies.

Other Conservative foreign-policy initiatives gained approval from specific interest groups. Human rights advocates praised Mulroney for his condemnation of racial discrimination in South Africa and vigorous support of sanctions against that country. French Canada approved of Mulroney's efforts to forge closer links with *la francophonie*, a loose association of the world's French-speaking states. Most Canadians took pride in Canada's commitment to international peacekeeping and to developmental assistance.

The strong job-creating economic recovery also aided the Conservatives. The decline in the inflation rate, from 12.5 percent in 1981 to only 4 percent in 1985, brought interest rates down, making it possible again for businesses and consumers to borrow. The omens appeared favourable for the construction of a new political consensus among Canadians.

Yet the Conservative honeymoon proved brief. The Mulroney government's frequent bouts with scandal and conflicts of interest, implicating several cabinet ministers, soon hurt its public image. Regionalism rose phoenix-like out of the country's flagrantly unequal economic recovery. While southern Ontario basked in virtually full employment, Quebec, the West, and the Atlantic provinces faced continued high jobless rates. The decline of oil and resource prices, coinciding with a severe farm crisis, hurt the economies of the western provinces in particular.

The Federal Deficit

Mulroney also found it difficult to reduce his government's huge budgetary deficit. As the national debt grew, Ottawa had to devote about one-quarter of its revenues simply to paying the interest on its borrowings. Mulroney promised "unyielding determination" to eradicate the deficit.

In spite of the government's valiant stands, the political necessity of maintaining federal expenditures hampered plans to control spending. When Ottawa reduced grants to the provinces, provincial governments accused it of pushing its deficit on to them. Ordinary Canadians, especially the worried middle classes, prevailed upon the government to reaffirm its somewhat wavering faith in the universality of social programs such as old-age pensions. Labour and the poorer provinces rallied to the defence of the much-maligned unemployment insurance program. Ottawa clearly understood the political risks of effecting drastic cuts in spending. Rather than reducing expenses, the government found it easier to raise income and sales taxes substantially, and to continue to borrow.

The Great Free-Trade Debate

The negotiation of a comprehensive trade agreement with the United States became the Mulroney government's most passionately debated initiative during its first mandate.

Canada has always sought wide access to foreign markets for its exports, while simultaneously using tariffs to reduce imports to protect Canadian jobs in industries unable to withstand competition from abroad. When multilateral trade negotiations discredited protective tariffs, Canada, like many other countries, erected a host of non-tariff barriers, such as quotas, in an effort to impede the entry of cheap imports of goods such as clothing and footwear. The downward slide of the Canadian dollar after 1976 helped less productive Canadians compete in foreign markets. It also meant that imports cost more.

As trade increased with the United States, Canada insistently proclaimed its belief in diversification. Yet by 1985, fully 80 percent of Canada's exports went to the United States, and 70 percent of its imports originated there. Prime Minister Brian Mulroney now argued in favour of even closer trade relations with the Americans. He asserted that a free-trade agreement with the United States would create jobs. Increased sales of goods in that market would also diminish Canada's burgeoning balance of payments deficit in relation to the flow of investment income, tourism, services, and interest payments to foreign lenders to finance the growing mountain of federal debt. Many sectors of the business community favoured free trade. Polls showed that, in the early stages of the debate, a solid majority of Canadians backed it, too. Consumers were generally convinced that free trade would bring lower prices.

Opposition to Free Trade

As the debate heated up, public support for free trade cooled. American protectionist measures weakened Canadian enthusiasm, though at the same time they seemed to make some form of agreement even more urgent. Labour unions, farmers, the churches, the federal New Democratic and Liberal parties, the government of Ontario, and several businesses warned that free trade would cost thousands of jobs. They argued that American companies might close their higher cost branch plants in Canada and serve the Canadian market from their more cost efficient American bases. Anti–free traders further warned that a deal could endanger Canada's more generous social programs, and that it even risked jeopardizing Canada's political sovereignty.

The Canada–U.S. Free Trade Agreement

Arduous negotiations culminated in an accord in 1987. By its terms, tariffs would end gradually, and Canada would gain enhanced access to most sectors of the American market. To resolve trade disputes, the agreement created a binational review panel that would simply ensure that each country's trade agencies made their decisions on the basis of existing law. (The United

States would later make frequent use of this measure to block or penalize imports from Canada.) In future, Canada could no longer bar most American takeovers of Canadian industries. Moreover, although Canada gained unrestricted access for energy exports to the United States, the deal also secured American access to Canadian supplies even in times of shortages. But Canada did obtain exemptions for its agricultural products sold through marketing boards and its threatened cultural enterprises.

WHERE SOCIAL SCIENTISTS DISAGREE

The Debate over Free Trade

In the late 1980s, economists and political scientists and even a few historians waded into the fray to debate the burning issue of free trade with the United States. Many expressed strong opposition. Economist Fred Lazar judged that the agreement virtually gave the American government the right to determine acceptable Canadian government policies.[1] For political scientist Garth Stevenson, free trade risked undermining the central government's raison d'être, since Ottawa could exercise "only minimal powers over the economy."[2] As for economist James Laxer, free trade was a "leap of faith" into the unknown that Canada would do well to avoid.[3] Other observers judged the project more favourably. Economist John Crispo reminded his opponents that an economically more dynamic Canada could also provide more support for culture, social security, and regional development.[4]

Many observers feared, or even hoped, that Canada would ultimately be obliged to harmonize its policies with American policies. In the opinion of political scientist Peter Cumming, it would be in Canada's own best interest if it forced the country to "revamp outdated policies."[5] For political scientist David Leyton-Brown, the real question was whether free trade would bring about a greater degree of "harmonization" than would have occurred without free trade. His modest reply: "That question is of course unanswerable."[6]

In the field of culture, negotiators contended that Canada's sovereignty was protected. For historian John Herd Thompson, however, Canada appeared to admit the American definition of culture, that cultural industries were a business like any other. Thompson saw this convergence of understandings of culture as holding "greater peril for Canada's cultural sovereignty than any threatened U.S. retaliation to specific Canadian policies of cultural protection and promotion."[7]

The Free Trade Agreement was signed in 1988. Trade policy analyst Michael Hart noted that, by the early 1990s, freer trade had become "the norm" while its critics had been "marginalized."[8] In 1994, Mexico joined Canada and the United States in launching the North American Free Trade Agreement (NAFTA). Cross-border trade and investment more than doubled in the years 1990–1995. In regard to culture and values, had free trade made Canadians more like Americans? Without a doubt, answered historian Jack Granatstein, provocatively, Canadians "are American in all but name."[9] Certainly not, replied pollster Michael Adams. Americans "have become a nation of God-fearing Darwinists, we have become a collection of tolerant social democrats."[10]

1. Fred Lazar, "The Trade Agreement: A Dissenting Opinion," in Marc Gold and David Leyton-Brown, eds., *Trade-Offs on Free Trade: The Canada–U.S. Free Trade Agreement* (Toronto: Carswell, 1988), p. 435.

2. Garth Stevenson, "The Agreement and Dynamics of Canadian Federalism," ibid., p. 140.

3. James Laxer, *Leap of Faith: Free Trade and the Future of Canada* (Edmonton: Hurtig, 1986).

4. John Crispo, *Free Trade: The Real Story* (Toronto: Gage, 1988), p. 204.

5. Peter Cumming, "Impact of the Free Trade Agreement on Public Policy," in Gold and Leyton-Brown, p. 433.

6. David Leyton-Brown, "The Canada–U.S. Free Trade Agreement," in Andrew B. Gollner and Daniel Salée, eds., *Canada under Mulroney: An End-of-Term Report* (Montreal: Véhicule Press, 1988), p. 117.

7. John Herd Thompson, "Canada's Quest for Cultural Sovereignty: Protection, Promotion, and Popular Culture," in Stephen J. Randall and Herman W. Konrad, eds., *NAFTA in Transition* (Calgary: University of Calgary Press, 1995), p. 410.

8. Michael Hart, *A Trading Nation: Canadian Trade Policy from Colonialism to Globalization* (Vancouver: UBC Press, 2002), p. 396.

9. Jack Granatstein, *Yankee Go Home? Canadians and Anti-Americanism* (Toronto: HarperCollins, 1996), p. 9.

10. Michael Adams, *Sex in the Snow: Canadian Social Values at the End of the Millennium* (Toronto: Penguin Books, 1998), p. 194.

By refusing to accept the accord, the Liberal-dominated Senate forced an election in late 1988. Discussion of free trade became the major issue. The victory of the Conservatives, though with a substantially reduced majority, ensured ratification of the agreement in early 1989. As plant closures brought steep job losses in 1989 and 1990, the labour movement blamed free trade. Other observers placed the responsibility on high interest rates, a rising Canadian dollar, a relative decline in productivity, increased taxes, and a deteriorating international economic situation. The Conservative government pushed on. Shortly after the election, it agreed to sign a new treaty with the United States and Mexico forming a North American free-trade zone. Canada had opted for a continentalist economy. There would be no turning back.

Demography

After 1970, Canada's population growth slowed to a rate of about 1 percent a year. High levels of immigration, not births, now explained much of the country's growth. Provinces whose population continued to expand rapidly, such as Alberta in the 1970s and Ontario in the 1980s, were those whose vigorous economies attracted newcomers both from abroad and from other Canadian provinces. Urban Canada continued to grow after 1970, though more slowly than in the 1950s and 1960s. Many rural areas and centres based on the exploitation of resources lost population.

The Birth Rate

By 1970, couples no longer had enough children to replace themselves. By the mid-1980s, the average Canadian family had shrunk to include a mere 1.6 children. Many women simply postponed having children. But sociologists noted an increase in "yuppie-style" marriages they called "dinks"—dual-income, no kids—as many couples found it difficult to juggle children and careers. After 1970, recourse to new birth-control methods became more frequent. For example, thousands of men and women in their thirties underwent voluntary sterilization.

The number of abortions also increased. That issue began to provoke passionate debate in Canada in the 1960s. Under a law adopted by Parliament in 1969, abortions remained illegal except when continued pregnancy threatened a woman's life or health. Discontented with the arbitrariness of the law, women's groups mobilized to demand the decriminalization of abortion. Finally, in 1988, the Supreme Court of Canada found the abortion law to be unconstitutional. Although the Mulroney government attempted to recriminalize abortion in a new bill in 1990, the Senate defeated the measure.

Changing Family Patterns

The revolution in family patterns continued through the 1970s and 1980s. Divorces became even more frequent, particularly after 1985, when new legislation made "marital breakdown," evidenced by a year or more of separation or by adultery or cruelty, the only grounds for divorce. Revised laws granting each spouse half of the property accumulated during the life of the marriage also contributed to making divorce a viable financial option for the spouse who owned no property independently—most often, the wife. Common-law unions gained in popularity, especially among younger Canadians. Governments moved to adapt legislation to this trend. Changing family patterns ensured that child care now became an important issue. Political scientist Rianne Mahon has noted that growing numbers of dual-earner couples and single-parent families produced a "crisis of care" that made non-parental child-care arrangements essential.[6]

Gays and Lesbians   Gays and lesbians increasingly worked for self-affirmation and liberation after 1970. They denounced what they viewed as police harassment and repression, and demanded better protection from "gay-bashing" and other forms of violence. They rallied to such cries as "Out of the closets and into the streets," and "Gay is just as good as straight."

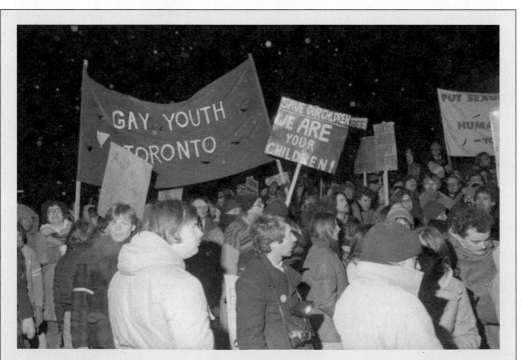

Gay community activists in Toronto, protesting a speech by right-wing family values advocate Anita Bryant, 1978.

Archives of Ontario/C193-3-0-3167, 78285-20, AO5290.

Gay groups pursued agendas of political and social activism. Television series began to portray homosexuals in less stereotypical terms. In 1977, Quebec became the first province to prohibit discrimination by reason of sexual orientation.

Canada's first Gay Pride celebration was staged discreetly in Toronto, in August 1972, with activities and a picnic on Toronto Island. A quarter-century later, 750 000 people attended a Gay Pride parade in Toronto, more than in any other North American city. Canadians did indeed begin to show greater tolerance, but gays hastened to point out that tolerance did not mean acceptance.

The Changing Role of Women

After 1970, relations between the sexes underwent a fundamental transformation. Twenty years later, though the goal of full equality was still far from being achieved, the male-dominated society of a generation earlier had been substantially eroded. Women worked within a multitude of organizations, and promoted a variety of visions, to bring about these changes.

Institutionalized Feminism

When the government failed to act quickly on the recommendations of the Royal Commission on the Status of Women, women established, in 1972, a National Action Committee embracing 600 associations representing more than five million women. Growing pressure brought Prime Minister Pierre Trudeau to appoint a minister responsible for the status of women and to establish the Canadian Advisory Council on the Status of Women. Most provinces appointed similar advisory councils. Quebec's Conseil du statut de la femme, equipped with funds for research, produced a detailed plan for change, *Égalité et indépendance*. Women's groups organized a multitude of conferences and workshops during 1975, the year the United Nations decreed to be International Women's Year.

The Home

In part, the home became the battleground for equality of the sexes. Change came slowly, and child care continued to be mainly women's work. Polls suggested that Canadians in general wanted men to take responsibility for a greater share of the housework; men themselves were not so sure.

The 1980s brought to the fore one very sombre element, hitherto seldom discussed openly: violence against women. In 1987, in response to a bleak report, *Battered but Not Beaten*, Ottawa announced major funding initiatives. Local women's groups opened shelters to assist homeless and battered women. They also set up rape crisis centres, fought for laws restricting pornography, and organized assistance for Aboriginal women, immigrant and refugee women, and women on welfare.

Editorial staff of Chatelaine, 1972. *Traditionally a home-makers' magazine,* Chatelaine *switched its emphasis to women's issues in the 1970s.*

Courtesy of *Chatelaine*. © Maclean Hunter Publishing Ltd.

Women in the Workforce

In the 1970s, union membership grew four times more quickly among females than it did among males. Unions themselves started to pay greater heed to women's needs. Women's committees succeeded in convincing some unions to adopt policies on child care, maternity benefits, equal pay for work of equal value, job safety, sexual harassment, and discrimination. The myth of female docility evaporated rapidly as women-dominated organizations such as nurses' unions waged bitter, sometimes illegal, strikes against what they judged to be unsatisfactory working conditions. Although women remained underrepresented as union executives, particularly in international unions, they began to play a greater role, as symbolized by the election in 1975 of Grace Hartman as president of the Canadian Union of Public Employees (CUPE), Canada's largest union. Yet the majority of women still worked in difficult-to-organize sectors such as banks, restaurants, offices, and retail stores. They often worked part-time as well.

By the 1970s, the principle of equal pay for men and women performing the same task had gained wide recognition. Yet, in the 1980s, the average woman's wage remained at approximately 65 percent of the average man's. Although women's lesser work experience and the generally lower educational levels of older women explained part of this difference, the continued concentration of women in low-paying occupations appeared to be the principal factor.

Challenges for Labour

While the claims of women moved forward rapidly after 1970, those of labour encountered serious obstacles. Union militancy, usually aimed at obtaining higher salaries and better working conditions, increased in the 1970s. In particular, the numerous strikes in the public sector during the 1970s alienated public opinion. Taxpayers quickly realized that they would have to foot the bill for what many viewed as excessive government generosity. Moreover, most Canadian workers did not belong to unions. They, as well as many workers affiliated to small organizations, resented the attempts of the most powerful unions to secure a greater share of the national wealth for their members.

The 1980s brought new challenges. A more conservative public approved governments that moved to restrain wages and limit strikes. Manufacturing industries and resource-sector companies laid off workers. Strong unions fought—sometimes quite successfully, as in the case of the autoworkers and the steelworkers—for job security and better pensions, and for wage protection against inflation and new taxes. Canadian autoworkers, favouring a less bureaucratic and more militant and democratic union, broke away from the American union in 1985 and then negotiated a made-in-Canada agreement with their employers. To reverse the decline in their numbers, unions signed up workers from outside their original jurisdictions.

Cultural Concerns

After 1970, university expansion slowed. Student enrolments increased more modestly, although the proportion of women grew rapidly. By the century's end, full-time women students were far more numerous than men in most university bachelor's and master's degree programs; men, however, were still a majority in doctoral programs.

A crisis in university financing appeared during the 1980s, as deficit-ridden provinces forced universities to accept real cuts in spending. Significantly, not one new university opened its doors in Canada between 1980 and 1994. Most provinces also imposed higher tuition fees and turned enthusiastically to corporate benefactors for additional financing. In his study of academic freedom, historian Michiel Horn worried that universities' closer relationships with business interests threatened "a fundamental university objective, one that academic freedom is meant to protect, namely, the disinterested pursuit of knowledge."[7]

New religious groups in Canada. A photo taken on Ste. Catherine Street, Montreal, May 1993. Religion had become both more personal and highly diversified. Sociologist Reginald Bibby claimed that Canadians now want "religion 'à la carte,' preferring to pick and choose ... from ... religious smorgasbords."

Michel Brunelle.

Contemporary Religion

Immigration from Asia diversified Canada's religious face, as sizable communities of Muslims, Buddhists, and Hindus became established. For most Canadians, however, the emphasis on individuality meant that religion became largely a personal matter. Canadians moved away from religions based on theology and denominational identification, and toward a view of religion as an inspiration for moral and ethical behaviour. The great majority said they still expected to turn to organized religion for rites such as baptisms, weddings, and funerals, but, with the notable exception of members of smaller Protestant conservative and evangelical churches, they attached less and less importance to regular attendance at worship services. While two Canadians in three attended weekly religious services in 1946, only one in five did so in 2001. Sociologist Reginald Bibby, a long-time observer of Canadian religious behaviour, judged that Canadians now wanted "religion 'à la carte,' preferring to pick and choose beliefs, practices, programs, and professional services from increasingly diversified religious smorgasbords."[8] At the same time, he viewed most churches as simply unable to "sell their product effectively."

Sports

Spectator sports dominated popular culture. Athletes basked in glory as long as they scored goals, hit runs, or won races on the slopes in the winter and on the speedways in the summer, and as long as they avoided the steroids that proved to be widely used in certain field sports. Hockey enjoyed immense interest, but it now had to share the spotlight with football, baseball, and, increasingly, basketball. Big-league baseball came to Montreal in 1969, when the Expos began to play. Toronto had to wait until 1977 for its team, the Blue Jays, which became the most financially successful enterprise in any sport.

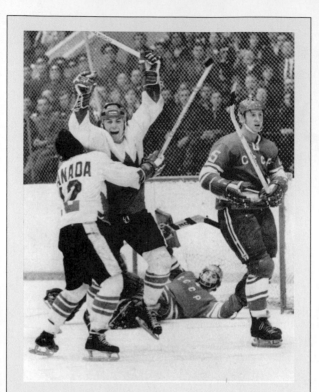

The most famous winning goal in Canadian hockey, scored by Paul Henderson in Moscow in the final game of the 1972 Canada–USSR hockey series, with just 34 seconds of play remaining. On the 25th anniversary of the goal in 1997, Canada Post issued a stamp honouring Henderson.

CP Photo (Toronto Star/Frank Lennon)

Hockey underwent an important expansion in the 1970s as the National Hockey League took in several franchises from the failed World Hockey Association. Although most players were Canadian, most new teams were American. Wayne Gretzky, undoubtedly the sport's brightest star of this era, attained the crowning glory of being pictured on the cover of *Time*. Shortly afterward the Edmonton Oilers relinquished their superstar to the Los Angeles Kings— an act akin to high treason in the eyes of many angry fans. As players' salaries soared, teams found survival more difficult in small Canadian markets. Some owners then sought to sell their teams. The Quebec Nordiques, for example, successful but playing in a small market, were transferred to Denver in 1995 where they promptly won the Stanley Cup.

In the late 1960s, Ottawa discovered the importance of sport as an instrument for promoting national unity and yielding political capital. It then began investing heavily in high-performance sports in order to produce more medal-winners in international competitions. The Canada–Soviet hockey series in 1972 showed that the return on such investments could be considerable. Watched by the largest Canadian television audience on record until that time, Team Canada won the series in the last seconds of the dramatic final encounter. One ecstatic Canadian university president suggested that the series probably did more to create a Canadian identity than ten years of Canada Council fellowships.

Montreal hosted the summer Olympic Games in 1976, the first time that this prestigious international gathering took place in Canada. (In 1988, Calgary welcomed the winter Olympics.) Provincial and municipal taxpayers were uneasy at the prospect of budget deficits, but Montreal mayor Jean Drapeau assured them there was no more possibility of incurring a deficit than there was of his becoming pregnant. After the Olympic lottery, Olympic coins, Olympic stamps, and other promotional paraphernalia failed to prevent a massive deficit, delighted cartoonists drew sketches of a pregnant mayor. The games themselves provided much excitement, though Canadian prowess would be much greater at the Los Angeles Olympics in 1984.

Cultural Industries

In the nationalist climate of the 1970s, cultural development came to be inextricably linked to the affirmation of national identity. For many English-speaking Canadians, the danger to survival came increasingly from the United States, mainly because many other Canadians avidly consumed that country's cultural products.

After 1970, the Americanization of Canadian broadcasting in English continued apace, although Canadian cultural industries did enjoy some protection through regulatory barriers. The regulatory agencies determined, for example, how much non-Canadian programming could be broadcast on Canadian television stations. Then cable television enabled almost all Canadians to gain access to the major U.S. networks. The arrival of satellite dish services in the late 1990s made protection in this area virtually impossible.

Statistics showed the extent of foreign domination of Canada's cultural industries. By 1990, for example, foreign-owned publishers had acquired 80 percent of Canada's book market. Nearly 85 percent of recording sales were foreign, as were 80 percent of magazines sold in Canada. When Canada moved to protect Canadian magazine publishers, the United States immediately threatened economic reprisals. In movie theatres, Canadian films had less than 5 percent of screen time, although a growing number of American producers, subsidized by the Canadian government, filmed in Toronto and Vancouver, considered a "Hollywood North." Yet some critics insisted that while Canadians consumed and borrowed American cultural products, they also reconstituted them and imprinted them with Canadian values. In this way, cultural anthropologist Frank Manning maintained, "the beaver can, and does, bite back," although Manning was uncertain whether the bite was serious or only a playful nip.[9]

Ottawa also provided subsidies for artists in all fields and funded cultural infrastructures. In spite of reduced financing, the CBC continued to affirm its objective of preserving and enriching Canadianism. The National Film Board (NFB), another important publicly supported institution, produced numerous high-quality documentaries, a field in which it excelled. The Canadian Film Development Corporation, later Telefilm Canada, gave financial backing to several critical successes, among them Peter Carter's *The Rowdyman* and Gilles Carle's *La vraie nature de Bernadette*. After the mid-1980s, it shifted its emphasis toward television production.

The late 1980s saw the production of several notable Canadian feature films. While Canadian films in English generally played to small audiences, Quebec films competed more successfully with American films. One blockbuster, Denis Arcand's *Decline of the American Empire*, portrayed decadent history teachers—an entirely fictional subject, of course.

Canadian Literature

After 1970, there were more Canadian writers and they wrote more. The growth of universities, as well as increased government funding and a larger population, help explain this significant growth. International acclaim gave many writers publicity, and established their reputations abroad as much as within Canada.

Literature mirrored Canadians' preoccupations, attitudes, and aspirations. Nationalist themes, for example, recurred frequently in novels in both English and French Canada, particularly during the 1970s. Many literary works presented the experience of minority groups such as Aboriginals and immigrants. For example, Joy Kogawa, in *Obasan*, poignantly evoked the fate of Japanese Canadians during World War II, while Acadian author Antonine Maillet painted a new image of Acadia and its people in her works. Other novels, such as those of Jane Rule and Timothy Findley, explored lesbian or gay themes. Historical settings were also common. *Les filles de Caleb*, Arlette Cousture's novel about the life of a family in the Mauricie region of Quebec a century ago, inspired a long-lasting television series that regularly attracted more than three million viewers.

Some writers set their works in small towns with closed societies. An example was Deptford, the scene of a powerful trilogy of novels by Robertson Davies featuring vivid central characters. Others dwelt upon the realities of urban living. Canadian literature also underlined the important role that regions have played in Canadian life. Atlantic writer David Adams Richards wrote of poverty and pride in northeastern New Brunswick in *The Coming of Winter* and *Blood Ties*, while W.O. Mitchell's *Roses Are Difficult Here* chronicled a year in the life of an Alberta foothills town called Shelby.

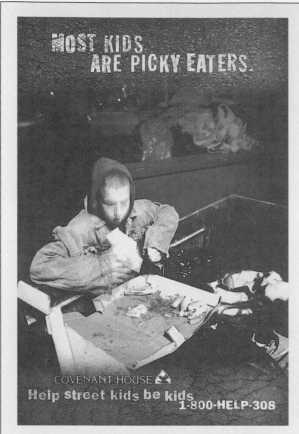

A Covenant House poster draws attention to the plight of Canadian cities' homeless youth.

Courtesy of Covenant House, Toronto.

New Challenges

The 1970s and 1980s defined new challenges. Increasingly aware of the risks of cancer and heart disease, many Canadians began to take preventive measures to ensure personal good health. In particular, they smoked less. Automobile associations and victims of drunk drivers successfully lobbied governments to take measures to reduce carnage on the highways. The use of seatbelts also contributed to the steady decline in the number of Canadians killed in accidents on the roads. The rapid spread of the deadly AIDS (acquired immune deficiency syndrome) virus after 1980 finally brought health authorities to launch campaigns promoting "safe sex" or abstinence. By 2000 the disease had already killed more than 15 000 Canadians, but medical advances were helping to prolong the lives of those afflicted.

Poverty

Throughout the 1980s, poverty remained a serious problem despite what was, generally, a growing economy. Governments revamped social programs in order to increase assistance to the poorest. At the same time, spending cuts pushed Canadians on social assistance below low-income cutoff lines. Marital breakdown, together with the trend to reject the institution of marriage, resulted in large numbers of single-parent families, most of them headed by women. Many of these families had very low incomes.

Rising crime rates also became a serious social concern in the 1970s and 1980s. Violent crime nearly doubled in the 1980s, although rates remained far lower than in the United States. Many offences were drug-related.

The Environment

Environmental issues gained increasing visibility after 1970 as Canadians discovered the negative aftermath of the unbridled, almost unregulated, development of past decades. They also learned that environmental issues were global in nature: the "greenhouse effect," the depletion of the ozone layer, the pollution of air and water, and the destruction of tropical and temperate rain forests all involved worldwide responsibility, and solutions required international cooperation. During the 1980s, Canada signed several multilateral agreements on the environment, notably those concerning climate change and ozone depletion.

More importantly, many Canadians came to see themselves as part of the problem. An expanding and wealthier population oriented toward consumption produced large quantities of wastes. It also made unsustainable demands upon natural resources. The burning of fossil fuels to heat homes, to run automobiles, and to drive industries fouled the air; an increasing number of scientists agreed that it also furthered climate change through the so-called "greenhouse gases" it produced. As numerous lakes and streams of the Canadian Shield became lifeless and as the surrounding vegetation showed increasing evidence of damage, Canadians realized the devastating effects of acid rain. Many industries also spewed chemical effluents into both air and water.

Prime agricultural land surrounding cities disappeared beneath low-density suburbs, roads, fast-food restaurants, shopping malls, and industrial parks. Agricultural methods, such as straightening streams and small watercourses, contributed to the erosion of topsoil and, through the abundant use of pesticides, herbicides, and fertilizers, to the pollution of water. Logging companies prepared to harvest the country's last old-growth stands of timber, and untouched wilderness receded still further north.

No easy solutions existed. Concerned citizens set up associations to publicize environmental dangers or to propose solutions. Some groups were Canadian creations. Greenpeace, a well-known environmental lobby, had its origins in Vancouver in 1970. Twenty years later the organization boasted 2.5 million members in forty countries. The Canadian Parks and Wilderness Society worked to establish new parks. Its Ontario partner won an important victory in 1973, when Quetico Park, on the north shore of Lake Superior, was reclassified as a primitive park from which all logging was banned. In the 1980s, Ontario doubled its park system.

Litigation also proved to be a useful weapon for environmentalists, Aboriginal peoples, and other concerned citizens. The Sierra Legal Defence Fund (now Ecojustice Canada), founded in 1990, took governments to court to force them to respect their own laws and regulations concerning the environment, and to force offenders to obey environmental laws. The Nature Conservancy of Canada pursued another line of action: it sought to protect ecologically sensitive lands through outright land purchases paid for by donations.

Governments and the Environment

Public pressure brought governments to take an interest in the environment. They established standards for clean air and clean water, and set up agencies to monitor compliance. They also provided for environmental assessments of important projects such as the construction of dams. To diminish pressure on landfill sites, municipalities gradually instituted recycling programs for glass, metals, paper, and plastics.

Controlling air and water pollution meant difficult and prolonged negotiations with the United States, whose industries and coal-fired power plants were major polluters of Canada's water and air. In 1987, however, Canada and the United States signed a tougher version of the Great Lakes Water Quality Agreement of 1978. Later, the U.S. Congress adopted the Clean Air Act. A Canadian lobby group played a significant role in the bill's passage by bringing constant pressure to bear on American legislators.

The battle for cleaner air and water involved tradeoffs. Pulp and paper mills polluted rivers and smelters poisoned the air, but they also provided jobs and revenues. When provincial governments attempted to impose costly pollution controls, companies often resisted and threatened to shut down operations.

Conflicting economic and environmental preoccupations were also in evidence in regard to the problem of preserving some of what remained of Canada's once-vast wilderness. In the name of protecting biodiversity for future generations, the United Nations urged member states to set aside 12 percent of their territory, which would be off limits for industrial and commercial activities; protected areas should be representative of all natural regions in each jurisdiction. The Canadian government took one important step in this direction in 1986, when it created the huge Ellesmere

Island National Park Reserve, Canada's thirty-second national park, thus protecting a biologically unique ecosystem situated close to the North Pole. It remained for the provinces to act.

Rapid change, begun in the 1960s, continued and even accelerated during the 1970s and 1980s. The women's rights movement, for example, boasted important accomplishments in the course of these two decades. Gays and lesbians, linguistic minorities, and ethnic minorities also achieved greater equality in these years.

Political decisions brought significant change to Canadian society as well as to the country's economy. The Charter of Rights and Freedoms, part of the Canadian constitution proclaimed in 1982, enabled women and minority groups to challenge laws that, in their view, prevented them from attaining greater equality. Free trade created even closer trade relations with the United States.

As the 1980s closed, new challenges presented themselves. Marked regional differences and rivalries profoundly influenced federal politics. Spending by Ottawa and by most of the provinces greatly exceeded revenues. After 1990, Canadians would be faced with the unpleasant realities of cuts in services as governments struggled to bring budget deficits under control.

NOTES

1. Paul Phillips, *Regional Disparities* (Toronto: James Lorimer, 1982), pp. 118–19.

2. Sylvia Bashevkin, *Toeing the Lines. Women and Party Politics in English Canada*, 2nd ed. (Toronto: Oxford University Press, 1993), p. vi.

3. Raymond M. Hébert, *Manitoba's French-Language Crisis: A Cautionary Tale* (Montreal/ Kingston: McGill-Queen's University Press, 2004), p. 208.

4. Robert Finbow, "Atlantic Canada: Forgotten Periphery in an Endangered Confedera- tion?," in Kenneth McRoberts, ed., *Beyond Quebec: Taking Stock of Canada* (Montreal/ Kingston: McGill-Queen's University Press, 1995), p. 67.

5. John Herd Thompson and Stephen J. Randall, *Canada and the United States: Ambivalent Allies*, 3rd ed. (Montreal/Kingston: McGill-Queen's University Press, 2002), p. 274.

6. Rianne Mahon, "Child Care as Citizenship Right? Toronto in the 1970s and 1980s," *Canadian Historical Review*, 86 (2005): 285–315.

7. Michiel Horn, *Academic Freedom in Canada: A History* (Toronto: University of Toronto Press, 1999), p. 338.

8. Reginald Bibby, *Mosaic Madness: The Poverty and Potential of Life in Canada* (Toronto: Stoddart, 1990), p. 84.

9. David H. Flaherty and Frank E. Manning, eds., *The Beaver Bites Back? American Popular Culture in Canada* (Montreal/Kingston: McGill-Queen's University Press, 1993), p. 4.

BEYOND THE BOOK

North American Free Trade Agreement

http://www.sice.oas.org/trade/nafta/naftatce.asp
Full text of the North American Free Trade Agreement.

Media Coverage of the New Constitution, 1982

http://archives.cbc.ca/politics/constitution/topics/1092
Television archival footage of the journey to Canada's new constitution in 1982.

Brian Mulroney

http://archives.cbc.ca/politics/prime_ministers/topics/1469
A video retrospective of the political career of Brian Mulroney, Canada's prime minister for much of the 1980s.

Gay and Lesbian Rights in Canada: The 1970s

http://www.uwo.ca/pridelib/bodypolitic/gaylib/70stimeline.htm
An historical timeline of gay and lesbian landmark events in Canada during the 1970s.

Young Women in Canada in the 1970s and Today

http://www.swc-cfc.gc.ca/pubs/pubspr/0662388976/index_e.html
A comparative look at the economic characteristics and cultural behaviours of young women in the 1970s and early 2000s.

In an Uncertain World

Canada: A People's History—Episode 17, In an Uncertain World. Directed by Susan Dando (CBC, 2001).

Between Men

Katherine Govier, *Between Men* (Markham, Ontario: Penguin Canada, 1987). A novel about Calgary during its boom in the late 1970s, with flashbacks to its history in the late 1880s.

RELATED READINGS

In R. Douglas Francis and Donald B. Smith, eds., *Viewpoints: Readings in Canadian History* (Toronto: Thomson Nelson, 2007), the article by Alain-G. Gagnon, "Québec-Canada's Constitutional Dossier," pp. 525–40, covers political aspects of this topic.

BIBLIOGRAPHY

On demography, see David K. Foot and Daniel Stoffman, *Boom, Bust and Echo: Profiting from the Demographic Shift in the 21st Century* (Toronto: Stoddart, 2000). Concerning the free-trade debate, see L. Ian MacDonald, *Free Trade: Risks and Rewards* (Montreal/Kingston: McGill-Queen's University Press, 2000); Michael Hart, *Decision at Midnight: Inside the Canada–US Free-Trade Negotiations* (Vancouver: UBC Press, 1994); and Stephen J. Randall and Herman W. Konrad, eds., *NAFTA in Transition* (Calgary: University of Calgary Press, 1995).

Business history is discussed in R.T. Naylor, *History of Canadian Business* (Montreal/Kingston: McGill-Queen's University Press, 2006). On western agriculture, see Barry Wilson, *Farming the System: How Politicians and Producers Shape Canadian Agricultural Policy* (Saskatoon: Western Producer Prairie Books, 1990). Writings on the environment include Chad Gaffield and Pam Gaffield, eds., *Consuming Canada: Readings in Environmental History* (Toronto: Copp Clark, 1995); Kathryn Harrison, *Passing the Buck: Federalism and Canadian Environmental Policy* (Vancouver: University of British Columbia Press, 1996); and Ken Drushka, *Canada's Forests: A History of Use and Conservation* (Montreal/Kingston: McGill-Queen's University Press, 2003).

Political issues are examined in Hugh G. Thorburn and Alain Whitehorn, eds., *Party Politics in Canada*, 8th ed. (Toronto: Prentice-Hall, 2001); and James Bickerton and Alain-G. Gagnon, *Canadian Politics*, 4th ed. (Peterborough, ON: Broadview Press, 2004). An excellent biography of Trudeau is Stephen Clarkson and Christina McCall, *Trudeau and Our Times*, vol. 1, *The Magnificent Obsession*; vol. 2, *The Heroic Delusion* (Toronto: McClelland & Stewart, 1990, 1994). On Trudeau's early years, see John English, *Citizen of the World: The Life of Pierre Elliott Trudeau*, vol. I, *1919–1968* (Toronto: Knopf Canada, 2006). Guy Laforest, *Trudeau and the End of a Canadian Dream* (Montreal/Kingston: McGill-Queen's University Press, 1995), is a critical evaluation. On Brian Mulroney, see the former prime minister's *Memoirs: 1939–1993* (Toronto: Douglas Gibson Books, 2007); and Stevie Cameron, *On the Take: Crime, Corruption and Greed in the Mulroney Years* (Toronto: Macfarlane Walter & Ross, 1994).

Books on federal–provincial relations include Garth Stevenson, *Unfulfilled Union: Canadian Federalism and National Unity*, 4th ed. (Montreal/Kingston: McGill-Queen's University Press, 2004); and Paul Brunner, ed., *Lougheed and the War with Ottawa* (Edmonton: History Book Publications, 2003). On constitutional issues, see David Milne, *The Canadian Constitution: From Patriation to Meech Lake*, new ed. (Toronto: James Lorimer, 1989). Among studies of foreign affairs are Robert Bothwell, *Alliance and Illusion: Canada and the World, 1945–1984* (Vancouver: UBC Press, 2007); J.L. Granatstein and Robert Bothwell, *Pirouette: Pierre Trudeau and Canadian Foreign Policy* (Toronto: University of Toronto Press, 1990); and Nelson Michaud and Kim Richard Nossal, eds., *Diplomatic Departures: The Conservative Era in Canadian Foreign Policy* (Vancouver: UBC Press, 2001).

On higher education, see Neil Tudiver, *Universities for Sale: Resisting Corporate Control over Canadian Higher Education* (Toronto: James Lorimer, 1999); and Paul Axelrod, *Values in Conflict: The University, the Marketplace, and the Trials of Liberal Education* (Montreal/Kingston: McGill-Queen's University Press, 2002). Studies of Canada's cultural originality include Ian Angus, *A Border Within: National Identity, Cultural Plurality, and Wilderness* (Montreal/Kingston: McGill-Queen's University Press, 1997); and David M. Thomas and Barbara Boyle Torrey, eds., *Canada and the United States: Differences That Count*, 3rd ed. (Peterborough, ON: Broadview Press, 2007). Canada's film industry is studied in George Melnyk, *One Hundred Years of Canadian Cinema* (Toronto: University of Toronto Press, 2004).

Books on the history of Canadian women include Alison Prentice et al., *Canadian Women: A History*, 2nd ed. (Toronto: Harcourt Brace, 1996); Ruth Roach Pierson et al., *Canadian Women's Issues*, vol. 1, *Strong Voices*; vol. 2, *Bold Visions* (Toronto: James Lorimer, 1993, 1995); and Sylvia B. Bashevkin, *Women on the Defensive: Living through Conservative Times* (Chicago: University of Chicago Press, 1998). On gays and lesbians, consult Miriam Smith, *Lesbian and Gay Rights in Canada: Social Movements and Equality-Seeking, 1971–1995* (Toronto: University of Toronto Press, 1999); and Tom Warner, *Never Going Back: A History of Queer Activism in Canada* (Toronto: University of Toronto Press, 2002). Social themes are explored Raymond B. Blake, Penny E. Bryden, and J. Frank Strain, eds., *The Welfare State in Canada: Past, Present and Future* (Concord, ON: Irwin Publishing, 1997); Duane Adams, ed., *Federalism, Democracy, and Health Policy in Canada* (Montreal/Kingston: McGill-Queen's University Press, 2001); and Peter Ward, *A History of Domestic Space: Privacy and the Canadian Home* (Vancouver: UBC Press, 1999).

Chapter Twenty-Six

CONTEMPORARY CANADA

TIME LINE

1991	Canadian troops participate in the Gulf War
1992	A devastating explosion at the Westray mine in Pictou County, Nova Scotia kills 26 miners
1993	The Liberal government of Jean Chrétien takes office
1994	The North American Free Trade Agreement (NAFTA)
1995	In Ontario, Mike Harris's new Conservative government begins to implement the "Common Sense Revolution"
1997	The Confederation Bridge linking Prince Edward Island and New Brunswick is opened
1998	The federal budget registers its first surplus in more than a quarter of a century
2001	Terrorist attacks are launched on New York City and Washington, DC
2002	Canada sends combat troops to Afghanistan Canada ratifies the Kyoto Protocol
2006	The Conservative Party wins a federal election
2008	Canada's economy is struck by a world-wide financial crisis, the collapse of commodities prices, and diminished exports

After the recession of the early 1990s, Canada's economy flourished, though regional imbalances were striking. Corporations improved their profits and business leaders were given handsome financial rewards. Most workers, however, saw their pay packets rise slowly, if at all, and adjustments to fierce global competition and then, after 2003, to a stronger Canadian dollar, cost many jobs, especially in manufacturing industries. After 2007, as housing prices declined dramatically in the United States, Canadian exports of forest products fell and many mills closed. Lower automobile sales caused widespread layoffs in southern Ontario and recession threatened that province. Worldwide demand for resources stagnated, and the prices of oil and minerals fell sharply.

The free trade election of 1988 and the failure of the Meech Lake Accord in 1990 contributed to the breakdown of political consensus. The Mulroney government's fortunes went from bad to worse. Voters showed more volatility, as old political loyalties dissolved. From 1993 to 2000, a divided and regionalized opposition helped the Liberals led by Jean Chrétien to win three consecutive majorities in the House of Commons. After 1998, budgetary surpluses, the first in more than a quarter-century, made more activist government again possible. Then scandal, internal strife, and a resurgent and united Conservative opposition led by Stephen Harper, from Alberta, undermined the Liberal governments of Chrétien and his successor, Paul Martin, paving the way for a Conservative victory in federal elections held in 2006.

As the numbers of elderly Canadians increased and those of young Canadians fell, health care became a major concern, much more so than education. Expenditures on health represented a constantly increasing share of provincial budgets. Environmental issues also worried Canadians and they heatedly discussed climate change, its likely consequences, and what they could do about it.

Technological innovation continued apace after 1990. The phenomenal development of the Internet linked Canadians and the rest of the world more closely. Companies and governments could now process and move data with speeds and efficiency unimaginable scarcely a few years earlier. Individuals could send messages electronically, obtain information on any subject, pay bills, purchase goods and services, and amuse themselves. The computer age also brought new and serious challenges to citizens' rights to privacy.

In 1999, Research in Motion, a Canadian company, launched the BlackBerry, a handheld wireless device used by some businesses to provide e-mail access to roaming employees. More and more Canadians acquired cellular phones; certainly they facilitated personal communication. Ringing cell phones were not so popular with teachers in classrooms, performers in concert halls, workers who did not want their bosses to be able to reach them 24 hours a day, and seatmates in buses and trains who preferred to read. Newer models of the phones could also be used to access the Internet, send text messages, watch movies and television, take pictures and videos, and play games. As one major service provider put it, "You'll be hooked!"

The Collapse of Consensus

The reelection of the Conservative government in 1988 soon brought about leadership changes in the two opposition parties. The NDP chose Audrey McLaughlin to succeed Ed Broadbent; she thus became the first woman to lead a federal political party. Jean Chrétien, a Quebecker who had occupied several cabinet posts under Trudeau, easily won the Liberal leadership in 1990, though his support in Quebec was weak, in part because of his perceived insensitivity to Quebec's exclusion from the constitutional agreement of 1982.

After the election of 1988, the Conservatives soon plummeted to third place in the polls. Scandals implicating cabinet ministers tarnished the government's image. Those who had fought free trade reviled Mulroney. Better-off Canadians complained when the government "clawed back" their family allowances and old-age pensions. The government's decision to replace the hidden manufacturers' sales tax with a fully visible goods and services tax (GST) of 7 percent, beginning in 1991, provoked vehement opposition. Cuts in subsidies to VIA Rail and to the Canadian Broadcasting Corporation (CBC) as well as the privatizing of Crown corporations also generated strong disapproval: critics accused Mulroney of dismantling national institutions. The deepening crisis in public finances limited the government's ability to respond to the demands placed on it.

High interest rates and much increased unemployment, particularly in the central provinces, only compounded the prevailing discontent. Recession descended upon Ontario in 1990 and the jobless rate rose dramatically, especially in manufacturing industries, construction, and retail sales. Premier Bob Rae's NDP government opted for massive spending in an effort to counteract the deleterious effects of the recession on Ontario's economy. Rapidly rising welfare and interest payments on the debt also contributed to huge budget deficits. Rae raised taxes and imposed a stringent restraint program designed to control public-sector wages while protecting jobs: employees were to take unpaid holidays, baptized "Rae days." Unions condemned the measures. Popular support for the NDP collapsed. A provincial election in 1995 brought victory to the Progressive Conservative party led by Mike Harris, who promised to implement a "Common Sense Revolution."

For their part, western Canadians saw the Mulroney government as overly attuned to the interests of central Canada. The meteoric rise in popularity of the western-based Reform Party after 1987 provided evidence of a powerful wave of dissatisfaction with the mainstream parties. Proclaiming that "the West wants in," the new party condemned the federal government's financial mismanagement, its "welfare-state approach" to meeting social needs, and its commitment to official bilingualism and multiculturalism as well as its immigration policy. It also opposed full gender equality, Aboriginal self-government, and civil rights for gays and lesbians, and engaged in much anti-Quebec rhetoric. Although the party soon toned down its West-oriented language in an effort to win support in Ontario and Atlantic Canada, Reform's major successes occurred in Alberta and British Columbia in the federal elections of 1993 and 1997.

Many Canadians outside Quebec also blamed Mulroney for the constitutional fiasco of the Meech Lake Accord, designed to bring Quebec to give its assent to the Constitution of 1982 (see Chapter 23). Within Quebec, support for sovereignty bounded upward in response to what most Quebeckers perceived as a rejection of the province's legitimate aspirations by Canadians outside Quebec. In Ottawa, several Conservative MPs from Quebec quit their party and formed a new grouping, the Bloc Québécois, committed to Quebec's independence.

The Conservatives tried again to achieve an agreement on constitutional reforms in 1991–1992. This time, wide consultations took place before the federal, provincial, and territorial first ministers, and the heads of Aboriginal organizations met at Charlottetown in 1992 and agreed on proposals that attempted to respond to a host of agendas for change, including Senate reform and Aboriginal self-government. A referendum held in October 1992 saw the voters of six provinces, including Quebec, reject the agreement. A Decima poll showed that "Quebec got too much" was the most favoured reason for voting no outside that province; Quebeckers in turn said that they believed Quebec had obtained too little, noting in particular the gutted distinct-society clause. Constitutional change appeared dead for the foreseeable future.

Election of 1993

The federal election of 1993 underlined the importance of Canada's regional divisions. The Progressive Conservatives, now led by Kim Campbell, Canada's first woman prime minister, met with a defeat of precedent-setting proportions: only two of their candidates were elected.

The Liberals won a majority, thanks in large part to Ontario. Their leader, Jean Chrétien, was the first French-speaking "old party" leader since Confederation to fail to take a majority of Quebec's seats. Quebec voters preferred to give their support to the Bloc Québécois, which became the official opposition in Parliament. Close behind came the West-based Reform Party. Finally, the unpopularity of provincial NDP governments in Ontario and British Columbia contributed heavily to that party's dismal performance.

The Chrétien Government

Once in power, the Chrétien government accepted most of the Conservative policies it had censured while in opposition. It did not repeal the GST. After vehemently criticizing free trade during the election campaign, it adopted the North American Free Trade Agreement (NAFTA) with the United States and Mexico.

In spite of a federal budget deficit that had climbed to a record $42 billion, the Liberal government did find money to launch a $6 billion infrastructure program, as it had promised during the election campaign. It sought instead to curtail other spending. It cut grants to the provinces for health, education, and social welfare, worsening budget crises in several provinces and forcing them to make reductions in their own programs. It reduced unemployment benefits and tightened eligibility rules, provoking strong reaction among the groups of workers concerned, particularly in eastern Canada. At the same time, it transferred into its general revenue fund most of the surplus that the Employment Insurance fund now accumulated because of high premiums and declining unemployment.

Government cuts to social programs signified the decline of the universal welfare state. Many Canadians regretted what they perceived as the disappearance of a widespread consensus on collective responsibility and shared risk. They blamed deficits not on excessive social spending but rather on the decreases in corporate taxation instituted by the Mulroney government and maintained by the Chrétien government.

Ottawa spent less elsewhere, too. It froze civil servants' wages. It devoted less money to foreign aid. It slashed defence spending, making it necessary to cut short several peacekeeping missions for lack of soldiers and equipment. Canada's international reputation suffered.

Political Success

When Chrétien left office in late 2003, in part as a result of pressure from the more popular Paul Martin, his former finance minister and heir apparent, his political successes were evident. He had won three general elections, each time with a majority of seats and about 40 percent of the votes. The opposition he faced in Parliament remained divided and regionalized. On the left, the NDP searched for new credibility and relevance, as voter support dwindled. In Quebec, the Bloc Québécois gradually weakened, as did sentiment for Quebec sovereignty generally.

Chrétien also benefited from disunity on the right, where two parties vied for conservative support. On the one hand, the old Progressive Conservatives attempted to regain lost popularity. On the other hand, the Reform Party replaced the Bloc as the official opposition in 1997 but, even reconstituted as the Canadian Alliance in 2000, it failed to expand its influence beyond the West. Party strife accompanied by a precipitous decline in membership resulted in the selection of a new leader, Stephen Harper, a former Reform Party MP. While continuing to advocate fiscal conservatism, smaller government, and greater autonomy for the provinces, the Alliance also defended Western positions such as opposition to federal gun registration and to environmental controls that might hurt the petroleum industry. At the same time it attempted to distance itself from the Reform Party's conservative views on abortion and gay rights. For many observers, the Alliance was simply experiencing the problems associated with any regionally based party attempting to widen its geographical base. More moderate Canadians preferred the centralist Liberals, particularly in Ontario, where the majority of Liberal seats were situated.

A lengthy list of costly administrative failures and mismanagement of public monies provoked strong criticism of the Liberal government. The auditor general drew attention to billions of dollars of corporate taxes that went unrecovered, to questionable grants made by the Department of Human Resources, and to a firearms registry program whose estimated costs of $100 million climbed to $1 billion. In addition, the government and even the prime minister were faulted for questionable ethics and political patronage. By the early 2000s, a strong majority of the population were telling pollsters that the Liberals were "arrogant and corrupt."

Still, voters proved ready to pardon Liberal faults. Chrétien appealed to many English-speaking Canadians for his uncompromising stand in regard to Quebec sovereignty. A prosperous economy also helped the party retain power. But the Liberal government could also boast of having finally brought order to government finances, certainly no mean feat after the failures of Trudeau and Mulroney. Thanks to spending cuts and especially to increased revenues from high taxation rates and economic growth, the federal budget finally registered a surplus in 1998. Additional surpluses enabled Ottawa to reduce income taxes, and to begin to pay down accumulated debt, which had now reached $580 billion.

Political Change

Chrétien's final months in power as well as Paul Martin's brief minority Liberal government were tarnished by the so-called "sponsorship scandal." Daily revelations at a commission of inquiry both titillated and shocked observers. Although Martin denied knowledge of government corruption, voters, particularly in Quebec, were not inclined to pardon. Nor were conservative voters divided as they had been in previous elections. In 2003 the Progressive Conservative party agreed to merge with Stephen Harper's Canadian Alliance, to form a new Conservative Party, of which Harper became leader. Harper's major challenge was to moderate Conservative rhetoric and positions. In particular, he sought to appeal to voters in Ontario and even in Quebec, where the collapse of Liberal support offered new opportunity. In the campaign of 2006, Harper played to voters' anger at Liberal corruption, adopted a conciliatory stance in Quebec, and made just a few specific promises such as reducing the sales tax, providing money for child care, and adopting tougher laws against gun and gang violence in Canadian cities. He won the election and formed a minority government. For the moment, pragmatism rather than ideology seemed to govern his actions.

Once in office, Harper attempted to attract voters in populous central Canada without losing his base of support in the western provinces. He promised to redress the "fiscal imbalance" that, in the opinion of many provinces, was evidenced by huge federal surpluses and tight provincial budgets. In his government's budget in 2007, he announced substantial spending increases, with more money for the equalization grants that enable poorer provinces to provide services comparable to those offered by richer provinces. These grants pleased Quebec, a major recipient of equalization, but displeased certain other recipient provinces, such as Nova Scotia, Newfoundland and Labrador, and Saskatchewan, which complained that Ottawa would not allow them to keep all of their resource revenues without losing equalization. He devoted more money to health, education, and welfare, to be granted on a per capita basis, thus pleasing the wealthy and populous provinces of Ontario and Alberta, which stood to make significant gains. Harper also announced new spending for public transit, notably in Toronto. Moreover, Harper saw no urgent need to act to ensure a substantial reduction of climate-changing greenhouse gases; his reticence in this regard pleased Alberta, Canada's major producer of such gases, whose economic dynamism and wealth were so largely based on the highly polluting extraction of oil from tar sands.

The Conservatives also sought to build new strength in Quebec without producing a backlash in the rest of Canada. In 2006, Harper had Parliament adopt a resolution that declared that "Québécois" formed a "nation within a united Canada." The use of the word "nation" in regard to Quebec strongly displeased many English-speaking voters who said they believed in "One Canada," but it represented at least a symbolic recognition of difference in Quebec. Harper himself assured that the motion had no concrete meaning. He hoped, as Mulroney before him, to attract so-called "soft nationalists" in Quebec, those who rejected both the reputedly uncompromising Liberals and the Bloc Québécois, which sought secession. Harper's attempts to woo Quebec failed to bring him additional seats in that province in federal elections held in October 2008. Yet thanks to increased support in Ontario and British Columbia, he was able to form a stronger minority government.

Canada and International Developments

In the 1990s and early 2000s, Canada's trade links with the United States intensified. Exports to the United States increased substantially, stimulated by free trade and a depreciating Canadian dollar that, by 2002, had fallen to a mere 62 cents (U.S.). Huge quantities of Albertan oil and gas flowed south. Several provinces exported electricity. The automotive industry in southern Ontario sent most of its production to the United States. Foreign ownership rose, and even business leaders expressed concern about the loss of head office jobs to that country. American protectionist measures, such as the punitive anti-dumping and anti-subsidy duties levied on softwood lumber imports from Canada, as well as Washington's decision to ignore the rulings of NAFTA's dispute settlement body in Canada's favour, embittered relations with the United States.

Globalization

Some Canadians joined critics across the world in denouncing the new global economic order, propelled by technological innovation, that undermined the sovereign powers of governments. In their view, governments were abdicating control to market forces through privatization, deregulation, and expenditure reduction. Multinational corporations now dwarfed many national governments in size. Increased global competition risked favouring reduced standards, resulting in increased poverty, diminished government services, weaker labour laws, swamped local cultures, and fewer environmental controls. Globalization, they argued, entailed more golden arches and branded clothing and footwear, while ignoring the real needs of citizens. These themes were given wide publicity in the protests and teach-ins held during the Free Trade Area of the Americas (FTAA) summit in Quebec City, in April 2001. However, globalization also had its defenders, who maintained that open trading nations tended to have higher labour and environmental standards than closed ones.

Terrorism

The terrorist attacks in the United States on September 11, 2001, which resulted in the deaths of some 3000 people, including 25 Canadians, had profound effects on Canada, too. When some American politicians portrayed Canadian border security as lax, Ottawa felt a need to prove otherwise in order to protect jobs and investment. The government's response was far-reaching and multifaceted. It improved aviation and airport security, and invested heavily in increased border security. It announced more spending on police and intelligence agencies, and

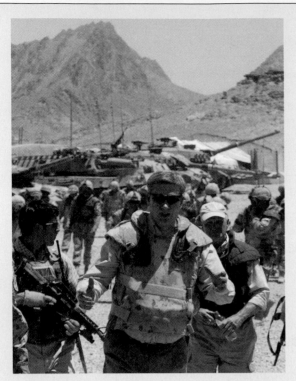

Canadian prime minister Stephen Harper touring a Canadian forward operation base in Kandahar province, Afghanistan, May 2007. By late 2008, Canada's participation in counterinsurgency operations in that country had already cost the lives of 100 soldiers.

CP Photo (Tom Hanson)

adopted an antiterrorism bill that gave new powers of investigation and detention to law enforcement authorities.

Civil libertarians worried that government actions taken to fight terrorism might erode citizens' basic rights. In one celebrated case, Maher Arar, a Syrian-born Canadian, was detained by American authorities while changing planes in New York in 2002, and then, instead of being sent to Canada (he was travelling on a Canadian passport), he was forcibly deported to Syria, where he was tortured and imprisoned in a tiny cell for almost a year. After Arar's return to Canada, some police and government officials made deliberate attempts to smear Arar's reputation by leaking false information to the media. A public inquiry absolved Arar of suspicion of any involvement in terrorist activities. Arar was awarded compensation for his ordeal, and received an official apology from the Canadian government.

Ottawa also took measures to improve infrastructure aimed at accelerating the flow of commercial traffic across the Canada–United States border. But a plan to establish a North American security perimeter and to harmonize Canadian visa requirements with those of the United States raised fears that Canada's sovereignty was in danger. Canada, however, could do nothing to stop the United States from requiring all persons crossing the border, including returning Americans, to present a passport, a measure that risked further deterring Americans from travelling to Canada.

Defence Abroad

Proud Canadians had traditionally viewed peacekeeping as one of their country's core values. In 1991, Canada contributed fully 10 percent of peacekeeping troops to United Nations missions. Its armed forces possessed important expertise in peacekeeping. By the 2000s, this image had become a myth, as few Canadian peacekeepers remained. In 2006, the Conservative government announced that huge amounts of money would be spent to upgrade military equipment and increase the armed forces' capabilities. For the government, Canada's new military objective was to be able to fight terrorist insurgencies militarily and show leadership in the world community.

The United Nations authorized the invasion of Afghanistan after the terrorist attacks in 2001. In 2002, Canada agreed to deploy combat troops to that country. By 2008, 2500 soldiers were fighting there, mostly in the perilous southern region of Kandahar, and 100 soldiers had already lost their lives. After minimal debate in Parliament, the Conservative government extended the hugely costly mission until at least 2011. However, when American and British troops invaded Iraq in March 2003 without the authorization of the world body, the Chrétien government refused to participate. Most Canadians, especially in Quebec, approved his decision.

Regional Imbalances

The early 1990s were difficult years for almost all the provinces; most suffered an economic recession that had a negative impact on their budgets. Severe cuts in federal transfers only exacerbated financial problems. Balancing budgets involved painful choices and unhappy voters often reacted negatively to declining services and higher taxes by turning governments out of office and electing new ones.

By the mid-1990s, the economies of most regions had improved. Oil brought significant new revenues to Newfoundland and Nova Scotia. Central Canada's manufacturing firms churned out goods for the voracious American market. In the West, the exploitation and sale of natural resources brought prosperity. Then, after 2002, the rising Canadian dollar, described as a "petro-dollar" by economists because it was pushed upward in part by higher oil prices, curtailed manufacturing exports by making them more expensive. Major American automobile makers closed plants in Ontario, but, for a time, losses were balanced by gains from new factories opened by Toyota and other foreign manufacturers. Then sharply higher gasoline prices hurt sales of large, gas-guzzling SUVs and light trucks. Forestry registered significant job losses, as a result of a dramatic slowdown in home construction in the United States. Western Canada, for its part, basked in prosperity, thanks to expensive oil, gas, and other resources. But then prices for these commodities crashed, putting development projects on hold.

The Hibernia oil platform ready to be towed out into the Atlantic Ocean, May 1997. Newfoundlanders hoped that oil production would stimulate the province's economy.

CP Photo (Jonathan Hayward)

Newfoundland and Labrador

On May 9, 1997, politicians and business people gathered at Bull Arm, northwest of St. John's, to christen the new Hibernia offshore oil production platform. The festive occasion was marred by a demonstration by hundreds of unemployed fishery workers, protesting against Ottawa's compensation program for the collapsed cod fishery. (Cod stocks, hitherto thought to be inexhaustible, had declined precipitously in the early 1990s as a result of overfishing, both domestic and foreign, and possibly, too, because of environmental factors.) That event seemed to dramatize the contrast between the Newfoundland of yesterday, a province of low incomes and a slowly dying fishing industry, and the Newfoundland of tomorrow, richer and more developed.

The exploitation of natural resources represented a substantial share of Newfoundland's economy. Major hydroelectric projects were planned in Labrador. Another megaproject involved the development of huge nickel deposits at Voisey's Bay, in northern Labrador. Production began in 2007. New jobs here were welcome, all the more so since oil and gas did not create large numbers of local jobs. Yet by 2008 resource revenues transformed

Newforundland into a "have" province, whose wealth made it possible to spend more per person on services than Ontario, a province which now began to receive equalization grants.

Maritime Provinces

High levels of unemployment also afflicted Nova Scotia, Prince Edward Island, and New Brunswick. Still, there were bright spots. In Nova Scotia, the building of the $2 billion Sable Island natural gas pipeline gave a strong boost to the construction industry, and offshore exploration continued. Prince Edward Island's economy benefited from the construction of the 13-km-long Confederation Bridge, opened in 1997. The "fixed link" across Northumberland Strait to New Brunswick stimulated tourism, a major industry on the island, and local agriculture now benefited from lower transportation costs. Job creation was also a priority for New Brunswick's Liberal government, headed by Frank McKenna. In particular, the "energizer premier," as one newspaper nicknamed McKenna, proved adroit at attracting telephone call centres to the province, though other provinces accused him of luring away their jobs.

Ontario and the "Common Sense Revolution"

Ontario's economy boomed after the mid-1990s, thanks to low interest rates, a dynamic U.S. economy that imported goods made in Ontario, especially automobiles, and a low Canadian dollar that favoured exports. In economist Thomas Courchene's words, Ontario was no longer a mere province, it had become, thanks in part to Conservative premier Mike Harris, "a North American region state."[1] Harris reduced provincial income taxes substantially—the highlight of his "Common Sense Revolution." To finance lower tax rates, he imposed radical spending cuts in education, health services, and welfare as well as substantial increases in university tuition costs. These actions caused considerable protest. Then the province took control of public education funding, partly removing financing from municipally levied, residential property taxes. In return, new responsibilities were devolved upon municipalities, including welfare, child care, care for the elderly, social housing, health programs, and public transit. The government also introduced a new market-value property tax assessment system, and it ordered the merger of Metro Toronto's six municipalities. These measures provoked some of the most acrimonious debates in the province's history among prospective winners and losers.

The West

Free trade boosted Manitoba's exports to the United States in the 1990s. New markets opened for industrial products. Large construction projects also produced economic stimulus. Saskatchewan also enjoyed impressive economic growth in the 1990s, assisted by strong oil and gas prices. Then, in the late 1990s, low grain prices as well as drought and competition from heavily subsidized American farmers provoked a serious farm crisis in both Saskatchewan and Manitoba.

Alberta's abundant oil revenues gave it financial latitude that other provinces lacked. Huge budget surpluses enabled the government to reduce income taxes to a flat rate of 10 percent for all workers and to eliminate the provincial debt. It also increased public spending substantially, granting large wage increases to health and education personnel, and earmarking billions of dollars for new schools, hospitals, bridges, and roads. At the same time, such rapid growth drove up prices and put tremendous pressure on infrastructure as well as on the environment.

In British Columbia, massive inflows of investment as well as large numbers of new immigrants, mainly from Asia, helped maintain an economic boom after 1990 while the rest of Canada slid into recession. Trade with Asia increased rapidly. Economic diversification continued. Then, the late 1990s saw the province struggle with hard times. Lost markets due to Asia's faltering economy, punitive American trade policies, rising international competition, and low prices brought sawmill closures and job losses. After 2000, soaring trade with China, especially the sale of natural resources such as coal, minerals, and lumber, brought new prosperity. Preparations for the Winter Olympics of 2010, to be held at sites near Vancouver, assured a booming construction industry.

Mining trucks with loads of oil-laden sand at the Albian Sands project, Fort McMurray, Alberta, August 2005. Such projects brought Alberta great wealth but also represented grave threats to the environment.

CP Photo (Larry MacDougal)

Population

Continued high levels of immigration explained most of Canada's population growth after 1990. By 2008, Canadians numbered 33 million, an increase of more than 10 million over 1971. Fully 80 percent of Canadians now lived in urban centres, and nearly one-half of them in just three areas: Toronto and the Golden Horseshoe region of southern Ontario; Montreal; and Vancouver. Alberta's population increased particularly rapidly during the 1990s and 2000s, as workers from other provinces flooded into the province in search of high-paying job opportunities.

Fort McMurray, Alberta, was one city that saw prodigious growth. Between 1999 and 2006 its population doubled to 80 000. Many new residents came from Newfoundland, a province whose population was declining. Median family income in Fort McMurray was $120 000, the highest in Canada. But new homes cost more than $500 000, and many newcomers had to stay in campgrounds and work camps.

Ontario, British Columbia, and Quebec also saw substantial population gains, celebrated by boosters in the media, in government, and in business. There were few discussions of what an ideal population for Canada might be and whether "healthy growth" in the numbers of Canadians, with their typically heavy impact on the environment and high consumption of resources, might take Canada even further away from the goal of sustainable development.

Cities and Suburbs

Many Canadians chose to live in the condominiums and highrise apartment buildings that altered the landscape of cities' inner suburbs or formed part of huge redevelopment projects in once-derelict port and industrial districts such as Vancouver's False Creek and Toronto's Harbourfront. But most preferred to inhabit the sprawling satellite communities that surrounded large cities. Costly infrastructures such as roads and sewer lines were necessary to serve these communities, and the use of automobiles was essential to commute to work or to find access to services. Traffic worsened. Dire predictions were made that, by 2025, drivers in the Greater Toronto Area would be facing total gridlock. Air pollution increased, too. By 2000, British Columbia's Fraser Valley had become one of the most polluted airsheds in Canada, as toxic smog from Vancouver funnelled directly into the area.

An Aging Population

While birth rates plummeted, advances in medicine and a decline in tobacco use enabled Canadians to live longer. Canadian society began to age rapidly. By 2000, the over-65s numbered 13 percent

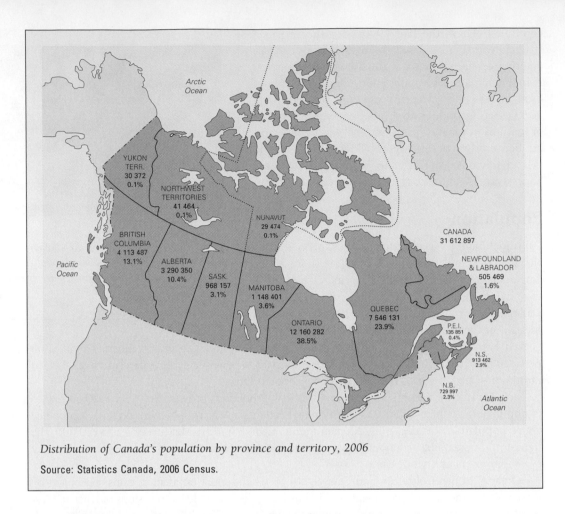

Distribution of Canada's population by province and territory, 2006

Source: Statistics Canada, 2006 Census.

of the population—a figure well above the 8 percent criterion used by the United Nations to signify an aging population.

In the 1990s, baby boomers embarked on a collective midlife crisis. In quest of their youth, some male boomers turned to Viagra and hair dye, while female boomers bought cosmetics to iron out the wrinkles. The "flower power" of the 1960s and 1970s now yielded to "grey power," forcing politicians to heed seniors' concerns, such as pensions and especially health care.

Health Care

For most Canadians, universal publicly funded health care was sacred, a defining feature of Canada that distinguished it from the United States, where health care, largely in private hands, was expensive and often inefficient and coverage blatantly unequal. They applauded when, in 1984, Parliament adopted the Canada Health Act, with all-party support, that curtailed hospital user fees and extra billing by doctors. And they worried, in the 1990s, when some provinces sought to increase the role of the private sector in an effort to control sharply expanding health costs. During the election campaign of 2000, the governing Liberals assured anxious citizens that they would never accept a two-tier public–private system.

Yet the health system was obviously in a state of crisis. In the late 1990s and early 2000s, dissatisfaction mounted as waiting lists for diagnostic tests and surgery lengthened, hospital emergency wards were overwhelmed, drug costs soared, services were disinsured, and shortages of doctors and nurses developed. Improved public finances enabled governments to put more money into health care, but the crisis deepened. In 2002, a federal report on the health-care system urged that public health care be retained, reinforced, and expanded. Private providers of medical services were to be excluded. Ottawa agreed to inject billions of dollars to fund primary care, home care, and catastrophic drug care. Still, was Canada's health system financially sustainable in the long term? Doubts grew as, each year, health expenses took an increasing share of provincial budgets. An aging population needed more care, and new medical treatments, while often wondrous, were also very costly. British Columbia's minister of health confessed that he went to bed each night "thanking the stars" that he was minister now and not in 25 years.

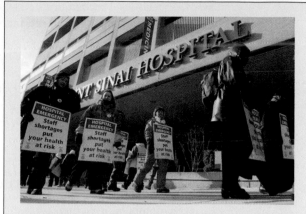

Hospital workers protest health-care cuts and staff shortages outside Toronto's Mount Sinai Hospital, February 2003.

CP Photo (Frank Gunn)

Poverty

Poverty was another important social problem that did not lend itself to easy solutions. As unemployment grew during the recession of 1990, rising demand overwhelmed food banks in urban areas. Canadian cities also saw the emergence of a homeless class that included refugees, people with mental and physical disabilities, Aboriginal people, single mothers with children, youth, and substance abusers. In 1998, in a highly political move, the city of Toronto declared homelessness a national disaster and sought disaster relief funds. After 2000, in spite of economic growth and reduced unemployment, poverty remained very much present in Canadian cities. Vancouver's Downtown East Side, an area of decrepit boarding houses, sleazy bars, and boarded-up shops, was plagued with Canada's highest rates of poverty and drug addiction. In Calgary, the numbers of homeless increased and shelters overflowed.

Gays and Lesbians

In 1995 the Supreme Court of Canada ruled that the Charter of Rights and Freedoms prohibited discrimination against gays and lesbians. Most provinces had already acted to protect homosexuals' legal rights. In 1999, a verdict of the court compelled Alberta, the last province, to ban discriminatory practices.

Gays and lesbians now turned their attention to obtaining recognition for same-sex unions. A series of court challenges established that gay couples possessed many of the rights and duties of married couples, and laws were rewritten to reflect this in such areas as spousal support, pension rights, adoption, and medical decision-making. In 1997, British Columbia became the first province to amend

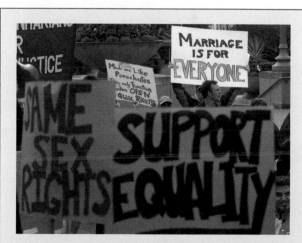

A demonstration held to show support for same-sex marriages takes place in Victoria, British Columbia, January 2005, outside a conference centre where Conservative Party leader Stephen Harper and his caucus, opposed to same-sex unions, were holding a retreat.

CP Photo (Don Denton)

laws to extend legal recognition to same-sex relationships. In 2003, Ontario courts ruled that prohibiting gays and lesbians from marrying violated the equality provisions of the Charter of Rights and Freedoms. Then, in 2005, the federal government drafted legislation to change the definition of marriage from a union between a man and a woman to a union between two persons. Religious institutions were free to decide whether to perform marriage ceremonies for same-sex couples. When the Conservatives took power in 2006, they introduced a motion asking that the question of same-sex marriage be reopened to support the traditional definition of marriage. In a free vote, most MPs from all three opposition parties combined to defeat the motion. The new definition of marriage would stand.

Women in the Workforce

As larger numbers of women took jobs outside the home, governments were called upon to make daycare facilities more affordable and available. Quebec innovated by setting up a system of publicly supported centres where parents paid just $5 a day per child; the highly popular system proved costly for taxpayers, and waiting lists were long. Across Canada, there were far more families with preschool children than there were spaces in licensed daycare centres.

Pay Equity

The notion of equal pay for work of equal value, or pay equity, became the battleground of the 1990s, as women argued that they were generally paid less than men for jobs requiring similar skills, effort, responsibility, and educational levels, and entailing similar working conditions. Ottawa and some provinces instituted pay-equity laws, in spite of hostility from the male-dominated business community.

The growing conservatism of the 1990s and early 2000s had implications for women. In Ontario, for example, Mike Harris's Conservative government repealed certain elements of the pay-equity legislation adopted by the previous NDP government. Moreover, women judged that budget cuts in health, welfare, and poverty relief programs by governments at all levels hit them disproportionately. Yet there was progress in many areas. Sixty percent of university students were women, and women outnumbered men in all fields except engineering and math. *Women in Canada 2000*, a report prepared by Statistics Canada, showed that the gap between higher men's pay and lower women's pay decreased substantially between 1985 and 1995. By 2000, women occupied about one-third of managerial positions, though usually on lower rungs. Not surprisingly, women experienced increased levels of stress and even depression as they attempted to hold down jobs while raising families.

Challenges for Labour

The 1990s proved difficult for unionized workers. In order to reduce expenditures and balance budgets, governments imposed layoffs, wage freezes, and even wage cuts.

Private-sector unions fared no better. Many high-paying manufacturing jobs disappeared as companies "rationalized" their operations, and union membership declined. New contracts often imposed wage rollbacks, or pegged wages to profitability, or brought a reduced pay scale for new employees. The recession of the early 1990s undermined the bargaining power of unions and thus sharply reduced the number of work stoppages. Unions themselves were often torn by internal strife.

Recruitment again increased in the late 1990s, thanks in part to an improving economy. But private-sector unions felt themselves under attack by the forces of globalization and cutthroat competition. Moreover, most of these unions were still based in the United States, and were often unresponsive to the needs of their Canadian membership. Labour attempted to reinvent itself, and to appeal to employees who now sought stress relief, schedules that did not disrupt family life, and greater control over their careers. Unions sought new members where they could find them. The United Steelworkers, for example, diversified into call centres, telemarketing, data processing, and other new-technology domains.

Spectator Sports

With the spread of the Internet in the 1990s, increasingly sedentary Canadians preferred spectator sports to active participation. Huge crowds cheered the astonishing Blue Jays of Toronto on to their victories in the World Series in 1992 and 1993. From that summit, baseball in Canada went downhill. Financial problems undermined the famed Montreal Expos, and the team finally moved to Washington, D.C. Younger Canadians preferred basketball, and soccer stirred rising interest. Football and hockey both remained popular.

The Olympic Games, summer but especially winter, created much enthusiasm and fostered pride in Canadian athletes' prowess. Canada's performance in the summer games was uneven; while results were disappointing at Sydney in 2000 and at Athens in 2004, Canada met its objectives by ranking fourteenth in the number of medals won at the Beijing games in 2008. Performances were truly outstanding at the winter Olympics held in Salt Lake City in 2002. The Canadian women's hockey team won a gold medal by triumphing over the American team. Then the largest audience in Canadian television history watched the men's hockey team defeat the United States and win the gold medal. Canadians felt good, and passionately Canadian. They celebrated enthusiastically in the streets and they waved flags. Globalization had not struck down nationalism. The giant American multinational firm, General Motors, describing itself as the Canadian Olympic team's proudest sponsor, had full-page Maple Leaf flags printed in newspapers, advising readers to post them in any window "to show how proud you are of our women's and men's national hockey teams." A consultant in sport policy called Canadian successes an emotional high-water mark for a generation. Proudly patriotic Canadian hockey stars then returned to their mostly American teams where they were paid, of course, in American dollars, highflying at the time.

In the Winter Games of 2006, Canada placed third among nations. In hockey, however, Canadian athletes' fortunes were mixed this time: as a Vancouver daily put it, "Canada's women were pure gold, the men were just plain old." The women won the gold medal, as in 2002, while the men's team was unimpressively beaten in the preliminaries. The hero of the Games was undoubtedly speed skater Cindy Klassen, from Winnipeg, who, with five medals won in the course of the games, skated her way into Olympic history.

Cultural Development

For cultural historian George Melnyk, Canadian films remain "a secondary cultural influence" in Canada, with two distinct and complementary national cinemas.[2] Hollywood has always overshadowed Canadian film-making in English. One Canadian filmmaker compared the difficulty of making a movie in Canada to climbing

The Canadian women's hockey team, with team coach Danièle Sauvageau (centre), just after winning the women's gold medal at the Salt Lake City Olympics in 2002.

CP Photo/COA (Mike Redwood)

Mount Everest without oxygen. He pointed to an indifferent public, harsh critics, tiny production budgets, promotional problems, and American-owned movie theatres. Various federal aid programs for filmmaking have existed since the 1940s, but budgets have always been modest. Canadian film directors such as Atom Egoyan and David Cronenberg have earned international reputations, but Canadian English-language films capture barely 1 percent of box office receipts. Most movies made in Canada were not Canadian movies at all: American majors filmed many productions in Vancouver, Toronto, and Montreal, attracted by generous federal and provincial tax credits.

French-speaking Canada boasted a far more successful movie-marketing machine and a distinctive filmmaking voice. In 2003, Canadian-made films occupied nearly 20 percent of Canada's French-language film market. *Les Boys, Les Boys II,* and *Les Boys III,* a series of comedies featuring a group of Montreal hockey players with much typical locker-room humour, were all top-grossing films. In 2002, more than one million Quebeckers flocked to see *Séraphin: Un homme et son péché,* an adaptation of a well-known novel by Claude-Henri Grignon, and shed a tear for the long-suffering Donalda, victim of her miserly husband. The film was set in St. Adèle, a village in the Laurentians north of Montreal, in the 1890s when landless pioneers were colonizing the region's poor farmlands. *Bon Cop, Bad Cop,* a police comedy, became the biggest blockbuster in Quebec's film history and the only Canadian-made movie in the country's Top 10 box office draws in 2006. The film featured two police officers, one a Quebecker, the other an anglophone from Toronto, forced to work together to outwit a serial murderer. Indeed, the years 1990–2006 represented a golden era for Quebec films.

Aboriginal Canada found a rare voice in the film *Atanarjuat (The Fast Runner),* directed by Zacharias Kunuk. This first feature film in the Inuktitut language proved a fascinating cultural document and also told an exciting story. Critics wrote glowingly about the film, which won many awards.

Canadian television had notable successes, too. In 2000, the CBC produced, in English and in French, the epic megaseries, *Canada: A People's History.* Using a narrative approach, it presented Canadian history as "one story" of "one people," earning praise from some historians who decried a tendency among other historians to give too much emphasis to differences among people, be they class, gender, ethnic, linguistic, or regional. Military topics in particular received much attention. For historian Lyle Dick, the CBC's presentation represented "a more activist deployment of history in the service of nation-building."[3]

Executive Producer Mark Starowicz just prior to filming the sequence on the Battle of the Plains of Abraham, in the television series Canada: A People's History.

Reproduced with permission from CBC Still Photo Collection

The 1990s saw the production by Radio-Canada of the series *Lance et compte,* centred on the professional and love lives of a group of hockey players; it proved an astounding success, attracting nearly half of the total French-language viewing public. The miniseries *Anne* and *Road to Avonlea,* based on Lucy Maud Montgomery's perennially and internationally popular novel *Anne of Green Gables,* enchanted more than five million nightly viewers in 1999. The "Anne industry" also attracted hundreds of thousands of foreign tourists, many of them from Japan, to Anne's supposed homestead in Prince Edward Island.

Popular Music

In music, such groups as the Philosopher Kings, the Tragically Hip, and the Barenaked Ladies carried off numerous awards, while Alanis Morissette's 1995 recording *Jagged Little Pill* sold millions of copies. In 2000, pop singer Nelly Furtado burst onto the scene with her CD *Whoa! Nelly*. In the 1990s, singers Céline Dion and Shania Twain gained international reputations. Gaspé native Kevin Parent's folk-tinged rock was a huge hit with Quebeckers, while Lac St. Jean native Pierre Lapointe's first album appeared in 2004 and soon brought him celebrity and a significant presence in Europe.

From 2005, sales of CD albums began to decline as music lovers could now download onto their computers the songs they preferred rather than buying entire albums. Canadian and especially Quebec musicians were slow to adapt to this new trend whose financial implications were worrying.

Canadian Literature

After 1990, an increasing number of Canadian authors wrote for international audiences. Margaret Atwood's novels saw phenomenal sales abroad. *The Blind Assassin*, which won the prestigious British Booker Prize in 2000, told the story of a woman growing up in a small Ontario town before World War I. Alice Munro's books of short stories, *The Love of a Good Woman* and *The View from Castle Rock*, full of insights about human behaviour and relationships, boosted that talented writer's reputation. In 2002, three of the finalists for the Booker prize, Yann Martel, Carol Shields, and Rohinton Mistry, were

Canadian pop star Alanis Morissette.
CP Photo (Andrew Wallace)

Canadian authors. Victor Lam's book of short stories, *Bloodletting and Miraculous Cures*, about the inner workings of hospitals inspired by his experiences in medical school and as a physician, won him the coveted Giller Prize in 2006. In the words of one critic, foreign attention proved a wonderful reinforcement for "neurotically insecure Canadians." Here, perhaps, was the globalization of Canadian culture.

COMMUNITY PORTRAIT

Clayoquot Sound and the Environmental Movement: The "War in the Woods"

On May 5, 2000, Canadian political leaders met at Clayoquot Sound, on the west coast of Vancouver Island, to unveil a plaque designating this area of great natural beauty as a United Nations biosphere reserve. Henceforth any logging in the area was to be carried out in an environmentally friendly manner. Forestry specialists described the project as the most significant ecosystem management experiment in British Columbia's history, and perhaps Canada's.

Traditionally, the forest industry showed little concern for environmental values. Priority went to short-term profit considerations. Then, in the early 1980s, many people began to worry about the accelerating destruction of the earth's last remaining rainforests, both tropical and temperate. Biologists argued that old-growth forests, with deep, multilayered canopies, standing dead trees, and centuries of accumulated deadfall on the forest floor, harboured an enormous diversity of species whose survival depended on the preservation of such rainforests. Clearcut logging, the method preferred by the forest industry, could not be reconciled with the preservation of biodiversity.

Clayoquot, an area of some 260 000 ha, was the last major unexploited watershed on Vancouver Island. In 1993, the provincial government gave forestry giant MacMillan Bloedel permission to clearcut most of the area's rainforest. Angry environmentalists formed a group, "Friends of Clayoquot Sound," which, in the summer of 1993, waged a "war in the woods," a nonviolent campaign of civil disobedience to protest against the government's action. They set up camp in the Black Hole clearcut, an area logged in the 1970s, replanted unsuccessfully four times and now badly eroded. Women were the key organizers of the protest. Fearing that concessions would encourage environmentalists to seek to protect other areas from logging, MacMillan Bloedel obtained an injunction banning demonstrations on company work sites. The government had 900 protestors arrested at the blockades, charged with criminal contempt of court for defying the injunction, and jailed or fined. Friends of Clayoquot continued their campaign, by targeting industrial consumers of British Columbia timber in Europe and threatening boycotts of their products. This tactic proved effec-

tive, and the battle at Clayoquot achieved international notoriety.

In October 1993, the British Columbia government appointed a panel composed of members of the region's First Nation, the Nuu-chah-nulth, and a team of scientists and technicians. The panel recommended an ecosystem approach that emphasized the maintenance of biological diversity, watershed integrity, and the protection of cultural, scenic, and recreational values. Clearcutting as a method of harvest was to be replaced by a method called "variable retention," an alternative silvicultural system whereby trees and patches of forest are retained to protect a variety of ecosystem components. The government agreed to implement all of the panel's recommendations. MacMillan Bloedel then negotiated with First Nations and environmentalists to find a mutually acceptable approach to some continued logging.

After the Clayoquot campaign, environmentalists won other victories. The provincial government set out a new Forest Practices Code that reduced the maximum size of clearcuts and mandated replanting of harvested areas. British Columbia also moved to place 13 percent of its land base in protected areas, in recognition of its responsibilities in regard to the United Nations Convention on Biological Diversity, which Canada had signed in 1992. Environmental critics asserted, however, that protected areas were often "rock and ice" where industry had no interest, and that old-growth forests were underrepresented. Nor were there any guarantees that a future, more business-oriented government would not roll back environmental protection, or fail to monitor and enforce forest management rules.

The initiatives of the environmental movement generated substantial opposition. Compromise between preservationist and economic imperatives seemed impossible. The logging industry accused environmentalists of increasing its costs and diminishing its profits. Forestry workers argued that restrictions on logging would lead to job losses. Some rural communities feared for their very existence. At times Aboriginal peoples and environmentalists differed in their attitudes toward nature. And governments wanted the attendant tax revenues and stumpage fees that the lumber industry provided.

Yet issues were undoubtedly more complex than they first appeared. Was it possible to assign a value in dollars to the maintenance of biodiversity? What would happen to jobs once all old-growth stands were cut? Was reforesta-tion of areas already harvested not a wiser option to assure a sustainable forest industry? Could other industries such as tourism and recreation offer new potential thanks to wilderness preservation? The environmental movement's activities brought all those interested in British Columbia's forests, and in forests elsewhere in Canada, to ask these questions, and to seek answers.

FURTHER READING

Benjamin Cashore, George Hoberg, Michael Howlett, Jeremy Rayner, and Jeremy Wilson, *In Search of Sustainability: British Columbia Forest Policy in the 1990s* (Vancouver: UBC Press, 2001).

Jeremy Wilson, *Talk and Log: Wilderness Politics in British Columbia, 1965–1996* (Vancouver: UBC Press, 1998).

The Environment

Opinion research shows that so-called bread-and-butter issues are usually citizens' primary concern. Job losses or sharp increases in energy costs threaten people's living standards. Health care is also a major preoccupation. Environmental issues have lower priority, because their impact on people is less visible and less immediate. Environmental interest groups have attempted to maintain such issues before the public, often by pointing out that they are closely linked to the health of people and that of the planet. They succeeded, from the late 1990s, in convincing many Canadians that global warming and climate change threatened Canada and the world, and that governments and people should act.

Actions taken to counter threats to the environment may have a negative impact on the economy that is more immediate and striking than the environmental threat itself. Moreover, when money is lacking and other priorities numerous, environmental issues appear clearly less important. In the 1990s, for example, deficit-ridden provincial governments found it politically easier to cut environmental spending than health care. Ontario, for example, reduced its spending on parks by fully 60 percent in the 1990s. Provincial governments also offloaded responsibilities onto regional and municipal governments, which frequently favoured economic interests over environmental concerns. With lower budgets, governments often failed to apply their own environmental laws and to monitor compliance. Although smog caused 5000 premature deaths each year, Ottawa's program for smog reduction, announced with great fanfare in 1990, remained a dead letter.

Habitat Conservation

As urbanization, agriculture, and resource exploitation occupied an ever-larger portion of the globe's surface, many wildlife species and plants faced the threat of extinction. Calling for immediate action, scientists warned that mankind's actions were leading to the disappearance of life forms at a rate that the world had not seen since the age of the dinosaurs. In 1992, at the Earth Summit at Rio de Janeiro, Canada signed a convention on biological diversity by which it agreed to take measures to protect threatened species and their habitats. Yet only in 2002, after a decade during which the number of species on the endangered list increased markedly, did Parliament adopt a Species at Risk Act. Four years later, wildlife conservation groups called upon NAFTA to launch an investigation into what they saw as Canada's failure to enforce endangered-species laws.

Ottawa and several provinces did take action to set aside and protect habitat necessary for the survival of ecosystems. In 2002, Ottawa announced the creation of ten new national parks and five marine conservation areas. Yet at the same time, forestry, mining, agriculture, and recreational activities in areas adjacent to existing parks caused increased ecological stress on the parks themselves. Provinces also moved to create new protected areas and take better care of existing ones. Yet many natural regions, particularly in heavily urbanized southern Canada, still had few or no protected areas. In partial remedy, in its budget of 2007, the Harper government attributed $225 million to the Nature Conservancy of Canada, to which it gave the responsibility for finding matching sums from private sources and then of purchasing and protecting ecologically important lands.

Air and Water Pollution

Waste disposal remained a serious issue. At one point, Torontonians were warned that they risked being buried beneath their own garbage if Michigan, northern Ontario, or Quebec refused to take it. Throughout the 1990s and the 2000s, environmental interest groups continued to point out that air and water pollution represented a grave health hazard for Canadians as well as a threat to the survival of natural ecosystems.

Industry continued to use the atmosphere for free waste disposal; it spewed out large quantities of contaminants, such as nitrogen oxides associated with smog, particulate matter

Wind power is a source of alternative energy. Here are generators at work on the Cowley Ridge Wind Farm project near the southern Alberta town of Cowley.

CP Photo (Larry MacDougal)

linked to respiratory illness, and toxic cancer-causing chemicals. A Hudson Bay Mining and Smelting facility in Flin Flon, Manitoba, was Canada's largest toxic polluter, while two Inco operations in Ontario, and Syncrude and Suncor plants in Alberta placed not far behind. With one-quarter of Canada's emissions, Alberta was the largest polluter. Much more populated Ontario, with its dirty coal-burning plants, placed second.

Water pollution remained a very current problem. In 2005, *Maclean's* published a report on sewage entitled "From Sea to Stinking Sea" in which it exposed Canada's lack of sewage treatment standards. The city of Victoria, for example, continued to flush raw sewage into the Juan de Fuca Strait. When studies showed that the lands around sewage outfalls had high levels of toxic chemicals that made them contaminated sites, the provincial government directed Victoria to come up with a plan to upgrade its sewage treatment levels.

Ontario and Ottawa promised to clean up and restore several polluted sites, among them Hamilton Harbour, the Niagara River, and Toronto Harbour, on the Canadian side of the Great Lakes, sites that had been contaminated over decades by the dumping of industrial waste, poorly treated municipal sewage, and agricultural runoff. In spite of huge sums spent since the 1970s by companies trying to improve water quality, industrial activities continued to pollute the Great Lakes. In 2007, Ecojustice Canada, an environmental advocacy group, issued its *Great Lakes Sewage Report Card*; it stated that 90 billion litres of raw sewage, containing human waste, pathogens, and hundreds of toxic chemicals, were still being dumped into the Great Lakes—the drinking-water supply for 24 million people—each year.

The Kyoto Protocol

During the 1990s and early 2000s, the international scientific community produced numerous studies that tended to demonstrate that the earth's climate was heating up and that human activities, principally the burning of fossil fuels—gas, oil, and coal—were the principal cause. Climate change, they said, would have disastrous consequences for the planet and its inhabitants.

Discussions of the issue appeared to pit environmental considerations against economic development. Canada's and the world's economy needed energy and most energy came from nonrenewable fossil fuels. Still, some provinces began encouraging alternative energies such as the creation of wind farms. Advocates for action to reduce emissions claimed that moving toward a greener economy would also create jobs, and that inaction would have, sooner or later, a disastrous impact on the world's economy and on human populations.

International agreement on the reduction of so-called greenhouse gases—carbon dioxide and methane—proved difficult, and the result, the Kyoto Protocol, which Canada signed in 1997, was a modest plan indeed. Objectives, agreed upon in 2001, were limited: by 2012 industrialized countries should reduce emissions of greenhouse gases to a level 6 percent below that of 1990. Developing nations such as China and India, whose gas emissions were mounting steadily, were exempted from obligations for the moment.

As time passed, opposition to Kyoto mounted in Canada. In Ontario, the automobile industry felt

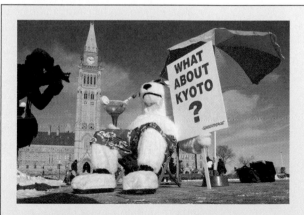

A Greenpeace activist dressed as a polar bear sunbathing on the front lawn of Parliament in Ottawa, January 2007. Greenpeace sought to publicize global warming and its effect on the environment.

CP Photo (Tom Hanson)

especially threatened. The sale to consumers of large, gas-guzzling sport-utility vehicles and light trucks brought far greater profits than compact automobiles. The truck transportation industry also feared the additional costs of any plan to reduce emissions.

Alberta, in particular, led the charge against the Protocol, fearful that any plan for reducing greenhouse gas emissions would hurt its petroleum and gas sector. Indeed, procedures used to extract oil from tar sands in northern Alberta explained why that province produced fully 40 percent of the country's greenhouse gases, helping to give Canada the worst record of the Group of Eight large industrial economies. Extracting oil from tar sands in open-pit mines necessitated huge amounts of energy, usually natural gas, as well as vast quantities of fresh water. New development projects, rapidly approved by the provincial government, assured that emissions would continue to spiral. After 2008, however, a slowing economy and sharply lower oil prices threatened to delay many of these projects.

Ottawa finally ratified the Kyoto Accord in 2002, although neither the government nor the public was ready for the tough measures required by the Kyoto plan. Between 2000 and 2005, Liberal governments put forward three plans for action. In the face of strong opposition from industry and petroleum-producing provinces, the plans set weak targets, often voluntary, and lacked implementation timelines. At the same time, Ottawa accorded huge subsidies to the oil and gas industry, a legacy of times when oil prices had been much lower.

The Conservative government of Stephen Harper, which took office in 2006, showed little enthusiasm for acting to reduce greenhouse gas production. Harper stated that Kyoto's targets were unreachable without shutting down Canada's economy. (By this time, instead of diminishing, Canadian emissions had increased by a hefty 35 percent over 1990 levels.) Instead of absolute reductions in emissions, his Clean Air Act proposed so-called "intensity targets" by which the oil industry, for example, would reduce emissions per barrel by developing new technology. Increasing production would, however, ensure that real emissions would keep rising. Moreover, it set reduction targets in the far-distant future—2050. In late 2007, at an international conference at Bali to discuss a successor agreement to Kyoto, the Canadian government objected to compulsory cuts in greenhouse gases unless all countries agreed to them. Disappointed environmentalists expressed shame that Canada was now perceived as an environmental laggard. Canadians showed ambivalence in their attitudes toward climate change. Polls showed that a majority were convinced that global warming existed, that it was having a negative impact on the earth, and that it was necessary to act; but at the same time, most Canadians showed much reticence toward solutions that risked changing their lifestyle or increasing living costs.

Since 1867, Canada has evolved into an increasingly complex society. The nation's population diversified ethnically and culturally in the nineteenth and, more rapidly, in the twentieth century. The role of the state increased greatly, especially after 1930, when governments came to play a role in virtually every aspect of human existence. Associations of all types proliferated as Canadians sought to counter the powerlessness of the individual acting alone. Material progress and improved living conditions, though by no means continuous, were generally apparent; their attendant costs, both human and environmental, were at first less apparent, except to their immediate victims. After 1960, however, many Canadians came to realize that high living standards and consumer choices often caused environmental degradation. Sustainability became a new byword.

Although Canada has undergone immense change, most of the basic themes of the country's early history remain operative today. In 1867, four major groups made up Canada's population—the Aboriginal peoples, French-speaking Canadians, English-speaking Canadians, and immigrants; today, the same four groups are evident, although not in the same proportion as in 1867. Canada in 1867 was a nation of regions; despite modern transportation and the communications revolution, it remains so today—indeed, to such an extent that doubts have often abounded about the survival of existing political arrangements. By the 1880s, federal–provincial affairs had become acrimonious; more than a century later, conflict often pervaded intergovernmental contacts. French–English relations were the source of bitter controversy in the nineteenth century; intercultural relations continued to generate passionate debate in the twentieth. Relations with the Aboriginal peoples were an important preoccupation in the nineteenth century as European settlement expanded westward; since 1950, Aboriginal issues have become complex but very present public policy questions.

In 1867, British and American influences weighed heavily on the new nation; today, the impact of the United States on Canada—culturally, politically, and economically—is in many ways far more weighty. Finally, despite the coming of the welfare state, flagrant social inequalities still distinguish Canadians from one another, much as they did in the past. Constant change, but equally apparent continuity—these are the two themes that reflect the past for Canadians in the early years of the twenty-first century.

NOTES

1. Thomas J. Courchene with Colin R. Telmer, *From Heartland to North American Region State: The Social, Fiscal and Federal Evolution of Ontario—An Interpretive Essay* (Toronto: Centre for Public Management, University of Toronto, 1998), pp. 268–96.

2. George Melnyk, *One Hundred Years of Canadian Cinema* (Toronto: University of Toronto Press, 2004), pp. 271–72.

3. "'A New History for the New Millennium': Canada: A People's History," *Canadian Historical Review*, 85 (2004), p. 109.

BEYOND THE BOOK

Canadian Heritage: Multiculturalism

http://www.canadianheritage.gc.ca/progs/multi/index_e.cfm
The Government of Canada's Web portal for information about national multiculturalism programs in Canada.

Canadian Federal Budgets: 1994–Present

http://www.fin.gc.ca/access/budinfoe.html
Official budgets of the Government of Canada from 1994 and onward.

Public Opinion Research Reports

http://www.porr-rrop.gc.ca/index-e.html
This site contains executive summaries of all public opinion research surveys undertaken by the Government of Canada since 2006. For example, select "Find a report" and search by department, such as "Health" or "Justice."

Federal Electoral History

http://www.elections.ca/intro.asp?section=pas&document=index&lang=e
A database of the results of all Canadian federal elections.

Media Concentration in Contemporary Canada

http://archives.cbc.ca/arts_entertainment/media/topics/790
CBC Archives clips review the history of media concentration in Canada to the present day.

Government of Canada

http://www.gc.ca/main_e.html
Official website of the Government of Canada. Links to resources about ministries, programs, and how the federal government works.

Between

Between: Living in the Hyphen. Directed by Anne Marie Nakagawa (National Film Board of Canada, 2005). Seven individuals share their stories and struggles of trying to find cultural identity when they are of multiethnic backgrounds.

RELATED READINGS

R. Douglas Francis and Donald B. Smith, eds., *Viewpoints: Readings in Canadian History* (Toronto: Thomson Nelson, 2007), contains the following articles relevant to this chapter: Alan C. Cairns, "Aboriginal Peoples in the Twenty-First Century: A Plea for Realism," pp. 545–71; Will Kymlicka, "The

Merits of Multiculturalism, pp. 562–71; and Rob Huebert, "Climate Change and Canadian Sovereignty in the Northwest Passage," pp. 571–81.

BIBLIOGRAPHY

Literature concerning aspects of contemporary Canada is abundant, and only a small sampling can be presented here. Studies of Canadian–American economic relations include John McDougall, *Drifting Together: The Political Economy of Canada–US Integration* (Peterborough, ON: Broadview Press, 2006); and Stephen Clarkson, *Uncle Sam and Us: Globalization, Neoconservatism, and the Canadian State* (Toronto: University of Toronto Press, 2002). See also Michael Adams, *Fire and Ice: The United States, Canada and the Myth of Converging Values* (Toronto: Penguin Canada, 2003). On business magnates, see Peter C. Newman, *Titans: How the New Canadian Establishment Seized Power* (Toronto: Penguin Books, 1998); and, on one controversial business leader, Richard Siklos, *Shades of Black: Conrad Black, His Rise and Fall* (Toronto: McClelland & Stewart, 2004). The energy question is discussed in G. Bruce Doern, ed., *Canadian Energy Policy and the Struggle for Sustainable Development* (Toronto: University of Toronto Press, 2005).

Among books on the environment, see Judith I. McKenzie, *Environmental Politics in Canada: Managing the Commons into the Twenty-First Century* (Toronto: Oxford, 2002); Mark Jaccard, John Nyboer, and Bryn Sadownik, *The Cost of Climate Policy* (Vancouver: UBC Press, 2002); Karen Bakker, ed., *Eau Canada: The Future of Canada's Water* (Vancouver: UBC Press, 2006); and Douglas Macdonald, *Business and Environmental Politics in Canada* (Peterborough, ON: Broadview Press, 2007).

Studies of Jean Chrétien include Lois Harder and Steve Patten, eds., *The Chrétien Legacy: Politics and Public Policy in Canada* (Montreal/Kingston: McGill-Queen's University Press, 2006); Jeffrey Simpson, *The Friendly Dictatorship*, rev. ed. (Toronto: McClelland and Stewart, 2002); and Lawrence Martin, *Iron Man: The Defiant Reign of Jean Chrétien*, vol. 2, rev. ed. (Toronto: Penguin Books Canada, 2003). Recent journalistic accounts of Canadian politics include Hugh Segal, *The Long Road Back: The Conservative Journey in Canada, 1993–2006* (Toronto: HarperCollins, 2006); Paul Wells, *Right Side Up: The Fall of Paul Martin and the Rise of Stephen Harper's New Conservatism* (Toronto: McClelland & Stewart, 2006); Bob Plamondon, *Full Circle: Death and Resurrection in Canadian Conservative Politics* (Toronto: Key Porter, 2006); William Johnson, *Steven Harper and the Future of Canada*, rev. ed. (Toronto: McClelland & Stewart, 2006); and Chantal Hébert, *French Kiss: Stephen Harper's Blind Date with Quebec* (Toronto: Knopf Canada, 2007).

On different strands composing Canada's foreign relations, see Roy Rempel, *Dreamland: How Canada's Pretend Foreign Policy Has Undermined Sovereignty* (Montreal/Kingston: McGill-Queen's University Press, 2006); Rosalind Irwin, ed., *Ethics and Security in Canadian Foreign Policy* (Vancouver: UBC Press, 2001); and Sean M. Maloney, *Canada and UN Peacekeeping: Cold War by Other Means* (St. Catharines, ON: Vanwell, 2002). Effects on Canada of the terrorist attacks of September 2001 are discussed in Kent Roach, *September 11: Consequences for Canada* (Montreal/Kingston: McGill-Queen's University Press, 2003); and in J.L. Granatstein's strongly opinionated essay, *Whose War Is It? How Canada Can Survive in the Post-9/11 World* (Toronto: HarperCollins, 2007). Relations between Ottawa and the provinces are examined in Richard Simeon, *Federal–Provincial Diplomacy: The Making of Recent Policy in Canada* (Toronto: University of Toronto Press, 2006). On the provinces, see Christopher Dunn, *Provinces: Canadian Provincial Politics*, 2nd ed. (Peterborough, ON: Broadview Press, 2006).

On sports history, consult Colin Howell, *Blood, Sweat, and Cheers: Sport and the Making of Modern Canada* (Toronto: University of Toronto Press, 2001). Reginald W. Bibby examines contemporary religion in *Restless Gods: The Renaissance of Religion in Canada* (Toronto: Stoddart, 2002). Sylvain Larocque, *Gay Marriage: The Story of a Canadian Social Revolution* (Toronto: James Lorimer, 2006), deals with a major gay rights issue. Gary Teeple criticizes government welfare policy in *Globalization and the Decline of Social Reform: Into the Twenty-First Century* (Toronto: Garamond, 2000). On poverty, see Jean Swanson, *Poor-Bashing: The Politics of Exclusion* (Toronto: Between the Lines Press, 2001). Child care is examined in Gordon Cleveland and Michael Krashinsky, eds., *Our Children's Future: Child Care Policy in Canada* (Toronto: University of Toronto Press, 2001).

Appendix

CANADIAN PRIME MINISTERS SINCE CONFEDERATION

Sir John Alexander Macdonald
Conservative
1867–1873, 1878–1891

Alexander Mackenzie
Liberal
1873–1878

Sir John Joseph Caldwell Abbott
Conservative
1891–1892

Sir John Sparrow David Thompson
Conservative
1892–1894

Sir Mackenzie Bowell
Conservative
1894–1896

Sir Charles Tupper
Conservative
1896

Sir Wilfrid Laurier
Liberal
1896–1911

Sir Robert Laird Borden
Conservative and Unionist
1911–1920

Arthur Meighen
Conservative and Unionist
1920–1921, 1926

William Lyon Mackenzie King
Liberal
1921–1926, 1926–1930, 1935–1948

Richard Bedford Bennett
Conservative
1930–1935

Louis Stephen St. Laurent
Liberal
1948–1957

John George Diefenbaker
Progressive Conservative
1957–1963

Lester Bowles Pearson
Liberal
1963–1968

Pierre Elliott Trudeau
Liberal
1968–1979, 1980–1984

Charles Joseph Clark
Progressive Conservative
1979–1980

John Napier Turner
Liberal
1984

Martin Brian Mulroney
Progressive Conservative
1984–1993

Kim Campbell
Progressive Conservative
1993

Jean Chrétien
Liberal
1993–2003

Paul Edgar Philippe Martin
Liberal
2003–2006

Stephen Joseph Harper
Conservative
2006–

Index

Abbaye d'Ardennes massacre, 428
Abella, Irving, 395
Abenakis, 78, 103–105
Aberhart, William
    ("Bible Bill"), 407
Aboîteau, 34
Aboriginal languages
    families of, 7–8
    modern retention, 505
Aboriginal peoples
    Acadia and, 64
    activism, 499
    artists, writers and performers, 506
    Bill C-31, 507
    Charter of Rights and Freedoms and, 563
    constitutional protection and, 499
    economic and social issues since the 1980s,
        505–507
    Expo 67 and, 497
    impact of industrialization on, 335
    land claims, 498, 503–504, 508, 510
    population figures, 505
    postwar attitudes toward, 493, 495–497
    protests in the 1990s, 500
    right to self-government, 499–500
    Royal Commission on, 500–501, 502, 503
    schools (*see* Aboriginal schools)
    slaves, 64
    White Paper of 1969, 497
    women (*see* Aboriginal women)
    World War II, 494–495
    Yale–Toronto Conference on the North Amer-
        ican Indian, 493–494
    See also First Nations; *individual peoples*
Aboriginal Peoples Television Network, 506
Aboriginal schools
    band-controlled, 496
    Jesuit-run, 38
    residential, 269, 496, 501–503
Aboriginal slaves, 63
Aboriginal women
    in the fur trade, 202
    Indian Act of 1867 and, 365
    Indian status and, 507
    in Iroquoian society, 15–16, 17
    in modern communities, 507
    suffrage and, 354
Abortion, 337, 569–570
Absentee landlordism, 244

Acadia
    becomes Nova Scotia, 64–65
    fall of, 83
    French settlement in, 34, 51
    location of, 51
    relations with Aboriginal peoples, 64
Acadians
    American Revolution and, 171
    bilingualism and, 564
    expulsion from Nova Scotia, 67–70
    identity of, 63, 64
    in Nova Scotia, 65–67
    return to Nova Scotia, 169–170
Acadien identity, 64
"Aces," 379–380
Acorn, Milton, 475
Acquired immune deficiency syndrome (AIDS),
    576
Act for the Temporary Government of Rupert's
    Land and the North-West Territory, 264–
    265
Action démocratique du Québec, 528
Action libérale nationale, 408
Act of Union of 1840, 114, 138, 143, 145, 146,
    148
Adams, Mary Louise, 458–459
Adams, Michael, 568
Afghanistan, 588
African American immigrants, 293
African Americans
    Loyalists, 176–177
    Underground Railway and, 155
    in Victoria, 226–228
African Canadians
    discrimination and, 547
    population in the Dominion of Canada, 251
    World War I and, 375
African Rifles, 227
African slaves
    Josiah Henson, 251–252
    in New France, 63
    See also Slaves and Slavery
Agawa Pictograph Site, 12
Agitprop theatre, 412
Agricultural equipment industry, 154
Agriculture
    in 1867, 249
    British Columbia, 330
    early nineteenth century, 110

the Great Depression and, 404–405
impact of industrialization on, 334–335
Iroquoians, 14
Maritimes, 181
New France, 58–59
Prairie Farm Rehabilitation Program, 410
Quebec, 332
United Canadas, 144
Upper Canada, 134
in the west, 150, 292, 561
Ahenakew, Edward, 201
AIDS, 576
Air Canada, 410
Aird Commission, 403
Aird Report, 403
Air pollution, 600–601
Aitken, Max (Lord Beaverbrook), 326
Akenson, Donald, 154
Alabama (C.S.S.), 237
Alaska boundary dispute, 318
Alaskan Panhandle, 216, 217
Albani, Emma (Marie Lajeunesse), 357
Alberta
    1970s, 561
    Aboriginal land-claims issues, 504
    economy in the 1960s, 482–483
    economy in the 1990s, 590
    greenhouse gas emissions and, 602
    National Energy Program and, 562
    prohibition and, 384
    recession of 1980–1981, 562–563
    schools issues, 314
Alderson, E.A.H., 375
Alexander, David, 451
Alger, Horatio, 326
Algonquian language group, 8, 11
Algonquians
    French settlement at Quebec and, 35
    fur trade, 32
    overview, 13–14
Algonquin Park, 351
Allan, Sir Hugh, 282, 284, 286
Allardyce, Gilbert, 184
All-Canadian Congress of Labour, 402
Alline, Henry, 171–172, 174
Alma Parish, 184
Alverstone, Lord, 318
Amateur Athletic Union of Canada, 362
Amateur sports clubs, 362
American Civil War, 237–238
American Federation of Labor, 340
American Fur Company, 207
American immigrants, 293
American Revolution
    First Nations and, 102–103
    invasion of Quebec, 100–102

Nova Scotia and, 169, 170–175, 189
persecution of the Loyalists, 172, 174–175
Amherst, Jeffery, 89, 97
Amherstburg, 155
Amiens, 384
Amor de Cosmos. *See* Smith, William
Anderson, Karen, 15
Angélique, Marie-Joseph, 63
Anglicans, 122, 254
Anglophones, Quebec and, 523, 524
Anglo-Saxon race, 315
Angus, R.B., 286
Anishinabeg, 103, 119, 130
Annedda, 27
Anne of Green Gables (Montgomery), 359, 596
Annexation movement, 149
Anse au Foulon, 87
Anticommunists, 456
Anti-Confederation League, 263
Anti-Semitism, 408, 449
"Apostle of Nova Scotia." *See* Alline, Henry
Appeasement, 419
Aquin, Hubert, 475
Arar, Maher, 588
Arbuckle, Franklin, 5, 10, 14
Arcand, Adrien, 408
Arcand, Denys, 476, 575
Archambault, Joseph-Papin, 384
Arctic Archipelago, 276
Arctic culture area, 13
Armed forces
    strength prior to World War II, 419
    women in, 424
    See also World War I; World War II
Armstrong, C., 332
Armstrong, M.W., 173
Art Association of Montreal, 357
Art magazines, 403
Asian immigrants, 295–296, 335, 544
Asian immigration, 540
Assembly. *See* Legislative Assembly
Assembly of First Nations, 497, 501
Assimilation, 268–269, 363–365, 501–503
Assiniboia, 202
Association catholique de la jeunesse canadienne-
    française, 317
Atanarjuat (The Fast Runner) (film), 596
Athapaskan language group, 8, 11
Atlantic, battle of, 427
Atlantic Canada
    Anti-Confederation sentiments, 304–305
    economy in the 1960s, 483–484
    economy in the early twentieth century, 329
    See also Maritimes; Newfoundland
Atlantic Canada Opportunities Agency, 566
Atlantic Development Board, 483

Atlantic salmon, 134
Atwood, Margaret, 475, 597
Aun, Karl, 539
Automotive industry, 400
Automotive Products Agreement, 479
"Auto Pact," 479
Avalon Peninsula, 29
Aviation, 400
Aztecs, 5

Baby boom, 458–459
Bacchi, Carol, 353
Back-to-nature movements, 350
Bagot, Sir Charles, 145, 146
Bains, Tara Singh, 546
Baird, Irene, 412
Baldwin, Robert, 135, 144, 146, 148
Balfour Declaration, 399
Balzer, Timothy, 429
Banff Park, 350–351
Banking, 184, 325
Bank of Canada, 406
"Banks," 26
Bannock, 202
Banting, Sir Frederick, 421
Barkham, Selma, 29
Barman, Jean, 224
Barnardo, Thomas, 294
Barnardo Homes, 294
Barnes, Viola, 173
Barr, Rev. Isaac, 293
Barrett, Dave, 560–561
Barrett, Stanley, 547
Barrett v. City of Winnipeg, 313
Baseball, 413, 573, 595
Bashevkins, Sylvia, 564
Basketball, women's, 404
Basque whaling, 29–31
Bastonnois, 102
Batoche, battle of, 309
Battered women, 571
    See also Domestic violence
Battle of the Atlantic, 427
Battle of the Boyne, 156
Battle of the Long Sault, The (film), 362
Battle of the Windmill, 136
Bay of Chaleur, 170
B.C. Electric Company, 483
Beaudé, Henri (Henri d'Arles), 69
Beauharnois, Marquis de, 63
Beaverbrook, Lord. See Aitken, Max
Beaver Dams, battle of, 128
Beck, Adam, 326
Beer, 58
Béique, Caroline, 355

Belany, Archie (Grey Owl), 351
Bell, Mathew, 108–109
Bennett, Charles Fox, 275
Bennett, R.B,, 393, 405, 406, 407
Bennett, W.A.C., 483, 560
Beothuks, 14, 188–189
Bercuson, David J., 285, 395–396, 430
Berger, Carl, 316
Berger, Thomas, 508
Berger Inquiry, 508
Beringia, 3
Bering Strait, 4, 5
Bernhardt, Sarah, 360
Berton, Pierre, 449, 467
Bessborough, Lord, 412
Best, Charles, 421
Bibby, Reginald, 573
Big Bear, 308, 309
Bilingualism
    in Quebec, 524
    school controversy in Ontario, 381
    during the Trudeau government, 564–565
Bill 22 (Quebec), 520
Bill 63 (Quebec), 519–520
Bill 101 (Quebec), 522, 524
Biological diversity, 600
Bird, Florence, 473
Bird Report, 473
Birth control, 337, 409–410, 471, 569
Birth rates
    1970s, 569–570
    New France, 55–56
Bishop, Billy, 379–380
Bishop, Morris, 25
Bishops, 56
Bissoondath, Neil, 551
Black, Conrad, 565
BlackBerry, 583
Black Death, 25
Blackfoot, 8, 195, 196, 207
Black Loyalists, 176–177
"Black Tuesday," 404
Blais, Marie-Claire, 475
Blake, Edward, 281, 282, 303
Bliss, Michael, 183, 285
Bloc Québécois, 527, 584, 585, 587
Blondin, George, 201
"Bloody Saturday," 394
Blue Jays, 595
Blue Quills school, 496
Board of Grain Supervisors, 377
Boers, 316
Bohemian Embassy, 475
Bolaria, B. Singh, 551
Bomber Command, 431

Bon Cop, Bad Cop (film), 596
"Boon-doggling," 405–406
Borden, Robert
    conscription during World War I and, 374,
      382
    Sam Hughes and, 377
    nationhood and, 398–399
    Naval Aid Bill, 320
    prohibition and, 384
    wartime recruitment and, 380
Border security, 587
Borduas, Paul-Émile, 461
Bouchard, Lucien, 89
Bougainville, Louis-Antoine de, 87
Boulay, Angélique Talon de, 88
Bourassa, Henri
    French-Canadian nationalism and, 318
    Naval Service Bill and, 320
    opposition to conscription, 383
    schools issues and, 314, 381
    the South African War and, 316
    World War I and, 373
Bourassa, Napoléon, 160
Bourassa, Robert, 517, 525, 526
Bourgeoys, Marguerite, 255, 256
Bourget, Ignace, 158, 243, 281, 282
Bowell, Mackenzie, 313
Braddock, Edward, 83
Brandt, Gail Cuthbert, 433
Brant, Joseph, 102, 120, 125
Brass bands, 357
Brébeuf, Fr. Jean de, 41, 45
Brebner, J.B., 173
Breweries, 58
Briand, Jean-Olivier, 98
Brightman, Robert, 198
British American Institute for Fugitive Slaves, 252
British-American League, 149
British Columbia
    Aboriginal land-claims issues and, 503–504
    Clayoquot Sound, 597–599
    Confederation and, 271, 274
    creation of, 222
    drinking restrictions and, 462
    economy in the 1960s, 483
    economy in the 1990s, 590–591
    economy in the late nineteenth century, 330
    economy in the mid-nineteenth century, 225
    historical overview, 228–229
    under James Douglas, 222–223
    New Democratic Party in the 1970s, 560–561
    population in the mid-nineteenth century, 226
    union with Vancouver Island, 228
British Columbia Packers Association, 330, 335
British Columbia Treaty Commission, 503
British common law, women under, 133

British Commonwealth Air Training Plan, 420
British immigrants, 128–129, 170, 293, 540
British imperialism, 315–316
British North America Act, 239, 246, 248
    See also Confederation
British Oxford Movement, 411
"British tariff," 284
Brittain, Donald, 476
Brittain, Miller, 403
Broadbent, Ed, 583
Broadcasting
    1970s, 574–575
    Aboriginal peoples and, 506
    See also Radio; Television
Brock, Isaac, 126
Bronfman family, 565
Brown, Craig, 285, 333
Brown, George, 153, 159, 239, 240, 242, 282
Brown, Jennifer, 198
Brown, Judith K., 15
Brown, Roy, 379
Brown, Wallace, 176
Brûlé, Étienne, 35, 37
Brunet, Michel, 333
Bubonic plague, 25
Buchignani, Norman, 550
Buck, Tim, 412
Buckler, Ernest, 461, 475
Buffalo, 11–12, 196, 205
Buffalo-hide trade, 206
Buffalo jumps, 12
Bumsted, J.M., 174
Bureau of Public Information, 424
Burns, Patrick, 326
Business
    emergence of corporations, 325
    entrepreneurs of the 1980s, 565
    "gilded age," 326–327
    See also Economy
Business schools, 331
Butler, Benjamin, 275
Byng, Sir Julian, 377, 379, 385–386

"Cabbagetown," 155
Cabot, John, 26
Cahokia, 6, 7
Caisse de dépôt et placement du Québec, 518
Caisses populaires, 349
"Cajun," 70
Calgary, 574
California, African Americans in, 227
Callaghan, Morley, 412
Campbell, Kim, 584
Campbell, Patrick, 120
Campeau, Lucien, 44
Camp Ipperwash, 494

Canada: A People's History (TV megaseries), 596
Canada and the Canadian Question (Smith), 314
Canada Assistance Act, 480
Canada Cement, 325
Canada Company, 129
Canada Council, 460
Canada East
  Confederation and, 242–243
  culture, 160
  education, 160
  migration and, 157
  politics, 153
  religion, 158–159
Canada First Movement, 281
Canada Grain Board Act, 406–407
Canada Health Act, 592
Canada Pacific Company, 282, 284, 286
Canada party, 265–266
Canada Pension Plan, 480
Canada–United State Migratory Birds Convention
  Treaty, 351
Canada–United States Free Trade Agreement,
  567–569
Canada West
  agriculture, 150
  annexation movement and, 149
  creation of, 138
  culture, 160
  education, 159–160
  immigration and the settlement of, 291–293
  industrial growth, 154
  migration and, 156–157
  politics, 153
  prohibition movement, 158
  religion, 158
  urban structure, 157
Canadian Academy of the Arts, 357
Canadian Advisory Council on the Status of
  Women, 571
Canadian Alliance, 585–586
Canadian–American relations
  under the Diefenbaker government, 478
  free trade agreement, 567–569
  reciprocity, 150–151, 185–186, 314–315,
    318–319
  World War II, 421–422
Canadian Authors' Association, 403
Canadian Bill of Rights, 542
Canadian Black Watch, 428
Canadian Broadcasting Corporation, 410, 459
Canadian Brotherhood of Railway Employees, 340
Canadian Centennial, 487
Canadian Congress of Labour, 456
Canadian Copper Company, 334
Canadian Corps, 384, 385–386
  See also Canadian Expeditionary Force

Canadian Council of Christians and Jews, 449
Canadian Courier (newspaper), 326
Canadian Defence Force, 380
Canadian dollar, 478, 587, 589
Canadian Expeditionary Force, 374–375
  See also Canadian Corps
Canadian Film Development Corporation, 575
Canadian Group of Painters, 412
Canadian Labour Congress, 456, 479
Canadian Light Infantry, 376
Canadian Manufacturers Association, 283
Canadian Mercury, 403
Canadian National Exhibition, 363
Canadian Nationalist Party, 408
Canadian National League, 319
Canadian National Railways, 378, 397
Canadian Northern Railway, 290, 377–378
Canadian Oil, 435
Canadian Pacific Railway, 284, 286–289
Canadian Pacific Railway Company, 286–289,
  361
Canadian Parks and Wilderness Society, 577
Canadian Patriotic Fund, 378
Canadian Radio Broadcasting Commission, 410
Canadian Seamen's Union, 456
Canadian Union of Public Employees, 572
Canadian Wheat Board, 377
Canadian Women's Army Corps, 424
Canadian Women's Peace Party, 382
Canadien-français, 63
Canadien identity, 63
Canadiens
  aftermath of the British Conquest, 99–100
  Royal Proclamation of 1763, 98
Canals, 135, 145
Candide (Voltaire), 89
Canoeists, 197
Caouette, Réal, 479
Cape Breton Island
  Acadians and, 65
  Fort Louisbourg, 64, 80
  Loyalists on, 176, 178
  See also Maritimes
Captain of militia, 56–57
Caraquet, 170
Caravels, 25
Card, Charles Ora, 292
Cardinal, Douglas, 506
Cardinal, Harold, 270
Caribbean immigrants, 544
Cariboo Road, 222
Carignan-Salières regiment, 46
Carillon, 84
Carle, Gilles, 575
Carleton, Guy, 99, 100, 105
Carman, Bliss, 359

Carr, Emily, 402
Carr, Lucien, 15
Carrier, Roch, 475
Carter, Peter, 575
Carter, Sarah, 269
Cartier, George-Étienne
 annexation concerns and, 149
 British Columbia negotiations and, 274
 campaign funds scandal, 282
 Charlottetown Conference, 239
 Confederation and, 242, 243, 247–248
 Grand Trunk Railway and, 151
 John Mcdonald and, 148, 153, 247
Cartier, Jacques, 27–28
Cartwright, Richard, 282
Casgrain, Thérèse, 473
Casinos, 506
Catherwood, Ethel, 404
Catholic Association of French-Canadian Youth, 317
Catholic unions, 341, 349, 402
Cayugas, 102, 103
CCF. See Co-operative Commonwealth Federation
Cellular phones, 583
Cens, 52
Censitaires, 51, 52
Censorship, 460
Chain Her by One Foot (Anderson), 15
Chamberlain, Joseph, 316
Champlain, Samuel de, 32–33, 34–37
"Chanson de la Grenouillère," 204
Chansonniers, 468
Chapais, Thomas, 89
Charbonneau, Joseph, 455
Charest, Jean, 528, 532
Charitable institutions, 339
Charlebois, Robert, 468
Charles II, 75
Charlottetown Accord, 500
Charlottetown Conference, 238–239, 240–241
Charter of Rights and Freedoms, 563, 564, 593
Châteauguay, battle of, 111
Château-Richer, 52
Chatelaine (magazine), 472
Chauveau, P.-J.-O., 250
Che-book-took, 66
Chemical warfare, 377
"Chemin du Roi," 58
Chénier, Jean-Olivier, 113
Chignecto–Cumberland region, 171
Chihoatenhwa, Joseph, 44
Chilcotins, 223
Children
 abuse, 336
 infanticide, 133

 in the mid-nineteenth century, 253
 mortality, 55–56, 337
 of the working class, 336–337
Children of Peace, 131–132
Child welfare, Aboriginal peoples and, 505
China, 544
Chinese Benevolent Association, 551
Chinese immigrants
 British Columbia, 226, 295
 railway construction, 287
 Vancouver, 547–548
Chiniquy, Charles, 158
"Chinook," 218
Chipewyans, 196
Chippewas, 14
Choice for Canada, A (Gordon), 480
Cholera epidemics, 109, 110
Choquette, Ernest, 359
Chown, Rev. S.D., 348
Chrétien, Jean, 527, 528, 583, 585–587
Churches. See Religion; Roman Catholic church; individual churches
Churchill, Winston, 429
Church of England, 122, 158
Church warden, 57
Cinema
 1902s, 404
 1930s, 411
 1960s, 476
 1970s, 575
 contemporary, 595–596
 early years of, 361–362
Cité libre (magazine), 485
Cities. See Urbanization
Civil Code, 56
Clancy, Francis, 413
Clark, Champ, 319
Clark, Greg, 386
Clark, Joe, 562, 563
Clark, S.D., 173–174, 394–395
Clarke, Austin, 553
Clayoquot Sound, 597–599
Clean Air Act (Canada), 602
Clean Air Act (U.S.), 577
"Clear Grits," 153
Clergue, Francis H., 326
Clerical work, 327, 338
Clifton, Rodney, 550
Climate change, 532
Coady, Moses, 411
Coaker, William Ford, 340
Cod fishery, 28–29, 589
Cohen, Leonard, 475
Colbert, Jean-Baptiste, 51, 54, 56–57
Colborne, Sir John, 113
Cold War, 452

Collège Marguerite Bourgeoys, 256
Colleges
    junior, 519
    women's, 256
    See also Higher education
Collèges d'enseignement général et professionnel, 519
"Colonist farmers," 249
Colquhoun, R.S., 375
Columbia country. *See* Oregon territory
Combines Investigation Act, 326
Commis, 56
Commission of Conservation, 336, 351
Committee for the Equality of Women in Canada, 473
Committee for the Original Peoples' Entitlement, 508, 510
Common-law unions, 570
Common School Act of 1846, 159
Common schools, 159
    See also Education; Schools
"Common Sense Revolution," 590
Commonwealth of Nations, 453
Communications
    1920s, 400
    1960s, 482
    Aboriginal peoples and, 506
    modern technology, 583
Communist Party of Canada, 408
Communists, 408, 456
Community of the Sisters of the Congregation of Notre Dame, 255–256
Compagnie des Cent-Associés, 37
Company of One Hundred Associates, 37, 51
Concordia University, 470
"Conductors," 155
Confederacy Council, 16
Confederate States of America, 237
Confederation
    American contribution to, 245–246
    British Columbia and, 271, 274
    British support for, 244
    Charlottetown Conference, 238–239, 240–241
    consideration of proposals, 242–243
    dominion–provincial relations and, 248
    final negotiations, 246–247
    final vote on, 243
    "Great Coalition of 1864," 238
    historical context, 237
    historical overview, 235
    nature of, 247–248
    New Brunswick and, 243, 246
    Newfoundland and, 275, 451
    Nova Scotia and, 263
    opposition in the Maritimes, 243–244

    Prince Edward Island and, 275–276
    Quebec Conference, 239, 241–242
Confederation Bridge, 590
Confédération des Travailleurs Catholiques du Canada, 341
"Confederation Poets," 359
Congregation of Notre Dame, 255–256
Congress of Aboriginal Peoples, 499
Congress of Industrial Organizations, 409
Connolly, Amelia, 220
Connolly, William, 220–221
Conscription
    World War I, 382
    World War II, 427, 428
Conservation
    1950s, 446
    1960s, 485
    contemporary, 599–600
    See also Environment and Environmentalism
Conservative Party
    in early Canada, 247
    election of 1891, 315
    election of 1896, 313
    origin of, 153
Consolidated companies, 325
Consolidated Lake Superior Company, 334
Constitution, The (newspaper), 135
Constitutional Act of 1791, 105–107, 112, 121–122
Constitution of 1982, 269, 499, 563
Consumerism, 445
Consumers Service, 423
Continentalism, 314–315
Contraception, 471
Convention of 1818, 181
Conversion, the Hurons and, 43–45
Cook, James, 216
Cook, Ramsay, 182, 333, 352
Co-operative Commonwealth Federation (CCF), 349, 407, 436, 479
Cooperatives, 411
Cormack, William, 189
Corn Laws, 149
Cornwallis, Edward, 66
Cornwallis, Lord, 174
Corporations
    emergence of, 325
    See also Business
Corvées, 57
Counter-Reformation, 38
Country born, 204–205
Courchene, Thomas, 590
Coureurs de bois, 37, 45–46
Cousture, Arlette, 575
Coutume de Paris, 56
Couture, Guillaume, 356
Crawford, Isabella Valancy, 359

Credit unions, 132, 349
Crees
    discontent with the federal government, 305
    James Bay and Northern Quebec Agreement,
        498
    land-claims issues, 504
    George Nelson and, 198
    smallpox vaccinations, 206
Creighton, Donald, 136–137, 285, 421
Crémazie, Octave, 160
Crerar, H.D.G., 429
Crerar, Thomas, 398
Crime rates, 576
Criminal Law Amendment Act, 339
Crispo, John, 568
Croll, David, 540
Cronon, William, 184
Crosby, Alfred, 7
Crosby, Thomas, 226
Cross, Richard, 520
Cultural industries, 1970s, 574–575
Culture
    1920s, 402–403
    1930s, 411–412
    1960s, 474–477
    1970s, 572–575
    Aboriginal, 363–365
    contemporary, 595–597
    defined, 356
    late nineteenth century, 356–360
    middle-class, 362
    modern Quebec, 530–532
    popular, 361–362
    postwar era, 459–462
    promotion of, 360–361
    working class, 363
Cumming, Peter, 568
Currie, Arthur, 379, 386
Custom of Paris, 56
Cut Knife Hill, 308

Dairy farming, 335
Dales, John, 285, 332
Dancocks, Daniel, 377
Dandurand, Josephine, 355
d'Arles, Henri (Henri Beaudé), 69
Dartmouth College, 104
Darwin, Charles, 347
Darwinian evolution, 347
Daughters of Marguerite Bourgeoys, 255
"Davidites," 131–132
Davies, Robertson, 461, 575
Davies, Thomas, 52
Davis, John, 32
Dawn, Ontario, 252
Dawson, William, 160

Day, Gordon, 104
Daycare centres, 350
Decarie, Graeme, 158
Dechêne, Louise, 53
Defence of Canada Regulations, 426
Deficit, federal, 566–567
Deforestation, 134
de Gaulle, Charles, 521
Delaney, Theresa, 310
Delgamuukw case (1997), 503
Demasduwit, 189
Demographics
    1960s, 471–472
    1970s, 569–571
    1990s, 591
    aging of the population, 591–592
    First Nations, 6–7
    mid-nineteenth century, 250–251
    urbanization and, 335
    See also Birth rates
Dempsey, Lotta, 473
Dene, 12, 508
Denendeh, 508–510
Denominational schools
    in Manitoba, 311–314
    See also Schools
Dent, J.M., 136
Department of Health, 386
Department of Indian Affairs, 268
Department of Labour, 341
Department of Manpower and Immigration, 542–
    543
Department of Regional Economic Expansion,
    483–484
Department of Soldiers' Civil Re-establishment,
    386
Desjardins, Alphonse, 349
Desjardins, Richard, 532
Detroit, 77, 97, 99, 126
Deutscher Bund Canada, 408
Dewdney, Edgar, 286
DEW Line, 453
Diamond Jubilee of Queen Victoria, 316
Dick, Lyle, 596
Dickason, Olive P., 7, 10, 201
Diefenbaker, John, 454–454, 458, 477–479
"Diefenbaker Party," 454–454
Dieppe Raid, 420, 429
Diet, in New France, 61
Dion, Céline, 531–532
Dionne, Ludger, 539
Dionne quintuplets, 411
Dionne Spinning Mill Company, 539
Diplomacy, postwar, 452–454
Dirks, Gerald, 548
Disallowance, 303–304, 305

Discovery (HMS), 216
Discrimination
    against ethnic minorities (*see* Ethnic minorities)
    gender, 338, 378, 473
    immigrants and, 547
    See also Racism
Diseases
    in the North West, 208
    Northwest Coast peoples and, 218, 225
    Plains First Nations and, 206–207
    Spanish influenza, 386
    See also Epidemics
Disenfranchisement, of women, 107, 133, 187
Distant Early Warning Line, 453
Divorce, 187, 472, 570
Documentaries, 411, 476, 575
Domagaya, 27
Dome Petroleum, 562
"Domesticity," 133
Domestics, 338
Domestic violence, 336, 571
Dominion Canner Limited, 325
Dominion Drama Festival, 412
Dominion Lands Act, 291
Dominion of Canada
    acquisition of the Arctic Archipelago, 276
    demographics in the mid-nineteenth century, 250–251
    early politics of, 247
    economy in 1867, 248–249
    naming of, 246–247
    nationalism, 281–282
    nationhood, 398–399
    relations with the First Nations, 267–269
    religion in the mid-nineteenth century, 254, 255–256
    schooling in the mid-nineteenth century, 254
    social life in 1867, 251–254
    urbanization in 1867, 249
Dominion–Provincial relations, 248
    See also Provincial rights
Donnacona, 27
Dorion, Antoine-Aimé, 242, 282
Douglas, James
    aboriginal policy, 221–222, 224–225
    ancestry, 227
    biographical overview, 220–221
    British Columbia and, 222–223
Douglas, Lord. *See* Selkirk, Fifth Earl of
Douglas, W.A.B., 429
Doukhobors, 295
Dower, 291
Dowries, 53
Draper, Henry "Sweet William," 147
Droit de corvée, 52

"Dry fishing," 28
Dubé, Marcel, 476
Dubinsky, Karen, 161
Duck Lake, 289, 308
Dudley, Margot Iris, 353
Duff, Wilson, 224
Dufferin, Lord, 361
Dumont, Gabriel, 308
Duncan, Norman, 359
Duncan, William, 226
Dundas, Henry, 122
Dundas Street, 122
Dunkards, 125
Duplessis, Maurice, 408, 515–517
Duquesne, Marquis, 82
Durham, Lord, 113–114, 138
Durham Report, 138
Durocher, René, 332–333
Duvernay, Ludger, 160

Earl Grey Musical and Dramatic Trophy Competition, 361
Earth Summit at Rio de Janeiro, 600
Eastern European immigrants, 295
Eastern Woodlands culture area, 13
Eaton, Timothy, 326–328
Eaton, Wyall, 358
Eccles, W.J., 53, 89
Ecojustice Canada, 577, 601
École d'enseignment supérieur, 256
École des Hautes Études Commerciales, 331
École littéraire de Montréal, 359
École Sociale Populaire, 349
Economic nationalism, 560
Economy
    1920s, 399–400
    1990s, 583, 589
    under the Diefenbaker government, 477–478
    early twentieth century, 325–330
    immigrants and, 545
    policies under the Pearson government, 479–480
    postindustrial era, 482
    postwar, 445–449, 449–450
    recessions, 477–478, 562, 584
    role of government in, 326
    World War II, 422–423
    See also individual provinces and territories
Eddy, Jonathan, 171
Edmonton Grads, 404
Edmonton Oilers, 574
Ed Sullivan Show, The (TV show), 460
Education
    Aboriginal peoples and assimilationist policies, 269, 506
    Canada East, 160

Canada West, 159–160
kindergartens, 350
language issues in Quebec, 520
mid-nineteenth century, 254
New France, 62
women and, 401
women teachers, 133, 338
the working class and, 336
See also Schools
Educational reform
early twentieth century, 349–350
Quebec, 517
Edwards, Murray, 360
Égalité et indépendance, 571
Egoyan, Atom, 552
Eight Men Speak (play), 412
Eiriksson, Leifr (Leif), 25
Election reform, 283
Electricity
service to homes, 448
See also Hydroelectric power
Elgin, Lord, 147–148, 150
Ellesmere Island National Park Reserve,
577–578
Emigration, 542
"Enemy aliens," 373
Engagés, 38, 39
England
early explorations, 26, 31–32
naval expeditions against Quebec, 79
Seven Years' War, 82–89
See also Great Britain
English, John A., 430, 454
English Canada, social gospel movement, 347–
349
English Canadian
imperialism, 315–316
nativism and, 296–297
English colonies
conflicts with New France, 76–78, 80–82
division among, 79
English criminal law, 99
English–French schools, 381
Ens, Gerhard, 307
Entertainment
1930s, 411
postwar era, 460–461
See also Cinema; Popular culture
Entrepreneurs, of the 1980s, 565
Environment and Environmentalism
1950s, 446
1960s, 485
1980s, 576–578
Clayoquot Sound, 597–599
contemporary issues, 599–602
habitat conservation, 599–600

Quebec and, 532–533
timber industry in New Brunswick, 182–184
Epidemics
First Nations and, 125
Huronia, 42–43, 44
North West, 208
Northwest Coast peoples and, 218, 225
Plains First Nations and, 206–207
Spanish influenza, 386
See also Diseases
Equal Opportunity Program (New Brunswick),
484
Equal Rights Association, 312
Erickson, Arthur, 469
Eskimo-Aleut language family, 7
Estonians, 539
Ethnic enclaves, 552
Ethnic minorities
World War I, 375, 381–382
World War II, 424–426
Eugenics movement, 348
European immigration, postwar, 537–539
European refugees, 537–539
Evangeline (film), 362
Executive Council, 105–106, 112, 138, 147
Expo 67, 487, 497
Exports, of the 1920s, 399–400

Factories
women in, 338
working conditions, 337
See also Labour and Labour unions
Fahrni, Magda, 448
Fairclough, Ellen, 458
Falardeau, Jean-Charles, 455
Falcon, Pierre, 204
Families
1960s, 472
1970s, 570–571
size of, 337
Family allowance, 432–433, 452
Family Compact, 130, 135, 136
"Farmers' Storehouse Company," 132
Farming. *See* Agriculture; Wheat farming
Farming equipment industry, 154
Fascists, 408
Fast Runner, The (film). *See* Atanarjuat
Faucher, Albert, 332
Federal deficit, 566–567
Federal disallowance, 303–304, 305
Federal government, powers given to, 239,
241–242
Federal income tax, 378
Federal–Provincial relations
postwar, 451
Rowell–Sirois Report, 434

Fédération des femmes du Québec, 473
Fédération nationale Saint-Jean-Baptiste, 355
Fellowship for a Christian Social Order, 411
Female Employees Fair Remuneration Act, 456
Feminism
   institutionalization of, 571
   "second wave," 472–473
Fenians, 245–246
Fenton, William N., 15
Ferland, J.B.A., 89
Ferron, Jacques, 475
Ferry Command, 421
Fielding, W.S., 284, 305
Fighter pilots, 379–380
Filles du roi, 53–54
Film. *See* Cinema
Findley, Timothy, 575
Firearms
   the Huron-Iroquois conflict and, 43, 45
   impact on the First Nations, 196
First Canadian Division, 374–375, 377, 378
First Nations
   in the 1920s, 401–402
   allies of New France, 78
   American Revolution and, 102–103, 171, 172
   Arctic culture area, 13
   assimilationist policies and, 268–269, 363–
      365, 501–503
   Canadian constitutional process and, 242
   civilizations of, 5–6
   culture area classification, 9–10
   discontent with the federal government, 305
   displacement by Loyalists, 177
   Dominion of Canada and, 267–269
   early contacts with Europeans, 27
   early relations with the French, 35, 37
   epidemics and (*see* Epidemics)
   French plans to convert, 38
   fur trade and (*see* Fur trade)
   impact of industrialization on, 335
   the Indian Act and (*see* Indian Act)
   land ownership and, 35
   linguistic classification, 7–8
   in the Maritimes, 188
   Mound Builders, 6
   in Newfoundland, 188–189
   in New France, 63
   Northeast culture area, 13
   Northwest Coast culture area, 10–11
   origins of, 3–4
   Plains culture area, 11–12
   Plateau culture area, 11
   population growth, 6–7
   racist attitudes toward, 297
   resistance to the British, 97
   Subarctic culture area, 12–13
   treaties and, 267, 269–270
   the United Canadas and, 148
   in Upper Canada, 123, 125, 129–130
   War of 1812 and, 126
   World War I and, 375
   See also Aboriginal peoples; Aboriginal women;
     individual peoples
Fish, Hamilton, 245
Fish Creek, 308
Fisher, Peter, 183
Fisher, Robin, 200, 201
Fisheries and the Fishing industry
   British Columbia, 330
   cod fishery, 28–29, 589
   early nineteenth century, 179
   Labrador fishery, 179
   Maritimes, 150
   Newfoundland, 28–29, 179, 181
   New France, 58
   origins of, 26
   Reciprocity Treaty of 1854 and, 181
   salmon processing, 330, 335
   sixteenth century, 28–29
Fishermen's Protective Union, 340
Fitzgerald, Lionel LeMoine, 403
Fitzpatrick, Charles, 314
Five Nations, 14, 16
Flanagan, Thomas, 306–307
Flavelle, Joseph W., 326
Fleming, Sandford, 287
Fletcher, Frederick J., 476
"Fluted point," 4
Flyers, World War I, 379–380
Folk singers, 468
Fontaine, Phil, 502
Forbes, Ernest, 353, 435
Ford Motor Company, 432
Foreign investment, 325, 449–450
Forest Practices Code, 598
Forestry. *See* Timber industry
Forke, Robert, 398
Forster, Ben, 285
Fort Beauséjour, 83
Fort Carillon, 83
Fort Cumberland, 171
Fort Duquesne, 82, 83, 84
Fort Frontenac, 84
Fortin, Marc-Aurèle, 412
Fortin, Pierre, 529
Fort Langley, 219
Fort McMurray, 591
Fort Necessity, 82
Fort Niagara, 85
Fortnightly Review, 403
Fort Oswego, 83, 85
Fort Rouillé, 85

Fort Saint-Frédéric, 80, 83
Fort Simpson, 219
Fort Vancouver, 219
Fort Victoria, 219, 220
Fort William Henry, 83
Fournier, Claude, 476
Fox nation, 80
France
    American Revolution and, 101
    Samuel de Champlain, 32–33
    early North Atlantic explorations, 26–28
Franceschini, James, 425
Francheville, François Poulin de, 58
Francis, Daniel, 200, 201
Francis, Robert, 294–295
Franciscans, 38
Franklin, Sir John, 208–209
Fraser, Blair, 446
Fraser, Simon, 218
Fraser River canyon, 215
Fraser River gold rush, 222
Fraternal organizations, 339
Fréchette, Louis, 360
Frederick's Town, 177
Fred Victor Mission, 348
Free Kindergarten Association, 350
Free trade, 149, 567–569
Free Trade Area of the Americas, 587
Frégault, Guy, 89
French Canada
    annexation movement and, 149
    World War II and, 426–427
French Canadians
    bilingual schools controversy in Ontario, 381
    Confederation and, 242–243
    industrialization and, 331–333
    language conflicts and, 519–520
    the Manitoba Act and, 266–267
    migration and, 157
    nationalism and, 281, 310–311, 317–318
    reformers during World War I, 384
    South African War and, 316–317
    in the United Canadas, 143–144
    World War I and, 380–381
French civil law, 99
French language
    bilingual schools controversy in Ontario, 381
    language laws, 520, 522–524, 564–565
    Quebec and, 520, 522–524
    teaching in Manitoba schools, 313
    the United Canadas and, 145
Frenchman's Butte, 308
French Métis
    overview, 205
    resistance of 1869–1870, 265–266

Seven Oaks skirmish and, 204
    See also Métis
French religious orders, 38–39
    See also Missionaries; individual orders
French Revolution, 111
Frideres, James S., 505
"Friends of Clayoquot Sound," 598
Frobisher, Martin, 31–32
Froebel, Friedrich, 349
Frog Lake, 308
Front de libération du Quebec, 520, 563
Frontenac, Comte de, 56, 75, 79
Fruit farming, 330
Fugitive Slave Act, 155
Fundy National Park, 184
Fur trade
    aboriginal women in, 202
    after the fall of New France, 197
    American Fur Company, 207
    Blackfoot and, 207
    "Chinook," 218
    decline in, 207
    expansion into the interior, 195–196
    First Nations' role in, 200–201
    impact of industrialization on, 335
    New France and, 77, 78
    Northwest Coast First Nations and, 217–218
    rise of, 32
    traders on Vancouver Island, 220
    See also Hudson's Bay Company; North West
        Company

Gadacz, Rene R., 505
Gagan, David, 156, 252
Gagné, Gilles, 528
Galicians, 295
Galt, Sir Alexander, 239, 292
Galt, Elliott, 287
Garment industry unions, 339
Garneau, François-Xavier, 53, 89, 160, 359
Gas emissions, 532, 601–602
Gasoline taxes, 562
Gathering Strength: Canada's Aboriginal Action
    Plan, 500
Gay Pride parade, 571
Gays, 472, 570–571, 593–594
Gélinas, Gratien, 412, 462
Gender discrimination, 338, 378, 473
General Agreement on Tariffs and Trade (GATT),
    449
General Motors, 474, 529, 595
Gentry. See Seigneurs
Gérin, Léon, 364
Gérin-Lajoie, Marie Lacoste, 355
Gérin-Lajoie, Paul, 517

Germany
   immigration and, 293
      World War I, 384
      World War II, 419
Ghettos, ethnic, 552
Gibbs, Mifflin, 227
Gift diplomacy, 80, 97, 171
Gill, Joseph-Louis, 104–105
Giraud, Marcel, 306
Gladstone, William, 271
Globalization, 587
Global warming, 510
Godbout, Adélard, 435
Gold mining, 334
Gold rushes, 222
Goodridge, Theodore, 359
Goods and services tax, 584
Gordon, Arthur, 244
Gordon, Walter, 480
Gouin, Paul, 408
Gouzenko, Igor, 452
Governor, in the United Canadas, 143, 146–148
Governor general, 56, 283
Gowanlock, Theresa, 310
Grainger, Martin Allen, 360
Grain (Stead), 403
Granatstein, J.L., 421–422, 429, 452, 568
Grand Banks, 26, 28–29
Grand Coteau, battle of, 205
Grand Trunk Pacific Railway, 290, 377–378
Grand Trunk Railway, 151, 153, 154, 290
Grant, Cuthbert, 204
Grant, George Munro, 357–358
Grant, John Webster, 41, 501
"Great Awakening," 173
Great Britain
   activity in the Northwest Coast, 216–217
   free trade, 149
   See also England
Great Coalition of 1864, 238
Great Depression
   advent and extent of, 404–405
   government response to, 405–407, 410–411
   impact of, 393
   relief, 405–406
   relief camps, 406
   third parties during, 407–408
"Great Exhibition," 357
Great Lakes Algonquians, 78
Great Lakes Water Quality Agreement, 577
Great Plains culture area, 11–12
Great Western Railway, 151
Greenhouse, Brereton, 429
Greenhouse gases, 532, 601–602
Greenland, 25

Greenpeace, 577
Greenway, Thomas, 305, 313
Greer, Allan, 16, 53–54
Gregg, Allan, 552
Grenfell, Wilfred, 310
Grenfell Mission, 348
Grenier, Robert, 30
Gretzky, Wayne, 574
Grey, Earl, 361, 362
Grey Nuns' Foundling Hospital, 158
Grey Owl. *See* Belany, Archie
Griffiths, Naomi, 68, 69
Grignon, Claude-Henri, 596
Groseilliers, Médard Chouart Des, 75
Grosse Île, 110
Groulx, Lionel, 317, 400–401
Group of Seven, 402
Grove, Frederick Philip, 403
Guard, Julia, 457
Guigues school, 381
Guns. *See* Firearms
Gwatkin, Willoughby, 375
Gwitch'in, 208

Habitants, 51, 61
Habitat conservation, 599–600
Habitation, 35
Haidas people, 8, 216
Haig-Brown, Celia, 502
Haitian immigrants, 547
Haldimand, Sir Frederick, 119
Halibut Treaty, 399
Halifax
   British fortification of, 179
   economic significance of, 185
   founding of, 66
   Nova Scotia's capital, 170
   urbanization, 249
Halpern, Monda, 354
Handler, Richard, 522
Harney, Robert A., 551, 552
Harper, Elijah, 500
Harper, Stephen, 501, 503, 585, 586, 602
Harris, Mike, 584, 590, 594
Harris, R. Cole, 53
Hart, Michael, 568
Hartman, Grace, 572
Harvey, D.C., 173
Head, Francis Bond, 130
Head-Smashed-In Buffalo Jump, 12
Health
   in contemporary society, 576
   See also Diseases; Epidemics; Public health
Health care, 452, 480, 583, 592–593
Health insurance, national, 452

Heavy industry
  New France, 58
  See also Industrialization
Hébert, Raymond, 565
Henday, Anthony, 196
Henry VII, 26
Henshaw, Peter, 429
Henson, Josiah, 251–252
Hérbert, Anne, 461
Heron, Craig, 396, 457
Héroux, Denis, 476
Hewitt, J.N.B., 15
Hiawatha (film), 362
Higher education
  1950s, 459
  1970s, 572
  Canada East, 160
  Canada West, 159–160
  expansion of, 469
  mid-nineteenth century, 254
  Quebec, 519
  women's colleges, 256
  women students, 459, 594
"High schools," 254
Hillmer, Norman, 421–422
Hind, Henry Youle, 207
Hindu immigrants, 546
Histoire du Canada (Garneau), 160, 359
Historical Landmark Association of Canada, 361
Historical Sites Board of Canada, 361
Histories, 160
Hitler, Adolf, 419
Hivernants, 206
HMS Discovery, 216
HMS Resolution, 216
Hockey, 404, 412–413, 574, 595
Holmes, John, 537
Holt, Herbert, 326
"Home Children," 293, 294–295
Home defence, 380
Home ownership, 445
  See also Housing
Homo erectus, 3
Homo habilis, 3
Homo sapiens neanderthalensis, 3
Homosexuals, 449, 472, 570–571, 593–594
Hong Kong, 420, 544
Hoodless, Adelaide, 351
Hopewell culture, 6
Horn, Michiel, 572
Horses
  Aboriginal peoples and, 12, 196–197
  in New France, 54
Hospital Insurance and Diagnostic Services Act, 452
Hospitalization insurance, Quebec, 517

Hospital nuns, 38
Housing
  World War II, 433
  See also Home ownership
Howe, C.D., 423, 449
Howe, Joseph, 189, 243–244, 246, 263
Hudson, Henry, 75
Hudson Bay, 75
Hudson's Bay Company
  the Blackfoot and, 207
  granted Rupert's Land, 75
  inland expeditions, 195–196
  in the Mackenzie River Valley, 208
  management of Vancouver Island, 220
  Northwest Coast fur trade and, 219
  North West Company and, 197, 199–200, 204
  recruitment from Orkney Islands, 204
  Red River Colony and, 202–203
  rivals, 197
  sale of Rupert's Land, 264
  Sayer trial and, 205
  Seven Oaks skirmish and, 204
  St. Paul, Minnesota and, 206
  vaccination of Cree against smallpox, 206
Hughes, James L., 350
Hughes, Sam, 374, 375, 377, 380–381
"Hughes's Boys," 374
Huguenots, 38
Humphrey, Jack, 403
"Hundred Days" campaign, 384
Hungarians, 541
Hunter, Adelaide. *See* Hoodless, Adelaide
Huron Confederacy, 37
Huronia
  epidemics, 42–43, 44
  fall of, 45–46
  missionaries and, 39–43
Hurons
  alliance of, 14
  conflict with the Iroquois, 43, 45
  conversion and, 43–45
  cultural differences with the French, 41–42
  early relations with the French, 35, 37
  Jesuits and, 41
  partners with the French, 39–40
  Wendake community, 364–365
Huron Tract, 129
Hutton, Edward, 316
Hyde Park Declaration, 422
Hydroelectric power
  1920s, 400
  British Columbia, 483
  Labrador, 485
  Ontario, 326
  Quebec, 332, 435, 517
  significance to industrialization, 331, 332

Hydro-Electric Power Commission of Ontario, 326
Hydro-Québec, 435, 517

Iacovetta, Frank, 539
Ile Royale, 64, 80
Île Saint-Jean, 68, 80
Illegal immigration, 548
Immigrant Act, 406
Immigrants
    adaptation and, 545–547
    "business-class," 543
    demographics, 544–545
    discrimination and, 547
    economic impact of, 543, 545
    French-speaking, 540–541
    labourers, 539
    later emigration from Canada, 542
    Loyalists, 105
    nonofficial languages, 552
    public health and, 109–110
    refugees, 548–549
    settlement areas, 543
    See also individual immigrant groups
Immigration
    demographics, 544–545, 553
    end of racial discrimination against, 542
    illegal, 548
    impact of, 552–554
    Maritimes and, 181, 187
    the North West and, 291–296
    postwar, 537–539
    postwar responses to, 540–541
    racial bias and quotas, 541
    reactions to, 547–549
    in recent years, 543–547
Immigration Appeal Board, 543
Immigration policy
    changes to increase immigration, 542–543
    evaluation of, 541–542
    postwar, 539–540
    refugees, 548–549
Immigration propaganda, 293
Imperial Federation League, 316
Imperialism, 315–316
Imperial Order of the Daughters of Empire, 315–316
Incas, 5–6
Income tax, 378, 590
Indentured workers, 38, 39
India, 544
Indian Act
    of 1876, 268, 364–365
    of 1880, 354
    of 1911, 297
    of 1951, 496

Indian Affairs Branch, 494
Indian Association of Alberta, 494, 496
Indian Brotherhood of the North West Territories, 508
Indian Exhibition, 358–359
Indian immigrants, 296
Indian policy
    assimilation (*see* Assimilation)
    treaties, 267, 269–270
    See also Indian Act
Indian Residential School Truth and Reconciliation Commission, 501
Indigenous people. *See* Aboriginal peoples; First Nations
Industrial Estates Limited, 484
Industrial Exhibition (Toronto), 363
Industrialization
    economic expansion and, 325
    effects of, 325
    factory working conditions, 337
    impact on Aboriginal people, 335
    impact on rural society, 334–335
    Ontario, 330–331, 332, 334
    Quebec Province, 331–333
    working-class life, 336–337
Industrial Workers of the World (IWW), 341
Industry and Humanity (King), 349
Infanticide, 133
Infant mortality, 55–56, 337
"In Flanders Fields," 377
Inflation, 559–560
Influenza, 207
Ingstad, Helge and Anne, 25
Innis, Harold, 33, 386
Innu, 14
Instruction 17, 381
Intendants, 51–52, 56
Intercolonial Railway, 263, 397
Interior Salish, 11
Internationalism, 436
International Ladies' Garment Workers Union, 339
International Nickel Company of Canada, 334
International Woodworkers of America, 455
Internment, 373, 425
Interoceanic Company, 284, 286
Interprovincial conferences, 311
Interventionist state, 471
In Times Like These (McClung), 352
Inuit language group, 13
Inuits
    early contact with Europeans, 31–32
    James Bay and Northern Quebec Agreement, 498
    land control and, 508
    during the mid-twentieth century, 495

relocation in the 1950s, 453
    Tapirisat of Canada, 499, 508
Inuit Tapirisat of Canada, 499, 508
Inuvialuit, 509, 510
Investment, 325, 449–450
Irish Catholics, 381
Irish immigrants
    farming and, 154
    Maritimes, 187
    Orange Community and, 155–156
    public health and, 109–110
Iron industry, 108–109
Ironworks, 57
Iroquoian language group, 8
Iroquois
    American Revolution and, 102–103
    attacks on New France, 46
    conflict with the French, 76–77
    conflict with the Hurons, 43, 45
    early contacts with Europeans, 27
    exodus from New York, 176
    overview, 14, 16–17
    peace with the French, 77
    population size, 6
    steel workers, 402
    Upper Canada, 125
    women, 15–16, 17
Irving, K.C., 484
Isbister, John, 332

James Bay and Northern Quebec Agreement, 498
Japanese Canadians
    World War I, 375
    World War II, 425–426
Japanese immigrants, 296
Jasen, Patricia, 161
Jefferson, Thomas, 126, 179
Jenness, Diamond, 493
Jesuit College at Quebec, 62
Jesuits
    Counter-Reformation, 38
    École Sociale Populaire, 349
    Estates controversy, 311
    Hurons and, 41–42
    Iroquoians and, 15
Jesuits' Estates Act, 311
Jeune-Canada, 408
Jewish immigrants, 292, 538
Joe Beef's Canteen, 363
Johnson, Daniel, 518–519
Johnson, Hugh, 546
Johnson, Leo, 137
Johnson, Lyndon B., 481
Johnson, Pauline (Tekahionwake), 359
Johnson, Sir William, 120
Jones, Leonard, 564

Jones, Peter, 121, 123
Junior colleges, 519

Kahkewaquonaby, 123
Kalm, Pehr, 61
Kandahar, Afghanistan, 588
Katz, Michael, 252
Kazimirski, Ann, 538
Kealey, Greg, 395
Kealey, Linda, 353
Kelsey, Henry, 195–196
Kenny, James, 484
Kerr, Illingworth, 403
Kerr, W.B., 173
Kindergartens, 350
King, James, 216–217
King, William Lyon Mackenzie
    approach to politics, 397
    Canadian autonomy and, 399
    conscription and, 427, 428
    federalism and, 434
    immigration and, 537, 539, 540
    Industry and Humanity, 349
    neutrality and, 419
    postwar economy and, 449
    retirement, 450
    return to power in 1935, 407, 410
    wartime relations with the United States and,
        421–422
Kin groups, 215
King's College, 159
"King's gift," 53
King's Highway, 58
Kinsey, Joseph, 306
Kirby, William, 160
Klassen, Cindy, 595
Klausen, Susanne, 433
Knights of Labor, 339, 363
Kogawa, Joy, 575
Kootenay, 11
Korean War, 453
Korinke, Valerie, 472
Krech, Shepard, III, 208
Kreighoff, Cornelius, 160, 357
Kroetsch, Robert, 475
Kropotkin, Peter, 295
Krotz, Elena, 539
Ktunaxa, 11
Kunuk, Zacharias, 596
Kutchin, 208
Kutenai, 11
Kyoto Protocol, 601–602

Labour and Labour unions
    1920s, 402
    1950s, 455–456

1960s, 474
1970s, 572
1990s, 594–595
Catholic, 349, 402
feuding between, 456
Great Depression, 408–409
historical overview, 339–341
immigrants and, 539, 543
limitations in the prewar era, 341
mid-nineteenth century, 253–254
Quebec, 515, 520
women and, 401, 457–458, 474, 571–572
World War II, 431–432
Labour Day, 341
Labrador
    Basque whaling, 29–31
    economy in the 1990s, 589
    hydroelectricity, 485
    Spanish influenza epidemic, 386
Labrador fishery, 179
Labyrinth (film), 476
Lachine, 76
Lachine Canal, 145, 158
Lac Ste. Anne, 206
Lafitau, Joseph-François, 15–16
Laflèche, Louis-François, 281, 282
LaFontaine, Louis-Hippolyte, 144, 146, 147, 148
Lajeunesse, Marie (Emma Albani), 357
Lake Témiscouata, 186
Lalemant, Fr. Gabriel, 45
Lam, David, 548
Lam, Victor, 597
Lamontagne, Maurice, 332
Lampman, Archibald, 359
Land claims, 498, 503–504, 508, 510
Land purchase agreements, 119, 129–130
Land survey, 291
Langlois, Simon, 528
Language families, indigenous, 7–8
Language laws, 145, 520, 522–524, 564–565
Lanphier, C. Michael, 550
L'Anse aux Meadows, 25
Laporte, Pierre, 520
La Salle, René-Robert Cavelier de, 75
Latvians, 539
Laurence, Margaret, 475
Laurendeau, André, 516
Laurentide Air Services, 400
Laurier, Wilfrid, 303, 387
    compromise on religious instruction, 313–314
    conscription during World War I and, 382
    French-Canadian nationalism and, 310
    National Policy and, 284
    national policy and, 281
    Naval Service Bill and, 320
    Prohibition Movement and, 355
    South African War and, 317
Laurier–Greenway controversy, 313–314
Lauvrière, Émile, 69
Laval, François de, 56
Lavallée, Calixa, 356
La Vérendrye, Pierre Gaultier de Varennes et de, 195
La Vérité (newspaper), 318
Law
    New France, 56
    Quebec Act of 1774 and, 99
    See also British common law
Lawrence, Charles, 66–67
Laxer, James, 568
Layton, Irving, 461, 475
Lazar, Fred, 568
Leacock, Stephen, 359–360
Leadership, 476
League of Hodenosaunee, 14
League of Nations, 399
Lee, David, 307
Lee-Enfield rifle, 377
Legal codes, 56
Legge, Francis, 173
Legislative Assembly
    established, 105
    versus the governor, 112
    Lord Durham's Report and, 138
    during the United Canadas, 143
Legislative Council, 105
Le Jeune, Fr. Paul, 32
Le Marquis de Montcalm (Chapais), 89
Lemelin, Roger, 461
Lemieux, Jean-Paul, 412
Lemieux, Vincent, 526
Le Nationaliste (newspaper), 317
Lend-Lease Act, 422
Le Nigog (arts magazine), 403
L'Erreur boréale (Desjardins), 532
Lesage, Jean, 517–518
Lesbians, 472, 570–571, 593–594
"Les Filles de Marguerite Bourgeoys," 255
Lévesque, René, 517, 521, 525
Levine, Marc V., 522–523
Lévis, Chevalier de, 87, 89
Leyton-Brown, David, 568
Li, Peter S., 551
Liberal party
    1873–1878, 282–283
    election of 1891, 315
    election of 1896, 313
Liberator bombers, 421
Lieutenant governor, 303–304
Life of Josiah Henson, The (Henson), 252

Lightfoot, Gordon, 468
Ligue d'Action, 408
Ligue nationaliste, 317
Lindsey, Charles, 136
Linguistic policy. *See* Language laws
Linteau, Paul-André, 157–158, 332–333
Literary journals, 403
Literature
   1920s, 403
   1930s, 412
   1960s, 475–476
   1970s, 575
   contemporary, 597
   late nineteenth century, 359–360
   postwar era, 461–462
Livesay, Dorothy, 461
Lloyd George, David, 379, 380
Locher, Uli, 523
Longhouses, 17
Loranger, Françoise, 475
Lorne, Marquis de, 357, 361
Lougheed, Peter, 561
Louisbourg, 64, 66, 80, 81–82, 84
Louisiana, 70, 75
Louis XIV, 46, 51, 56, 77
Louis XVI, 101
Lower, A.R.M., 150
Lower, Arthur R.M., 183
Lower Canada
   Act of Union of 1840, 114
   professional elite, 111–112
   public health, 109–110
   rebellions, 111, 112–114
   urban life in the early nineteenth century, 107–109
Lower Canadian School Act of 1846, 160
Low-income housing, 471
Loyalists
   African American, 176–177
   emigration to Quebec province, 105
   Maritimes, 176–178
   persecution of, 172, 174–175
   Thirteen Colonies, 172
Loyola, Ignatius, 38
Lundy's Lane, battle of, 128
Lunenburg, 66

MacBeth, R.G., 306
Macdonald, Angus L., 451
Macdonald, John A.
   assimilation of First Nations peoples and, 268
   British Columbia and, 271
   Canadian Pacific Railway and, 284, 286, 287, 289
   George-Étienne Cartier and, 148, 153, 247
   Confederation and, 238, 239, 246, 257

Manitoba schools issue, 312–313
   National Policy, 281, 283–284
   negotiations with Prince Edward Island, 275
   negotiations with the Métis, 265, 266
   Nova Scotia's anti-confederation politics and, 263
   Ontario–Manitoba boundary dispute, 303
   opposition to unrestricted reciprocity, 314–315
   "Pacific Scandal," 282, 286
   political conventions established by, 247
   as Prime Minister, 270
   Louis Riel's execution, 310
Macdonald, Margaret, 378
Macdonell, Rev. D.J., 348
Macdonell, Miles, 203
MacDowell, Laurel Sefton, 432
MacEwen, Gwendolyn, 475
Machias, 171
MacKay, R.A., 137
Mackenzie, Alexander, 197, 218, 282–283
Mackenzie, Isabel, 133–134
Mackenzie, William, 290
Mackenzie, William Lyon, 135, 137
Mackenzie River Valley, 208
Mackenzie Valley Aboriginal peoples, 495
Mackenzie Valley pipeline, 508
Mackey, Joseph, 421
MacLennan, Hugh, 461
MacMechan, Archibald McKellar, 68
MacMillan Bloedel, 598
Macoun, John, 287
Macphail, Agnes, 401
Macpherson, David, 284, 286
Madelaine de Verchères (film), 362
Madison, James, 126
Magazines, 403, 411, 461, 575
Maillet, Antonine, 575
Maine, 186
Maisonneuve, Paul de Chomedey de, 39
Maliseets, 171, 177, 188
Managerial class, 327
"Manifest destiny," 219
Manitoba
   1970s, 561
   bilingualism and, 565
   boundary dispute with Ontario, 303
   disallowance policy and, 305
   discontent with the federal government, 305
   economy in the 1960s, 482
   economy in the 1990s, 590
   prohibition and, 384
   schools issues, 311–314
Manitoba Act, 266–267, 291
Mann, Donald, 290
Mann, Susan, 461, 515

Manning, Frank, 575
"Maple Leaf Forever, The" (song), 356–357
Marean, Ada, 350
Marie de l'Incarnation, 38
Maritime Art, 403
Maritime Rights movement, 397
Maritimes
    Confederation and, 238, 243–244, 304–305
    demographics, 189–190
    economy in the 1990s, 590
    economy in the early nineteenth century, 181–184
    economy in the early twentieth century, 329
    economy to 1812, 179
    First Nations in, 188
    fisheries, 150
    immigrants and, 181, 187
    Loyalist communities in, 176–178
    Maritime Rights movement, 397
    overview, 169
    railways, 186
    Reciprocity Treaty and, 186
    relationship to New England, 169–170
    responsible government, 189
    social life in the mid-nineteenth century, 252–253
    timber industry, 181, 182–184
    United States and, 185–186
    urbanization, 249
    War of 1812, 189
    women in, 187
    World War II, 435
Marois, Pauline, 528
Marriage
    mid-nineteenth century, 253
    postwar era, 458–459
    same-sex, 594
Marshall, Donald, Jr., 497
Marshall decision (1999), 504
Marshall Plan, 449
Martin, Chester, 264
Martin, Joseph, 312
Martin, Paul, 501, 528, 585, 586
Massachusetts colony, 79
Massey, Daniel, 154
Massey, Hart, 154, 361
Massey, Vincent, 459
Massey Commission, 459, 460
Massey Hall, 361
Massey Manufacturing Company, 361
Mass media, impact on politics, 476
Masters, D.C., 394
Mathias, 215–216
Maugerville, 171
Mavor, James, 295
Mayas, 5

McAree, John, 155, 156
McCallum, John, 249
McCarthy, D'Alton, 311–312
McClung, Nellie, 351, 352
McCrae, John, 377
McDougall, William, 265
McGee, Thomas D'Arcy, 239, 245
McGhee, Robert, 10, 46
McGill University, 160
McInnis, Peter, 456
McKenna, Brian and Terence, 430
McKenna, Frank, 590
McKiernan, Charles, 363
McLachlan, James Bryson, 340
McLaughlin, Audrey, 583
McMullen, John, 160
McMurchy, Helen, 409
McNaughton, A.G.L., 428, 429
Measles, 7, 206–207
Medical care. *See* Health care
Meech Lake Accord, 500, 526, 584
Meighen, Arthur, 394, 397
Melnyk, George, 595
Memorandum (documentary), 476
Mennonites, 291–292, 538
Merchandising, 327
Mercier, Honoré, 310, 311
Metcalfe, Sir Charles, 145, 147
Methodists, 122, 131
Métis
    1920s, 401
    Charter of Rights and Freedoms and, 563
    conflicts with the Sioux, 205
    Constitution of 1982 and, 499
    discontent with the federal government, 305
    federal recognition of, 507
    French-speaking, 204, 205
    land-claims issues, 510
    the North-West Rebellion and, 305–310
    origins, 76
    rebellion of, 289
    at the Red River, 200, 202
    resistance of 1869–1870, 265–266
    rise of, 200
    Sayer trial and, 205
    Seven Oaks skirmish and, 204
Métis Association of the North West Territories, 508
Michilimackinac, 75–76, 126
Micmac. *See* Mi'kmaqs
Micone, Marco, 532
Middle class
    culture, 363
    postwar, 446–448
    women, 338, 401
Middleton, Frederick, 308

Migration
    early peoples, 3, 4
    United Canadas, 156–157
Mikisew Cree, 506
Mi'kmaqs (Micmacs)
    Acadians and, 64
    American Revolution and, 171
    displacement by Loyalists, 177
    displacement in the Maritimes, 188
    the English and, 66
    fur trade, 32
    land-claims issues, 504
    linguistic family, 8
    location of, 13
Military
    in New France, 60
    See also Armed forces; World War I; World
        War II
Military Service Act, 382
Military Voters Act, 383
Militia, 56–57
Miller, J.R., 502
Milloy, John S., 502
Mining industry
    1920s, 399
    British Columbia, 330
    Ontario, 334
Minorities
    unions and, 339–340
    World War I, 375, 381–382
    World War II, 424–426
Minto, Lord, 316
Mishipeshu, 12
Missionaries
    arrival in Huronia, 39–43
    Northwest Coast First Nations and, 226
    See also individual religious orders
"Mission" First Nations, 78
Missions, 63, 348
Mississaugas, 103, 119, 120–121, 125, 130
Mistry, Rohinton, 553
Mitchell, W.O., 461, 575
Mixed-bloods, 200, 265
    See also Country born; Métis
Mnjikning, 506
Mohawks, 102, 103, 500
Mohawk Saint (Greer), 16
Molson, William, 149
Mons, 384
Montagnais, 14
Montcalm, Louis-Joseph de, 84, 87, 88, 89–90
Monte Verde, 4
Montgomery, Lucy Maud, 359, 596
Montreal
    annexation movement and, 149
    burning of, 63

economic development, 331
fall of, 97
founding of, 39
growth of, 107–109, 154
Olympic Games, 574
population growth, 99, 335
urban development, 157–158
urbanization and segregation, 249
working-class life in, 336–337
"Montreal group," 403
Mont Royal, 108
Moodie, Susanna, 160
Moore, Elizabeth, 15
Moor's Indian Charity School, 104
Morality, state regulation, 348–349
Morantz, Toby, 200
Moraviantown, battle of, 128
Morenz, Howie, 413
Mormons, 292
Morton, Desmond, 420
Morton, W.L., 306
"Mothers of Confederation," 240
Mound Builders, 6
Mountbatten, Lord Louis, 429
Movies. See Cinema
Mowat, Oliver, 303, 304
Mulroney, Brian
    chosen Conservative party leader, 563
    federal deficit, 566–567
    free-trade debate, 567–569
    government of, 559, 565–566, 583, 584
    Meech Lake Accord, 526
Multiculturalism, 549–552
Multiculturalism Act, 549
Municipal Improvements Assistance Act, 410
Munro, Alice, 475, 597
Murdoch, Beamish, 173
Murray, James, 87, 97, 98, 99
Murray, Margaret Polson, 315
Musgrave, Anthony, 271, 274
Music
    Aboriginal peoples and, 506
    contemporary, 596–597
    late nineteenth century, 356–357
    mid-nineteenth century, 160
Muslim immigrants, 548
Mussolini, Benito, 419
Mutchmor, Rev. James, 458, 467

Napoleonic Wars, 179
National Council of Women of Canada, 355
National debt, World War I, 378
National Employment Commission, 410
National Energy Program, 562–563, 565
National Film Board, 424, 459, 476, 575
National health care. See Health care

National Health Program, 452
National Hockey League, 404
National Housing Act, 410
National Indian Brotherhood, 497, 499
Nationalism
    Canada First Movement, 281
    French-Canadian, 281, 310–311, 317–318
    imperialism and, 316
    Quebec and, 516, 521
    Trudeau and, 563
    ultramontane movement, 281–282
    World War I and, 399
Nationalization, 560
National policy, 281, 284, 285–286
National Policy (tariff), 281, 283–284, 285–286
National Progressive Party, 398
National Service Board, 380
National Social Christian Party, 408
National tariff, 281, 283–284, 285–286
National Transcontinental railway, 290
Native Council of Canada, 499
Nativism, 296–297
Natural Products and Marketing Act, 406
Nature Conservancy of Canada, 577, 600
Naval Aid Bill, 320
Naval Service Bill, 320
Navigation Laws, 149
Neale, Greg, 385
Neanderthal man, 3
Nègres blancs d'Amérique (Vallières), 521
Nelles, H.V., 332
Nelligan, Émile, 359
Nelson, George, 198–199
Nelson, Robert, 112, 113, 198, 199
Nelson, Wolfred, 112, 113, 198, 199
Neutrality, 419
New Brunswick
    Acadians and, 70
    agriculture, 181
    banking, 184
    border controversy with Maine, 186
    Confederation and, 243, 246
    displacement of First Nations, 177
    economy in the 1960s, 484
    economy in the 1990s, 590
    Fenian raids and, 245–246
    founding, 177
    Loyalist settlements, 176
    reciprocity with America and, 185–186
    timber industry, 182–184
    women in, 187
    See also Maritimes
New Democratic Party, 474, 479, 560–561, 584, 585
New England, Acadia and, 64

Newfoundland
    1860s, 190
    Beothuks, 188–189
    Confederation and, 244, 451
    economy in the 1960s, 484–485
    economy in the 1990s, 589–590
    economy in the early twentieth century, 329
    fishery, 28–29, 179, 181
    Loyalist settlements, 176
    Meech Lake Accord and, 526
    missions, 348
    opposition to Confederation, 275
    population growth, 187
    unions, 340
    World War II, 435
Newfoundland Regiment, 379
New France
    in 1645, 39
    administrative reforms, 56–57
    birth rates and child mortality, 55–56
    Canadien identity, 64
    Samuel de Champlain and, 37
    the church in, 61–62
    Company of One Hundred Associates, 37
    conflicts with English colonies, 76–78, 80–82
    conflicts with the Iroquois, 46, 76–77
    early French-aboriginal relations, 35, 37
    economic development, 58–59
    education and social work in, 62
    English challenge from the north, 75
    expansion north and west, 75–76
    failure as a "compact colony," 57–58
    filles du roi, 53–54
    First Nations allies, 78
    First Nations population, 63
    founding of Montreal, 39
    founding of Quebec, 34–37
    habitants, 61
    immigration figures, 55
    military operations, 1713–1755, 80
    North American strategy of 1701, 77
    population growth, 55
    religious orders and, 38–39
    royal government, 51
    seigneurial system, 51–52, 53–54
    settlement of St. Lawrence Valley, 55–56
    Seven Years' War, 82–89
    slaves, 63
    society of, 59–61
    Treaty of Utrecht, 79–80
    war against the Fox, 80
    wartime strengths and weaknesses, 78
New Light Movement, 171–172
Newman, Peter, 478, 565
"New Ontario," 334

Newspapers, 160, 189, 403, 461
Newton, Janice, 354
New York colony, 79
Niagara Falls, 161
Niagara Peninsula, 246
Nielsen, Marianne O., 505
Ninety-Two Resolutions, 112
Nipissings, 14
No. 2 Construction Battalion (Coloured), 375
Nobel Peace Prize, 454
Noble, Charles, 410
Noble plough, 410
Noel, S.J.R., 143, 148
"No Man's Land," 376
Nonofficial languages, 552
Nootka Sound, 216, 217
Normal schools, 160, 187
Normandy invasion, 428
Norrie, Kenneth, 286
Norse, 25
North American Air Defence Agreement, 453
North American Air Defence Command, 478
North American Free Trade Agreement (NAFTA),
    568, 569, 585
North Atlantic Trading Company, 293
North Atlantic Treaty Organization (NATO),
    452
North Canada
    Aboriginal peoples in the mid-twentieth
        century, 495
    Cold War interest in, 453
Northeast culture area, 13
Northern Railway, 151
North Vietnam, 481
North West Canada
    administrating, 264–265
    discontent and rebellion, 305–310
    Dominion's strategy for, 290–297
    early history, 215
    European exploration, 216–217
    immigration, 291–296
    land surveys, 291
    World War II, 435
    See also North West Territories
Northwest Coast First Nations
    description of, 10–11
    early history of, 215
    economic conditions in the mid-nineteenth
        century, 226
    impact of the gold rushes on, 225
    impressions of Europeans, 215–216
    maritime fur traders and, 217–218
    missionaries and, 226
    notions of property, 215
    policies of James Douglas toward, 221–222,
        224–225

North West Company
    emergence, 197
    Hudson's Bay Company and, 199–200, 204
    in the Mackenzie River Valley, 208
    Red River settlement and, 203–204
    the search for a route to the Pacific and, 218
North-West Mounted Police, 291
Northwest Passage, 26, 75, 208–209, 510
North-West Rebellion
    causes and origins, 305–307
    military campaign, 308–309
    significance of, 310
    trials, 309–310
North West Territories
    Aboriginal land-claims issues, 508
    on the eve of Canadian settlement, 207–209
    the Manitoba Act and, 266
    territorial division, 508–510
    See also North West Canada
Nor'Wester, The (newspaper), 265
Notman, William, 160, 357
Notre-Dame-de-la-Victoire, 79
Notre-Dame-des-Victoires, 79
Nova Scotia
    Acadia becomes, 64–65
    Acadian history in, 65–67
    Acadians expelled from, 67–70
    Acadians return to, 169–170
    agriculture, 181
    American Revolution and, 169, 170–175, 189
    banking, 184
    British immigrants, 170
    Confederation and, 243–244, 246, 263
    economy in the 1960s, 484
    economy in the 1990s, 590
    economy in the early twentieth century, 329
    New Englanders and, 169
    repeal movement, 263
    responsible government, 189
    secession threats, 305
    women in, 187
    See also Maritimes
Novascotian (newspaper), 189
Nova Scotia Party, 263
Nunavut, 493, 508–510
Nunavut Land Claims Agreement, 510
Nurses, 338, 378

O'Brien, Lucius R., 357
"O Canada" (song), 356
"October Crisis," 520
Odanak, 103–105
Odawa, 14
Oddfellows, 339
Official Languages Act, 484, 522, 564
Offshore oil production, 589

Ogdensburg Agreement, 421–422
Ohio country, 82
Ohio Mound Builders, 6
Oil industry, 562–563
Ojibwas, 14, 103, 198
Oka Crisis, 500
Oliver, Frank, 295, 297
Olympic Games, 574, 595
Ondaathe, Michael, 553
Onderdonk, Andrews, 287
One Big Union, 393, 394–395
Oneidas, 102, 130
Onondagas, 102, 103
Ontario
    bilingual schools and, 381
    boundary dispute with Manitoba, 303
    "Common Sense Revolution," 590
    economy in the 1960s, 482
    emigration to Manitoba, 267
    industrialization, 330–331, 332, 334
    provincial-rights movement, 303–304
    recession of 1990, 584
    schooling in the mid-nineteenth century, 254
    social life in the mid-nineteenth century, 251–252
    World War II, 435
Ontario Hydro, 326
Ontario–Manitoba boundary dispute, 303
Ontario Society of Artists, 357
Opera, 357
Orange Community, 155–156
Orange Lodge, 381
Orange Order, 145
Order of Sleeping Car Porters, 340
Ordinances, religious, 61–62
Ordonnances, 61–62
Oregon territory, 218–220
Organs, 132
Orkney Islands, 204
Ormsby, Margaret, 223–224
Ortona, battle of, 428
Osgoode, William, 122
Ostenso, Martha, 403
Ottawa
    Aboriginal land-claims issues, 504
    chosen as capital, 154
    Confederation and, 248
Ottawa Hockey Club, 362
Ottawas, 14
Otter, William, 308
Ouellet, Fernand, 53, 333
Ouellette, Fernand, 475
Owram, Doug, 445, 462, 468

Pacific Fur Company, 218
"Pacific Scandal," 286

"Padlock Law," 408
Painters. See Visual arts
Palliser, John, 207
Palmer, Bryan, 396, 457
Palmer, Howard, 550
Panama Canal, 330
Panis, 64
Panneton, Philippe (Ringuet), 412
Paper industry, 331, 399, 405
Papineau, Louis-Joseph, 112, 113, 149
Papineau, Talbot, 385
Papineau (Fréchette), 360
Paquet, Gilles, 551
Parent, Madeleine, 455
Parishes, in New France, 62
Paris Peace Conference, 398–399
Parker, Gilbert, 359
Parkman, Francis, 89
Parks, 446
Parr, Joy, 457
Parti bleu, 148
Parti canadien, 112
Parti national, 310
Parti patriote. See Parti canadien
Parti Québécois, 469, 474, 517, 521, 527, 528
Parti rouge, 153, 242
Passchendale, battle of, 384
Pastedechouan, Pierre, 32
Paterson, A.P., 397
Patronage, 516
Patterson, Stephen E., 69
Pawnees, 64
Pay equity, 594
Payment, Diane, 307
Peacekeeping, 453–454, 588
Peace River Dam, 483
Pearson, Lester B.
    immigration and, 542
    Indian Act and, 497
    Liberal party and, 454, 477
    on media and politics, 476
    Nobel Prize, 454
    as Prime Minister, 478, 479–481
    Pierre Trudeau and, 485
    United Nations and, 436
Peasant settlers, 51, 52
Peel, Paul, 358
Peel County, 156
Péladeau, Pierre, 565
Pellatt, Henry, 326
Penner, Norman, 395
Pensions, 480, 517–518
People of the Longhouse, 14
Pérez, Juan, 216
Permanent Joint Board of Defence, 421

Perrault, Pierre, 476
"Persons Case," 401
Petit Séminaire, 62
Petroleum industry, 562–563
Phillips, Paul, 564
Phips, Sir William, 79
Photography, 160
Pickersgill, J.W., 540
Picturesque Canada, 357–358
Pinard, Maurice, 526
Pinsent, R.J., 244
Pioneer Rifle Corps, 227
Pipelines, 508
Pitt, William (the Elder), 84
Plains Cree, 197
Plains culture area, 11–12
Plains First Nations
    firearms and, 196
    mid-nineteenth century, 206–207
Plains of Abraham, battle of, 87, 88
Planned corporate suburbs, 471
Planned suburbs, 471
Planters, 169
Plateau culture area, 11
Plebiscite of 1942, 427
Plessis, Msg. Joseph-Octave, 111
Poetry, 160, 359, 403, 475
"Policy of Progress," 329
Polk, James, 219–220
Pollution, 532, 577, 600–601
Pollution Probe, 485
Pond, Peter, 197
Pontbriand, Bishop, 98
Pontiac, 97
Pope, J.C., 276
Pope, J.H., 289
Popular culture
    1920s, 403–404
    1930s, 411
    late nineteenth century, 361–362
    postwar era, 460–461
    tourism, 161
Popular music, 596–597
Porters, 340
Port Royal, 34, 64
Portuguese exploration, 25–26
Potlach, 10, 268–269
Poundmaker, 308, 309
Pour la patrie (Tardivel), 318
Poverty
    1980s, 576
    Aboriginal peoples and, 505
    contemporary trends, 593
Prairie Farm Rehabilitation Act, 410
Prairie Farm Rehabilitation Program,
    410

Prairies
    economic development and urbanization, 330
    World War II, 436
Pratt, E.J., 403
Presbyterians, 130–131, 254
Preston, W.T.R., 293
Price, Richard, 270
Prince Edward Island, 80
    Acadians and, 68
    agriculture, 181
    banking, 184
    Confederation and, 244, 275–276
    disenfranchisement of women, 187
    economy in the 1960s, 483
    economy in the 1990s, 590
    Loyalists in, 176, 177–178
    See also Maritimes
Proclamation of 1763, 97–98, 119
Professional elite, early nineteenth century,
    111–112
Progressive Conservative Party, 561, 585, 586
Progressive movement, 397–398
Prohibition, 158, 355–356, 384
Propaganda
    World War I, 381–382
    World War II, 424
Property
    Northwest Coast peoples and, 215
    voting qualification and, 107
    women's rights in the West and, 291
Prophetic Bible Institute, 407
Prostitution, 348
Protective tariffs, 283–284, 285–286
Protestants
    1960s, 467
    mid-nineteenth century, 254
Proulx, Maurice, 411
Province of Canada, 138
Province of Quebec
    Act of Union, 114
    American invasion, 100–102
    Constitutional Act of 1791, 105–107
    creation of, 97
    economy in the early nineteenth century,
        107
    immigration of Loyalists, 105
    Royal Proclamation of 1763, 98
    rural life in the early nineteenth century, 110
    urban life, 99
    See also Quebec
Province of the Canadas
    economy of, 144–145
    See also United Canadas
Provincial-compact theory, 303
Provincial rights, 248, 303–304
Provincial Workmen's Association, 340

Public health
    contemporary society, 576
    early nineteenth century, 109–110, 337
    See also Diseases; Epidemics
Public schools
    Canada West, 159
    See also Education; Schools
Public sector unions, 474, 520
Pulp industry, 331, 399, 405
Purdy, Al, 475

Quakers, 131
Quarter-sections, 291
Quebec
    after World War II, 515–517
    agriculture, 249, 332
    anglophones and, 523, 524
    bilingualism in, 524
    Bill 22, 520
    Bourassa governments, 520, 525
    Catholic social action movement, 349
    constitutional issue and, 526–528
    Constitution of 1982 and, 563
    contemporary politics, 528–529
    culture, 530–532
    demographic trends, 529
    Duplessis government, 515–517
    economy since 1990, 529
    environmental issues and, 532–533
    future challenges facing, 533
    Stephen Harper and, 587
    independence and, 524, 584
    industrialization, 331–333
    Johnson government, 518–519
    language issues, 519–520, 525–526, 529–530
    language laws, 520, 522–524
    literature, 359, 403, 475
    Meech Lake Accord and, 526
    nationalism and, 516, 521, 525–526
    "October Crisis," 520
    under the Parti Québécois, 522–524
    prohibition and, 384
    "Quiet Revolution," 517–518
    referendum debate on sovereignty, 524
    Roman Catholic Church in, 254
    schooling in the mid-nineteenth century, 254
    Social Credit and, 478–479
    social life in the mid-nineteenth century, 251
    social reform and, 400–401
    student protests and, 469
    Union Nationale, 408
    unions, 341, 402
    urban development, 157–158
    women reformers, 355
    World War II, 435
    See also Province of Quebec

Quebec Act of 1774, 99–100
Quebec City
    American attack on, 100
    early years, 37
    economy in the early nineteenth century, 107
    English naval expeditions against, 79
    fall of, 84–87, 88
    founding of, 34–37
    growth of, 107
    population figures, 99
    public health, 110
    urban development, 157
    urban life, 99
Quebec Conference, 239, 241–242
Quebec Nordiques, 574
"Québécois," 587
Quebec Seminary, 62
Queen Charlotte Islands, 220
Queen's Rangers, 122
Queenston Heights, battle of, 126
Quetico Park, 577
Quiberon Bay, battle of, 87
"Quiet Revolution," 517–518

Race theory, imperialism and, 315–316
Racism, 296–297, 541
Radio, 400, 403, 411, 596
Radio-Canada, 596
Radisson, Pierre-Esprit, 75
Rae, Bob, 584
Railways
    British Columbia, 271
    early nineteenth century, 109
    Maritimes, 186
    nationalization during World War I, 377–378
    transcontinental, 284, 286–290
    United Canadas, 151–153
    See also individual railways
Ralston, J.L., 428
Ramsay, David, 120–121
Rand, Ivan, 432
Randall, Stephen, 178
Rand Formula, 432
Rationing, 423
Rawlyk, George, 169, 174
Ray, Arthur J., 200
Raynauld, André, 332
Rea, Kenneth, 482
Read, Colin, 137
Rebekahs, 339
Rebellion Losses Bill, 147
Rebellions
    Lower Canada, 111, 112–114, 132
    Upper Canada, 135–138

Recessions
    1960–1961, 477–478
    1980–1981, 562
    1990, 584
Reciprocity, 150–151, 185–186, 314–315,
    318–319
Reciprocity Treaty, 143, 150–151, 154, 181, 186,
    245
Récollets, 38
Red Bay, Labrador, 29–31
Redekop, Maria, 538
Redpath, John, 149
Red River carts, 202
Red River Colony
    end of isolation, 205–206
    the Métis and, 200, 202
    origin and settling of, 202–204
Réductions, 63
Reed, William, 356
Reformers. See "Clear Grits"
Reform Movement, 135–136, 145, 147, 148
Reform Party, 584, 585
Refugees, 537–539, 548–549
Regina Trench, 379
"Regulation 17," 381
Reichmann, Albert and Paul, 565
Relations, 15, 38
Relief, 405–406
Relief camps, 406
Religion
    1930s, 411
    1950s, 462
    1960s, 467
    Children of Peace, 131–132
    Constitutional Act of 1791 and, 121–122
    contemporary, 573
    immigrants and, 546
    mid-nineteenth century, 254, 255–256
    United Canadas, 158–159
    United Church of Canada, 400
    Upper Canada, 122–123, 125, 130–131
    women and, 458
    See also individual churches
Religious instruction
    Manitoba schools issue, 313–314
    North-West Territory, 314
Religious revivals
    "Great Awakening," 173
    New Light Movement, 171–172
Rentes, 52
Research in Motion, 583
Residential schools, 269, 496, 501–503
Resolution (HMS), 216
Responsible government
    Maritimes, 189
    United Canadas, 146–148

Retour de l'exilé (Fréchette), 360
Rich, E.E., 200
Richards, Cara E., 15
Richards, David Adams, 575
Richelieu, Cardinal, 37, 38
Richler, Mordecai, 461
Richmond, Anthony H., 550
Richthofen, Baron von ("Red Baron"), 379
Rideau Canal, 135
Ridley, Ethel, 378
Riel, Louis
    battle of Duck Lake and, 289
    defence of Rupert's Land, 265
    execution of Thomas Scott and, 266
    North-West Rebellion and, 305, 306,
        309–310
    Wolseley expedition and, 267
Right to vote. See Suffrage
Ringuet. See Panneton, Philippe
Road systems
    United Canadas, 145
    Upper Canada, 122, 134–135
Road to Washington, The (pamphlet), 319
Robert, Jean-Claude, 332–333
Roberts, Charles G.D., 359
Roberts, Lance W., 550
Robertson, Gideon, 394
Roberval, Jean-François de La Rocque de, 28
Robichaud, Louis, 484
Robson, John, 271
Rocher, Guy, 518
Rock music, 468
Rocky Mountains Park, 350–351
Rogers, A.B., 287
Rogers, Robert, 104
Roman Catholic church
    1960s, 467
    under the British in Quebec, 98
    Canada East, 158–159
    early nineteenth century, 110–111
    independence from government dictates, 111
    Manitoba schools issue and, 312–314
    mid-nineteenth century, 254
    New France, 61–62
    Quebec nationalism and, 317
    schools in Canada West, 159
    social action movement, 349
    social reform in the 1920s and, 400–401
    theatre and, 412
    ultramontane movement, 281–282
    unions and (see Catholic unions)
Roosevelt, Franklin Delano, 421, 422
Ross rifle, 377
Roth, Lorna, 506
Rotures, 61
Rouges, 153

Rowell–Sirois Commission on Dominion–
    Provincial Relations, 434
Rowell–Sirois Report, 434
Rowley, Kent, 455
Roy, Gabrielle, 448
Roy, Patricia, 426
Royal Air Force, 379–380
Royal Canadian Academy of the Arts, 357, 361
Royal Canadian Air Force, 420, 431
Royal Canadian Navy
    crisis in the early twentieth century, 319–320
    World War I, 374, 380
    World War II, 427
Royal Commission on Aboriginal peoples,
    500–501, 502, 503
Royal Commission on Bilingualism and
    Biculturalism, 480–481
Royal Commission on Dominion–Provincial
    Relations, 411
Royal Commission on Price Spreads, 407
Royal Commission on the Relations of Labour
    and Capital, 341
Royal Commission on the Status of Women, 473,
    571
Royal Military College, 380
Royal Navy, 84
Royal Proclamation of 1763, 97–98
Royal Twenty-second Regiment ("Vandoos"), 379
Rule, Jane, 472, 575
Rupert, Prince, 75
Rupert's Land, 75, 264–265, 303
Rural depopulation, 335
Russia, 216, 217
Rutledge, Joseph Lister, 68
Ryan, Claude, 524
Ryerson, Egerton, 131, 159, 254
Ryerson, Stanley, 137

Sabia, Laura, 473
Sacred Feathers, 123
Saddle Island, 30
Saint-Jean-Baptiste Society, 360
Saint John, 177, 185, 249
Saint John River valley, 169, 170, 171, 177
Saint John's Island, 169, 177
    See also Prince Edward Island
Salaberry, Charles-Michel de, 111
Salles d'asile, 350
Salmon processing, 330, 335
Salt, 28
Salvation Army, 348
Same-sex unions and marriages, 472, 593–594
Sangster, Charles, 160
Sangster, Joan, 353, 457
San Juan Island, 228
Saratoga, New York, 101

Saskatchewan
    Aboriginal land-claims issues, 504
    economy in the 1960s, 482
    economy in the 1970s, 561
    prohibition and, 384
    schools issues, 314
Saskatchewan River, 195
Saskatchewan Treaty Land Entitlement Frame-
    work, 504
Sauvé, Paul, 516
Sayer, Pierre-Guillaume, 205
Sayer trial, 205
Scarlet fever, 206
Schools
    bilingualism and, 381
    Canada West, 159
    Confederation and, 246
    economic development and, 327
    Manitoba and, 311–314
    in the mid-nineteenth century, 254
    in New France, 62
    residential, 269, 496, 501–503
    technical and business, 331
    See also Aboriginal schools; Education;
        English–French schools
Schools Act (Manitoba), 312
Schoolteachers. See Teaching
Schultz, John, 265, 266
"Scientific management," 327
Scott, Duncan Campbell, 269, 359
Scott, Frank, 450
Scott, Thomas, 266
Scott Act, 355
Scottish immigrants, 178, 187
Scurvy, 27
Seal fishery, 181
Sea otter trade, 217
"Second wave" feminism, 472–473
Secord, Laura, 128
Sections, 291
Séguin, Maurice, 333
Seigneurial system, 51–52, 53–54, 99
Seigneurs, 51, 52, 99
Selkirk, Fifth Earl of (Lord Douglas), 202
Semaines sociales, 384
Semple, Robert, 204
Senate, creation of, 241
Senecas, 102
Senior, Hereward, 176
Separate schools, 246
Séraphin: Un homme et son péché (film), 596
Serpent burial mounds, 6
Service, Robert, 360
Service industries, 482
Seton, Ernest, 350
Settlement houses, 348

Settlers of the Marsh (Grove), 403
Seven Oaks skirmish, 204
Seventy-Two Resolutions, 239, 246
Seven Years' War, 82–89, 97
Sewage, 601
Sex segregation, in the workplace, 473
Sexual control, the state and, 348
Sharp, Mitchell, 480
Shawnadithit, 189
Shipbuilding industry
    in 1867, 248–249
    decline in, 304–305
    Maritimes, 182
    New France, 57
    Quebec City, 107
Shirley, William, 81
Shore, Eddie, 412–413
Sicily invasion, 428
Sierra Legal Defence Fund, 577
Sifton, Clifford, 292–293, 295, 314
Simcoe, John Graves, 119, 122, 123
Simon Fraser University, 469
Simpson, Sir George, 219
Singer-songwriters, 468
Siouan language family, 7–8, 11
Sioux, 205
Sir George Williams University, 470
Sisters of the Congregation of Notre Dame,
    255–256
Six Nations, 14, 102–103
Six Nations Confederacy, 102
Slaves and Slavery
    Josiah Henson, 251–252
    New France, 63
    revolts, 63
    Underground Railway, 155
    Upper Canada, 123
Smallpox, 7, 42, 206
Smallwood, Joey, 451, 485
Smith, A.J., 243
Smith, Donald A., 265, 286, 289
Smith, Elijah, 508
Smith, Goldwin, 314
Smith, William, 134
Smith, William (Amor de Cosmos), 271
Smuggling, 179
Sobey, Frank, 484
Social action movement, 349
Social Credit Party, 407, 436, 478–479,
    483, 561
Social Darwinism, 315, 326
Social gospel movement, 347–349, 400
Social reform
    decline in the 1920s, 400–401
    women and, 351–355
    World War I, 383–384

Social welfare
    New France, 62
    World War II, 432–433
    See also Welfare state
Société de Notre-Dame de Montreal, 39
Société Saint-Jean-Baptiste de Montréal, 160
Society of Canadian Artists, 357
Society of Friends, 131
Society of Jesus. *See* Jesuits
Soirées de famille, 360
Somme, battle of, 379
"Song of Frog Plain," 204
Sons of Freedom, The, 295
Soroki nation, 103
Sorrel, battle of, 378
Souster, Raymond, 475
South African War, 316–317
South Asian immigrants, 546, 547
South Vietnam, 481
Sovereign Council, 56
Soviet Union, 452
Spain, 216, 217
Spanish Armada, 30–31
Spanish influenza epidemic, 386
Sparrow case (1990), 499
Species at Risk Act, 600
Spence, Mrs. Jacob, 356
Spies, 452
"Sponsorship scandal," 586
Sporting clubs, 339
Sports
    1930s, 412–413
    1970s, 573–574
    contemporary, 595
    early twentieth century, 362–363
    television and, 461
    women's basketball, 404
Sprague, D.N., 307
Squamish, 215
Squires. *See* Seigneurs
Sri Lanka, 544
St. Alban's raids, 237–238
St. Andrews Institute, 348
St. Charles, battle of, 113
St. Croix River, 34
St. Denis, battle of, 113
St. Eloi, battle of, 376
St. Eustache, battle of, 113
St. Laurent, Louis, 450–451
St. Lawrence and Atlantic railway, 151
St. Lawrence Iroquoians, 16, 27–28, 32, 33
St. Lawrence River, 55
St. Lawrence Valley, settlement of, 55–56
St. Maurice Forges, 58, 108–109
St. Paul, Minnesota, 205–206
Stacey, C.P., 85, 90

Stadacona, 27
Stagflation, 479
Stanfield, Robert, 560
Stanley, George F.G., 89–90, 269, 270, 306
Stanley, Lord, 362
Stanley Cup, 362
State interventionism, 471
Statement of Apology to the Aboriginal Peoples
    for Residential Schools, 503
Status Indians, 507
Statute of Westminster, 399
Ste. Foy, 87
Stead, R.J.C., 403
Steamships, 182
Steckley, John, 44
Steel Company of Canada (Stelco), 325, 455
Stegner, Wallace, 291
Stelco (Steel Company of Canada), 325, 455
Stephen, George, 286, 289
Sterilization, 569
Stevens, G.R., 153
Stevenson, Garth, 523, 568
Stewart, Gordon, 174
Stoney Creek, battle of, 128
Storck, Peter L., 3
Stowe, Harriet Beecher, 252
Strachan, John, 130, 160
Strait of Belle Isle, 29
Strange, Thomas Bland, 308
Strikes
    1920s, 402
    1950s, 455
    1960s, 474
    1970s, 572
    mid-nineteenth century, 158
    prior to World War I, 341
    Winnipeg General Strike, 393–396
    World War II, 432
Strong-Boag, Veronica, 352, 353, 448
Struthers, James, 452
Student Christian Movement, 411
Student revolt, 468–469, 470
Subarctic Algonquians, 12
Subarctic culture area, 12–13
Suburbs, 471, 591
Suez Canal Crisis, 454
Suffrage
    Aboriginal peoples, 496
    Constitutional Act of 1791, 106–107
    women, 148, 351–352, 353, 383–384, 435
Sugiman, Pam, 457–458
Sullivan, Ed, 460
Sullivan, John, 102
Sulpicians, 39
Sulte, Benjamin, 53
"Sun King." See Louis XIV

Superior Council, 56
Supreme Court of Canada, 283
Susquehannock, 46
Sutherland, Daniel, 375
Sutherland, David, 361
Swettenham, John, 376–377
Sydenham, Lord (Charles Poulett Thomson),
    143–144, 145

T. Eaton Company, 327–328
Taché, Alexander, 265
Tadoussac, 32, 37
Taft, William, 319
Taignoagny, 27
Taiwan, 544
Talbot, Thomas, 129
Talon, Jean, 51–52, 57, 58
Tardivel, Jules-Paul, 318
Tariffs, 281, 283–284, 285–286, 567
Taxation, 242, 378
Taylor, Charles, 523
Taylor, Frederick W., 327
Teaching, women and, 133, 338
Team Canada, 574
Technical schools, 331
Tecumseh, 125, 126, 128
Tekahionwake (Pauline Johnson), 359
Telecommunications, 583
Telefilm Canada, 575
Telephones, 400
Television, 460–461, 476, 506,
    574–575, 596
Temple of Peace, 131–132
Tennant, Paul, 224
Ten Resolutions, 112
Terrorism
    contemporary concerns, 587–588
    "October Crisis," 520
Tessier, Albert, 411
Theatre
    1930s, 412
    1960s, 476
    late nineteenth century, 360
Thériault, Yves, 461, 475
Third parties, 407–408
Thirty Acres (Ringuet), 412
Thistle, Paul C., 200
Thompson, David, 218
Thompson, John Herd, 478, 566, 568
Thomson, Charles Poulett (Lord Sydenham),
    143–144, 145
Thomson, Dale C., 518
Thule, 13
Tilley, Charles, 263
Tilley, Samuel Leonard, 243, 246–247
Tillotson, Shirley, 456

Timber industry
 British Columbia, 330
 Clayoquot Sound and, 597–599
 early nineteenth century, 107
 Maritimes, 181, 182–184
 United Canadas, 144, 150
 Upper Canada, 134
 urban development in Quebec and, 157
Tolstoy, Leo, 295
Tompkins, Jimmy, 411
Tooker, Elisabeth, 16
Tories, 145, 147, 149
Toronto
 "Cabbagetown," 155
 Gay Pride parade, 571
 growth of, 154
 immigrant population, 545
 Orange Community, 155–156
 population growth, 335
 Sunday sports and, 462
 working-class life in, 336–337
Toronto Annexation Association, 149
Toronto Declaration, 135
Toronto Stock Exchange, 154
Totem poles, 218
Tourism, 161
Townships, 291
Trade
 in New France, 60
 postwar, 449
 See also Free trade
Trades and Labor Congress, 340, 341, 393, 402, 456
Trade Union Act, 339
Trade unions
 mid-nineteenth century, 253–254
 See also Labour and Labour unions
Traill, Catharine Parr, 160
Trans-Canada Air Lines, 410
Transcontinental railways, 284, 286–290
Transportation industry, 482
"Trash farming," 410
Travois, 12
Treaties, with the First Nations, 267, 269–270
Treaty of Aix-la-Chapelle, 82
Treaty of Ghent, 181
Treaty of Paris, 97, 103, 175
Treaty of Utrecht, 58, 64, 66, 79–80, 196
Treaty of Washington, 274
Tremblay, Michel, 472, 476
Tremblay, Thomas, 379
Trent affair, 237
Trente Arpents (Ringuet), 412
Trevithick, Scott, 502
Trigger, Bruce G., 14, 33, 44, 45
Trinity University, 160

Trudeau, Pierre Elliott, 455
 background of, 485–486
 Constitution of 1982 and, 563
 critics of, 560, 561–562
 Maurice Duplessis and, 516
 gasoline taxes and, 562
 government of, 559–560
 linguistic equality and, 519
 multiculturalism and, 549
 National Energy Program, 562–563
 program of, 486–487
 Quebec sovereignty debate and, 524
 record of, 563–564
 student protests and, 469
 White Paper of 1969, 497
 women's rights and, 571
Tsimshians, 8
Tuberculosis, 207
Tubman, Harriet, 155
Tuck, James, 29–30
Tungavik Federation of Nunavut, 508, 510
Tupper, Charles, 243, 263, 313
Turner, Frederick Jackson, 306
Turner, John, 565
Tuscaroras, 102
Tyrer, A.H., 409
Tyson, Ian and Sylvia, 468

Ukrainians immigrants, 295
Ultramontanism, 159, 281–282
Uncle Tom's Cabin (Stowe), 252
Underground Railway, 155
Underhill, Frank, 419
Unemployment Assistance Act, 452
Unemployment insurance plan, 432
Unemployment Relief Act, 405
Union Nationale, 408, 516, 518–519
Unions. See Labour and Labour unions
United Auto Workers, 409, 457–458
United Canadas
 annexation movement and, 149
 British free trade and, 149
 capital city chosen, 153–154
 culture, 160
 economy of, 144–145
 education, 159–160
 First Nations and, 148
 French Canadians and, 143–144
 migrant mobility in, 156–157
 overview, 143
 politics in, 153–154
 population figures, 154
 prohibition movement, 158
 reciprocity with the United States, 150–151
 Reform coalition, 145
 religion, 158–159

responsible government, 146–148
social developments, 154–158
tourism, 161
urban and commercial development, 154
United Church of Canada, 400, 411, 458
United Electrical, Radio and Machine Workers'
    Union, 457
United Empire Loyalists, 316
United Farmers of Alberta, 398
United Mine Workers of America, 340
United Nations, 436, 588
United States
    Alaska boundary dispute, 318
    Canadian immigration, 542
    Canadian relations with, 318–319
    Confederation and, 245–246
    economic ties with Canada, 399
    Manifest Destiny, 219
    the Maritimes and, 185–186
    Marshall Plan, 449
    reciprocity and, 150–151, 185–186, 314–315,
      318–319
    See also American Civil War; American
      Revolution
United States Magazine and Democratic Review,
    The (newspaper), 219
Universal medical care. *See* Health care
Université du Quebec, 519
Université Laval, 160
Universities
    1970s, 572
    growth of, 469
    mid-nineteenth century, 254
    student radicals, 470
    women and, 459, 594
    See also Higher education
University of Toronto, 159–160, 469
Upper Canada
    British immigrants and, 128–129
    Constitutional Act of 1791, 121–122
    displacement of the First Nations, 123, 125
    economic growth, 134
    Family Compact, 130, 135, 136
    the First Nations in, 129–130
    founding of, 119
    growth of, 125
    land purchases from the Anishinabeg, 119
    Lord Durham's report, 138
    Loyalist settlements, 121
    Loyalist women in, 123
    population growth, 119
    rebellion of 1837, 135–138
    Reform Movement, 135–136
    religion and religious disputes, 122–123, 125,
      130–131
    under John Simcoe, 122–123

slavery and, 123
transportation, 134–135
War of 1812, 125–128
women in, 123, 133 134
Urbanization
    in 1867, 249
    contemporary trends, 591
    effects of, 325
    life in industrial cities, 336–337
    population growth in cities, 335
    in the Prairies, 330
Urban proletariat, 157, 158
Urban reform movement, 350
Uruslines, 38

Vaccination programs, 206
Valcartier military camp, 374
Vallières, Pierre, 521
Valour and the Horror, The (television series), 430
Vance, Jonathan, 399
Vancouver
    Chinatown, 550, 551
    Chinese immigrants and, 547–548, 551
    immigrant population, 545, 551
    poverty, 593
Vancouver, George, 217
Vancouver Island
    Aboriginal land and, 274
    James Douglas as governor, 220
    economic development, 330
    population growth, 335
    union with British Columbia, 228
Van Horne, William Cornelius, 287
Van Kirk, Sylvia, 198
Vaudreuil, Marquis de, 97
Vaudreuil, Philippe de Rigaud de, 63, 80, 83, 84,
    88
Veregin, Peter, 295
Verrazzano, Giovanni da, 26
Verrières Ridge, battle of, 428
Victoria, Queen, 316
Victoria, Vancouver Island, 226–228
Victoria Bridge, 153
Victoria Charter, 520
Victorian Order of Nurses, 338, 351
Victoria Pioneer Rifle Corps, 227
Victory Bonds, 378, 423
Vietnam War, 481
Vietnam War protests, 468
Vigneault, Gilles, 468
Villa, Brian Loring, 429
Ville-Marie, 39
Vimy Ridge, battle of, 379, 386
"Vinland," 25
Violent crime, 576
Virtuosos, 357

"Visible minorities," 544–545
Visual arts
    1920s, 402–403
    1930s, 412
    late nineteenth century, 357–359
    mid-nineteenth century, 160
Voice of Women, 473
Voltaire, 89
Volunteering, during World War I, 378
Voting rights. *See* Suffrage

"Wabanki," 103
Waddell, Eric, 522
Wage labourers, 157, 158
Walcheren Island, battle of, 428
Walker, Horatio, 358
Walker, Sir Hovenden, 79
Walpole Island band council, 496
Walters, Angus, 404
Ward, Peter, 425
War Measures Act, 373, 411, 425,
    520, 563
War of 1812, 125–128, 179, 189
War Pigeon, The (film), 362
Wars of Religion, 28
Wartime Elections Act, 383
Washington, George, 82, 100
Waste disposal, 600–601
Water pollution, 600–601
    See also Pollution
Watson, Homer, 358
Way, Charles Jones, 357
Webster–Ashburton Treaty of 1842, 186
Welfare state
    1960s, 480
    decline of, 585
    development of, 451–452
    See also Social welfare
Welland Canal, 135, 145, 158
Wendake, 364–365
West, John, 204
Western Canada
    1970s, 560–562
    economy in the 1960s, 482–483
    economy in the 1990s, 590–591
    See also Canada West
Western Labour Conference, 393
West Indian immigrants, 544
Weston, Galen, 565
Wetlands, 533
Whaling, 29–31
Wheat farming
    advances in the early twentieth century, 292
    the Great Depression and, 404–405
    in the mid-nineteenth century, 249

United Canadas, 134
    Upper Canada, 144
Wheelock, Rev. Eleazar, 104
Whisky traders, 207
Whitaker, Denis and Sheilagh, 429
White Paper of 1969, 497
Whitney, James, 381
Whitton, Charlotte, 458
Whooping cough, 207
Wiebe, Rudy, 475
Wife-beating, 336
Wildcat strikes, 474
Wilderness conservation, 350–351
Wild Geese (Ostenso), 403
Wildlife conservation, 350–351
William of Orange, 156
Williams, Percy, 404
Williston Lake, 483
Willson, David, 131
Wilson, Lois, 458
Windigo, 198
Windmill, battle of the, 136
Wineland, 25
Winnipeg, 330, 335
Winnipeg General Strike, 393–396
"Winterers," 206
Wise, S.F., 430
Wiseman, Adele, 461
Wolfe, James, 85–86
Wolfe's Cove, 87
Wolseley, Garnet, 267
Wolseley expedition, 267
Woman's Christian Temperance Union, 356
Women
    1920s, 401
    1930s, 409–410
    1960s, 472–473
    armed services, 424
    colleges, 256
    disenfranchisement, 107, 133, 187
    domestic violence, 336, 571
    filles du roi, 53–54
    higher education and, 459, 594
    immigration to New France, 52–54
    imperialism and, 315–316
    institutionalized feminism, 571
    life in the mid-nineteenth century, 253
    in the Maritimes, 187
    middle-class postwar life, 447–448
    "Mothers of Confederation," 240
    in New France, 60
    pay equity and, 594
    in postwar Canada, 433
    postwar status, 456–459
    Prohibition movement and, 355

property rights in the North West, 291
refugees entering Canada, 539
in rural Canada, 401
"second wave" feminism, 472–473
social reform and, 351–353
suffrage and, 148, 351–352, 353, 383–384, 435
during the Trudeau government, 564
unions and, 339, 457–458, 474
in Upper Canada, 123, 133–134
in the workforce, 109, 327, 337–338, 378, 423–424, 433, 456, 458, 473, 571–572, 594
World War I, 378
World War II, 423–424
writers in the 1960s, 475
Women's Art Association, 357
Women's basketball, 404
Women's Equal Employment Opportunity Act, 473
Women's Institute, 351
Wood, Henry Wise, 398
Woodland Assiniboine, 197, 200
Woodland Cree, 196, 197, 200
Woodland First Nations, 196–197
Woodsworth, J.S., 349, 394, 407
Workers' Experimental Theatre, 412
Workers' Unity League, 408–409
Working class
    charitable and social institutions for, 339
    life in industrial cities, 336–337
    women, 337–338
Working-class consciousness, 158
Working-class culture, 363
World War I
    British treatment of Canada during, 380
    Canadian Corps, 384, 385–386
    Canadian Expeditionary Force, 374–375
    conscription crisis, 382
    demobilization, 386
    end of, 384
    ethnic tensions during, 381–382
    impact of, 373, 387
    initial Canadian response to, 373
    interventionist government during, 377–378
    key battles of, 378–379, 384
    national disunity during, 380–382
    nationalism and, 399
    nature of, 376–377
    origins of, 373
    recruitment, 380
    social reform and, 383–384
    Union government and the election of 1917, 382–383
    as a "white man's war," 375
    women and, 378
World War II
    Aboriginal peoples during, 494–495
    appeasement and neutrality preceding, 419
    beginning of, 419
    British Commonwealth Air Training Plan, 420
    Canadian–American relations, 421–422
    casualties, 431
    conscription and, 428
    economy during, 422–423
    French Canada and, 426–427
    impact of, 419, 431, 434, 436–437
    industrial conflicts during, 432
    plebiscite of 1942, 427
    the provinces during, 434–436
    rationing, 423
    treatment of ethnic minorities during, 424–426
    war effort in the first years, 420–421
    war effort in the later years, 427–428
    women and the war effort, 423–424
Wright, Sidney, 295
Wynn, Graeme, 183–184

Yale–Toronto Conference on the North American Indian, 493–494
Yellowhorn, Eldon, 3
Yonge, Sir George, 122
Yonge Street, 122
York boats, 197
York Factory, 79
Yorktown, Virginia, 174
York University, 469
Young, George, 404
Youth protest, 467–469, 470
Ypres, battle of, 377
Ypres Salient, 378
Yukon Native Brotherhood, 508
Yukon Territory
    Aboriginal land-claims issues, 508
    Alaska boundary dispute, 318

Zouaves, 281